Language and Composition

The Art of Voice

2nd Edition

Gilbert H. Muller

The City University of New York
LaGuardia College

Melissa E. Whiting

University of Arkansas–Fort Smith

Reinforced Binding What does it mean?
Since high schools frequently adopt for several years, it is important that a textbook can withstand the wear and tear of usage by multiple students. To ensure durability, McGraw-Hill has elected to manufacture this textbook with a reinforced binding.

AP®, Advanced Placement®, and Advanced Placement Program® are trademarks registered by the College Board, which was not involved in the production of, and does not endorse, these products.

COVER: EyeEm/Alamy Stock Photo

About the Cover: The cover shows a quirky-looking tree isolated on a tiny island. Or maybe not so isolated. Look closer and you'll see birds concealed within the branches. The tree seems to be bowing to its reflection—leading the viewer to wonder what lies below the surface of the water. Notice how trees on the shoreline and their reflections connect the lone tree to a larger whole. You might experience an entirely different visual response if the connections surrounding the tree were removed from the image. As an AP Language and Composition student, you will learn how to search for "connections" in a similar manner. The AP English Language and Composition course will teach you to understand WHAT authors are saying, as well as HOW and WHY they are saying it. You will also learn how to create meaning and connections in your own writing.

The Internet addresses listed in the text were accurate at the time of publication. The inclusion of a website does not indicate an endorsement by the authors or McGraw-Hill Education, and McGraw-Hill Education does not guarantee the accuracy of the information presented at these sites.

mheducation.com/prek-12

Send all inquiries to:
McGraw-Hill Education
8787 Orion Place
Columbus, OH 43240

ISBN: 978-0-07-691932-1
MHID: 0-07-691932-3

Printed in the United States of America.

2 3 4 5 6 QVS 23 22 21 20 19

About the Authors

Gilbert H. Muller is professor emeritus of English at the LaGuardia campus of the City University of New York. He has also taught at Stanford University, where he received a Ph.D. in English and American Literature; Vassar College; and several universities overseas. Dr. Muller is the author of the award-winning *Nightmares and Visions: Flannery O'Connor and the Catholic Grotesque; Chester Himes; New Strangers in Paradise: The Immigrant Experience and Contemporary American Fiction; William Cullen Bryant: Author of America*; and other critical studies. His essays and reviews have appeared in *The New York Times, The New Republic, The Nation, The Sewanee Review, The Georgia Review*, and elsewhere. He has written and edited best-selling textbooks in English and composition, including McGraw-Hill's *The Short Prose Reader*, with Harvey Wiener, now in its twelfth edition, and *The McGraw-Hill Reader*, now in its twelfth edition. Among Dr. Muller's awards are fellowships from the National Endowment for the Humanities, the Fulbright Commission, the Ford Foundation, and the Mellon Foundation.

Melissa E. Whiting is a retired professor of English and Rhetoric at the University of Arkansas Fort Smith, where she also served as Department Head. She has also taught at the University of Southern Mississippi and the University of Oklahoma, where she received a Ph.D. in English Education. Dr. Whiting was an English teacher at Vinita High School in Vinita, Oklahoma, where she taught Advanced Placement Language and Composition. She also serves as a Reader and Table Leader at the AP Language and Composition scoring. Dr. Whiting is the co-author of *How English Teachers Get Taught* and other pedagogical studies. Her publications have appeared in the *English Journal, Teaching Writing Teachers, The International Journal of Learning, Research in Rural Education, The Oklahoma English Journal*, and *The Tennessee English Journal*. She wrote the *Advanced Placement Instructor's Manual* that accompanies the eighth edition of the *Prentice-Hall Reader* (Ed. G. Miller). She continues to be involved with AP workshops and task forces, served as a Senior Reviewer for the AP textbook audit, and has contributed textbook reviews to AP Central. She continues to serve as a scorer for the edTPA, SAT, and various state writing tests. She continues to conduct high school writing workshops, focusing on AP Language and Composition in the four-state area of Oklahoma, Arkansas, Missouri, and Kansas.

Contributing Writer and Reviewers

Contributing Writer

Stephanie Ferree Hyatt teaches AP English Language and Composition and AP English Literature and Composition at Lee High School in Huntsville, Alabama. In 2012, Hyatt was named Teacher of the Year for both Lee High School and Huntsville City Schools. Hyatt is actively involved with the A+ College Ready Initiative and the National Math and Science Institute, for whom she teaches AP exam prep sessions for students and curriculum workshops for teachers. Hyatt has served on the Teacher Engagement Committee of the Council of Chief State School Officers and serves on the Teacher Cabinet for the Alabama State Department of Education. Hyatt holds a Master's Degree in English from the University of Alabama Huntsville, an Educational Specialist Degree in Teaching and Learning from Liberty University, and is currently writing her doctoral dissertation for an Educational Doctorate in Curriculum and Instruction. "I owe a debt of gratitude to the countless teachers who have posted their brilliant lesson plans online and to the many professional development workshop leaders who have influenced my teaching over the years."

Reviewers

Ann Jackson, Kingwood, Texas

Lynn Knowles, formerly of Flower Mound, Texas

Christine Kingsolver Palmer, Colorado Springs, Colorado

Katie Stueart, Fayetteville, Arkansas

Patricia Vandever, Charlottesville, Virginia

Contents in Brief

Table of Contents

CHAPTER 6

History, Culture, and Civilization: Are We Citizens of the World? 234

Table of Contents *continued*

Rhetorical Table of Contents

Essays in *Language and Composition:
The Art of Voice* by Rhetorical Mode

Illustration

Causal Analysis

Argumentation and Persuasion

Developing Critical Readers and Masterful Writers

Language and Composition: The Art of Voice was created specifically to meet the needs of today's AP English Language and Composition classroom. This blended rhetoric/reader provides a solid framework for students to fine-tune their foundational skills as they successfully move on to more rigorous critical reading, thinking, and writing and learn to master the art of rhetoric in its many forms. The text engages students with the finest classic and contemporary essays—works that span myriad ages, cultures, and disciplines—and prepares students for an expanded universe of literacies, encouraging fluency with print, visual, digital, audio, and interactive texts. Eudora Welty speaks of reading as "a sweet devouring," and this book invites students to participate in—and enjoy—the vast and varied pleasures of responding to texts in any form.

Crafted in 5 parts and 13 chapters, *Language and Composition: The Art of Voice* covers the major modes of writing and many of the disciplines that high school students will encounter on the AP Exam and as college students.

The organization scaffolds instruction from skills and processes; to critical reading, thinking, and writing; and on to AP-level application and mastery. In addition, expansive coverage of rhetorical analysis, argumentation, and synthesis provide the necessary depth and breadth of coverage students need to prepare for the AP Exam.

Examples throughout the book illustrate concepts and serve as meaningful models that students can draw on as they develop their craft and apply their newly acquired skills.

The text, paired with the digital resources in the *AP advantage*, delivers accessible and adaptive support to help students prepare for the course, keep pace with the course, and succeed on the AP Exam.

Organization

PART 1 Close Reading and Writing Skills

CHAPTER 1 teaches sound and actionable reading skills to build a strong foundation.

CHAPTER 2 focuses on the writing process—planning/prewriting, drafting, and revising/editing.

CHAPTER 3 provides extensive coverage of argument and synthesis, skills that are critical for developing a deeper understanding of and engagement with texts.

PART 2 Issues Across the Disciplines

CHAPTERS 4–10 explore core disciplines, including education, the social sciences, the humanities, and the sciences. These chapters ask a key question designed to elicit constructive class discussion, thoughtful analysis, and sound critical writing. Each chapter offers 5 to 8 prose models that encourage students to practice skills they will need throughout life: analysis, criticism, argumentation, and synthesizing a variety of sources.

PART 3 AP Favorites

CHAPTER 11 includes 23 diverse essays encompassing discourses, speeches, sermons, ponderings, and proposals. These selections were chosen based on a survey of more than 250 AP English Language and Composition teachers, ensuring that the essays will seamlessly integrate into instructional plans.

CHAPTER 12 includes 3 sample student essays submitted as "excellent" by AP teachers. These provide exemplars on which students can model their own essays.

PART 4 Research Paper

CHAPTER 13 offers up-to-date coverage of 21st-century research writing, including citation and documentation to guide students in writing research papers regardless of the subject matter.

PART 5 AP Language and Composition Practice Exam

A complete practice exam gives students the opportunity to experience first-hand what they will encounter in May after completing the AP Language and Composition course.

Chapter 1

- Examples of annotation and questioning the text to identify, understand, and interact with arguments
- Coverage of the reader's rhetorical triangle and how readers/listeners use it as they interact with a text/speech to analyze the author's meaning or intention
- Extended coverage and examples of appeals—ethos, pathos, and logos—for students to recognize how writers/speakers connect to their audience
- Examples of rhetorical devices to help students understand the effects of the tools great writers use in their works—such as adding tone, depth, and interest
- Instruction on analyzing visual texts—paintings, advertisements, cartoons, graphs, and so on—to help students effectively read and respond to images as texts

Chapter 2

- Coverage of the writer's rhetorical triangle and how students can consider that dynamic and apply it to their own writing
- Examples of strategies for writing introductory, body, and concluding paragraphs—and how to make connections between them for students to use as models

Chapter 3

- Detailed instructions on how to approach the argument and synthesis essays on the AP Exam

Part 2 Issues Across the Disciplines

- Multiple-choice questions in the Chapter Assessment model the types of questions students will answer on the AP Exam.
- Chapter 7's new theme focuses on essays and visuals related to business and economics, subject areas that are increasingly relevant.

Part 3 AP Favorites

- Chapter 12 includes 3 sample student essays submitted as "excellent" by AP teachers that students can use as models for their own essays.

Part 5 AP Language and Composition Practice Exam

- A complete Practice Exam gives students the opportunity to experience first-hand what they will encounter in May after completing the AP Language and Composition course.

Key Features

Informed by the comments and suggestions from teachers across the country, *Language and Composition: The Art of Voice* offers the following proven and significant features:

A Rich Selection of Readings

The essays and images in this book address themes of current and enduring interest. Topics like social networking, the legacy of Michael Jackson, the appeal of Wonder Woman, globalization, and cultural challenges should elicit lively student response and effective writing. The essays have been selected carefully to embrace a rich assortment of authors, to achieve balance among constituencies, to cover major historical periods, and to provide prose models and styles for class analysis, discussion, and imitation. The authors in this text— from Frederick Douglass to Margaret Atwood, Rachel Carson to Jared Diamond, and Julia Alvarez to David Sedaris—all have high visibility as writers and thinkers of value. All of these authors—writing from such vantage points as literature, journalism, anthropology, sociology, art history, biology, and philosophy—start from the perspective that ideas exist in the world, that we should be alert to them, and that we should be able to deal with them in our own discourse. These essays have been chosen to engage students and sustain their interest as they become deeper readers of texts in a variety of formats and from multiple perspectives.

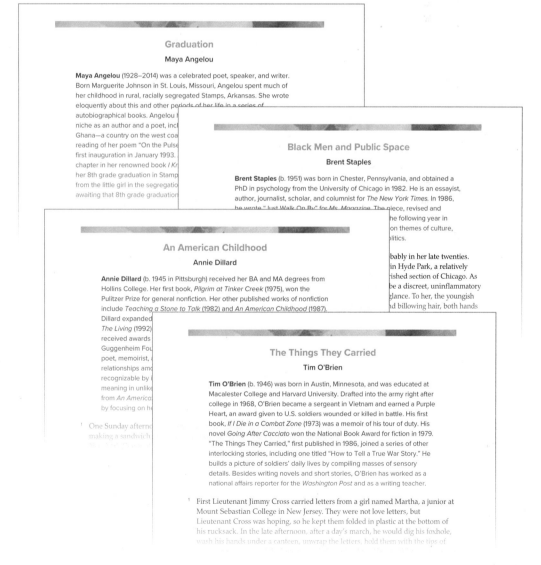

Graduation
Maya Angelou

Maya Angelou (1928–2014) was a celebrated poet, speaker, and writer. Born Marguerite Johnson in St. Louis, Missouri, Angelou spent much of her childhood in rural, racially segregated Stamps, Arkansas. She wrote eloquently about this and other periods of her life in a series of autobiographical books. Angelou [...] niche as an author and a poet, incl[...] Ghana—a country on the west coa[...] reading of her poem "On the Pulse[...] first inauguration in January 1993.[...] chapter in her renowned book *I Kn[...] her 8th grade graduation in Stamp[...] from the little girl in the segregatio[...] awaiting that 8th grade graduation[...]

Black Men and Public Space
Brent Staples

Brent Staples (b. 1951) was born in Chester, Pennsylvania, and obtained a PhD in psychology from the University of Chicago in 1982. He is an essayist, author, journalist, scholar, and columnist for *The New York Times*. In 1986, he wrote "Just Walk On By" for *Ms. Magazine*. The piece, revised and [...] he following year in [...] on themes of culture, [...]litics.

[...]bably in her late twenties. [...] in Hyde Park, a relatively [...]ished section of Chicago. As [...] be a discreet, uninflammatory [...]glance. To her, the youngish [...]d billowing hair, both hands

An American Childhood
Annie Dillard

Annie Dillard (b. 1945 in Pittsburgh) received her BA and MA degrees from Hollins College. Her first book, *Pilgrim at Tinker Creek* (1975), won the Pulitzer Prize for general nonfiction. Her other published works of nonfiction include *Teaching a Stone to Talk* (1982) and *An American Childhood* (1987). Dillard expanded [...] *The Living* (1992) [...] received awards [...] Guggenheim Fou[...] poet, memoirist, [...] relationships amo[...] recognizable by [...] meaning in unlike[...] from *An America*[...] by focusing on he[...]

[1] One Sunday afterno[...] making a sandwich[...]

The Things They Carried
Tim O'Brien

Tim O'Brien (b. 1946) was born in Austin, Minnesota, and was educated at Macalester College and Harvard University. Drafted into the army right after college in 1968, O'Brien became a sergeant in Vietnam and earned a Purple Heart, an award given to U.S. soldiers wounded or killed in battle. His first book, *If I Die in a Combat Zone* (1973) was a memoir of his tour of duty. His novel *Going After Cacciato* won the National Book Award for fiction in 1979. "The Things They Carried," first published in 1986, joined a series of other interlocking stories, including one titled "How to Tell a True War Story." He builds a picture of soldiers' daily lives by compiling masses of sensory details. Besides writing novels and short stories, O'Brien has worked as a national affairs reporter for the *Washington Post* and as a writing teacher.

[1] First Lieutenant Jimmy Cross carried letters from a girl named Martha, a junior at Mount Sebastian College in New Jersey. They were not love letters, but Lieutenant Cross was hoping, so he kept them folded in plastic at the bottom of his rucksack. In the late afternoon, after a day's march, he would dig his foxhole, wash his hands under a canteen, unwrap the letters, hold them with the tips of

Key Features *continued*

Flexible Instruction for Diverse Learners, Levels, and Styles

Because the selections range from simple essays to more abstract and complex modes of discourse, teachers and students will be able to use *Language and Composition: The Art of Voice* at virtually all levels of a program. It can be used with any of the major pedagogical perspectives common to the practice of composition today: as a writing-across-the-curricula text, as the basis for a rhetorically focused course, as a thematic reader, as a multicultural anthology, or as an in-depth reader. Teachers can pair and sequence essays to suit their instructional style and to increasingly challenge students with more rigorous texts at a comfortable pace.

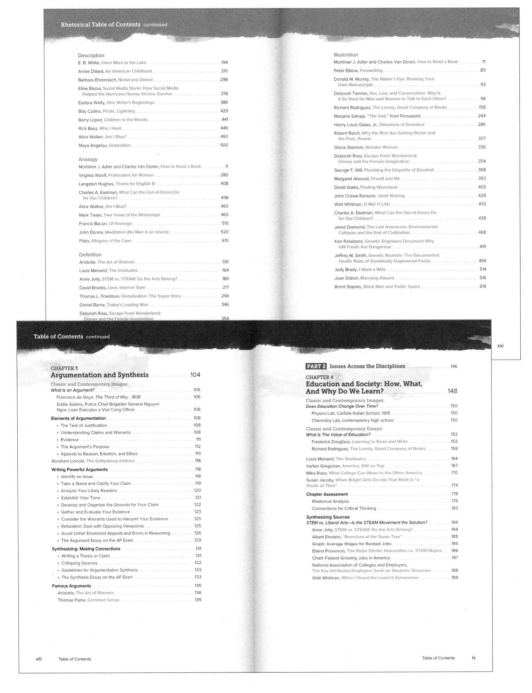

Chapter Introductions That Encourage Students to Reflect on Major Issues

The introduction to each disciplinary chapter gives students a broad perspective on the field at hand by putting major issues and concerns in context. Each introduction begins with a preview section that alerts students to strategies for reading, discussion, and writing.

As you read the essays in this chapter, consider the following questions:

- According to the author, what should our relationship to the natural world be?
- What claims or arguments does the author make about the importance of nature? Do you agree or disagree with these claims and arguments?
- What specific ecological problem does the author investigate?
- How does the author think that nature influences human behavior?
- What cultural factors are involved in our approach to the environment?
- Is the writer's tone optimistic, pessimistic, or neutral in the assessment of our ability to conserve nature?
- Do you find that the author is too idealistic or sentimental in the depiction of nature? Why?
- Based on the author's essay, how does he or she qualify as a nature writer?
- What rhetorical strategies do the authors employ?
- How have you been challenged or changed by the essays in this chapter?

◄ Questions in the chapter opener lead students to discover through critical thinking how to interact with each text and how to contextualize them within the core discipline.

Key Features *continued*

Integrated and Focused Treatment of Argument

Argumentation is a critical skill required for entering into conversations that have a wide range of positions. Developing the ability to take a position and build, support, and sustain an effective argument helps student become critical readers and thinkers as well as informed citizens.

A focused chapter on persuasive writing is reinforced throughout the book by "Writing an Argument" essay assignments accompanying each reading.

CHAPTER 3

Argumentation and Synthesis

Traditionally, we think of an argum[ent] argument *can* be a quarrel or a di[s] which participants express oppos[i] reasons for or against a position o[r] examples, the purpose is the sam[e] persuade or convince the audien[ce]

In their book *Metaphors We Live By*, [

Writing an Argument   Argue for or against the proposition that an effective parent should have—at least—a touch of unconventionality. Alternatively, take a position on the role of conformity in life.

Writing an Argument   Think about the numerous action heroes or superheroes that young children and adolescents encounter today in various media forms. Write an essay in which you contend that exposure to such superheroes either does or does not encourage violent behavior in young people.

The Synthesizing Sources ▶ features in Chapters 4–10 prompt students to examine a variety of textual and visual arguments from different points of view to identify patterns of agreement and disagreement. *Language and Composition: The Art of Voice* encourages students to consider complex, multiple perspectives, moving beyond pro/con thinking.

≫ SYNTHESIZING SOURCES

Social Media—Has It Empowered Us or Disenfranchised Us?

Social media could be arguably one of greatest influences on society today. Increasingly, we turn to social media to get our information. Instant information also becomes instant susceptibility to many dark Internet interferences connected to what we read and believe. Connected people have the opportunity to be empowered or disenfranchised by this form of media. Critically read and analyze the texts and images here, and then answer the questions that follow.

▼ **SOURCE A**

Millennials Using Social Media

Monkey Business Images/Shutterstock.com

Current Coverage of Plagiarism, Summary, Documentation, and the Research Process

The chapters in Part 1 provide integrated guidelines on each of these topics. Chapter 13 offers an up-to-date tour of research, writing research papers, and MLA/APA documentation in this age of new media.

Avoiding Plagiarism

It is your responsibility to present honest written work. When you employ summary, paraphrase, and quotation in an essay or a research paper, you must avoid **plagiarism**—the attempt to pass off the work of others as your own. The temptation to plagiarize is not only one of the oldest "crimes" in academia but also an unfortunate by-product of computers, for there are numerous opportunities for harried, enterprising, or—let's face it—dishonest students to download bits of information or entire texts and appropriate them without acknowledgment. At the same time,
the most inv
writing rese
warned: Co
you can fail

Plagiarism i
research pa

- Cite (p
  inform
  unders
  George

- Cite al
  anothe
  this bo
  belong

- Work I
  Consta
  and sy
  particularly help
  close t

If you are ir
legitimate to
on any infor

34   C

Paraphrasing, Summarizing, Quoting

As you prepare to respond to the writing of others, you need to develop skills so your own writing will reflect the hard work that went into the reading process. To this end, you can benefit from learning some shortcuts that will assist you in garnering information about what you have read. These skills include paraphrasing, summarizing, ar

Paraphra

Paraphrasing m
Students might
own words are t
serves two mai
plagiarizing, eve
paraphrasing
rewrite it. As yo
improve your al
you have read a
often leads you
the paraphrasin

It is important w
while not using
numbers or hea
to never use thr
danger of not us
you can keep wo
the end of a par

The following ai
outside source f
successful appli
text, it does not

Original

But, press
gives rise,
composed
ethnic and
assimilatio

Unsuccess

But, press
suggests t
racial grou
integration

30   Chapt

APA (American Psychological Association) Documentation

The samples below show how to use APA style for citing a source in the text and in the References section at the end of a paper.

APA Parenthetical Documentation

The basic APA p
publication, info
list. Although re
should add the p
information is lc
numbers or hea
danger of not us
the end of a par

Direct Quot

One argue
of the Sup
and histor
protect no

Direct Quot

Rostron (2
for the ma
textual arg
Amendme

How to Use Paraphrase

Clarke (20
Hurricane
support fo

The city's
two altern

In 2008, V
(Conclusio

690   Chap

MLA (Modern Language Association) Documentation

Make it as clear as possible to your reader where a source begins (with a signal phrase) and ends (with a parenthetical citation) in your paper. When you cannot provide specific parenthetical information (such as when a source does not have page numbers), make it as easy as possible for your reader to find the citation on your Works Cited page by including key identification elements like the source's name within the sentence. The following examples illustrate how to cite some of the most common sources in the text and in the list of Works Cited at the end of a paper.

MLA Parenthetical Documentation

Book

A basic MLA in-text citation includes the author's last name and the page number (for sources that use numbered pages), identifying exactly where the quotation or information is located. This in-text citation leads readers to an entry on the Works Cited page, which provides more complete information about the source.

> In the conclusion, he offers a gruesome description of the dying man's physical and emotional struggles (Tolstoy 1252–53).

If the author's name is included in the text, it does not need to be repeated in the citation.

> Garcia Marquez uses another particularly appealing passage as the opening of the story (105).

If citing a quotation longer than four typed lines, set it off from the text of the paper and indented one-half inch (1/2") from the left margin. Double-space the quote and move the period before the parenthetical citation.

Work with Three or More Authors

If you mention the authors' names in your sentence narrative, you may include all the last names or write just the first author's name followed by "and others." In the parenthetical citation, however, include only the first author's name followed by *et al.*

> Most political revolutions have been instigated by people in the middle class (Bentley et al. 634).

Work Without an Author

Use the full title of the work if it is brief; if the title is longer, however, use a shortened version, beginning with the word you will use to alphabetize the work on the Works Cited page.

> *Computerworld* has developed a thoughtful editorial on the issue of government and technology ("Uneasy Silence" 54).

684   Chapter 13 | Writing a Research Paper

Key Features *continued*

Uniform Apparatus That Reinforces Close Reading and Writing

Support is provided for every essay to ensure students get the maximum benefit from their reading.

Each selection in this text is preceded by a brief introduction that offers biographical information about the author.

The questions that follow each essay are organized in a consistent format created to reinforce essential reading, writing, and oral communication skills. Arranged in three categories—**Comprehension**, **Rhetorical Analysis**, and **Writing**— these questions reflect current compositional theory as they move students from audience analysis to various modes, processes, and media of composition. The integrated design of these questions makes each essay— simple or complex, short or long, old or new—accessible to students who possess varied reading and writing abilities.

Comprehension

1. One of the most important points Woolf makes is why women have been limited by their lack of ways of making money. How does she make the argument that by lacking rooms of their own, women have been prevented from making money and being more of a literary force?

2. What do Woolf's musings about Shakespeare's sister and "Judith's" belief that she would not have been considered a genius, even if she shared the same mental capacities of her brother, prove in aiding Woolf's thesis?

3. What makes the one major character in this essay so uncanny?

Rhetorical Analysis

4. What is the effect of the repetition of the word *without* when describing what life might be like today for Shakespeare's sister in the closing paragraph?

5. What does Woolf's rhetoric suggest about the literature women did write at the time, and its connection to men?

6. "A Room of One's Own," by the words alone, is a metaphor for independent and respected living. Come up with some other metaphors that have similar meanings.

7. Explain the irony presented in paragraph 7.

Writing

8. Write an analytic essay in which you analyze Woolf's attitude about the role of money. Use the text to support your analysis.

9. Woolf says, "Of the two—the vote and the money—the money, I own, seemed infinitely the more important." In a comparison essay, compare and contrast the benefits and drawbacks of choosing money over the right to vote.

10. **Writing an Argument** Woolf argues that, "Great bodies of people are never responsible for what they do. They are driven by instincts which are not within their control." Do you agree with this statement? Write an argumentative essay defending your position.

Rhetorical Analysis

4. Why does Atwood begin on a personal note: "I grew up with George Orwell"? What is the effect of beginning the essay this way?

5. What is Atwood's main claim? What premises or warrants does she establish, and how sound is the logic? Justify your response.

6. Consider the appeal of ethos. Atwood seems to speak from a position of authority. How does she establish this sense of authority in the essay?

7. Why does Atwood summarize Orwell's two novels at considerable length? How does she use comparison and contrast to frame her discussion of the novels?

8. What causes and effects does Atwood analyze in this essay? In each, what is her purpose?

9. How does Atwood conclude her discussion of Orwell? How successful do you find the ending, and why?

A Variety of Synthesis Activities

Synthesizing multiple texts and images leads to a comprehensive understanding of an issue or topic and provides a broader contextual range for evaluation. Three types of Synthesis practice are found throughout the book to help students as they prepare for the Synthesis question on the AP Exam.

Synthesizing the Classic + Contemporary Essays

1. Compare and contrast the tone of each writer. How does tone affect purpose? How does it affect mood? Select at least three passages from White and three from Kingsolver that demonstrate how their tones differ. Do they offer any hints as to the "voice" or personality of the writers? Why or why not?

2. What contemporary issues does Kingsolver address that White either ignores or is unaware of? Consider that White was born 58 years before Kingsolver, so his world was quite a different one. Are there other variables that might help us distinguish their concerns and outlooks—for example, gender, class, and environment?

3. What central values does each author have regarding the family? How are they similar? How do they differ? How do their values reflect their times?

◄ Each pairing of Classic & Contemporary Essays has a group of Synthesis questions that require students to analyze, compare, and contrast.

At the end of Chapters 4-10, ► the Connections for Critical Thinking questions in the Chapter Assessment help students gain practice in synthesizing, critiquing, and making comparative assessments of various groups of essays.

Connections for Critical Thinking

1. Both Annie Dillard's "An American Childhood" and E. B. White's "Once More to the Lake" explore the experience of childhood from a different perspective. Do they share a common voice or mood? What is distinctive about each essay? Which essay do you prefer, and why? Consider the style and emotional impact of the writing.

2. Argue for or against the claim that Alvarez's portrayal of a quinceañera and Brooks's take on online dating are biased.

3. Argue for or against the idea that the presentation of relatively new types of relationships like those described in the essays by Kingsolver and Brooks seem more highly romanticized than the "traditional" relationships described by White and Alvarez.

4. Argue for or against the view that changes in society and its norms—specifically, increased geographical mobility, an evolving workplace, ideas about economic class, individual liberties—have resulted in new forms of identity. Use examples from the work of Brooks, Kingsolver, and others.

In these same chapters, the ► feature Synthesizing Sources provides students with multiple sources of excerpts, cartoons, graphs, poetry, and more about a particular topic—social media, women's rights, helicopter parenting, online shopping, GMOs, and so on. A cadre of questions and activities require students to synthesize the pieces within each of these Synthesis groupings.

≫SYNTHESIZING SOURCES

STEM vs. Liberal Arts—Is the STEAM Movement the Solution?

≫SYNTHESIZING SOURCES

GMOs—Are They Good for the World or Not?

≫SYNTHESIZING SOURCES

Online Shopping: Has It Affected Our Lives for Better or Worse?

French author Alphonse Karr (1849) observed "The more things change, the more they stay the same." Many people would argue, however, that online shopping has completely changed the way shoppers shop. The social aspects of shopping have disappeared, and companies such as Amazon have taken the place of malls, big box stores, mom-and-pop shops, and open-air markets. Has online shopping signaled the demise of retail? Critically read and analyze these sources,

Key Features *continued*

Visual Rhetoric

Paired visuals—Classic and Contemporary Images—appear in Chapters 1-10. These photographs, paintings, and other visual texts, along with the accompanying "Using a Critical Perspective" and "Analyzing Visuals and Their Rhetoric" questions, serve to interest students in the chapter's central topics and get them thinking about the relationship between the juxtaposed images.

An entirely **NEW!** section in Chapter 1—**Analyzing Visual Texts**—provides in-depth instruction in visual rhetoric to help students understand that images, like texts, are a channel for communication.

Assessment

 The thematic chapters include NEW! **Chapter Assessments** that mimic Section I of the AP Exam, giving students the opportunity to practice deep analysis and evaluation skills required on the actual test. ▼

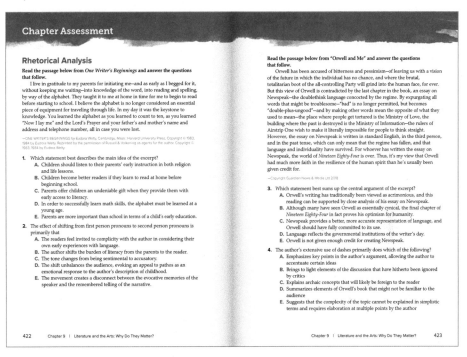

Chapter Assessment

Rhetorical Analysis

Read the passage below from *One Writer's Beginnings* and answer the questions that follow.

I live in gratitude to my parents for initiating me—and as early as I begged for it, without keeping me waiting—into knowledge of the word, into reading and spelling, by way of the alphabet. They taught it to me at home in time for me to begin to read before starting to school. I believe the alphabet is no longer considered an essential piece of equipment for traveling through life. In my day it was the keystone to knowledge. You learned the alphabet as you learned to count to ten, as you learned "Now I lay me" and the Lord's Prayer and your father's and mother's name and address and telephone number, all in case you were lost.

—ONE WRITER'S BEGINNINGS by Eudora Welty, Cambridge, Mass.: Harvard University Press, Copyright © 1983, 1984 by Eudora Welty. Reprinted by the permission of Russell & Volkening as agents for the author. Copyright © 1983, 1984 by Eudora Welty.

1. Which statement best describes the main idea of the excerpt?
   A. Children should listen to their parents' early instruction in both religion and life lessons.
   B. Children become better readers if they learn to read at home before beginning school.
   C. Parents offer children an undeniable gift when they provide them with early access to literacy.
   D. In order to successfully learn math skills, the alphabet must be learned at a young age.
   E. Parents are more important than school in terms of a child's early education.

2. The effect of shifting from first person pronouns to second person pronouns is primarily that
   A. The readers feel invited to complicity with the author in considering their own early experiences with language.
   B. The author shifts the burden of literacy from the parents to the reader.
   C. The tone changes from being sentimental to accusatory.
   D. The shift unbalances the audience, evoking an appeal to pathos as an emotional response to the author's description of childhood.
   E. The movement creates a disconnect between the evocative memories of the speaker and the remembered telling of the narrative.

Read the passage below from "Orwell and Me" and answer the questions that follow.

Orwell has been accused of bitterness and pessimism—of leaving us with a vision of the future in which the individual has no chance, and where the brutal, totalitarian boot of the all-controlling Party will grind into the human face, for ever. But this view of Orwell is contradicted by the last chapter in the book, an essay on Newspeak—the doublethink language concocted by the regime. By expurgating all words that might be troublesome—"bad" is no longer permitted, but becomes "double-plus-ungood"—and by making other words mean the opposite of what they used to mean—the place where people get tortured is the Ministry of Love, the building where the past is destroyed is the Ministry of Information—the rulers of Airstrip One wish to make it literally impossible for people to think straight. However, the essay on Newspeak is written in standard English, in the third person, and in the past tense, which can only mean that the regime has fallen, and that language and individuality have survived. For whoever has written the essay on Newspeak, the world of *Nineteen Eighty-Four* is over. Thus, it's my view that Orwell had much more faith in the resilience of the human spirit than he's usually been given credit for.

—Copyright Guardian News & Media Ltd 2018.

3. Which statement best sums up the central argument of the excerpt?
   A. Orwell's writing has traditionally been viewed as acrimonious, and this reading can be supported by close analysis of his essay on Newspeak.
   B. Although many have seen Orwell as essentially cynical, the final chapter of *Nineteen Eighty-Four* in fact proves his optimism for humanity.
   C. Newspeak provides a better, more accurate representation of language, and Orwell should have fully committed to its use.
   D. Language reflects the governmental institutions of the writer's day.
   E. Orwell is not given enough credit for creating Newspeak.

4. The author's extensive use of dashes primarily does which of the following?
   A. Emphasizes key points in the author's argument, allowing the author to accentuate certain ideas
   B. Brings to light elements of the discussion that have hitherto been ignored by critics
   C. Explains archaic concepts that will likely be foreign to the reader
   D. Summarizes elements of Orwell's book that might not be familiar to the audience
   E. Suggests that the complexity of the topic cannot be explained in simplistic terms and requires elaboration at multiple points by the author

422   Chapter 9 | Literature and the Arts: Why Do They Matter?

Chapter 9 | Literature and the Arts: Why Do They Matter?   423

 A complete NEW! **Practice Exam** in Part 5 prepares students to take the AP Exam by reflecting on the content and format of the exam.

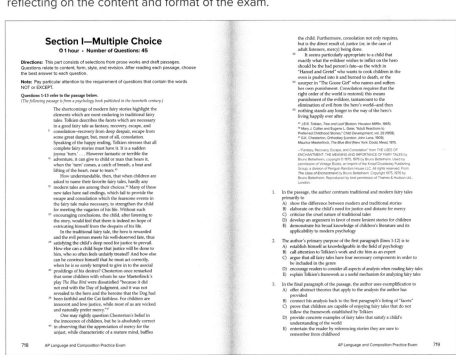

Section I—Multiple Choice

⏱ 1 hour • Number of Questions: 45

Directions: This part consists of selections from prose works and draft passages. Questions relate to content, form, style, and revision. After reading each passage, choose the best answer to each question.

Note: Pay particular attention to the requirement of questions that contain the words NOT or EXCEPT.

Questions 1–13 refer to the passage below.
(The following passage is from a psychology book published in the twentieth century.)

The shortcomings of modern fairy stories highlight the elements which are most enduring in traditional fairy tales. Tolkien describes the facets which are necessary in a good fairy tale as fantasy, recovery, escape, and
5 consolation—recovery from deep despair, escape from some great danger, but, most of all, consolation. Speaking of the happy ending, Tolkien stresses that all complete fairy stories must have it. It is a sudden joyous 'turn.'. . . However fantastic or terrible the
10 adventure, it can give to child or man that hears it, when the 'turn' comes, a catch of breath, a beat and lifting of the heart, near to tears.[40]
    How understandable, then, that when children are asked to name their favorite fairy tales, hardly any
15 modern tales are among their choices.[44] Many of these new tales have sad endings, which fail to provide the escape and consolation which the fearsome events in the fairy tale make necessary, to strengthen the child for meeting the vagaries of his life. Without such
20 encouraging conclusions, the child, after listening to the story, would feel that there is indeed no hope of extricating himself from the despairs of his life.
    In the traditional fairy tale, the hero is rewarded and the evil person meets his well-deserved fate, thus
25 satisfying the child's deep need for justice to prevail. How else can a child hope that justice will be done to him, who so often feels unfairly treated? And how else can he convince himself that he must act correctly, when he is so sorely tempted to give in to the asocial
30 proddings of his desires? Chesterton once remarked that some children with whom he saw Maeterlinck's play *The Blue Bird* were dissatisfied "because it did not end with the Day of Judgment, and it was not revealed to the hero and the heroine that the Dog had
35 been faithful and the Cat faithless. For children are innocent and love justice, while most of us are wicked and naturally prefer mercy."[47]
    One may rightly question Chesterton's belief in the innocence of children, but he is absolutely correct
40 in observing that the appreciation of mercy for the unjust, while characteristic of a mature mind, baffles

the child. Furthermore, consolation not only requires, but is the direct result of, justice (or, in the case of adult listeners, mercy) being done.
45   It seems particularly appropriate to a child that exactly what the evildoer wishes to inflict on the hero should be the bad person's fate—as the witch in "Hansel and Gretel" who wants to cook children in the oven is pushed into it and burned to death, or the
50 usurper in "The Goose Girl" who names and suffers her own punishment. Consolation requires that the right order of the world is restored; this means punishment of the evildoer, tantamount to the elimination of evil from the hero's world—and then
55 nothing stands any longer in the way of the hero's living happily ever after.

[40] J.R.R. Tolkien, *Tree and Leaf* (Boston: Houghton Mifflin, 1965).
[44] Mary J. Collier and Eugene L. Gaier, "Adult Reactions to Preferred Childhood Stories," *Child Development*, vol. 29 (1958).
[47] G.K. Chesterton, *Orthodoxy* (London: John Lane, 1909).
Maurice Maeterlinck, *The Blue Bird* (New York: Dodd, Mead, 1911).

—"Fantasy, Recovery, Escape, and Consolation" from THE USES OF ENCHANTMENT: THE MEANING AND IMPORTANCE OF FAIRY TALES by Bruno Bettelheim, copyright © 1975, 1976 by Bruno Bettelheim. Used by permission of Vintage Books, an imprint of the Knopf Doubleday Publishing Group, a division of Penguin Random House LLC. All rights reserved. From *The Uses of Enchantment* by Bruno Bettelheim. Copyright 1975, 1976 by Bruno Bettelheim. Reproduced by kind permission of Thames & Hudson Ltd., London.

1. In the passage, the author contrasts traditional and modern fairy tales primarily to
   A) show the difference between modern and traditional stories
   B) elaborate on the child's need for justice and distaste for mercy
   C) criticize the cruel nature of traditional tales
   D) develop an argument in favor of more lenient stories for children
   E) demonstrate his broad knowledge of children's literature and its applicability to modern psychology

2. The author's primary purpose of the first paragraph (lines 1–12) is to
   A) establish himself as knowledgeable in the field of psychology
   B) call attention to Tolkien's work and cite him as an expert
   C) argue that all fairy tales have four necessary components in order to be included in the genre
   D) encourage readers to consider all aspects of analysis when reading fairy tales
   E) explain Tolkien's framework as a useful mechanism for analyzing fairy tales

3. In the final paragraph of the passage, the author uses exemplification to
   A) offer abstract theories that apply to the analysis the author has provided
   B) connect his analysis back to the first paragraph's listing of "facets"
   C) prove that children are capable of enjoying fairy tales that do not follow the framework established by Tolkien
   D) provide concrete examples of fairy tales that satisfy a child's understanding of the world
   E) entertain the reader by referencing stories they are sure to remember from childhood

718   AP Language and Composition Practice Exam

AP Language and Composition Practice Exam   719

Key Features *continued*

AP Favorites and Sample Student Essays

The **23 essays** in Chapter 11 are texts highly valued by AP Language and Composition teachers. Providing these essays in one place saves time and effort on the part of teachers so they can focus on instructional planning and actual teaching instead of spending time searching through multiple sources for their favorite essays.

Chapter 12 provides real student essays deemed "excellent" by their teachers: **Synthesis Essay**, **Analysis Essay**, and **Argument Essay**. These essays can be used as models as students develop their essay writing skills. Knowing that these essays were written by their peers helps students develop confidence by demonstrating how this level of writing is achievable.

Contents

Sample Student Rhetorical Analysis Essay

By Arianna Kholanjani
New Century Technology High School
Huntsville, Alabama

Written as a response to Question 2 from the 2017 Released Exam, this
essay analyzes th
to her speech to

In Luce's speech
sets up her argum
sensationalist stor
Luce's use of re
for her argument
which will remind
argument. In para
In this context, "y
By repeating and
the journalists and
starts with the me
manner immediate
that they are the p
to come. Repeatin
hand—the journal

Sample Student Argument Essay

By Emma Perkins
Boulder High School
Boulder, Colorado

Responding to Question 3 from the 2005 Released Exam, this essay
evaluates the pro
spending on luxu

For a world so a
world that is starti
the world, it can b
in addressing the
worlds. While som
whether to buy a l
struggle to decide
time to gather wat
There are, of cou
advocated for the
income to oversea
size, there are bot
On the one han
would undoubtedl
wealthiest 1% of t

Sample Student Synthesis Essay

By Ariel Carter
White Bear Lake High School South Campus
White Bear Lake, Minnesota

Responding to Question 1 from the 2009 Released Exam, this essay offers
a documented opinion on the considerations the United States government
should take in funding space exploration.

When it comes to making decisions regarding space exploration, financial issues should be considered above all others. Money and government's allocation of that money leads to additional discussion of resources, determines the quality of life for regular citizens.

Since the beginning of space exploration, people have looked to the stars in wonder, asking what could be out there, but also questioning whether or not space exploration is the best use of tax payer money—especially since there has been little found. According to Source E, the United States spent 17 billion dollars in 2006 alone on space exploration. This may be an obvious statement, but that's a lot of money, and one has to ask, what else could that money have gone to? 2006 was two years before the Great Recession, and that same 17 billion dollars could have been used to support American citizens in more direct ways. See, space exploration does not financially help many people. Yes, it helps engineers and those directly involved in space exploration, but it does little for everyone else besides take money away

AP advantage
McGraw-Hill Education

The Pathway to Success for Today's AP® Students

AP advantage helps students navigate the rigors of Advanced Placement® coursework with accessible, engaging, and fully aligned resources designed specifically for today's learners.

From pre-course skill mastery, through comprehensive core curriculum, to targeted and adaptive test prep, **AP advantage** tailors the learning experience to students' diverse needs and learning styles.

AP Success Starts With:

- Self-paced, diagnostic AP course prep
- Fully aligned core curriculum
- Clear, accessible, skills-based pedagogy
- A robust digital platform with customizable resources designed for today's AP teachers and students
- Flexible implementation with print, digital or hybrid options
- Personalized AP test prep

All your resources, all in one place with *AP advantage*

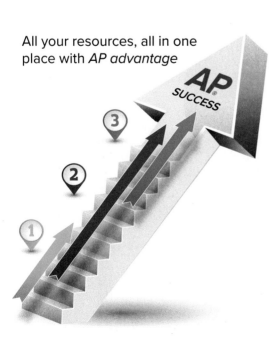

① ONboard

AP Course Prep

- Self-paced, diagnostic, interactive AP course prep
- Builds prerequisite skills and knowledge
- Great for first weeks of school assignments

② APcore

AP Course Resources

- Robust online platform that extends class instruction
- Interactive, engaging pedagogy tied to the text
- Powerful reporting tools and customizable content

③ SCOREboard

AP Test Prep

- Personalized, adaptive AP content review
- Complete, auto-graded AP practice exams
- Builds mastery and confidence for AP Exam success

Digital Resources for Students

Personalized, Adaptive, Dynamic

Language and Composition: The Art of Voice is enriched with resources including interactivities, reading and writing practice, and adaptive learning tools that enhance the teaching and learning experience both inside and outside of the classroom.

Authored by the world's leading subject matter experts, and organized by chapter level, the resources provide students with multiple opportunities to contextualize and apply their understanding. Teachers can save time, customize lessons, monitor student progress, and make data-driven decisions in the classroom with the flexible, easy-to-navigate instructional tools.

Intuitive Design

Resources are organized at the chapter level. To enhance core content, teachers can add assignments, activities, and instructional aids to any lesson. The chapter landing page gives students access to:

- Assigned activities
- Resources and assessments
- Interactive eBook
- Composition Essentials 3.0

Interactive Core Skill Development

The instructional chapters offer step-by-step online practice of the foundational skills vital to understanding and interacting with any form of communication. Each interactive instructional module includes four parts:

- Concept: The skill is introduced and explained.
- Model: An illustrative example demonstrates effective application.
- Practice: Independent application activities reinforce understanding.
- Assess: Measure students' depth of understanding and skill proficiency.

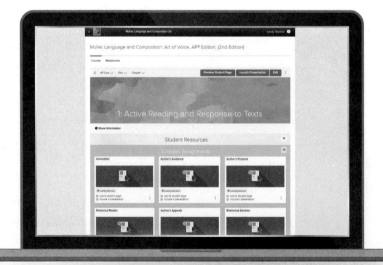

Skills Covered:

1 **Active Reading**
   - Annotation
   - Author's Audience
   - Author's Purpose
   - Appeals

   - Rhetorical Modes
   - Rhetorical Devices
   - Visual Analysis

2 **Writing Process**
   - Considering Purpose and Audience
   - Choosing an Appropriate Tone
   - Developing the Thesis
   - Writing Introductory Paragraphs

   - Writing Body Paragraphs
   - Writing End Paragraphs
   - Revising

3 **Argumentation and Synthesis**
   - Identify an Issue
   - Clarify Your Claim
   - Analyze Your Likely Readers
   - Establish Your Tone

   - Develop the Grounds for Your Claim
   - Refutation: Deal with Opposing Viewpoints
   - Critiquing Sources

Rhetorical Analysis and Assessment

Each major essay in Chapters 4-11 includes online rhetorical analysis, assessment, and additional content about the author to provide support and context that enable students to gain a deeper and broader understanding of why and when these essays were written and the reason they are important.

Digital Resources for Students *continued*

Composition Essentials 3.0

Composition Essentials 3.0 is included in the *AP advantage* suite of resources to support core skill mastery for developing writers. The results of a customizable diagnostic test create a personalized learning plan for each student that continually adapts as the student further engages with the content. Students have access to extensive resources to practice, apply, and assess their proficiency including: more than 4,500 exercises with feedback on grammar, punctuation, and usage; electronic peer review utilities; a database of sample student projects; tutorials on avoiding plagiarism, using document design, and understanding visual rhetoric; and more.

Contents

Teacher Resources

Teachers have access to the interactive eBook, adaptive *Composition Essentials 3.0*, plus a wealth of customizable chapter resources and powerful gradebook tools.

Teacher Manual, available in print and online, includes:

- Lesson plans and strategies for teaching close reading and writing skills, rhetorical analysis, synthesis, and argument
- Strategies for teaching individual essays
- Sample rhetorical analyses
- Answers to questions in the Student Edition
- Additional thought-provoking questions to ignite classroom discussion
- Comparative essay discussion formats
- Tips for pre-writing and guided writing activities
- Sample syllabus to help organize the course
- Pacing guides for 50-minute classes and 90-minute blocks

Additional digital resources to support instruction include:

- Student Performance reports help teachers identify gaps, make data-driven decisions, and adjust instruction
- Assignable interactive learning tools to support rhetorical analysis, developing an argument, and synthesizing
- Online assessments
- Customizable assignments— interactive activities and printouts

Harness technology, unlock success with the digital resources for this text.
Visit My.MHEducation.com

PART

1

CLOSE READING AND WRITING SKILLS

CHAPTERS AT A GLANCE

CHAPTER 1

Active Reading and Response to Texts

Welcome to Advanced Placement* English Language and Composition! Much of what you will learn here mirrors the readings and activities in a first-year college composition course. This textbook will help you read and write effectively, not only in academic settings, but in settings encompassing the workplace and beyond. Many reading and writing skills—such as the ability to analyze, critique, and synthesize information—are seemingly timeless. To gain a voice in this 21st-century Information Age, however, you also must know how to read and write several different kinds of texts in both print and electronic formats, and learn how to apply these skills in new and developing ways. Changes in technology and society itself are continuously transforming the way we read and respond to texts.

You read and write in numerous print and digital environments. In all likelihood, you are texting, tweeting, and blogging (or at least reading others' blogs); maintaining websites of your own; creating and uploading podcasts; sharing video clips on YouTube or audio files through peer-to-peer programs; and interacting in multiple formats on social networking sites. And you are probably making electronic presentations in the classroom while still using pen and paper to take notes or to create journal entries. So, as you can see, your literacy environment is far more complex than it was for previous generations.

* Advanced Placement Program and AP are registered trademarks of the College Board, which was not involved in the production of, and does not endorse, this product.

According to the National Council of Teachers of English, a literate person in the 21st century must be able to

- use the tools of technology,
- work with others to solve problems,
- design and share information with people from anywhere in the world for many purposes,
- manage multiple streams of information,
- create or evaluate multimedia texts, and
- make responsible, ethical choices based on this complex information.

As a 21st-century student, you are swimming in an ocean of information sources, and you will need to approach them with both focus and skills that go beyond casual reading—the type you may do for leisure or escapism. Even in non-English courses—computer science, mathematics, or biochemistry, for example—you are sure to find a healthy amount of reading that supplements other classroom or laboratory activities. And increasingly, the literacy universe that awaits you will require active engagement from you.

The reading and writing skills you develop this year will help you in your future profession (or professions). Consider, for example,

- a lawyer reviewing the legal history of a case or preparing a brief,
- a doctor reviewing current literature on medical innovations or writing a detailed progress report on a patient's recovery, or
- an environmental researcher reading and writing about issues pertaining to pollution and global warming.

All of these activities require the ability to think, read, and write about complex material. You must learn to read actively to see the difference between established facts versus pure speculation; rational arguments versus emotional ones; and organized essays versus structurally deficient ones.

The reading selections in this textbook have been chosen specifically to assist you in developing and sharpening such skills. As you tackle these pieces, you will realize that sound and engaged reading habits enable you to understand the fine points of logic, reasoning, analysis, argumentation, evaluation, and synthesis.

Reading Actively ("Close Reading")

Active reading suggests that you, as a reader, have an obligation to yourself and the author to bring an alert, responsive perspective to whatever you read. You are not an empty glass to be filled with the knowledge and opinions of the authors, but rather an active learner who can bring to bear your own reflections on what you read. Active reading means learning to annotate (a strategy discussed later in this chapter), to reflect on what you read, and to develop personal responses to prepare yourself for writing the essays your teacher assigns. This process is not merely an academic exercise; it is a skill that enriches you as a person throughout your life and career.

Active reading leads you to identify and understand the arguments present in our world today. Keep in mind that an "argument" does not mean the words are loud and volatile. Almost everything you read is an argument. When writers communicate their views with the goal of swaying or influencing the reader, they are writing arguments. Active reading also leads you to question—but not necessarily wholly reject—the statements of politicians; the promises of advertisements; or the speculations of teachers, philosophers, or scientists. As a result, active reading allows you to successfully participate in the national conversation, leading to responsible citizenship.

You can always find reasons to rationalize your failure to read actively and "closely." You are hungry. The material is boring. Your friends are discussing an interesting topic on social media. Fortunately, various techniques can guide you through this maze of distractions. Consider these five essential strategies to overcome the barriers to active reading:

1. **Develop an attitude of "active consciousness."** In other words, do not be passive, wholly-accepting, or completely hostile to the writer or the text. Instead, be actively engaged with the text as if you were in a conversation with the writer.

2. **Read attentively.** Give your full attention to the text in order to understand and respond to it. Take personal responsibility and work to understand what you are reading.

3. **Paraphrase.** Periodically restate in your own words what you have just read. Learn to process bits of key information. Keep a running inventory of key points. Take mental or actual notes on the text's main points. (More information on paraphrasing and summarizing appears later in this chapter and in Chapter 13.)

4. **Ask questions.** If for any reason you are uncertain about any aspect of the text, pose a question about it and try to answer it yourself. If you are unable to answer your question, seek help from an Internet search or a classmate, or ask for clarification from the teacher.

5. **Control your biases.** Recognize that you (and everyone else) have biases and prejudices—and then work to control and correct any prejudices that might interfere with your fair evaluation of the text's ideas. For example, you might have misgivings about a liberal or conservative writer. Strong emotions can affect your ability to keep an open mind and your power to think fairly about a subject or issue.

Questioning the Text

Posing key questions about a text (item 4 on the previous page) and then answering them to the best of your ability is a helpful means of not only reading actively, but of understanding an essay's substance and structure. Certain basic questions, like the ones listed below, are applicable for nearly any text you confront, and answering them for yourself can be a powerful means of enhancing your comprehension. As you read an essay, such questions help you spot the significant issues.

- What is the thesis (the main point or a statement set forth as a premise) of the text?
- What methods does the author use to support the main point—examples, descriptions, personal experience, or history, for instance? Does he or she cite authorities, studies, or statistics?
- What values does the author present? In other words, is the author directly or indirectly presenting her or his moral framework on an issue, or is she or he summarizing or describing an issue?
- Does the author use any special terms or expressions you need to define to understand the essay?
- Does the author use any terms or expressions in the essay that cause an emotional response from you?
- Who is the implied audience for the essay? Is it written for a specialized profession (such as scientists or educators)? Is it written for individuals with a focus on their particular role in society; for example, as parents or consumers or citizens?

Example: Questioning the Text

The essay that follows on pages 6-8, "From Ancient Greece to Iraq, the Power of Words in Wartime," by Robin Tolmach Lakoff, appeared in *The New York Times* on May 18, 2004. Read the essay and its annotations. Also consider and apply the questions above as you read the selection.

From Ancient Greece to Iraq, The Power of Words in Wartime

Robin Tolmach Lakoff

Robin Tolmach Lakoff is a <u>linguistics professor</u> at the University of California at Berkeley and the author of *The Language War*. This particular article appeared in *The New York Times* on <u>May 18, 2004</u>.

Is the author (professor) writing for college students? ▶

Who is the intended audience for this piece? (Who reads *The New York Times*?) ▶

What was happening in the United States in May 2004? ▶

Does paragraph 2 contain the thesis? ▶

"Social animals" in paragraph 3 gives me an uncomfortable mixed message. ▶

What does the author mean by "normal conditions" in paragraph 3? ▶

Is the first sentence in paragraph 5 the thesis, or is it related to the thesis? ▶

Look up this vocabulary: demeaning, etymologically, reclamation, derogatory, ethologist, connotation ▶

1   An American soldier refers to an Iraqi prisoner as "it." A general speaks not of "Iraqi fighters" but of "the enemy." A weapons manufacturer doesn't talk about people but about "targets."

2   <u>Bullets and bombs are not the only tools of war. Words, too, play their part.</u>

3   Human beings are <u>social animals</u>, genetically hard-wired to feel compassion toward others. Under <u>normal conditions</u>, most people find it very difficult to kill.

4   But in war, military recruits must be persuaded that killing other people is not only acceptable but even honorable.

5   <u>The language of war is intended to bring about that change, and not only for soldiers in the field.</u> In wartime, language must be created to enable combatants and noncombatants alike to see the other side as killable, to overcome the innate queasiness over the taking of human life. Soldiers, and those who remain at home, learn to call their enemies by names that make them seem not quite human—inferior, contemptible and not like "us."

6   The specific words change from culture to culture and war to war. The names need not be obviously **demeaning**. Just the fact that we can name them gives us a sense of superiority and control. If, in addition, we give them nicknames, we can see them as smaller, weaker and childlike—not worth taking seriously as fully human.

7   The Greeks and Romans referred to everyone else as "barbarians"—**etymologically** those who only babble, only go "bar-bar." During the American Revolution, the British called the colonists "Yankees," a term with a history that is still in dispute. While the British intended it disparagingly, the Americans, in perhaps the first

historical instance of **reclamation**, made the word their own and gave it a positive spin, turning the derisive song "Yankee Doodle" into our first, if unofficial, national anthem.

8   In World War I, the British gave the Germans the nickname "Jerries," from the first syllable of German. In World War II, Americans referred to the Japanese as "Japs."

9   The names may refer to real or imagined cultural and physical differences that emphasize the ridiculous or the repugnant. So in various wars, the British called the French "Frogs." Germans have been called "Krauts," a reference to weird and smelly food. The Vietnamese were called "slopes" and "slants." The Koreans were referred to simply as "gooks."

10   The war in Iraq has added new examples. Some American soldiers refer to the Iraqis as "hadjis," used in a **derogatory** way, apparently unaware that the word, which comes from the Arabic term for a pilgrimage to Mecca, is used as a term of respect for older Muslim men.

11   The Austrian **ethologist** <u>Konrad Lorenz</u> suggested that the more clearly we see other members of our own species as individuals, the harder we find it to kill them.

◄ Does Konrad Lorenz make a valid point in supporting the author's claim? Look up Lorenz's background.

12   So some terms of war are collective nouns, encouraging us to see the enemy as an <u>undifferentiated mass</u>, rather than as individuals capable of suffering. Crusaders called their enemy "the Saracen," and in World War I, the British called Germans "the Hun."

◄ Not sure I understand what the author means here. Are we supposed to view the enemy as both different from us AND as an "undifferentiated mass"?

13   American soldiers are trained to call those they are fighting against "the enemy." It is easier to kill an enemy than an Iraqi.

14   The word "enemy" itself provides the facelessness of a collective noun. Its non-specificity also has a fear-inducing **connotation**; enemy means simply "those we are fighting," without reference to their identity.

15   The terrors and uncertainties of war make learning this kind of language especially compelling for soldiers on the front. But civilians back home also need to believe that what their country is doing is just and necessary, and that the killing they are supporting is in some way different from the killing in civilian life that is rightly punished by the criminal justice system. <u>The use of the language developed for military purposes by civilians reassures them that war is not murder.</u>

◄ Is this sentence in paragraph 15 an exaggeration? How does the author know?

16   The linguistic habits that soldiers must absorb in order to fight make atrocities like those at <u>Abu Ghraib</u> virtually inevitable. The same language that creates a

◄ What actually happened at Abu Ghraib? Where is it located?

psychological chasm between "us" and "them" and enables American troops to kill in battle, makes enemy soldiers fit subjects for torture and humiliation. <u>The reasoning is: They are not really human, so they will not feel the pain.</u>

17   Once language draws that line, all kinds of mistreatment become imaginable, and then justifiable. To make the abuses at Abu Ghraib unthinkable, we would have to abolish war itself.

How did the author come to this reasoning in paragraph 16? Isn't torture meant to cause pain? ▶

Comprehension

1. Assume that the major question raised by Lakoff's essay is "How is language a tool of war?" Summarize her answer, which is the main point. HINT: Her point in this essay is NOT "we can or should abolish war," as even the author likely does not believe this.

2. Evidence typically consists of direct observations (verifiable facts) combined with the writer's interpretation of those observations to establish the main point. What types of evidence does Lakoff use? Distinguish her observations from her interpretations.

Rhetorical Analysis

3. What is the tone of the essay? What can you infer from this tone about Lakoff's emotional relationship to language used in wartime?

4. How does Lakoff's diction—the words she herself uses rather than the authors she quotes—contribute to her tone?

Writing

5. Research what the term *collective noun* means. Identify examples of nouns that are and are not collective. Synthesize from these sources your own definitions of *collective noun* and *non-collective noun*.

6. **Writing an Argument**   Argue for or against the proposition from paragraph 11: Is it always true that people find it hard to kill other people they know well?

Preparing to Read

This textbook contains essays covering a variety of subjects by writers from a wealth of backgrounds, cultures, and historical periods. All, however, have something to say and a way of saying it that others have found significant. Many have stood the test of time, whether a year, a decade, or centuries. The finest essays have staying power. As Ezra Pound said, "Literature is news that stays news," and great essays convey this sense of permanent value.

When you are given a reading assignment from the textbook, a good reading preparation strategy is to understand who wrote the essay, when and where he or she wrote it, and why he or she wrote it. The *who, when, where,* and *why* behind any text is the **context**. You can gather such information by reading the brief biographical notes that precede each essay. Study the authors' personal and educational backgrounds, their beliefs and credos, and some of the significant moments of their lives. You often will find logical connections between writers' lives and the topics they have written about.

Focus on the title of the essay. What can you infer from the title? How long is the essay? Although you may delight at the thought of reading shorter rather than longer texts, you may find this variable is not always the deciding factor in determining how easily you "get through" the essay. Short essays can be intricate and difficult; long ones can be simpler and more transparent. A long essay on a topic that interests and engages you may be more rewarding than a shorter essay you find irrelevant.

Other basic prereading activities include a quick scan of the text, noting whether section breaks exist in the essay, whether subheadings are included, and whether the author has used references such as footnotes. Other preliminary questions could be: What is the date of the original publication of the essay? In what medium was it originally published? Is the essay a fully contained work, or is it an excerpt from a larger text? Are visual aids included, such as graphs, charts, diagrams, or lists?

Because authors often use typographical signals to highlight or to help organize what they have written, you might ask: Does the author use quotation marks to signal certain words? Are italics used, and if so, what are their purpose? Are other books and authors cited in the essay? Does the author use organizational tools such as Arabic or Roman numerals? After you have answered these questions regarding mechanics, you will be prepared to deal more substantively with the essay as a unit of meaning and communication.

Preparing to read also means tapping into your own background knowledge. Often we do not realize how much we know about a topic until we actively respond to what others introduce in their writings. By tackling the reading assignments in the text, you will not only learn new information, but will also find that reading frees your ability to express your opinions. For this reason, most English teachers look upon reading as a two-way process: an exchange between writer and reader. Although the credentials and experiences of a professional writer may seem impressive, they should not deter you from considering your own talents as you read. But first, you must find a way to harness those abilities.

The following is a summary for reading and responding to texts actively.

▶ *Who* is the author? Look for connections about his or her life experiences and the topic of the piece. (*Headnotes*, or author introductions that appear at the start of the essays in this book, provide some of this information.) If there is more than one author, what is the personal or professional relationship between these writers?

▶ Note *when* the selection first appeared. How is that significant?

▶ Note *where* the selection first appeared. (This information often appears at the end of the selection in the *copyright* line.) What do you know about this publication? Is the text an entire selection, an excerpt, or part of a chapter? What difference might that make to you, the reader?

▶ What is significant about the title? Does the title present the author's general subject in a straightforward way, hint at the topic, or create a sense of mystery, irony, or humor?

▶ Determine the author's purpose *(why)*: to entertain; to evoke emotion or provoke action; to promote, teach, or investigate an idea; or some combination of these.

▶ How does the author organize the essay? What constitutes the introductory section, the body or middle of the essay, and the conclusion? Do subdivisions or numbered sections exist, and how are they linked logically? Do there appear to be any missing links?

▶ What is the author's main point, or the stated or implied answer to whatever question the essay poses or explores? The author may state the main point (also termed a *thesis* or *claim*) clearly and concisely in the introduction, place it elsewhere in the text, permit it to evolve slowly, or require you to infer it after reading the entire essay.

▶ Determine how well other assertions or narratives in the essay support the main point. What evidence does the author use? Does sufficient information or evidence support the main point?

▶ Visualize the author's original readers or "audience," and notice how the author adjusts both the argument and the elements of *style*—language, sentence structure, and complexity of thought—to this audience.

▶ Become conscious of how your personal experience affects your response to the author's ideas. Everyone approaches reading with a set of assumptions and biases. How do your own assumptions and biases influence your response?

Annotating and Note Taking

It should be evident by now that you should not just passively absorb whatever information an author conveys. Instead, you should feel comfortable with engaging the author as you might a friend in a lively conversation or argument. And just as a talk with a friend involves active listening, rebuttal, and the use of facts and logic, the interaction between yourself and an author needs to be dynamic as well.

Interacting with a text is so important in the learning process that a well-known American philosopher and intellectual, Mortimer Adler, wrote an essay that has become a classic on this topic: "How to Read a Book." Like most of the essays in this book, the essay that follows contains a headnote providing information about the author and is followed by questions for response and writing.

How to Read a Book

Mortimer J. Adler and Charles Van Doren

Mortimer Jerome Adler (1902–2001) was born in New York City and received his Ph.D. from Columbia University in 1928. A staunch advocate for classical philosophy, Adler believed that there are unshakable truths—an idea rejected by most contemporary philosophers. Many of his more than 75 books attempt to edify the general reader by explaining basic philosophical concepts in everyday language. He was also chairman of the editorial board of the *Encyclopaedia Britannica*. This excerpt from "How to Read a Book" is typical of his didactic, pragmatic approach to education. **Charles Van Doren** (1926–), Columbia University English instructor and son of a prize-winning poet, is best known for his participation in the NBC television network's 1950s trivia quiz show *Twenty One* where, in the winter of 1956–1957, he claimed a final victory over Herb Stempel with millions of viewers watching. Van Doren parlayed his fame into a job as a cultural correspondent for the network's *Today* show. Ultimately, the show *Twenty One* proved to be a scam with Van Doren and Stempel being exposed as willing participants. Van Doren has spent his later years quietly writing a variety of texts.

1   If you have the habit of asking a book questions as you read, you are a better reader than if you do not. But . . . merely asking questions is not enough. You have to try to answer them. And although that could be done, theoretically, in your mind only, it is much easier to do it with a pencil in your hand. The pencil then becomes the sign of your alertness while you read.

2   It is an old saying that you have to read "between the lines" to get the most out of anything. The rules of reading are a formal way of saying this. But we want to persuade you to "write between the lines," too. Unless you do, you are not likely to do the most efficient kind of reading.

3   When you buy a book, you establish a property right in it, just as you do in clothes and furniture when you buy and pay for them. But the act of purchase is

actually only the prelude to possession in the case of a book. Full ownership of a book only comes when you have made it a part of yourself, and the best way to make yourself a part of it—which comes to the same thing—is by writing in it.

4   Why is marking up a book indispensable to reading it? First, it keeps you awake—not merely conscious, but wide awake. Second, reading, if it is active, is thinking, and thinking tends to express itself in words, spoken or written. The person who says he knows what he thinks but cannot express it usually does not know what he thinks. Third, writing your reactions down helps you to remember the thoughts of the author.

5   Reading a book should be a conversation between you and the author. Presumably he knows more about the subject than you do; if not, you probably should not be bothering with his book. But understanding is a two-way operation; the learner has to question himself and question the teacher. He even has to be willing to argue with the teacher, once he understands what the teacher is saying. Marking a book is literally an expression of your differences or your agreements with the author. It is the highest respect you can pay him.

6   There are all kinds of devices for marking a book intelligently and fruitfully. Here are some devices that can be used:

   1. UNDERLINING—of major points, of important or forceful statements.
   2. VERTICAL LINES AT THE MARGIN—to emphasize a statement already underlined or to point to a passage too long to be underlined.
   3. STAR, ASTERISK, OR OTHER DOO-DAD AT TIIE MARGIN—to be used sparingly, to emphasize the ten or dozen most important statements or passages in the book. You may want to fold a corner of each page on which you make such marks or place a slip of paper between the pages. In either case, you will be able to take the book off the shelf at any time and, by opening it to the indicated page, refresh your recollection.
   4. NUMBERS IN THE MARGIN—to indicate a sequence of points made by the author in developing an argument.
   5. NUMBERS OF OTHER PAGES IN THE MARGIN—to indicate where else in the book the author makes the same points, or points relevant to or in contradiction of those here marked; to tie up the ideas in a book, which, though they may be separated by many pages, belong together. Many readers use the symbol "Cf" to indicate the other page numbers; it means "compare" or "refer to."
   6. CIRCLING OF KEY WORDS OR PHRASES—This serves much the same function as underlining.
   7. WRITING IN THE MARGIN, OR AT THE TOP OR BOTTOM OF THE PAGE—to record questions (and perhaps answers) which a passage raises in your mind; to reduce a complicated discussion to a simple statement; to record the sequence of major points right through the book. The end-papers at the back of the book can be used to make a personal index of the author's points in the order of their appearance.

7   To inveterate book-markers, the front endpapers are often the most important. Some people reserve them for a fancy bookplate. But that expresses only their financial ownership of the book. The front endpapers are better reserved for a record of your thinking. After finishing the book and making your personal index

on the back endpapers, turn to the front and try to outline the book, not page by page or point by point (you have already done that at the back), but as an integrated structure, with a basic outline and an order of parts. That outline will be the measure of your understanding of the work; unlike a bookplate, it will express your intellectual ownership of the book.

Comprehension

1. Summarize what Adler means by "marking up a book."

2. In your own words, explain how you believe Adler would define the phrase "reading a book" in our modern age.

3. What does Adler suggest the reader use the front and back endpapers for?

Rhetorical Analysis

4. What is the tone of the essay? What can you infer from this tone about Adler's emotional relationship to books?

5. Paragraph 6 lists devices for marking a book. What if Adler had written the list in paragraph form rather than numbering them? What if he had listed them with bullets? Would the tone have changed? Would your perception have changed? Why?

6. Study the rhetorical format of paragraph 4. What strategy is Adler employing?

7. Adler uses the analogy that "reading a book should be a conversation between you and the author." What other analogies can you find in the essay?

Writing

8. Photocopy and mark up Adler's piece in the same manner he recommends that you mark up any good piece of writing. Then write a process analysis essay to summarize the various methods you used.

9. Compare and contrast two books: one that Adler would regard as "light reading" and one he would regard as worthy of marking up. Indicate the primary differences between these books in terms of their diction, level of discourse, insight, purpose, and scholarship.

10. **Writing an Argument**   Argue for or against the proposition that Adler's essay has lost its relevance owing to the introduction of new forms of educational media such as electronic media.

Annotating

In many ways, annotating is "talking" to the text. As Adler discussed in his essay, annotating refers to marking the text with notes about content or personal reactions, and with symbols such as question marks and exclamation points. Annotating is not merely underlining or highlighting, however. Those markings alone often serve little purpose in helping you comprehend a text. Most likely, when you return to passages you have underlined or highlighted, you will have forgotten why you felt they were important. If you do underline or highlight, be sure to link these markings with a note in the margin. Learning is best accomplished by restating ideas in your own words. An example of an annotated essay is found on page 26.

If you are not given permission to mark this textbook, mark up a photocopy of the essay being analyzed instead. Or attach sticky notes to the textbook pages, and write your annotations on those. A third option is to use the eBook version of the textbook, which has highlighting capabilities. A fourth option is to copy and paste an essay from the eBook into a new document. Then turn on "Track Changes" or click "New Comment" in your word-processing program, and use these features to annotate the article electronically.

Taking Notes

To fully comprehend many of the essays in this book, or to respond to them in depth, take notes to supplement your annotations, just as you might take notes during a classroom lecture. You may wish, for example, to type key excerpts from an essay into one document so you can see critical quotations together. Or you may opt to summarize the essay by outlining its key points—a reversal of the process you would use to develop your own essay, wherein you begin with an outline and expand it into paragraphs. By collapsing an essay into an outline, you have a handy reference of the author's thesis and supporting points, and the methods used to develop them. Another function of note taking is overcoming the belief that you will remember ideas without jotting them down, only to find out later that you cannot recall significant information from memory. You will appreciate the benefits of taking notes when you tackle lengthy essays, which may run 15 or 20 pages.

The Art of Rhetorical Analysis

Rhetoric is the art of discourse, or communication—both speaking and writing. In AP English Language and Composition, you will learn and apply rhetorical skills in your own essays. You will also learn how to conduct rhetorical analysis. This occurs when you analyze the writing or speech of *someone else*.

You might have heard someone refer to a politician's words as "rhetoric," or worse yet "empty rhetoric." When people refer to *rhetoric* in this way, they imply a negative connotation—that the speaker is spouting meaningless words. In its true sense, however, "rhetoric" refers to the methods a writer or speaker uses to persuade a reader or audience.

Aristotle and the Rhetorical Triangle

The study of rhetoric is not new. The Greek philosopher Aristotle lived from 384 B.C. to 322 B.C. His book, often referred to as *The Art of Rhetoric,* is considered the foundation for all studies of rhetoric and persuasion. Aristotle stated that in any rhetorical situation–that is, in any argument–three elements are in constant communication with one another: the writer (or speaker), the subject (or topic), and the reader (or audience). We refer to these elements as the rhetorical triangle—see the "points" of the triangle below.

Simply put, when an author writes, she must consider the subject of the piece and make sure she is presenting that topic in the most persuasive light. At the same time, she must know her audience and how to appeal to it. Similarly, the audience is interpreting the writer's words as well as interacting with the topic, either because they are being persuaded or because they are rejecting the writer's arguments.

Aristotelian or Rhetorical Triangle

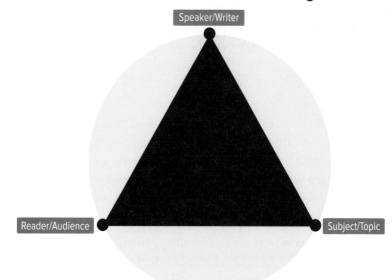

An essayist attempts to communicate a message to his or her audience. This message includes the **exigence**—the issue or situation that prompted the writer to write now—and the content. But "message making" is a process—the exchange of information and ideas through verbal or visual symbols. Your goal in reading actively is to understand not just the informational content of a text but also the author's perception of the audience, the author's purpose for writing, and how the author presents words and uses sentence structure to create meaning and influence your beliefs and behavior. A good writer, to paraphrase Plato in *Phaedrus*, tries to "enchant" your mind.

Author's Perception of Audience

Understanding an author's perception of his or her audience can aid the reader by providing context. As you learned earlier, one prereading step is to gain clues to the author's perception by learning about his or her background. But you also want to understand whom the writer wants to impact with the message. Is the writer attempting to influence an individual, a particular group, or the public at large? What an author says and how he or she says it depends on whom the author perceives will be receiving the message—the intended audience.

Writing intended for a specific person may be more personal in nature, and usually includes information that tackles a narrow subject. Examples include a letter to the principal asking for changes to the dress code, a request to the president of a corporation, or a complaint to the mayor.

Writing for a specific group will be broad enough to interest all members of the group but specific enough to give the audience the information they need. Examples include an article for high school seniors heading off to college, a newsletter for employees at a specific corporation, or an instruction manual for users of a particular product.

The third type of audience is the general public. This audience can be the most difficult to address. The language, information, and subject matter must be widely accessible. Examples include newspapers, bestselling novels, and popular magazines.

Author's Purpose

As you read an essay (or any text, including blogs and tweets), you should consider the author's *purpose* for writing. In most basic terms, the purpose is the writer's reason for writing. Identifying the purpose can be as easy as asking a simple question: What does the writer hope to accomplish? To answer this question, you need to know information about the speaker, the subject, and the audience—the three points of Aristotle's rhetorical triangle.

These are the more common purposes for writing: to inform, to instruct, to persuade, to disprove, to describe, to narrate, to demonstrate, to compare and contrast, to seek a solution to a problem, to explain a process, to classify, to define, to warn, to evaluate, to entertain, and to summarize. Although most essays contain a variety of purposes, often one will stand out among the others.

Look for indicators of purpose. Sometimes authors will state their purposes outright. An author of a geography textbook might write this sentence: "The purpose of this section is to explain what sunspots are." The purpose of this writing is obviously to *inform* the audience about sunspots. Another purpose is to *instruct*: "There are several things you can do to reduce your carbon footprint." When a writer wants to instruct the reader, he or she gives directions or a set of steps to follow.

Suppose a citizen sent the following email to her state senator: "I urge you to vote against the proposed change in the tax bill." This writer's purpose is to *persuade* the senator to vote against a particular action. An author of a short story, features column, or blog may write something like this: "Although I didn't think it was very funny at the time, I now look back and laugh when I recall the Thanksgiving turkey catching on fire." This passage hopes to *entertain* the audience with a funny story.

Author's Presentation

Be mindful of an author's tone or attitude as you read an essay. This awareness is as important as the content itself. In fact, tone communicates as clearly as words do. The tone depends on the author's purpose and audience, and it is created by using presentation tools—or rhetorical tools—which include *appeals, modes,* and *devices.* As mentioned earlier, these are the tools good writers use to "enchant" the reader.

Appeals

Aristotle claims that when a speaker delivers an argument, he or she must *appeal* to audience members in a way that will persuade them. Aristotle identifies three types of appeals, which he calls *ethos, pathos,* and *logos.*

ETHOS   Aristotle's first appeal, **ethos**, is defined as an ethical appeal. When an author employs ethos, he or she is giving the audience a reason to trust. In a sense, he is asking the audience to have faith in his message because he is an honorable and ethical individual. In President Dwight D. Eisenhower's farewell address, for example, he warns against the increasing collusion between the U.S. military and industrial leaders. Eisenhower uses ethos to sway the audience to agree with him on the basis of his credibility and character.

> Three days from now, after half a century in the service of our country, I shall lay down the responsibilities of office as, in traditional and solemn ceremony, the authority of the Presidency is vested in my successor. . . . In the councils of government, we must guard against the acquisition of unwarranted influence, whether sought or unsought, by the military-industrial complex. The potential for the disastrous rise of misplaced power exists and will persist. We must never let the weight of this combination endanger our liberties or democratic processes.

Farewell Address by President Dwight D. Eisenhower, January 17, 1961. www.ourdocuments.gov

PATHOS   The second of Aristotle's appeals is **pathos**, or an appeal to emotion. Some have said that pathos is an appeal to "motherhood and apple pie." What they mean is that pathos asks us to feel patriotic, or to empathize with a certain position.

Appeals to pathos must be done carefully. For pathos to be effective, it must have *gravitas*—seriousness or dignity. A deep universal truth, such as freedom or equality, must be attached to the argument. In the following excerpt, Thomas Paine uses pathos to persuade American colonists to fight for independence from British rule:

> [T]he harder the conflict, the more glorious the triumph. . . . I call not upon a few, but upon all: not on *this* state or *that* state, but on *every* state; up and help us; lay your shoulders to the wheel; better to have too much force than too little, when so great an object is at stake.
>
> "The Crisis" in *The Writings of Thomas Paine.* Collected and edited by Moncure Daniel Conway. Vol. I, 1774-1779. G.P. Putnam's Sons, ©1894

LOGOS   Aristotle's final appeal is to **logos**, or logic. When writers or speakers use numbers or facts to back up their argument, they are appealing to *logos*. In many ways, this is considered the purest appeal. It does not rely on the audience to make a value judgment as to whether the speaker is ethical—as with ethos. Nor is the audience looking at whether the speaker has established sufficient *gravitas* for the argument—as with pathos. Instead, logos simply provides the facts. In the following passage, the writer supports her argument with facts from a government source.

> Driver training must be revised to include a demonstration that reveals the dangers of texting while driving. The National Highway Traffic Safety Administration reports that, due to distracted driving, 9 people are killed and more than 1,000 are injured every day* in the United States.
>
> *Source: Centers for Disease Control and Prevention

Many if not most writers use all three types of appeals in their works. You will learn more about appeals in Chapter 3.

Rhetorical Modes

The patterns of writing that help writers develop their ideas are called **rhetorical modes**. Rhetorical modes are linked to the writer's purpose for writing. Some common rhetorical modes include:

- Narration
- Description
- Definition
- Classification
- Process Analysis
- Exemplification
- Cause and Effect
- Comparison and Contrast
- Persuasion/Argumentation

If an author wants to narrate a plot or tell a story, she would write a narrative. If an author wants to explain what caused a result—such as actions that led to the

Civil War—the rhetorical mode of cause and effect would be used. To present a process such as constructing a birdhouse or decorating a cake, an author would write a process analysis. Suppose you want to write about different models of e-readers. You would use the rhetorical mode of exemplification.

Although you may not think of essays in terms of genre as you do literature (poetry, short fiction, drama), the mode used can help you understand the motivation behind a writer's work and to seek out significant passages. If the essay is written using the rhetorical mode of persuasion or argumentation, for example, you should focus on the supporting points the author has provided, determining whether they offer adequate support for the author's point of view. In an essay arguing for the return to traditional family values, for instance, the use of one anecdote to prove a point would probably not be enough to persuade most readers. You will learn more about rhetorical modes, or patterns of writing, in Chapter 2.

Rhetorical Devices

In addition to appeals and varied modes of writing, successful writers use **rhetorical devices** to create tone and add depth or layers of meaning to their writing. In short, rhetorical devices are the tools necessary to differentiate truly good writing from mediocre writing. They make the text interesting. Rhetorical devices include word choice, syntax, figurative language, and other stylistic features. For example, how an author chooses to punctuate a certain text can alter the meaning. Read this sentence: "Rachael Ray finds inspiration in cooking, her family, and her dog." Notice how using variations in punctuation changes the meaning: "Rachael Ray finds inspiration in cooking her family and her dog."

Sentence fragments, usually frowned upon, can actually be stylistic choices. A sentence fragment could be used to: (1) create a sense of immediacy; (2) create pictures that stand out in a reader's mind; (3) convey the pacing of an action—to speed up or slow down the story; and (4) make readers pay more attention to certain details that are significant. As long as fragments are used for a purpose and as intentional rhetorical devices, there is no reason to see them as wrong.

Here are several other common rhetorical devices:

ALLUSION An **allusion** is a literary, biographical, or historical reference, whether real or imaginary. Writers and speakers use allusions to connect their words to larger symbols or global issues, and to stir emotions in the reader. Writers also use allusions to illuminate an idea by using a creative, useful comparison. There are many sources of allusions. Some of the most common are the Bible, famous historical events or persons, mythology, classic pieces of literature and art, and even popular culture. For an allusion to be effective, it must be common enough for the audience to know it.

In the excerpt that follows, the author compares preparing to win a chess match to preparing for success in life. He mentions "Sisyphean task," which is an allusion to Sisyphus, a cruel king in Greek mythology who was forced to eternally roll a huge boulder up a hill, only to have it always roll back down upon reaching the top.

It begins with intense preparation, which requires that you motivate yourself to work long, grueling, lonely hours. It often feels like a Sisyphean task, since you know that perhaps only ten percent of your analysis will ever see the light of day.

How Life Imitates Chess by Garry Kasparov. Bloomsbury Publishing USA, © 2007/2008 by Garry Kasparov

ALLITERATION **Alliteration** is the repetition of the same sounds in neighboring words or stressed syllables. This creates sound awareness and a cadence. Alliteration can take many poetic forms. Read the passage below from Eudora Welty. Notice how repetition of the *s* sound in the second sentence resonates with you, the reader.

Ever since I was first read to, then started reading to myself, there has never been a line read that I didn't *hear*. As my eyes followed the sentence, a voice was saying it silently to me.

ONE WRITER'S BEGINNINGS by Eudora Welty, Cambridge, Mass.: Harvard University Press, Copyright © 1983, 1984 by Eudora Welty. Reprinted by the permission of Russell & Volkening as agents for the author. Copyright © 1983, 1984 by Eudora Welty.

ANALOGY An **analogy** shows the relationship of one thing to another thing. We often analyze an analogy by stating that Item A is related to Item B in the same manner as Item C is related to Item D. In the passage below, an analogy is made between students and oysters, as opposed to students and sausages.

Pupils are more like oysters than sausages. The job of teaching is not to stuff them and then seal them up, but to help them open and reveal the riches within. There are pearls in each of us, if only we knew how to cultivate them with ardor and persistence.

"What True Education Should Do" from ON THE CONTRARY by Sydney J. Harris. Boston: Houghton Mifflin Company, The Riverside Press Cambridge. Copyright © 1964 by Sydney J. Harris

DICTION **Diction,** or word choice, is a very conscious rhetorical device. When writers choose specific words, they are the defining the tone, or attitude, of their writing. Every word has two definitions: a *denotative* definition, which is its dictionary definition, and a *connotative* definition, which refers to the feelings associated with the word, or the ideas the word suggests beyond the literal meaning. Ask yourself why a writer chose *that* particular word to convey his or her meaning.

President Franklin D. Roosevelt spoke to Congress and the American people after Japan bombed Pearl Harbor, Hawaii, on December 7, 1941. In this closing portion of the speech, reflect on how the underlined word choices, or diction, affect you emotionally.

I believe that I interpret the will of the Congress and of the people when I <u>assert</u> that we will not only defend ourselves to the uttermost, but will make it very certain that this form of <u>treachery</u> shall never again <u>endanger</u> us. <u>Hostilities</u> exist. There is <u>no blinking</u> at the fact that our people, our territory, and our interests are in <u>grave</u> danger. With confidence in our armed forces, with the <u>unbounding</u> determination of our people, we will gain the <u>inevitable</u> <u>triumph</u>—so help us God.

Address by Franklin D. Roosevelt to Congress Asking That a State of War Be Declared Between the United States and Japan. December 8, 1941. www.loc.gov

HYPERBOLE   **Hyperbole** is an exaggeration, usually of great proportions, to set a tone. Pay attention to how the use of hyperbole creates meaning in the following excerpt.

A day was twenty-four hours long but seemed longer. There was no hurry, for there was nowhere to go, nothing to buy and no money to buy it with, nothing to see outside the boundaries of Maycomb County.

To Kill a Mockingbird by Harper Lee. Grand Central Publishing, Hachette Book Group, New York, NY. © 1960 by Harper Lee

The description is seen through the eyes of a young girl living in Maycomb County. Living in a small Alabama town is frustrating for her, but days do not last longer than twenty-four hours, nor is there really "nowhere to go."

IMAGERY   **Imagery** appeals to the five senses. Authors use imagery to help the reader see, feel, smell, hear, or taste something. Think about the mental images created when reading the following passage by American short story writer Washington Irving.

[Ichabod Crane] was tall, but exceedingly lank, with narrow shoulders, long arms and legs, hands that dangled a mile out of his sleeves, feet that might have served for shovels, and his whole frame most loosely hung together. His head was small, and flat at top, with huge ears, large green glassy eyes, and a long snipe nose, so that it looked like a weather-cock, perched upon his spindle neck, to tell which way the wind blew. To see him striding along the profile of a hill on a windy day, with his clothes bagging and fluttering about him, one might have mistaken him for the genius of famine descending upon the earth, or some scarecrow eloped from a cornfield.

"The Legend of Sleepy Hollow, and the Spectre Bridegroom" from *The "Sketch Book"* by Washington Irving. Philadelphia: J.B. Lippincott Company, © 1889

IRONY   Another rhetorical device to look for in your reading is **irony**. Irony can be seen when a contradiction occurs in action or in speech. There are different kinds of irony. In *verbal irony,* a person says one thing but means something else, often just the opposite. For example: "Just texting and checking email doesn't give drivers enough to do. Automakers would really help if they built videogames into the dashboard." The writer believes the opposite—that drivers should stop being distracted and focus only on driving. Irony is used to get across the true point.

Another type of irony is *situational irony,* in which an unforeseen reversal of events occurs, or something happens that is different from what the reader expects. Situational irony is found in O. Henry's short story "The Gift of the Magi": Della's greatest possession is her long hair. Jim's greatest possession is his father's watch.

Della cuts and sells her hair to purchase a gold chain for Jim's watch. He, in an ironic twist, sells his watch to purchase a jeweled comb for Della's hair.

JUXTAPOSITION   **Juxtaposition** is the placement of two words or ideas next to each other for emphasis or contrast. This famous quote by President John F. Kennedy uses juxtaposition: "Ask not what your country can do for you—ask what you can do for your country."

In the passage below, Charles Dickens uses juxtaposition to set the tone of uncertainty leading up to the French Revolution. In this excerpt, juxtaposition is enhanced by parallel structure (discussed on the next page). The two rhetorical devices often work together.

> It was the best of times, it was the worst of times, it was the age of wisdom, it was the age of foolishness, it was the epoch of belief, it was the epoch of incredulity, it was the season of Light, it was the season of Darkness, it was the spring of hope, it was the winter of despair, we had everything before us, we had nothing before us, we were all going direct to Heaven, we were all going direct the other way. . . .

A Tale of Two Cities by Charles Dickens. Leipzig: Bernhard Tauchnitz, © 1859

METAPHOR AND SIMILE   **Metaphors** compare two unlike things to help provide the reader with a mental image. Find the metaphor in this passage by President John F. Kennedy.

> To those new states whom we welcome to the ranks of the free, we pledge our word that one form of colonial control shall not have passed away merely to be replaced by a far more iron tyranny. We shall not always expect to find them supporting our view. But we shall always hope to find them strongly supporting their own freedom—and to remember that, in the past, those who foolishly sought power by riding the back of the tiger ended up inside.

Inaugural Address, John F. Kennedy, January 20, 1961. www.ourdocuments.gov

Kennedy compares dictatorships to a tiger. The metaphor is used to remind those who back or promote brutal regimes—represented by the tiger—that they often end up getting consumed by the regime.

A **simile** is a type of metaphor but uses the words *like* or *as* to make the comparison. In the excerpt below, George Orwell describes the result of using too many foreign terms, pretentious words, and long-winded phrases when writing. Notice how the simile in the excerpt provides imagery to help the reader see or feel something.

> A mass of Latin words falls upon the facts like soft snow, blurring the outline and covering up all the details.

"Politics and the English Language" from SHOOTING AN ELEPHANT AND OTHER ESSAYS by George Orwell. Copyright 1950 by Sonia Brownell Orwell. Copyright © renewed 1978 by Sonia Pitt-Rivers. Reprinted by permission of Houghton Mifflin Harcourt Publishing Company. All rights reserved. *Politics and the English Language* by George Orwell (Copyright © George Orwell, 1946). Reproduced by permission of Bill Hamilton as the Literary Executor of the Estate of the Late Sonia Brownell Orwell.

PARALLEL STRUCTURE   **Parallel structure** uses similar patterns of sentence structure. Ideas are presented in similar grammatical constructs. Authors use parallel structure either to compare and contrast or to list items. Analyze the parallel structure in William Jennings Bryan's "Cross of Gold" speech:

> We have petitioned, and our petitions have been scorned; we have entreated, and our entreaties have been disregarded; we have begged, and they have mocked when our calamity came. We beg no longer; we entreat no more; we petition no more. We defy them.

> William Jennings Bryan, Democratic National Convention, July 9, 1896. From *Harper's Encyclopedia of United States History.* Harper & Brothers Publishers, 1906.

PERSONIFICATION   Writers use **personification** to give inanimate objects human characteristics and abilities. In the passage below, Maya Angelou personifies the sun by giving it the ability to "speak."

> The depths had been icy and dark, but now a bright sun spoke to our souls.

> "Chapter 23" from I KNOW WHY THE CAGED BIRD SINGS by Maya Angelou, copyright © 1969 and renewed 1997 by Maya Angelou. Used by permission of Random House, an imprint and division of Penguin Random House LLC. All rights reserved. Reprinted by permission of Little Brown Book Group Limited.

REPETITION   **Repetition** occurs when authors repeat a remark to emphasize its importance. British Prime Minister Winston Churchill uses repetition in this famous speech to instill hope for citizens to defeat their enemies in World War II.

> We shall go on to the end, we shall fight in France, we shall fight on the seas and oceans, we shall fight with growing confidence and growing strength in the air, we shall defend our Island, whatever the cost may be, we shall fight on the beaches, we shall fight on the landing grounds, we shall fight in the fields and in the streets, we shall fight in the hills; we shall never surrender.

> Winston Churchill, 1940. www.winstonchurchill.org

SATIRE   **Satire** is used to ridicule people, policies, and institutions—not only to make us laugh but also to help us see our political and social follies. Its purpose is to point out flaws in humanity's foolishness and to bring about change. Jonathan Swift, the most famous satirist, pointed out that satire is like a glass "wherein beholders do generally discover everybody's face but their own."

Mark Twain, the king of American satire, satirizes the U.S. jury system here:

> We have a criminal jury system which is superior to any in the world; and its efficiency is only marred by the difficulty of finding twelve men every day who don't know anything and can't read.

> "After-Dinner Speech" from *Sketches New and Old* by Mark Twain. Harper & Brothers Publishers, © 1875

Twain is saying that the idea of an "impartial" jury—the foundation of fair trials—is superior. But he is criticizing the notion that to be truly impartial means the jurors have not read a newspaper or kept abreast of what's happening in the world—which makes the jurors uneducated. Twain wants the jury selection system to change so juries are made up of educated people who are influenced more by knowledge and true justice than by a lawyer's tactics.

SYMBOLISM   **Symbolism** uses concrete items to represent abstract ideas. For example, eagles are symbols of the American spirit. Doves are symbols of peace. Writers use symbols to creatively refer to foundational elements. In the proverb "The pen is mightier than the sword," the *pen* is a symbol for writing and free speech. The *sword* is a symbol for military action or violence.

In the following passage, President Barack Obama uses the term *anchor* to symbolize America as the foundation for strengthening democracy around the world.

> America will remain the anchor of strong alliances in every corner of the globe. And we will renew those institutions that extend our capacity to manage crisis abroad, for no one has a greater stake in a peaceful world than its most powerful nation.

Second Inaugural Address, Barack Obama, January 21, 2013. obamawhitehouse.archives.gov

SYNTAX   **Syntax** is simply the arrangement of words within a sentence. Sometimes an author will use a long sentence to show the logical aspect of a situation. In contrast, a writer can use a short sentence or fragment to make a strong statement or to show urgency. Sometimes the writer will purposely place the subject and the verb at the end of a sentence to build suspense.

In the passage below, Ralph Waldo Emerson tells teachers how they should educate their students. Notice how he changes the cadence from longer sentences to shorter sentences when he wants to stress a point.

> I believe that our own experience instructs us that the secret of Education lies in respecting the pupil. It is not for you to choose what he shall know, what he shall do. It is chosen and foreordained, and he only holds the key to his own secret. By your tampering and thwarting and too much governing he may be hindered from his end and kept out of his own. Respect the child. Wait and see the new product of Nature. Nature loves analogies, but not repetitions. Respect the child. Be not too much his parent. Trespass not on his solitude.

"Education" from *Lectures and Biographical Sketches* by Ralph Waldo Emerson. Boston: Houghton, Mifflin and Company, 1884

Using the Rhetorical Triangle

We can now expand the rhetorical triangle to include not just the "points" but the sides and interior as well. These are the elements you should look for when analyzing and annotating an essay.

Recall the three *points* of the rhetorical triangle. At the top of the triangle is the writer or speaker. In order to write, the writer needs something to discuss—a subject or topic. The writer must also be aware of who is going to read the work—the audience or reader. These three points are the First Triad of the triangle.

The three *sides* of the triangle are the Second Triad. To say something meaningful about a topic, a writer needs to have a point. Therefore, the writer develops an assertion, a thesis, or a main idea about the subject.

On the other side of the triangle, the writer needs to get the audience's attention—and keep it. To do so, the writer has to decide how best to appeal to the audience. The writer might establish an authoritative appeal through *ethos* by showing that he is credible and trustworthy. If the audience appears to be very rational and logical, the writer may choose to appeal with *logos*—using logic, facts, statistics, data, graphs, and charts. If the audience can be swayed by emotional appeals, the writer will consider using *pathos*.

At the bottom of the triangle, the writer needs to consider the context, which is the time, place, and occasion of the composition. Context provides a basis for understanding how the targeted audience is receiving the writer's message about this subject.

The *inner group* is the Third Triad. The author's tone is his or her attitude or feeling toward the subject. The rhetorical modes are the patterns and methods the writer uses to structure the writing—the purpose. Rhetorical devices are the tools the writer uses to create meaning and to deliver his or her message.

Aristotelian or Rhetorical Triangle

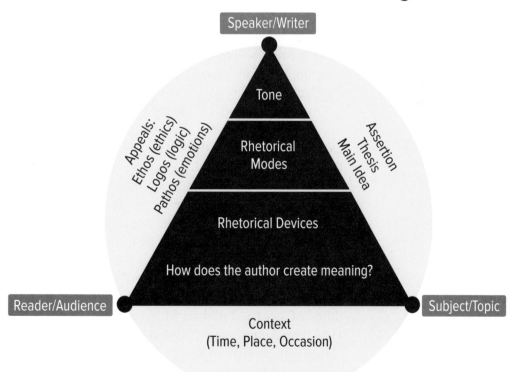

Example: Rhetorical Analysis

The following essay, "The Cult of Ethnicity," by the influential historian Arthur M. Schlesinger, Jr., has been "questioned" and annotated to demonstrate how a student might rhetorically analyze it. Schlesinger's essay also will be used to explain aspects of the reading and writing process as we move through the rest of this chapter and into Chapter 2.

The Cult of Ethnicity

Arthur M. Schlesinger, Jr.

The word *cult* in the title has a negative connotation, and by being associated with "ethnicity," we are given a clue to where Schlesinger is going with this essay: He believes promoting ethnicity is wrong.

1   The history of the world has been in great part the history of the mixing of peoples. Modern communication and transport accelerate mass migrations from one continent to another. Ethnic and racial diversity are more than ever a salient fact of the age.

2   But what happens when people of different origins, speaking different languages and professing different religions, inhabit the same locality and live under the same political sovereignty? Ethnic and racial conflict— far more than ideological conflict—is the explosive problem of our times.

This sentence in paragraph 2 is an appeal to pathos. *Conflict* and *explosive problems of our times* give urgency to the problem that belongs to all of us. This seems like the thesis. If so, where are the supports? Or is it the thesis?

3   On every side today ethnicity is breaking up nations. The Soviet Union, India, Yugoslavia, Ethiopia, are all in crisis. Ethnic tensions disturb and divide Sri Lanka, Burma, Indonesia, Iraq, Cyprus, Nigeria, Angola, Lebanon, Guyana, Trinidad—you name it. Even nations as stable and civilized as Britain and France, Belgium and Spain, face growing ethnic troubles. Is there any large multiethnic state that can be made to work?

Look up these countries listed in paragraph 3. The list of names is an appeal to logos. Demonstrates knowledge on the part of the author, an appeal to ethos.

4   The answer to that question has been, until recently, the United States. "No other nation," Margaret Thatcher has said, "has so successfully combined people of different races and nations within a single culture." How have Americans succeeded in pulling off this almost unprecedented trick?

What is the effect of this rhetorical question in paragraph 4?

5   We have always been a multiethnic country. Hector St. John de Crevecoeur, who came from France in the 18th century, marveled at the astonishing diversity of the settlers—"a mixture of English, Scotch, Irish, French,

Historical figure "Hector St. John de Crevecoeur"—who was he?

Dutch, Germans and Swedes . . . this promiscuous breed." He propounded a famous question: "What then is the American, this new man?" And he gave a famous answer: "Here individuals of all nations are melted into a new race of men." *E pluribus unum*.

6   The United States escaped the divisiveness of a multiethnic society by a brilliant solution: the creation of a brand-new national identity. The point of America was not to preserve old cultures but to forge a new, American culture. "By an intermixture with our people," President George Washington told Vice President John Adams, immigrants will "get assimilated to our customs, measures and laws: in a word, soon become one people." This was the ideal that a century later Israel Zangwill crystallized in the title of his popular 1908 play *The Melting Pot*. And no institution was more potent in molding Crevecoeur's "promiscuous breed" into Washington's "one people" than the American public school.

7   The new American nationality was inescapably English in language, ideas, and institutions. The pot did not melt everybody, not even all the white immigrants; deeply bred racism put black Americans, yellow Americans, red Americans and brown Americans well outside the pale. Still, the **infusion** of other **stocks**, even of nonwhite stocks, and the experience of the New World reconfigured the British legacy and made the United States, as we all know, a very different country from Britain.

8   In the 20th century, new immigration laws altered the composition of the American people, and a cult of ethnicity erupted both among non-Anglo whites and among nonwhite minorities. This had many healthy consequences. The American culture at last began to give shamefully overdue recognition to the achievements of groups subordinated and spurned during the high noon of Anglo dominance, and it began to acknowledge the great swirling world beyond Europe. Americans acquired a more complex and invigorating sense of their world—and of themselves.

9   But, pressed too far, the cult of ethnicity has unhealthy consequences. It gives rise, for example, to the conception of the United States as a nation composed not of individuals making their own choices but of **inviolable** ethnic and racial groups. It rejects the historic American goals of assimilation and integration.

◄ Imagery: individuals all melted into a new race. Latin phrase, meaning "out of many, one." Provides positive tone of enlightenment holding promise for the future.

◄ Is this just an American phenomenon? "creation of a brand-new national identity"

◄ What is this new American culture mentioned in paragraph 6? Does the author define it?

◄ Paragraph 6 highlights Schlesinger's credibility as a historian, an appeal to ethos.

◄ What is the definition of "melting pot" used in paragraph 6?

◄ Note Schlesinger's use of historical process analysis in paragraph 7

◄ Vocabulary to Check: **Infusion, stocks, inviolable, zeal, Eurocentric, apocalyptic, ferment, Kleagle, crucible**

◄ "shamefully" in paragraph 8 is an appeal to pathos

◄ Allusion to old western movies "high noon"

◄ Imagery: a swirling world that is shaking up one dominant culture

◄ "Pressed too far" signals a warning—danger. Provokes the emotion of fear

◄ Is this sentence in paragraph 9 the thesis?

Is this phrase in paragraph 10 ▶
related to the thesis?

Diction. Term "hullabaloo" ▶
ridicules multiculturalism and
political correctness

This sentence in paragraph 11 is ▶
supporting evidence against
multiculturalism.

Sentence beginning with ▶
"Europe—the unique source" is a
general statement—where are the
specific examples?

Diction. "Apocalyptic"—fears ▶
that minorities will suffer if schools
foster separatism

Is this sentence in paragraph 12 ▶
an exaggeration? How does
author know?

Author shifts from instilling ▶
fear to finding optimism in
paragraph 13

Alliteration—"eruption of ▶
ethnicity." What is the effect of
this alliteration?

Who are these people— ▶
"romantic ideologues"? Author
doesn't mention specific names

Reality is stronger than ▶
"ideology." Is this author's
"solution"?

"Children of the crucible" ▶
ties back to melting pot
mentioned at the beginning

10   And, in an excess of **zeal**, well-intentioned people seek to transform our system of education from a means of creating "one people" into a means of promoting, celebrating and perpetuating separate ethnic origins and identities. The balance is shifting from *unum* to *pluribus*.

11   That is the issue that lies behind the hullabaloo over "multiculturalism" and "political correctness," the attack on the "**Eurocentric**" curriculum and the rise of the notion that history and literature should be taught not as disciplines but as therapies whose function is to raise minority self-esteem. Group separatism crystallizes the differences, magnifies tensions, intensifies hostilities. Europe—the unique source of the liberating ideas of democracy, civil liberties and human rights—is portrayed as the root of all evil, and non-European cultures, their own many crimes deleted, are presented as the means of redemption.

12   I don't want to sound apocalyptic about these developments. Education is always in **ferment**, and a good thing too. The situation in our universities, I am confident, will soon right itself. But the impact of separatist pressures on our public schools is more troubling. If a **Kleagle** of the Ku Klux Klan wanted to use the schools to disable and handicap black Americans, he would hardly come up with anything more effective than the "Afrocentric" curriculum. And if separatist tendencies go unchecked, the result can only be the fragmentation, resegregation and tribalization of American life.

13   I remain optimistic. My impression is that the historic forces driving toward "one people" have not lost their power. The eruption of ethnicity is, I believe, a rather superficial enthusiasm stirred by romantic ideologues on the one hand and by unscrupulous con men on the other: self-appointed spokesmen whose claim to represent their minority groups is carelessly accepted by the media. Most American-born members of minority groups, white or nonwhite, see themselves primarily as Americans rather than primarily as members of one or another ethnic group. A notable indicator today is the rate of intermarriage across ethnic lines, across religious lines, even (increasingly) across racial lines. "We Americans," said Theodore Roosevelt, "are children of the crucible."

¹⁴ The growing diversity of the American population makes the quest for unifying ideals and a common culture all the more urgent. In a world savagely bereft by ethnic and racial antagonisms, the United States must continue as an example of how a highly differentiated society holds itself together.

▶ A sharp conclusion. Argument? United States must be example. This is the thesis.

SOAPSTone

Another way of remembering how to focus on a writer's words is to apply SOAPSTone, an acronym developed by the College Board for teaching rhetorical analysis. It stands for:

Speaker Who is speaking (narrating the essay)? What is his/her "occupation:" observer, participant, critic?

Occasion What is the occasion? Determine the context of the writing.

Audience Who is the intended audience for the essay?

Purpose What is the author's purpose in writing the essay?

Subject What is the general subject matter of the essay? (Summarize the essay in 15 words or less.)

Tone What is the tone of the essay? What specific rhetorical devices contribute to the tone?

Paraphrasing, Summarizing, Quoting

As you prepare to respond to the writing of others, you need to develop skills so your own writing will reflect the hard work that went into the reading process. To this end, you can benefit from learning some shortcuts that will assist you in garnering information about what you have read. These skills include paraphrasing, summarizing, and quoting directly.

Paraphrasing

Paraphrasing means taking what you have read and putting it in your own words. Students might initially feel it is a waste of time to paraphrase when the author's own words are the best way to articulate his or her ideas. Paraphrasing, however, serves two main purposes. The more obvious one is that it prevents you from plagiarizing, even inadvertently, what you have read. In terms of learning, it is particularly helpful because it requires you to digest what you have read and then rewrite it. As you do so, you will develop writing patterns that over time will improve your ability to communicate. Paraphrasing forces you to think about what you have read and reinforces what you have read. You may find that paraphrasing often leads you to challenge the text or think more deeply about it simply because the paraphrasing process requires that you fully comprehend what you read.

It is important while paraphrasing to retain all the essential information of the original while not using any of the author's original vocabulary or style. One rule to follow is to never use three or more words that appeared together in the original. However, you can keep words such as articles (*a, an, the*) and conjunctions (*and, for, but*).

The following are two examples of paraphrasing that demonstrate unsuccessful and successful application of the technique.

Original

> But, pressed too far, the cult of ethnicity has unhealthy consequences. It gives rise, for example, to the conception of the United States as a nation composed not of individuals making their own choices but of inviolable ethnic and racial groups. It rejects the historic American goals of assimilation and integration.

👎 Unsuccessful Paraphrase

> But, pressed too far, the focus on ethnicity has dangerous consequences. It suggests that the United States is a nation made up of separate ethnic and racial groups rather than individuals. It goes against the American ideals of integration and assimilation.

There are several problems in the unsuccessful paraphrase. Rather than changing key words, the writer has merely rearranged them. The sentence structure is very similar to that of the original, as is the ordering of ideas. If you incorporate this paraphrase into your own essay, the teacher would probably consider it a form of plagiarism. It is simply too close to the original. To truly paraphrase, you must substitute vocabulary, rearrange sentence structure, and change the length and order of sentences. These strategies are more evident in the successful paraphrase.

 Successful Paraphrase

> Our country is made up of both individuals and groups. The recent trend to focus on the idea that one's ethnic background should have a major influence on one's perspective as a citizen goes against the moral foundations of the United States. It is the very concept of accepting American culture as one's own that has made our country strong and relatively free from cultural conflict.

Summarizing

A summary is a short, cohesive paragraph or paragraphs that are faithful to the structure and meaning of the original essay, but developed in your own words and including only the most essential elements of the original. Summaries are particularly helpful when you are planning to write lengthy assignments that require you to compare two or more sources. Because a good summary requires you to use many of the skills of active reading, it helps you to "imprint" the rhetorical features and content of what you have read in your memory, and also provides you with a means of communicating the essence of the essay to another person or group.

To summarize successfully, you need to develop the ability to know what to leave out as much as what to include. As you review your source, the annotations and notes you made should help immensely. Since you want to work with only the essentials of the original, you must delete all unimportant details and redundancies. Unlike paraphrasing, however, most summaries require you to stick to the general order of ideas as they are presented in a text. They should not be mere retellings of what you have read, but should present the relationships among the ideas. It may be helpful to think of a summary as a news story—the essential details of what happened are presented in an orderly chronological fashion. Another strategy in summarizing is to imagine that the audience for which you are summarizing has not read the original. This places a strong responsibility on you to communicate the essentials of the text accurately.

The six steps on the next page should help you in preparing a summary. After you have reviewed the steps, read the summary that follows and consider whether it fulfills these suggestions.

1. Read the entire source at least twice and annotate it at least once before writing.
2. Write an opening sentence that states the author's thesis.
3. Explain the author's main supporting ideas, reviewing your notes to make sure you have included all of them. Be careful not to plagiarize, and use quotations only where appropriate.
4. Restate important concepts, key terms, main principles, and so on. Do not include your opinion or judge the essay in any way.
5. Present the ideas in the order in which they originally appeared. Note that in this sense summarizing is different from paraphrasing, in which staying too close to the original order of words may be detrimental to the process.
6. Review your summary after you complete it. Consider whether someone who has not read the original would find your summary sufficient to understand the essence of the original work. You may wish to have classmates or friends read the essay and share their verbal understanding of what you have written.

Now review the following summary of Schlesinger's essay and note how it adheres to the points listed above.

Sample Summary

Schlesinger argues that the surge of interest in ethnic separatism being hyped by some people for various ethnic groups threatens the unifying principle of our country's founders and undermines the strength of our society. This principle is that the American identity forged by its creators would be adopted by all peoples arriving here through a process of assimilation to our culture, values, and system of government so that cultural conflict could be avoided. Although he finds some merit in the idea that recognizing the contributions of certain groups who have been kept out of the national focus, for example, "nonwhite minorities," is a positive move, he fears this can be taken to an extreme. The result could be the development of antagonism between ethnic groups solely on the basis of overemphasizing differences rather than recognizing similarities. He further argues that efforts to fragment American culture into subgroups can have the effect of jeopardizing their own empowerment, the opposite of the movement's intention. He gives the example of "Afrocentric" schooling, which he claims could harm students enrolled in its curriculum. Despite this new interest in the "cult of ethnicity," the author is optimistic that its effects are limited. He claims that most Americans still strive toward unity and identify themselves as Americans first, and members of ethnic or racial groups second. He buttresses this belief by explaining that intermarriage is growing across racial, religious, and ethnic lines. This striving toward unity and identification with America among groups is particularly important today since their diversity is continuously increasing.

Quoting

Direct quotations often have a unique power because they capture the essence of an idea accurately and briefly. They are also stylistically powerful. When reading an essay, you may find a sentence worded so eloquently that you save it to use in a future writing assignment. Or you may wish to use direct quotations to demonstrate the effectiveness of an original essay or the authoritative voice of the author. It may be necessary to quote an author because her or his vocabulary simply cannot be changed without injuring the meaning of the original. Review the following quotations taken from the Schlesinger essay, and consider how paraphrasing them would diminish their rhetorical power.

Direct Quotations Reflecting the Conciseness of the Original

"The history of the world has been in great part the history of the mixing of peoples."

"On every side today ethnicity is breaking up nations."

"And if separatist tendencies go unchecked, the result can only be the fragmentation, resegregation and tribalization of American life."

Direct Quotations Having Particular Stylistic Strength

"The pot did not melt everybody."

"The balance is shifting from *unum* to *pluribus*."

Direct Quotations Establishing the Writer's Authority (Ethos)

"The point of America was not to preserve old cultures but to forge a new, American culture. 'By an intermixture with our people,' President George Washington told Vice President John Adams, immigrants will 'get assimilated to our customs, measures and laws: in a word, soon become one people.'"

"A notable indicator today is the rate of intermarriage across ethnic lines, across religious lines, even (increasingly) across racial lines."

Direct Quotation Demonstrating Conceptual Power

"The eruption of ethnicity, is, I believe, a rather superficial enthusiasm stirred by romantic ideologues on the one hand and by unscrupulous con men on the other."

Avoiding Plagiarism

It is your responsibility to present honest written work. When you employ summary, paraphrase, and quotation in an essay or a research paper, you must avoid **plagiarism**—the attempt to pass off the work of others as your own. The temptation to plagiarize is not only one of the oldest "crimes" in academia but also an unfortunate by-product of computers, for there are numerous opportunities for harried, enterprising, or—let's face it—dishonest students to download bits of information or entire texts and appropriate them without acknowledgment. At the same time, numerous websites and software programs allow teachers to locate even the most inventive forms of plagiarism—right down to words and phrases. When writing research papers, you may be required to attach all downloaded materials. Be warned: College instructors treat plagiarism as academic treason. If you plagiarize, you can fail a course, be suspended from college, and even be expelled.

Plagiarism is discussed again in Chapter 13, which presents information on writing research papers. For now, you can avoid plagiarism by following these basic rules:

- Cite (provide a reference for) all quoted, summarized, or paraphrased information in your paper, unless that information is commonly known or understood. (For example, you would not have to cite the information that George Washington was our first president, because it is common knowledge.)

- Cite all special phrases or unique stylistic expressions that you derive from another writer's work. You might love a phrase by one of the famous writers in this book—say, E. B. White or Maya Angelou—but that writer invented it, and it belongs to him or her. You cannot use it without acknowledging the source.

- Work hard to summarize and paraphrase material in your own words. Constantly check your language and sentence structure against the language and syntax in the source you are using. If your words and sentences are too close to the original, change them.

If you are in doubt about whether to cite a source, cite it. In addition, it is perfectly legitimate to ask your teacher or a tutor to look at your draft and render an opinion on any information you have summarized, paraphrased, or quoted.

Analyzing Visual Texts

We are immersed in a visual culture. This culture requires us to contend with and think actively about the constant flow of images encountered. In addition, courses in the humanities, fine arts, English, engineering, social science, computer science, media communications, and others require you to analyze and understand visual elements. Some visual elements—graphs, tables, and diagrams, for example—may be integral to an understanding of written texts. Other visuals—photographs, paintings, advertisements, graphic novels, political cartoons, and even graffiti—may function as instruments of persuasion, commentaries on current events, perspectives on the past, portals to psychological understandings, humor, and occasions for enjoyment.

Visual images convey messages that often are as powerful as well-composed written texts. Consider, for example, Eddie Adams's potent photograph of the execution of a prisoner by the notorious chief of the Saigon national police, General Nguyen Ngoc Loan (see Chapter 3, page 106). The chief of police aims his pistol at the head of the prisoner and presses the trigger. The viewer, in that captured instant, sees the jolt of the prisoner's head and a sudden spurt of blood. Reproduced widely in the American press in February 1968, Adams's image did as much as any written editorial to transform the national debate over the Vietnam War.

Questions to Guide Visual Analysis

Just as you analyze or parse a verbal text during the process of active reading, you also have to think actively about visual images or elements. In general, when you assess a visual, you are usually looking for three things:

1. **The purpose of the visual**—for example, to inform, instruct, persuade, entertain

2. **The context of the subject matter**—cultural ideas associated with people or items in the image

3. **The overall emotion conveyed by the image**—pride, attraction, revulsion, fear, amusement, and so on—and how that emotional effect is created (shapes, colors, textures, and symbols used; how lines, shapes, and colors focus attention in the image)

The following questions can guide your analysis of such visual texts as paintings, photographs, advertisements and propaganda, political cartoons, and charts and graphs:

- What are the design elements, format, and structure of the visual? Is it black and white, or are other colors used? How does the placement of design elements affect the message?

- Is the image abstract or realistic—or both? What is the relationship among the elements making up the image?

- Does the image have a historical or cultural context necessary to understand it?

- Who is the intended audience? Does the image call for a specific audience response?

- What textual information do you immediately notice? What is the relationship between image and text?

- What is the purpose of the visual? What emotions or attitudes does the image convey?
- What thesis or point of view does the information in the visual suggest?
- What is the nature of the evidence, and how can it be verified?
- What emphases and relationships do you detect among the visual details?

Paintings

Apply some of the questions listed to Johannes Vermeer's painting *The Love Letter*, which was created c. 1669–1670. *The Love Letter* shows a seated woman dressed in fine golden clothing. Her fur-lined jacket is a symbol of wealth. Vermeer is showing us how upper-class women in Amsterdam dressed. A servant girl has just walked into

The Love Letter (c. 1669–1670), Johannes Vermeer (1632–1675)
Rijksmuseum, Amsterdam

the room, set down her clothing basket, and handed a letter to the woman. There is a mood of expectation. The woman has stopped playing her lute and holds the letter but has not opened it. You know the letter is important by the expression on the woman's face. She looks inquiringly at the servant, as if she is nervous about opening the letter. At first, you fear that the letter holds bad news. Then you notice the servant girl is smiling. Do you think the letter holds bad news after all? Study the rest of the visual. Do you see the painting of a ship on the wall? Perhaps Vermeer used this as a clue that the person who wrote the letter is far away, or is coming home.

Notice how you, as the viewer, appear to be standing inside a closet looking out at the action. The doorway and the curtain serve as a frame for the two women. Light contrasts with dark. The painting would not be nearly as interesting if you weren't standing in the closet eavesdropping on a private moment.

The artist has used bright white and yellow textures to draw attention to the seated woman. The white tiles on the floor provide a visual path to the seated woman. Notice how your eye follows the direction of the woman's eyes, up along the line of the servant's bent arm, to the servant's face. The artist added these visual elements to direct your view.

What is the purpose of the painting? It does not seem to be a persuasive piece, urging you to take action or change your beliefs. Emotionally, the viewer might feel expectant—but not really a stronger emotion such as awe, anger, or patriotic. When viewing *The Love Letter*, are you supposed to learn that servants were mistreated during this time period? Apparently not. The woman and her servant appear to be friendly toward each other. Are you supposed to appreciate the vast wealth of the upper class? No, or the artist would not have included items in the painting that show typical daily life, such as the pair of shoes on the floor or the broom. This painting is just trying to tell a story and leave you guessing about who wrote the letter and its contents.

Migrant Mother (1936), Dorothea Lange (1895–1965) Library of Congress Prints and Photographs Division [LC-DIG-fsa-8b29516]

All the elements in this painting are similar to the rhetorical strategies used by an author in a narrative text. Every painting has a particular tone (an artist's attitude toward his or her subject), just as an essayist adopts a tone in his or her writing.

Photographs

Recall that the *who, when, where,* and *why* behind any text is the context. A photograph has context too, and knowing the context helps you better analyze and understand what you are viewing. The photograph at left was taken in 1936. The Great Depression, which had begun in 1929, was one of the most shattering experiences in the economic history of the modern world. Farmers faced even more devastation when droughts and destructive agricultural techniques turned once-fertile regions in the Great Plains into a massive Dust Bowl. Many farmers had no choice but to leave the lands their families had farmed for generations. The Farm Security Administration (FSA) hired a group of photographers to record the social and economic problems faced by the farmers and migrant workers living in rural sections of the country. Among these photographers was Dorothea Lange.

On one of her assignments for the FSA, Lange came across a temporary camp set up on the edge of a pea field, where the crop had failed. In a small tent, she found a young mother and her three children dressed raggedly and clustered together. Lange's famous photo communicates a powerful portrayal of hopelessness and anxiety. The strong upward movement created by the woman's forearm leads the viewer's eye directly to her face. The viewer can tell that worry plagues the woman—lines are etched in her forehead and at the corners of her eyes. The woman seems lost in her thoughts—she stares vacantly into the distance and does not look at the camera. Her hand, posed at the corner of her expressionless mouth, hints at the uncertainty she is experiencing about her family's future. Nothing distracts us from the woman's anxiety—especially because the children on either side of the woman are facing away from the viewer.

Advertisements

The visual elements used by advertisers take advantage of our innate capacity to be affected by symbols—from McDonald's golden arches to a pickup truck framed by an eagle or the American flag. When viewing advertisements from an active perspective, learn to detect the explicit and implicit messages being conveyed by certain images and symbols, and identify the design strategies that condition your response. Such visual emblems convey unspoken ideas and have enormous power to promote products, personalities, and ideas.

Advertisements, like other visuals, combine many different elements, so be sure to consider all details:

- color, light, and shadow;
- the number and arrangement of objects and the relationships among them;
- the foreground and background images within the frame;
- the impact of typography;
- the impact of language if it is employed;
- the medium in which the visual appears;
- the inferences and values you draw from the overall composition.

Find an example of each detail listed above in the advertisements here. Also

John Flournoy/McGraw-Hill Education

National Archives and Records
Administration (593691)

Alasdair Drysdale

John Flournoy/McGraw-Hill Education

©Lars A. Niki

consider the purpose of the advertisements, and the appeals used to persuade the audience. Which advertisement(s) uses pathos to make an emotional appeal to the viewer? Which uses logos to persuade using facts? Which relies on ethos to gain the trust of the viewer?

Propaganda

Although propaganda can be analyzed like other visuals, its overriding purpose is to persuade and create a personal reaction. Propaganda, like advertisements, uses words or symbolic images to make you think a certain way, adopt a certain opinion, or take a certain action. The following propaganda posters appeared in the United States during World War I and World War II. The purpose of the poster on the left is obvious. The U.S. government—as symbolized by Uncle Sam—wanted young men to enlist in the army. The use of the colors red, white, and blue symbolizes patriotism. The stern, serious look of Uncle Sam uses ethos to gain the viewer's trust. Notice that the white background causes no distractions from the poster's message.

In contrast, the poster on the right uses pathos—the emotions of fear and horror—to convince viewers to buy bonds to fund the war. Monstrous hands and claws symbolize the enemy during World War II: Nazi Germany and Japan. Notice the dark background and black type. The innocent woman and child—in bright colors— appear unsuspecting of the danger surrounding them.

(l) Library of Congress Prints and Photographs Division [LC-USZC4-595]

(r) National Archives and Records Administration (NWDNS-44-PA-97)

Although the next visual is a historical painting, it is also propaganda. It shows Napoleon Bonaparte, the emperor of France in the early 1800s who conquered much of Europe. Even without knowing the historical context of the painting,

Napoleon Crossing the Alps (1801), Jacques-Louis David (1748–1825)
John Parrot/Stocktrek Images/Getty Images

however, we recognize it as propaganda because it completely ignores the bloodshed and destruction of war. The calm, determined expression on Napoleon's face instills trust (ethos) in the viewer. Emotion (pathos) is elicited by the "movement" of the painting: a fierce wind whips the cloak and horse's tail and mane up the steep incline, suggesting that even nature is on the side of the heroic military leader. What French citizen of 1800 could fail to admire—and want to join—the courageous actions of Napoleon as communicated by this painting?

Political Cartoons

Political cartoons engage in serious fun. They express opinions about public figures, political issues, or economic and social conditions. Most political cartoons are connected with the main news stories of the day. Viewing cartoons helps you understand which current issues are considered important, as well as the diversity of opinion surrounding them. The purpose of most political cartoons is to expose the gap between appearance and reality, or to show the difference between what *is* and what *should* or *could* be. Through their drawings, political cartoonists often expose hypocrisy, point out pretentiousness, laugh at arrogance, deflate the powerful, and give voice to the underdog. Political cartoonists get their message across through satire. Recall that satire is a type of humor meant to expose human folly in order to suggest change or make room for improvement. Satire in political cartoons comes in many forms, including caricature, symbolism, allusion, irony, metaphor, and stereotyping.

The political cartoon below alludes to the famous painting shown here: *Writing the Declaration of Independence, 1776*. Benjamin Franklin is reading Thomas Jefferson's draft of the Declaration of Independence. Irony is found in the words "That's beautiful Tom." The cartoonist is pointing out that the famous words in the Declaration of Independence—"all men are created equal"—are "beautiful" only if a person was a white male when the Declaration was written. The cartoon satirizes the Founders' neglect in addressing women's and other minorities' issues. Further, by drawing the scrubwoman with a stoic expression and placing her "outside" the black background, the cartoonist has disconnected the woman in every way from the exalted moment occurring for the smiling men— declaring independence, freedom, and equality.

Library of Congress Prints and Photographs Division (LC-USZC4-9904)

Mike Peters (c) Distributed by King Features Syndicate, Inc.

Graphs and Tables

If you encounter graphs and tables in a text, analyze the information these visuals present, the implications of the numbers or statistics, the emphases and highlights conveyed, and the way the visual elements shape your understanding of the material and its relationship to the text. Sometimes the material presented in such visuals is technical, requiring you to carefully analyze its structure, the relationship of parts to the whole, the assertions that are advanced, and the validity of the evidence conveyed. In short, active reading of graphs and tables is as demanding as active reading of the printed word. Just as you often have to reread text, you also might need to return to graphs and tables, perhaps from a fresh perspective, to comprehend the content of the visual.

BAR GRAPHS   Bar graphs compare quantities at a glance. Each bar represents an amount—the longer the bar, the larger the amount. Read the title to learn the subject of the graph, and then study the information on the axes to see what the bars are measuring. The *vertical axis* (Y-axis) is the line on the side. It usually has numbers or percentages, and you often measure the lengths of the bars with these numbers. The *horizontal axis* (X-axis) is the line across the bottom. Depending on the orientation of the graph, what you are comparing is usually labeled here. A key may be necessary to explain what the bars represent. Compare the lengths of the bars to draw conclusions about the topic. What is being compared in the bar graph below? Which age group commits the most piracy? Which gender? What percentage of the total accesses music through copyright infringement?

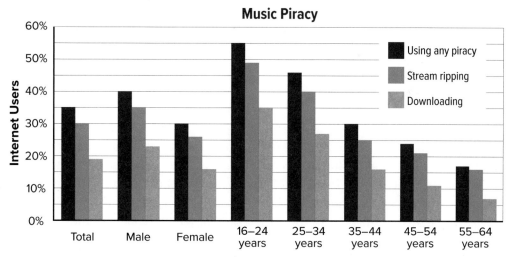

Based on a survey of 12,610 internet users in 13 countries
Source: IFPI Ipsos I Music Consumer Insight Report 2016

LINE GRAPHS   Line graphs show how amounts change over time. Start by reading the title, and then study the information on the vertical or Y-axis. Amounts being compared usually appear on this axis. Then study the information along the horizontal or X-axis. Time (in years, months, or days, for example) usually appears along this axis. Select a point on a line, and then note the year on the horizontal axis below this point and the quantity measured on the vertical axis. Analyze the movement of the line and whether it increases or decreases over time. Consider the causes of the changes. By how much has the cost of public colleges increased from 1980 to 2015? How does this increase differ from the increase in private college tuition? What do you think might account for the difference?

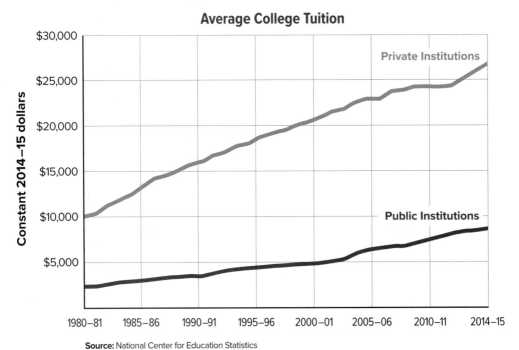

Source: National Center for Education Statistics

TABLES   The information listed in a table is categorized in two ways—by columns and by rows. Read the title to find out the subject of the table. Read the top of each column. These headings define the groups or categories of information to be compared. Examine the labels in the left-hand column. These describe ranges or subgroups and are often organized chronologically or alphabetically. Then compare the data presented in the body of the table. Look for patterns, trends, and consistencies as well as inconsistencies. Note high and low ranges—and consider reasons for those. Determine if you need more information to understand a trend.

Study the table on the next page. Do any of the percentages surprise you? Which country has the highest percentage of people who use a computer, the Internet, and a mobile device? Does knowing that the population of Qatar is 2.6 million, with a per capita income of $125,000, help explain the data? Why is the computer and mobile data for the United States not available?

Country	Percentage of Individuals Using Online Services and Devices					
	Computer	Year of Data	Internet	Year of Data	Mobile	Year of Data
Austria	81.0	2014	80.6	2013	92.7	2012
Azerbaijan	48.0	2011	75.0	2014	83.3	2011
Bangladesh	5.6	2013	6.6	2013	81.2	2013
Colombia	54.2	2013	52.6	2014	85.9	2013
Cuba	29.2	2013	27.9	2013	11.3	2013
Egypt	36.9	2013	25.6	2011	77.7	2013
El Salvador	27.1	2013	23.1	2013	76.2	2013
France	81.7	2014	81.9	2013	89.7	2012
Hong Kong	75.9	2013	74.2	2013	61.1	2013
Israel	74.2	2013	70.9	2013	91.3	2010
Japan	61.8	2013	89.7	2013	71.4	2013
Kenya	9.1	2010	7.2	2010	59.8	2010
Lithuania	72.2	2014	68.5	2013	95.2	2012
Mexico	46.7	2013	44.4	2014	62.0	2013
Qatar	95.1	2013	97.6	2013	99.8	2013
Russian Federation	69.3	2013	70.5	2014	...	
Spain	73.3	2014	71.6	2013	94.3	2012
Sweden	93.3	2014	94.8	2013	96.6	2012
Thailand	35.0	2013	34.9	2014	73.3	2013
Tunisia	24.6	2012	17.1	2010	96.8	2014
United Kingdom	91.2	2014	89.8	2013	94.2	2012
United States	...		74.7	2012	...	

... Data not available
Sources: ITU World Telecommunication/ICT Indicators Database. http://data.un.org/DocumentData.aspx?id=374

Learn to treat visuals in any medium as texts that need to be "read" actively. Every visual requires its own form of annotation, where you analyze the selection and how its parts are arranged, then interpret the emotional effects and significant ideas and messages it presents. Throughout this textbook, paired "classic and contemporary" images such as the two on pages 46–47 give you opportunities to read visual texts with an active eye.

Pulitzer Prize–winning combat photographer Joe Rosenthal captured this scene of U.S. Marines raising the American flag on the Pacific Island of Iwo Jima on February 25, 1945. The campaign to capture the island from Japanese troops cost nearly 7,000 American lives. Rosenthal's photo has been reproduced widely in the media and served as the model for the Marine Corps War Memorial in Washington, D.C.

Photographer Thomas E. Franklin captured a memorable moment in the wake of the terrorist attack on the World Trade Center in New York City in September 2001.

How Do We Communicate?

Using a Critical Perspective Carefully examine these two photographs. What is your overall impression of these images? What details and objects in each scene capture your attention? What similarities and differences do you detect? How does each image communicate ideas and values about the culture that has produced it? Does one appeal to you more than the other? Why or why not?

Analyzing Visuals and Their Rhetoric

1. How does Rosenthal's photo show movement? Does Franklin's photo show the same movement? Explain.

2. Where does the use of diagonal lines draw your eyes to the centerpiece of each photo?

3. How do the men in each photo reveal "determination" in different ways?

4. Study the setting surrounding the group of people in each photo. What effect does the setting have on your emotional response to each image?

CHAPTER 2

The Writing Process

The active reading tools discussed earlier in Chapter 1 provide a foundation for embarking on writing assignments. All good writing starts by reading—which ultimately provides you with information to support your own writing. Make it a daily habit to read articles and books about a wide variety of topics—and keep a journal of reactions to what you have read.

After you have gathered sources to inform what you will write, you must create your own content. You will do this through:

1. **Planning/Prewriting** You decide what points you will cover—and in what order—from various sources as well as from your own observations, ideas, and interpretations. You also decide what tone you will use, and whom you will address in your writing.
2. **Drafting** Write according to your plan, not worrying about making your writing perfect at first—just get it all down!
3. **Revising/Editing** Look over your writing again. Find ways to make your sentences clearer and support for your main point more compelling. Often, this means editing or even deleting parts of your draft entirely.

These three steps are generally referred to as the *writing process*. You will move back and forth within the different steps of the writing process as you generate the raw materials of composition and gradually refine them. We therefore acknowledge at the outset that everyone approaches the writing process somewhat differently. To illuminate these varied processes, we will examine strategies employed by professional writers and several students, including student Jamie Taylor as she read and responded to the essay by Arthur M. Schlesinger, Jr., presented in Chapter 1.

But first we begin with an overview of the writing process, starting with the origin and development of a writer's ideas. Think of the process of writing as a craft. In Old English, the word *craft* signifies strength and power. If you write using the processes of planning/prewriting, drafting, and revising/editing, you can create strong, powerful, and effective essays and documents.

We will be discussing a formal style of writing in this chapter, but acknowledging that you are already a writer is essential. Many of you write and send text messages, for example. You decide what to text, how to make it succinct and interesting, and perhaps even edit your texts before you send them—or should have. How many of us have *not* edited texts, tweets, and other forms of social media but wish we had?

You also know the power of textual visuals. For instance, the use of emojis is one way we communicate without words. As emojis become more sophisticated, they provide an even sharper way to show our emotions. Emojis signal responses, the end of a conversation, a bit of levity, and a spot-on way to show our feelings about any subject. Emojis even have their own dictionary at sites such as https:// emojipedia.org/. GIFs (Graphic Interchange Format) help us communicate visually as well. Sometimes using a GIF just "says it all." Hashtags have also become a form of communication. Tagging with hashtags points readers to thematic content and styles (#writing, #communicationskills). Added to *The Oxford English Dictionary* in 2014, hashtags are officially recognized as part of our vocabulary. All three—emojis, GIFs, and hashtags—are just a small representation of valid informal ways of communication, given the right context.

American novelist Edith Wharton (1862–1937) writes at her desk.

How Do We Compose?

Using a Critical Perspective   Consider these two images of authors engaged in the writing process. What is the dominant impression in each photo? What similarities and differences do you see? Which setting seems more conducive to your writing process, and why?

Analyzing Visuals and Their Rhetoric

1. What would you consider the dominant impression of the writing process in each of the settings in the two photographs?

2. What impressions do you get from the body language of the authors in both pictures?

3. How has new technology changed the way most writers write? What do these photos tell us about how formal writing has changed for most people?

4. What similarities are shared by the two photographs? Which is the strongest?

American novelist Edith Wharton (1862–1937) writes at her desk.

Writer and cinematographer Charlie Craighead, watched by his cat, works in his office in Moose, Wyoming.

Planning/Prewriting

Planning/prewriting is typically the first stage of the writing process. It is the stage in which you discover a reason to write, select and narrow a topic, consider audience and purpose, determine the tone or personal voice you wish to use, and engage in preliminary writing activities to generate content for your essay. Content is the vital element of a composition. "Content" is what you say. Tone and diction determine how you say it.

Get in the mood to write. Ernest Hemingway used to sharpen all his pencils as preparation for a day's writing. French philosopher Voltaire soaked his feet in cold water to get the creative juices flowing. You might want to text a classmate regarding a topic, bounce ideas around in group chats, search for and read articles about the topic, or consult a relevant e-book or blog. During prewriting, you are free to let ideas and thoughts flow.

The Rhetorical Triangle Revisited

Recall the Aristotelian or rhetorical triangle you learned about in Chapter 1. Just as you identified the elements of the triangle when you analyzed another person's writing, you need to keep in mind these same elements in your own writing.

Aristotelian or Rhetorical Triangle

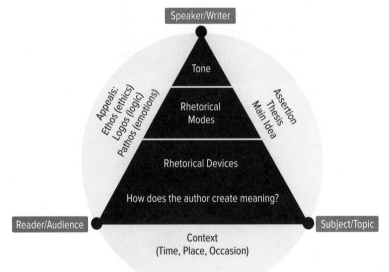

The First Triad refers to the three *points* of the rhetorical triangle.

- At the top of the triangle is you—the writer.
- In order to write, you need something to discuss—a subject or topic as well as its exigency: why the information is important, and why now.
- You also must be aware of who is going to read the work—the audience or reader.

The three *sides* of the triangle are the Second Triad.

- To say something meaningful about a topic, you need to have a point. Therefore, you as a writer must develop an assertion, a thesis, or a main idea about a particular subject.

- On the other side of the triangle, you need to get the audience's attention. To do so, you must decide how best to appeal to the audience. You might establish an authoritative appeal through *ethos* by showing that you are credible and trustworthy. If the audience appears to be very rational and logical, you may choose to appeal with *logos*—using facts, statistics, data, graphs, and charts. If the audience can be swayed by emotional appeals, consider using *pathos*.

- At the bottom of the triangle, you need to consider the context—the time, place, and occasion of your composition (who, when, where, why). Context provides a basis for understanding how your targeted audience is receiving your message about this subject.

The *inner group* of terms is the Third Triad. These can be completed as you write.

- Your tone is your attitude or feeling toward the subject.

- The rhetorical modes are the patterns or methods you use to structure your writing.

- Rhetorical devices are the tools you use to create tone and meaning as you deliver your message.

Considering Purpose and Audience

Before you create content, you should ask yourself *why* you are writing. Determining your purpose or goal—the reason you are writing—forces you to ask: What do I hope to accomplish with my writing? With a specific purpose in mind, you start to anticipate the type of composing task ahead of you.

Your AP English Language and Composition teacher will put forth writing assignments that require you to answer a question. This type of assignment is called a "prompt" because it *prompts* you to answer the question in a certain way. Most prompts ask you either to analyze another writer's works or to persuade your own audience about a topic. (See Chapter 12 for a sample student analysis essay.) But there are many other reasons for writing. You might narrate a story or describe a beautiful sunset. You might explain how to program a video game or classify movies according to genre. You might explain the cause of a problem in your community or compare and contrast two groups of friends. Or, in a journal entry, you might explore your own identity.

The purpose of your writing should be linked to the rhetorical mode you choose. Recall from Chapter 1 that rhetorical modes are methods or patterns of writing that help a writer develop his or her ideas. Most writing actually combines more than one of these rhetorical modes, but the following basic categories can help shape your writing to a specific, overall purpose. More information about and examples of rhetorical modes will be covered in the "Drafting" stage of the writing process. (See p. 59.)

Purpose	Rhetorical Mode (Type of Writing)
To narrate; to tell a story	Narration
To define; to explain what a concept means	Definition
To describe	Description
To classify	Classification
To present a process; to show how something is done	Process Analysis
To give examples	Exemplification
To explain what causes a result	Causal Analysis
To compare and contrast	Comparison/Contrast
To analyze; to show how separate parts work to create the whole	Analysis
To convince or persuade	Persuasion; Argumentation

As you determine your purpose, you must also create common ground between yourself and your audience. In fact, defining your audience is essential to defining your purpose. Think of your audience as the readers of your message. What do they already know about the topic? What do you know about their opinions and backgrounds? Are they likely to agree or disagree with you? (This last question is especially important in argumentative writing, which will be discussed in Chapter 3.) By anticipating who your readers are, you can begin to craft your writing. In an academic setting, your primary audience might be your teacher, but secondary readers might be classmates, or a school newsletter interested in reprinting your essay.

Choosing an Appropriate Tone

Tone is the attitude of a writer toward his or her subject matter. It is the *voice* your readers will hear when they read your essay. Part of the task of prewriting is to select a voice that is appropriate to the purpose, the situation, and the audience you address. The casual voice you use when texting a friend would not be the appropriate tone in an essay composed for your English teacher.

Different writing situations demand different tones. If you are presenting how to do something (process analysis) or explaining what causes a result (causal analysis), you want to project a balanced, objective, largely dispassionate tone. In contrast, if you are writing a narrative essay on the life and death of a family pet, your tone might be humorous or poignant. The tone of a persuasive/argumentative piece should be logical, insistent, compelling, and even satirical.

Recall from Chapter 1 that tone is created through diction, or word choice. It is also created through syntax, or sentence structure, as well as various other rhetorical devices such as analogy, alliteration, hyperbole, repetition, and irony.

Tone is integral to the social dimension of the writing process. It requires a degree of self-awareness, for tone at all times should inspire trust: you should sound reasonable, well informed about your subject, and fair. Above all, you do not want to sound abrupt, long-winded, sarcastic, or confused. Your tone has everything to do with whether your intended purpose is effective. You determine your intentions—and then proceed with stylistic choices, keeping your audience in mind.

Generating Ideas

When you start a writing project, you need to generate ideas as you search for something to say. Some writers doodle, others create cluster trees of ideas, and still others prefer extensive lists. If your task is to write an essay analyzing another writer's work, you can and should annotate the work with notes and observations—this is called questioning the text. (See Chapter 1, p. 5.)

Freewriting and Brainstorming

Two other useful methods of connecting with what you already know or believe are freewriting and brainstorming. Freewriting is quite simple. Select an amount of time, say from 5 to 15 minutes, and jot down or type everything you can think of regarding the subject at hand. Do not worry about punctuation or grammar. This activity is all about getting your cognitive wheels rolling. (See Peter Elbow's essay "Freewriting" at the end of this chapter.) Brainstorming is basically the same thing as freewriting. In brainstorming, however, you might jot down ideas and questions in a bulleted list.

When you have finished freewriting and/or brainstorming, review what you have written. These methods can help you generate ideas. For example, examine the following freewriting and brainstorming exercises by a student, James Moore, which he wrote after reading Arthur M. Schlesinger, Jr.'s "The Cult of Ethnicity." (See the entire essay in Chapter 1, p. 26.)

Freewriting Sample

This essay shows that the author really knows his history because he cites so many historical figures, places, and can quote word for word authorities that back up his argument. He makes a great argument that America's strength is in its diversity and at the same time its unity. I never thought of these two things as being able to complement one another. I always thought of them as being separate. It opens my mind to a whole new way of thinking. One thing that would have strengthened his argument, though, is the fact that although he criticizes people who want to separate themselves into subgroups, he doesn't really mention them by name. He's great when it comes to advancing his own argument but he seems to be a bit too general when he comes to attacking the opposition. I would have liked it if he had mentioned by name people who are undermining America's strengths.

Brainstorming Sample

- Author says ideological conflict isn't such a big problem, but what about gap between rich and poor? If no gap, maybe people wouldn't look for "false idols."
- Schlesinger seems white mainstream. Does this mean he doesn't understand reasons why people on margins of society get tempted to join "cults"?
- He uses supporting points well but doesn't exactly explain why "multiculturalism" and "political correctness" are happening now. What is it about today that's opened the door to these ideas?

- Many references to places with ethnic tensions. It'd be great to study one place and see if it has similarities to same issues in U.S.
- Seems to be writing for academic audience. Can he reach most people with this sophisticated writing? I don't know about most places he mentions.
- What's the solution? I don't think author offers any. That could be start of topic for my paper.

Consider the benefits of freewriting and brainstorming. You can comment on the subject matter of the piece you're reading without censoring your thoughts. This prepares you for the second reading by marshaling a more coherent idea of your perspective. Freewriting and brainstorming can help you contribute to the writer-reader "conversation" or help you see a topic in a new way. For example, in Moore's freewriting sample, he discovered for himself the idea that the strength of American society is a combination of commonality and diversity. In addition, during the brainstorming process, you might come up with a potential idea for a response essay, as Moore did in the example.

Here is the prewriting process Jamie Taylor followed when first reading Arthur M. Schlesinger, Jr.'s "The Cult of Ethnicity."

Brainstorming Notes

- Schlesinger seems to be saying that multiculturalism poses a danger because it threatens to create ethnic divisiveness rather than healthy identification.
- This not only undermines us now, but threatens the very democratic principles upon which the United States was founded.
- He says America must set an example for the rest of the world, which is torn with racial and ethnic strife.
- He believes there is a small group of individuals with a "hidden agenda" who are trying to create this divisiveness. These individuals are self-centered and have their own interests at heart, not the interests of the people they represent.
- One flaw in the essay was that it seemed vague. He didn't mention any names or give specific examples. Only generalities.
- He suggests the "battle" will be won by ordinary citizens; for example, he cites the many intermarriages occurring today.
- Although he sees danger, he is optimistic because he thinks democracy is a strong institution.
- He writes from a position of authority. He cites many historical figures and seems very well read.
- The major problem I see in his essay is that he seems to lump everyone together in the same boat. He doesn't give enough credit to the average person to see through the hollowness of false idols. You don't need a Ph.D. to see the silliness of so many ideas floating around out there.

- So many things to consider—how should I focus my essay??? What should be my theme??

- Hmmm. Idea!!! Since I agree with his basic points, but find he doesn't provide specifics, and doesn't give most people enough credit to see through the emptiness of cult rhetoric, why not use my personal observations to write a response paper in which I show just how reasonable we are in distinguishing rhetoric from substance?

Outlining

After freewriting and brainstorming, consider creating a sketch outline—yet another prewriting strategy. Essays have a beginning, a middle, and an end. Therefore, for a formal essay where you have time to create purposeful paragraphs, you can assume you will have to write an introductory paragraph, at least one body paragraph (but probably more), and a conclusion paragraph. For many years, composition was traditionally taught using only the five-paragraph essay, but today the choice to use five paragraphs can be considered a type of starting block when initially organizing an essay.

Traditional Outline

I. Introductory Paragraph

II. Body paragraph

III. Body paragraph

IV. Body paragraph

V. Conclusion Paragraph

Jamie Taylor developed a preliminary outline to guide her into the drafting stage of the composing process.

Sample Outline

I. Introduction: Summarize essay and thesis; provide counter thesis

II. University life as a demonstration of "ethnic" democracies

III. The emptiness and false promises of self-styled ethnic leaders

IV. The rejection of "home-grown" cults

V. Conclusion

Organic Essays

Although Taylor employed brainstorming and a preliminary outline to organize her thoughts prior to writing her essay, not everyone uses these prewriting activities. Some students need to go through a series of prewriting activities, while others can dive into a first draft. In fact, many teachers encourage their students to practice writing "organic" essays—essays that flow more naturally without following the five-paragraph rule. Turn the page to see a prompt (in bold type) followed by a student draft of an organic essay.

Concerning the lack of proper communication between men and women, Deborah Tannen states, "Once the problem is understood, improvement comes naturally." Apply Tannen's statement to other issues, and develop a position on whether "once a problem is understood, improvement comes naturally."

Tannen has it all wrong.

If problems were understood, and improvement occurred naturally, we wouldn't be in the mess we are in today. Problems exist globally and locally. Syria, for example, has faced the problem of civil war for years, yet I doubt the people of Syria would agree that they live in a world of improvement. Syrian refugees have faced oppression and disregard from all sides of the world. Frankly, they are like orphaned children who have nowhere to go and no one to protect them.

And Syria isn't alone. North Korea is ruled by an inflamed tyrant who has made the country a worldwide tinderbox. Other nations "understand" the problem, but oppressiveness is just not going to go away. Nothing happens "naturally" as Tannen asserts.

Local problems are characterized by inertia, too. For example, teacher pay is appalling in my state. Our teachers continue to flock to other states where the pay is better and support for education is valued. Those teachers who do stay in my state have had to protest or boycott to receive even a marginal standard-of-living increase in their pay. Nothing has improved "naturally" for them. There are many more examples I could use, but it is clear that Tannen has it all wrong.

Nevertheless, the process of developing content for both formal and organic essays includes a search for ideas, a willingness to discard ideas and strategies that do not work, an ability to look at old ideas in a fresh way, and a talent for moving back and forth across a range of composing activities. Rarely does that flash of insight or first draft produce the ideal flow of words resulting in a well-written essay.

Drafting

Everyone approaches the drafting—or composing—process differently. There are, however, certain basic principles for this stage. Drafting begins the minute the prompt is assigned. It starts in your mind as you begin to weigh what you have been assigned to read (or respond to). It segues into a type of inner conversation with yourself that expands into a "conversation" with the author and others who will be reading and possibly scoring your essay. You may be tempted to start writing your essay immediately, but even in a timed writing, give careful consideration and credence to your own gut reactions to what you have just read. Annotate the source material with your reactions. Even if you forgo a formal outline, do not skip the preliminary writing activities in the planning/prewriting phase. These will provide you with some notes to help you get out of the proverbial "starting gate."

Developing the Thesis

Every essay requires a thesis or assertion—the main point that holds all your information together and from which all other elements of the essay develop. A thesis is not just *any* idea relevant to the bulk of your topic, but the *underlying* idea that best expresses your purpose in writing the essay. Your thesis is the controlling idea for the entire essay. Think of the thesis as the overriding point you want to make. It is your assertion about the topic at hand. And keep in mind that your intended audience must be considered when you choose how to develop your thesis.

Functions of the Thesis

The thesis statement, which often appears as a single sentence in the first paragraph of your essay, serves several important functions:

- It introduces the topic to the reader.
- It expresses your approach to the topic—the opinion, attitude, or outlook that creates your special angle of interpretation for the topic.
- It provides the reader with hints about the way the essay will develop.
- It should arouse the reader's interest by revealing your originality and your genuine commitment to the topic.

Your thesis cannot always be captured in a single sentence. Indeed, professional writers often offer an implied or unstated thesis, or they articulate a thesis statement that permeates an entire paragraph. Look to your reading for models about placement of these statements.

Always ask if a thesis hooks you. Do you find it provocative? Do you know where the author is coming from? Does the author offer a map for the entire essay? These are questions to consider as you compose your own thesis statements.

Taking a Stand

The thesis requires you to take a stand on your topic. It is your reason for wanting to inform or persuade your audience. In the thesis below, the writer has staked out a position, limited the topic, and given the reader an idea of how the essay will develop.

Sample Thesis Statement—Argument Essay

> A certain level of conformity is important to a functioning society, but without some level of individualism, society will cease to thrive.

Not all thesis statements involve arguments. Nevertheless, you cannot have a thesis unless you have something to demonstrate, explore, or prove.

Sample Thesis Statement—Analysis Essay

> In the short story "Reason," science fiction author Isaac Asimov reveals his skeptical attitude toward technology by creating an eerie situation, making the protagonist doubtful, and ending the story with an ironic statement.

Writing Introductory Paragraphs

"Beginnings," wrote the English novelist George Eliot, "are always troublesome." A good introduction should be like a door that entices readers into the world of your essay, arousing their curiosity about the topic and thesis with carefully chosen material developed through a variety of techniques.

Functions of the Introduction

A solid introduction informs, orients, interests, and engages the audience. The introduction, which is usually a single paragraph composed of several sentences, serves several important functions:

- It introduces the topic.
- It states the writer's attitude toward the subject, normally in the form of a thesis statement.
- It offers readers a guide to the essay.
- It draws readers into the topic.

Strategies for Writing the Introduction

However you choose to capture your readers' attention depends on your purpose for writing, your subject, and the audience you want to reach. Keep in mind, however, that the overarching purpose of an introductory paragraph is to get to the main idea, or the point of your essay. This "point" is your thesis statement.

You may want to start your introduction with a general or broad statement about the subject. This broad statement should not only present the topic to the reader but also engage your audience. Each sentence after that will narrow the subject until you reach the focus of the essay—or the thesis statement. (See the diagram on next page.)

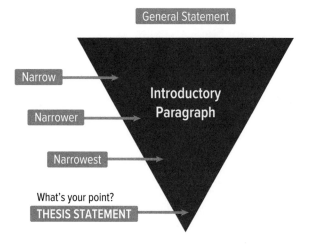

General Statement

Narrow

Narrower

Narrowest

What's your point?
THESIS STATEMENT

Introductory Paragraph

The introduction paragraph below follows the pattern as shown above.

> People have made amazing technological progress within the last century. Decades before astronauts landed on the moon and long before the International Space Station, Isaac Asimov was writing about space stations and humanlike robots. Asimov was an author and biochemist but also a futurist, predicting some amazing achievements such as housing people in outer space. Yet Asimov poses some questions about humans and the machines they build. The title of his book of short stories—*I, Robot*—hints at the idea of a machine with a mind of its own. In the short story "Reason," Asimov reveals his skeptical attitude toward technology by creating an eerie situation, making the protagonist doubtful, and ending the story with an ironic statement.

Other strategies for the introduction paragraph include the following:

Describe a brief story or incident that sets the stage for your topic and frames your thesis. In the following paragraph, Judith Ortiz Cofer uses a personal incident to introduce the topic of ethnic stereotyping. (See the entire essay in Chapter 6.)

> On a bus trip to London from Oxford University where I was earning some graduate credits one summer, a young man, obviously fresh from a pub, spotted me and as if struck by inspiration went down on his knees in the aisle. With both hands over his heart he broke into an Irish tenor's rendition of "María" from *West Side Story*. My politely amused fellow passengers gave his lovely voice the round of gentle applause it deserved. Though I was not quite as amused, I managed my version of an English smile: no show of teeth, no extreme contortions of the facial muscles—I was at this time of my life practicing reserve and cool. Oh, that British control, how I coveted it. But "María" had followed me to London, reminding me of a prime fact of my life: You can leave the island, master the English language, and travel as far as you can, but if you are a Latina, especially one like me who so obviously belongs to Rita Moreno's gene pool, the island travels with you.

Start with a shocking, controversial, or intriguing statement or opinion. The startling introduction to Brent Staples's essay "Black Men and Public Space" leads to his thesis that racism has the "ability to alter public space in ugly ways." (See the entire essay in Chapter 11.)

> My first victim was a woman—white, well dressed, probably in her late twenties. I came upon her late one evening on a deserted street in Hyde Park, a relatively affluent neighborhood in an otherwise mean, impoverished section of Chicago. As I swung onto the avenue behind her, there seemed to be a discreet, uninflammatory distance between us. Not so. She cast back a worried glance. To her, the youngish black man—a broad six feet two inches with a beard and billowing hair, both hands shoved into the pockets of a bulky military jacket—seemed menacingly close. After a few more quick glimpses, she picked up her pace and was soon running in earnest. Within seconds she disappeared into a cross street.

> Brent Staples writes editorials on politics and culture for *The New York Times* and is author of "Parallel Time," a memoir.

Begin with a comparison or contrast. In the following introduction, Robert Reich uses contrast to point out the economic stability of American workers *then* and *now*. (See the entire essay in Chapter 7.)

> All Americans used to be in roughly the same economic boat. Most rose or fell together, as the corporations in which they were employed, the industries comprising such corporations, and the national economy as a whole became more productive—or languished. But national borders no longer define our economic fates. We are now in different boats, one sinking rapidly, one sinking more slowly, and the third rising steadily.

> "Why the Rich are Getting Richer and the Poor Poorer" from THE WORK OF NATIONS: PREPARING OURSELVES FOR 21ST-CENTURY CAPITALISM by Robert B. Reich, copyright © 1991 by Robert B. Reich. Used by permission of Alfred A. Knopf, an imprint of the Knopf Doubleday Publishing Group, a division of Penguin Random House LLC. All rights reserved.

Ask a thoughtful question or series of questions directed toward establishing your thesis. Deborah Ross evaluates the Disney ideology as it affects the imaginative and actual lives of girls. She uses questions to make her point. (See the entire essay in Chapter 8.)

> In 1989, Disney's little mermaid first asked the musical question, "When's it my turn?" She asked it again in 1996, when her movie was re-released in theaters, and she continues to ask it, frequently, in many of our living rooms. Never has a protagonist had so many turns to demand a turn: Yet, seemingly, she remains unsatisfied. If even the heroine in a Disney "girls' movie" does not enjoy being a girl, how must the girls watching her feel about it?

> Reprinted from "Escape from Wonderland: Disney and the Female Imagination" by Deborah Ross, in *Marvels & Tales: Journal of Fairy-Tale Studies* Vol. 18 No. 1, © 2004 Wayne State University Press, with the permission of Wayne State University Press.

Offer several relevant examples to support your thesis. David Gates provides examples in the introduction to his essay about the life, death, and career of music legend Michael Jackson. (See the entire essay in Chapter 9.)

> True, for a while he was the king of pop—a term apparently originated by his friend Elizabeth Taylor—and he's the last we're ever likely to have. Before Michael Jackson came Frank Sinatra, Elvis Presley, and the Beatles; after him has come absolutely no one, however brilliant or however popular, who couldn't be ignored by vast segments of an ever-more-fragmented audience. Not Kurt Cobain, not Puffy, not Mariah Carey, not Céline Dion, not Beyoncé, not Radiohead—not even Madonna, his closest competitor. When the news of his death broke, the traffic on Twitter caused the site to crash, even though he hadn't had a hit song for years.

Begin with a vivid description that supports your main idea. The paragraph below introduces Nancy Mairs's essay "On Being a Cripple," in which she describes her life with multiple sclerosis. (See the entire essay in Chapter 11.)

> The other day I was thinking of writing an essay on being a cripple. I was thinking hard in one of the stalls of the women's room in my office building, as I was shoving my shirt into my jeans and tugging up my zipper. Preoccupied, I flushed, picked up my book bag, took my cane down from the hook, and unlatched the door. So many movements unbalanced me, and as I pulled the door open I fell over backward, landing fully clothed on the toilet seat with my legs splayed in front of me: the old beetle-on-its-back routine. Saturday afternoon, the building deserted, I was free to laugh aloud as I wriggled back to my feet, my voice bouncing off the yellowish tiles from all directions. Had anyone been there with me, I'd have been still and faint and hot with chagrin. I decided that it was high time to write the essay.

Cite a statistic or provide data. Jared Diamond uses data in the following introduction to his essay about the environmental crises of previous civilizations. (See the entire essay in Chapter 10.)

> One of the disturbing facts of history is that so many civilizations collapse. Few people, however, least of all our politicians, realize that a primary cause of the collapse of those societies has been the destruction of the environmental resources on which they depended. Fewer still appreciate that many of those civilizations share a sharp curve of decline. Indeed, a society's demise may begin only a decade or two after it reaches its peak population, wealth, and power.

Use a quotation or reference to clarify and illustrate your topic and thesis. In the introduction below, Paul Krugman refers to an outside article to lead into his article about economic status. (See the entire essay in Chapter 7.)

> The other day I found myself reading a leftist rag that made outrageous claims about America. It said that we are becoming a society in which the poor tend to stay poor, no matter how hard they work; in which sons are much more likely to inherit the socioeconomic status of their father than they were a generation ago. The name of the leftist rag? *Business Week*, which published an article titled "Waking Up From the American Dream." The article summarizes recent research showing that social mobility in the United States (which was never as high as legend had it) has declined considerably over the past few decades. If you put that research together with other research that shows a drastic increase in income and wealth inequality, you reach an uncomfortable conclusion: America looks more and more like a class-ridden society.

Correct a false assumption. In the following introduction, Amartya Sen points out that using generalizations about "civilization" tends to blur the realities of complex cultures. (See the entire essay in Chapter 6.)

> When people talk about clashing civilizations, as so many politicians and academics do now, they can sometimes miss the central issue. The inadequacy of this thesis begins well before we get to the question of whether civilizations must clash. The basic weakness of the theory lies in its program of categorizing people of the world according to a unique, allegedly commanding system of classification. This is problematic because civilizational categories are crude and inconsistent and also because there are other ways of seeing people (linked to politics, language, literature, class, occupation, or other affiliations).

All of these strategies are ways to introduce your topic and state your thesis. They should be relatively brief and should direct the reader into the body of the essay. Finally, they should reveal your perspective and your tone or voice. In your introductory paragraph, the reader—your audience—should sense that you are prepared to address your topic in an honest, revealing, and perhaps provocative manner.

Writing Body Paragraphs

The body is the middle of the essay. Usually, the body consists of a series of paragraphs whose purpose is to satisfy your readers' expectations or questions about the topic and thesis statement you presented in the introduction. The body of an essay gives substance, stability, balance, and a clear argument supporting your thesis. It offers facts, details, explanations, and claims as a foundation to your main idea. It keeps the reader intellectually intrigued.

Effective Paragraph Development

So how do you start writing body paragraphs? The good news is you already have. During the planning/prewriting stage, you took notes, created annotations, did some freewriting or brainstorming, and created some type of outline. Then you wrote a thesis statement and an introductory paragraph. Referring back to all of these items will help guide you as you create body paragraphs.

Recall that an essay is controlled by its thesis statement. Before you start working on the body paragraphs, you need to look at your thesis statement again. This will remind you of the overarching point of your essay. For example, your thesis statement might be:

Sample Thesis Statement

> Social media has had adverse effects on American culture, including a rise in teen anxiety, a reduction in social skills, and, ironically, greater feelings of isolation.

Topic sentences are relatively general ideas, and they often are generated from the thesis statement—but not word-for-word. Thus, three topic sentences for body paragraphs supporting the thesis statement above could be:

- Teen anxiety—often a normal part of post-adolescence—has risen in the United States since the emergence of social media.
- Using social media has resulted in a loss of social skills learned previously through face-to-face interaction.
- Ironically, mass communication through social media has resulted in people feeling more rather than less isolated.

Just as the thesis statement serves to focus and hold together the entire essay, a topic sentence—or claim—serves to focus and sustain each body paragraph. Keep the topic sentence clearly in mind as you plan the rest of a body paragraph to ensure you maintain unity. Additional sentences in the paragraph must elaborate on or support the topic sentence (general idea) with explanations, examples, facts, details, and evidence. For example, a body paragraph using the first topic sentence above might follow a structure like that shown on the next page.

Structure for a Body Paragraph

> Teen anxiety has risen in the United States since the emergence of social media. This **second sentence** might describe examples of anxious behavior that has risen due to social media. The **third sentence** could identify statistics or evidence that illustrate and verify the rise of the behavioral examples in the second sentence. The **fourth sentence** might discuss the causes of the behaviors—as related to social media—described in the second sentence. The **fifth sentence** might include a quotation from an expert who analyzes anxious behavior. The **sixth sentence** could explain how such behaviors were lacking, different, or minimized before social media emerged. The **final sentence** might tie the main idea of the paragraph back to the thesis, and connect to the main idea of the next paragraph.

Effective paragraph development depends on your ability to create a block of thought that is *unified* and *coherent,* and that presents ideas that flesh out the topic sentence, thereby informing or convincing the reader. To achieve a sense of completeness as you develop body paragraphs, be sure to have enough topic sentences (typically at least three points you want to make) and sufficient examples or evidence for each key point.

Making Artful Connections

In addition to being unified and coherent, your writing needs to be inviting enough to lure your reader to follow the path you want them to take. Strong writers do not normally plod along, going from point A to point B as they make their points, with the conclusion as the final goal. Instead, they go back and read what they have written so they can make artful connections both between and within paragraphs.

Consider the texts or song lyrics that move you. What makes them so intriguing? Certainly the content appeals to you, but the writers probably use interesting words or a play on words, and may apply unusual methods to return to the chorus or main idea. They are making artful and alluring connections.

There are many ways to make artful connections. Add transition words and phrases to move fluently from one sentence to the next, and from one paragraph to another. Perhaps move the topic sentence in one of the body paragraphs so it is the closing statement instead of the first statement. Always check your syntax to avoid repetitious sentence patterns, unless you have done this intentionally for figurative purposes. For example, starting each sentence with the word *The* is boring. Combine some sentences so you do not have a repetitive string of simple sentences in a row. Be sure to connect the main idea in a paragraph back to the thesis statement—and to adjacent paragraphs as well.

Writing Patterns (Rhetorical Modes)

Different topics lend themselves to different types of development. Rhetorical modes—patterns or approaches—are essentially writing and reasoning strategies designed to support your presentation of a topic or hypothesis. Among the major rhetorical approaches are description, narration, illustration, process analysis, comparison and contrast, causal analysis, definition, classification, and argumentation. Keep in mind that these strategies are templates for successful writing, but not every "good" essay follows the forms of these templates exactly.

DESCRIPTION   Descriptive writing is often the best tool for explaining observations about objects, people, scenes, and events. Description is the creation of a "picture" using words. Many professions rely on descriptive writing. Psychologists, for example, might need to describe the behavior of an autistic child. Archaeologists may describe how a section of an excavated area looks. Botanists might describe a particular plant in detail. Effective description depends on several characteristics:

- It conveys ideas through images that appeal to our various senses: sight, hearing, touch, smell, and taste. It selects and organizes details carefully in a clearly identifiable spatial ordering—left to right, top to bottom, near to far, and so forth.
- It creates a dominant impression, a particular mood or feeling.

In the following paragraph from her book *Spanish Harlem*, Patricia Cayo Sexton captures through description the sights, sounds, and rhythms of life in New York City's East Harlem:

> Clusters of men, sitting on orange crates on the sidewalks, will play checkers or cards. The women will sit on the stoop, arms folded, and watch the young at play; and the young men, flexing their muscles, will look for some adventure. Vendors, ringing their bells, will hawk hot dogs, orange drinks, ice cream; and the caressing but often jarring noise of honking horns, music, children's games, and casual quarrels, whistles, singing, will go on late into the night.

Spanish Harlem by Patricia Cayo Sexton. Harper & Row Publishers. Copyright © 1965 by Patricia Cayo Sexton.

NARRATION   Narration answers the question "What happened?" It can be used to tell real or fictional stories, to relate historical events, to present personal experience, or to support an analysis of events. Telling stories—or narration—is a basic pattern of organizing your thoughts. You employ narration on a daily basis—to tell what happened at work, in the cafeteria, or on a Saturday night. Narration is also essential to many forms of academic writing, ranging from history, to sociology, to science. When planning and writing narration, keep in mind the following guidelines:

- Present the events of your narration in a logical and coherent order. Make certain you link events through the use of appropriate transitional words.
- Select the narrative details carefully to suit the purpose of the essay. Narrate only those aspects of the event that serve to illustrate and support your thesis.
- Choose a point of view and perspective suitable for your topic and audience. Narrative point of view may be either first or third person. A first-person narrative (*I, we*) is suitable for stories about yourself. A third-person narrative (*he, she, it, they*) conveys stories about others. The narrative perspective you use

depends on your audience and purpose. Obviously, you would use a different perspective and tone to narrate a laboratory experiment than you would to narrate a soccer match.

- Use dialogue, if appropriate to your topic, to add realism and interest to your narrative.
- Limit the scope of the event you are narrating, and bring it to a suitable conclusion or climax.

When narration is used for informational or expository purposes, the story makes a point, illustrates a principle, or explains something. In other words, the event tends to serve as evidence in support of your thesis. Here is a sample student paragraph based on narration:

> Like most little girls I thought it would be very grown up to get my hair done in a beauty parlor instead of by my mother or older sister. For more than a month I cried and badgered my family. Finally, after hearing enough of my whining, my mother gave in and made an appointment for me. At the beauty parlor, I sat with my mother and a few older women, naively waiting for my transformation into another Shirley Temple. Finally the hairdresser placed me in a chair and began to chop a mass of hair onto the floor and then subject me to a burning sensation as rollers wound my remaining hair tight. The result was a classic example of the overworked permanent. At home later that day, I tried washing and rewashing my hair to remove the tangled mess. It took a week until I would see anyone without a scarf or hat over my head and a month before I could look at someone without feeling that they were making fun of me the minute I turned my back. In a way, I feel that such a fruitless journey to the hairdresser actually helped me along the road to adulthood since it was a perfect example of a disappointment that only time and patience, rather than tantrums and senseless worrying, can overcome.

ILLUSTRATION   Illustration develops your paragraph beyond the topic sentence. By *illustration*, we mean various types of examples and supporting evidence. Such illustration or examples may be short or extended. Here are some types of illustration that will help you write well-developed paragraphs and essays:

- *Fact:* Many schools have established programs that promote, and in some cases, require, student community service in order to graduate.
- *Statistic:* In 2011, 19 states allowed districts to award credit toward graduation for volunteering or service learning, and seven states allowed districts to require service for graduation.
- *Example:* Maryland is the only state that requires service learning to graduate, although the District of Columbia and several large school districts (Atlanta, Chicago, and Philadelphia) also require community service to graduate.
- *Quotation:* According to the *National Center for Education Statistics* in the U.S. Department of Education, "Females (50 percent) are more likely than males (38 percent) to volunteer in high school."

- *Process:* Society recognized that inspiring volunteerism would help if programs were set up to do so, and thus the federal government created programs such as the Peace Corp and VISTA. Then state governments thought the same idea could be applied to high school students. . . .

- *Comparison and contrast:* Before the service requirement, Maryland seniors were 8 percent more likely than students nationally to volunteer. After the service requirement, Maryland seniors were 9 to 17 percent less likely to volunteer.

- *Personal experience:* I volunteered much more before it became mandatory for me to do so.

- *Case study:* Dave, as an eighth grader, enthusiastically logged his service hours weekly at the humane society. By the time he was a senior and involved in sports and work, he relied on monthly tasks from his parents to fulfill his service hours.

It is not enough to just present examples, however. Illustration should be cited, and it should be as effective as possible. Watch out for weak or poorly presented illustration. For every main idea or topic sentence in a paragraph, use specific supporting evidence that sufficiently proves or amplifies your point. If you do not have the right amount of evidence, your paragraph and essay will be underdeveloped, as in the following case:

> High school students should be given the choice whether or not to provide community service. Maryland's students who were forced to provide community service in order to graduate reduced their hours of volunteerism.

The two-sentence paragraph above has promise but does not follow through with the main idea adequately. The concept at the heart of the topic sentence is clearer and more complete in the revised version:

> High school students should be given the choice whether or not to provide community service. Many schools have established programs that promote, and in some cases, require, student community service in order to graduate. In Maryland, for example, all students must complete service learning to graduate, while the District of Columbia and several large school districts throughout the country also require community service to graduate. To inspire volunteerism in much the same way as the federal government did when creating the Peace Corp and VISTA, some school districts began requiring mandatory community service. But the requirement seems to have backfired. Before the service requirement, Maryland seniors were 8 percent more likely than students nationally to volunteer. After the service requirement, Maryland seniors were 9 to 17 percent *less* likely to volunteer.

In the revision above, the student chose to use evidence, specific in nature, to provide adequate support for the topic sentence. Other details and illustrative strategies might have been selected. In selecting illustrative material, you should always ask: Are there other examples that are more lively, specific, concrete, revealing, or interesting? All of the evidence should work together to support the thesis.

PROCESS ANALYSIS   When you describe how something works, you are explaining a process. The complexity of your explanation will depend on how complex the process itself is, how detailed you want your explanation to be, and what you want your audience to be able to do or understand as a result of reading your explanation. Are you providing how-to-do-it instructions for a relatively simple task like boiling water, or are you attempting to explain a complicated laboratory experiment or computer program?

Before you write a process analysis, you must first determine how much information your audience already has. For example, if you are explaining how to make a peanut butter and jelly sandwich, it is fair to assume the reader will know where to get the bread.

Using the rhetorical mode of process analysis requires analytical and problem-solving abilities because you have to break down operations into parts and actions. Process analysis always involves the systematic presentation of step-by-step procedures, often using signal words such as *after, before, first, second, then,* and *next*. You must show *how* the steps or parts in a process lead to its completion or resolution.

Your analysis of a process can occur at the paragraph level, or it can control the development of an entire essay. Note how Laurence J. Peter, author of the book *The Peter Prescription,* uses process analysis to structure the following paragraph:

> If you are inexperienced in relaxation techniques, begin by sitting in a comfortable chair with your feet on the floor and your hands resting easily in your lap. Close your eyes and breathe evenly, deeply, and gently. As you exhale each breath let your body become more relaxed. Starting with one hand direct your attention to one part of your body at a time. Close your fist and tighten the muscles in your forearm. Feel the sensation of tension in your muscles. Relax your hand and let your forearm and hand become completely limp. Direct all your attention to the sensation of relaxation as you continue to let all tension leave your hand and arm. Continue this practice once or several times each day, relaxing your other hand and arm, your legs, back, abdomen, chest, neck, face, and scalp. When you have this mastered and can relax completely, turn your thoughts to scenes of peaceful beauty. Begin, if you wish, by recalling pleasant scenes of natural tranquility from your past. Stay with your inner self as long as you wish, either thinking of nothing or visualizing only the loveliest of images. Often you will become completely unaware of your surroundings. When you open your eyes you will find yourself refreshed in mind and body.

> *The Peter Prescription: How to Be Creative, Confident, & Competent* by Laurence J. Peter. William Morrow & Company, Inc. Copyright © 1972 by Laurence J. Peter.

Peter establishes his relationship and his purpose with his audience in the very first sentence, and then offers step-by-step procedures that move readers toward a full understanding of the process. Remember that you are the expert when writing about a process, and you have to think carefully about the degree of knowledge your audience possesses. To develop a process essay, follow these guidelines:

1. Select an appropriate topic.
2. Decide whether your primary purpose is to direct or explain.
3. Determine the knowledge gap between you and your audience.
4. Explain necessary equipment or define specific terms.
5. Organize paragraphs in a complete sequence of steps.
6. Explain each step clearly and completely.
7. State results or outcomes.

COMPARISON AND CONTRAST   Comparison and contrast is a method of organizing similarities and differences between two persons, places, things, or ideas. In English class, you might compare and contrast two writers' views on a single topic. Make sure that what you are comparing is narrow enough for the length of your essay. You would do better, for example, to compare two jazz pianists than to compare a jazz pianist and Dixieland jazz as a whole. In addition, there needs to be a *purpose* for your comparison. This purpose should be given in your thesis statement, or main assertion.

As you research your two subjects of comparison, use a graphic organizer such as a Venn diagram to help you list the information. Try to find a central idea between the two subjects that you can analyze. With a tentative central idea in mind, begin to organize your notes in an outline, which will help you stay focused and on topic.

The organization of comparison and contrast essays generally follows two basic patterns, or methods: the *block method* and the *alternating method.* Use the block method when you want to write about one entire subject before writing about the other subject. Use the alternating or point-by-point method when you want to write about one feature of both subjects, followed by a second feature of both subjects; and so on. In both methods, follow through in an orderly manner, stating clearly the main thesis or reason for establishing the comparison, and providing clear transitions as you move from idea to idea. Consider the following paragraph written by a student:

> The story of Noah and the Great Flood is probably the best known story of a deluge in the Mesopotamian Valley. However, there are several other accounts of a large flood in the valley. Of these, the Akkadian story of Utnapishtim, as told by Gilgamesh, is the most interesting due to its similarities to the biblical story of Noah. Utnapishtim is a king who is forewarned of the coming of a great flood. He is advised to build an ark and does so. After many days the waters recede and Utnapishtim exits the ark and is turned into a god. The stories of Noah and Utnapishtim bear a striking resemblance in several parts: a god or gods cause a flood to punish men and women; arks, of certain dimensions, are built; animals are taken on board; birds are released to find land; and the arks come to rest on mountains. These parallels are so striking that many think the two to be the same tale.

Given the design of this paragraph, the student could develop body paragraphs that deal in detail with each of the key resemblances in the order they are mentioned: the coming of the flood, the building of the ark, the animals taken on board, the release of the birds, and the lodging of both arks on mountains. By employing the alternating method, the student constructs a well-organized comparative framework for analyzing the story of Noah and the story of Utnapishtim.

CAUSAL ANALYSIS   In both high-school and college-level writing, you frequently must explain the causes or effects of some event, situation, or phenomenon. This type of investigation is termed *causal analysis.* When you analyze something, you divide it into its logical parts or processes for the purpose of close examination. Thus, phenomena as diverse as divorce in America, the Civil War, carcinogens in asbestos, the death of Martin Luther King, Jr., or the 2010 earthquake in Haiti can be analyzed in terms of their causes and effects.

With causal analysis, you cannot simply tell a story, summarize an event, or describe an object or phenomenon. Instead, you must explain the *why* and *what* of a topic. The analysis of causes seeks to explain why a particular condition occurred. The analysis of effects seeks to explain what the consequences or results were, are, or will be. Some essays and reports focus on causes, others on effects, and still others on both causes and effects. The following paragraph from a student's sociology paper focuses on a cause-and-effect relationship:

> My parents came to New York with the dream of saving enough money to return to Puerto Rico and buy a home with some land and fruit trees. Many Puerto Ricans, troubled by the problem of life on the island, find no relief in migration to New York City. They remain poor, stay in the barrio, are unable to cope with American society and way of life, and experience the destruction of their traditionally close family life. My parents were fortunate. After spending most of their lives working hard, they saved enough to return to the island. Today they tend their orange, lemon, banana, and plantain trees in an area of Puerto Rico called "El Paraíso." It took them most of a lifetime to find their paradise—in their own backyard.

Here the writer blends personal experience with a more objective analysis of causes and effects, presenting the main cause-effect relationship in the first sentence, analyzing typical effects, providing an exception to this conventional effect, and describing the result.

Sometimes you will want to focus exclusively on causes or on effects. For example, in a history course, the topic might be to analyze why World War II occurred, as this student sought to do:

> It is popularly accepted that Hitler was the major cause of World War II, but the ultimate causes go much deeper than one personality. There were long-standing German grievances against reparations levied on the nation following its defeat in World War I. Moreover, there were severe economic strains that caused resentment among the German people. Compounding these problems was the French and English reluctance to work out a sound disarmament policy and American noninvolvement in the matter. Finally, there was the European fear that Communism was a much greater danger than National Socialism. All these factors contributed to the outbreak of World War II.

Note that in his attempt to explain fully the causes of an event, the writer goes beyond *immediate* causes—the most evident causes that trigger the event being analyzed. He tries to identify the *ultimate* causes, the deep-rooted reasons that completely explain the problem. In order to present a sound analysis of a problem, you need to be able to trace events logically to their underlying origins. Similarly, you have to engage in strategic thinking about immediate and ultimate effects in order to explain fully an event's results.

Writing about cause-and-effect relationships demands attention to logic and thorough preparation. To write effective and logical essays of causal analysis, follow these guidelines:

1. Be honest, objective, and reasonable when establishing your thesis (the point you are making). As an active thinker, you have to recognize and then avoid prejudices and logical fallacies, including unsupportable claims, broad generalizations and overstatements, and false relationships. (For a discussion of logical fallacies, see page 127.)
2. Distinguish between causes and effects, and decide whether you plan to focus on causes, effects, or both. As a prewriting strategy, draw up a list of causes and a corresponding list of effects. You can then organize your paper around the central causes and effects.
3. Distinguish clearly between immediate and ultimate causes and effects. Explore those causes and effects that best serve the purpose of your paper and your audience's expectations.
4. Provide illustration in the form of evidence. Do not rely on simple assertions. Statistics and testimony from reliable authorities are especially effective types of evidence to support your analysis.
5. Establish links between causes or effects. Seek a logical sequence of related elements, a chain of causality that helps readers understand the totality of your topic.

There are many ways to write about causes and effects, depending on whether you are looking for explanations, reasons, consequences, connections, results, or any combination of these elements.

DEFINITION   Some ideas and concepts require definition if readers are to make sense of them. You cannot discuss supply and demand in economic theory, for example, without defining the concept of the "invisible hand" (people acting in their own rational self-interest improve the economy and general welfare). Because concepts are often abstract, they may mean different things to different readers. In order to make ourselves understood, we must be able to specify their meaning in a particular context.

There are three types of definitions. The simple *lexical* definition, or dictionary definition, is useful when briefly identifying concrete, commonplace, or uncontroversial terms for the reader. Many places, persons, and things can be defined in this manner. The *extended* definition is an explanation that might involve a paragraph or an entire essay. It is frequently used for abstract, complex, or controversial terms. In a *stipulative* definition, you offer a special definition of a term, or set limitations on your use of the term. A solid definition, whether it is lexical, extended, or stipulative, involves describing the essential nature and characteristics of a concept that distinguish it from related ideas.

Consider the following paragraph by a student:

> The degree of loneliness that we feel can range from the mild or temporary case to a severe state which may eventually lead to depression or other psychological disorders. Being able to recognize the signs and signals of loneliness may help you to avoid it in the future. Do you find yourself unable to communicate with others? If so, you might be lonely. Do you find it difficult to put your faith in other human beings? If so, then you are setting up a situation that may be conducive to loneliness because you are preventing yourself from becoming too close to another person. Do you find yourself spending great amounts of time alone on a regular basis? Do you find that you are never invited to parties or other social events? Are you unable to love or care for another human being because you are afraid of permanent responsibilities and commitments? These are all signs and signals of either loneliness or situations that may eventually lead to loneliness. Loneliness is the feeling of sadness or grief experienced by a person at the realization that he or she lacks the companionship of other people.

Notice how the student introduces and emphasizes the central concept—loneliness—that is defined in this paragraph. She adds to the definition through a series of rhetorical questions and answers—a strategy that permits her to analyze the qualities or manifestations of the concept. These symptoms serve as examples that reveal what is distinctive or representative about the condition of loneliness.

Definition can be used for several purposes. It may explain a difficult concept like phenomenology or a lesser-known activity like cricket. Definition can be used to identify and illustrate the special nature of a person, object, or abstract idea.

CLASSIFICATION   Classification is a mode of active thinking and writing based on the division of a concept into groups and subgroups, and the examination of important elements within these groups. As a pattern of writing, classification enables you to make sense of large and potentially complex concepts. You divide a concept into groups and subgroups, and you classify elements within categories. Assume, for instance, that your government teacher asks for an analysis of the branches of the U.S. federal government. You divide the federal government into the executive, legislative, and judicial branches and, depending on your purpose, you subdivide even further into departments, agencies, and so forth. Then, according to some consistent principle or thesis—say, a closer look at the erosion of the division of powers—you develop information for each category reflecting common characteristics. Essentially, if you classify in a rigorous and logical way, you sort out the parts and ideas within a scheme, progressing from general to specific in your treatment of the topic.

In developing a classification essay, you also have to determine the *system* of classification that works best for the demands of the assignment. The system you select depends to an extent on your reader's expectations and the nature of the subject. Imagine that you have been asked to write an essay on sports by a health teacher, a psychology teacher, or a sociology teacher. Your system might be types of sports injuries for the health teacher, behavior patterns of football players for your psychology teacher, or levels of violence and aggression in team sports for your sociology teacher. For a broad concept like sports, there are many possible classificatory systems depending on the purpose of your paper.

Although several classification and division strategies might be appropriate for any given concept, the following guidelines should be reviewed and applied for any classification essay:

1. Think about the controlling principle for your classification. *Why* are you classifying the concept? *What* is the significance? Create a thesis statement that gives your reader a clear perspective on your classification scheme.
2. Divide the subject into major categories, and subdivide categories consistently. Make certain you isolate all important categories and that these categories do not overlap excessively.
3. Arrange the classification scheme in an effective order—as a chronology, in spatial terms, in order of importance, or from simple to complex.
4. Present and analyze each category in a clear sequence, proceeding through the categories until the classification scheme is complete.
5. Define or explain any difficult concepts within each category, providing relevant details and evidence.
6. Combine classification with other appropriate writing strategies—comparison and contrast, process analysis, definition, and so forth.

Examine this student paragraph:

> To many people, fishing is finding a "fishy-looking" spot, tossing a hooked worm into the water, and hoping that a hungry fish just happens to be nearby. Anyone who has used this haphazard method can attest to the fact that failures usually outnumber successes. The problem with the "bait and wait" method is that it is very limited. The bait has less chance of encountering a fish than it would if it were presented in different areas of water. A more intelligent approach to fishing is to use the knowledge that at any given moment fish can be in three parts of a lake. Assuming that a lake has fish, anglers will find them on the surface, in the middle, or on the bottom of the lake. Fishing each of these areas involves the use of a separate technique. By fishing the surface, fishing the middle, or fishing the bottom, you greatly increase the chances of catching a fish.

This example is the student's introductory paragraph to a classification essay that blends description, process analysis, comparison and contrast, and the use of evidence to excellent effect. From the outset, however, the reader knows that this will be a classification essay.

ARGUMENTATION   Argumentation is a form of active thinking in which you try to convince an audience to accept your position on a topic, or persuade members of this audience to act in a certain way. In a sense, everything is an argument, for much of what you read and write, see and hear, is designed to elicit a desired response. Whether reading written words, viewing various media forms, or listening to the spoken word (especially of politicians), you know that just about anything is potentially debatable.

Argumentation in writing, however, goes beyond ordinary disagreements. With an argumentative essay, your purpose is to convince or persuade readers in a logical, reasonable, and appealing way. In other words, with formal argumentation, you must distinguish mere personal opinion from opinions based on reasons derived from solid evidence. An argumentative essay has special features and even step-by-step processes that will be treated in greater detail in Chapter 3. For now, it is worth noting that solid argumentative writing can combine many of the forms and purposes that have been discussed in this chapter. Your understanding of such forms and purposes of discourse as narration, illustration, analysis, and comparison and contrast, and how these strategies can combine in powerful ways, will help you compose solid argumentative essays.

Above all, with argumentation, you must develop what Virginia Woolf called "some fierce attachment to an idea." Once you commit yourself to a viewpoint on a topic or issue, you will find it easy to bring an argumentative edge to your writing. Consider the following excerpt from an essay by Caroline Bird that begins with the provocative title "College Is a Waste of Time and Money":

> A great majority of our nine-million college students are not in school because they want to be or because they want to learn. They are there because it has become the thing to do or because college is a pleasant place to be; because it's the only way they can get parents or taxpayers to support them without working at a job they don't like; because Mother wanted them to go, or some other reason entirely irrelevant to the course of studies for which college is supposedly organized.

"College Is a Waste of Time and Money" by Caroline Bird. *Psychology Today,* May 1975, Vol. 6, No. 12. Copyright © 1975 by Ziff-Davis Publishing Company.

Clearly, Bird's claim has that argumentative edge you encounter in essays designed to convince readers of a particular viewpoint or position on an issue. Do you agree or disagree with Bird's claim? How would you respond to her assertions? What evidence would you provide to support your claim?

Argumentation is a powerful way to tap into the aspirations, values, and conduct of your audience. It makes demands on readers and writers to do something, believe something, or even become somebody different—say, a more tolerant person or a more active citizen. True, argument can provoke conflict, but it can also resolve it. In fact, many experts today emphasize the value of argument in solving problems and defusing or managing conflicts.

At the outset of any argument process, you must recognize that you have a problem to solve and decisions to make. Problem solving often is at the heart of argumentation; it is a process in which situations, issues, and questions are analyzed and debated, and decisions are made. The basic steps to problem solving in argumentation are these:

1. Define and analyze the problem. Examine all available information to identify the problem precisely.
2. Interpret the facts and review alternative approaches.
3. Make a claim or a decision—that is, assert the best course of action.
4. Implement the decision in order to persuade or convince your audience that the problem has been addressed and solved.
5. Evaluate the outcome in follow-up documents.

At times, it will be hard to diagnose a problem and find solutions for it. At other times, there is no ideal solution to a problem.

Argumentation is not a simple academic exercise but rather an indispensable tool in personal and professional situations. It is indispensable in addressing increasingly complex political, economic, social, and technological trends on both a domestic and a global scale. Moreover, argument can produce ethically constructive and socially responsible results. Argument makes special demands on a writer that will be treated comprehensively in Chapter 3.

Writing End Paragraphs

If an essay does not have a strong, appropriate ending, it may leave the reader feeling confused or dissatisfied. In contrast, an effective closing paragraph leaves the reader with the impression that the main point is well-made.

A closing, like your introduction, should be relatively brief. It is your one last attempt at clarity, one final chance to illuminate your topic. It often helps readers get a sense of closure if you are careful to reiterate a specific idea mentioned in the introduction. Here are some ways to end your essay successfully:

Review the question you raised and your answer, and then summarize what your support for that answer has been. For example, in the beginning of an article titled "Delusions of Grandeur," Henry Louis Gates, Jr., asks his friends how many African American professional athletes they think are at work today. In the essay, he discusses the limited career choices presented as viable to African American youth and public misconceptions about blacks in sports. Here is his concluding paragraph (See the entire essay in Chapter 7.):

> Of course, society as a whole bears responsibility as well. Until colleges stop using young blacks as cannon fodder in the big-business wars of so-called nonprofessional sports, until training a young black's mind becomes as important as training his or her body, we will continue to perpetuate a system akin to that of the Roman gladiators, sacrificing a class of people for the entertainment of the mob.

Gates, Henry Louis, Jr. "Delusions of Grandeur." Sports Illustrated. 19 August 1991: Print. Copyright © 1991 by Henry Louis Gates, Jr. Reprinted with the permission of the author; all rights reserved.

Discuss what is implied if your point is correct. How might that change how people perceive and act in the world? In an essay titled "The Globalization of Eating Disorders," Susan Bordo takes aim at Western media images of "beauty" and how they affect cultures around the world. Here is her conclusion (See the entire essay in Chapter 8.):

> What is to be done? I have no easy answers. But I do know that we need to acknowledge, finally and decisively, that we are dealing here with a cultural problem. If eating disorders were biochemical, as some claim, how can we account for their gradual "spread" across race, gender, and nationality? And with mass media culture increasingly providing the dominant "public education" in our children's lives—and those of children around the globe—how can we blame families? Families matter, of course, and so do racial and ethnic traditions. But families exist in cultural time and space—and so do racial groups. In the empire of images, no one lives in a bubble of self-generated "dysfunction" or permanent immunity. The sooner we recognize that—and start paying attention to the culture around us and what it is teaching our children—the sooner we can begin developing some strategies for change.
>
> Copyright © Susan Bordo.

Show the outcome or effects of the facts and ideas of the essay. In his essay "Education," for example, Ralph Waldo Emerson gives advice to teachers, arguing that the "secret of Education lies in respecting the pupil." In the conclusion, he describes what can happen if teachers follow his advice (See the entire essay in Chapter 11.):

> The beautiful nature of the world has here blended your happiness with your power. Work straight on in absolute duty, and you lend an arm and an encouragement to all the youth of the universe. Consent yourself to be an organ of your highest thought, and lo! suddenly you put all men in your debt, and are the fountain of an energy that goes pulsing on with waves of benefit to the borders of society, to the circumference of things.
>
> "Education" from *Lectures and Biographical Sketches* by Ralph Waldo Emerson. Boston: Houghton, Mifflin and Company, 1884

Ask a thought-provoking question that sums up the main point of the essay. Virginia Woolf uses this strategy in an essay titled "Professions for Women," in which she argues that women must overcome several "angels," or phantoms, to succeed in professional careers. Here is how she concludes her message (See the entire essay in Chapter 7.):

You have won rooms of your own in the house hitherto exclusively owned by men. You are able, though not without great labour and effort, to pay the rent. You are earning your five hundred pounds a year. But this freedom is only a beginning; the room is your own, but it is still bare. It has to be furnished; it has to be decorated; it has to be shared. How are you going to furnish it, how are you going to decorate it? With whom are you going to share it, and upon what terms? These, I think are questions of the utmost importance and interest. For the first time in history you are able to ask them; for the first time you are able to decide for yourselves what the answers should be.

Suggest a solution to some problem you have discussed. In her essay "When Bright Girls Decide that Math is 'a Waste of Time'," Susan Jacoby examines the reasons girls are often deficient in math and science. She provides a solution in her conclusion (See the entire essay in Chapter 4.):

Since there is ample evidence of such feelings in adolescence, it is up to parents to see that their daughters do not accede to the old stereotypes about "masculine" and "feminine" knowledge. Unless we want our daughters to share our intellectual handicaps, we had better tell them no, they can't stop taking mathematics and science at the ripe old age of 16.

Offer an anecdote, allusion, or lighthearted point that sums up your thesis. This strategy is evident in Barbara Kingsolver's conclusion to her essay "Stone Soup." In the essay, Kingsolver eschews the idea of the nuclear family as the standard by which the healthy family should be judged (See the entire essay in Chapter 5.):

Any family is a big empty pot, save for what gets thrown in. Each stew turns out different. Generosity, a resolve to turn bad luck into good, and respect for variety—these things will nourish a nation of children. Name-calling and suspicion will not. My soup contains a rock or two of hard times, and maybe yours does too. I expect it's a heck of a bouillabaisse.

Use a quotation that supports your main point or illuminates an aspect of the topic. In the essay "Wonder Woman," Gloria Steinem explains why the comic book heroine Wonder Woman was such a formative influence during her childhood. She uses an appropriate quotation in her conclusion (See the entire essay in Chapter 8.):

> Perhaps that's the appeal of Wonder Woman, Paradise Island, and this comic book message. It's not only a child's need for a lost independence, but an adult's need for a lost balance between women and men, between humans and nature. As the new Wonder Woman says to Vanessa, "Remember your *power,* little sister."
>
> However simplified, that is Wonder Woman's message: Remember Our Power.
>
> "Wonder Woman" by Gloria Steinem. Reprinted by permission of Gloria Steinem, feminist activist.

Use a full-circle pattern by echoing or repeating a phrase, idea, or detail that you presented in your introductory paragraph. In the introduction to his essay about economic inequality "The Death of Horatio Alger," Paul Krugman mentions the American Dream. Here, in his concluding paragraph, he mentions it again (See the entire essay in Chapter 7.):

> Where is this taking us? Thomas Piketty, whose work with Saez has transformed our understanding of income distribution, warns that current policies will eventually create "a class of rentiers in the U.S., whereby a small group of wealthy but untalented children controls vast segments of the US economy and penniless, talented children simply can't compete." If he's right—and I fear that he is—we will end up suffering not only from injustice, but from a vast waste of human potential.
>
> Goodbye, Horatio Alger. And goodbye, American Dream.
>
> From *The Nation*, December 18, 2003 © 2003 The Nation Company. All rights reserved. Used by permission and protected by the Copyright Laws of the United States. The printing, copying, redistribution, or retransmission of this Content without express written permission is prohibited. www.thenation.com

Here is the essay Jamie Taylor wrote in response to Arthur M. Schlesinger, Jr.'s "The Cult of Ethnicity." Consider the strategies she used to make her composing process a success.

Student Essay

Jamie Taylor

Humanities 101, sec. 008

Professor Fred Segal

4 November 2009

Cultist Behavior or Doltish Behavior?

In Arthur M. Schlesinger's "The Cult of Ethnicity," the author warns that there are forces at work within our nation that undermine our principles of democracy. These forces come in the guise of individuals and groups who claim that they know what's right for the people whom they represent. Although he doesn't mention them all specifically, one can infer he means that certain leaders from the African American community, the Latino community, the Native American community, the Asian community, and so forth are advocating strong identification within groups to keep their identities alive since they claim Eurocentric culture has had a history of stealing and suppressing their own historic roots. But Schlesinger seems to fear that only divisiveness can result. In this regard, he does not give the individual enough credit. Rather than have a paternalistic attitude

◀ The introductory paragraph presents Schlesinger's main argument, amplifies Schlesinger's inferred claims, and then presents the writer's counterargument.

about what he fears these groups are doing, he should give more credit to the members of these groups to be able to discern which messages regarding ethnicity to accept as being benign and which to reject as being downright silly.

The first body paragraph presents ▶ Taylor's first point supported with evidence and examples.

Take, for example, the many clubs in the average college or university. Nearly every ethnic group is represented by one of these organizations. For example, my university has many groups that represent African Americans, Latinos, Asians, Native Americans, even subgroups like the Korean Society, the Chinese Student Association, and so on. Belonging to these groups gives students a healthy place to socialize, discuss common areas of interest and concern, and assist with community outreach. For example, many of these clubs sponsor programs to give demonstrations of cultural traditions such as cooking, dance, clothing, and so on to civic and business groups. They also assist the needy in gaining access to social services, particularly for shut-ins and the elderly who may not speak English. Also, there is strength in numbers, and the fact that these clubs are popular attests to the fact that they tolerate a range of ideas so that no one "ideology" is promoted over another. Besides, if that were to happen, it is the right of the organization to vote a person out of office or membership. To say that these clubs promote divisiveness would be like saying that the Newman Society for Catholic students or Hillel House for Jewish students promotes religious intolerance.

Second, self-styled leaders of various racial and ethnic groups—in their efforts to be divisive—actually help people to see through their rhetoric, or at least, to apply only that which is reasonable and reject that which is intolerable. Because of today's media, such leaders cannot "hide" their views and thus can become their own worst enemies when presenting them in front of a national audience. For example, Louis Farrakhan has not only alienated Jewish individuals owing to his open anti-Semitism, and many among the gay population for his antigay sentiments, but many African Americans as well, particularly women, who often condemn him for his patriarchal views regarding the family and society. A simple proof of his lack of power is the fact that he has been presenting these antidemocratic ideals for decades now, and there is little evidence that anyone is listening to them. Another example is the late Rabbi Meyer Kahane, who advocated the expulsion of all Arabs from Israel. An open opponent of democracy, he was condemned by Jewish leaders in the United States to

◄ The second point offers a unique slant on divisive ethnic and racial leaders and the ability of Americans to reject their claims. Again, specific examples and evidence buttress Taylor's argument.

the point where he was shunned from any discussion regarding religious issues.

The writer's third and final point encompasses a variety of "antidemocratic" groups and rejects their "postures." ▶

Finally, one can feel confident that even within the margins of mainstream America, cultist groups are their own worst enemy. Take, for example, the various groups of extremists. The philosophy and tactics of these groups are condemned by the vast majority of Americans owing to their antidemocratic postures, not to mention their often violent, even murderous activities. They may capture the headlines for a while, but they will never capture the hearts of Americans so long as we stay true to the "measures and laws" that Washington spoke of in his discussion with John Adams.

The conclusion returns to Schlesinger, while recapping Taylor's main points. ▶

In conclusion, the open democratic society we have created is just too strong a force to be weakened or undermined by "romantic ideologies" or "unscrupulous con men" as Schlesinger puts it. Mr. Schlesinger has little to worry about. Just look around your school cafeteria. There's no white section or Latino section or Asian section: Nowadays, it's just one big American section.

Revising

Revising—the rethinking and rewriting of material—takes place during every stage of the composing process. It is integral to the quest for clarity and meaning. "Writing and rewriting are a constant search for what one's saying," declares celebrated American author John Updike. Similarly, the famous essayist E. B. White admits, "I rework a lot to make it clear." If these two great prose stylists revise material in order to seek clarity for their ideas, then you too should adopt the professional attitude that there is always room for improvement. In fact, one trait that distinguishes experienced from inexperienced writers is that experienced writers understand fully the need to revise.

Revision is an art, and it is a skill that can be developed. It is the only way to make your writing match the vision of what you want to accomplish. At all levels—word, sentence, paragraph, and essay—you should develop a repertoire of choices that will permit you to solve writing problems and sharpen your ideas. You might also share your draft with another reader who can let you know what is or is not working and give you suggestions for improvement. To make the process of revision worthwhile, you should ask yourself the following questions during your prewriting and drafting activities:

- Is the essay long enough (or too long) to meet the demands of the assignment?
- Is the topic suitable for the assignment?
- Do you have a clear thesis statement?
- Does your writing make sense? Are you communicating with your reader instead of just with yourself?
- Have you included everything that is important to the development of your thesis or argument?
- Is there anything you should discard?
- Do you offer enough examples or evidence to support your key ideas?
- Have you ordered and developed paragraphs logically?
- Do you have a clear beginning, middle, and end?

Once you have answered these questions, you will be able to judge the extent to which you have to revise your first draft.

Proofreading

Proofreading is part of the revision process. You do not have final copy until you have carefully checked your essay for mistakes and inconsistencies. Proofreading differs from the sort of revision that moves you from an initial draft to subsequent versions of an essay in that it does not offer the opportunity to make major changes in content or organization. It does give you a last chance to correct typos and other minor errors that arise from carelessness, haste, or inaccuracy during the writing process.

When you proofread, do so word by word and line by line. Concentrate on spelling, punctuation, grammar, mechanics, and paragraph form. Read each sentence aloud—from the computer screen or a printed hard copy. If something sounds or looks wrong to you, consult a handbook, dictionary, or other reliable references. Then make corrections accordingly.

Here are some basic guidelines for proofreading your essay:

1. Check the title. Are words capitalized properly?
2. Check the rest of the words in the essay that should be capitalized.
3. Check the spelling of any word you are uncertain about.
4. Check the meaning of any word you think you might have misused.
5. Check to see if you have unintentionally omitted or repeated any words.
6. Check paragraph format. Have you indented each paragraph?
7. Check to make certain you have smooth, grammatically correct sentences. This is your last chance to eliminate awkward grammar errors.
8. Check to make sure your paper follows your teacher's formatting guidelines, such as appropriate margins, font size, and documentation style. (See Chapter 13 for more on documentation.)

Responding to Editorial Comments

Even when you submit what you *think* is the final version of your essay, your teacher might not agree that the essay has reached its best possible form. Teachers are experienced in detecting essays' strengths and weaknesses, pinpointing mistakes, and suggesting how material can be improved. Their comments are not attacks; they want you to pay attention to them, to recognize and correct errors, and possibly to revise your essay once again—most likely for a higher grade. If you receive editorial comments in an objective manner and respond to them constructively, you will become a more effective writer.

Ultimately, refinement is integral to the entire writing process. From reading materials that you confront at the outset and respond to in various ways, you move through many composing stages to create a finished product. Your best writing will occur after you refine and tweak and further refine. This process involves the many strategies covered in this book that are designed to help you acquire greater control over the art of active reading and writing.

Journaling

The art of keeping a journal is an advantage as you work on your writing skills. Journals can take on many forms and will normally require thoughtful responses to assigned material, although the forms of the response might be very different.

One type of journaling is the reader-response journal entry. This type of journal entry often includes three paragraphs, and can be a starting point for rhetorical analysis. The first paragraph of this type of journaling focuses on *what* the author says—a brief summary. The second paragraph focuses on *why* the author says it—a single paragraph analysis of the author's purpose. The third paragraph focuses on *how* the author makes his or her claims. Write quickly and keep your analysis to one page. Again, this is only one way to approach reader-response journaling. Take your lead from the way your teacher wants you to structure the journal entry.

Another use of journals is to identify your interpretation of or gut reaction to the topic of the essay, as well as your reaction to the literal words used in the essay itself. You may also want to add information about previously read essays on the same topic.

Journaling gives you a way to respond in an authentic way, and it is a crucial component of the writing process. Journaling can empower your own voice. Often journals become a welcome method of negotiating differing meanings and interpretations if you share them in groups.

John Donne aptly observed that "No man is an island." Collaborative classroom work furthers and empowers any endeavor that matters. Writing with others is a very dramatic way for you to see that there are many ways to say something. When you write alone, a temptation exists to believe that you must find one right word for the idea you have in your head. Writing with others accentuates the rich possibilities for interpreting phenomena in diverse ways because everyone has to talk about the choices they have made and comment on the choices the members of your writing community have made. Talking through these choices achieves clarification, because fused ideas add to the overall progress of the writing purpose.

Collaborative Writing

Collaborative writing adds a much needed dimension in sharpening your own writing skills. Collaborative writing is not a patchwork of group members' contributions—it is a flowing work in progress until the final draft is turned in. Much collaborative writing takes the shape of editing through the responses of group members.

When working collaboratively directly in the classroom or through such sites as Google Docs, you need to be prepared to share (not dominate or avoid) the work in your group, as well as work off group members' strengths. In collaborative writing, people are joined for a similar cause, they have one another to depend upon, they are not looking for clone-like answers, and they discover diverse outcomes that lead to stronger writing and understanding.

Many theorists have attested that "knowledge is socially learned"; thus, it would be remiss not to recognize the power that collaborative writing holds. We exchange ideas and, if we remain receptive to others' opinions, we grow intellectually and personally through these exchanges. Because we bring many culturally charged beliefs to the table, we in turn confront others' opinions and contemplate the impact of those viewpoints.

Collaborative writing goes far beyond the classroom as well. Real-world demands make collaborative writing essential. Think of the multitude of businesses that depend on colleagues working together to present common reports and recommendations. Popular political leaders would not be successful without a collaboration of skilled writers helping them shape every speech and document. Even mundane tasks, such as correcting sentences, become occasions for generating an awareness of the importance of decision making by group reflective practices. Follow the guidelines below to increase the success of your collaborative group:

Guidelines for Successful Collaborative Writing

▶ Know that each member of your group is as important as the next.

▶ Be sure you have important contact information for each member.

▶ Your first group meeting needs to address and establish guidelines (also called norms) as well as form a timetable. Follow the agreed-upon timetable, but leave room for flexibility.

▶ Agree on the group's purpose and goals (as outlined by the teacher in many circumstances) and determine how best to meet them.

▶ Identify each member's responsibilities, but allow for individual talents and skills.

▶ Establish the time, place, and length of group meetings. Internet use such as wikis, emails, and blogs (to name a few) often play a big part in collaboration.

▶ **Provide clear and precise feedback to members.** This is usually the most important collaborative effort.

▶ Be an active listener. Be an active participant. Be engaged.

▶ Use a standard reference guide for matters of style, documentation, and format.

Three Brief Essays on Writing and Communication

You have just learned how to compose an essay in a three-part process: planning/prewriting, drafting, and revising/editing. You also read that, in actual practice, these stages should not be treated as strictly linear or clear-cut "steps," and that you may wish to complete some steps collaboratively. Everyone approaches the writing process somewhat differently, and the three authors that follow are evidence of that. Read the various strategies for writing and communication each author presents.

Freewriting

Peter Elbow

Peter Elbow (b. 1935) was born in New York and received degrees from Williams College, Exeter College, Oxford, and Brandeis University. He has taught at the University of Massachusetts at Amherst, the State University of New York at Stony Brook, the Massachusetts Institute of Technology, Franconia College, and Evergreen State College. He is considered by some writing teachers to have revolutionized the teaching of writing through his popularization of the concept and practice called "freewriting." He is the author or editor of more than 15 books on writing, including *Writing without Teachers, Writing with Power, Embracing Contraries, What Is English?* and, most recently, *Everyone Can Write: Essays toward a Hopeful Theory of Writing and Teaching Writing* (2000). In "Freewriting," taken from *Writing without Teachers*, Elbow explains an exercise for writing students that he helped popularize in American colleges, universities, and writing workshops.

1   The most effective way I know to improve your writing is to do freewriting exercises regularly. At least three times a week. They are sometimes called "automatic writing," "babbling," or "jabbering" exercises. The idea is simply to write for ten minutes (later on, perhaps fifteen or twenty). Don't stop for anything. Go quickly without rushing. Never stop to look back, to cross something out, to wonder how to spell something, to wonder what word or thought to use, or to think about what you are doing. If you can't think of a word or a spelling, just use a squiggle or else write, "I can't think of it." Just put down something. The easiest thing is just to put down whatever is in your mind. If you get stuck it's fine to write "I can't think what to say, I can't think what to say" as many times as you want; or repeat the last word you wrote over and over again; or anything else. The only requirement is that you *never* stop.

2   What happens to a freewriting exercise is important. It must be a piece of writing which, even if someone reads it, doesn't send any ripples back to you. It is like writing something and putting it in a bottle in the sea. The teacherless class helps your writing by providing maximum feedback. Freewritings help you by

providing no feedback at all. When I assign one, I invite the writer to let me read it. But also tell him to keep it if he prefers. I read it quickly and make no comments at all and I do not speak with him about it. The main thing is that a freewriting must never be evaluated in any way; in fact there must be no discussion or comment at all.

3   Here is an example of a fairly coherent exercise (sometimes they are very incoherent, which is fine):

I think I'll write what's on my mind, but the only thing on my mind right now is what to write for ten minutes. I've never done this before and I'm not prepared in any way—the sky is cloudy today, how's that? now I'm afraid I won't be able to think of what to write when I get to the end of the sentence—well, here I am at the end of the sentence—here I am again, again, again, again, at least I'm still writing—Now I ask is there some reason to be happy that I'm still writing—ah yes! Here comes the question again—What am I getting out of this? What point is there in it? It's almost obscene to always ask it but I seem to question everything that way and I was gonna say something else pertaining to that but I got so busy writing down the first part that I forgot what I was leading into. This is kind of fun oh don't stop writing—cars and trucks speeding by somewhere out the window, pens clittering across people's papers. The sky is cloudy—is it symbolic that I should be mentioning it? Huh? I dunno. Maybe I should try colors, blue, red, dirty words—wait a minute—no can't do that, orange, yellow, arm tired, green pink violet magenta lavender red brown black green—now that I can't think of any more colors—just about done—relief? maybe.

Freewriting may seem crazy but actually it makes simple sense. Think of the difference between speaking and writing. Writing has the advantage of permitting more editing. But that's its downfall too. Almost everybody interposes a massive and complicated series of editings between the time words start to be born into consciousness and when they finally come off the end of the pencil or typewriter onto the page. This is partly because schooling makes us obsessed with the "mistakes" we make in writing. Many people are constantly thinking about spelling and grammar as they try to write. I am always thinking about the awkwardness, wordiness, and general mushiness of my natural verbal product as I try to write down words.

4   But it's not just "mistakes" or "bad writing" we edit as we write. We also edit unacceptable thoughts and feelings, as we do in speaking. In writing there is more time to do it so the editing is heavier: when speaking, there's someone right there waiting for a reply and he'll get bored or think we're crazy if we don't come out with *something*. Most of the time in speaking, we settle for the catch-as-catch-can way in which the words tumble out. In writing, however, there's a chance to try to get them right. But the opportunity to get them right is a terrible burden: you can work for two hours trying to get a paragraph "right" and discover it's not right at all. And then give up.

5   Editing, *in itself*, is not the problem. Editing is usually necessary if we want to end up with something satisfactory. The problem is that editing goes on *at the same time* as producing. The editor is, as it were, constantly looking over the

shoulder of the producer and constantly fiddling with what he's doing while he's in the middle of trying to do it. No wonder the producer gets nervous, jumpy, inhibited, and finally can't be coherent. It's an unnecessary burden to try to think of words and also worry at the same time whether they're the right words.

6   The main thing about freewriting is that it is *nonediting*. It is an exercise in bringing together the process of producing words and putting them down on the page. Practiced regularly, it undoes the ingrained habit of editing at the same time you are trying to produce. It will make writing less blocked because words will come more easily. You will use up more paper, but chew up fewer pencils.

7   Next time you write, notice how often you stop yourself from writing down something you were going to write down. Or else cross it out after it's written. "Naturally," you say, "it wasn't any good." But think for a moment about the occasions when you spoke well. Seldom was it because you first got the beginning just right. Usually it was a matter of a halting or even garbled beginning, but you kept going and your speech finally became coherent and even powerful. There is a lesson here for writing: trying to get the beginning just right is a formula for failure—and probably a secret tactic to make yourself give up writing. Make some words, whatever they are, and then grab hold of that line and reel in as hard as you can. Afterwards you can throw away lousy beginnings and make new ones. This is the quickest way to get into good writing.

8   The habit of compulsive, premature editing doesn't just make writing hard. It also makes writing dead. Your voice is damped out by all the interruptions, changes, and hesitations between the consciousness and the page. In your natural way of producing words there is a sound, a texture, a rhythm—a voice—which is the main source of power in your writing. I don't know how it works, but this voice is the force that will make a reader listen to you, the energy that drives the meanings through his thick skull. Maybe you don't *like* your voice; maybe people have made fun of it. But it's the only voice you've got. It's your only source of power. You better get back into it, no matter what you think of it. If you keep writing in it, it may change into something you like better. But if you abandon it, you'll likely never have a voice and never be heard.

9   Freewritings are vacuums. Gradually you will begin to carry over into your regular writing some of the voice, force, and connectedness that creep into those vacuums.

WRITING WITHOUT TEACHERS by Elbow (1975) pp. 3-7 © 1973, 1998 by Peter Elbow. By permission of Oxford University Press, USA.

Comprehension

1. What is the thesis of the essay? Is it implied or stated directly in the text?

2. In paragraph 5, Elbow refers to the "producer" and the "editor." Who are they? Where are they located? How did they develop?

3. In paragraph 8, the author makes a connection between one's personal "voice" and the idea of "power." Why does Elbow focus so strongly on this connection?

4. Elbow frequently uses the "imperative" (or command) sentence format in the opening paragraph. Why? What would have been the effect had he used the simple declarative format?

5. Writers often use examples to help illustrate their point. Does the example of a freewriting exercise Elbow provides in paragraph 3 help you to understand the method? Why or why not?

6. The author uses colloquial terms such as "squiggle" (paragraph 1), "crazy" and "mushiness" (paragraph 3), and "lousy" (paragraph 7). How does his use of such words affect the tone of the essay? How would you describe his tone?

7. Are there any elements in Elbow's own style that suggest his essay may have started as a freewriting exercise? Consider the reasons he provides for the importance of freewriting—for example, generating ideas, discovering one's own voice, or expressing oneself succinctly and naturally.

8. Elbow is himself a college writing teacher. Based on your assessment of the tone of the essay, who do you think is his intended audience? Is it broad or narrow? Specialized or general? Or could he have in mind more than one type of audience? Explain your answer.

9. Note the number of times Elbow begins his sentences with coordinating conjunctions ("but," "and," "or"). For example, in paragraph 4, he makes this syntactical choice three times. Many writing teachers frown on this method of structuring sentences. Why does Elbow employ it?

10. Compare the essay's introduction to its conclusion. Note how the introduction is rather long and the conclusion is quite short (two sentences, in fact). How do these two elements contribute to the overall "pace" of the essay?

Writing

11. During one week, complete three freewriting exercises. Wait one week, and then review what you have written. Explore any insights your freewriting gives you into your writer's "voice"—your concerns, interests, style, and power.

12. Write an expository paper explaining the difficulties you have when writing an essay homework assignment or writing an essay-length response during an exam.

13. Write a comparison and contrast essay wherein you examine the similarities and differences of speaking and writing.

14. **Writing an Argument** Write an essay in which you support or refute the value of freewriting.

The Maker's Eye: Revising Your Own Manuscripts

Donald M. Murray

Donald M. Murray (1917–2006) combined a career as teacher, journalist, fiction writer, poet, and author of several important textbooks on writing. He worked as a teacher, journalist, and editor for *Time* magazine. His books include *A Writer Teaches Writing, Write to Learn, Read to Write,* and more recently *Shoptalk: Learning to Write with Writers* (1991), *Crafting a Life in Essay, Story, Poem* (1996), and *The Craft of Revision* (1997). In this essay, originally published in the magazine *The Writer,* Murray argues for the absolute importance of the revision process to the writer. As he presents the stages of the revision process, Murray illustrates their usefulness to any writer—whether beginner or experienced—and offers his personal views and those of other authors.

1 When students complete a first draft, they consider the job of writing done—and their teachers too often agree. When professional writers complete a first draft, they usually feel that they are at the start of the writing process. When a draft is completed, the job of writing can begin.

2 That difference in attitude is the difference between amateur and professional, inexperience and experience, journeyman and craftsman. Peter F. Drucker, the prolific business writer, calls his first draft "the zero draft"—after that he can start counting. Most writers share the feeling that the first draft, and all of those which follow, are opportunities to discover what they have to say and how best they can say it.

3 To produce a progression of drafts, each of which says more and says it more clearly, the writer has to develop a special kind of reading skill. In school we are taught to decode what appears on the page as finished writing. Writers, however, face a different category of possibility and responsibility when they read their own drafts. To them the words on the page are never finished. Each can be changed and rearranged, can set off a chain reaction of confusion or clarified meaning. This is a different kind of reading, which is possibly more difficult and certainly more exciting.

4 Writers must learn to be their own best enemy. They must accept the criticism of others and be suspicious of it; they must accept the praise of others and be even more suspicious of it. Writers cannot depend on others. They must detach themselves from their own pages so that they can apply both their caring and their craft to their own work.

5 Such detachment is not easy. Science fiction writer Ray Bradbury supposedly puts each manuscript away for a year to the day and then rereads it as a stranger. Not many writers have the discipline or the time to do this. We must read when our judgment may be at its worst, when we are close to the euphoric moment of creation.

6 Then the writer, counsels novelist Nancy Hale, "should be critical of everything that seems to him most delightful in his style. He should excise what he most

admires, because he wouldn't thus admire it if he weren't . . . in a sense protecting it from criticism." John Ciardi, the poet, adds, "The last act of the writing must be to become one's own reader. It is, I suppose, a schizophrenic process, to begin passionately and to end critically, to begin hot and to end cold; and, more important, to be passion-hot and critic-cold at the same time."

7   Most people think that the principal problem is that writers are too proud of what they have written. Actually, a greater problem for most professional writers is one shared by the majority of students. They are overly critical, think everything is dreadful, tear up page after page, never complete a draft, see the task as hopeless.

8   The writer must learn to read critically but constructively, to cut what is bad, to reveal what is good. Eleanor Estes, the children's book author, explains: "The writer must survey his work critically, coolly, as though he were a stranger to it. He must be willing to prune, expertly and hard-heartedly. At the end of each revision, a manuscript may look . . . worked over, torn apart, pinned together, added to, deleted from, words changed and words changed back. Yet the book must maintain its original freshness and spontaneity."

9   Most readers underestimate the amount of rewriting it usually takes to produce spontaneous reading. This is a great disadvantage to the student writer, who sees only a finished product and never watches the craftsman who takes the necessary step back, studies the work carefully, returns to the task, steps back, returns, steps back, again and again. Anthony Burgess, one of the most prolific writers in the English-speaking world, admits, "I might revise a page twenty times." Roald Dahl, the popular children's writer, states, "By the time I'm nearing the end of a story, the first part will have been reread and altered and corrected at least 150 times. . . . Good writing is essentially rewriting. I am positive of this."

10   Rewriting isn't virtuous. It isn't something that ought to be done. It is simply something that most writers find they have to do to discover what they have to say and how to say it. It is a condition of the writer's life.

11   There are, however, a few writers who do little formal rewriting, primarily because they have the capacity and experience to create and review a large number of invisible drafts in their minds before they approach the page. And some writers slowly produce finished pages, performing all the tasks of revision simultaneously, page by page, rather than draft by draft. But it is still possible to see the sequence followed by most writers most of the time in rereading their own work.

12   Most writers scan their drafts first, reading as quickly as possible to catch the larger problems of subject and form, then move in closer and closer as they read and write, reread and rewrite.

13   The first thing writers look for in their drafts is *information*. They know that a good piece of writing is built from specific, accurate, and interesting information. The writer must have an abundance of information from which to construct a readable piece of writing.

14   Next writers look for *meaning* in the information. The specifics must build a pattern of significance. Each piece of specific information must carry the reader toward meaning.

15   Writers reading their own drafts are aware of *audience.* They put themselves in the reader's situation and make sure that they deliver information which a reader wants to know or needs to know in a manner which is easily digested. Writers try to be sure that they anticipate and answer the questions a critical reader will ask when reading the piece of writing.

16   Writers make sure that the *form* is appropriate to the subject and the audience. Form, or genre, is the vehicle which carries meaning to the reader, but form cannot be selected until the writer has adequate information to discover its significance and an audience which needs or wants that meaning.

17   Once writers are sure the form is appropriate, they must then look at the *structure,* the order of what they have written. Good writing is built on a solid framework of logic, argument, narrative, or motivation which runs through the entire piece of writing and holds it together. This is the time when many writers find it most effective to outline as a way of visualizing the hidden spine by which the piece of writing is supported.

18   The element on which writers may spend a majority of their time is *development.* Each section of a piece of writing must be adequately developed. It must give readers enough information so that they are satisfied. How much information is enough? That's as difficult as asking how much garlic belongs in a salad. It must be done to taste, but most beginning writers underdevelop, underestimating the reader's hunger for information.

19   As writers solve development problems, they often have to consider questions of *dimension.* There must be a pleasing and effective proportion among all the parts of the piece of writing. There is a continual process of subtracting and adding to keep the piece of writing in balance.

20   Finally, writers have to listen to their own voices. *Voice* is the force which drives a piece of writing forward. It is an expression of the writer's authority and concern. It is what is between the words on the page, what glues the piece of writing together. A good piece of writing is always marked by a consistent, individual voice.

21   As writers read and reread, write and rewrite, they move closer and closer to the page until they are doing line-by-line editing. Writers read their own pages with infinite care. Each sentence, each line, each clause, each phrase, each word, each mark of punctuation, each section of white space between the type has to contribute to the clarification of meaning.

22   Slowly the writer moves from word to word, looking through language to see the subject. As a word is changed, cut, or added, as a construction is rearranged, all the words used before that moment and all those that follow that moment must be considered and reconsidered.

23   Writers often read aloud at this stage of the editing process, muttering or whispering to themselves, calling on the ear's experience with language. Does this sound right—or that? Writers edit, shifting back and forth from eye to page to ear to page. I find I must do this careful editing in short runs, no more than fifteen or twenty minutes at a stretch, or I become too kind with myself. I begin to see what I hope is on the page, not what actually is on the page.

24   This sounds tedious if you haven't done it, but actually it is fun. Making something right is immensely satisfying, for writers begin to learn what they are

writing about by writing. Language leads them to meaning, and there is the joy of discovery, of understanding, of making meaning clear as the writer employs the technical skills of language.

25   Words have double meanings, even triple and quadruple meanings. Each word has its own potential for connotation and denotation. And when writers rub one word against the other, they are often rewarded with a sudden insight, an unexpected clarification.

26   The maker's eye moves back and forth from word to phrase to sentence to paragraph to sentence to phrase to word. The maker's eye sees the need for variety and balance, for a firmer structure, for a more appropriate form. It peers into the interior of the paragraph, looking for coherence, unity, and emphasis, which make meaning clear.

27   I learned something about this process when my first bifocals were prescribed. I had ordered a larger section of the reading portion of the glass because of my work, but even so, I could not contain my eyes within this new limit of vision. And I still find myself taking off my glasses and bending my nose towards the page, for my eyes unconsciously flick back and forth across the page, back to another page, forward to still another, as I try to see each evolving line in relation to every other line.

28   When does this process end? Most writers agree with the great Russian writer Tolstoy, who said, "I scarcely ever reread my published writings, if by chance I come across a page, it always strikes me: all this must be rewritten; this is how I should have written it."

29   The maker's eye is never satisfied, for each word has the potential to ignite new meaning. This article has been twice written all the way through the writing process, and it was published four years ago. Now it is to be republished in a book. The editors make a few small suggestions, and then I read it with my maker's eye. Now it has been re-edited, re-revised, re-read, re-re-edited, for each piece of writing to the writer is full of potential and alternatives.

30   A piece of writing is never finished. It is delivered to a deadline, torn out of the typewriter on demand, sent off with a sense of accomplishment and shame and pride and frustration. If only there were a couple more days, time for just another run at it, perhaps then . . . .

Comprehension

1. In paragraph 1, what does Murray mean by the statement "When a draft is completed, the job of writing can begin"? Isn't a draft a form of writing? Do you agree with his notion of a "zero draft"?

2. According to Murray, what are the major differences between student and professional writers? Why do the differences help make the "professional" more accomplished at his or her work?

3. What are the differences between the reading styles of novice and experienced writers? How do the differences affect their own writings?

4. Compare the introduction of this essay to that of Elbow's "Freewriting." How do they differ in tone and structure?

5. Murray begins to classify various aspects of the writer's concern in paragraph 13. Why does he wait so long to begin this analysis? Why are certain key words in paragraphs 13–20 italicized?

6. Murray uses analogy, comparing one thing with another, very different thing, to make the writing process concrete and familiar. Identify some of these analogies. Why are they models of clarity?

7. Murray refers to a writer as "the maker" several times in the essay. What does he imply by this usage? What other professions might be included in this category?

8. What is the purpose of the essay? Is it to inform? To persuade? To serve as a model? Anything else? Explain your response.

9. Murray ends the essay with ellipses. Why?

10. Notice the sentence in paragraph 29 that has four consecutive words with the prefix *re-*. What is the purpose and effect of this rhetorical device?

Writing

11. Murray focuses on the process, craft, and purpose of the writer, but he does not define "writer." Write an extended definition essay explaining what he means by this occupation or profession.

12. Write an essay explaining your own writing process. Do not be intimidated if it is not like the one described by Murray. Compare and contrast your method with that of one or more of your classmates.

13. **Writing an Argument**   Murray suggests that revision is actually "fun" (paragraph 24). Do you agree or disagree? Write an essay defending your position.

Sex, Lies and Conversation: Why Is It so Hard for Men and Women to Talk to Each Other?

Deborah Tannen

Deborah Tannen (b. 1945), born in Brooklyn, New York, holds a Ph.D. in linguistics from the University of California at Berkeley. She is a Professor of Linguistics at Georgetown University. Tannen published numerous specialized articles and books on language and linguistics before becoming nationally known as a best-selling author. She publishes regularly in such magazines as *Vogue* and *New York,* and her book *That's Not What I Meant: How Conversational Style Makes or Breaks Your Relations with Others* (1986) drew national attention to her work on interpersonal communication. Her other popular books on communication include *You Just Don't Understand: Women and Men in Conversation* (1990), *Talking from 9 to 5: How Women's and Men's Conversational Styles Affect Who Gets Heard, Who Gets Credit, and What Gets Done at Work* (1994), and *I Only Say This Because I Love You: How the Way We Talk Can Make or Break Family Relationships Throughout Our Lives* (2001). The following essay was published in the *Washington Post* in 1990.

1   I was addressing a small gathering in a suburban Virginia living room—a women's group that had invited men to join them. Throughout the evening, one man had been particularly talkative, frequently offering ideas and anecdotes, while his wife sat silently beside him on the couch. Toward the end of the evening, I commented that women frequently complain that their husbands don't talk to them. This man quickly concurred. He gestured toward his wife and said, "She's the talker in our family." The room burst into laughter; the man looked puzzled and hurt. "It's true," he explained. "When I come home from work I have nothing to say. If she didn't keep the conversation going, we'd spend the whole evening in silence."

2   This episode crystallizes the irony that although American men tend to talk more than women in public situations, they often talk less at home. And this pattern is wreaking havoc with marriage.

3   The pattern was observed by political scientist Andrew Hacker in the late '70s. Sociologist Catherine Kohler Riessman reports in her new book *Divorce Talk* that most of the women she interviewed—but only a few of the men—gave lack of communication as the reason for their divorces. Given the current divorce rate of nearly 50 percent, that amounts to millions of cases in the United States every year—a virtual epidemic of failed conversation.

4   In my own research, complaints from women about their husbands most often focused not on tangible inequities such as having given up the chance for a career to accompany a husband to his, or doing far more than their share of daily life-support work like cleaning, cooking, social arrangements and errands. Instead, they focused on communication: "He doesn't listen to me," "He doesn't talk to

me." I found, as Hacker observed years before, that most wives want their husbands to be, first and foremost, conversational partners, but few husbands share this expectation of their wives.

5   In short, the image that best represents the current crisis is the stereotypical cartoon scene of a man sitting at the breakfast table with a newspaper held up in front of his face, while a woman glares at the back of it, wanting to talk.

Linguistic Battle of the Sexes

6   How can women and men have such different impressions of communication in marriage? Why the widespread imbalance in their interests and expectations?

7   In the April [1990] issue of *American Psychologist*, Stanford University's Eleanor Maccoby reports the results of her own and others' research showing that children's development is most influenced by the social structure of peer interactions. Boys and girls tend to play with children of their own gender, and their sex-separate groups have different organizational structures and interactive norms.

8   I believe these systematic differences in childhood socialization make talk between women and men like cross-cultural communication, heir to all the attraction and pitfalls of that enticing but difficult enterprise. My research on men's and women's conversations uncovered patterns similar to those described for children's groups.

9   For women, as for girls, intimacy is the fabric of relationships, and talk is the thread from which it is woven. Little girls create and maintain friendships by exchanging secrets; similarly, women regard conversation as the cornerstone of friendship. So a woman expects her husband to be a new and improved version of a best friend. What is important is not the individual subjects that are discussed but the sense of closeness, of a life shared, that emerges when people tell their thoughts, feelings, and impressions.

10   Bonds between boys can be as intense as girls', but they are based less on talking, more on doing things together. Since they don't assume talk is the cement that binds a relationship, men don't know what kind of talk women want, and they don't miss it when it isn't there.

11   Boys' groups are larger, more inclusive, and more hierarchical, so boys must struggle to avoid the subordinate position in the group. This may play a role in women's complaints that men don't listen to them. Some men really don't like to listen, because being the listener makes them feel one-down, like a child listening to adults or an employee to a boss.

12   But often when women tell men, "You aren't listening," and the men protest, "I am," the men are right. The impression of not listening results from misalignments in the mechanics of conversation. The misalignment begins as soon as a man and a woman take physical positions. This became clear when I studied videotapes made by psychologist Bruce Dorval of children and adults talking to their same-sex best friends. I found that at every age, the girls and women faced each other directly, their eyes anchored on each other's faces. At every age, the boys and men sat at angles to each other and looked elsewhere in the room, periodically glancing at each other. They were obviously attuned to

each other, often mirroring each other's movements. But the tendency of men to face away can give women the impression they aren't listening even when they are. A young woman in college was frustrated: Whenever she told her boyfriend she wanted to talk to him, he would lie down on the floor, close his eyes, and put his arm over his face. This signaled to her, "He's taking a nap." But he insisted he was listening extra hard. Normally, he looks around the room, so he is easily distracted. Lying down and covering his eyes helped him concentrate on what she was saying.

13   Analogous to the physical alignment that women and men take in conversation is their topical alignment. The girls in my study tended to talk at length about one topic, but the boys tended to jump from topic to topic. The second-grade girls exchanged stories about people they knew. The second-grade boys teased, told jokes, noticed things in the room and talked about finding games to play. The sixth-grade girls talked about problems with a mutual friend. The sixth-grade boys talked about 55 different topics, none of which extended over more than a few turns.

Listening to Body Language

14   Switching topics is another habit that gives women the impression men aren't listening, especially if they switch to a topic about themselves. But the evidence of the 10th-grade boys in my study indicates otherwise. The 10th-grade boys sprawled across their chairs with bodies parallel and eyes straight ahead, rarely looking at each other. They looked as if they were riding in a car, staring out the windshield. But they were talking about their feelings. One boy was upset because a girl had told him he had a drinking problem, and the other was feeling alienated from all his friends.

15   Now, when a girl told a friend about a problem, the friend responded by asking probing questions and expressing agreement and understanding. But the boys dismissed each other's problems. Todd assured Richard that his drinking was "no big problem" because "sometimes you're funny when you're off your butt." And when Todd said he felt left out, Richard responded, "Why should you? You know more people than me."

16   Women perceived such responses as belittling and unsupportive. But the boys seemed satisfied with them. Whereas women reassure each other by implying, "You shouldn't feel bad because I've had similar experiences," men do so by implying, "You shouldn't feel bad because your problems aren't so bad."

17   There are even simpler reasons for women's impression that men don't listen. Linguist Lynette Hirschman found that women make more listener-noise, such as "mhm," "uhuh," and "yeah," to show "I'm with you." Men, she found, more often give silent attention. Women who expect a stream of listener-noise interpret silent attention as no attention at all.

18   Women's conversational habits are as frustrating to men as men's are to women. Men who expect silent attention interpret a stream of listener-noise as overreaction or impatience. Also, when women talk to each other in a close, comfortable setting, they often overlap, finish each other's sentences and anticipate what the other is about to say. This practice, which I call "participatory

listenership," is often perceived by men as interruption, intrusion and lack of attention.

19   A parallel difference caused a man to complain about his wife, "She just wants to talk about her own point of view. If I show her another view, she gets mad at me." When most women talk to each other, they assume a conversationalist's job is to express agreement and support. But many men see their conversational duty as pointing out the other side of an argument. This is heard as disloyalty by women, and refusal to offer the requisite support. It is not that women don't want to see other points of view, but that they prefer them phrased as suggestions and inquiries rather than as direct challenges.

20   In his book *Fighting for Life,* Walter Ong points out that men use "agonistic" or warlike, oppositional formats to do almost anything; thus discussion becomes debate, and conversation a competitive sport. In contrast, women see conversation as a ritual means of establishing rapport. If Jane tells a problem and June says she has a similar one, they walk away feeling closer to each other. But this attempt at establishing rapport can backfire when used with men. Men take too literally women's ritual "troubles talk," just as women mistake men's ritual challenges for real attack.

The Sounds of Silence

21   These differences begin to clarify why women and men have such different expectations about communication in marriage. For women, talk creates intimacy. Marriage is an orgy of closeness: you can tell your feelings and thoughts, and still be loved. Their greatest fear is being pushed away. But men live in a hierarchical world, where talk maintains independence and status. They are on guard to protect themselves from being put down and pushed around.

22   This explains the paradox of the talkative man who said of his silent wife, "She's the talker." In the public setting of a guest lecture, he felt challenged to show his intelligence and display his understanding of the lecture. But at home, where he has nothing to prove and no one to defend against, he is free to remain silent. For his wife, being home means she is free from the worry that something she says might offend someone, or spark disagreement, or appear to be showing off; at home she is free to talk.

23   The communication problems that endanger marriage can't be fixed by mechanical engineering. They require a new conceptual framework about the role of talk in human relationships. Many of the psychological explanations that have become second nature may not be helpful, because they tend to blame either women (for not being assertive enough) or men (for not being in touch with their feelings). A sociolinguistic approach by which male-female conversation is seen as cross-cultural communication allows us to understand the problem and forge solutions without blaming either party.

24   Once the problem is understood, improvement comes naturally, as it did to the young woman and her boyfriend who seemed to go to sleep when she wanted to talk. Previously, she had accused him of not listening, and he had refused to change his behavior, since that would be admitting fault. But then she learned about and explained to him the differences in women's and men's habitual ways of

aligning themselves in conversation. The next time she told him she wanted to talk, he began, as usual, by lying down and covering his eyes. When the familiar negative reaction bubbled up, she reassured herself that he really was listening. But then he sat up and looked at her. Thrilled she asked why. He said, "You like me to look at you when we talk, so I'll try to do it." Once he saw their differences as cross-cultural rather than right and wrong, he independently altered his behavior.

25   Women who feel abandoned and deprived when their husbands won't listen to or report daily news may be happy to discover their husbands trying to adapt once they understand the place of small talk in women's relationships. But if their husbands don't adapt, the women may still be comforted that for men, this is not a failure of intimacy. Accepting the difference, the wives may look to their friends or family for that kind of talk. And husbands who can't provide it shouldn't feel their wives have made unreasonable demands. Some couples will still decide to divorce, but at least their decisions will be based on realistic expectations.

26   In these times of resurgent ethnic conflicts, the world desperately needs cross-cultural understanding. Like charity, successful cross-cultural communication should begin at home.

Deborah Tannen. "Sex, Lies and Conversation." *The Washington Post,* June 24, 1990. Copyright © Deborah Tannen. Adapted from *You Just Don't Understand: Women and Men in Conversation,* HarperCollins. Reprinted with Permission.

Comprehension

1. What is the thesis or claim of this essay? Where does Tannen most clearly articulate it?

2. To advance her argument, the author cites political scientists and sociologists, while she herself is a linguist. What do professionals in the first two fields do? Why does Tannen use their observations in developing her argument?

3. Why does the author employ a question in her title? What other device does she employ in her title to capture the reader's attention?

Rhetorical Analysis

4. Tannen begins her essay with an anecdote. Is this an effective way of opening this particular essay? Why or why not?

5. Besides anecdotes, the author uses statistics, social science research, appeals to authority, and definition in advancing her argument. Find at least one example of each device. Explore the effectiveness of each.

6. Where and how does the author imply that she is an authority on the subject? How does this contribute to or detract from her ability to win the reader's confidence?

7. Tannen divides her essay into four sections: one untitled and three with headings. How does each section relate to the others structurally and thematically?

8. Concerning the lack of proper communication between men and women, Tannen states, "Once the problem is understood, improvement comes naturally" (paragraph 24). Is this statement supported with evidence? Explain.

Writing

9. Two other linguists, Dr. Eva Berger and Isaac Berger, wrote a book titled *The Communication Panacea: Pediatrics and General Semantics,* which argues that much of what is blamed on lack of communication actually has economic and political causes. Argue for or against this proposition in light of the ideas advanced in Tannen's essay.

10. Using some of the observational methods described in the essay, conduct your own research by observing a couple communicating. Write a short essay discussing your findings.

11. **Writing an Argument** Tannen states, "Once the problem is understood, improvement comes naturally." Argue for or against this proposition.

Connections for Critical Thinking

1. Examine the "how-to" aspect of the essays by Elbow and Murray. What general strategies do they use to develop a comprehensive process analysis of an expansive subject—for example, reading or writing? Write an essay in which you compare the tactics these writers employ to demonstrate their processes.

2. Study the tone of Schlesinger's essay "The Cult of Ethnicity" (in Chapter 1). How does he remain "civil" while arguing against a contemporary view he seems to abhor? Next, study Tannen's "Sex, Lies and Conversation" and examine the tone she uses in addressing the complex subject of language. Make some general observations about how the stylistic elements of an essay contribute to the ability of the author to communicate difficult subjects in a manner that is appealing to the reader.

3. Synthesize the ideas in Elbow's "Freewriting" and those in Murray's "The Maker's Eye: Revising Your Own Manuscripts" so that you can write a coherent essay on writing that takes into account the transition from inspiration to craft.

CHAPTER 3

Argumentation and Synthesis

Traditionally, we think of an argument as a verbal fight. And yes, an argument *can* be a quarrel or a dispute. But it is also a formal debate in which participants express opposing viewpoints on a topic, or a series of reasons for or against a position or an issue. Notice that in all of these examples, the purpose is the same: the speaker or the writer aims to persuade or convince the audience of his or her position.

In their book *Metaphors We Live By*, George Lakoff and Mark Johnson discuss the idea of an argument as "war." Indeed, if we have a verbal "battle," we see anyone who does not agree with our point as an opponent or enemy. Then we attack their claims and defend our own. We try to shoot down their weak points. We target their indefensible claims, and then we try to rebut their argument. It is little wonder that our discussions are heated at times.

In this chapter, you'll learn to think of an argument essay not as a fight but instead as civilized discourse. Like a dance in which you take the lead, you want to *persuade* your reader to follow you. Or, like a lawyer, you build a position and subject your opponent's position to dissection in an effort to win the case.

An argument asserts an opinion based on evidence. You find arguments everywhere: blogs, editorials, scientific articles, and so on. People can use argument to sift through competing viewpoints to achieve a consensus everyone can live with.

You must learn argument as a mode of thinking, reading, and writing in classroom situations, but you should use it in your civic and social life as well. When you engage in argumentation, you offer reasons to support a position, belief, or conclusion. You also communicate your opinions in ways that are thoughtful, considerate, and interesting.

A typical argument essay makes a point not everyone agrees with and defends it by presenting widely accepted facts or direct personal observations, combined with interpretation in support of the debated point. Closely allied with argumentation is *persuasion*, in which the writer appeals to readers' intelligence, emotions, and beliefs in order to influence them to adopt a position or act in a certain way. Logic and persuasive appeal often combine when a writer tries to convince an audience that his or her position is valid and that other perspectives, while understandable perhaps, require reconsideration.

It is important to distinguish between oral arguments and written ones. Admittedly, both spoken and written arguments have a common purpose in their attempt to convince someone to agree with a particular position, make a certain decision, or take a specific action. In both your oral and written arguments, you will usually invoke reasons and attempt to manipulate language skillfully. However, with an oral argument, you rarely have access to factual evidence needed to support your reasons. Nor will you often have time to organize an oral argument the way you would organize a written one. Oral arguments therefore tend to be more emotional and less organized.

Unlike most oral arguments, effective written arguments can be carefully planned, organized, researched, and revised. You as the writer can consider your likely audience, and anticipate and answer objections to the assertions being made. Moreover, you can also take time to assess the validity of the logic (interpretation of evidence) and other persuasive techniques used. Finally, you have time to choose the appropriate language and style for your argument, exploring rhetorical devices you learned about in Chapters 1 and 2: the use of striking diction, figurative language, rhythmic sentence patterns, and various tones and shades of meaning during the prewriting, drafting, and revision stages.

A. Burkatovski/Fine Art Images 11805/SuperStock

Eddie Adams/AP Images

Horrified by the excesses of the Napoleonic invasion of his homeland and the Spanish war for independence, the Spanish artist Francisco de Goya (1746–1828) painted *The Third of May, 1808*, a vivid rendition of an execution during wartime.

What Is an Argument?

Using a Critical Perspective What images and strategies do the Spanish artist Francisco de Goya and the American photographer Eddie Adams employ to construct an argument about war? What exactly is their argument? Comment on the nature and effectiveness of the details they use to illustrate their position. Which work do you find more powerful or engaging? Explain.

Analyzing Visuals and Their Rhetoric

1. In the Goya painting, why do you think that the man being executed is illuminated?

2. Is the "enemy" clearly defined in either image? Explain.

3. Thinking about question 2, give several reasons why the persecuted are portrayed as sympathetic figures.

4. What "argument" do the painter and the photographer make about war?

Another wartime execution, this time captured on film by Eddie Adams in an image that won the Pulitzer Prize for spot news photography in 1969, brought home to Americans the horrors and ambiguities of the Vietnam War.

Elements of Argumentation

Constructing an effective argument depends on the careful arrangement of claims, evidence, and refutation—steps we will cover more thoroughly in the pages that follow. The list below, however, shows at a glance what an argument might include:

- This is what I believe (claim—introductory paragraph).
- This is the *first* reason I believe what I do, plus my supporting evidence (body paragraph).
- This is the *second* reason I believe what I do, plus my supporting evidence (body paragraph).
- These are some things YOU believe, and they are valid points, but here is some information that explains why you are wrong (concession; followed by refutation, rebuttal, and counterargument).
- These are some conclusions that support why I am right (concluding paragraph).

The Test of Justification

Before you can begin any argument or persuasive essay, you need a controversial topic, or at least an opinion that seems worth defending. Whether a writer can construct an argument or not hinges on the concept of *justification*—the recognition that a subject lends itself to legitimate differences of opinion.

Not all statements require justification. A statement that is a verifiable fact or a commonly accepted assumption or belief—what we term a *warrant*—generally does not need justification. To test the concept of justification, consider the following four statements.

1. President John F. Kennedy was assassinated on November 22, 1963.
2. Children should not smoke.
3. The death penalty is fair retribution for murderers.
4. Only people between the ages of 18 and 75 should be able to receive a driver's license.

Which of these statements require justification? The first statement about President Kennedy is a verifiable fact, and the second statement strikes any reasonable audience as common sense. Thus, the first two statements do not require justification and consequently could not be the subject of an argument essay. In contrast, the third statement, concerning the death penalty, offers an opinion that would elicit either agreement or disagreement but in either case would demand substantiation. Similarly, the fourth statement, about drivers' licenses, is an issue that is debatable from a variety of positions. Therefore, statements 3 and 4 require justification: They are open to argumentation.

Understanding Claims and Warrants

A useful approach to argument appears in *An Introduction to Reasoning* and *The Uses of Argument* by British logician and philosopher Stephen Toulmin. In his studies, Toulmin observes that any argument involves a *claim* supported by *reasons/evidence* (facts, examples, statistics, and expert testimony). Underlying the claims and evidence are warrants. As mentioned on the previous page, *warrants* are commonly accepted assumptions or beliefs, and they lead from reason/evidence to claim. Here is the way Toulmin presents his model:

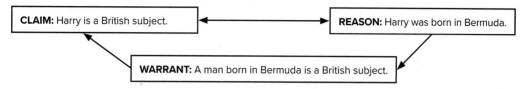

In truth, Toulmin's example is too simplistic. The claims you wrestle with when reading or writing arguments typically are more complex and controversial than Toulmin's diagram suggests, and the need for extensive evidence is more demanding. Nevertheless, Toulmin's model offers a useful way to understand the fundamental nature of argumentative reasoning.

Claims

When you formulate an argument in writing, you make a specific claim, which is an assertion you plan to prove. You present this claim, or major proposition, as truth, and you support the claim with a series of logically related statements. Think of a claim as the thesis or main point of the argument that holds all other logically related statements together. The claim is the main idea you set out to prove, and in a well-reasoned argument, everything makes the claim seem inevitable. Any paper you write that fails to state a claim—your position in an argument—will leave readers wondering if you actually have an argument to present.

As mentioned earlier, a claim must be an arguable point, one you can build a carefully reasoned paper around. For example, to say "Turn down that techno music" to your friend is a command but doesn't qualify as a claim, although it could get you involved in a heated conversation. The argument below fails the test of justification because there is no credible evidence and interpretation:

 Fails the Test of Justification

> **Claim:** Techno music is awful (so turn it down!)
> **Evidence:** I hate it.
> **Interpretation:** If I hate something, it must be awful.
> **Fallacy:** Weak definition of *awful* as "everything that I happen to hate."

To transform the command into a legitimate claim or an arguable point, you would have to state a proposition that expresses your main idea about techno music. The version of the argument below passes the test of justification:

 Passes the Test of Justification

> **Claim:** A considerate friend would not play loud techno music, *unless alone in the apartment.*
> (Why? asks the friend.)
> **Evidence:** Techno music irritates *some* people because techno is too repetitive and the bass is overpowering, and we're all sharing the same space.

Interpretation: Anything shared *should* be kept acceptable to everyone sharing it (like a pizza: if you pick up every piece with your bare hands, nobody else can really feel good about sharing it).

A complex, extended argument essay often reveals several types of claims. A *claim about meaning* (What is techno music?) is a proposition that defines or interprets a subject as it establishes an arguable point. A *claim about value* (Techno music is good or bad) advances an ideally open-minded view of the subject based on a coherent framework of aesthetic or ethical values. A *claim about policy* (Music stations should be forced to limit playing techno music) advances propositions concerning laws, regulations, and initiatives designed to produce specific outcomes. Finally, *claims about consequences* (People who listen to techno music lose appreciation for authentic instruments) are rooted in propositions involving various forms of cause-and-effect relationships. Constructing an argument around one or more of these types of claims is essential to gaining an audience's acceptance.

Qualifiers

Many claims, of course, cannot be presented as absolute propositions. You as a writer must seek common ground with readers, and foster a degree of trust by anticipating that some members of any audience will disagree with your claim, treat it with skepticism, and perhaps even respond with hostility. For this reason, it is important to *qualify* or clarify the nature of your claim. The words shown in italics in the sample arguments above are qualifiers. A *qualifier* restricts the absolute nature of a claim by using such cue words and phrases as *sometimes, probably, usually,* and *in most cases.* Qualifiers can also explain certain circumstances or conditions under which the claim might not be true: The friend can play techno as loud as he/she wants if alone, for example. The use of qualifiers enables a writer to anticipate certain reactions and handle them in an effective and subtle way. When you take the AP Exam, you may be asked to "agree, disagree, or qualify" your position regarding an issue, so qualifiers are important.

Warrants

Even more important than the possible need to qualify a claim is the need to justify it. This is done by linking the claim to reasons/evidence in such a way that the audience sees the train of thought leading from the evidence to the claim. If you look again at the model Toulmin provides, you see that the reason "Harry was born in Bermuda" does not completely support the claim "Harry is a British subject." What is required is a *warrant*—a general belief, principle, or rule—that underscores the claim and the reason/evidence. Thus, the warrant "Since a man born in Bermuda is a British subject" explains *why* the claim follows from the reason/evidence.

Think of warrants as the assumptions that lead writers to hold the opinions they present. From this perspective, we can see that a weak or unclear warrant will undermine an argument and render it invalid. For example, review the claim, reason, and warrant at the top of the next page.

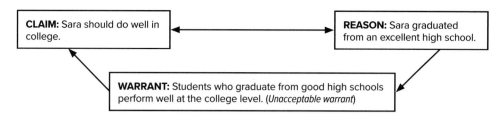

The warrant above is not satisfactory: To state that college success is based solely on the quality of one's high school education is to base the argument on a warrant few readers would find acceptable. Now read the claim supported by the following reason/evidence and new warrant:

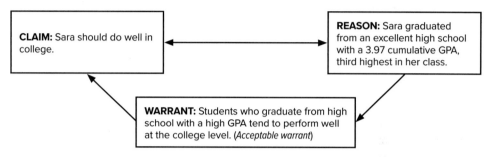

We see that the new warrant establishing the link between reason/evidence and claim becomes more acceptable. There is, in fact, a general belief among experts that a person's grade point average (GPA) in high school is a sound predictor—perhaps sounder than SAT scores—of his or her potential for success in college.

If you disagree with a writer's assumptions, you are questioning the warrants underlying the argument. An effective argument should rest on an acceptable warrant.

Even if a warrant, stated or unstated, is clear, understood, and backed with support, however, readers might still disagree with it. For example, one could argue that Sara might have obtained her lofty GPA in high school by taking easy courses, and consequently we cannot readily predict her success in college. Not everyone will accept even the most reasonable of warrants.

Evidence

One of the pleasures in reading mysteries is the quest for evidence. The great writers of crime and mystery fiction—Edgar Allan Poe, Sir Arthur Conan Doyle, Agatha Christie—were adept at creating a chain of clues, or evidence, leading to the solution to the crime. Whether it is a letter lying on a desk in Poe's "The Purloined Letter" or a misplaced chair in Christie's *The Murder of Roger Ackroyd*, it is evidence we seek to solve the crime.

When writing arguments, evidence is used more to prove a point than to solve a mystery. Good writers must know what constitutes evidence—examples, facts, statistics, quotations, information from authoritative sources, personal experience, careful reasoning—and how to use it to support certain claims. Writers must also determine if the evidence and interpretations accompanying the evidence are valid and relevant.

Evidence is the data, or *grounds*, used to make claims clear, concrete, and convincing. In argumentation, the presentation of evidence must be examined from the perspective of logic or sound reasoning. Central to logic is the relationship of evidence to a *generalization*, a statement or conclusion that what is applicable in one situation also applies to similar situations. You cannot think and write clearly unless you test evidence to see that it supports your claims, assumptions, or general statements.

Here are some basic questions about evidence to consider when reading and writing argument essays:

- **Is the evidence typical and representative?** Examples must fairly represent the condition or situation if your claim is to be valid. If evidence is distorted or unrepresentative, a claim will not be logical or convincing.

- **Is the evidence relevant?** The evidence should speak directly to the claim. It should not utilize peripheral or irrelevant data.

- **Is the evidence specific and detailed?** In reading and writing arguments, do not trust broad, catchall statements presented as "evidence." Valid evidence should involve accurate quotations, paraphrases, and presentations of data from authoritative, legitimate sources.

- **Is the evidence accurate and reliable?** A claim is only as valid as the data supporting it. Facts should come from reliable sources. Current evidence, rather than outdated evidence, should predominate in a current argument. Sources should be cited accurately for the convenience of the reader. Although personal observation and experience are admissible as types of evidence, such testimony rarely serves as conclusive proof for a claim.

- **Is the evidence sufficient?** There must be enough evidence to support claims and reasons. One piece of evidence, no matter how carefully selected, is rarely sufficient to win an argument.

Argument essays should provide a clear, logical link between the evidence and the writer's claim, assertion, generalization, or conclusion. If an argument essay reveals false or illogical reasoning—that is, if the step from the evidence to the generalization is misleading, confusing, or deceptive—readers will not accept the truth of the claim or the validity of the evidence.

The Argument's Purpose

Whether you are reading another writer's argument or starting to plan one of your own, you need to consider the purposes of the argument. As an AP student, your general aim is to communicate in essay form to a literate and knowledgeable audience of teachers. When thinking about the subject for an essay, you also have to consider a more specialized *purpose*—the specific nature or aim—behind your composition. You might have to report the result of an experiment in animal behavior, analyze a poem, compare and contrast Mario Puzo's novel *The Godfather* with its film adaptation, or assert the need for capital punishment. In each instance, your essay requires a key rhetorical strategy or set of strategies. These strategies reflect your purpose—your intention—in developing the essay. An argument essay may serve one or more purposes:

- To present a position, belief, or conclusion in a rational and effective way
- To defend a position against critics or detractors
- To persuade people to agree with a position or take a certain action
- To attack a position, with or without presenting an alternative or opposing viewpoint

An effective argument essay often combines a variety of forms and purposes. For example, an argument essay on legalizing marijuana might explain effects, analyze laws, or evaluate data. When you take time to consider your purpose before you even begin to write, the decisions you make will help you to think more clearly about both the design and intention of your essay.

Appeals to Reason, Emotion, and Ethics

You must establish rapport with your audience in an argument essay. Recall the rhetorical triangle from Chapters 1 and 2. According to Aristotle, you can utilize three types of appeals: logos, pathos, and ethos. The first type, *logos*, is the logical appeal in which you use reason and present evidence. The second type, *pathos*, is an appeal to the emotions of your audience. You can present specific anecdotes and evidence to produce a desired emotional reaction toward your position on the topic. The third type, *ethos*, is an ethical appeal that helps you establish your credibility, either through your own credentials or through those of your sources. Aristotle thought the best and most effective argumentative writing blended logical, emotional, and ethical appeals to move an audience to a desired action. Let's take a closer look at each appeal and how it can be utilized.

Appeals to Reason (Logos)

The *appeal to reason* or logic is the primary instrument of effective argument. The most common way of developing an argument according to the principles of sound reasoning is *deduction*, or an ordering of ideas from the general to the particular. With deduction, you move from a general assertion or claim to reasons/evidence and other support focused on the assertion. Consider the following student paragraph, which uses the deductive method:

> Anti-marijuana laws make people contemptuous of the legal system. This contempt is based in part on the key fact that there are too many contradictions and inconsistencies in criminal penalties for marijuana use. Laws vary radically from state to state. In Texas, you can be sentenced to 180 days in jail, a $2,000 fine, and two years of probation for possession of fewer than two ounces of marijuana. In contrast, marijuana is legal in California and Colorado.

Deduction is a convincing way of arranging ideas and information logically. By stating the proposition or generalization first, you present the most important idea. Then, as in the paragraph above, you move to more specific ideas and details.

Examined more rigorously, deductive reasoning involves a process of critical thinking known as *syllogism*, in which you move from a major statement or premise, then through a minor premise, to a third statement or conclusion. Aristotle's famous syllogism captures this mental process:

Major premise: All human beings are mortal.

Minor premise: Socrates is a human being.

Conclusion: Socrates is mortal.

The soundness of any deductive argument rests on the *truth* of the premises and the *validity* of the syllogism itself. In other words, if you grant the truth of the premises, you must also grant the conclusion.

Inductive reasoning reverses the process of deduction by moving from particular ideas to general ones. In the following excerpt from a speech, Abraham Lincoln presents various ideas and evidence that lead to a major proposition at the end:

> The real issue in this controversy—the one pressing upon every mind—is the sentiment on the part of one class that looks upon the institution of slavery in this country as a wrong, and of another class that does not look upon it as a wrong. . . . On this subject of treating it as a wrong, and limiting its spread, let me say a word. Has anything ever threatened the existence of this Union save and except this very institution of slavery? What is it that we hold most dear amongst us? Our own liberty and prosperity. What has ever threatened our liberty and prosperity, save and except this institution of slavery? If this is true, how do you propose to improve the condition of things by enlarging slavery—by spreading it out and making it bigger?

> Lincoln-Douglas Debates. From *Abraham Lincoln: Complete Works*, Volume One. Edited by John G. Nicolay and John Hay. New York: The Century Co. 1920

By presenting his supporting idea first, Lincoln is able to interest us before we reach the climactic argument at the end of the paragraph. Of course, whether we accept Lincoln's argument or are prepared to debate his claim depends on the strength of the reasons and evidence he offers.

Many of the argument essays you read and much of the argumentative writing you undertake will reflect the mental processes of deduction and induction. Constructing an argument through the use of logos, or logical reasoning, is a powerful way to convince or persuade a particular audience about the validity of your claims.

Appeals to Emotion (Pathos)

In addition to developing your argument logically using the appeal to reason, you should consider the value of incorporating *appeals to emotion*. A letter home asking for more money would in all likelihood require a certain carefully modulated emotional appeal. Dr. Martin Luther King, Jr.'s famous "I Have a Dream" speech at the 1963 March on Washington (see Chapter 6), is one of the finest contemporary examples of emotional appeal. King's speech ends with this invocation:

> When we let freedom ring, when we let it ring from every village and every hamlet, from every state and every city, we will be able to speed up that day

when all of God's children, black men and white men, Jews and Gentiles, Protestants and Catholics, will be able to join hands and sing in the words of the old Negro spiritual, "Free at last! Free at last! Thank God almighty, we are free at last!"

King's skillful application of balanced biblical cadences, connotative and figurative language, and a strong, almost prophetic tone demonstrates the value of carefully crafted emotional appeal in the hands of an accomplished writer of argument.

Of course, in constructing an argument, you should avoid the sort of cynical manipulation of emotion that is common in the world of spoken discourse and the media in general. (A list of unfair emotional appeals appears later in this chapter.) But honest emotional appeal provides a human context for the rational ideas and evidence you present in an argument essay—ideas that might otherwise be uninteresting to your audience. Assuredly, if you want to persuade your audience to undertake a particular course of action, you must draw members of this audience closer to you as a person, and inspire them by skillfully using your feelings about the subject or issue.

Appeals to Ethics (Ethos)

For an emotional appeal to achieve maximum effectiveness, it must reinforce not only the rational strength of your argument but also the ethical basis of your ideas. When you use *ethical appeal*, you present yourself as a well-informed, fair-minded, honest person. Aristotle acknowledged the importance of *ethos*, or the character of the writer, in the construction of an argument. If you create a sense that you are trustworthy, your readers or listeners will be inspired or persuaded. The "sound" or "voice" of your essay, which you convey to the reader through your style and tone, will help in convincing the audience to share your opinion.

President Franklin D. Roosevelt spoke to Congress and the American people after Japan bombed Pearl Harbor, Hawaii, on December 7, 1941. In the following portion of the speech, he uses his credentials—ethos—to appeal to Congress to declare war.

> As commander in chief of the Army and Navy, I have directed that all measures be taken for our defense. But always will our whole nation remember the character of the onslaught against us.

Address by Franklin D. Roosevelt to Congress Asking That a State of War Be Declared Between the United States and Japan. December 8, 1941. www.loc.gov

In an appeal to ethics, you try to convince the reader that you are a person of sound character—that you possess good judgment and values. As a person of goodwill and good sense, you also demonstrate an ability to empathize with your audience, to understand their viewpoints and perspectives. The psychologist Carl Rogers suggests that a willingness to embrace a potentially adversarial audience, to treat this audience more like an ally in an ethical cause, is a highly effective way to establish both goodwill and credibility. In Rogerian argument, your willingness to understand an opposing viewpoint and actually rephrase it reflectively for mutual understanding enables you to further establish your ethical and personal qualities.

Analyze the powerful combination of rational, emotional, and ethical appeals in Abraham Lincoln's 1863 Gettysburg Address.

The Gettysburg Address

Abraham Lincoln

Abraham Lincoln (1809–1865) was born the son of a pioneer in 1809 in Hodgesville, Kentucky, and moved to Illinois in 1831. After brief experiences as a clerk, postmaster, and county surveyor, he studied law and was elected to the state legislature in 1834. A prominent member of the newly formed Republican Party, Lincoln became president on the eve of the Civil War. In 1862, after the Union victory at Antietam, Lincoln issued the Emancipation Proclamation freeing the slaves—the crowning achievement of an illustrious presidency. Although he was an outstanding orator and debater throughout his political career, the Gettysburg Address is one of his greatest speeches—and certainly his most famous. It was delivered at the dedication of the Gettysburg National Cemetery in 1863. Its form and content reflect the philosophical and moral views of the time as well as the rhetorical skill of its speaker. Lincoln was assassinated by John Wilkes Booth in 1865, shortly after Robert E. Lee's surrender and the end of the Civil War.

1 Fourscore and seven years ago our fathers brought forth on this continent a new nation, conceived in liberty, and dedicated to the proposition that all men are created equal.

2   Now we are engaged in a great civil war, testing whether that nation, or any nation so conceived and so dedicated, can long endure. We are met on a great battle-field of that war. We have come to dedicate a portion of that field as a final resting-place for those who here gave their lives that that nation might live. It is altogether fitting and proper that we should do this.

3   But, in a larger sense, we cannot dedicate—we cannot consecrate—we cannot hallow—this ground. The brave men, living and dead, who struggled here, have consecrated it far above our poor power to add or detract. The world will little note nor long remember what we say here, but it can never forget what they did here. It is for us, the living, rather, to be dedicated here to the unfinished work which they who fought here have thus far so nobly advanced. It is rather for us to be here dedicated to the great task remaining before us—that from these honored dead we take increased devotion to that cause for which they gave the last full measure of devotion; that we here highly resolve that these dead shall not have died in vain; that this nation, under God, shall have a new birth of freedom; and that government of the people, by the people, for the people, shall not perish from the earth.

"The Gettysburg Address" by Abraham Lincoln. From *Abraham Lincoln: Complete Works*, Volume One. Edited by John G. Nicolay and John Hay. New York: The Century Co. 1920

Comprehension

1. Although this speech was supposed to be a "dedication," Lincoln states that "we cannot dedicate." What does he mean by this?

2. Lincoln uses abstract words such as *liberty*, *freedom*, and *nation*. What does he mean specifically by each of these terms?

3. What exactly happened "Fourscore and seven years ago" in the context of the speech? Why is this reference so significant to the purpose of Lincoln's address?

Rhetorical Analysis

4. Note the progression of imagery from that of "death" to that of "birth." How does this structure contribute to the claim and coherence of the speech?

5. How do the syntax (arrangement of words within a sentence), punctuation, and choice of the first-person plural form of address contribute to our understanding that this message was intended to be spoken rather than written?

6. Note how Lincoln refers to the combatants as "brave" and "honored." How does he suggest that their struggle differed from that of "us the living"? How does this comparison and contrast create clear similarities and differences between those who fought and those who are present to carry on the soldiers' work?

7. The American Civil War was a battle between the North and the South, as were the opponents at the Battle of Gettysburg. However, Lincoln does not mention this. What is the reason behind this omission? How does it create a speech focused on more comprehensive issues?

8. Besides being president, Lincoln was by definition a politician. In what ways can we determine that this is a political speech as well as a dedication?

9. Speeches are intended to be heard. What are some elements in this speech—for example, vocabulary, syntax, length or brevity of the sentences, and juxtaposition of sentences—that appeal to the reader's sense of sound?

10. Does this speech appeal primarily to the intellect or the emotions, or equally to the two? What are two or three sentences that demonstrate one or both of these appeals? What is the rationale behind your selections? Does Lincoln include any ethical appeals?

Writing

11. Research the actual historical events that occurred during the Battle of Gettysburg. Write an argument essay in which you discuss the significance of this particular speech at this point in the Civil War. Use a minimum of two secondary source materials.

12. Read the speech three times. Then write a paraphrase of it. Examine your paraphrase to discover what elements you recalled. Then reread the speech and write an expository essay focusing on how the structure of the speech contributed to your understanding of the subject.

Writing Powerful Arguments

One of the most common writing assignments is the argument essay. Unlike narrative essays, descriptive essays, and the major forms of expository writing—comparison and contrast, definition, classification, process, and causal analysis—an argument essay requires you to take a stand and to support a position. You must present your ideas as powerfully as possible to advance your point of view and convince readers to accept your position or take a specific course of action. Before you start writing, consider the questions below. Knowing the answers will help you hook and persuade the reader.

- **To whom are you writing?** Are you writing to authorities? Power elites? Teachers? Average readers? Yourself?

- **What is your attitude?** Are you angry? Pleased? Perplexed? What tone will you project?

- **What, exactly, are you trying to accomplish?** An official response? A change of attitude? An explanation? Entertainment?

- **What are you contributing to the debate?** What's the added value here? Just your opinion? New facts? A solution? New arguments, contexts, or dimensions to consider?

- **Have you sincerely questioned your own assumptions?** Will your position survive scrutiny? How would your opponents answer your most compelling arguments?

The process for writing powerful arguments that appears in this section is useful, but it is not a formula. Ultimately, you can construct powerful arguments in numerous ways, but you always must consider the relationship between your ideas, your purpose, and your audience.

Identify an Issue

Not every subject lends itself to useful or necessary argument. Certain subjects—for example, playing soccer—might appeal to you personally and powerfully, but are they worth arguing about? Consequently, your first step in writing an effective argument essay is to identify a rhetorical exigence (issue or situation requiring attention now) that will elicit differing opinions and pass the test of justification.

Not all issues in argument essays must be of national or global concern. In fact, issues like capital punishment, gay marriage, or global climate change might not be of special interest to you. However, if your teacher requires an argument essay on one of these broad hot-button topics, you will need to prepare by first establishing an argumentative perspective on it—in other words, by choosing your side on the issue. Fortunately, you often have opportunities to select issues of more immediate, personal, or local concern: Should fast-food franchises be permitted in the student cafeteria? Should there be a school policy on mandatory community service? Whether dealing with an issue assigned by the teacher or selecting your own issue for an argument essay, ask yourself at the outset what your position on the issue is and how it can be developed through logic and evidence.

Take a Stand and Clarify Your Claim

After you have identified an issue that lends itself to argumentation, you must take a clear stand on the issue. During this prewriting stage, you want to begin to articulate and pinpoint your claim, and thereby start to limit, control, and clarify the scope of your argument. Consequently, the first step at this stage is to establish as clearly as possible what your claim is going to be. You might want to experiment with one or more of the following strategies:

- List some preliminary reasons for your response. By listing reasons, as well as the types of evidence you will need to support those reasons, you will be able to determine at an early stage whether you have enough material for a solid argument essay and what forms of research you will have to conduct.

- Gather and explore information on the issue from debates on radio, television, or the Internet. Keep notes of examples, facts, and ideas that might support your claim.

- Write informally about the issue, considering your immediate response to it—how it makes you feel or what you think about it. If the issue provokes an emotional response, what are the causes? What are your more thoughtful or intellectual responses to the issue?

- Begin to think about possible objections to your position, and list these opposing viewpoints.

After you have developed a preliminary approach to an issue, you should be prepared to state your claim in the form of a thesis statement. Recall from Chapter 2 that you must limit the scope and purpose of your thesis or claim. Too broad a claim will be hard to cover in a convincing fashion in a standard argument essay. One useful way to limit and clarify your claim is to consider the purpose of your argument:

- Do you want to argue a position on a particular issue?

- Do you want to argue that a certain activity, belief, or situation is good or bad, harmful or beneficial, effective or ineffective?

- Do you want to persuade readers to undertake or avoid a particular course of action?

- Do you want readers to consider an issue in a new light?

- Do you want readers to endorse your interpretation or evaluation of an artistic or literary work?

By narrowing your primary purpose, you will arrive at the main point of your argument—your claim.

Read the statement below. This is typical wording for an argument prompt on an AP exam:

Prompt: Consider the issues surrounding cell phone use, and develop a position on whether cell phones should be allowed in the classroom.

Good essays explore the complexity of the issue, including the gray areas, and develop a nuanced position. They qualify their position by showing it is valid under certain conditions. For example, a qualified claim on this issue might state, "With a teacher's supervision, students could use their cell phones to enhance learning in a classroom."

Analyze Your Likely Readers

All writing can be considered a conversation with an audience of readers. In argumentative writing, it is especially important to establish a common ground of belief with your readers if you expect them to accept your claim or undertake a certain course of action. To establish common ground, it is important to know your audience well so you can steer them favorably to your claim and the reasons and evidence supporting it. You also want to know your audience so you can select the best type of evidence to appeal to them in the body paragraphs of your essay. If you determine the nature of your audience *before* you compose the first draft of your essay, you will be able to tailor the appeal, style, content, and tone to a specific person or group.

Try to anticipate audience expectations by asking basic questions about your readers:

- How much do readers know about the issue? Is it an audience of experts or a general audience with only limited knowledge of the issue?
- What does the audience expect from you in terms of your purpose? Do the readers expect you to prove your claim or persuade them to accept it, or both?
- Will the readers be friendly, hostile, or neutral toward your argument? What political, cultural, ethical, or religious factors contribute to the audience's probable position on this issue?
- What else do you know about the readers' opinions, attitudes, and values? How might these factors shape your approach to the argument?

Suppose you are planning to write an argument essay on pollution. What common expectations would an English teacher, a psychology teacher, and a chemistry teacher have concerning your argument? What differences in approach and content would be dictated by your decision to write for one of these teachers? Now consider the following different audiences for a paper on the topic of pollution: a group of grade-school children in your hometown; the Environmental Protection Agency; the manager of a landfill operation; or a relative whose town has been experiencing chemical pollution. In each instance, the type and nature of the audience will influence your approach to the issue and even your purpose.

Remember that through your purpose you find the proper context for your argument. See this connection between the topic and the audience in the rhetorical triangle on the next page. In addition, any writer who wants to communicate effectively with his or her audience will adjust the content and tone of an argument so as not to lose, confuse, or mislead the reader.

Aristotelian or Rhetorical Triangle

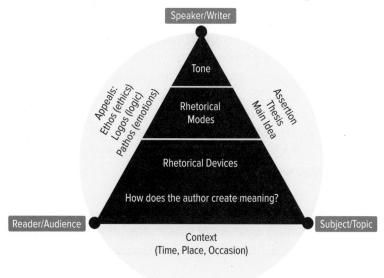

Establish Your Tone

Recall from Chapters 1 and 2 that by *tone* we mean the attitude you take toward your subject. Tone is the personal *voice* a reader "hears" in your writing. This voice will vary depending on the situation, your purpose, and your audience. It may be personal or impersonal and range across a spectrum of attitudes: serious or humorous, subjective or objective, straightforward or ironic, formal or casual, and so on. Your tone derives from your word choice (diction), sentence structure (syntax), figurative language such as metaphor and symbolism, and other rhetorical devices such as analogy, allusion, and repetition.

You adjust your tone to match your purpose in writing. In argumentation, an effective tone will be a true and trustworthy reflection of the writing situation. After all, you are writing an argument essay to convince and persuade, and consequently you need to sound like a reasonable, well-organized, and rational individual. When writing for teachers, you must be especially careful to maintain a reasonable and principled tone and attend to ethical responsibilities, including the need to document sources with integrity. You do not have to sound scholarly, legalistic, or overly technical in presenting your argument, but you do have to employ a personal voice that is appropriate to the writing occasion and audience expectations.

To achieve an appropriate tone in argumentative writing, you will often need to be forceful in presenting your ideas. You are staking out a position, perhaps on a controversial issue, and you must seem willing to defend it. Try to maintain a consistent voice of authority, but do not be overbearing. A voice that is too emotional, overblown, or irrational will in all likelihood alienate the reader and erode your claim.

Develop and Organize the Grounds for Your Claim

You establish the validity of your claim by setting out the *grounds*—evidence and interpretation or commentary—that support your main point. Whereas the claim presents your general or major proposition, as you develop your grounds you organize the argument into *minor propositions*, evidence, commentary, and *refutation* (counterargument). By establishing the grounds for your claim, you explain your particular perspective or point of view on an issue. The grounds for your claim permit the reader to "see" the strength of your position. Keep in mind the difference between your *opinions*, which are beliefs you cannot verify logically, versus *reasons*, which are based on logic, evidence, and direct proof.

There are numerous ways to state the primary reasons or grounds for holding your position. Think of these primary reasons as minor propositions underlying the basis of your claim—reasons that readers would find it difficult to rebut or reject. Three possible models for organizing claims and grounds in an essay can be considered:

Model 1

- ▶ Introduction: statement and clarification of claim
- ▶ First minor proposition and evidence
- ▶ Second minor proposition and evidence
- ▶ Third minor proposition and evidence
- ▶ Refutation of opposing viewpoints for minor propositions
- ▶ Conclusion

Model 2

- ▶ Introduction: statement and clarification of claim
- ▶ First minor proposition and evidence; refutation
- ▶ Second minor proposition and evidence; refutation
- ▶ Third minor proposition and evidence; refutation
- ▶ Conclusion

Model 3

- ▶ Statement and clarification of claim
- ▶ Summary of opposing viewpoints and refutation
- ▶ First minor proposition and evidence
- ▶ Second minor proposition and evidence
- ▶ Third minor proposition and evidence
- ▶ Conclusion

You can arrange your argument in numerous ways. Sometimes you may need more than the three minor propositions illustrated in these models to support your claim. Certainly only a single reason will not provide sufficient grounds to prove an argument. The models can serve a useful purpose, however, especially as a handy template in exams that require argumentative responses to a question.

Gather and Evaluate Your Evidence

After you have established your claim and your reasons, you can turn your attention to developing evidence for your claim. Collecting evidence is a bit like the strategies for successful fishing presented on page 75: You want to fish the top, the middle, and the bottom of your subject. Phrased somewhat differently, you want to cast a wide net as you seek evidence designed to support your claim and reasons.

Gathering Evidence Online

At the outset, a carefully designed online search can yield ample evidence, permitting you to establish links to sites and listservs where you can download or print full or abstracted texts from periodicals, books, documents, and reports. Searching online, however, can be like navigating a minefield. Useless "facts," misinformation, hoaxes, and informational marketing ploys are sometimes presented alongside serious research, honest reporting, and critical analysis. Sometimes the title of a source for the topic you are researching may seem quite appealing, but that does not mean it is a reliable source. Look at the domain name, and then, if you decide to read on, be aware of biases. Researching online requires you to consider qualifications, compare and contrast information, evaluate depth of coverage, check and review data, look elsewhere, and more. The chart below lists basics you should check when engaging with materials online.

Guidelines for Assessing Websites

A good website:

▶ Clearly states the author and/or organizational **source** of the information

▶ Clearly states the **date** the material was written and when the site was last revised

▶ Provides **accurate** data whose parameters are clearly defined

▶ Keeps **bias** to a minimum, and clearly indicates point of view

▶ Provides live **links** to related high-quality websites

▶ Is clearly **organized** and designed for ease of use

▶ Keeps advertising separate from content, and does not permit advertisers to determine content

Gathering Evidence at the Library

To guard against the pitfalls involved in relying exclusively on browser-based searching, you should also make a trip to the library. Research librarians can help you evaluate websites and direct you to the best sources—both traditional and electronic—for the types of evidence you are seeking. (See Chapter 13 for more on library and online research.)

Gathering Expert Testimony

Depending on your subject, you might consider interviewing individuals who can provide expert testimony designed to support your claim and reasons. Finally, your personal experience and the experiences of your friends and acquaintances might provide useful evidence, although such kinds of anecdotal or firsthand support should be treated judiciously and not serve as the entire basis of your paper. For instance, you and your friends might claim a current horror movie is great, but such personal evidence must be tempered by a willingness to consult established critics for additional support.

Utilize Unintended Evidence

If you cast a wide net, you will almost always catch more than you require. Yet the very process of searching comprehensively for evidence can produce exciting, unintended consequences. You might discover that certain evidence suggests a need to revise or qualify your claim. Evidence can also help you articulate or confirm the warrants that are the foundation of your argument. The insights gained by considering other evidence might cause you to develop a new reason for your claim you had not considered initially. You might also discover evidence that helps you refute the ideas of your anticipated opposition. Skillfully exploit the wealth of evidence at your disposal.

Refine Your Evidence

After you have collected adequate evidence to bolster your claim and the key reasons supporting that claim, the next necessary step is to evaluate and select the *best* evidence. Writers who carefully evaluate and select their evidence produce effective arguments. At the outset, the nature of the writing situation—an exam, a term paper, a letter to the editor—will dictate to an extent the type of evidence you need to evaluate. In most instances, however, your evidence should be *credible, comprehensive,* and *current.* Your evidence is *credible* when your sources are reliable and the evidence itself is representative. Your evidence is *comprehensive* when you provide a broad range of facts, information, and data designed to cover all aspects of your argument. In presenting evidence comprehensively, you also make certain there is sufficient support for each of your reasons—not too much evidence for one and too little for another, but an even balance between and among the minor propositions. Finally, always try to locate the most *current* evidence available to support your claim. Data and statistics often do not age well and tend to lose their relevance. In some arguments, however, older evidence can be compared with newer information. For example, a paper arguing that immigration to the United States is out of control could make skillful use of data from the 1960 Census *and* the 2020 Census.

Evidence is the heart of any argument. Without evidence, readers will not be interested in your claim and support. Make certain that your evidence—facts, examples, and details—is accurate and skillfully presented so readers become interested in your more abstract propositions, identify with your position, and come away convinced of your argument's validity.

Consider the Warrants Used to Interpret Your Evidence

Even as you clarify your claim and assemble your reasons and evidence, you must also consider the warrants, or unstated assumptions, underlying your argument. Sometimes these assumptions are stated, but often they remain unstated. In either instance, they are not necessarily self-evident or universally accepted. They are significant, nevertheless, for warrants serve as the bedrock of an argument; as generalizations, they are far broader than claims and evidence.

When you are writing for a friendly or supportive audience, you can usually assume your readers will accept the warrants or unstated assumptions supporting your claim, so you might not even need to state them. For example, if you claim in a report for your biology teacher that creationism should not be taught in high school science classrooms, your argument is based on several assumptions or warrants: that there is no scientific basis for creationism, for example; or that the U.S. Constitution requires the separation of church and state.

But what if you were to make your claim in a letter to a local school board, several of whose members want to revise the ninth-grade earth science curriculum to emphasize creationism and evolution equally? In this instance, you would be presenting your argument to a skeptical audience, so you would have to state your assumptions or warrants clearly, bolster them with adequate support, and back up your assumptions with further arguments—evidence and interpretation supporting them.

Develop the habit of looking for and evaluating warrants behind the argument. If you are reading an argument essay, and the assumptions are stated, that will make this task easier. If the warrants are unstated, you will have to detect and evaluate them. If you are writing an argument essay, you should consider whether your audience will understand and consent to the warrants that serve as the foundation of your paper. If you have any doubt, then you should include the warrants.

Refutation: Deal With Opposing Viewpoints

Any controversial issue is going to have more than one viewpoint, and you must recognize contending claims and handle them fairly. As suggested in the section on audience analysis, you can enhance your credibility by describing these opposing viewpoints fully and accurately, with a respectful rather than hostile tone, even as you demonstrate that your position is the most reasonable and valid.

As a prewriting strategy for *refutation*, or counterargument, you might try dividing a sheet of paper or your computer screen into three columns, labeling them, from left to right, "Supporting Viewpoints," "Opposing Viewpoints," and "Refutation." Then list the main supporting points for your claim, thinking of possible opposing responses and writing them down as you go. Foretelling how the opposition will respond to your supporting reasons will help you develop counterarguments. You can use the resulting chart as a guide to organize sections of your argument essay.

This technique for counterarguments forces you to acknowledge opposing viewpoints and also to refute them in a systematic way. It is perfectly appropriate—and even necessary—to demonstrate the weakness or insufficiency of opposing arguments. Refutation strengthens your position. Any complex argument you present will not be complete unless you skillfully refute all predictable opposing viewpoints, using one of the following techniques:

- **Question the opposition's claim.** Is it too flimsy or broad, overstated, or improperly grounded in minor propositions?

- **Question the opposition's evidence.** Is it insufficient, outdated, or inaccurate?

- **Question the warrants of an opposing argument.** What assumptions and beliefs wrongly underpin the opposition's claim?

- **Concede (accept) some part of the opposition's viewpoint.** This is a subtle but extremely attractive strategy that shows you are a courteous and unbiased thinker and writer (and constitutes an appeal to ethics).

Avoid Unfair Emotional Appeals and Errors in Reasoning

When you write and revise an argument essay, you need to avoid certain temptations and dangers unique to this form of discourse. You must make certain your argumentative strategies are fair and appropriate and that you have avoided oversimplifying your argument. You also need to resist the temptation to use persuasive appeals that distort or falsify logical reasoning.

Unfair Emotional Appeals

Emotional appeals are effective when used appropriately in argumentation, but used unfairly they can distort your logical reasoning. Such loaded arguments are filled with appeals to the reader's emotions, fears, and prejudices. Here are some of the most common fallacies of emotional argumentation to avoid:

TRANSFER   Transfer is the association of a proposition with a famous person. Transfer can be either positive ("In the spirit of President Franklin D. Roosevelt, we should pass a jobs program for the nation's unemployed") or negative ("The president's immigration policy resonates with Hitler's Nazism"). Another term for negative transfer is *name calling*. In both the positive and negative types of transfer, there is no logical basis for the connection.

AD HOMINEM   *Ad hominem* ("against the man" or, literally, "to the person") is a strategy that discredits a person in an effort to discredit his or her argument. It attacks the person rather than the position: "Richards is a liberal and consequently cannot understand the dangers of unchecked immigration." In this instance, the individual becomes a false issue.

GLITTERING GENERALITIES **Glittering generalities** is a strategy that deliberately arouses an audience's emotions about certain institutions and ideas. Certain words have strong positive or negative connotations. Such words as *patriotism* and *motherhood* are *virtue* words. Suggestive words can be used to distort meaning by illogical association and to manipulate an audience to take a stand for or against a proposition: "The school should not take the *totalitarian* step of requiring athletes to maintain a full course load."

BANDWAGON **Bandwagon** is a related strategy in which the writer generalizes falsely that the crowd or majority is always right: "Everyone is voting for Erikson and you should too." This strategy taps into many people's fear of missing out (FOMO).

These unfair emotional appeals are often found in political speech writing, advertising, and propaganda. When you write argument essays, you should use persuasive appeal to *reinforce* rather than *distort* the logical presentation of your ideas, blending reasonable claims and valid emotional and ethical appeals to convince rather than trick your audience into agreeing with you.

Errors in Reasoning (Logical Fallacies)

Equally important is the need to avoid errors in reasoning in the construction of an argument. Here are some types of errors in reasoning, or *logical fallacies*, common in argumentative writing:

HASTY GENERALIZATIONS A **hasty generalization** is a conclusion based on insufficient, unrepresentative, or untrue evidence: "Our tennis team won at state, so the other school teams should be able to do the same." When you indulge in hasty generalizations, you jump to false conclusions. Hasty generalizations are also at the heart of stereotyping—the oversimplified generalization to a group or to individual members of the group. Make certain you have adequate and accurate evidence to support any claim or conclusion.

BROAD GENERALIZATIONS A **broad generalization** typically employs words like *all, never,* and *always* to state something absolutely or categorically. It is actually a form of overstatement, as in the sentence "Freud always treated sexuality as the basis of human behavior." Usually, readers can easily find exceptions to such sweeping statements, so it is best to qualify them.

OVERSIMPLIFICATION **Oversimplification** reduces alternatives. Several forms of oversimplification might be used:

> *Either/Or* Assuming there are only two sides to an issue, or only two possibilities, or only yes or no, or only right or wrong: "Either we make English a four-year requirement or students will not be able to write well."

> *No Choice* Assuming there is only one possibility: "The United States has no other alternative than to build a missile defense system." Parents and politicians are prone to no-other-choice propositions.

No Harm or Cost Assuming a potential benefit will not have significant harms, consequences, or costs: "We should impose tariffs on all goods imported from China." No-harm generalizations or arguments may overlook significant implications. Always consider alternative evidence.

One Solution Assuming a complicated issue has only one solution: "Embryonic stem cells should not be used for research, for using them in this way will lead to the destruction of human life." Always consider evidence for other solutions or alternative approaches to issues and problems.

BEGGING THE QUESTION   The logical fallacy labeled **"begging the question"** occurs when a claim is stated without supporting evidence. For example, if you argue that vandalism by teenagers is unavoidable because teenagers are young and irresponsible, you are begging the question because you are not proving your premise—you are only making another claim. Another form of begging the question is to take a conclusion for granted before it is proved.

FALSE CAUSE-AND-EFFECT RELATIONSHIPS   Perhaps the most common error in trying to establish causal relationships is known as the ***post hoc, ergo propter hoc*** fallacy ("after this, therefore because of this"). The fact that one event *follows* another is not proof the first *caused* the second. If you maintain there is an increase in the crime rate every time a full moon occurs, for example, you are falsely identifying an unrelated event as a cause. Many superstitions—popular, political, and otherwise—illogically assume that one event somehow causes another.

DISCONNECTED IDEAS   Termed ***non sequitur*** ("it does not follow"), this fallacy in reasoning arises when there is no logical connection between two or more ideas. Put differently, an argument's conclusion is not related to its premises: "Barack Obama was a good president because he worked out every morning." Sometimes you perceive a connection exists but you fail to state it in writing. For example, you may think presidents need to stay in shape to be effective leaders. In other words, *you* may see the logical connection between your ideas, but if you do not make it explicit, readers may think there is a *non sequitur*.

WEAK OR FALSE ANALOGIES   An *analogy* is a type of comparison. A **weak or false analogy** explains a subject by comparing it to the features of another essentially dissimilar subject: "Unless we learn to think critically about the Niagara of information that washes over us every day, we will be lost in a flood of rumors and gossip." Analogies can be used to illustrate or explain a point, although they should always be used carefully and with discretion. More significantly, an analogy can *never* function as evidence or logical proof of a position.

The Argument Essay on the AP Exam

You will be asked to write an argument essay on the AP Language and Composition exam. Below is a prompt for an argument essay similar to what you will see on the exam:

> An American economist recently defended the existence of sweatshops (low-paying factories) in developing countries, stating that they provide a path for laborers to rise out of poverty.
>
> Consider the economist's claim about sweatshops; then develop a position on the assertion that everyone benefits when multinational corporations set up factories (sweatshops) in developing countries. Support your argument with appropriate evidence from your reading, observation, and experience.

This chapter has discussed how to clarify your claim (thesis), consider your warrants, and gather and evaluate evidence as you create an argument essay. When you take the AP exam, however, you will not be able to research your topic. Without access to research, how should you approach responding to the prompt with "appropriate evidence"? As the prompt above states, you need to create your argument from prior reading, observation, and experience. Although every topic is different, several general issues can be applied to any topic to reveal the complexity and possible views that can be addressed in your argument. The mnemonic, or memory device, "HELPS ME" is an easy way to remember the sort of evidence that "helps me" develop an argument.

HELPS ME

History
Current Events
Literature and Arts
Personal Experience
Science and Technology
Money
Ethics

History

Look at a controversial topic from a historical perspective, or events over time. What evidence throughout history affects your argument on the topic? Or, how will a topic's history impact your position? Consider this evidence of how multinationals have impacted the world throughout recent history: Multinationals lead to interdependence, English as an international language, and the U.S. dollar as the global currency.

Current Events

If you get stuck wondering how to expand your argument, ask yourself: How does your proposal on the topic, or your opponent's proposal, apply to current events? These could be political, social, or environmental events. You might support your argument regarding multinationals with current events this way: Lack of regulations in developing countries has led to pollution and catastrophic factory collapses. Reduced regulations lead to lower costs for consumers, but they also endanger employees.

Literature and Arts

Supportive examples can be found in literature and visual arts such as paintings, photos, and theater. Using literary examples will not automatically gain you additional credit with scorers at the AP exam, but many argument topics can be handled adroitly with the incorporation of a literature example. If you have read Upton Sinclair's *The Jungle,* for instance, imagine the connections you could make between his analysis of the meatpacking industry and the sweatshop conditions the workers experienced. When incorporating literature in your essay, it is not necessary to provide a summary of the book you are referencing. Instead, consider the overall purpose of the author's writing and incorporate specific details to further your argument.

Personal Experience

Personal experience is probably the most common type of evidence used in the argument essay. But be cautious and narrate experiences that carry gravitas and are truly relevant to the argument. You will have much more credibility if you detail a time when you truly developed as a human being (learning to cook when a parent was ill) than when you simply struggled to get what you wanted (finding the right outfit for homecoming). For this prompt, it is not likely you have had personal experience with a sweatshop. If you have visited a developing country and witnessed poor labor conditions, however, those details provide compelling evidence to your argument.

Science and Technology

Consider scientific and technological evidence as you approach the issue and your argument. How do scientific advancements impact the topic? How might your position change based on the speed and efficiency of technology? Part of an argument and supporting evidence regarding multinationals could support this claim: Technology and education offered by multinationals can help create or improve the middle class.

Money

One issue that concerns most controversial topics is money. Some money questions you might raise include: How is this proposal to be funded? What will it cost in dollars and employees? The bottom line for most arguments is the dollar. In an argument about multinational corporations, a money issue might be: Multinationals pay low wages in developing countries, keeping prices of products low in the U.S.

Ethics

To present a position effectively, consider not only your beliefs, values, and morals, but also those of your audience. As you take a position on a controversial topic, establish right from wrong and abide by a code of ethics. An ethical issue regarding multinationals might be: Unethical low wages are counterbalanced by offering available jobs.

The hallmark of argumentation is sound critical thinking. A successful argument essay reveals a writer who is able to reason well, judge opinions on the basis of evidence, and back up ideas in a convincing and valid way. If you present your claims, grounds, and evidence carefully, and treat the opposition with respect, you are on your way to constructing a solid argument essay. See Chapter 12 to review a sample student argument essay.

Synthesizing: Making Connections

Synthesizing is a necessary skill for you to master in AP Language and Composition as well as in life. Throughout your academic and professional careers, you will be asked to gather information to make decisions. More often than not, the information you encounter will be diverse and contradictory. Your task will be to digest the differing sources before you make a valid, compelling argument for some sort of conclusion.

When you synthesize, you create a coherent whole from separate elements. The combination of the elements must be polished and purposeful, and create a valuable end product. Synthesizing information is an advanced form of analysis that involves understanding multiple sources of information, identifying how those sources vary, and combining the information into a cohesive argument.

You synthesize information every day, even though you may not realize it. Suppose you are trying to decide whether to buy a new videogame. You would probably watch a trailer or advertisement for the game, and you might read a review of the game on a favorite website. You may ask your friends about their experience with the game, and each friend might have a different opinion. You would consider all of this information—these arguments—before you make a decision about purchasing the game. You would synthesize all of the messages you received and then form a coherent argument, which would then guide your decision-making. This process is synthesis.

In a synthesis essay, you enter into a "conversation" with two or more writers, attempting to understand their main ideas or arguments, to analyze the evidence they provide, and to evaluate their conclusions. As with any academic conversation, you must present the writers' ideas with accuracy and respect—but also with an eye to the purpose or aim of your own writing.

When synthesizing, then, what begins as an isolated moment (actively reading a single text) spirals into a series of moments (reading several texts), which demands your powers of comparative analysis and the ability to evaluate relationships among sources. In addition, synthesizing requires you to consider the sources' biases.

Writing a Thesis or Claim

There are several types of synthesis. With *explanatory synthesis*, you try to accurately identify the key ideas and purposes of various writers or sources, but you do not argue for or against a certain viewpoint. For example, here is a student's thesis based on the essays by Peter Elbow and Donald Murray from Chapter 2:

> Both Peter Elbow and Donald Murray stress the importance of process in the craft of composition, but approach the process from different perspectives.

In the example above, the student makes a modest but useful attempt to convey information accurately through explanatory synthesis.

With *argumentative synthesis*, the writer takes a side. Consider the shift from explanation to argument as the writer now assumes a position in presenting the ideas of Elbow and Murray:

Although Peter Elbow's theory of freewriting might be useful to certain students with basic writing problems, Donald Murray in his stress on revision offers far more useful advice for high school students who want to improve their writing.

Observe how the writer moves from explanatory to argumentative synthesis as she critiques the two readings and their authors. She takes sides. She presents a claim (which she will have to support with convincing grounds or evidence). She wants us to agree with her interpretation and assessment.

Argumentative synthesis, like all types of argumentative writing, presents a claim about which reasonable people might agree or disagree. The challenge is to formulate your synthesis in such a way that it convinces or persuades your audience to agree with your assessment and fundamental viewpoint.

Critiquing Sources

Obviously, before you can synthesize various sources, you must read and analyze those sources. In doing so, you should rely on the strategies for active reading and writing outlined in Chapters 1 and 2. At the outset, it is wise to focus on *critiquing*—the evaluation of each separate source's quality or worth based on a clearly defined set of guidelines. With critiquing, you cannot rely on a personal opinion or preference. Critiquing demands clear criteria and objective assessment of the text. It is a necessary aspect of successful argumentative synthesis.

When critiquing sources in AP and college composition courses, you will consider issues such as: style, organization, importance of subject, effectiveness of a writer's claim, and quality of evidence. You will agree, disagree, or (in certain cases) agree *and* disagree to varying degrees with a writer—but do so from the vantage point of informed judgment.

The formal demands of critiquing are neither mysterious nor intimidating. In everyday situations, we engage in critiquing: arguing over the merits of two recent films, evaluating the skills of various sports stars, praising our favorite musicians, or supporting one candidate for political office over all others. Writing a formal critique is perhaps more of a challenge than situations from everyday life, but if you follow basic steps, the process of critiquing becomes manageable.

1. **Carefully read and annotate each source.** Cite the source of the article and the author's intended audience, look for the thesis or claim, identify the author's purpose (to inform, argue, or entertain), highlight the evidence, and consider the style and organization of the piece.

2. **Briefly summarize your findings.** Your summary should focus on the author's main points.

3. **Evaluate the source.** Consider the overall validity of the author's presentation: Has the writer achieved his or her purpose? What is the quality of the supporting evidence? Is the information or evidence convincing and representative? Has the author interpreted the material correctly and argued logically?

Guidelines for Argumentative Synthesis

Consider the synthesis essay as an argument essay with sources. Your conversation with other writers/source material is used to bolster your own claim—your assertion that you plan to prove and with which other readers can agree or disagree. To support your argument, you seek evidence from relevant sources, analyze and evaluate the merits of that evidence, and use it to support your argument.

1. **Consider your purpose.** Is your purpose to *explain* or to *argue*—or perhaps a combination of both? How will this purpose affect your search for sources?

2. **Select and identify your sources.** Where and when did the article first appear, and what might this publication tell you about the writer's perspective? Identify the author, noting his or her credentials, publications, and occupation. How does the title or subtitle reveal the writer's purpose? Does the title seem to align to your purpose? Why or why not?

3. **Read actively.** What is the writer's primary purpose? What is the main idea or argument? What are the minor points? How do the subpoints relate to the central point? What is the structure of the text—the introduction, middle sections, and conclusion? How does the text reinforce a key idea that you may have in mind for an essay?

4. **Take notes and summarize.** Use the techniques of print and/or electronic annotation. Identify the writer's main point and rewrite it in one or two sentences.

5. **Establish connections among readings.** What relationships do you detect as you move from text to text? How do major and minor points stressed by the writers in their texts overlap or diverge? What elements of their arguments are similar and dissimilar? Draw up a list of similar and dissimilar points for handy reference.

6. **Write your synthesis.** First, write down your thesis or claim, and develop it in an introductory paragraph. Next, draft body paragraphs that offer support for the thesis or claim; write topic sentences for all paragraphs; incorporate explanatory or argumentative details drawn from the sources that you synthesize; and document your sources properly in order to avoid any charge of plagiarism. Finally, write a conclusion that grows organically from the preceding paragraphs and reinforces your main idea. Then revise your essay.

The Synthesis Essay on the AP Exam

One of the three essays on the AP Language and Composition exam will ask you to synthesize multiple sources and create a compelling argument based on a prompt. For the synthesis essay question, you will receive a packet of six to eight different sources introduced by a set of guiding thoughts. Each source will have bibliographic information, letting you know the author, publisher, and publication date. Additional context information may be provided for some of the sources as well. Each source is usually several paragraphs to a full page, and some of the sources will be a photograph, chart, political cartoon, or other type of visual. Usually, you are required to use a minimum of only three different sources in your essay. You will be given 15 minutes to review the sources, and 40 minutes to write the essay.

Read the introductory information thoroughly *before* you examine the sources. An introductory page to the synthesis question will give you context for the situation you will write about. This background information may be broad or specific. The introduction will also provide a description of the specific issue at hand, and it will present different viewpoints on the issue as well. The introduction also provides the prompt as well as information on how to write the essay. You will be told to consider an argument or a statement. You will basically agree or disagree with a statement, idea, or viewpoint—and then explore the topic and support your position with a discussion of the sources. Here is a sample introduction to the AP synthesis essay. The prompt (or task) is bolded:

> War seems to be an inevitable part of the human experience. Depending on the circumstances, war is considered ennobling, necessary, and just. However, it may also be seen as corrupt, irrational, or even evil. Must war be an unavoidable part of human civilization? Is the sacrifice of war worth it? Do the casualties outweigh the causes?
>
> Read the following sources (including any introductory information) carefully. **Then develop a position about what issues should be considered most important in making the decision to declare war.**
>
> Make sure that your argument is central; use the sources to illustrate and support your reasoning. Avoid merely summarizing the sources. Indicate clearly which sources you are drawing from, whether through direct quotation, paraphrase, or summary. You may cite the sources as Source A, Source B, etc., or by using the descriptions in parentheses.
>
> Source A (Wilson)
> Source B (Kennedy)
> Source C (Political Cartoon)
> Source D (Bush)
> Source E (Reagan)
> Source F (Department of Veterans Affairs)
> Source G (Chart: Department of Defense)

Notice that the prompt wants you to *develop a position*. This means you must state an opinion that someone else can disagree with. If your main argument does not have an opposing viewpoint, then you do not have a strong position. Always connect your argument to a clear, arguable thesis statement. For example, the prompt above asks you to "develop a position about what issues should be considered most important in making a decision to go to war." Although not explicitly stated, this prompt wants you to create a hierarchy of important factors. In your notes, write your own sentence about what the prompt actually wants you to do.

Very briefly, brainstorm your ideas about each side of the issue. What you do *not* want to do is simply list and briefly discuss each of the factors that should be considered. That structure would lead you straight to a summary, which you want to avoid. You do not want or need to explain the sources at any point in your essay. Knowledge of the sources is assumed—the reader grading your essay has seen and is familiar with the source material. Instead, create an argument that focuses on one or two issues that should be considered, but then clearly argue for *one* issue that trumps all others. This structure keeps your essay focused and your argument effective.

Now you are ready to read and analyze the sources. Each source comes with an "information box" that tells you about the author, origin, publication, date, and so on. Examine this information carefully. Look for context, the intended audience, bias, authority of the author, the source of the author's information, and the type of evidence the author presents. Your task, remember, is to use the sources to strengthen your *own* argument. You do not want to summarize the sources, and you do not have to agree with them in order to use them in your essay. You must "converse" with the sources. Use what works with your argument. In addition, form an argument *against* the sources on the opposite side of the issue. Remember, your voice should be the loudest in the "room."

As you analyze the first source, consider its most convincing arguments:

- Which part of the text would you be most likely to use in an essay?
- Could this piece be used to negate an argument?
- Do you find faulty reasoning in this piece? If so, how could you use this information to strengthen your own argument?
- Is there any bias in the source? If so, discussing the bias will add sophistication to your argument.
- If you like the source, make a mental note to come back to it and possibly use it when writing your essay. If you don't like the source or don't find it particularly useful, you don't have to use it. You are only required to use three of the six to eight sources you are given.

As you analyze the second source, ask the same questions as above—but also compare it to the first source.

After you've analyzed the assignment page, dissected the prompt, and examined the sources, you will then craft your synthesis essay. Understand that the prompt has no right or wrong answer. The exam reader cares only about how well you argue your position, not which side of the issue you take. Organize your argument around your own ideas, and then construct your paragraphs around the major points of your argument, using the sources only as supportive evidence or as springboards for discussion.

If you do quote or paraphrase any of the sources, use quotes and paraphrase judiciously and acknowledge the sources with the correct citations. (See Chapter 1 for a refresher on how to use quotations or paraphrase.) Writers who fail to acknowledge their sources correctly—even by accident—commit plagiarism. You may cite the information you use in one of two ways. You can refer to the source by the letter ascribed to it in the prompt: Source A, Source B, and so on. Or you may refer to the source by the author's last name or the title. Be consistent. Do not switch back and forth between citation styles. See Chapter 12 to review a sample student synthesis essay.

Famous Arguments

Read and analyze the two sources that follow. Study how Aristotle defines and explains the necessity of rhetoric. See argumentation in action through Thomas Paine's words.

The Art of Rhetoric

Aristotle

The city-state of Athens saw a surfacing of democracy in the years around 460 B.C.E., when public speaking became an essential skill for politicians in the assemblies and councils and even for ordinary citizens in the courts of law. Thus, skills in rhetorical technique rapidly developed, laying the groundwork for a host of practical manuals for the layman. Unlike the books giving "tricks" for successful debating, "The Art of Rhetoric" held a far deeper purpose. In it, Aristotle (384–322 B.C.E.) establishes the methods of informal reasoning, provides the first artistic and visual evaluation of prose style, and offers detailed observations on character and the emotions. Extremely influential upon later Western culture, "The Art of Rhetoric" is a fascinating consideration of the forces of persuasion and literalism, and a compelling guide to the principles behind oratorical skills. What follows is an excerpt from Aristotle's treatise.

1 Rhetoric is useful (1) because things that are true and things that are just have a natural tendency to prevail over their opposites, so that if the decisions of judges are not what they ought to be, the defeat must be due to the speakers themselves, and they must be blamed accordingly. Moreover, (2) before some audiences not even the possession of the exactest knowledge will make it easy for what we say to produce conviction. For argument based on knowledge implies instruction, and there are people whom one cannot instruct. Here, then, we must use, as our modes of persuasion and argument, notions possessed by everybody, as we observed in the *Topics* when dealing with the way to handle a popular audience. Further, (3) we must be able to employ persuasion, just as strict reasoning can be employed, on opposite sides of a question, not in order that we may in practice employ it in both ways (for we must not make people believe what is wrong), but in order that we may see clearly what the facts are, and that, if another man argues unfairly, we on our part may be able to confute him. No other of the arts draws opposite conclusions: dialectic and rhetoric alone do this. Both these arts draw opposite conclusions impartially. Nevertheless, the underlying facts do not lend themselves equally well to the contrary views. No; things that are true and things that are better are, by their nature, practically always easier to prove and easier to believe in. Again, (4) it is absurd to hold that a man ought to be ashamed of being unable to defend himself with his limbs, but not of being unable to defend himself with speech and reason, when the use of rational speech is more distinctive of a human being than the use of his limbs. And if it be objected that one who uses such power of speech unjustly

might do great harm, *that* is a charge which may be made in common against all good things except virtue, and above all against the things that are most useful, as strength, health, wealth, generalship. A man can confer the greatest of benefits by a right use of these, and inflict the greatest of injuries by using them wrongly.

2   It is clear, then, that rhetoric is not bound up with a single definite class of subjects, but is as universal as dialectic; it is clear, also, that it is useful. It is clear, further, that its function is not simply to succeed in persuading, but rather to discover the means of coming as near such success as the circumstances of each particular case allow. In this it resembles all other arts. For example, it is not the function of medicine simply to make a man quite healthy, but to put him as far as may be on the road to health; it is possible to give excellent treatment even to those who can never enjoy sound health. Furthermore, it is plain that it is the function of one and the same art to discern the real and the apparent means of persuasion, just as it is the function of dialectic to discern the real and the apparent syllogism. What makes a man a "sophist" is not his faculty, but his moral purpose. In rhetoric, however, the term "rhetorician" may describe either the speaker's knowledge of the art, or his moral purpose. In dialectic it is different: a man is a "sophist" because he has a certain kind of moral purpose, a "dialectician" in respect, not of his moral purpose, but of his faculty.

3   Let us now try to give some account of the systematic principles of Rhetoric itself—of the right method and means of succeeding in the object we set before us. We must make as it were a fresh start, and before going further define what rhetoric is.

4   Rhetoric may be defined as the faculty of observing in any given case the available means of persuasion. This is not a function of any other art. Every other art can instruct or persuade about its own particular subject-matter; for instance, medicine about what is healthy and unhealthy, geometry about the properties of magnitudes, arithmetic about numbers, and the same is true of the other arts and sciences. But rhetoric we look upon as the power of observing the means of persuasion on almost any subject presented to us; and that is why we say that, in its technical character, it is not concerned with any special or definite class of subjects.

5   Of the modes of persuasion some belong strictly to the art of rhetoric and some do not. By the latter I mean such things as are not supplied by the speaker but are there at the outset—witnesses, evidence given under torture, written contracts, and so on. By the former I mean such as we can ourselves construct by means of the principles of rhetoric. The one kind has merely to be used, the other has to be invented.

6   Of the modes of persuasion furnished by the spoken word there are three kinds. The first kind depends on the personal character of the speaker; the second on putting the audience into a certain frame of mind; the third on the proof, or apparent proof, provided by the words of the speech itself. Persuasion is achieved by the speaker's personal character when the speech is so spoken as to make us think him credible. We believe good men more fully and more readily than others: this is true generally whatever the question is, and absolutely true where exact certainty is impossible and opinions are divided. This kind of persuasion, like the others, should be achieved by what the speaker says, not by what people think of his character before he begins to speak. It is not true, as some writers assume in

their treatises on rhetoric, that the personal goodness revealed by the speaker contributes nothing to his power of persuasion; on the contrary, his character may almost be called the most effective means of persuasion he possesses. Secondly, persuasion may come through the hearers, when the speech stirs their emotions. Our judgements when we are pleased and friendly are not the same as when we are pained and hostile. It is towards producing these effects, as we maintain, that present-day writers on rhetoric direct the whole of their efforts. This subject shall be treated in detail when we come to speak of the emotions. Thirdly, persuasion is effected through the speech itself when we have proved a truth or an apparent truth by means of the persuasive arguments suitable to the case in question.

7 There are, then, these three means of effecting persuasion. The man who is to be in command of them must, it is clear, be able (1) to reason logically, (2) to understand human character and goodness in their various forms, and (3) to understand the emotions—that is, to name them and describe them, to know their causes and the way in which they are excited. It thus appears that rhetoric is an offshoot of dialectic and also of ethical studies. Ethical studies may fairly be called political; and for this reason rhetoric masquerades as political science, and the professors of it as political experts—sometimes from want of education, sometimes from ostentation, sometimes owing to other human failings. As a matter of fact, it is a branch of dialectic and similar to it, as we said at the outset. Neither rhetoric nor dialectic is the scientific study of any one separate subject: both are faculties for providing arguments. This is perhaps a sufficient account of their scope and of how they are related to each other.

The Works of Aristotle: Rhetorica, by W. R. Roberts. De rhetorica ad Alexandrum, by E. S. Forster. De poetica, by I. Bywater. Volume 11 of *The Works of Aristotle*, William David Ross. Clarendon Press, 1924.

Comprehension

1. The last paragraph points out skills a person must hold to effectively persuade. What are other words for the three listed abilities that a person must hold?

2. What does Aristotle believe to be the most important means for a person to be able to persuade others?

3. Where is rhetoric's place when considering the arts?

4. Aristotle begins and ends this portion of "The Art of Rhetoric" with one clear point about the misuse of rhetoric. What is that point?

Rhetorical Analysis

5. How does Aristotle use exemplification to assert his position?

6. Aristotle uses the rhetorical strategy of repetition in paragraph 3 (and once in paragraph 7). Identify it and explain why it is effective.

7. What effect do the numerical lists add to Aristotle's rhetorical style?

8. Why does Aristotle choose to write this piece in the first person?

9. Write a short paraphrase of this excerpt.

10. Consider areas of expertise where you could be successfully persuasive. Choose three and write three premises for your arguments.

11. Now consider three stumbling blocks to the arguments you listed in answer 2, and write how you would address each stumbling block.

Common Sense (1776)

Thomas Paine

Thomas Paine (1737–1809) was an influential 18th-century writer of essays and pamphlets, including *The Age of Reason*, an essay regarding the place of religion in society; *Rights of Man*, a piece defending the French Revolution; and *Common Sense*, a pamphlet that was published in 1776 during the American Revolution. *Common Sense* is credited with bringing Paine's ideas to the larger audience of the Colonies, swaying the "undecided" public opinion to the view that independence from the British was a necessity. His plain speaking style was one the masses could follow and act upon.

1   IN the following pages I offer nothing more than simple facts, plain arguments, and common sense: and have no other preliminaries to settle with the reader, than that he will divest himself of prejudice and prepossession, and suffer his reason and his feelings to determine for themselves that he will put on, or rather that he will not put off, the true character of a man, and generously enlarge his views beyond the present day.

2   Volumes have been written on the subject of the struggle between England and America. Men of all ranks have embarked in the controversy, from different motives, and with various designs; but all have been ineffectual, and the period of debate is closed. Arms as the last resource decide the contest; the appeal was the choice of the King, and the Continent has accepted the challenge.

3   It hath been reported of the late Mr. Pelham (who tho' an able minister was not without his faults) that on his being attacked in the House of Commons on the score that his measures were only of a temporary kind, replied, "THEY WILL LAST MY TIME." Should a thought so fatal and unmanly possess the Colonies in the present contest, the name of ancestors will be remembered by future generations with detestation.

4   The Sun never shined on a cause of greater worth. 'Tis not the affair of a City, a County, a Province, or a Kingdom; but of a Continent—of at least one-eighth part of the habitable Globe. 'Tis not the concern of a day, a year, or an age; posterity are virtually involved in the contest, and will be more or less affected even to the end of time, by the proceedings now. Now is the seed-time of Continental union,

faith and honour. The least fracture now will be like a name engraved with the point of a pin on the tender rind of a young oak; the wound would enlarge with the tree, and posterity read in it full grown characters.

5   By referring the matter from argument to arms, a new era for politics is struck—a new method of thinking hath arisen. All plans, proposals, &c. prior to the nineteenth of April, i.e. to the commencement of hostilities, are like the almanacks of the last year; which tho' proper then, are superseded and useless now. Whatever was advanced by the advocates on either side of the question then, terminated in one and the same point, viz. a union with Great Britain; the only difference between the parties was the method of effecting it; the one proposing force, the other friendship; but it hath so far happened that the first hath failed, and the second hath withdrawn her influence.

6   As much hath been said of the advantages of reconciliation, which, like an agreeable dream, hath passed away and left us as we were, it is but right that we should examine the contrary side of the argument, and enquire into some of the many material injuries which these Colonies sustain, and always will sustain, by being connected with and dependent on Great Britain. To examine that connection and dependence, on the principles of nature and common sense, to see what we have to trust to, if separated, and what we are to expect, if dependent.

7   I have heard it asserted by some, that as America has flourished under her former connection with Great Britain, the same connection is necessary towards her future happiness, and will always have the same effect. Nothing can be more fallacious than this kind of argument. We may as well assert that because a child has thrived upon milk, that it is never to have meat, or that the first twenty years of our lives is to become a precedent for the next twenty. But even this is admitting more than is true; for I answer roundly that America would have flourished as much, and probably much more, had no European power taken any notice of her. The commerce by which she hath enriched herself are the necessaries of life, and will always have a market while eating is the custom of Europe.

8   But she has protected us, say some. That she hath engrossed us is true, and defended the Continent at our expense as well as her own, is admitted; and she would have defended Turkey from the same motive, viz.—for the sake of trade and dominion.

9   Alas! we have been long led away by ancient prejudices and made large sacrifices to superstition. We have boasted the protection of Great Britain, without considering, that her motive was INTEREST not ATTACHMENT; and that she did not protect us from OUR ENEMIES on OUR ACCOUNT; but from HER ENEMIES on HER OWN ACCOUNT, from those who had no quarrel with us on any OTHER ACCOUNT, and who will always be our enemies on the SAME ACCOUNT. Let Britain waive her pretensions to the Continent, or the Continent throw off the dependence, and we should be at peace with France and Spain, were they at war with Britain. The miseries of Hanover last war ought to warn us against connections.

10   It hath lately been asserted in parliament, that the Colonies have no relation to each other but through the Parent Country, i.e. that Pennsylvania and the Jerseys and so on for the rest, are sister Colonies by the way of England; this is certainly a

very roundabout way of proving relationship, but it is the nearest and only true way of proving enmity (or enemyship, if I may so call it.) France and Spain never were, nor perhaps ever will be, our enemies as AMERICANS, but as our being the SUBJECTS OF GREAT BRITAIN.

[11]   But Britain is the parent country, say some. Then the more shame upon her conduct. Even brutes do not devour their young, nor savages make war upon their families. Wherefore, the assertion, if true, turns to her reproach; but it happens not to be true, or only partly so, and the phrase PARENT OR MOTHER COUNTRY hath been jesuitically adopted by the King and his parasites, with a low papistical design of gaining an unfair bias on the credulous weakness of our minds. Europe, and not England, is the parent country of America. This new World hath been the asylum for the persecuted lovers of civil and religious liberty from EVERY PART of Europe. Hither have they fled, not from the tender embraces of the mother, but from the cruelty of the monster; and it is so far true of England, that the same tyranny which drove the first emigrants from home, pursues their descendants still.

[12]   In this extensive quarter of the globe, we forget the narrow limits of three hundred and sixty miles (the extent of England) and carry our friendship on a larger scale; we claim brotherhood with every European Christian, and triumph in the generosity of the sentiment.

[13]   It is pleasant to observe by what regular gradations we surmount the force of local prejudices, as we enlarge our acquaintance with the World. A man born in any town in England divided into parishes, will naturally associate most with his fellow parishioners (because their interests in many cases will be common) and distinguish him by the name of NEIGHBOR; if he meet him but a few miles from home, he drops the narrow idea of a street, and salutes him by the name of TOWNSMAN; if he travel out of the county and meet him in any other, he forgets the minor divisions of street and town, and calls him COUNTRYMAN, i.e. COUNTYMAN; but if in their foreign excursions they should associate in France, or any other part of EUROPE, their local remembrance would be enlarged into that of ENGLISHMEN. And by a just parity of reasoning, all Europeans meeting in America, or any other quarter of the globe, are COUNTRYMEN; for England, Holland, Germany, or Sweden, when compared with the whole, stand in the same places on the larger scale, which the divisions of street, town, and county do on the smaller ones; Distinctions too limited for Continental minds. Not one third of the inhabitants, even of this province, [Pennsylvania], are of English descent. Wherefore, I reprobate the phrase of Parent or Mother Country applied to England only, as being false, selfish, narrow and ungenerous.

[14]   But, admitting that we were all of English descent, what does it amount to? Nothing. Britain, being now an open enemy, extinguishes every other name and title: and to say that reconciliation is our duty, is truly farcical. The first king of England, of the present line (William the Conqueror) was a Frenchman, and half the peers of England are descendants from the same country; wherefore, by the same method of reasoning, England ought to be governed by France.

[15]   Much hath been said of the united strength of Britain and the Colonies, that in conjunction they might bid defiance to the world. But this is mere presumption;

the fate of war is uncertain, neither do the expressions mean anything; for this continent would never suffer itself to be drained of inhabitants, to support the British arms in either Asia, Africa, or Europe.

16   Besides, what have we to do with setting the world at defiance? Our plan is commerce, and that, well attended to, will secure us the peace and friendship of all Europe; because it is the interest of all Europe to have America a free port. Her trade will always be a protection, and her barrenness of gold and silver secure her from invaders.

17   I challenge the warmest advocate for reconciliation to show a single advantage that this continent can reap by being connected with Great Britain. I repeat the challenge; not a single advantage is derived. Our corn will fetch its price in any market in Europe, and our imported goods must be paid for buy them where we will.

18   But the injuries and disadvantages which we sustain by that connection, are without number; and our duty to mankind at large, as well as to ourselves, instruct us to renounce the alliance: because, any submission to, or dependence on, Great Britain, tends directly to involve this Continent in European wars and quarrels, and set us at variance with nations who would otherwise seek our friendship, and against whom we have neither anger nor complaint. As Europe is our market for trade, we ought to form no partial connection with any part of it. It is the true interest of America to steer clear of European contentions, which she never can do, while, by her dependence on Britain, she is made the makeweight in the scale of British politics.

19   Europe is too thickly planted with Kingdoms to be long at peace, and whenever a war breaks out between England and any foreign power, the trade of America goes to ruin, BECAUSE OF HER CONNECTION WITH BRITAIN. The next war may not turn out like the last, and should it not, the advocates for reconciliation now will be wishing for separation then, because neutrality in that case would be a safer convoy than a man of war. Every thing that is right or reasonable pleads for separation. The blood of the slain, the weeping voice of nature cries, 'TIS TIME TO PART. Even the distance at which the Almighty hath placed England and America is a strong and natural proof that the authority of the one over the other, was never the design of Heaven. The time likewise at which the Continent was discovered, adds weight to the argument, and the manner in which it was peopled, encreases the force of it. The Reformation was preceded by the discovery of America: As if the Almighty graciously meant to open a sanctuary to the persecuted in future years, when home should afford neither friendship nor safety.

20   The authority of Great Britain over this continent, is a form of government, which sooner or later must have an end: And a serious mind can draw no true pleasure by looking forward, under the painful and positive conviction that what he calls "the present constitution" is merely temporary. As parents, we can have no joy, knowing that this government is not sufficiently lasting to ensure any thing which we may bequeath to posterity: And by a plain method of argument, as we are running the next generation into debt, we ought to do the work of it, otherwise we use them meanly and pitifully. In order to discover the line of our duty rightly, we should take our children in our hand, and fix our station a few years farther into life; that eminence will present a prospect which a few present fears and prejudices conceal from our sight.

21   Though I would carefully avoid giving unnecessary offence, yet I am inclined to believe, that all those who espouse the doctrine of reconciliation, may be included within the following descriptions. Interested men, who are not to be trusted, weak men who CANNOT see, prejudiced men who will not see, and a certain set of moderate men who think better of the European world than it deserves; and this last class, by an ill-judged deliberation, will be the cause of more calamities to this Continent than all the other three.

22   It is the good fortune of many to live distant from the scene of present sorrow; the evil is not sufficiently brought to their doors to make them feel the precariousness with which all American property is possessed. But let our imaginations transport us a few moments to Boston; that seat of wretchedness will teach us wisdom, and instruct us for ever to renounce a power in whom we can have no trust. The inhabitants of that unfortunate city who but a few months ago were in ease and affluence, have now no other alternative than to stay and starve, or turn out to beg. Endangered by the fire of their friends if they continue within the city and plundered by the soldiery if they leave it, in their present situation they are prisoners without the hope of redemption, and in a general attack for their relief they would be exposed to the fury of both armies.

23   Men of passive tempers look somewhat lightly over the offences of Great Britain, and, still hoping for the best, are apt to call out, "Come, come, we shall be friends again for all this." But examine the passions and feelings of mankind: bring the doctrine of reconciliation to the touchstone of nature, and then tell me whether you can hereafter love, honour, and faithfully serve the power that hath carried fire and sword into your land? If you cannot do all these, then are you only deceiving yourselves, and by your delay bringing ruin upon posterity. Your future connection with Britain, whom you can neither love nor honour, will be forced and unnatural, and being formed only on the plan of present convenience, will in a little time fall into a relapse more wretched than the first. But if you say, you can still pass the violations over, then I ask, hath your house been burnt? Hath your property been destroyed before your face? Are your wife and children destitute of a bed to lie on, or bread to live on? Have you lost a parent or a child by their hands, and yourself the ruined and wretched survivor? If you have not, then are you not a judge of those who have. But if you have, and can still shake hands with the murderers, then are you unworthy the name of husband, father, friend or lover, and whatever may be your rank or title in life, you have the heart of a coward, and the spirit of a sycophant.

24   This is not inflaming or exaggerating matters, but trying them by those feelings and affections which nature justifies, and without which, we should be incapable of discharging the social duties of life, or enjoying the felicities of it. I mean not to exhibit horror for the purpose of provoking revenge, but to awaken us from fatal and unmanly slumbers, that we may pursue determinately some fixed object. It is not in the power of Britain or of Europe to conquer America, if she do not conquer herself by *delay* and *timidity*. The present winter is worth an age if rightly employed, but if lost or neglected, the whole continent will partake of the misfortune; and there is no punishment which that man will not deserve, be he who, or what, or where he will, that may be the means of sacrificing a season so precious and useful.

25   It is repugnant to reason, to the universal order of things to all examples from former ages, to suppose, that this continent can longer remain subject to any external power. The most sanguine in Britain does not think so. The utmost stretch of human wisdom cannot, at this time, compass a plan short of separation, which can promise the continent even a year's security. Reconciliation is *now* a falacious dream. Nature hath deserted the connexion, and Art cannot supply her place. For, as Milton wisely expresses, "never can true reconcilement grow where wounds of deadly hate have pierced so deep."

26   Every quiet method for peace hath been ineffectual. Our prayers have been rejected with disdain; and only tended to convince us, that nothing flatters vanity, or confirms obstinacy in Kings more than repeated petitioning—and nothing hath contributed more than that very measure to make the Kings of Europe absolute: Witness Denmark and Sweden. Wherefore, since nothing but blows will do, for God's sake, let us come to a final separation, and not leave the next generation to be cutting throats, under the violated unmeaning names of parent and child.

27   To say, they will never attempt it again is idle and visionary, we thought so at the repeal of the stamp act, yet a year or two undeceived us; as well may we suppose that nations, which have been once defeated, will never renew the quarrel.

28   As to government matters, it is not in the power of Britain to do this continent justice: The business of it will soon be too weighty, and intricate, to be managed with any tolerable degree of convenience, by a power, so distant from us, and so very ignorant of us; for if they cannot conquer us, they cannot govern us. To be always running three or four thousand miles with a tale or a petition, waiting four or five months for an answer, which when obtained requires five or six more to explain it in, will in a few years be looked upon as folly and childishness—There was a time when it was proper, and there is a proper time for it to cease.

29   Small islands not capable of protecting themselves, are the proper objects for kingdoms to take under their care; but there is something very absurd, in supposing a continent to be perpetually governed by an island. In no instance hath nature made the satellite larger than its primary planet, and as England and America, with respect to each other, reverses the common order of nature, it is evident they belong to different systems: England to Europe, America to itself.

30   I am not induced by motives of pride, party, or resentment to espouse the doctrine of separation and independence; I am clearly, positively, and conscientiously persuaded that it is the true interest of this continent to be so; that every thing short of *that* is mere patchwork, that it can afford no lasting felicity,—that it is leaving the sword to our children, and shrinking back at a time, when, a little more, a little farther, would have rendered this continent the glory of the earth.

Common Sense by Thomas Paine. Philadelphia: W. & T. Bradford, February 14, 1776.
http://www.gutenberg.org/files/147/147-h/147-h.htm

Comprehension

1. Paine's major complaint with the current political system between Great Britain and America centers on what idea?

2. How does Paine feel about "every quiet method for peace"?

3. What is one of the largest obstacles for Great Britain to remain in control of America?

Rhetorical Analysis

4. Why was Paine's *Common Sense* so effective in getting people to act?

5. Why does Paine include the quote by Milton in paragraph 25?

6. How does the title influence the emotions of the readers?

7. What would you consider Paine's greatest emotional appeal?

Writing

8. Think about a situation in which you have felt oppressed. Then write a logical appeal to right the wrongs of that oppression.

9. Brainstorm other political situations that could create a document such as *Common Sense*. Give the historical, sociocultural, or economic background of a chosen political situation and justify why the wrongs should be righted.

10. **Writing an Argument**   Write an essay in which you support or discourage political acts that endanger lives.

PART
2

ISSUES ACROSS THE DISCIPLINES

CHAPTERS AT A GLANCE

CHAPTER 4

Education and Society: How, What, and Why Do We Learn?

As you read the essays in this chapter, consider the following questions:

- What is the main educational issue that the author deals with?
- What tone does the author establish? Does the author take a positive or a negative position?
- Does the author define *education*? If so, how? If not, how does the author allude to a definition?
- What forms of evidence do the authors use to support their views on education?
- How do the rhetorical features of the essays that focus on personal experience differ from those of the essays that examine education from a more global perspective?
- What have you learned about the value of education from reading these selections?
- Which essays persuaded you the most? Which the least? Why?

In "Learning to Read and Write," a chapter from his autobiography, Frederick Douglass offers a spirited affirmation of the rights we all should have to pursue an education. For Douglass, who was born into slavery, knowledge began not only with experience but also with the need to articulate that experience through literacy. Because Douglass believed everyone deserved to learn to read and write, he was willing to risk punishment—even death—to gain that ability. Today, all over the globe, as ethnic and political conflicts arise, men and women face the same challenge of expressing themselves. For even with a tool like the Internet, if one does not have the tools to express oneself or if the expression of thought is suppressed, the vehicle for conveying ideas, no matter how powerful, is rendered useless.

Perhaps the struggle for an education always involves a certain amount of effort and risk, but the struggle also conveys excitement and the deep, abiding satisfaction that derives from achieving knowledge of oneself and of the world. Time and again in the essays in this chapter, we discover there is always a price to be paid for acquiring knowledge, developing intellectual skills, and attaining wisdom. However, numerous task forces and national commissions tell us students today are not willing to pay this price and that, as a consequence, we have become academically mediocre. Is it true we no longer delight in educating ourselves through reading, as Richard Rodriguez recounts in "The Lonely, Good Company of Books"? Is it true we take libraries for granted—we expect them to be available but never visit them? A democratic society requires an educated citizenry, people who refuse to commit intellectual suicide or self-neglect. The writers in this chapter, who take many pathways to understanding, remind us that we cannot afford to be passive or compliant when our right to an education is challenged.

Today we are in an era of dynamic change in attitudes toward education. Such issues as multiculturalism, racism, sexism, and immigration suggest the liveliness of the educational debate. Any debate over contemporary education touches on the themes of politics, economics, religion, or the social agenda, forcing us to recognize that configurations of power are at the heart of virtually all educational issues in society today.

Without education, many of our ideas and opinions can be stereotyped or prejudiced, bearing no relationship to the truth. It is easy to understand how such views can arise if we are merely passive vessels for others' uninformed opinions rather than active learners who seek true knowledge. If we judge the tenor of the essayists in this section, we discover that many of them are subversives, waging war against both ignorance *and* dogma. These writers treat education as the key to upsetting the status quo and effecting change. Operating from diverse backgrounds, they challenge many assumptions about our educational system and invite us to think critically about its purpose.

CLASSIC ▼

akg-images/The Image Works

CONTEMPORARY ▼

Hill Street Studios/Blend Images LLC

Founded in 1879, the Carlisle Indian School in Carlisle, Pennsylvania, was intended to acculturate and educate Native Americans. This photograph shows both male and female students in a physics lab in 1915. Among the comments published in the school paper was one by Miss W., teacher of the Juniors: "[H]er pupils show superior ability in solving for themselves problems in physics and physical geography. She thinks that, 'with sufficient training, some will be found to have special gifts for original research.'"

At the beginning of the 21st century, most high schools and universities in the United States were coeducational, and it is not unusual to see both male and female students in a laboratory setting, as shown in this contemporary photo of a high school biology lab.

Does Education Change Over Time?

Using a Critical Perspective Consider these two photographs of students in science laboratories, the first from the early 20th century and the second from the present. What is the setting of each laboratory like? Who are the people? What does each photographer frame and leave out of the scene? Which educational setting seems more conducive to scientific or educational inquiry? Why?

Analyzing Visuals and Their Rhetoric

1. How are the settings for the photographs different, and what does that imply, if anything, about the level of education exhibited in each photo?

2. How are the photos similar, and what do those similarities show about education?

3. Are there gender divisions in the photos? Explain.

4. How do the visual elements and the perspective of each photograph reveal expressive content, or purpose?

5. Give descriptive titles for each of the photos and explain why you decided on those titles.

What Is the Value of Education?

A famous adage proclaims that "the pen is mightier than the sword." In Frederick Douglass's narrative and the excerpt from the work of Richard Rodriguez, we get two portraits that demonstrate the truth of the adage. Douglass's efforts at becoming fully literate freed him from what would have been a life of slavery. No weapon could have done that for him. It is obvious that Douglass learned his lesson well, for his prose is stately, clear, direct, and precise. His story speaks of a determined youth and man who had a powerful motivation in learning to read and write. Would he have done so without this motivation? Perhaps, because he seems to be a very self-directed individual, as is evident from the anecdotes he relates. Rodriguez, too, has a strong motivation to master, and even to excel at, reading and writing. Writing nearly 150 years after Douglass, and at a time when he needn't fear slavery looming over him, Rodriguez nevertheless perceived that by emulating his teachers, who promoted book reading, his own reading would make him a better person. He, like Douglass, sensed that there was something about acquiring knowledge and about expanding one's view of the world by learning how others viewed it that would provide him with a certain amount of independence. As you read the following two essays, you may wish to consider whether the quiet, modest tone each author projects may have something to do with the subject matter. For reading, although active and mind-opening, is still a private and "lonely" activity.

Learning to Read and Write

Frederick Douglass

Frederick Douglass (1817–1895) was an American abolitionist, orator, and journalist. Born of the union between a slave and a white man, Douglass later escaped to Massachusetts. An impassioned antislavery speech brought him recognition as a powerful orator; thereafter he was much in demand for speaking engagements. He described his experience as a black man in America in *Narrative of the Life of Frederick Douglass* (1845). After managing to buy his freedom, Douglass founded *The North Star*, a newspaper he published for the next 17 years. In the following excerpt from his stirring autobiography, Douglass recounts the tremendous obstacles he overcame in his efforts to become literate.

1   I lived in Master Hugh's family about seven years. During this time, I succeeded in learning to read and write. In accomplishing this, I was compelled to resort to various stratagems. I had no regular teacher. My mistress, who had kindly commenced to instruct me, had, in compliance with the advice and direction of her husband, not only ceased to instruct, but had set her face

against my being instructed by any one else. It is due, however, to my mistress to say of her, that she did not adopt this course of treatment immediately. She at first lacked the depravity indispensable to shutting me up in mental darkness. It was at least necessary for her to have some training in the exercise of irresponsible power, to make her equal to the task of treating me as though I were a brute.

2 My mistress was, as I have said, a kind and tender-hearted woman; and in the simplicity of her soul she commenced, when I first went to live with her, to treat me as she supposed one human being ought to treat another. In entering upon the duties of a slaveholder, she did not seem to perceive that I sustained to her the relation of a mere chattel, and that for her to treat me as a human being was not only wrong, but dangerously so. Slavery proved as injurious to her as it did to me. When I went there, she was a pious, warm, and tender-hearted woman. There was no sorrow or suffering for which she had not a tear. She had bread for the hungry, clothes for the naked, and comfort for every mourner that came within her reach. Slavery soon proved its ability to divest her of these heavenly qualities. Under its influence, the tender heart became stone, and the lamb-like disposition gave way to one of tiger-like fierceness. The first step in her downward course was in her ceasing to instruct me. She now commenced to practise her husband's precepts. She finally became even more violent in her opposition than her husband himself. She was not satisfied with simply doing as well as he had commanded; she seemed anxious to do better. Nothing seemed to make her more angry than to see me with a newspaper. She seemed to think that here lay the danger. I have had her rush at me with a face made all up of fury, and snatch from me a newspaper, in a manner that fully revealed her apprehension. She was an apt woman; and a little experience soon demonstrated, to her satisfaction, that education and slavery were incompatible with each other.

3 From this time I was most narrowly watched. If I was in a separate room any considerable length of time, I was sure to be suspected of having a book, and was at once called to give an account of myself. All this, however, was too late. The first step had been taken. Mistress, in teaching me the alphabet, had given me the *inch*, and no precaution could prevent me from taking the *ell*.

4 The plan which I adopted, and the one by which I was most successful, was that of making friends of all the little white boys whom I met in the street. As many of these as I could, I converted into teachers. With their kindly aid, obtained at different times and in different places, I finally succeeded in learning to read. When I was sent on errands, I always took my book with me, and by doing one part of my errand quickly, I found time to get a lesson before my return. I used also to carry bread with me, enough of which was always in the house, and to which I was always welcome; for I was much better off in this regard than many of the poor white children in our neighborhood. This bread I used to bestow upon the hungry little urchins, who, in return, would give me

that more valuable bread of knowledge. I am strongly tempted to give the names of two or three of those little boys, a testimonial of the gratitude and affection I bear them; but prudence forbids—not that it would injure me, but it might embarrass them; for it is almost an unpardonable offence to teach slaves to read in this Christian country. It is enough to say of the dear little fellows, that they lived on Philpot Street, very near Durgin and Bailey's shipyard. I used to talk this matter of slavery over with them. I would sometimes say to them, I wished I could be as free as they would be when they got to be men. "You will be free as soon as you are twenty-one, *but I am a slave for life!* Have not I as good a right to be free as you have?" These words used to trouble them; they would express for me the liveliest sympathy, and console me with the hope that something would occur by which I might be free.

5   I was now about twelve years old, and the thought of being a *slave for life* began to bear heavily upon my heart. Just about this time, I got hold of a book entitled "The Colombian Orator." Every opportunity I got, I used to read this book. Among much of other interesting matter, I found in it a dialogue between a master and his slave. The slave was represented as having run away from his master three times. The dialogue represented the conversation which took place between them, when the slave was retaken the third time. In this dialogue, the whole argument in behalf of slavery was brought forward by the master, all of which was disposed of by the slave. The slave was made to say some very smart as well as impressive things in reply to his master—things which had the desired though unexpected effect; for the conversation resulted in the voluntary emancipation of the slave on the part of the master.

6   In the same book, I met with one of Sheridan's mighty speeches on and in behalf of Catholic emancipation. These were choice documents to me. I read them over and over again with unabated interest. They gave tongue to interesting thoughts of my own soul, which had frequently flashed through my mind, and died away for want of utterance. The moral which I gained from the dialogue was the power of truth over the conscience of even a slaveholder. What I got from Sheridan was a bold denunciation of slavery, and a powerful vindication of human rights. The reading of these documents enabled me to utter my thoughts, and to meet the arguments brought forward to sustain slavery; but while they relieved me of one difficulty, they brought on another even more painful than the one of which I was relieved. The more I read, the more I was led to abhor and detest my enslavers. I could regard them in no other light than a band of successful robbers, who had left their homes, and gone to Africa, and stolen us from our homes, and in a strange land reduced us to slavery. I loathed them as being the meanest as well as the most wicked of men. As I read and contemplated the subject, behold! that very discontentment which Master Hugh had predicted would follow my learning to read had already come, to torment and sting my soul to unutterable anguish. As I writhed under it, I would at times feel that learning to read had been a curse rather than a blessing.

It had given me a view of my wretched condition, without the remedy. It opened my eyes to the horrible pit, but to no ladder upon which to get out. In moments of agony, I envied my fellow-slaves for their stupidity. I have often wished myself a beast. I preferred the condition of the meanest reptile to my own. Any thing, no matter what, to get rid of thinking! It was this everlasting thinking of my condition that tormented me. There was no getting rid of it. It was pressed upon me by every object within sight or hearing, animate or inanimate. The silver trump of freedom had roused my soul to eternal wakefulness. Freedom now appeared, to disappear no more forever. It was heard in every sound, and seen in every thing. It was ever present to torment me with a sense of my wretched condition. I saw nothing without seeing it, I heard nothing without hearing it, and felt nothing without feeling it. It looked from every star, it smiled in every calm, breathed in every wind, and moved in every storm.

7   I often found myself regretting my own existence, and wishing myself dead; and but for the hope of being free, I have no doubt but that I should have killed myself, or done something for which I should have been killed. While in this state of mind, I was eager to hear anyone speak of slavery. I was a ready listener. Every little while, I could hear something about the abolitionists. It was some time before I found what the word meant. It was always used in such connections as to make it an interesting word to me. If a slave ran away and succeeded in getting clear, or if a slave killed his master, set fire to a barn, or did any thing very wrong in the mind of a slaveholder, it was spoken of as the fruit of *abolition.* Hearing the word in this connection very often, I set about learning what it meant. The dictionary afforded me little or no help. I found it was "the act of abolishing"; but then I did not know what was to be abolished. Here I was perplexed. I did not dare to ask any one about its meaning, for I was satisfied that it was something they wanted me to know very little about. After a patient waiting, I got one of our city papers, containing an account of the number of petitions from the north, praying for the abolition of slavery in the District of Columbia, and of the slave trade between the States. From this time I understood the words *abolition* and *abolitionist,* and always drew near when that word was spoken, expecting to hear something of importance to myself and fellow-slaves. The light broke in upon me by degrees. I went one day down on the wharf of Mr. Waters; and seeing two Irishmen unloading a scow of stone, I went, unasked, and helped them. When we had finished, one of them came to me and asked me if I were a slave. I told him I was. He asked, "Are ye a slave for life?" I told him that I was. The good Irishman seemed to be deeply affected by the statement. He said to the other that it was a pity so fine a little fellow as myself should be a slave for life. He said it was a shame to hold me. They both advised me to run away to the north; that I should find friends there, and that I should be free. I pretended not to be interested in what they said, and treated them as if I did not understand them; for I feared they might be treacherous. White men have been known to encourage slaves to escape,

and then, to get the reward, catch them and return them to their masters. I was afraid that these seemingly good men might use me so; but I nevertheless remembered their advice, and from that time I resolved to run away. I looked forward to a time at which it would be safe for me to escape. I was too young to think of doing so immediately; besides, I wished to learn how to write, as I might have occasion to write my own pass. I consoled myself with the hope that I should one day find a good chance. Meanwhile, I would learn to write.

8   The idea as to how I might learn to write was suggested to me by being in Durgin and Bailey's ship-yard, and frequently seeing the ship carpenters, after hewing, and getting a piece of timber ready for use, write on the timber the name of that part of the ship for which it was intended. When a piece of timber was intended for the larboard side, it would be marked thus—"L." When a piece was for the starboard side, it would be marked thus—"S." A piece for the larboard side forward, would be marked thus—"L. F." When a piece was for starboard side forward, it would be marked thus—"S. F." For larboard aft, it would be marked thus—"L. A." For starboard aft, it would be marked thus— "S. A." I soon learned the names of these letters, and for what they were intended when placed upon a piece of timber in the ship-yard. I immediately commenced copying them, and in a short time was able to make the four letters named. After that, when I met with any boy who I knew could write, I would tell him I could write as well as he. The next word would be, "I don't believe you. Let me see you try it." I would then make the letters which I had been so fortunate as to learn, and ask him to beat that. In this way I got a good many lessons in writing, which it is quite possible I should never have gotten in any other way. During this time, my copy-book was the board fence, brick wall, and pavement; my pen and ink was a lump of chalk. With these, I learned mainly how to write. I then commenced and continued copying the Italics in Webster's Spelling Book, until I could make them all without looking on the book. By this time, my little Master Thomas had gone to school, and learned how to write, and had written over a number of copy-books. These had been brought home, and shown to some of our near neighbors, and then laid aside. My mistress used to go to class meeting at the Wilk Street meetinghouse every Monday afternoon, and leave me to take care of the house. When left thus, I used to spend the time in writing in the spaces left in Master Thomas's copy-book, copying what he had written. I continued to do this until I could write a hand very similar to that of Master Thomas. Thus, after a long, tedious effort for years, I finally succeeded in learning how to write.

From *Narrative of the Life of Frederick Douglass: An American Slave*, Written by Himself. 1845.

Comprehension

1. What strategies does Douglass use to continue his education after his mistress's abandonment?

2. Why did the author's mistress find his reading newspapers particularly threatening?

3. Why does Douglass call learning to read "a curse rather than a blessing" (paragraph 6)?

Rhetorical Analysis

4. What is Douglass's thesis? Paraphrase two points Douglass makes to support his thesis.

5. The first couple of sentences in the story, though simple, are very powerful. How do they serve to set up the mood of the piece and the reader's expectations?

6. Cite examples of Douglass's use of metaphors, and discuss how they help Douglass achieve his purpose.

7. How would you describe Douglass's writing style and level of language? Does it reveal anything about his character? Justify your response.

8. Explain the way in which the author uses comparison and contrast.

9. What is Douglass's definition of *abolition*, and how does he help the reader define it? How does this method contribute to the reader's understanding of the learning process?

Writing

10. What does Douglass mean when he writes that "education and slavery were incompatible with each other" (paragraph 2)? Write an essay in which you consider the relationship between the two.

11. Both Douglass and his mistress were in inferior positions to Master Hugh. Write an essay in which you compare and contrast their positions in society at the time.

12. Illiteracy is still a problem in the United States. Write an account of what your day-to-day life would be like if you couldn't write or read. What impact would this deficiency have on your life? Use concrete examples to illustrate your narrative.

13. **Writing an Argument** Write an essay in which you argue for or against the proposition that American education continues to discriminate against minority groups.

The Lonely, Good Company of Books

Richard Rodriguez

Richard Rodriguez (b. 1944) was born in San Francisco and received degrees from Stanford University and Columbia University. He also did graduate study at the University of California, Berkeley, and at the Warburg Institute, London. Rodriguez became a nationally known writer with the publication of his autobiography, *Hunger of Memory: The Education of Richard Rodriguez* (1982). In it, he describes the struggles of growing up biculturally—feeling alienated from his Spanish-speaking parents yet not wholly comfortable in the dominant culture of the United States. He opposes bilingualism and affirmative action as they are now practiced in the United States, and his stance has caused much controversy in educational and intellectual circles. Rodriguez continues to write about social issues such as acculturation, education, and language in *Days of Obligation: An Argument with My Mexican Father* (1992) and *Brown: The Last Discovery of America* (2002). In the following essay, Rodriguez records his childhood passion for reading.

1   From an early age I knew that my mother and father could read and write both Spanish and English. I had observed my father making his way through what, I now suppose, must have been income tax forms. On other occasions I waited apprehensively while my mother read onion-paper letters air-mailed from Mexico with news of a relative's illness or death. For both my parents, however, reading was something done out of necessity and as quickly as possible. Never did I see either of them read an entire book. Nor did I see them read for pleasure. Their reading consisted of work manuals, prayer books, newspapers, recipes. . . .

2   In our house each school year would begin with my mother's careful instruction: "Don't write in your books so we can sell them at the end of the year." The remark was echoed in public by my teachers, but only in part: "Boys and girls, don't write in your books. You must learn to treat them with great care and respect."

3   OPEN THE DOORS OF YOUR MIND WITH BOOKS, read the red and white poster over the nun's desk in early September. It soon was apparent to me that reading was the classroom's central activity. Each course had its own book. And the information gathered from a book was unquestioned. READ TO LEARN, the sign on the wall advised in December. I privately wondered: What was the connection between reading and learning? Did one learn something only by reading it? Was an idea only an idea if it could be written down? In June, CONSIDER BOOKS YOUR BEST FRIENDS. Friends? Reading was, at best, only a chore. I needed to look up whole paragraphs of words in a dictionary. Lines of type were dizzying, the eye having to move slowly across

the page, then down, and across. . . . The sentences of the first books I read were coolly impersonal. Toned hard. What most bothered me, however, was the isolation reading required. To console myself for the loneliness I'd feel when I read, I tried reading in a very soft voice. Until: "Who is doing all that talking to his neighbor?" Shortly after, remedial reading classes were arranged for me with a very old nun.

4   At the end of each school day, for nearly six months, I would meet with her in the tiny room that served as the school's library but was actually only a storeroom for used textbooks and a vast collection of *National Geographics.* Everything about our sessions pleased me: the smallness of the room; the noise of the janitor's broom hitting the edge of the long hallway outside the door; the green of the sun, lighting the wall; and the old woman's face blurred white with a beard. Most of the time we took turns. I began with my elementary text. Sentences of astonishing simplicity seemed to me lifeless and drab: "The boys ran from the rain. . . . She wanted to sing. . . . The kite rose in the blue." Then the old nun would read from her favorite books, usually biographies of early American presidents. Playfully she ran through complex sentences, calling the words alive with her voice, making it seem that the author somehow was speaking directly to me. I smiled just to listen to her. I sat there and sensed for the very first time some possibility of fellowship between a reader and a writer, a communication, never *intimate* like that I heard spoken words at home convey, but one nonetheless *personal.*

5   One day the nun concluded a session by asking me why I was so reluctant to read by myself. I tried to explain; said something about the way written words made me feel all alone—almost, I wanted to add but didn't, as when I spoke to myself in a room just emptied of furniture. She studied my face as I spoke; she seemed to be watching more than listening. In an uneventful voice she replied that I had nothing to fear. Didn't I realize that reading would open up whole new worlds? A book could open doors for me. It could introduce me to people and show me places I never imagined existed. She gestured toward the bookshelves. (Bare-breasted African women danced, and the shiny hubcaps of automobiles on the back covers of the *Geographic* gleamed in my mind.) I listened with respect. But her words were not very influential. I was thinking then of another consequence of literacy, one I was too shy to admit but nonetheless trusted. Books were going to make me "educated." *That* confidence enabled me, several months later, to overcome my fear of the silence.

6   In fourth grade I embarked upon a grandiose reading program. "Give me the names of important books," I would say to startled teachers. They soon found out that I had in mind "adult books." I ignored their suggestion of anything I suspected was written for children. (Not until I was in college, as a result, did I read *Huckleberry Finn* or *Alice's Adventures in Wonderland.*) Instead, I read *The Scarlet Letter* and Franklin's *Autobiography.* And whatever I read I read for extra credit. Each time I finished a book, I reported the achievement to

a teacher and basked in the praise my effort earned. Despite my best efforts, however, there seemed to be more and more books I needed to read. At the library I would literally tremble as I came upon whole shelves of books I hadn't read. So I read and I read and I read: *Great Expectations;* all the short stories of Kipling; *The Babe Ruth Story;* the entire first volume of the *Encyclopaedia Britannica* (A–ANSTEY); the *Iliad; Moby Dick; Gone with the Wind; The Good Earth; Ramona; Forever Amber; The Lives of the Saints; Crime and Punishment; The Pearl. . . .* Librarians who initially frowned when I checked out the maximum ten books at a time started saving books they thought I might like. Teachers would say to the rest of the class, "I only wish the rest of you took reading as seriously as Richard obviously does."

7   But at home I would hear my mother wondering, "What do you see in your books?" (Was reading a hobby like her knitting? Was so much reading even healthy for a boy? Was it the sign of "brains"? Or was it just a convenient excuse for not helping around the house on Saturday mornings?) Always, "What do you see . . . ?"

8   What *did* I see in my books? I had the idea that they were crucial for my academic success, though I couldn't have said exactly how or why. In the sixth grade I simply concluded that what gave a book its value was some major idea or theme it contained. If that core essence could be mined and memorized, I would become learned like my teachers. I decided to record in a notebook the themes of the books that I read. After reading *Robinson Crusoe,* I wrote that its theme was "the value of learning to live by oneself." When I completed *Wuthering Heights,* I noted the danger of "letting emotions get out of control." Rereading these brief moralistic appraisals usually left me disheartened. I couldn't believe that they were really the source of reading's value. But for many years, they constituted the only means I had of describing to myself the educational value of books.

9   In spite of my earnestness, I found reading a pleasurable activity. I came to enjoy the lonely, good company of books. Early on weekday mornings, I'd read in my bed. I'd feel a mysterious comfort then, reading in the dawn quiet—the blue-gray silence interrupted by the occasional churning of the refrigerator motor a few rooms away or the more distant sounds of a city bus beginning its run. On weekends I'd go to the public library to read, surrounded by old men and women. Or, if the weather was fine, I would take my books to the park and read in the shade of a tree. Neighbors would leave for vacation and I would water their lawns. I would sit through the twilight on the front porches or in backyards, reading to the cool, whirling sounds of the sprinklers.

10   I also had favorite writers. But often those writers I enjoyed most I was least able to value. When I read William Saroyan's *The Human Comedy,* I was immediately pleased by the narrator's warmth and the charm of his story. But as quickly I became suspicious. A book so enjoyable to read couldn't be very "important." Another summer I determined to read all the novels of Dickens.

Reading his fat novels, I loved the feeling I got—after the first hundred pages— of being at home in a fictional world where I knew the names of the characters and cared about what was going to happen to them. And it bothered me that I was forced away at the conclusion, when the fiction closed tight, like a fortune-teller's fist—the futures of all the major characters neatly resolved. I never knew how to take such feelings seriously, however. Nor did I suspect that these experiences could be part of a novel's meaning. Still, there were pleasures to sustain me after I'd finish my books. Carrying a volume back to the library, I would be pleased by its weight. I'd run my fingers along the edge of the pages and marvel at the breadth of my achievement. Around my room, growing stacks of paperback books reinforced my assurance.

11   I entered high school having read hundreds of books. My habit of reading made me a confident speaker and writer of English. Reading also enabled me to sense something of the shape, the major concerns, of Western thought. (I was able to say something about Dante and Descartes and Engels and James Baldwin in my high school term papers.) In these various ways, books brought me academic success as I hoped that they would. But I was not a good reader. Merely bookish, I lacked a point of view when I read. Rather, I read in order to acquire a point of view. I vacuumed books for epigrams, scraps of information, ideas, themes—anything to fill the hollow within me and make me feel educated. When one of my teachers suggested to his drowsy tenth-grade English class that a person could not have a "complicated idea" until he had read at least two thousand books, I heard the remark without detecting either its irony or its very complicated truth. I merely determined to compile a list of all the books I had ever read. Harsh with myself, I included only once a title I might have read several times. (How, after all, could one read a book more than once?) And I included only those books over a hundred pages in length. (Could anything shorter be a book?)

12   There was yet another high school list I compiled. One day I came across a newspaper article about the retirement of an English professor at a nearby state college. The article was accompanied by a list of the "hundred most important books of Western Civilization." "More than anything else in my life," the professor told the reporter with finality, "these books have made me all that I am." That was the kind of remark I couldn't ignore. I clipped out the list and kept it for the several months it took me to read all of the titles. Most books, of course, I barely understood. While reading Plato's *Republic,* for instance, I needed to keep looking at the book jacket comments to remind myself what the text was about. Nevertheless, with the special patience and superstition of a scholarship boy, I looked at every word of the text. And by the time I reached the last word, relieved, I convinced myself that I had read *The Republic.* In a ceremony of great pride, I solemnly crossed Plato off my list.

Comprehension

1. What was Rodriguez's parents' attitude toward reading? How did it influence his attitude? Cite examples from the essay that support your opinion.

2. What does Rodriguez mean by the "fellowship between a reader and a writer" (paragraph 4)? Why does he differentiate between "intimate" and "personal" forms of communication?

3. Rodriguez hoped that reading would fill "the hollow" inside him. What was the cause of his emptiness? Why did he find reading a lonely experience?

Rhetorical Analysis

4. What is the thesis of Rodriguez's essay? Is it stated or implied? Explain.

5. How does the author's use of narrative advance his views on reading and education?

6. What is the writer's tone? How effective is it in conveying his point of view?

7. Rodriguez uses uppercase letters (small capitals) when referring to signs advocating reading. Why does he use this device? How does it support his point of view?

8. The essay ends with an ironic anecdote. Why did Rodriguez choose to conclude this way? Does it satisfactorily illustrate his attitude? Explain how it ties into his earlier question, "Did one learn something only by reading it?"

9. What words or phrases imply that there is an ethnic component in Rodriguez's conflict? Is the subtlety effective? Justify your response.

Writing

10. Rodriguez's parents had a pragmatic attitude toward reading. What was the attitude in your home as you were growing up? Did your parents encourage your interest in reading? Did they read themselves? What is the first book you remember reading by yourself? Write an essay in which you describe your reading history, and how it has impacted your life.

11. Is reading still a significant source of information and entertainment, or has it been usurped by television or the Internet? Write an essay explaining why it is important (or necessary) to be a reader today.

12. **Writing an Argument** Rodriguez believed reading would make him "educated." Do you agree or disagree? Is reading vital to a person's education? How do you define *education?* Can it be acquired only through reading, or are there other contributing factors? Write an argumentative essay on this topic.

Synthesizing the Classic + Contemporary Essays

1. Both Rodriguez and Douglass were motivated to educate themselves in a society inimical to this achievement. Compare and contrast their struggles and attitudes in their quests for knowledge.

2. Pretend you are Rodriguez, and write a letter to Douglass addressing the issues of minorities and education in present-day America. What would Rodriguez say about the progress of minorities in our society?

3. Although Rodriguez and Douglass treat a similar theme, they communicate their messages differently. Which narration do you consider more powerful, and why?

4. Rodriguez explores the theme of isolation in his story. Is there any evidence that this feeling was shared by Douglass in his efforts to learn how to read? Use proof from both narratives to support your view.

5. Slavery was an obvious obstacle to Douglass's attempt to educate himself. What impeded Rodriguez's progress? Were similar forces at work? Cite examples from Rodriguez's narrative to prove your point.

The Graduates

Louis Menand

Louis Menand (b. 1951) is an influential contemporary educator and writer. He has degrees from Pomona College (BA, 1973; MA, 1975) and Columbia University (PhD, 1980), and he is a professor of English and American literature at Harvard. Menand has written and edited books on modernism, academic freedom, and pragmatism, receiving the Pulitzer Prize in history for *The Metaphysical Club: A Story of Ideas in America* (2001). Menand has also been a contributing editor to the *New Republic* and *New York Review of Books* and a staff writer for *The New Yorker*. "I don't think of there being any division between my academic career and my career in journalism," he writes; "it happens that some of my interests are relatively scholarly and some are not." In the following "unscholarly," or popular essay, published in *The New Yorker* in 2007, Menand offers a dissenting opinion on the value of a college education.

1   On your first sleepover, your best friend's mother asks if you would like a tuna-fish-salad sandwich. Your own mother gives you tuna-fish-salad sandwiches all the time, so you say, "Sure." When you bite into the sandwich, though, you realize, too late, that your best friend's mother's tuna-fish salad tastes nothing like the tuna-fish salad your mother makes. You never dreamed that it was possible for there to be more than one way to prepare tuna-fish salad. And what's with the bread? It's brown, and appears to have tiny seeds in it. What is more unnerving is the fact that your best friend obviously considers his mother's tuna-fish salad to be perfectly normal and has been eating it with enjoyment all his life. Later on, you discover that the pillows in your best friend's house are filled with some kind of foam-rubber stuff instead of feathers. The toilet paper is pink. What kind of human beings are these? At two o'clock in the morning, you throw up, and your mother comes and takes you home.

2   College, from which some 1.5 million people will graduate this year, is, basically, a sleepover with grades. In college, it is not so cool to throw up or for your mother to come and take you home. But plenty of students do throw up, and undergo other forms of mental and bodily distress, and plenty take time off from school or drop out. Almost half the people who go to college never graduate. Except in the case of a few highfliers and a somewhat larger number of inveterate slackers, college is a stressful experience.

3   American colleges notoriously inflate grades, but they can never inflate them enough, because education in the United States has become hypercompetitive and every little difference matters. In 1960, Harvard College had around five thousand applicants and accepted roughly thirty percent; this year, it had almost twenty-three thousand applicants and accepted nine percent. And the narrower the funnel, the finer applicants grind themselves in order to squeeze through it. Perversely, though, the competitiveness is a sign that the system is doing what Americans want it to be doing. Americans want education to be two things, universal and meritocratic. They

want everyone to have a slot who wants one, and they want the slots to be awarded according to merit. The system is not perfect: Children from higher-income families enjoy an advantage in competing for the top slots. But there are lots of slots. There are more than four thousand institutions of higher education in the United States, enrolling more than seventeen million students. Can you name fifty colleges? Even if you could name a thousand, there would be three thousand you hadn't heard of. Most of these schools accept virtually all qualified applicants.

4   What makes for the stress is meritocracy. Meritocratic systems are democratic (since, in theory, everyone gets a place at the starting line) and efficient (since resources are not wasted on the unqualified), but they are huge engines of anxiety. The more purely meritocratic the system—the more open, the more efficient, the fairer—the more anxiety it produces, because there is no haven from competition. Your mother can't come over and help you out—that would be cheating! You're on your own. Everything you do in a meritocratic society is some kind of test, and there is never a final exam. There is only another test. People seem to pick up on this earlier and earlier in their lives, and at some point it starts to get in the way of their becoming educated. You can't learn when you're afraid of being wrong.

5   The biggest undergraduate major by far in the United States today is business. Twenty-two percent of bachelor's degrees are awarded in that field. Eight percent are awarded in education, five percent in the health professions. By contrast, fewer than four percent of college graduates major in English, and only two percent major in history. There are more bachelor's degrees awarded every year in Parks, Recreation, Leisure, and Fitness Studies than in all foreign languages and literatures combined. The Carnegie Foundation for the Advancement of Teaching, which classifies institutions of higher education, no longer uses the concept "liberal arts" in making its distinctions. This makes the obsession of some critics of American higher education with things like whether Shakespeare is being required of English majors beside the point. The question isn't what the English majors aren't taking; the question is what everyone else isn't taking.

6   More than fifty percent of Americans spend some time in college, and American higher education is the most expensive in the world. The average annual tuition at a four-year private college is more than twenty-two thousand dollars. What do we want from college, though? It is hard to imagine that there could be one answer that was right for each of the 1.5 million or so people graduating this year, one part of the college experience they all must have had. Any prescription that had to spread itself across that many institutions would not be very deep. One thing that might be hoped for, though, is that, somewhere along the way, every student had a moment of vertigo (without unpleasant side effects). In commencement speeches and the like, people say that education is all about opportunity and expanding your horizons. But some part of it is about shrinking people, about teaching them that they are not the measure of everything. College should give them the intellectual equivalent of their childhood sleepover experience. We want to give graduates confidence to face the world, but we also want to protect the world a little from their confidence. Humility is good. There is not enough of it these days.

Comprehension

1. What is Menand's opinion of the American system of education? Do you think he is biased? Why or why not?

2. According to Menand, what are some of the reasons why a college education has become devalued?

3. Explain what Menand means by *meritocracy*. Would you say that the fact that he teaches at Harvard and refers to this institution in his essay explains his focus on this concept? Justify your response by referring to the text.

Rhetorical Analysis

4. Menand wrote this brief essay for a well-known and decidedly urbane publication. How does he address his audience? What elements of Menand's style would appeal to *The New Yorker* readers?

5. What is Menand's purpose in creating an analogy in his introductory paragraph? Do you find this strategy effective? Why or why not?

6. Where does Menand state his claim? What are his main supporting points, and what types of evidence does he present?

7. Does Menand rely largely on appeals to reason, emotion, or ethics, or does he combine these approaches? Justify your response.

8. How does Menand link his opening and concluding paragraphs? Why does he use the word *vertigo* in the last paragraph?

Writing

9. Write a causal essay in which you analyze the reasons why college can be a stressful experience.

10. Compose your own extended definition of meritocracy and how this relates to the American educational system.

11. **Writing an Argument** Write a rebuttal to Menand, arguing that a college education is in no way comparable to one's first sleepover.

America, Still On Top

Vartan Gregorian

Vartan Gregorian (b. 1934), a celebrated educator, foundation head, and public intellectual, was born in Tabriz, Iran. He immigrated with his parents to the United States in 1956 and studied at Stanford University (BA, 1958; PhD, 1964), majoring in history. Gregorian was a popular professor of history at San Francisco State University, the University of Texas, the University of Pennsylvania, and several other institutions before embarking on a distinguished career as an administrator. Known for his fund-raising prowess, Gregorian has been provost of the University of Pennsylvania, president of the New York Public Library in the 1980s, president of Brown University in the 1990s, and since 1997 president of the Carnegie Corporation of New York. He has written several books, including *The Emergence of Modern Afghanistan, 1880–1946* (1969), *Islam: A Mosaic, Not a Monolith* (2003), and *The Road to Home: My Life and Times* (2003). In this essay, which appeared in *Newsweek International* in 2007, Gregorian compares American colleges with competing educational systems abroad.

1   One of the great strengths of U.S. higher education is that it grew by informal design. Following the 1862 Morrill Act, which gave federal land to the states to found colleges, the states created not only universities but also state, junior, city and county colleges, some of them two-year. Without a formal national plan, there emerged a template for public higher education—affordable schooling for all, close to home, paid for by both state and federal governments. Today American higher education is a more than $200 billion enterprise, enrolling nearly 18 million students in almost 4,000 public and private colleges and universities.

2   Elsewhere, higher education grew in a much more top-down manner. In communist societies from the Soviet Union to China and throughout most of Asia and Latin America, a central bureaucracy ran universities, and often still does. Typically, these systems have been unprepared for changing expectations, as even the most remote and repressed populations have begun to develop—via the media and the Internet—a perception of how the other half lives. Many view education as a way to get their fair share. When they see countrymen returning with degrees from the United States or Europe and getting the best jobs, they begin to demand quality improvements in their own universities, for which resources are often lacking. The result is a growing gap between expectations and reality. That's one reason that after a falloff following 9/11, the United States has regained its status as the destination of choice for international students.

3   To catch up, countries in Europe—not to mention Asia, Africa and Latin America—have welcomed a proliferation of private universities, including "virtual" online entities. But many of these institutions are of questionable legitimacy. In the central Indian state of Chattisgarh, private colleges are springing up rapidly, but most are "universities only in name," run out of flats and thus quite literally

"a cottage industry," reported the local Tribune newspaper. Faculty is also an issue: in many countries, professors are poorly paid and institutions rely on temporary adjuncts, lecturers and part-timers.

4   Providing poor-quality schools will likely backfire, because students are increasingly unwilling to accept substandard fare. In an era of global brand awareness, everyone wants the "right name" on clothes, cars and diplomas, too. In China, students at second-tier schools have been known to pay extra to have their diplomas bear the name of a better university—and to riot if that promise is not met.

5   Many universities are looking to America as a model for how to survive. That means raising or introducing tuition, increasing enrollment (including the number of foreign students who pay full fare) and boosting endowments through fund-raising. Money, however, is not enough to build a quality university. In many countries, for example, professors are members of the civil service and do not enjoy the status, or salary, that will draw the best talent. In centralized systems like China's, authorities can order up any number of engineers or scientists, but that does not mean they will be any good. Other nations are expanding bureaucracies to accommodate unemployed graduates, especially in the humanities and social science—an obvious recipe for disaster.

6   Today, free markets are on a collision course with state ownership or sponsorship of universities. The main challenge for each nation is to meet not only the aspirations of its citizens but the demands of its job markets as well. Countries that fail will face a debilitating brain drain. Even America is not immune. In the past, the United States relied on the many international students who came to study—especially science, math and technology—and then stayed. It also gave preferential treatment to immigrants with specialized skills. Today, as many societies advance economically, they are better able to retain talent and even attract professionals from the United States. Now America must increasingly rely on its own population to produce the necessary engineers, teachers, scientists and other professionals. It can no longer afford, for example, to accept the fact that last year, Maryland's entire 11-campus university system produced only 46 secondary math and science teachers. Or that the proportion of foreign-born doctoral students in engineering at U.S. universities is close to 60 percent.

7   The United States needs to redouble its efforts, particularly by investing more to improve education in the K-through-12 years and at the university level, too. There is no room for complacency in the global competition, even though America's diverse and hybrid system of public and private schools has solved the challenges of higher education better than most.

Gregorian, Vartan, "America, Still on Top," *Newsweek*, August 20-27, 2007. Reprinted by permission of the author.

Comprehension

1. According to Gregorian, what are the strengths of American higher education? What are the weaknesses?

2. According to Gregorian, why is American higher education, on balance, superior to those in Europe, Asia, Africa, and Latin America?

3. Explain the "collision course" that Gregorian mentions in this essay.

Rhetorical Analysis

4. What is the purpose of Gregorian's introductory paragraph? How effective do you find this strategy? Justify your response with reference to the text.

5. What is Gregorian's claim, and where does he present it most clearly?

6. How does Gregorian use comparison and contrast to structure this essay? What points of comparison does he develop?

7. What types of evidence does Gregorian provide to support his argument? Do you find this evidence to be sufficient? Why or why not?

8. What is Gregorian's purpose in referring to the post-9/11 and increasingly globalized world? Does this motif reinforce his argument or detract from it? Explain.

Writing

9. Write a brief essay on what you perceive as the strengths of American higher education.

10. Compare and contrast the thesis of Gregorian's essay with the thesis of Louis Menand's "The Graduates."

11. **Writing an Argument**   Argue for or against the proposition that in a globalized world, foreign educational systems will ultimately catch up with American higher education.

What College Can Mean to the Other America

Mike Rose

Mike Rose (b. 1944) is a nationally recognized writer, educator, and specialist in composition. He was born in Altoona, Pennsylvania, to Italian immigrants, and moved with his parents to a working-class neighborhood in south Los Angeles when he was seven years old. Based on his own experience of having been tracked into a vocational slot in high school, Rose advocates a reevaluation of remedial writers in such books as *Writer's Block* (1984), *When a Writer Can't Write* (1985), and other texts. He also is a prominent spokesperson for the value of public education in a democracy. Rose received a PhD in education from UCLA and has taught there for nearly forty years. In this essay he wrote for *The Chronicle of Higher Education* in 2011, Rose argues for educational policy initiatives that will benefit the poor.

1   The stakes go beyond the economic to the basic civic question: What kind of society do we want to become?

2   It has been nearly 50 years since Michael Harrington wrote *The Other America*, pulling the curtain back on invisible poverty within the United States. If he were writing today, Harrington would find the same populations he described then: young, marginally educated people who drift in and out of low-pay, dead-end jobs, and older displaced workers, unable to find work as industries transform and shops close. But he would find more of them, especially the young, their situation worsened by further economic restructuring and globalization. And while the poor he wrote about were invisible in a time of abundance, ours are visible in a terrible recession, although invisible in most public policy. In fact, the poor are drifting further into the dark underbelly of American capitalism.

3   One of the Obama administration's mantras is that we need to "out-innovate, out-educate, and out-build" our competition in order to achieve fuller prosperity. The solution to our social and economic woes lies in new technologies, in the cutting edge. This is our "Sputnik moment," a very American way to frame our problems. However, the editors of *The Economist* wrote a few months back that this explanation of our economic situation is "mostly nonsense."

4   Instead, the business-friendly, neoliberal magazine offered a sobering—at times almost neo-Marxist—assessment of what it considers the real danger in our economy, something at the core of Harrington's analysis: chronic, ingrained joblessness that is related to our social and economic structure. We are looking toward the horizon of innovation when we should be looking straight in front of us at the tens of millions of chronically unemployed Americans and providing comprehensive occupational, educational, and social services. Otherwise, to cite an earlier issue of *The Economist* that also dealt with American inequality, we risk "calcifying into a European-style class-based society." For people without school or work, we already have.

5   There are a few current policy initiatives that are aimed at helping the disadvantaged gain economic mobility, mostly through some form of postsecondary education. Sadly, the most ambitious of these—the federal American Graduation Initiative—was sacrificed during the health-care negotiations, although some smaller projects remained in the stimulus package and the Department of Education. Private foundations, notably Gates and Lumina, have been sponsoring such efforts as well. These efforts reach a small percentage of poor and low-income Americans and, on average, are aimed at the more academically skilled among them—although many still require remedial English and mathematics. A certificate or degree alone will not automatically lift them out of hard times—there is a bit of magic-bullet thinking in these college initiatives—but getting a decent basic education could make a significant difference in their lives. At the least, these efforts are among the few antipoverty measures that have some degree of bipartisan support.

6   For the last year and a half, I have been spending time at an inner-city community college that serves this population, and I have seen firsthand the effects of poverty and long-term joblessness. Although some students attend the college with the goal of transfer, the majority come for its well-regarded occupational programs. More than 90 percent must take one or more basic-skills courses; 60 percent are on financial aid. A fair number have been through the criminal-justice system.

7   As I have gotten to know these students, the numbers have come alive. Many had chaotic childhoods, went to underperforming schools, and never finished high school. With low-level skills, they have had an awful time in the labor market. Short-term jobs, long stretches of unemployment, no health care. Many, the young ones included, have health problems that are inadequately treated if treated at all. I remember during my first few days on the campus noticing the number of people who walked with a limp or irregular gait.

8   What really strikes me, though, is students' level of engagement, particularly in the occupational programs. There are a few people who seem to be marking time, but most listen intently as an instructor explains the air-supply system in a diesel engine or the way to sew supports into an evening dress. And they do and redo an assignment until they get it right. Hope and desire are brimming. Many of the students say this is the first time school has meant anything to them. More than a few talk about turning their lives around. It doesn't take long to imagine the kind of society we would have if more people had this opportunity.

9   But right at the point when opportunity is offered, it is being threatened by severe budget cuts in education and social services. For several years, the college— like so many in the United States—has been able to offer only a small number of summer classes, and classes are being cut during the year. Enrollment in existing classes is growing. Student-support services are scaled back. And all the while, more people are trying to enroll at the college; some will have to be turned away, and those who are admitted will tax an already burdened system.

10   Given the toll the recession has taken on state and local governments, policy makers face "unprecedented challenges" and say they "have no other choice" but to make cuts in education. Secretary of Education Arne Duncan, borrowing a now-ubiquitous phrase, has called the necessity to do more with less "the new normal."

11   I don't dispute the difficulty of budgeting in the recession, nor the fact that education spending includes waste that should be cut. But we need to resist the framing of our situation as inevitable and normal. This framing makes the recession a catastrophe without culpability, neutralizing the civic and moral dimensions of both the causes of the recession and the way policy makers respond to it.

12   The civic and moral dimensions also are diminished by the powerful market-based orientation to economic and social problems. Antigovernment, anti-welfare-state, antitax—this ideology undercuts broad-scale public responses to inequality.

13   If the editors of *The Economist* are right, the deep cuts in education—especially to programs and institutions that help poor people connect to school or work—will have disastrous long-term economic consequences that far outweigh immediate budgetary gains. And rereading *The Other America* reminds us that the stakes go beyond the economic to the basic civic question: What kind of society do we want to become? Will there be another Michael Harrington 50 years from now writing about an America that has a higher rate of poverty and even wider social divides?

"What College Can Mean to the Other America" by Mike Rose for *The Chronicle of Higher Education,* September 11, 2011. Reprinted by permission of the author.

Comprehension

1. Note all references that Rose makes to Michael Harrington and his book. Explain the importance that Rose gives to Harrington's study and its relevance to his topic.

2. Summarize Rose's perception of the current state of educational policy for the poor in the United States.

Rhetorical Analysis

3. Examine Rose's introductory paragraph. How does he structure this opening unit?

4. How does Rose tailor his message to his audience of college administrators?

5. Explain Rose's tone and voice in this essay. Where does he personalize his argument, and what is the effect?

6. How does Rose use a problem-solution pattern of organization in developing his argument? Point to specific passages where this pattern becomes apparent.

7. What is the relationship of Rose's concluding paragraph to his claim and to the evidence that he offers in the body of his essay?

8. In a personal essay, explore your own place in American society—or in the nation where you were born and raised—and how this molded your educational experience.

9. **Writing an Argument**   Argue for or against the proposition that the U.S. Congress should provide a solid education for the poor.

When Bright Girls Decide That Math Is "a Waste of Time"

Susan Jacoby

Susan Jacoby (b. 1945) has worked as an educator and as a reporter for the *Washington Post* and a columnist for *The New York Times*. As a freelance journalist in the former Soviet Union (from 1969 to 1971), she produced two books about her experiences. Jacoby has contributed to a number of publications, including *The Nation* and *McCall's*; her books include *The Possible She* (1979), a collection of autobiographical essays; *Wild Justice: The Evolution of Revenge* (1983); *Half-Jew: A Daughter's Search for Her Buried Past* (2000); and *The Age of American Unreason* (2008). In this essay from *The New York Times*, Jacoby examines the reasons girls are often deficient in math and science.

1 Susannah, a 16-year-old who has always been an A student in every subject from algebra to English, recently informed her parents that she intended to drop physics and calculus in her senior year of high school and replace them with a drama seminar and a work-study program. She expects a major in art or history in college, she explained, and "any more science or math will just be a waste of my time."

2 Her parents were neither concerned by nor opposed to her decision. "Fine, dear," they said. Their daughter is, after all, an outstanding student. What does it matter if, at age 16, she has taken a step that may limit her understanding of both machines and the natural world for the rest of her life?

3 This kind of decision, in which girls turn away from studies that would give them a sure footing in the world of science and technology, is a self-inflicted female disability that is, regrettably, almost as common today as it was when I was in high school. If Susannah had announced that she had decided to stop taking English in her senior year, her mother and father would have been horrified. I also think they would have been a good deal less sanguine about her decision if she were a boy.

4 In saying that scientific and mathematical ignorance is a self-inflicted female wound, I do not, obviously, mean that cultural expectations play no role in the process. But the world does not conspire to deprive modern women of access to science as it did in the 1930s, when Rosalyn S. Yalow, the Nobel Prize–winning physicist, graduated from Hunter College and was advised to go to work as a secretary because no graduate school would admit her to its physics department. The current generation of adolescent girls—and their parents, bred on old expectations about women's interests—are active conspirators in limiting their own intellectual development.

5 It is true that the proportion of young women in science-related graduate and professional schools, most notably medical schools, has increased significantly in the past decade. It is also true that so few women were studying advanced science and mathematics before the early 1970s that the percentage increase in female enrollment does not yet translate into large numbers of women actually working in science.

6   The real problem is that so many girls eliminate themselves from any serious possibility of studying science as a result of decisions made during the vulnerable period of midadolescence, when they are most likely to be influenced—on both conscious and subconscious levels—by the traditional belief that math and science are "masculine" subjects.

7   During the teen-age years the well-documented phenomenon of "math anxiety" strikes girls who never had any problem handling numbers during earlier schooling. Some men, too, experience this syndrome—a form of panic, akin to a phobia, at any task involving numbers—but women constitute the overwhelming majority of sufferers. The onset of acute math anxiety during the teen-age years is, as Stalin was fond of saying, "not by accident."

8   In adolescence girls begin to fear that they will be unattractive to boys if they are typed as "brains." Science and math epitomize unfeminine braininess in a way that, say, foreign languages do not. High-school girls who pursue an advanced interest in science and math (unless they are students at special institutions like the Bronx High School of Science where everyone is a brain) usually find that they are greatly outnumbered by boys in their classes. They are, therefore, intruding on male turf at a time when their sexual confidence, as well as that of the boys, is most fragile.

9   A 1981 assessment of female achievement in mathematics, based on research conducted under a National Institute for Education grant, found significant differences in the mathematical achievements of 9th and 12th graders. At age 13 girls were equal to or slightly better than boys in tests involving algebra, problem solving and spatial ability; four years later the boys had outstripped the girls.

10   It is not mysterious that some very bright high-school girls suddenly decide that math is "too hard" and "a waste of time." In my experience, self-sabotage of mathematical and scientific ability is often a conscious process. I remember deliberately pretending to be puzzled by geometry problems in my sophomore year in high school. A male teacher called me in after class and said, in a baffled tone, "I don't see how you can be having so much trouble when you got straight A's last year in my algebra class."

11   The decision to avoid advanced biology, chemistry, physics and calculus in high school automatically restricts academic and professional choices that ought to be wide open to anyone beginning college. At all coeducational universities women are overwhelmingly concentrated in the fine arts, social sciences and traditionally female departments like education. Courses leading to degrees in science- and technology-related fields are filled mainly by men.

12   In my generation, the practical consequences of mathematical and scientific illiteracy are visible in the large number of special programs to help professional women overcome the anxiety they feel when they are promoted into jobs that require them to handle statistics.

13   The consequences of this syndrome should not, however, be viewed in narrowly professional terms. Competence in science and math does not mean one is going to become a scientist or mathematician any more than competence in writing English means one is going to become a professional writer. Scientific and mathematical illiteracy—which has been cited in several recent critiques by panels studying

American education from kindergarten through college—produces an incalculably impoverished vision of human experience.

14 Scientific illiteracy is not, of course, the exclusive province of women. In certain intellectual circles it has become fashionable to proclaim a willed, aggressive ignorance about science and technology. Some female writers specialize in ominous, uninformed diatribes against genetic research as a plot to remove control of childbearing from women, while some well-known men of letters proudly announce that they understand absolutely nothing about computers, or, for that matter, about electricity. This lack of understanding is nothing in which women or men ought to take pride.

15 Failure to comprehend either computers or chromosomes leads to a terrible sense of helplessness, because the profound impact of science on everyday life is evident even to those who insist they don't, won't, can't understand why the changes are taking place. At this stage of history women are more prone to such feelings of helplessness than men because the culture judges their ignorance less harshly and because women themselves acquiesce in that indulgence.

16 Since there is ample evidence of such feelings in adolescence, it is up to parents to see that their daughters do not accede to the old stereotypes about "masculine" and "feminine" knowledge. Unless we want our daughters to share our intellectual handicaps, we had better tell them no, they can't stop taking mathematics and science at the ripe old age of 16.

Comprehension

1. What reasons does Jacoby give for girls' deficiency in math and science?

2. Why does Jacoby call it a "self-inflicted female disability" (paragraph 3)?

3. According to Jacoby, what are the consequences of being math- and science-illiterate?

Rhetorical Analysis

4. Explain the main idea of Jacoby's essay in your own words.

5. Does the writer use abstract or concrete language in her essay? Cite examples to support your response.

6. What technique does Jacoby use in paragraphs 1 and 2? How does it aid in setting up her argument?

7. What rhetorical strategies does the writer use in her essay?

8. How does the use of dialogue aid in developing paragraph 10? What effect does the general use of dialogue have on Jacoby's point?

9. How is Jacoby's conclusion consistent in tone with the rest of the essay? Does it supply a sense of unity? Why or why not?

10. Write an essay describing a school-related phobia you once had or continue to have (for example, in math, writing, physical education, or biology). Explain where you think that fear came from, how it affected your performance in school, and what you did (or are doing) to cope with the issue.

11. Write an essay about the need for math and science literacy in today's world. Use support from Jacoby's essay.

12. **Writing an Argument** Write an argumentation essay proposing that math and science phobia is not "self-inflicted" but is caused primarily by the continued presence of sexism in society.

Chapter Assessment

Rhetorical Analysis

Read the paragraph below from "Learning to Read and Write" and answer the questions that follow.

My mistress was, as I have said, a kind and tender-hearted woman; and in the simplicity of her soul she commenced, when I first went to live with her, to treat me as she supposed one human being ought to treat another. In entering upon the duties of a slaveholder, she did not seem to perceive that I sustained to her the relation of a mere chattel, and that for her to treat me as a human being was not only wrong, but dangerously so. Slavery proved as injurious to her as it did to me. When I went there, she was a pious, warm, and tender-hearted woman. There was no sorrow or suffering for which she had not a tear. She had bread for the hungry, clothes for the naked, and comfort for every mourner that came within her reach. Slavery soon proved its ability to divest her of these heavenly qualities. Under its influence, the tender heart became stone, and the lamb-like disposition gave way to one of tiger-like fierceness. The first step in her downward course was in her ceasing to instruct me. She now commenced to practise her husband's precepts. She finally became even more violent in her opposition than her husband himself. She was not satisfied with simply doing as well as he had commanded; she seemed anxious to do better. Nothing seemed to make her more angry than to see me with a newspaper. She seemed to think that here lay the danger. I have had her rush at me with a face made all up of fury, and snatch from me a newspaper, in a manner that fully revealed her apprehension. She was an apt woman; and a little experience soon demonstrated, to her satisfaction, that education and slavery were incompatible with each other.

—From *Narrative of the Life of Frederick Douglass: An American Slave*, Written by Himself. 1845.

1. The effect of the author's use of figurative language in the line that reads, "Under its influence, the tender heart became stone, and the lamb-like disposition gave way to one of tiger-like fierceness" primarily serves to
   A. Juxtapose the kinder actions of the mistress at a previous time to her increasing cruelty.
   B. Employ imagery to help the reader envision the treatment of the slave.
   C. Describe the mistress's animal-like tendencies.
   D. Illustrate the changes that a slave must necessarily go through in order to survive the ordeal of slavery.
   E. Establish a visual connection between the treatment of slaves and the characteristics of specific animals.

2. The author most likely assumes which of the following about his audience?
   A. They are abolitionists working to free the slaves.
   B. They are slave-owners, themselves.
   C. They will most likely sympathize with the "mistress's" predicament.
   D. They, too, have been slaves.
   E. They are opposed to slavery.

Read the passage below from "The Lonely, Good Company of Books" and answer the questions that follow.

OPEN THE DOORS OF YOUR MIND WITH BOOKS, read the red and white poster over the nun's desk in early September. It soon was apparent to me that reading was the classroom's central activity. Each course had its own book. And the information gathered from a book was unquestioned. READ TO LEARN, the sign on the wall advised in December. I privately wondered: What was the connection between reading and learning? Did one learn something only by reading it? Was an idea only an idea if it could be written down? In June, CONSIDER BOOKS YOUR BEST FRIENDS. Friends? Reading was, at best, only a chore. I needed to look up whole paragraphs of words in a dictionary. Lines of type were dizzying, the eye having to move slowly across the page, then down, and across. . . . The sentences of the first books I read were coolly impersonal. Toned hard. What most bothered me, however, was the isolation reading required. To console myself for the loneliness I'd feel when I read, I tried reading in a very soft voice. Until: "Who is doing all that talking to his neighbor?" Shortly after, remedial reading classes were arranged for me with a very old nun.

—"The Lonely, Good Company of Books" by Richard Rodriguez. Copyright © 1981 by Richard Rodriguez. Reprinted by permission of Georges Borchardt, Inc., on behalf of the author.

3. The author's use of multiple questions in this excerpt serves primarily to
   A. Illustrate his lack of understanding as a young student.
   B. Exemplify the author's keen intellect that led to his eventual scholarly success.
   C. Pose questions that will be answered later in the passage.
   D. Create a contrast between the nun and the author.
   E. Establish context for the phrase "toned hard."

4. The effect of the capitalized poster captions primarily
   A. Catches the reader's attention and reminds them of posters they have also seen in classrooms.
   B. Demonstrates the author's early difficulty with reading.
   C. Parallels the author's early disconnect with reading by creating a similarly jarring sensation for the reader.
   D. Satirizes the modern education system for trite attempts to reach students.
   E. Provides evidence that the author was able to read far better than the nuns believed him capable.

Chapter Assessment

Read the passage below from "The Graduates" and answer the question that follows.

On your first sleepover, your best friend's mother asks if you would like a tuna-fish-salad sandwich. Your own mother gives you tuna-fish-salad sandwiches all the time, so you say, "Sure." When you bite into the sandwich, though, you realize, too late, that your best friend's mother's tuna-fish salad tastes nothing like the tuna-fish salad your mother makes. You never dreamed that it was possible for there to be more than one way to prepare tuna-fish salad. And what's with the bread? It's brown, and appears to have tiny seeds in it. What is more unnerving is the fact that your best friend obviously considers his mother's tuna-fish salad to be perfectly normal and has been eating it with enjoyment all his life. Later on, you discover that the pillows in your best friend's house are filled with some kind of foam-rubber stuff instead of feathers. The toilet paper is pink. What kind of human beings are these? At two o'clock in the morning, you throw up, and your mother comes and takes you home.

—Louis Menand/The New Yorker © Condé Nast

5. The primary purpose of opening the passage with second person point of view is to
   A. Draw the audience into the essay with a humorous hook.
   B. Create a sense of complicity with an inclusive anecdotal scenario.
   C. Exclude any reader who has not experienced childhood sleepovers.
   D. Suggest that narrative writing is the cornerstone to a successful college education.
   E. Define a uniquely American experience in a particularly jarring mode.

Read the passage below from "America, Still on Top" and answer the questions that follow.

Many universities are looking to America as a model for how to survive. That means raising or introducing tuition, increasing enrollment (including the number of foreign students who pay full fare) and boosting endowments through fund-raising. Money, however, is not enough to build a quality university. In many countries, for example, professors are members of the civil service and do not enjoy the status, or salary, that will draw the best talent. In centralized systems like China's, authorities can order up any number of engineers or scientists, but that does not mean they will be any good. Other nations are expanding bureaucracies to accommodate unemployed graduates, especially in the humanities and social science—an obvious recipe for disaster.

—Gregorian, Vartan, "America, Still on Top," *Newsweek*, August 20-27, 2007. Reprinted by permission of the author.

6. The tone of the paragraph can best be described as
    A. Scholarly and erudite.
    B. Didactic and authoritarian.
    C. Matter of fact and pragmatic.
    D. Critical yet emotional.
    E. Blunt yet charismatic.

7. The author develops this paragraph in which of the following ways?
    A. By analyzing a process and determining the next steps necessary
    B. By identifying a problem and implicitly comparing that problem to ancillary problems that exist elsewhere
    C. Through direct comparison and contrast of Eastern and Western education systems
    D. By establishing a claim and supporting that claim with examples of potential future scenarios
    E. Through a causal analysis of the development of the identified problem

Read the passage below from "What College Can Mean to the Other America" and answer the questions that follow.

It has been nearly 50 years since Michael Harrington wrote *The Other America,* pulling the curtain back on invisible poverty within the United States. If he were writing today, Harrington would find the same populations he described then: young, marginally educated people who drift in and out of low-pay, dead-end jobs, and older displaced workers, unable to find work as industries transform and shops close. But he would find more of them, especially the young, their situation worsened by further economic restructuring and globalization. And while the poor he wrote about were invisible in a time of abundance, ours are visible in a terrible recession, although invisible in most public policy. In fact, the poor are drifting further into the dark underbelly of American capitalism.

—"What College Can Mean to the Other America," by Mike Rose for *The Chronicle of Higher Education,* September 11, 2011. Reprinted by permission of the author.

8. What is the primary effect of the colon in the sentence, "If he were writing today, Harrington would find the same populations he described then: young, marginally educated people who drift in and out of low-pay, dead-end jobs, and older displaced workers, unable to find work as industries transform and shops close."

    A. It creates a more complicated sentence, thereby creating an appeal to ethos.
    B. It allows the author to provide his own working definition for Harrington's academically known term.
    C. It is a direct allusion to Harrington's scholarly research and establishes the author within the continuum of this discourse.
    D. It separates an otherwise run-on sentence into meaningful parts.
    E. It allows the author to show the clear distinction between his own work and Harrington's.

9. How does the following sentence relate to the sentences that precede it? "And while the poor he wrote about were invisible in a time of abundance, ours are visible in a terrible recession, although invisible in most public policy."

    A. It presents the essential paradox of the position the group he defines find themselves in.
    B. It completes the definition Rose offers in the second sentence in the paragraph.
    C. It illustrates the economic problems established with globalization.
    D. It allows him to connect to the preceding sentences through the use of multiple conjunctions at the beginnings of sentences.
    E. It establishes the complete contradiction from the world Harrington described and the world Rose currently writes about.

Read the passage below from "When Bright Girls Decide That Math is a Waste of Time" and answer the question that follows.

During the teen-age years the well-documented phenomenon of "math anxiety" strikes girls who never had any problem handling numbers during earlier schooling. Some men, too, experience this syndrome—a form of panic, akin to a phobia, at any task involving numbers—but women constitute the overwhelming majority of sufferers. The onset of acute math anxiety during the teen-age years is, as Stalin was fond of saying, "not by accident."

10. Placing the term "math anxiety" in quotation marks does which of the following?

    A. It makes clear that the "syndrome" defined in the second sentence is fact and crucial to the argument of the essay.

    B. It conveys to the audience that the author does not believe this syndrome actually exists.

    C. It acknowledges that the concept is likely one that the audience will implicitly understand even without a definition.

    D. It sets the term apart as important and invites the audience to consider its definition before the author presents one directly.

    E. It shows that the term has been used by the author in other writing.

Connections for Critical Thinking

1. Compare and contrast the rhetorical devices of a personal essay as represented in Rodriguez's "The Lonely, Good Company of Books" with the rhetoric of an argumentative essay like Rose's "What College Can Mean to the Other America."

2. Analyze an event in your education when you had a disagreement with a teacher, administrator, or another authority figure. Explain and explore whether the differences in viewpoint were based on emotional perspective, intellectual perspective, or both.

3. Select the essay in this chapter you find most pertinent to your life as a student. Explain why you selected the essay, and explore your intellectual and emotional responses to it.

4. Does your high school seem to support Jacoby's views regarding the educational lives of women? Explain why or why not.

5. It is 2050. Write an essay in which you explore the demographics of a typical high school classroom. Refer to the ideas contained in the Gregorian and Jacoby essays.

6. Write an essay that categorizes at least three educational issues that the authors in this chapter examine. Establish a clear thesis to unify the categories you establish.

7. Analyze the patterns and techniques Menand, Rose, and Jacoby use to advance their claims about education today.

STEM vs. Liberal Arts—Is the STEAM Movement the Solution?

Historically, a degree from STEM (Science, Technology, Engineering, Math) has appeared far more lucrative than a Liberal Arts degree, which includes language arts, philosophy, and social sciences. The majors in each degree have experienced a great divide in the areas of financial rewards and highly regarded societal values. A movement—STEAM (with "Art" added)—has gained momentum since many believe the arts should be a recognized part of STEM. But will this signal the end of the Liberal Arts major? Is the Liberal Arts major relevant in this world of increasing technology? Should STEM include the "A" to make a Liberal Arts degree more valid?

▼ SOURCE A

"STEM vs. STEAM: Do the Arts Belong?" by Anne Jolly

—Anne Jolly, STEM curriculum developer and consultant, and author of *STEM by Design: Strategies & Activities for Grades 4–8*.

A tug of war is currently looming between proponents of STEM education (science, technology, engineering, and math) and advocates for STEAM lessons, which add art to the mix. Whichever side you come down on, here are some ideas for you to mull over.

STEM   First, consider the why and what of STEM education. Both private and public sectors report that 21st-century workers require skills that many of today's graduates don't have. Students need more in-depth knowledge of math and science, plus the ability to integrate and apply that knowledge to solve the challenges facing our nation.

STEM, then, is a specific program designed for a specific purpose—to integrate and apply knowledge of math and science in order to create technologies and solutions for real-world problems, using an engineering design approach. It's no surprise that STEM programs need to maintain an intense focus.

STEAM   Recently, the idea of adding the arts to STEM programs has been gaining momentum. Surprisingly, I've heard push-back from both camps:

1. **From STEM proponents:** STEM lessons naturally involve art (for example, product design), language arts (communication), and social studies and history (setting the context for engineering challenges). STEM projects do not deliberately exclude the arts or any other subject; rather, these subjects are included incidentally as needed for engineering challenges. The focus of STEM is developing rigorous math and science skills through engineering. How can you focus on other subjects (such as art) without losing the mission of STEM or watering down its primary purpose?

2. **From arts proponents:** Engineering and technology can certainly serve the artist and help create art. But if we're talking about how one can use art in engineering . . . as an artist, it seems we're missing the point and devaluing, or not realizing, art's purpose and importance. We have it backwards.

▼ SOURCE B

"Branches of the Same Tree" Quotation by Albert Einstein

—From *Out of My Later Years: The Scientist, Philosopher, and Man Portrayed Through His Own Words* by Albert Einstein. New York: Open Road Integrated Media. Copyright ©1956 by the Estate of Albert Einstein.

All religions, arts and sciences are branches of the same tree. All these aspirations are directed toward ennobling man's life, lifting it from the sphere of mere physical existence and leading the individual toward freedom.

▼ SOURCE C

Average Wages for Related Jobs

—Source: Bureau of Labor Statistics, www.bls.gov/oes/current

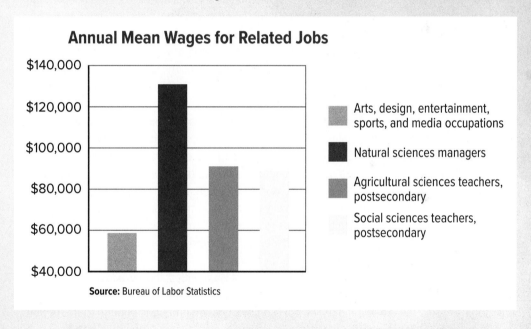

Annual Mean Wages for Related Jobs

- Arts, design, entertainment, sports, and media occupations
- Natural sciences managers
- Agricultural sciences teachers, postsecondary
- Social sciences teachers, postsecondary

Source: Bureau of Labor Statistics

▼ SOURCE D

"The Major Divide: Humanities vs. STEM Majors" by Elaina Provencio

—Elaina N. Provencio (2015)

"Oh the humanity!" The popularity of Humanities majors is declining. Recent studies have found that the percentage of students earning degrees in this field is lower than it has been in previous years. What is to blame?

College students these days live in a society and economy that demand modernization and technological advances. As a nation we are competing with countries that have an edge in these fields that we do not possess. The job market is being exported, and in this modern-industrial age there is a societal pressure to keep up, to have a skill in the STEM realm. However, while our nation is in need of another great wave of science and innovation, this national obsession has had an effect on the pursuits of Liberal Arts and Humanities.

These days, it is difficult to see an advantage in majors that fall under this umbrella. When I tell people that I am an intended English major, the usual reaction is, "Are you going to be a teacher?" or, "Why did you go to Berkeley for that?" Humanities majors are at the butt of the career jokes. To most, a degree in Liberal Arts or Humanities is a wasted piece of paper and a job at a fast-food chain. This could not be further from the truth. There are strengths and advantages that a degree in fields such as History, Linguistics, and Political Science hold that STEM degrees do not. Humanities majors encourage analysis, critical-thinking, and a vast knowledge of various topics. These majors look deeper into varied texts that affect media, culture, society, literature, and politics. It is not the major specification that is applied in the workforce, but it is the work ethic and skills that are gained in earning the degree. English majors work well with close readings and analysis, as well as grammar and writing, which can be applied to media professions, law, business, creative professions, and politics. If our country focuses only on the drive to be a technologically advanced nation, our culture and society will follow in suit. We need the Humanities majors to run our schools, social services, and political centers. Who will write future great films and literature? Where does art come into play in a STEM filled world? Engineers do not fit at the UN table.

While this is a dramatic view of the disintegration of Humanities, it does allow for a different perspective. What would this nation be without the pursuit of knowledge in these topics? It is easy to push aside the old and make way for the new, but when there is enough room for both, whom do we hurt? STEM majors are very valuable to our society and foundation as a nation, but our current obsession with them will lead to a pool of laborers in a modern workforce that all serve the same function.

An apparent myth is leading many millennials to believe that specific degrees guarantee income and job security. While there is research to support certain career paths that are profitable, no graph or survey can determine your future. Every individual is just that, an individual. You define yourself by the work and advantages that you bring to the table. Not every Software Engineer is successful, and not every Philosophy major is unemployed. One's major does not define one's future.

▼ SOURCE E

Fastest Growing Jobs in America

—Source: Occupational Outlook Handbook, Bureau of Labor Statistics, https://www.bls.gov/ooh/fastest-growing.htm

Occupation	Growth Rate, 2016–2026	2017 Median Pay
Solar photovoltaic installers	105%	$39,490
Wind turbine service technicians	96%	$53,880
Home health aides	47%	$23,210
Personal care aides	39%	$23,100
Physician assistants	37%	$104,860
Nurse practitioners	36%	$103,880
Statisticians	34%	$84,060
Physical therapist assistants	31%	$57,430
Software developers, applications	31%	$101,790
Mathematicians	30%	$103,010
Physical therapist aides	29%	$25,730
Bicycle repairers	29%	$28,390
Medical assistants	29%	$32,480
Genetic counselors	29%	$77,480
Occupational therapy assistants	29%	$59,310
Information security analysts	28%	$95,510
Physical therapists	28%	$86,850
Operations research analysts	27%	$81,390
Forest fire inspectors and prevention specialists	27%	$37,380
Massage therapists	26%	$39,990

▼ SOURCE F

"The Key Attributes Employers Seek on Students' Resumes" from the National Association of Colleges and Employers (NACE), November 30, 2017

Reprinted from the *2018 Job Outlook*, with permission of the National Association of Colleges and Employers, copyright holder.

College students who are conducting their job search and want to impress employers with their resumes should emphasize their abilities to solve problems and work as part of a team, according to a new survey report from the National Association of Colleges and Employers (NACE).

When NACE asked employers participating in its *Job Outlook 2018* survey which attributes—beyond a strong GPA—they most value, employers indicated that problem-solving skills and an ability to work in a team are the most desired attributes and are of equal importance. (See Figure 1.) This is the second consecutive year that the largest percentage of employers will search for these attributes on students' resumes.

Following problem-solving skills and teamwork abilities, written communication skills, leadership, and a strong work ethic are also highly valued attributes that employers want to see evidence of on resumes.

Figure 1: Attributes Employers Seek on a Candidates Resume

- Problem-solving skills
- Ability to work in a team
- Communication skills (written)
- Leadership
- Strong work ethic
- Analytical/quantitative skills
- Communication skills (verbal)
- Initiative
- Detail-oriented
- Flexibility/adaptability
- Technical skills
- Interpersonal skills (relates well to others)
- Computer skills
- Organizational ability
- Strategic planning skills
- Creativity
- Friendly/outgoing personality
- Tactfulness
- Entrepreneurial skills/risk-taking
- Fluency in a foreign language

"When I Heard the Learn'd Astronomer" by Walt Whitman

—From *Leaves of Grass*. Philadelphia: Rees Welsh & Co. © 1881

When I heard the learn'd astronomer,

When the proofs, the figures, were ranged in columns before me,

When I was shown the charts and diagrams, to add, divide, and measure them,

When I sitting heard the astronomer where he lectured with much applause in the lecture-room,

How soon unaccountable I became tired and sick,

Till rising and gliding out I wander'd off by myself,

In the mystical moist night-air, and from time to time,

Look'd up in perfect silence at the stars.

Applying Your Synthesis Skills

Comprehension

1. Summarize the inferred arguments made in each source.

Rhetorical Analysis

2. How does Source A personify STEM and STEAM?

3. What is the metaphorical effect of Source B, and how is this achieved?

4. How do Sources C and E make a convincing argument using logos?

5. Source D provides a paradoxical argument. What is this argument?

6. How does the arrangement of the material in Source F give greater clarity?

7. Compare and contrast the "learn'd astronomer's" evidence to Whitman's visual epiphany when he leaves the lecture and walks outside (Source G).

Writing an Argument

8. Using examples from the sources, write an essay explaining why you do or do not support the STEAM movement.

CHAPTER 5

Family Life: How Do We Become Who We Are?

As you read the essays in this chapter, consider the following questions:

- What rhetorical mode is the author using: narration, exposition, or argumentation? Why is this mode appropriate for the author's purpose?
- What perspective does the writer take on the subject of identity formation? Is the writer optimistic, pessimistic, or something else? What is the writer's tone?
- What are the cultural, social, and economic issues addressed in the essay?
- How do you regard the authority of the author? Does she or he seem to be speaking from experience and knowledge? In essays that explain or argue, does the evidence appear substantial or questionable? Explain.
- What stylistic devices does the author employ to re-create a memory, explain a function, or argue a stance regarding an issue of identity?
- Which essays appear alike in purpose and method, and why?
- What have you learned or discovered about your own identity from reading these essays?
- Do you prefer one rhetorical mode over another—for example, personal narration over argumentation? If so, why?

Every culture has its own ideas about what identity is, how it is formed, and where it comes from. What is the influence of family on the creation of identity? Families nourish us during childhood, and the values our families seek to maintain usually affect our identities in powerful ways, whether we adopt them wholly, modify them, or reject them outright. Writers have always been aware of the importance of the family in human development and behavior, and have written about it from various perspectives, using narration, sociological and psychological analysis, and cultural criticism, among other approaches. Tolstoy wrote that "happy families are all alike; every unhappy family is unhappy in its own way." But we shall discover that Tolstoy had a limited view of family life and its values—probably circumscribed by the mores of the time he lived in. Some of our finest essayists and observers of social life today demonstrate in this chapter that what constitutes the definition of a family is up for grabs.

The family is one of the few institutions we find in every society throughout the world—at least every thriving society. Anthropologists, sociologists, and psychologists tell us that family patterns are exceedingly diverse even in the same societies. In the past and even more so today, children grow up in many ways: in nuclear and in nontraditional households; in single-parent and in dual-parent arrangements; in extended families and in blended families; and in patriarchal and matriarchal, heterosexual and homosexual, monogamous and polygamous situations. And the dynamics of family life assume added dimension as we move across cultures, studying European families, African American families, Hispanic families, Asian families, and so forth. Even within these groups, we find variables that affect family life and values, such as economic class, social class, and educational levels.

Americans today seem to be groping for a definition of what constitutes the happy family. With the influences of the media and of peer pressure on children, the rise in the number of latchkey children, and the fact that there is a growing diversity of cultures in America owing to the new wave of immigration, the family appears to be less of a traditional haven than it was even a generation ago. This chapter contains vivid accounts of the long-standing bonds within the family that have been treasured for their capacity to build values of love and sharing. It also contains essays that demonstrate how family life is filled with emotional complexities and conflicts that the child must negotiate as she or he finds meaning and attempts to construct an identity. Each writer, whether writing narration, exposition, or argumentation, shows how significant the family is for the development of our values, personalities, and lifestyles.

CLASSIC ▼

Fine Art Images/age fotostock

CONTEMPORARY ▼

Kent Meireis/The Image Works

How Do We Respond to Marriage?

Using a Critical Perspective Analyze the two images of weddings. What was your first impression of Flemish artist Pieter Brueghel's *Peasant Wedding Dance* and the photograph of the contemporary wedding? What details do you see? What senses do the artist and the photographer draw on to convey the atmosphere of the wedding? What does each want to say about the institution of marriage? How do you know?

Analyzing Visuals and Their Rhetoric

1. Describe the settings and perspective of each wedding.

2. Compare and contrast the tone of each visual text.

3. Note where each person is standing in the contemporary wedding photograph and explain the significance of each person's position and stance.

4. What do weddings say about culture?

CLASSIC ▼

How Much Do Families Matter?

E. B. White and Barbara Kingsolver represent two generations, each raised with different values regarding the function, structure, and role of the family. Both authors are master stylists, but each reflects a style of writing, an intellectual universe, and an external world that views the healthy family differently. White writes in clear, concise, elegiac prose. It marches on in a quiet, evenly patterned rhythm. Perhaps it is a metaphor of his view of life in general and family life in particular. Tradition is to be treasured; continuity is to be celebrated. He attends to the details of a nature outing and suggests that the sights, sounds, and smells that imbue the events he and his son experience are the same as those he experienced years before with his own father. For White, it seems, pleasure is derived from connectivity and permanence.

Kingsolver is passionate about her perspective on what constitutes a healthy family structure, but it is a family transformed, reconfigured, and rearranged by contemporary events and values. Kingsolver's notion of family is various while White's view is archetypal. Kingsolver seems to believe that change in families creates security, particularly if one is moving from a dysfunctional environment to a more coherent one. Is White conservative in his views? Is Kingsolver a liberal? Perhaps a better way to get a sense of their differences is to inquire whether our amorphous contemporary world requires us to be more flexible and critical. And, of course, we must consider that Kingsolver adds a woman's voice to the conversation about family, a voice that was not as frequently heard by the members of White's generation.

Once More to the Lake

E. B. White

E(lwyn) B(rooks) White (1899–1985), perhaps the finest American essayist of the 20th century, was at his most distinctive in his treatments of people and nature. A recipient of the National Medal for Literature, and associated for years with *The New Yorker*, White is the author of *One Man's Meat* (1942), *Here Is New York* (1949), and *The Second Tree from the Corner* (1954), among numerous other works. He was also one of the most talented writers of literature for children, the author of *Stuart Little* (1945), *Charlotte's Web* (1952), and *The Trumpet of the Swan* (1970). In this essay, White combines narration and description to make a poignant and vivid statement about past and present, youth and age, life and death.

1   One summer, along about 1904, my father rented a camp on a lake in Maine and took us all there for the month of August. We all got ringworm from some

kittens and had to rub Pond's Extract on our arms and legs night and morning, and my father rolled over in a canoe with all his clothes on; but outside of that the vacation was a success and from then on none of us ever thought there was any place in the world like that lake in Maine. We returned summer after summer—always on August 1st for one month. I have since become a saltwater man, but sometimes in summer there are days when the restlessness of the tides and the fearful cold of the sea water and the incessant wind which blows across the afternoon and into the evening make me wish for the placidity of a lake in the woods. A few weeks ago this feeling got so strong I bought myself a couple of bass hooks and a spinner and returned to the lake where we used to go, for a week's fishing and to revisit old haunts.

2   I took along my son, who had never had any fresh water up his nose and who had seen lily pads only from train windows. On the journey over to the lake I began to wonder what it would be like. I wondered how time would have marred this unique, this holy spot—the coves and streams, the hills that the sun set behind, the camps and the paths behind the camps. I was sure the tarred road would have found it out and I wondered in what other ways it would be desolated. It is strange how much you can remember about places like that once you allow your mind to return into the grooves which lead back. You remember one thing, and that suddenly reminds you of another thing. I guess I remembered clearest of all the early mornings, when the lake was cool and motionless, remembered how the bedroom smelled of the lumber it was made of and of the wet woods whose scent entered through the screen. The partitions in the camp were thin and did not extend clear to the top of the rooms, and as I was always the first up I would dress softly so as not to wake the others, and sneak out into the sweet outdoors and start out in the canoe, keeping close along the shore in the long shadows of the pines. I remembered being very careful never to rub my paddle against the gunwale for fear of disturbing the stillness of the cathedral.

3   The lake had never been what you would call a wild lake. There were cottages sprinkled around the shores, and it was in farming country although the shores of the lake were quite heavily wooded. Some of the cottages were owned by nearby farmers, and you would live at the shore and eat your meals at the farmhouse. That's what our family did. But although it wasn't wild, it was a fairly large and undisturbed lake and there were places in it which, to a child at least, seemed infinitely remote and primeval.

4   I was right about the tar: It led to within half a mile of the shore. But when I got back there, with my boy, and we settled into a camp near a farmhouse and into the kind of summertime I had known, I could tell that it was going to be pretty much the same as it had been before—I knew it, lying in bed the first morning, smelling the bedroom, and hearing the boy sneak quietly out and go off along the shore in a boat. I began to sustain the illusion that he was I, and therefore, by simple transposition, that I was my father. This sensation

persisted, kept cropping up all the time we were there. It was not an entirely new feeling, but in this setting it grew much stronger. I seemed to be living a dual existence. I would be in the middle of some simple act, I would be picking up a bait box or laying down a table fork, or I would be saying something, and suddenly it would be not I but my father who was saying the words or making the gesture. It gave me a creepy sensation.

5   We went fishing the first morning. I felt the same damp moss covering the worms in the bait can, and saw the dragonfly alight on the tip of my rod as it hovered a few inches from the surface of the water. It was the arrival of this fly that convinced me beyond any doubt that everything was as it always had been, that the years were a mirage and there had been no years. The small waves were the same, chucking the rowboat under the chin as we fished at anchor, and the boat was the same boat, the same color green and the ribs broken in the same place, and under the floor-boards the same fresh-water leavings and débris—the dead hellgrammite, the wisps of moss, the rusty discarded fishhook, the dried blood from yesterday's catch. We stared silently at the tips of our rods, at the dragonflies that came and went. I lowered the tip of mine into the water, tentatively, pensively dislodging the fly, which darted two feet away, poised, darted two feet back, and came to rest again a little farther up the rod. There had been no years between the ducking of this dragonfly and the other one—the one that was part of memory. I looked at the boy, who was silently watching his fly, and it was my hands that held his rod, my eyes watching. I felt dizzy and didn't know which rod I was at the end of.

6   We caught two bass, hauling them in briskly as though they were mackerel, pulling them over the side of the boat in a businesslike manner without any landing net, and stunning them with a blow on the back of the head. When we got back for a swim before lunch, the lake was exactly where we had left it, the same number of inches from the dock, and there was only the merest suggestion of a breeze. This seemed an utterly enchanted sea, this lake you could leave to its own devices for a few hours and come back to, and find that it had not stirred, this constant and trustworthy body of water. In the shallows, the dark, water-soaked sticks and twigs, smooth and old, were undulating in clusters on the bottom against the clean ribbed sand, and the track of the mussel was plain. A school of minnows swam by, each minnow with its small individual shadow, doubling the attendance, so clear and sharp in the sunlight. Some of the other campers were in swimming, along the shore, one of them with a cake of soap, and the water felt thin and clear and unsubstantial. Over the years there had been this person with the cake of soap, this cultist, and here he was. There had been no years.

7   Up to the farmhouse to dinner through the teeming, dusty field, the road under our sneakers was only a two-track road. The middle track was missing, the one with the marks of the hooves and the splotches of dried, flaky manure. There had always been three tracks to choose from in choosing which track to

walk in; now the choice was narrowed down to two. For a moment I missed terribly the middle alternative. But the way led past the tennis court, and something about the way it lay there in the sun reassured me; the tape had loosened along the backline, the alleys were green with plantains and other weeds, and the net (installed in June and removed in September) sagged in the dry noon, and the whole place steamed with midday heat and hunger and emptiness. There was a choice of pie for dessert, and one was blueberry and one was apple, and the waitresses were the same country girls, there having been no passage of time, only the illusion of it as in a dropped curtain—the waitresses were still fifteen; their hair had been washed, that was the only difference—they had been to the movies and seen the pretty girls with the clean hair.

8   Summertime, oh summertime, pattern of life indelible, the fade-proof lake, the woods unshatterable, the pasture with the sweetfern and the juniper forever and ever, summer without end; this was the background, and the life along the shore was the design, the cottagers with their innocent and tranquil design, their tiny docks with the flagpole and the American flag floating against the white clouds in the blue sky, the little paths over the roots of the trees leading from camp to camp and the paths leading back to the outhouses and the can of lime for sprinkling, and at the souvenir counters at the store the miniature birch-bark canoes and the post cards that showed things looking a little better than they looked. This was the American family at play, escaping the city heat, wondering whether the newcomers in the camp at the head of the cove were "common" or "nice," wondering whether it was true that the people who drove up for Sunday dinner at the farmhouse were turned away because there wasn't enough chicken.

9   It seemed to me, as I kept remembering all this, that those times and those summers had been infinitely precious and worth saving. There had been jollity and peace and goodness. The arriving (at the beginning of August) had been so big a business in itself, at the railway station the farm wagon drawn up, the first smell of the pine-laden air, the first glimpse of the smiling farmer, and the great importance of the trunks and your father's enormous authority in such matters, and the feel of the wagon under you for the long ten-mile haul, and at the top of the last long hill catching the first view of the lake after eleven months of not seeing this cherished body of water. The shouts and cries of the other campers when they saw you, and the trunks to be unpacked, to give up their rich burden. (Arriving was less exciting nowadays, when you sneaked up in your car and parked it under a tree near the camp and took out the bags and in five minutes it was all over, no fuss, no loud wonderful fuss about trunks.)

10   Peace and goodness and jollity. The only thing that was wrong now, really, was the sound of the place, an unfamiliar nervous sound of the outboard motors. This was the note that jarred, the one thing that would sometimes break the illusion and set the years moving. In those other summertimes all motors were inboard; and when they were at a little distance, the noise they

made was a sedative, an ingredient of summer sleep. They were one-cylinder and two-cylinder engines, and some were make-and-break and some were jump-spark, but they all made a sleepy sound across the lake. The one-lungers throbbed and fluttered, and the twin-cylinder ones purred and purred, and that was a quiet sound too. But now the campers all had outboards. In the daytime, in the hot mornings, these motors made a petulant, irritable sound; at night, in the still evening when the afterglow lit the water, they whined about one's ears like mosquitoes. My boy loved our rented outboard, and his great desire was to achieve singlehanded mastery over it, and authority, and he soon learned the trick of choking it a little (but not too much), and the adjustment of the needle valve. Watching him I would remember the things you could do with the old one-cylinder engine with the heavy flywheel, how you could have it eating out of your hand if you got really close to it spiritually. Motor boats in those days didn't have clutches, and you would make a landing by shutting off the motor at the proper time and coasting in with a dead rudder. But there was a way of reversing them, if you learned the trick, by cutting the switch and putting it on again exactly on the final dying revolution of the flywheel, so that it would kick back against compression and begin reversing. Approaching a dock in a strong following breeze, it was difficult to slow up sufficiently by the ordinary coasting method, and if a boy felt he had complete mastery over his motor, he was tempted to keep it running beyond its time and then reverse it a few feet from the dock. It took a cool nerve, because if you threw the switch a twentieth of a second too soon you would catch the flywheel when it still had speed enough to go up past center, and the boat would leap ahead, charging bull-fashion at the dock.

11   We had a good week at the camp. The bass were biting well and the sun shone endlessly, day after day. We would be tired at night and lie down in the accumulated heat of the little bedrooms after the long hot day and the breeze would stir almost imperceptibly outside and the smell of the swamp drift in through the rusty screens. Sleep would come easily and in the morning the red squirrel would be on the roof, tapping out his gay routine. I kept remembering everything, lying in bed in the mornings—the small steamboat that had a long rounded stern like the lip of a Ubangi, and how quietly she ran on the moonlight sails, when the older boys played their mandolins and the girls sang and we ate doughnuts dipped in sugar, and how sweet the music was on the water in the shining night, and what it had felt like to think about girls then. After breakfast we would go up to the store and the things were in the same place—minnows in a bottle, the plugs and spinners disarranged and pawed over by the youngsters from the boys' camp, the fig newtons and the Beeman's gum. Outside, the road was tarred and cars stood in front of the store. Inside, all was just as it had always been, except there was more Coca-Cola and not so much Moxie and root beer and birch beer and sarsaparilla. We would walk out with a bottle of pop apiece and sometimes the pop would backfire up our noses

and hurt. We explored the streams, quietly, where the turtles slid off the sunny logs and dug their way into the soft bottom, and we lay on the town wharf and fed worms to the tame bass. Everywhere we went I had trouble making out which was I, the one walking at my side, the one walking in my pants.

12   One afternoon while we were there at that lake a thunderstorm came up. It was like the revival of an old melodrama that I had seen long ago with childish awe. The second-act climax of the drama of the electrical disturbance over a lake in America had not changed in any important respect. This was the big scene, still the big scene. The whole thing was so familiar, the first feeling of oppression and heat and a general air around camp of not wanting to go very far away. In midafternoon (it was all the same) a curious darkening of the sky, and a lull in everything that had made life tick; and then the way the boats suddenly swung the other way at their moorings with the coming of a breeze out of the new quarter, and the premonitory rumble. Then the kettle drum, then the snare, then the bass drum and cymbals, then crackling light against the dark, and the gods grinning and licking their chops in the hills. Afterward the calm, the rain steadily rustling in the calm lake, the return of light and hope and spirits, and the campers running out in joy and relief to go swimming in the rain, their bright cries perpetuating the deathless joke about how they were getting simply drenched, and the children screaming with delight at the new sensation of bathing in the rain, and the joke about getting drenched linking the generations in a strong indestructible chain. And the comedian who waded in carrying an umbrella.

13   When the others went swimming my son said he was going in too. He pulled his dripping trunks from the line where they had hung all through the shower, and wrung them out. Languidly, and with no thought of going in, I watched him, his hard little body, skinny and bare, saw him wince slightly as he pulled up around his vitals the small, soggy, icy garment. As he buckled the swollen belt suddenly my groin felt the chill of death.

CLASSIC AND CONTEMPORARY ESSAYS

CLASSIC ▼

Comprehension

1. At what point in the essay do you begin to sense White's main purpose? What is his purpose? What type of reader might his purpose appeal to?

2. What motivates White to return to the lake in Maine? Explain the "simple transposition" that he mentions in paragraph 4. List the illustrations that he gives of this phenomenon. What change does he detect in the lake?

3. Explain the significance of White's last sentence. Where are there foreshadowings of this statement?

Rhetorical Analysis

4. Explain the effect of White's use of figurative language in paragraphs 2, 10, and 12.

5. Identify those words and phrases that White invokes to establish the sense of mystery about the lake. Why are these words and their connotations important to the nature of the illusion that he describes?

6. Explain the organization of the essay in terms of the following paragraph units: 1–4, 5–7, 8–10, and 11–13. Explain the function of paragraphs 8 and 12.

7. There are many vivid and unusual descriptive details in this essay—for example, the dragonfly in paragraph 5 and the two-track road in paragraph 7. How does White create symbolic overtones for these descriptive details and others? Why is the lake itself a complex symbol? Explain with reference to paragraph 6.

8. Describe the persona that White creates for himself in the essay. How does this persona function?

9. What is the relation between the introductory and concluding paragraphs, specifically in terms of irony of statement? Explain the irony between the two paragraphs.

Writing

10. Explore in an essay the theme of nostalgia, such as the nostalgia apparent in "Once More to the Lake." What are the beauties and the dangers of nostalgia? Can the past ever be recaptured or relived? Justify your answer.

11. Referring to revisiting a site on the lake that he had visited years before with his father, White remarks in paragraph 4, "I could tell that it was going to be pretty much the same as it had been before." In an essay, analyze the strategies White uses to indicate the unchanging role and function of the family.

12. **Writing an Argument** Argue for or against the proposition that nostalgia can obscure the true nature of family relationships and even suppress painful memories that should be confronted.

CONTEMPORARY ▶

Stone Soup

Barbara Kingsolver

Barbara Kingsolver (b. 1955) was born in Annapolis, Maryland; grew up in rural Kentucky, and was educated at DePauw University and the University of Arizona. Her fiction includes *The Bean Trees* (1988); *Homeland* (1990); *Animal Dreams* (1991), for which she won a PEN fiction prize and an Edward Abbey Ecofiction Award; *Pigs in Heaven* (1993), which won a Los Angeles Times Book Award for Fiction; and *The Poisonwood Bible* (1998). Kingsolver's nonfiction includes *High Tide in Tucson: Essays from Now or Never* (1995), *Last Stand: America's Virgin Lands* (2002), and *Animal, Vegetable, Miracle: A Year of Food Life* (2007). She has also worked as a biologist, is active in the field of human rights, and plays keyboard with an amateur rock 'n' roll band. The following essay, first published in the January 1995 issue of *Parenting*, eschews the idea of the nuclear family as the standard by which the healthy family should be judged.

1   In the catalog of family values, where do we rank an occasion like this? A curly-haired boy who wanted to run before he walked, age seven now, a soccer player scoring a winning goal. He turns to the bleachers with his fists in the air and a smile wide as a gap-toothed galaxy. His own cheering section of grown-ups and kids all leap to their feet and hug each other, delirious with love for this boy. He's Andy, my best friend's son. The cheering section includes his mother and her friends, his brother, his father and stepmother, a stepbrother and stepsister, and a grandparent. Lucky is the child with this many relatives on hand to hail a proud accomplishment. I'm there too, witnessing a family fortune. But in spite of myself, defensive words take shape in my head. I am thinking: I dare *anybody* to call this a broken home.

2   Families change, and remain the same. Why are our names for home so slow to catch up to the truth of where we live?

3   When I was a child, I had two parents who loved me without cease. One of them attended every excuse for attention I ever contrived, and the other made it to the ones with higher production values, like piano recitals and appendicitis. So I was a lucky child too. I played with a set of paper dolls called "The Family of Dolls," four in number, who came with the factory-assigned names of Dad, Mom, Sis, and Junior. I think you know what they looked like, at least before I loved them to death and their heads fell off.

4   Now I've replaced the dolls with a life. I knit my days around my daughter's survival and happiness, and am proud to say her head is still on. But we aren't the Family of Dolls. Maybe you're not, either. And if not, even though you are

statistically no oddity, it's probably been suggested to you in a hundred ways that yours isn't exactly a real family, but an impostor family, a harbinger of cultural ruin, a slapdash substitute—something like counterfeit money. Here at the tail end of our century, most of us are up to our ears in the noisy business of trying to support and love a thing called family. But there's a current in the air with ferocious moral force that finds its way even into political campaigns, claiming there is only one right way to do it, the Way It Has Always Been.

5   In the face of a thriving, particolored world, this narrow view is so pickled and absurd I'm astonished that it gets airplay. And I'm astonished that it still stings.

6   Every parent has endured the arrogance of a child-unfriendly grump sitting in judgment, explaining what those kids of ours really need (for example, "a good licking"). If we're polite, we move our crew to another bench in the park. If we're forthright (as I am in my mind, only, for the rest of the day), we fix them with a sweet imperious stare and say, "Come back and let's talk about it after you've changed a thousand diapers."

7   But it's harder somehow to shrug off the Family-of-Dolls Family Values crew when they judge (from their safe distance) that divorced people, blended families, gay families, and single parents are failures. That our children are at risk, and the whole arrangement is messy and embarrassing. A marriage that ends is not called "finished," it's called *failed.* The children of this family may have been born to a happy union, but now they are called *the children of divorce.*

8   I had no idea how thoroughly these assumptions overlaid my culture until I went through divorce myself. I wrote to a friend: "This might be worse than being widowed. Overnight I've suffered the same losses—companionship, financial and practical support, my identity as a wife and partner, the future I'd taken for granted. I am lonely, grieving, and hard-pressed to take care of my household alone. But instead of bringing casseroles, people are acting like I had a fit and broke up the family china."

9   Once upon a time I held these beliefs about divorce: that everyone who does it could have chosen not to do it. That it's a lazy way out of marital problems. That it selfishly puts personal happiness ahead of family integrity. Now I tremble for my ignorance. It's easy, in fortunate times, to forget about the ambush that could leave your head reeling: serious mental or physical illness, death in the family, abandonment, financial calamity, humiliation, violence, despair.

10   I started out like any child, intent on being the Family of Dolls. I set upon young womanhood believing in most of the doctrines of my generation: I wore my skirts four inches above the knee. I had that Barbie with her zebra-striped swimsuit and a figure unlike anything found in nature. And I understood the Prince Charming Theory of Marriage, a quest for Mr. Right that ends smack dab where you find him. I did not completely understand that another whole story *begins* there, and no fairy tale prepared me for the combination of bad

luck and persistent hope that would interrupt my dream and lead me to other arrangements. Like a cancer diagnosis, a dying marriage is a thing to fight, to deny, and finally, when there's no choice left, to dig in and survive. Casseroles would help. Likewise, I imagine it must be a painful reckoning in adolescence (or later on) to realize one's own true love will never look like the soft-focus fragrance ads because Prince Charming (surprise!) is a princess. Or vice versa. Or has skin the color your parents didn't want you messing with, except in the Crayola box.

11   It's awfully easy to hold in contempt the straw broken home, and that mythical category of persons who toss away nuclear family for the sheer fun of it. Even the legal terms we use have a suggestion of caprice. I resent the phrase "irreconcilable differences," which suggests a stubborn refusal to accept a spouse's little quirks. This is specious. Every happily married couple I know has loads of irreconcilable differences. Negotiating where to set the thermostat is not the point. A nonfunctioning marriage is a slow asphyxiation. It is waking up despised each morning, listening to the pulse of your own loneliness before the radio begins to blare its raucous gospel that you're nothing if you aren't loved. It is sharing your airless house with the threat of suicide or other kinds of violence, while the ghost that whispers, "Leave here and destroy your children," has passed over every door and nailed it shut. Disassembling a marriage in these circumstances is as much *fun* as amputating your own gangrenous leg. You do it, if you can, to save a life—or two, or more.

12   I know of no one who really went looking to hoe the harder row, especially the daunting one of single parenthood. Yet it seems to be the most American of customs to blame the burdened for their destiny. We'd like so desperately to believe in freedom and justice for all, we can hardly name that rogue bad luck, even when he's a close enough snake to bite us. In the wake of my divorce, some friends (even a few close ones) chose to vanish, rather than linger within striking distance of misfortune.

13   But most stuck around, bless their hearts, and if I'm any the wiser for my trials, it's from having learned the worth of steadfast friendship. And also, what not to say. The least helpful question is: "Did you want the divorce, or didn't you?" Did I want to keep that gangrenous leg, or not? How to explain, in a culture that venerates choice: two terrifying options are much worse than none at all. Give me any day the quick hand of cruel fate that will leave me scarred but blameless. As it was, I kept thinking of that wicked third-grade joke in which some boy comes up behind you and grabs your ear, starts in with a prolonged tug, and asks, "Do you want this ear any longer?"

14   Still, the friend who holds your hand and says the wrong thing is made of dearer stuff than the one who stays away. And generally, through all of it, you live. My favorite fictional character, Kate Vaiden (in the novel by Reynolds Price), advises: "Strength just comes in one brand—you stand up at sunrise and meet what they send you and keep your hair combed."

15   Once you've weathered the straits, you get to cross the tricky juncture from casualty to survivor. If you're on your feet at the end of a year or two, and have begun putting together a happy new existence, those friends who were kind enough to feel sorry for you when you needed it must now accept you back to the ranks of the living. If you're truly blessed, they will dance at your second wedding. Everybody else, for heavens sake, should stop throwing stones.

16   Arguing about whether nontraditional families deserve pity or tolerance is a little like the medieval debate about left-handedness as a mark of the devil. Divorce, remarriage, single parenthood, gay parents, and blended families simply are. They're facts of our time. Some of the reasons listed by sociologists for these family reconstructions are: the idea of marriage as a romantic partnership rather than a pragmatic one; a shift in women's expectations, from servility to self-respect and independence; and longevity (prior to antibiotics no marriage was expected to last many decades—in Colonial days the average couple lived to be married less than twelve years). Add to all this, our growing sense of entitlement to happiness and safety from abuse. Most would agree these are all good things. Yet their result—a culture in which serial monogamy and the consequent reshaping of families are the norm—gets diagnosed as "failing."

17   For many of us, once we have put ourselves Humpty-Dumpty–wise back together again, the main problem with our reorganized family is that other people think we have a problem. My daughter tells me the only time she's uncomfortable about being the child of divorced parents is when her friends say they feel sorry for her. It's a bizarre sympathy, given that half the kids in her school and nation are in the same boat, pursuing childish happiness with the same energy as their married-parent peers. When anyone asks how she feels about it, she spontaneously lists the benefits: our house is in the country and we have a dog, but she can go to her dad's neighborhood for the urban thrills of a pool and sidewalks for roller-skating. What's more, she has three sets of grandparents!

18   Why is it surprising that a child would revel in a widened family and the right to feel at home in more than one house? Isn't it the opposite that should worry us—a child with no home at all, or too few resources to feel safe? The child at risk is the one whose parents are too immature themselves to guide wisely; too diminished by poverty to nurture; too far from opportunity to offer hope. The number of children in the U.S. living in poverty at this moment is almost unfathomably large: twenty percent. There are families among us that need help all right, and by no means are they new on the landscape. The rate at which teenage girls had babies in 1957 (ninety-six per thousand) was twice what it is now. That remarkable statistic is ignored by the religious right—probably because the teen birth rate was cut in half mainly by legalized abortion. In fact, the policy gatekeepers who coined the phrase "family values" have steadfastly ignored the desperation of too-small families, and since 1979 have steadily

reduced the amount of financial support available to a single parent. But, this camp's most outspoken attacks seem aimed at the notion of families getting too complex, with add-ons and extras such as a gay parent's partner, or a remarried mother's new husband and his children.

19 To judge a family's value by its tidy symmetry is to purchase a book for its cover. There's no moral authority there. The famous family comprised by Dad, Mom, Sis, and Junior living as an isolated economic unit is not built on historical bedrock. In *The Way We Never Were*, Stephanie Coontz writes, "Whenever people propose that we go back to the traditional family, I always suggest that they pick a ballpark date for the family they have in mind." Colonial families were tidily disciplined, but their members (meaning everyone but infants) labored incessantly and died young. Then the Victorian family adopted a new division of labor, in which women's role was domestic and children were allowed time for study and play, but this was an upper-class construct supported by myriad slaves. Coontz writes, "For every nineteenth-century middle-class family that protected its wife and child within the family circle, there was an Irish or German girl scrubbing floors . . . a Welsh boy mining coal to keep the home-baked goodies warm, a black girl doing the family laundry, a black mother and child picking cotton to be made into clothes for the family, and a Jewish or an Italian daughter in a sweatshop making 'ladies' dresses or artificial flowers for the family to purchase."

20 The abolition of slavery brought slightly more democratic arrangements, in which extended families were harnessed together in cottage industries; at the turn of the century came a steep rise in child labor in mines and sweat-shops. Twenty percent of American children lived in orphanages at the time; their parents were not necessarily dead, but couldn't afford to keep them.

21 During the Depression and up to the end of World War II, many millions of U.S. households were more multigenerational than nuclear. Women my grandmother's age were likely to live with a fluid assortment of elderly relatives, in-laws, siblings, and children. In many cases they spent virtually every waking hour working in the company of other women—a companionable scenario in which it would be easier, I imagine, to tolerate an estranged or difficult spouse. I'm reluctant to idealize a life of so much hard work and so little spousal intimacy, but its advantage may have been resilience. A family so large and varied would not easily be brought down by a single blow: It could absorb a death, long-illness, an abandonment here or there, and any number of irreconcilable differences.

22 The Family of Dolls came along midcentury as a great American experiment. A booming economy required a mobile labor force and demanded that women surrender jobs to returning soldiers. Families came to be defined by a single breadwinner. They struck out for single-family homes at an earlier age than ever before, and in unprecedented numbers they raised children in suburban isolation. The nuclear family was launched to sink or swim.

23   More than a few sank. Social historians corroborate that the suburban family of the postwar economic boom, which we have recently selected as our definition of "traditional," was no panacea. Twenty-five percent of Americans were poor in the mid-1950s, and as yet there were no food stamps. Sixty percent of the elderly lived on less than $1,000 a year, and most had no medical insurance. In the sequestered suburbs, alcoholism and sexual abuse of children were far more widespread than anyone imagined.

24   Expectations soared, and the economy sagged. It's hard to depend on one other adult for everything, come what may. In the last three decades, that amorphous, adaptable structure we call "family" has been reshaped once more by economic tides. Compared with fifties families, mothers are far more likely now to be employed. We are statistically more likely to divorce, and to live in blended families or other extranuclear arrangements. We are also more likely to plan and space our children, and to rate our marriages as "happy." We are less likely to suffer abuse without recourse, or to stare out at our lives through a glaze of prescription tranquilizers. Our aged parents are less likely to be destitute, and we're half as likely to have a teenage daughter turn up a mother herself. All in all, I would say that if "intact" in modern family-values jargon means living quietly desperate in the bell jar, then hip-hip-hooray for "broken." A neat family model constructed to service the Baby Boom economy seems to be returning gradually to a grand, lumpy shape that human families apparently have tended toward since they first took root in the Olduvai Gorge. We're social animals, deeply fond of companionship, and children love best to run in packs. If there is a *normal* for humans, at all, I expect it looks like two or three Families of Dolls, connected variously by kinship and passion, shuffled like cards and strewn over several shoeboxes.

25   The sooner we can let go the fairy tale of families functioning perfectly in isolation, the better we might embrace the relief of community. Even the admirable parents who've stayed married through thick and thin are very likely, at present, to incorporate other adults into their families—household help and baby-sitters if they can afford them or neighbors and grandparents if they can't. For single parents, this support is the rock-bottom definition of family. And most parents who have split apart, however painfully, still manage to maintain family continuity for their children, creating in many cases a boisterous phenomenon that Constance Ahrons in her book *The Good Divorce* calls the "binuclear family." Call it what you will—when ex-spouses beat swords into plowshares and jump up and down at a soccer game together, it makes for happy kids.

26   Cinderella, look, who needs her? All those evil stepsisters? That story always seemed like too much cotton-picking fuss over clothes. A childhood tale that fascinated me more was the one called "Stone Soup," and the gist of it is this: Once upon a time, a pair of beleaguered soldiers straggled home to a village empty-handed, in a land ruined by war. They were famished, but the villagers had so little they shouted evil words and slammed their doors. So the soldiers

dragged out a big kettle, filled it with water, and put it on a fire to boil. They rolled a clean round stone into the pot, while the villagers peered through their curtains in amazement.

27   "What kind of soup is that?" they hooted.

28   "Stone soup," the soldiers replied. "Everybody can have some when it's done."

29   "Well, thanks," one matron grumbled, coming out with a shriveled carrot. "But it'd be better if you threw this in."

30   And so on, of course, a vegetable at a time, until the whole suspicious village managed to feed itself grandly.

31   Any family is a big empty pot, save for what gets thrown in. Each stew turns out different. Generosity, a resolve to turn bad luck into good, and respect for variety—these things will nourish a nation of children. Name-calling and suspicion will not. My soup contains a rock or two of hard times, and maybe yours does too. I expect it's a heck of a bouillabaisse.

Comprehension

1.   What is the essay's thesis?

2.   According to Kingsolver, why is our society so apt to condemn divorce?

3.   What is the author's view of family symmetry (paragraph 19)?

Rhetorical Analysis

4.   What rhetorical function does the opening anecdote serve in introducing the essay's subject matter?

5.   What is Kingsolver's purpose in capitalizing, italicizing, and placing quotation marks around certain phrases—for example, the Way It Has Always Been (paragraph 4), *failed* and *the children of divorce* (paragraph 7), and "family values" (paragraph 18)?

6.   What is the author's purpose in creating a gap between paragraphs 15 and 16? What is the focus of her argument after this break?

7.   Compare the introductory paragraph with the concluding one. How do they differ? How are they similar? How do they help set the boundaries of the essay?

8.   This essay contains personal observations, personal experiences, historical data, and anecdotes. How would you describe the author's rhetorical mode to a person who has not read the essay?

9. Unlike the titles of most essays, the title "Stone Soup" gives no hint at the essay's content. What is the rhetorical purpose in keeping the meaning of the title a mystery until the very end?

10. In paragraph 2, Kingsolver asks the question, "Why are our names for home so slow to catch up to the truth of where we live?" Does the author suggest an answer to this question either implicitly or explicitly during the course of the essay? If so, where?

Writing

11. Interview two individuals at least 25 years apart in age. Compare and contrast their views on divorce and/or family.

12. Describe the dynamics of a blended family with which you are familiar. It may be your own or a friend's.

13. **Writing an Argument**   Kingsolver makes many positive assertions in the essay. In a well-written essay, take a position on one of Kingsolver's claims. Use evidence from your reading, personal experience, and observation.

Synthesizing the Classic + Contemporary Essays

1. Compare and contrast the tone of each writer. How does tone affect purpose? How does it affect mood? Select at least three passages from White and three from Kingsolver that demonstrate how their tones differ. Do they offer any hints as to the "voice" or personality of the writers? Why or why not?

2. What contemporary issues does Kingsolver address that White either ignores or is unaware of? Consider that White was born 56 years before Kingsolver, so his world was quite a different one. Are there other variables that might help us distinguish their concerns and outlooks—for example, gender, class, and environment?

3. What central values does each author have regarding the family? How are they similar? How do they differ? How do their values reflect their times?

4. At what point in Kingsolver's essay does the life experience E.B. White writes about enter into her essay? Explain.

An American Childhood

Annie Dillard

Annie Dillard (b. 1945 in Pittsburgh) received her BA and MA degrees from Hollins College. Her first book, *Pilgrim at Tinker Creek* (1975), won the Pulitzer Prize for general nonfiction. Her other published works of nonfiction include *Teaching a Stone to Talk* (1982) and *An American Childhood* (1987). Dillard expanded her range of writing with the publication of her first novel, *The Living* (1992), and her latest novel, *The Maytrees* (2007). She has received awards from the National Endowment for the Arts and the Guggenheim Foundation as well as many other sources. As an essayist, poet, memoirist, and literary critic, she focuses her themes on the relationships among the self, nature, religion, and faith. Her writing is recognizable by its observations of the minutiae of life and its search for meaning in unlikely places, such as a stone or an insect. In this passage from *An American Childhood*, the author gives us a portrait of her mother by focusing on her idiosyncrasies of speech, gesture, and attitude.

1   One Sunday afternoon Mother wandered through our kitchen, where Father was making a sandwich and listening to the ball game. The Pirates were playing the New York Giants at Forbes Field. In those days, the Giants had a utility infielder named Wayne Terwilliger. Just as Mother passed through, the radio announcer cried—with undue drama—"Terwilliger bunts one!"

2   "Terwilliger bunts one?" Mother cried back, stopped short. She turned. "Is that English?"

3   "The player's name is Terwilliger," Father said. "He bunted."

4   "That's marvelous," Mother said. "'Terwilliger bunts one.' No wonder you listen to baseball. 'Terwilliger bunts one.'"

5   For the next seven or eight years, Mother made this surprising string of syllables her own. Testing a microphone, she repeated, "Terwilliger bunts one"; testing a pen or a typewriter, she wrote it. If, as happened surprisingly often in the course of various improvised gags, she pretended to whisper something else in my ear, she actually whispered, "Terwilliger bunts one." Whenever someone used a French phrase, or a Latin one, she answered solemnly, "Terwilliger bunts one." If Mother had had, like Andrew Carnegie, the opportunity to cook up a motto for a coat of arms, hers would have read simply and tellingly, "Terwilliger bunts one." (Carnegie's was "Death to Privilege.")

6   She served us with other words and phrases. On a Florida trip, she repeated tremulously, "That . . . is a royal poinciana." I don't remember the tree; I remember the thrill in her voice. She pronounced it carefully, and spelled it. She also liked to say "portulaca."

7   The drama of the words "Tamiami Trail" stirred her, we learned on the same Florida trip. People built Tampa on one coast, and they built Miami on another. Then—the height of visionary ambition and folly—they piled a slow, tremendous

road through the terrible Everglades to connect them. To build the road, men stood sunk in muck to their armpits. They fought off cottonmouth moccasins and six-foot alligators. They slept in boats, wet. They blasted muck with dynamite, cut jungle with machetes; they laid logs, dragged drilling machines, hauled dredges, heaped limestone. The road took fourteen years to build up by the shovelful, a Panama Canal in reverse, and cost hundreds of lives from tropical, mosquito-carried diseases. Then, capping it all, some genius thought of the word Tamiami: they called the road from Tampa to Miami, this very road under our spinning wheels, the Tamiami Trail. Some called it Alligator Alley. Anyone could drive over this road without a thought.

8   Hearing this, moved, I thought all the suffering of road building was worth it (it wasn't my suffering), now that we had this new thing to hang these new words on—Alligator Alley for those who liked things cute, and, for connoisseurs like Mother, for lovers of the human drama in all its boldness and terror, the Tamiami Trail.

9   Back home, Mother cut clips from reels of talk, as it were, and played them back at leisure. She noticed that many Pittsburghers confuse "leave" and "let." One kind relative brightened our morning by mentioning why she'd brought her son to visit: "He wanted to come with me, so I left him." Mother filled in Amy and me on locutions we missed. "I can't do it on Friday," her pretty sister told a crowded dinner party, "because Friday's the day I lay in the stores."

10   (All unconsciously, though, we ourselves used some pure Pittsburghisms. We said "tele pole," pronounced "telly pole," for that splintery sidewalk post I loved to climb. We said "slippy"—the sidewalks are "slippy." We said, "That's all the farther I could go." And we said, as Pittsburghers do say, "This glass needs washed," or "The dog needs walked"—a usage our father eschewed; he knew it was not standard English, nor even comprehensible English, but he never let on.)

11   "Spell 'poinsettia,'" Mother would throw out at me, smiling with pleasure. "Spell 'sherbet.'" The idea was not to make us whizzes, but, quite the contrary, to remind us—and I, especially, needed reminding—that we didn't know it all just yet.

12   "There's a deer standing in the front hall," she told me one quiet evening in the country.

13   "Really?"

14   "No. I just wanted to tell you something once without your saying, 'I know.'"

15   Supermarkets in the middle 1950s began luring, or bothering, customers by giving out Top Value Stamps or Green Stamps. When, shopping with Mother, we got to the head of the checkout line, the checker, always a young man, asked, "Save stamps?"

16   "No," Mother replied genially, week after week, "I build model airplanes." I believe she originated this line. It took me years to determine where the joke lay.

17   Anyone who met her verbal challenges she adored. She had surgery on one of her eyes. On the operating table, just before she conked out, she appealed feelingly to the surgeon, saying, as she had been planning to say for weeks, "Will I be able to play the piano?" "Not on me," the surgeon said. "You won't pull that old one on me."

18   It was, indeed, an old one. The surgeon was supposed to answer, "Yes, my dear, brave woman, you will be able to play the piano after this operation," to

which Mother intended to reply, "Oh, good, I've always wanted to play the piano." This pat scenario bored her; she loved having it interrupted. It must have galled her that usually her acquaintances were so predictably unalert; it must have galled her that, for the length of her life, she could surprise everyone so continually, so easily, when she had been the same all along. At any rate, she loved anyone who, as she put it, saw it coming, and called her on it.

19   She regarded the instructions on bureaucratic forms as straight lines. "Do you advocate the overthrow of the United States government by force or violence?" After some thought she wrote, "Force." She regarded children, even babies, as straight men. When Molly learned to crawl, Mother delighted in buying her gowns with drawstrings at the bottom, like Swee'pea's, because, as she explained energetically, you could easily step on the drawstring without the baby's noticing, so that she crawled and crawled and crawled and never got anywhere except into a small ball at the gown's top.

20 When we children were young, she mothered us tenderly and dependably; as we got older, she resumed her career of anarchism. She collared us into her gags. If she answered the phone on a wrong number, she told the caller, "Just a minute," and dragged the receiver to Amy or me, saying, "Here, take this, your name is Cecile," or, worse, just, "It's for you." You had to think on your feet. But did you want to perform well as Cecile, or did you want to take pity on the wretched caller?

21   During a family trip to the Highland Park Zoo, Mother and I were alone for a minute. She approached a young couple holding hands on a bench by the seals, and addressed the young man in dripping tones: "Where have you been? Still got those baby-blue eyes; always did slay me. And this"—a swift nod at the dumbstruck young woman, who had removed her hand from the man's—"must be the one you were telling me about. She's not so bad, really, as you used to make out. But listen, you know how I miss you, you know where to reach me, same old place. And there's Ann over there—see how she's grown? See the blue eyes?"

22   And off she sashayed, taking me firmly by the hand, and leading us around briskly past the monkey house and away. She cocked an ear back, and both of us heard the desperate man begin, in a high-pitched wail, "I swear, I never saw her before in my life . . ."

23 On a long, sloping beach by the ocean, she lay stretched out sunning with Father and friends, until the conversation gradually grew tedious, when without forethought she gave a little push with her heel and rolled away. People were stunned. She rolled deadpan and apparently effortlessly, arms and legs extended and tidy, down the beach to the distant water's edge, where she lay at ease just as she had been, but half in the surf, and well out of earshot.

24   She dearly loved to fluster people by throwing out a game's rules at a whim—when she was getting bored, losing in a dull sort of way, and when everybody else was taking it too seriously. If you turned your back, she moved the checkers around on the board. When you got them all straightened out, she denied she'd touched them; the next time you turned your back, she lined them up on the rug or hid them under your chair. In a betting rummy game called Michigan, she routinely

played out of turn, or called out a card she didn't hold, or counted backward, simply to amuse herself by causing an uproar and watching the rest of us do double-takes and have fits. (Much later, when serious suitors came to call, Mother subjected them to this fast card game as a trial by ordeal; she used it as an intelligence test and a measure of spirit. If the poor man could stay a round without breaking down or running out, he got to marry one of us, if he still wanted to.)

25 She excelled at bridge, playing fast and boldly, but when the stakes were low and the hands dull, she bid slams for the devilment of it, or raised her opponents' suit to bug them, or showed her hand, or tossed her cards in a handful behind her back in a characteristic swift motion accompanied by a vibrantly innocent look. It drove our stolid father crazy. The hand was over before it began, and the guests were appalled. How do you score it, who deals now, what do you do with a crazy person who is having so much fun? Or they were down seven, and the guests were appalled. "Pam!" "Dammit, Pam!" He groaned. What ails such people? What on earth possesses them? He rubbed his face.

26 She was an unstoppable force; she never let go. When we moved across town, she persuaded the U.S. Post Office to let her keep her old address—forever—because she'd had stationery printed. I don't know how she did it. Every new post office worker, over decades, needed to learn that although the Doaks' mail is addressed to here, it is delivered to there.

27 Mother's energy and intelligence suited her for a greater role in a larger arena—mayor of New York, say—than the one she had. She followed American politics closely; she had been known to vote for Democrats. She saw how things should be run, but she had nothing to run but our household. Even there, small minds bugged her; she was smarter than the people who designed the things she had to use all day for the length of her life.

28 "Look," she said. "Whoever designed this corkscrew never used one. Why would anyone sell it without trying it out?" So she invented a better one. She showed me a drawing of it. The spirit of American enterprise never faded in Mother. If capitalizing and tooling up had been as interesting as theorizing and thinking up, she would have fired up a new factory every week, and chaired several hundred corporations.

29 "It grieves me," she would say, "it grieves my heart," that the company that made one superior product packaged it poorly, or took the wrong tack in its advertising. She knew, as she held the thing mournfully in her two hands, that she'd never find another. She was right. We children wholly sympathized, and so did Father; what could she do, what could anyone do, about it? She was Samson in chains. She paced.

30 She didn't like the taste of stamps so she didn't lick stamps; she licked the corner of the envelope instead. She glued sandpaper to the sides of kitchen drawers, and under kitchen cabinets, so she always had a handy place to strike a match. She designed, and hounded workmen to build against all norms, doubly wide kitchen counters and elevated bathroom sinks. To splint a finger, she stuck it in a lightweight cigar tube. Conversely, to protect a pack of cigarettes, she carried it in a Band-Aid box. She drew plans for an over-the-finger toothbrush for babies, an oven rack that slid up and down, and—the family favorite—Lendalarm.

Lendalarm was a beeper you attached to books (or tools) you loaned friends. After ten days, the beeper sounded. Only the rightful owner could silence it.

31   She repeatedly reminded us of P. T. Barnum's dictum: You could sell anything to anybody if you marketed it right. The adman who thought of making Americans believe they needed underarm deodorant was a visionary. So, too, was the hero who made a success of a new product, Ivory soap. The executives were horrified, Mother told me, that a cake of this stuff floated. Soap wasn't supposed to float. Anyone would be able to tell it was mostly whipped-up air. Then some inspired adman made a leap: Advertise that it floats. Flaunt it. The rest is history.

32   She respected the rare few who broke through to new ways. "Look," she'd say, "here's an intelligent apron." She called upon us to admire intelligent control knobs and intelligent pan handles, intelligent andirons and picture frames and knife sharpeners. She questioned everything, every pair of scissors, every knitting needle, gardening glove, tape dispenser. Hers was a restless mental vigor that just about ignited the dumb household objects with its force.

33   Torpid conformity was a kind of sin; it was stupidity itself, the mighty stream against which Mother would never cease to struggle. If you held no minority opinions, or if you failed to risk total ostracism for them daily, the world would be a better place without you.

34   Always I heard Mother's emotional voice asking Amy and me the same few questions: "Is that your own idea? Or somebody else's?" "*Giant* is a good movie," I pronounced to the family at dinner. "Oh, really?" Mother warmed to these occasions. She all but rolled up her sleeves. She knew I hadn't seen it. "Is that your considered opinion?"

35   She herself held many unpopular, even fantastic, positions. She was scathingly sarcastic about the McCarthy hearings while they took place, right on our living-room television; she frantically opposed Father's wait-and-see calm. "We don't know enough about it," he said. "I do," she said. "I know all I need to know."

36   She asserted, against all opposition, that people who lived in trailer parks were not bad but simply poor, and had as much right to settle on beautiful land, such as rural Ligonier, Pennsylvania, as did the oldest of families in the finest of hidden houses. Therefore, the people who owned trailer parks, and sought zoning changes to permit trailer parks, needed our help. Her profound belief that the country-club pool sweeper was a person, and that the department-store saleslady, the bus driver, telephone operator, and house-painter were people, and even in groups the steelworkers who carried pickets and the Christmas shoppers who clogged intersections were people—this was a conviction common enough in democratic Pittsburgh, but not altogether common among our friends' parents, or even, perhaps, among our parents' friends.

37   Opposition emboldened Mother, and she would take on anybody on any issue—the chairman of the board, at a cocktail party, on the current strike; she would fly at him in a flurry of passion, as a songbird selflessly attacks a big hawk.

38   "Eisenhower's going to win," I announced after school. She lowered her magazine and looked me in the eyes: "How do you know?" I was doomed. It was fatal to say, "Everyone says so." We all knew well what happened. "Do you consult

this Everyone before you make your decisions? What if Everyone decided to round up all the Jews?" Mother knew there was no danger of cowing me. She simply tried to keep us all awake. And in fact it was always clear to Amy and me, and to Molly when she grew old enough to listen, that if our classmates came to cruelty, just as much as if the neighborhood or the nation came to madness, we were expected to take, and would be each separately capable of taking, a stand.

Comprehension

1. Dillard creates a picture of her mother's personality through a number of anecdotes and explanations. How would you sum up the mother's personality?

2. Dillard's mother appears to have a special appreciation for words and language. What effect does this appreciation have on her family and acquaintances?

3. What values does the mother hold? What behaviors and attitudes does she abhor and discourage?

Rhetorical Analysis

4. In paragraph 7, Dillard explains that the highway from Tampa to Miami is referred to either as "Tamiami Trail" or "Alligator Alley." What is the connotation of each of these terms? Why does her mother prefer to call it "Tamiami Trail"?

5. The author herself seems to have inherited a special fascination for language. Study her use of dashes and semicolons in paragraphs 26 and 27. How do they help contribute to energetic writing?

6. What are the functions of the spaces between paragraphs 19 and 20, 22 and 23, and 32 and 33? How do these divisions contribute to the structure of the essay as a whole?

7. How does Dillard use her writing talents to create paragraph 8 out of one long sentence? What other examples can you provide of long sentences in the essay? What is her purpose in using these long sentences? How do they contribute to the overall style of the writing?

8. What is the overall emotional "tone" of the writer toward her subject— admiring, or loving, or cautionary? What adjectives does she use in describing her mother that provide the reader with clues to the tone?

9. Dillard quotes her mother directly on several occasions. Can we assume that she is quoting precisely, given that the essay was written years after the incidents described? Does it matter?

10. The final paragraph not only provides closure to the essay but transmits a lesson the mother wants her family to learn. How do the style and structure of this paragraph contribute to the ultimate message of the essay? In other words, how does the form help convey the meaning?

Writing

11. Write a descriptive essay about someone you know very well, using at least five anecdotes from that person's life, so that by the end of the essay, we have a mental picture of your subject's personality, values, and attitudes. This could be someone in your family, or someone else you are or were very close to.

12. Describe an incident or person in your life when the unconventional taught you an important lesson.

13. **Writing an Argument** Argue for or against the proposition that an effective parent should have—at least—a touch of unconventionality. Alternatively, take a position on the role of conformity in life.

Love, Internet Style

David Brooks

David Brooks (b. 1961) is a columnist for the op-ed page of *The New York Times*. Prior to joining the *Times*, he was a senior editor at the *Weekly Standard*, an op-ed page editor at the *Wall Street Journal*, and a contributing editor to *Newsweek*. He is also a weekly guest on the *PBS NewsHour*. A graduate of the University of Chicago, Brooks writes on a wide range of topics, often from a conservative perspective; he has edited *Backward and Upward: The New Conservative Writing*. Brooks's recent books *Bobos in Paradise: The New Upper Class and How They Got There* (2000) and *On Paradise Drive* (2004), which explores the lives of people living in the suburbs, offer fascinating and often amusing insights into contemporary American culture. In this essay, which appeared in *The New York Times* in 2003, Brooks examines the ways in which the Internet facilitates personal relationships.

1   The Internet slows things down.

2   If you're dating in the Age of the Hook-Up, sex is this looming possibility from the first moment you meet a prospective partner. But couples who meet through online dating services tend to exchange e-mail for weeks or months. Then they'll progress to phone conversations for a few more weeks. Only then will there be a face-to-face meeting, almost always at some public place early in the evening, and the first date will often be tentative and Dutch.

3   Online dating puts structure back into courtship. For generations Americans had certain courtship rituals. The boy would call the girl and ask her to the movies. He might come in and meet the father. After a few dates he might ask her to go steady. Sex would progress gradually from kissing to petting and beyond.

4   But over the past few decades that structure dissolved. And human beings, who are really good at adapting, found that the Internet, of all places, imposes the restraints they need to let relationships develop gradually. So now 40 million Americans look at online dating sites each month, and we are seeing a revolution in the way people meet and court one another.

5   The new restraints are not like the old restraints. The online dating scene is like a real estate market where people go to fulfill their most sensitive needs. It is at once ruthlessly transactional and strangely tender.

6   It begins with sorting. Online daters can scan through millions of possible partners in an evening and select for age, education, height, politics, religion and ethnic background. JDate is a popular site for Jews. EHarmony insists that members fill out a long, introspective questionnaire, and thus is one of the few sites where most members are women. Vanity Date is for the South Beach crowd. "At Vanity Date," the Web site declares, "we have a vision of creating the largest database of the world's most good-looking, rich and superficial people."

7   Most of the sites have programs that link you up with people like yourself. One of the side effects of online dating is that it is bound to accelerate social

stratification, as highly educated people become more efficient at finding and marrying one another.

8   Each member at a dating site creates his or her own Web page. The most important feature on the page is the photo; studies show that looks are twice as powerful as income in attracting mates.

9   But there are also autobiographical essays. If you judge by these essays, skinny-dipping with intellectuals is the most popular activity in America. All the writers try to show they are sensual yet smart.

10   The women on these sites are, or project themselves as being, incredibly self-confident. "I am a vivacious, intelligent, warm-hearted, attractive, cool chick, with a sharp, witty, and effervescent personality," writes one on Match.com. Another says: "I am a slender, radiantly beautiful woman on fire with passion and enthusiasm for life. I am articulate, intelligent and routinely given the accolade of being brilliant."

11   Still, men almost always make the first contact. Prospective partners begin a long series of e-mail interviews. Internet exchanges encourage both extreme honesty (the strangers-on-a-train phenomenon) and extreme dishonesty, as people lie about their ages, their jobs, whether they have kids and, most often, whether they are married. (About a fifth of online daters are married men.)

12   Whatever else has changed, men are more likely to be predators looking for sex, while women try to hold back. Men will ask women for more photos "from different angles." A woman, wanting to be reassured that this guy is not some rapist, will shut off anyone who calls her "hottie" or who mentions sex first. Women generally control the pace of the relationship.

13   But despite all the crass competition, all the marketing, all the shopping around, people connect. Studies by Katelyn McKenna at N.Y.U. and others indicate that Internet relationships are at least as powerful as relationships that begin face to face. Many people are better at revealing their true selves through the keyboard than through conversation. And couples who slow down and prolong the e-mail phase have a better chance of seeing their relationships last than people who get together more quickly.

14   The online dating world is superficially cynical. The word "love" will almost never appear on a member's page, because it is so heavy and intimidating. But love is what this is all about. And the heart, even in this commercial age, finds a way.

Comprehension

1. How does Brooks describe Internet "love"? What does he mean by his opening sentence, "The Internet slows things down"?

2. What features of Internet culture does the writer identify as facilitating human relationships?

3. According to Brooks, how do men and women differ in their approach to online relationships?

Rhetorical Analysis

4. What is Brooks's purpose in beginning his essay with a single-sentence paragraph? Is this sentence the thesis? Why or why not?

5. How would you describe the writer's stance? What is his attitude toward his subject? Offer examples to support your answer.

6. What are Brooks's main reasons in support of his thesis or claim? What forms of evidence does he offer to support his claim?

7. How does the writer develop an extended definition of Internet "love"?

8. Brooks frequently structures his essay by means of comparison and contrast. Why do you think he uses this strategy? Do you find the method effective? Why or why not?

9. Does the final paragraph provide a solid conclusion? Justify your answer.

Writing

10. Write a definition essay on "Internet love." Be certain to provide examples and utilize other rhetorical strategies like comparison and contrast to develop this extended definition.

11. **Writing an Argument**   Write a persuasive essay about the dangers and/ or harmless effects of online dating. Provide at least three minor propositions and sufficient evidence to support your position.

Once Upon a Quinceañera

Julia Alvarez

Julia Alvarez (b. 1950), a novelist, poet, and nonfiction writer, was born in New York City but raised until age 10 in the Dominican Republic. She was forced to flee with her family after her father, a physician, was implicated in a plot to overthrow the dictator Rafael Trujillo, an event alluded to in her semiautobiographical novel, *How the Garcia Girls Lost Their Accents* (1991). (A second novel, *Yo!*, which continues the Garcia/Alvarez family saga, appeared in 1997.) Alvarez attended Middlebury College (BA, 1971) and Syracuse University (MFA, 1975), and she is currently on the English and American Literatures faculty at Middlebury. In addition to her fiction, Alvarez has published several volumes of poetry, books for children, a collection of essays, and numerous articles for major magazines. One of her latest books is *Saving the World* (2006), in which Alvarez examines the global attempt to eradicate smallpox. In this selection from *Once Upon a Quinceañera* (2007), Alvarez provides readers with insight into one of the most common and compelling rituals that frame the lives of young Latinas.

1 I'm sitting in my room at the Pan American Hotel feeling pretty much like Cinderella before her fairy godmother shows up. I drove down from Vermont early this morning, a five-hour drive that had taken me six hours since I'm not used to finding my way through the urban labyrinths of parkways and expressways with exits popping up out of nowhere to this multicultural, multilingual, multimulti area of Queens where forty years ago my own immigrant adolescence was spent.

2 I've driven down here to attend Monica Ramos's quinceañera. The plan was that I would phone the Ramoses as soon as I arrived and they would come and get me so I could follow the quinceañera in the last few hours of her preparations. But I've been calling the family home number and Monica's father's cell number for the last half hour and nobody answers. Maybe it's the busy floral pattern of the hotel bedspread or the scented air freshener recently sprayed in the room, but I'm beginning to feel lightheaded with misgivings. Did I come this far just to spend a night in my overpriced room at the Pan American, only to have to turn around tomorrow morning and drive back to Vermont without even a glimpse of this Queens quinceañera?

3 Like many USA-born Latinas, Monica, whose parents were both born in the Dominican Republic, is actually celebrating her quinceañera on her sixteenth birthday. This is just one more adaptation of the old-country tradition which has now survived more than four decades on American soil. But with a persistence unique to this immigrant group that seems to retain at least some of its Spanish and its feeling that "home" is still south of the Rio Grande even into a second and third generation, Monica calls her sweet sixteen a "quinceañera sort of."

4 Monica's quinceañera had sounded great over the phone. It was going to be so special, she told me during several long-distance conversations. Open, friendly,

easy to talk to, Monica was one of the most verbal and forthcoming quinceañeras I interviewed. She didn't want a party at first, but she was finally won over by two things: the chance to dress up in a beautiful princess gown and the opportunity to give a speech in front of her whole family and all her friends. Monica's party will include the lighting of seventeen candles, each one dedicated to a special person with a little speech about why this person is so special to her.

5   "There's always an added candle, dedicated to someone absent," Monica explains about the extra candle. "Mine's going to be dedicated to God for giving me such a special life."

6   Monica has told me that she is a devoted Catholic. I have to bite my tongue so as not to point out that a candle meant for someone absent is perhaps not the best category for a God who I'm sure Monica believes is everywhere. But it's hard enough to get these young ladies to confide in a virtual stranger without peppering them with prickly questions. As one young lady told me when I pursued a line of questioning about how exactly she thought she was going to go from being a girl to being a woman by having a quinceañera, "This is becoming annoying."

7   Instead I asked Monica if her quinceañera was going to have a theme. Themes are popular: The quinceañera is a butterfly, emerging from a flower. The quinceañera is a princess, sitting on a throne. The quinceañera is a cowgirl, with a court of boys sporting lassos. The quinceañera, like a magician's trick, rises up out of a trapdoor in a puff of smoke.

8   "Mine is all based on Disney characters," Monica announced excitedly. The girlfriends in her court were going to be Sleeping Beauty, Snow White, Jasmine, Belle . . . "We're going to do like a little play where my prince is going to find my heels on the dance floor and bring them to my dad to put on my feet," Monica gushed on.

9   Before hanging up, I asked Monica what her quinceañera meant to her. Although she had been quite garrulous about the party details, Monica seemed stumped by the question. Every quinceañera I've asked has given me the same pat answer. Claudia in Lawrence, Massachusetts, a short, stocky girl in sweat pants, pressured by her mami to have a quince party; Ashley in San Antonio, a popular, petite girl with a string of girlfriends who had celebrated or were in line to celebrate their quinces; Leticia in East L.A., who ran off with her chambelán seven months later—all of them echoed Monica as if reciting the mantra of quinceañeras: "I'm going from being a girl to being a woman." When I pressed Monica about what this meant, she answered vaguely: "It's like part of my culture."

10   "So, did your mother have a quinceañera back in the D.R.?" I wondered.

11   Monica wasn't sure. "Mami!" she called out from her end of the phone. "Did you have a quinceañera?" The answer came back, "A quinceañera, no, mi'ja."

12   I found out about Monica's quinceañera only four days ago in that word-of-mouth way so reminiscent of our home cultures. A Dominican student's Colombian friend has a mother who owns a flower shop in Queens that does a lot of quinceañeras, and she (the mother) was doing Monica's flowers and also providing some of the props, and she told the Ramoses about me. By the time I got word back that the Ramoses would be happy to have me attend Monica's party and, phone number in hand, I called them, they were into that forty-eight-hour countdown usually

associated with weddings in which everyone is racing around, hyperventilating, arguing, bursting into tears, and the bride is threatening to call the whole thing off. In fact, Monica's party is taking place soon after the headline story about the runaway bride, Jennifer Wilbanks, who disappeared days before her wedding in Duluth, Georgia. As I sit in my hotel room, waiting to get through to the Ramoses, I wonder if no one is answering because Monica has run off. Perhaps she will be the first runaway quinceañera to get national media attention.

13   On the phone, a very generous Mr. Ramos ("José, por favor!") had offered to pick me up at the airport should I come by plane. "I wouldn't think of it with as much as you have to do," I declined. In part, I thought it wise to have a way to get from the church, where a Mass or blessing would precede the party, to the Dance Club, where the ceremony, supper, and dance would take place, and back to the hotel at a reasonable hour, as these parties tend to go on past the Cinderella stroke of midnight. Bringing my own wheels will turn out to be an inspired decision in more ways than I would ever have anticipated. But at the moment, I am wondering if the long drive has been in vain as none of the messages I've left on Mr. Ramos's cell phone or home phone have been returned. Foolishly, I have no address, no other way to contact the family. I look out the grimy picture window of the Pan American past the back parking lot toward street after street of fenced-in row houses, and I know, with a sinking heart, that this is not the kind of neighborhood where everyone knows everybody else.

14   An hour goes by. It's Friday, so back in Vermont, my husband is still at work. I had suggested we both fly down, wimpy city driver that I am, and make a weekend of it, but before I could finish outlining the fun of two nights at the Pan American Hotel, my husband was shaking his head. He'd had enough of quinceañeras, thank you. "You've only been to a few," I argued, feeling vaguely wounded at his obvious disenchantment with one of *my* cultural traditions. "I've been to four and that's three too many," he countered. I don't know if it's his thrifty German-Lutheran roots, but from the beginning he has looked askance at these over the top celebrations, many of them costing much more than working-class families can afford.

15   His skepticism about this tradition is also my own. The incredible expense; a girl encouraged in the dubious fantasy of being a princess as if news of feminism had never reached her mami; the marketing of a young lady as attractive, marriageable goods. Why not save the money for education? I've snuck in that question in all of my interviews. Why not have coming-of-age celebrations for boys as well as girls? But still, every time the young lady makes an entrance through her archway, or curtains part and there she is, sitting on her swing or a throne or a carousel horse, while the whole familia and roomful of friends applaud her, my eyes tear up and my throat catches. The tradition, whatever its trappings, is homing in on a need to acknowledge and celebrate these new arrivals in the field of time. From my spot in the crowd I am torn between optimism for this tender, young being emerging from the cocoon of her childhood and a sense of dread that the world she is entering, unlike the fantasy she is enjoying this one night, will not allow for such winged flight.

Comprehension

1. Why does Alvarez inject herself into this story?

2. Why, according to Alvarez, is quinceañera so important in Latino/Hispanic culture?

3. What, ultimately, is Alvarez's attitude toward quinceañera? How do you know? Why doesn't Alvarez's husband want to accompany her as she attends the quinceañera?

Rhetorical Analysis

4. Although she writes in various literary modes, Alvarez is best known as a novelist. What elements of fiction—foreshadowing and characterization, for example—do you detect in this essay? Identify specific passages to support your analysis. How effective are these strategies, and why?

5. How would you describe Alvarez's audience for this essay? How successful is she in tailoring the tone and content of the selection to this audience? Does she present herself as an authority on the subject or an investigator, and what is the importance of this stance?

6. Does Alvarez establish a thesis or claim about quinceañeras? Why or why not?

7. Alvarez gradually establishes an extended or working definition of quinceañera. Locate passages where the reader receives information about this custom or ritual.

8. How does Alvarez link her introductory and concluding paragraphs? How do these two paragraphs serve as a framing device for the body of the selection?

Writing

9. Write a narrative essay in which you tell about a ritual, custom, or celebration that is important to your family or culture.

10. In an analysis essay, compare/contrast two coming-of-age celebrations, such as quinceañeras and sweet sixteen celebrations, or bar/bat mitzvahs.

11. **Writing an Argument**   Argue for or against the proposition that coming-of-age celebrations have become too expensive and ostentatious in contemporary American culture.

Rhetorical Analysis

Read the passage below from "Once More to the Lake" and answer the questions that follow.

One summer, along about 1904, my father rented a camp on a lake in Maine and took us all there for the month of August. We all got ringworm from some kittens and had to rub Pond's Extract on our arms and legs night and morning, and my father rolled over in a canoe with all his clothes on; but outside of that the vacation was a success and from then on none of us ever thought there was any place in the world like that lake in Maine. We returned summer after summer—always on August 1st for one month. I have since become a saltwater man, but sometimes in summer there are days when the restlessness of the tides and the fearful cold of the sea water and the incessant wind which blows across the afternoon and into the evening make me wish for the placidity of a lake in the woods. A few weeks ago this feeling got so strong I bought myself a couple of bass hooks and a spinner and returned to the lake where we used to go, for a week's fishing and to revisit old haunts.

—Copyright ©1941 by E. B. White. Reprinted by permission of ICM Partners.

1. What is the significance of the final sentence in the paragraph?
   A. The author shifts from a description of the past to the present, suggesting a tone of nostalgia and a desire to capture lessons of childhood.
   B. The author recollects activities that were meaningful in his youth, suggesting that by recapturing these activities, he will recapture the joy of his youth.
   C. The author moves into a descriptive mode, having completed his work in the narrative mode.
   D. The author enters into causal analysis, suggesting that there is a relationship between the "cold of the sea water" and his strong desire "for a week's fishing."
   E. The author utilizes diction associated with fishing in order to "hook" the reader.

2. The author's treatment of summer lake vacations as "a success" despite skin irritation and boating accidents suggest which of the following?
   A. His father was a terrible boater who put the family in danger while vacationing at the lake.
   B. The kittens the children played with were rabid and could have caused the children to become permanently ill.
   C. The minor inconveniences of the lake evoke a feeling of relative freedom and nostalgia for the author.
   D. The author is employing a facetious tone and did not really find the vacations to be a success at all.
   E. The author is still angry that the children were not allowed to take the kittens home.

Read the passage below from "Stone Soup" and answer the questions that follow.

When I was a child, I had two parents who loved me without cease. One of them attended every excuse for attention I ever contrived, and the other made it to the ones with higher production values, like piano recitals and appendicitis. So I was a lucky child too. I played with a set of paper dolls called "The Family of Dolls," four in number, who came with the factory-assigned names of Dad, Mom, Sis, and Junior. I think you know what they looked like, at least before I loved them to death and their heads fell off.

3. In calling herself "a lucky child" the author is referencing
   A. Her overly attentive parents.
   B. Her complete set of well-loved paper dolls.
   C. The variation in her parents' parenting styles.
   D. The fact that she lived through appendicitis.
   E. Her success as a pianist.

4. Which of the following most clearly indicates the rhetorical effect of the last sentence of the passage?
   A. The audience is drawn into the essay with the use of the second person pronoun "you" and an invitation to envision a commonality the author presumes for the audience's childhood.
   B. The author suggests a shift to violence that she will likely continue to discuss in the following paragraphs.
   C. The paper dolls are described as being "loved to death," foreshadowing the disintegration of the author's idyllic family.
   D. The author underscores the discrepancy in her family experience with that of her audience who would not know what the paper dolls looked like.
   E. The author breaks convention by using the pronoun "you," thereby destroying any sense of ethos she has established with the audience.

Chapter Assessment

Read the passage below from "An American Childhood" and answer the questions that follow.

She dearly loved to fluster people by throwing out a game's rules at a whim—when she was getting bored, losing in a dull sort of way, and when everybody else was taking it too seriously. If you turned your back, she moved the checkers around on the board. When you got them all straightened out, she denied she'd touched them; the next time you turned your back, she lined them up on the rug or hid them under your chair. In a betting rummy game called Michigan, she routinely played out of turn, or called out a card she didn't hold, or counted backward, simply to amuse herself by causing an uproar and watching the rest of us do double-takes and have fits. (Much later, when serious suitors came to call, Mother subjected them to this fast card game as a trial by ordeal; she used it as an intelligence test and a measure of spirit. If the poor man could stay a round without breaking down or running out, he got to marry one of us, if he still wanted to.)

—Excerpt from pp. 110-17 from AN AMERICAN CHILDHOOD by ANNIE DILLARD. Copyright © 1987 by Annie Dillard. Reprinted by permission of HarperCollins Publishers. Reprinted by the permission of Russell & Volkening as agents for the author. Copyright © 1987 by Annie Dillard.

5. In this excerpt in which the author describes her mother, which personal characteristics does the mother most clearly portray?
    A. She is an obligate cheater at games, showing she cannot be trusted.
    B. She is a rule-follower, insisting that those around her learn new games as quickly as she does in order to maintain her interest.
    C. She is not as intelligent as the other members of her family, as evidenced by her becoming bored with games she does not understand.
    D. She is a free spirit, becoming bored easily but insisting on treating life with a sort of wild abandon.
    E. She is a devoted albeit overbearing mother who makes it difficult for anyone to earn the right to marry her daughter.

6. How does the first sentence ("She dearly loved to fluster people . . . when everybody else was taking it too seriously.") relate to the subsequent sentences in the paragraph?
    A. The author makes a claim about her mother, and then offers proof of this claim by quoting her mother's friends.
    B. The author begins by stating an observable behavior by her mother, and then subsequently provides anecdotal support for her observation.
    C. The author describes a character flaw in her mother, and then analyzes possible causes for this flaw.
    D. The author explains her mother's charm with all of the guests that visited their home, and then describes fun and joyful events from her childhood.
    E. The author decries her mother's apathy toward rules, and then describes the difficulties this apathy caused when it came time for the author to marry.

Read the passage below from "Love, Internet Style" and answer the questions that follow.

It begins with sorting. Online daters can scan through millions of possible partners in an evening and select for age, education, height, politics, religion and ethnic background. JDate is a popular site for Jews. EHarmony insists that members fill out a long, introspective questionnaire, and thus is one of the few sites where most members are women. Vanity Date is for the South Beach crowd. "At Vanity Date," the Web site declares, "we have a vision of creating the largest database of the world's most good-looking, rich and superficial people."

7. A central strategy of the author is
    A. To provide specific examples of the phenomena of Internet dating in order to establish the ubiquity of the practice.
    B. To describe in-depth a specific example in order to focus the article on the superficiality of those who engage in Internet dating.
    C. To use terminology ("sorting") associated with popular fiction in order to show that the practice is not real.
    D. To provide identifiers associated with race and class in order to suggest the limitations of Internet dating.
    E. To quote a single specific website in order to generalize the inadvisability of using all Internet dating websites.

8. The tone of the paragraph can best be described as
    A. Scholarly and erudite.
    B. Didactic and authoritarian.
    C. Matter of fact and pragmatic.
    D. Critical yet emotional.
    E. Blunt yet charismatic.

Chapter Assessment

Read the passage below from "Once Upon a Quinceañera" and answer the questions that follow.

Before hanging up, I asked Monica what her quinceañera meant to her. Although she had been quite garrulous about the party details, Monica seemed stumped by the question. Every quinceañera I've asked has given me the same pat answer. Claudia in Lawrence, Massachusetts, a short, stocky girl in sweat pants, pressured by her mami to have a quince party; Ashley in San Antonio, a popular, petite girl with a string of girlfriends who had celebrated or were in line to celebrate their quinces; Leticia in East L.A., who ran off with her chambelán seven months later—all of them echoed Monica as if reciting the mantra of quinceañeras: "I'm going from being a girl to being a woman." When I pressed Monica about what this meant, she answered vaguely: "It's like part of my culture."

9. The author's use of Spanish words that may be unfamiliar to the audience suggests which of the following?
   A. The author does not know English words that would suffice in this situation.
   B. The concept of "quinceañera" is indelibly linked to Latin cultures, and therefore an audience reading about "quinceañeras" must be open to the language associated with the event.
   C. The audience for this essay is primarily a Spanish-speaking audience.
   D. The author believes that everyone should be bilingual.
   E. The author does not want to offend her audience by translating the words into English.

10. Which of the following best describes the development of the argument in this paragraph?
    A. The author provides inferential definitions of several terms associated with quinceañeras in order to inform the reader of the importance of the tradition.
    B. The author details the stories of several quinceañeras in order to establish the ubiquity of their experiences.
    C. The author builds to a climax in which she identifies the important rite of passage of the quinceañera.
    D. The author describes several quinceañera experiences that ended in disaster, including a girl running away after learning to view herself as a grown woman.
    E. The author suggests that she has interviewed multiple quinceañeras and determined that the significance of the quinceañera is unclear to the participants.

Connections for Critical Thinking

1. Both Annie Dillard's "An American Childhood" and E. B. White's "Once More to the Lake" explore the experience of childhood from a different perspective. Do they share a common voice or mood? What is distinctive about each essay? Which essay do you prefer, and why? Consider the style and emotional impact of the writing.

2. Argue for or against the claim that Alvarez's portrayal of a quinceañera and Brooks's take on online dating are biased.

3. Argue for or against the idea that the presentation of relatively new types of relationships like those described in the essays by Kingsolver and Brooks seem more highly romanticized than the "traditional" relationships described by White and Alvarez.

4. Argue for or against the view that changes in society and its norms—specifically, increased geographical mobility, an evolving workplace, ideas about economic class, individual liberties—have resulted in new forms of identity. Use examples from the work of Brooks, Kingsolver, and others.

5. Write a classification essay analyzing the women presented in the essays by Kingsolver, Dillard, and Alvarez.

Helicopter Parenting

There has been an increasing focus on the role that parents play in their children's academic and social lives. When do concerned parents become hovering "helicopter" parents (or "snowplow" parents who want to remove *all* obstacles from their children's paths)? The following sources present different views about where the line should be drawn for over-parenting. Critically read and analyze the text and images, and then answer the questions that follow.

▼ SOURCE A

"Helicopter Parenting Earns Its Wings" by Fred Lee

Fred Lee, WiseBread.com

Whether you love them or loathe them, helicopter parents are back in the news, and the findings may surprise you. As reported in an article in the *Boston Globe*, a recent study determined that there may actually be benefits to helicopter parenting, and as much as we'd like to malign the practice when we see it, being overly involved in your kid's life just might have its merits.

Helicopter parenting is the mildly pejorative term for those moms and dads you see on playgrounds and libraries (you probably know a few of them personally) who hover incessantly, much like a helicopter, over their children. Taken a step further, they go out of their way to over-parent their kids, making sure they never get hurt, never lose or fail, and intervene in as much of their children's lives as they can. . . .

Whatever be the case, as a parent, you've probably heard all the arguments against the practice of over parenting; how it might encourage poor behavior (can you say spoiled?); instill children with fear of taking chances; deny them their own sense of self; make them too reliant on other people to solve their problems; and make it difficult if not impossible for them to set out and create a life of their own. Furthermore, being heavily dependent on mom or dad to make your big life decisions surely can't bode well for any future intimate relationships that your kids might develop when they're older.

The take home message? Helicopter parenting should be avoided because it is simply bad for your kids. Or is it?

When you really get down to it, it just seems like common sense that you're not doing your kids any favors by holding their hand all the time, and yet, the findings discussed in the *Globe* actually paint a different picture: that college age children whose parents fit their definition of being helicopter parents, had actually grown into capable, well adjusted college students who were "more engaged in learning and reported greater satisfaction with their colleges." The findings were so unexpected that even the researchers conducting the study were taken by surprise, to the point where they had to go back and take a second look (so much objective inquiry).

And they also make the point that most of our impressions of helicopter parents are in the extreme. We think of them as those people who have completely taken control of their kids' lives and keep track of their every movement, when in fact, many who fit the definition are in fact simply more involved. So maybe it's not a bad idea to take the negativity about over-parenting with a grain of salt, and keep in mind that it's really a question of degrees.

A father helps his son with homework.

Hero/Corbis/Glow Images

▼ **SOURCE C**

"The Effects of 'Helicopter Parenting'" by Joel L. Young, M.D.

Joel L. Young, MD, Medical Director, Rochester Center for Behavioral Medicine, Clinical Associate Professor of Psychiatry: Wayne State University School of Medicine, The Effects of "Helicopter Parenting": How you might be increasing your child's anxiety, January 25, 2017, *Psychology Today*, https://www.psychologytoday.com/us/blog/when-your-adult-child-breaks-your-heart/201701/the-effects-helicopter-parenting.

As it turns out, so-called helicopter parenting does kids no favors. It can be challenging to watch a child fail—or to wonder if they will succeed—but this is a necessary ingredient in the recipe for successful adulthood. A new study suggests that helicopter parenting can trigger anxiety in certain kids, adding to a small pile of data suggesting that helicopter parenting stunts kids' emotional and cognitive development. . . .

Some other research, as well as anecdotal data from college counseling centers, also points to the ability of helicopter parenting to induce anxiety. College-aged students whose parents are overly involved in their academic lives, or whose parents created rigidly structured childhood environments, are more likely to experience anxiety and depression. They may also experience academic difficulties.

▼ SOURCE D

CARTOON: "Helicopter Parenting"

McGraw-Hill Education

▼ SOURCE E

"For Some, Helicopter Parenting Delivers Benefits" by Don Aucoin

"There is this stereotypical, oversensationalized, negative portrait, where they use 'over-parenting' and 'helicopter parenting' synonymously," says Barbara Dafoe Whitehead, a social historian and author who studies family issues. "Over-parenting is not letting your kids take the consequences of their actions, swooping down to rescue them, and the result would be a spoiled brat. But helicopter parenting is entirely different, and I think it is a positive style of child-rearing. . . ."

That was what Jillian Kinzie found—to her astonishment—when she helped conduct a national survey in 2007 at 750 colleges and universities. . . . The survey found that college students whose parents fit the survey's definition of helicopter parents—they had met frequently with campus officials to discuss issues involving their children—were more engaged in learning and reported greater satisfaction with their colleges, even though they had slightly lower grades than other students.

. . . [T]he line between helicopter parenting and over-parenting is a porous one, often crossed. Susan Newman, the author of "Nobody's Baby Now: Reinventing Your Adult Relationship With Your Mother and Father," maintains that helicopter parents "do their children an extreme disservice. When parents are making decisions for their children all the time and protecting them, when they get out on their own they don't know a thing about disappointment," Newman says. "I've seen a lot of these children who are parented in the helicopter manner who can't make a decision. They are calling home constantly: 'I don't get along with my roommate, what should I do? My roommate ate my food, what should I do'?"

Student Mental Health

American College Health Association. American College Health Association-National College Health Assessment II: Reference Group Executive Summary Spring 2018. Silver Spring, MD: American College Health Association, 2018.

Percentage of College Students Who Experienced Mental Health Symptoms (in the last 12 months)			
Symptom	Male	Female	Total
Felt things were hopeless	45.1	56.1	53.4
Felt overwhelmed by all you had to do	77.8	91.4	87.4
Felt exhausted (not from physical activity)	75.2	87.9	84.3
Felt very lonely	55.1	65.5	62.8
Felt very sad	58.1	72.6	68.7
Felt so depressed that it was difficult to function	34.3	44.0	41.9
Felt overwhelming anxiety	48.8	68.9	63.4
Felt overwhelming anger	36.5	43.8	42.1

Applying Your Synthesis Skills

Comprehension

1. Write a definition of *helicopter parenting* based on the sources. Which two sources give the most compelling viewpoint of helicopter parenting that best portray your own thoughts on this issue? Why were these sources the most successful?

Rhetorical Analysis

2. How did the writer of Source A view helicopter parenting? How does his diction develop his point of view?

3. Compare and contrast the visuals in Sources B and D. Explain their similarities and differences.

4. How does the information in Source F support the argument in both Sources C and E? Do you believe the data in Source F is reliable? Why or why not?

5. Based on these sources, where would you draw the line between what is considered helping children and becoming intrusive?

Writing an Argument

6. Write an essay detailing your views on this topic. Incorporate text evidence from all six sources as you synthesize your thoughts.

CHAPTER 6

History, Culture, and Civilization: Are We Citizens of the World?

As you read the essays in this chapter, consider the following questions:

- On what specific events does the author concentrate? What is the time frame?
- Does the author define *culture, history,* or *civilization?* How? Is this definition stated or implied? Is it broad or narrow? Is the writer hopeful or pessimistic? Explain.
- Is the author's tone objective or subjective? What is his or her purpose? Does the author have a personal motive in addressing the topic in the way he or she does?
- Which areas of knowledge—for example, history, philosophy, and political science—does the author bring to bear on the subject?
- What is the author's purpose in addressing events and personalities—to explain, to instruct, to amuse, to criticize, or to celebrate?
- What cultural problems and historical conflicts does the author raise?
- How does the medium the author writes in contribute to his or her perspective on culture?
- Which authors altered your perspective on a topic, and why?
- After reading, how would you define *civilization?* Are you hopeful about its state?
- What rhetorical devices do the authors use in presenting their ideas?

We seem to be at a crossroads in history, culture, and civilization, but does the future hold great promise or equally great danger—or both? Skilled writers can bring history and culture to life, enabling us to develop a sense of the various processes that have influenced the development of civilizations over time. By studying the course of history and cultures, we develop causal notions of how events are interrelated and how traditions have evolved. The study of history and issues can be an antidote to the continuous "present tense" of the media, which often have the power to make us believe we live from moment to moment, discouraging reflection on why we live the way we do and how we came to be the people we are.

The future assuredly holds peril as well as promise. History tells us that while there has never been complete absence of barbarism and nonrational behavior in human affairs, there have been societies, cultures, and nations committed to harmonious, or civil, conduct within various social realms. While it is clear that we have not attained an ideal state of cultural or world development, at the same time, we have advanced beyond the point in primitive civilization at which someone chipped at a stone in order to make a better tool.

As we consider the course of contemporary civilization, we must contend with our own personal histories and cultures as well as with the interplay of contradictory global forces. When, for example, Martin Luther King, Jr., approaches the subject of oppression from a theological perspective, we are reminded of how important the concept of freedom is to our heritage and the various ways it can be addressed. But we must also become concerned with finding a purpose beyond the parameters of our very limiting personal and nationalistic identities, something the Czech writer and statesman Václav Havel calls the "divine revolution." Indeed, we have entered an era of renewed ethnic strife in which a preoccupation with cultural differences seems stronger than the desire for universal civilization. The writers assembled here grapple with these contradictions; they search for those constituents of history and culture that might hasten the advent of a civilized world.

The idea of civilization suggests a pluralistic ethos whereby people of diverse histories and backgrounds can maintain cultural identities but also coexist with other cultural representatives in a spirit of tolerance and mutual respect. The wars, upheavals, and catastrophes of the 20th century were spawned by a narrow consciousness. Hopefully, in this century, all of us can advance the goal of a universal civilization based on the best that we have been able to create for humankind.

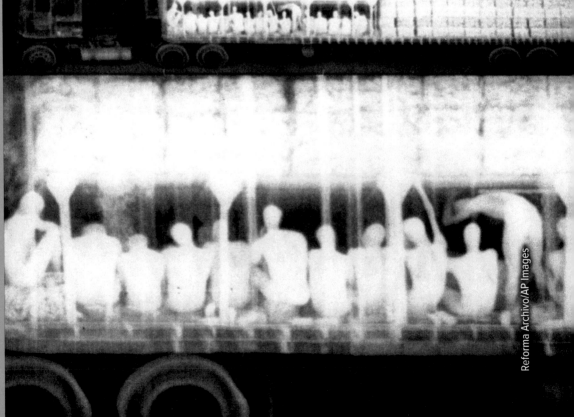

From the time of the first European settlers, the North American continent has experienced wave after wave of immigration from every part of the world. One period of heavy immigration occurred in the late 19th and early 20th centuries, when millions of people from Eastern and Southern Europe entered the United States through Ellis Island in New York City, as shown in this classic photograph.

More recently, immigrants continue to come to the United States from all over the world, often entering the country illegally. This X-ray photo shows a wide shot and a close-up image of people being smuggled across Mexico's border with Guatemala.

How Do We Become Americans?

Using a Critical Perspective Compare the scene of early 20th-century immigrants at New York City's Ellis Island with the March 1999 X-ray photo taken by Mexican authorities of human forms and cargo in a truck. What mood is conveyed by each representation? Does each photograph have a thesis or argument? Explain. Which photo do you find more engaging and provocative, and why?

Analyzing Visuals and Their Rhetoric

1. What is your major impression of the two shots of the second photo?

2. How is the issue of health and personal space differentiated in the classic photo as compared to the contemporary photo?

3. Immigrants are divided into legal and illegal aliens. How do these photos support those labels?

4. Examine the elements physically surrounding the people in each photo. Write a paragraph describing how these elements reflect immigration policy of the time.

CLASSIC ▼

What Is the American Dream?

Both Thomas Jefferson and Dr. Martin Luther King, Jr., are now safely ensconced within the pantheon of American historical figures. The following two writing samples help indicate why. Both are concerned with perhaps the most significant issue that concerns contemporary humankind: freedom. Jefferson creates a doctrine that is powerful owing to his use of concise and powerful language, which he employs both to enumerate British offenses and to call on his fellow Americans to revolt if need be. While his list of grievances may seem unquestionably correct to the contemporary mind, one must consider that Jefferson was a product of the Enlightenment, when philosophers had finally turned their attention to the primacy of individual rights after millennia of living under monarchic rule. King also provides us with the powerful theme of freedom in his famous speech; while his reflections address the peculiarly American racial divide, his style contains many biblical references, and his rhetoric is that of the sermon. You should consider why these two documents, regardless of their historical context, are seen as milestones in our nation's history.

The Declaration of Independence
In Congress, July 4, 1776

Thomas Jefferson

Thomas Jefferson (1743–1826) was governor of Virginia during the American Revolution, America's first secretary of state, and the third president of the United States. He had a varied and monumental career as politician, public servant, scientist, architect, educator (he founded the University of Virginia), and man of letters. Jefferson attended the Continental Congress in 1775, where he wrote the rough draft of the Declaration of Independence. Other hands made contributions to the document that was signed on July 4, 1776, but the wording, style, structure, and spirit of the final version are distinctly Jefferson's. Like Thomas Paine, Benjamin Franklin, James Madison, and other major figures of the Revolutionary era, Jefferson was notable for his use of prose as an instrument for social and political change. In the Declaration of Independence, we see the direct, precise, logical, and persuasive statement of revolutionary principles that makes the document one of the best-known and best-written texts in world history. Jefferson died in his home at Monticello on July 4, 50 years to the day from the signing of the Declaration of Independence.

1   When in the Course of human events it becomes necessary for one people to dissolve the political bands which have connected them with another, and to

assume among the powers of the earth, the separate and equal station to which the Laws of Nature and of Nature's God entitle them, a decent respect to the opinions of mankind requires that they should declare the causes which impel them to the separation.

2   We hold these truths to be self-evident, that all men are created equal, that they are endowed by their Creator with certain unalienable Rights, that among these are Life, Liberty and the pursuit of Happiness.—That to secure these rights, Governments are instituted among Men, deriving their just powers from the consent of the governed.—That whenever any Form of Government becomes destructive of these ends, it is the Right of the People to alter or to abolish it, and to institute new Government, laying its foundation on such principles and organizing its powers in such form, as to them shall seem most likely to effect their Safety and Happiness. Prudence, indeed, will dictate that Governments long established should not be changed for light and transient causes; and accordingly all experience hath shewn that mankind are more disposed to suffer, while evils are sufferable, than to right themselves by abolishing the forms to which they are accustomed. But when a long train of abuses and usurpations, pursuing invariably the same Object evinces a design to reduce them under absolute Despotism, it is their right, it is their duty, to throw off such Government, and to provide new Guards for their future security.—Such has been the patient sufferance of these Colonies; and such is now the necessity which constrains them to alter their former Systems of Government. The history of the present King of Great Britain is a history of repeated injuries and usurpations, all having in direct object the establishment of an absolute Tyranny over these States. To prove this, let Facts be submitted to a candid world.

3   He has refused his Assent to Laws, the most wholesome and necessary for the public good.

4   He has forbidden his Governors to pass Laws of immediate and pressing importance, unless suspended in their operation till his Assent should be obtained; and when so suspended, he has utterly neglected to attend to them.

5   He has refused to pass other Laws for the accommodation of large districts of people, unless those people would relinquish the right of Representation in the Legislature, a right inestimable to them and formidable to tyrants only.

6   He has called together legislative bodies at places unusual, uncomfortable, and distant from the depository of their public Records, for the sole purpose of fatiguing them into compliance with his measures.

7   He has dissolved Representative Houses repeatedly, for opposing with manly firmness his invasions on the rights of the people.

8   He has refused for a long time, after such dissolutions, to cause others to be elected; whereby the Legislative powers, incapable of Annihilation, have returned to the People at large for their exercise; the State remaining in the mean time exposed to all the dangers of invasion from without, and convulsions within.

9   He has endeavored to prevent the population of these States; for that purpose obstructing the Laws for Naturalization of Foreigners; refusing to pass others to encourage their migrations hither, and raising the conditions of new Appropriations of Lands.

10   He has obstructed the Administration of Justice, by refusing his Assent to Laws for establishing Judiciary powers.

11   He has made Judges dependent on his Will alone, for the tenure of their offices, and the amount and payment of their salaries.

12   He has erected a multitude of New Offices, and sent hither swarms of Officers to harass our people, and eat out their substance.

13   He has kept among us, in times of peace, Standing Armies without the Consent of our legislatures.

14   He has affected to render the Military independent of and superior to the Civil power.

15   He has combined with others to subject us to a jurisdiction foreign to our constitution, and unacknowledged by our laws; giving his Assent to their Acts of pretended Legislation:

16   For quartering large bodies of armed troops among us:
For protecting them, by a mock Trial, from punishment for any Murders which they should commit on the Inhabitants of these States:
For cutting off our Trade with all parts of the world:
For imposing Taxes on us without our Consent:
For depriving us in many cases, of the benefits of Trial by jury:
For transporting us beyond Seas to be tried for pretended offences:
For abolishing the free System of English Laws in a neighboring Province, establishing therein an Arbitrary government, and enlarging its Boundaries so as to render it at once an example and fit instrument for introducing the same absolute rule into these Colonies:
For taking away our Charters, abolishing our most valuable Laws and altering fundamentally the Forms of our Governments:
For suspending our own Legislatures, and declaring themselves invested with power to legislate for us in all cases whatsoever.

17   He has abdicated Government here, by declaring us out of his Protection and waging War against us.

18   He has plundered our seas, ravaged our Coasts, burnt our towns, and destroyed the lives of our people.

19   He is at this time transporting large Armies of foreign Mercenaries to complete the works of death, desolation and tyranny, already begun with circumstances of Cruelty & Perfidy scarcely paralleled in the most barbarous ages, and totally unworthy the Head of a civilized nation.

20   He has constrained our fellow Citizens taken Captive on the high Seas to bear Arms against their Country, to become the executioners of their friends and Brethren, or to fall themselves by their Hands.

21   He has excited domestic insurrections amongst us, and has endeavored to bring on the inhabitants of our frontiers, the merciless Indian Savages, whose known rule of warfare, is an undistinguished destruction of all ages, sexes and conditions.

22   In every stage of these Oppressions We have Petitioned for Redress in the most humble terms: Our repeated Petitions have been answered only by repeated injury. A Prince, whose character is thus marked by every act which may define a Tyrant, is unfit to be the ruler of a free people.

23   Nor have We been wanting in attentions to our British brethren. We have warned them from time to time of attempts by their legislature to extend an unwarrantable jurisdiction over us. We have reminded them of the circumstances of our emigration and settlement here. We have appealed to their native justice and magnanimity, and we have conjured them by the ties of our common kindred to disavow these usurpations, which would inevitably interrupt our connections and correspondence. They too have been deaf to the voice of justice and of consanguinity. We must, therefore, acquiesce in the necessity, which denounces our Separation, and hold them, as we hold the rest of mankind, Enemies in War, in Peace Friends.

24   We, therefore, the Representatives of the United States of America, in General Congress, Assembled, appealing to the Supreme Judge of the world for the rectitude of our intentions, do, in the Name, and by Authority of the good People of these Colonies, solemnly publish and declare, That these United Colonies are, and of Right ought to be Free and Independent States; that they are Absolved from all Allegiance to the British Crown, and that all political connection between them and the State of Great Britain, is and ought to be totally dissolved; and that as Free and Independent States, they have full Power to levy War, conclude Peace, contract Alliances, establish Commerce, and to do all other Acts and Things which Independent States may of right do. And for the support of this Declaration, with a firm reliance on the protection of divine Providence, we mutually pledge to each other our Lives, our Fortunes and our sacred Honor.

—From www.archives.gov/founding-docs/declaration-transcript

Comprehension

1. Explain Jefferson's main and subordinate purposes in this document.

2. What is Jefferson's key assertion or argument? Mention several reasons that he gives to support his argument.

3. Summarize Jefferson's definition of human nature and government.

Rhetorical Analysis

4. There are many striking words and phrases in the Declaration of Independence, notably in the beginning. Locate three such examples, and explain their connotative power and effectiveness.

5. Jefferson and his colleagues had to draft a document designed for several audiences. What audiences did they have in mind? How do their language and style reflect their awareness of multiple audiences?

6. The Declaration of Independence is a classic model of syllogistic reasoning and deductive argument. What is its major premise, and where is this premise stated? The minor premise? The conclusion?

7. What sort of inductive evidence does Jefferson offer?

8. Why is the middle portion, or body, of the Declaration of Independence considerably longer than the introduction or conclusion? What holds the body together?

9. Explain the function and effect of parallel structure in this document.

Writing

10. Discuss the relevance of the Declaration of Independence to politics today.

11. Explain in an essay why the Declaration of Independence is a model of effective prose. Analyze the choices Jefferson makes to achieve his purpose in the Declaration of Independence.

12. **Writing an Argument** Write your own declaration of independence—from family, employer, required courses, or the like. Develop this declaration as an op-ed piece for a newspaper.

I Have a Dream

Martin Luther King, Jr.

Martin Luther King, Jr., (1929–1968) was born in Atlanta, Georgia, and received degrees from Morehouse College, Crozer Theological Seminary, Boston University, and Chicago Theological Seminary. As Baptist clergyman, civil rights leader, founder and president of the Southern Christian Leadership Conference, and 1964 Nobel Peace Prize winner, King was a celebrated advocate of nonviolent resistance to achieve equality and racial integration in the world. King was a gifted orator and a highly persuasive writer. His books include *Stride Toward Freedom* (1958), *Letter from Birmingham City Jail* (1963), *Strength to Love* (1963), *Why We Can't Wait* (1964), and *Where Do We Go from Here: Chaos or Community?* (1967), a book published shortly before he was assassinated on April 4, 1968, in Memphis, Tennessee. This selection, a milestone of American oratory, was the keynote address at the March on Washington, August 28, 1963.

1   I am happy to join with you today in what will go down in history as the greatest demonstration for freedom in the history of our nation.

2   Fivescore years ago, a great American, in whose symbolic shadow we stand today, signed the Emancipation Proclamation. This momentous decree came as a great beacon light of hope to millions of Negro slaves who had been seared in the flames of withering injustice. It came as a joyous daybreak to end the long night of their captivity.

3   But one hundred years later, the Negro still is not free; one hundred years later, the life of the Negro is still sadly crippled by the manacles of segregation and the chains of discrimination; one hundred years later, the Negro lives on a lonely island of poverty in the midst of a vast ocean of material prosperity; one hundred years later, the Negro is still languishing in the corners of American society and finds himself in exile in his own land.

4   So we've come here today to dramatize a shameful condition. In a sense we've come to our nation's capital to cash a check. When the architects of our republic wrote the magnificent words of the Constitution and the Declaration of Independence, they were signing a promissory note to which every American was to fall heir. This note was the promise that all men, yes, black men as well as white men, would be guaranteed the unalienable rights of life, liberty, and the pursuit of happiness.

5   It is obvious today that America has defaulted on this promissory note in so far as her citizens of color are concerned. Instead of honoring this sacred obligation, America has given the Negro people a bad check; a check which

has come back marked "insufficient funds." We refuse to believe that there are insufficient funds in the great vaults of opportunity of this nation. And so we've come to cash this check, a check that will give us upon demand the riches of freedom and the security of justice.

6   We have also come to this hallowed spot to remind America of the fierce urgency of now. This is no time to engage in the luxury of cooling off or to take the tranquilizing drug of gradualism. Now is the time to make real the promises of democracy; now is the time to rise from the dark and desolate valley of segregation to the sunlit path of racial justice; now is the time to lift our nation from the quicksands of racial injustice to the solid rock of brotherhood; now is the time to make justice a reality for all God's children. It would be fatal for the nation to overlook the urgency of the moment. This sweltering summer of the Negro's legitimate discontent will not pass until there is an invigorating autumn of freedom and equality.

7   Nineteen sixty-three is not an end, but a beginning. And those who hope that the Negro needed to blow off steam and will now be content, will have a rude awakening if the nation returns to business as usual.

8   There will be neither rest nor tranquility in America until the Negro is granted his citizenship rights. The whirlwinds of revolt will continue to shake the foundations of our nation until the bright day of justice emerges.

9   But there is something that I must say to my people who stand on the warm threshold which leads into the palace of justice. In the process of gaining our rightful place we must not be guilty of wrongful deeds.

10   Let us not seek to satisfy our thirst for freedom by drinking from the cup of bitterness and hatred. We must forever conduct our struggle on the high plane of dignity and discipline. We must not allow our creative protest to degenerate into physical violence. Again and again we must rise to the majestic heights of meeting physical force with soul force.

11   The marvelous new militancy which has engulfed the Negro community must not lead us to a distrust of all white people, for many of our white brothers, as evidenced by their presence here today, have come to realize that their destiny is tied up with our destiny and they have come to realize that their freedom is inextricably bound to our freedom. This offense we share mounted to storm the battlements of injustice must be carried forth by a biracial army. We cannot walk alone.

12   And as we walk, we must make the pledge that we shall always march ahead. We cannot turn back. There are those who are asking the devotees of civil rights, "When will you be satisfied?" We can never be satisfied as long as the Negro is the victim of the unspeakable horrors of police brutality.

13   We can never be satisfied as long as our bodies, heavy with fatigue of travel, cannot gain lodging in the motels of the highways and the hotels of the cities. We cannot be satisfied as long as the Negro's basic mobility is from a smaller ghetto to a larger one.

14   We can never be satisfied as long as our children are stripped of their selfhood and robbed of their dignity by signs stating "for whites only." We cannot be satisfied as long as a Negro in Mississippi cannot vote and a Negro in New York believes he has nothing for which to vote. No, we are not satisfied, and we will not be satisfied until justice rolls down like waters and righteousness like a mighty stream.

15   I am not unmindful that some of you have come here out of excessive trials and tribulation. Some of you have come fresh from narrow jail cells. Some of you have come from areas where your quest for freedom left you battered by the storms of persecution and staggered by the winds of police brutality. You have been the veterans of creative suffering. Continue to work with the faith that unearned suffering is redemptive.

16   Go back to Mississippi; go back to Alabama; go back to South Carolina; go back to Georgia; go back to Louisiana; go back to the slums and ghettos of the northern cities, knowing that somehow this situation can, and will be changed. Let us not wallow in the valley of despair.

17   So I say to you, my friends, that even though we must face the difficulties of today and tomorrow, I still have a dream. It is a dream deeply rooted in the American dream that one day this nation will rise up and live out the true meaning of its creed—we hold these truths to be self-evident, that all men are created equal.

18   I have a dream that one day on the red hills of Georgia, sons of former slaves and sons of former slave-owners will be able to sit down together at the table of brotherhood.

19   I have a dream that one day, even the state of Mississippi, a state sweltering with the heat of injustice, sweltering with the heat of oppression, will be transformed into an oasis of freedom and justice.

20   I have a dream my four little children will one day live in a nation where they will not be judged by the color of their skin but by the content of their character. I have a dream today!

21   I have a dream that one day, down in Alabama, with its vicious racists, with its governor having his lips dripping with the words of interposition and nullification, that one day, right there in Alabama, little black boys and black girls will be able to join hands with little white boys and white girls as sisters and brothers. I have a dream today!

22   I have a dream that one day every valley shall be exalted, every hill and mountain shall be made low, the rough places shall be made plain, and the crooked places shall be made straight and the glory of the Lord will be revealed and all flesh shall see it together.

23   This is our hope. This is the faith that I go back to the South with.

24   With this faith we will be able to hew out of the mountain of despair a stone of hope. With this faith we will be able to transform the jangling discords of our nation into a beautiful symphony of brotherhood.

25   With this faith we will be able to work together, to pray together, to struggle together, to go to jail together, to stand up for freedom together, knowing that we will be free one day. This will be the day when all of God's children will be able to sing with new meaning—"my country 'tis of thee; sweet land of liberty; of thee I sing; land where my fathers died, land of the pilgrims' pride; from every mountain side, let freedom ring"—and if America is to be a great nation, this must become true.

26   So let freedom ring from the prodigious hilltops of New Hampshire.

27   Let freedom ring from the mighty mountains of New York.

28   Let freedom ring from the heightening Alleghenies of Pennsylvania.

29   Let freedom ring from the snow-capped Rockies of Colorado.

30   Let freedom ring from the curvaceous slopes of California.

31   But not only that.

32   Let freedom ring from Stone Mountain of Georgia.

33   Let freedom ring from Lookout Mountain of Tennessee.

34   Let freedom ring from every hill and molehill of Mississippi, from every mountainside, let freedom ring.

35   And when we allow freedom to ring, when we let it ring from every village and hamlet, from every state and city, we will be able to speed up that day when all of God's children—black men and white men, Jews and Gentiles, Catholics and Protestants—will be able to join hands and to sing in the words of the old Negro spiritual, "Free at last, free at last; thank God Almighty, we are free at last."

Comprehension

1.   What is the main purpose of this speech? Where does King state this purpose most clearly?

2.   Why does King make use of "fivescore years ago" (paragraph 2)? How is this more appropriate than simply saying "a hundred years ago"?

3.   Who is King's audience? Where does he acknowledge the special historical circumstances influencing his speech?

Rhetorical Analysis

4.   Identify several allusions King includes. From what sources does King adapt phrases to give his work allusive richness?

5.   What do the terms *interposition* and *nullification* (paragraph 21) mean? What is their historical significance?

6. Why does King make use of repetition? Does this technique work well in print? Explain.

7. What is the purpose of the extended metaphor in paragraphs 4 and 5? Which point in paragraph 3 does it refer to?

8. Why is this selection titled "I Have a Dream"? How do dreams serve as a motif for this speech?

Writing

9. Many people consider "I Have a Dream" to be among the greatest speeches delivered by an American. In an essay, explain how King's speech is effective.

10. Write your own "I Have a Dream" essay, basing it on your vision of America.

11. **Writing an Argument** Prepare a newspaper editorial advocating a solution to one aspect of racial, ethnic, or sexual injustice.

Synthesizing the Classic + Contemporary Essays

1. Compare the Declaration of Independence with King's speech in terms of language, style, and content. Are they equally powerful and resonant? Cite specific passages from the essays to illustrate your response.

2. Rewrite the Declaration of Independence in modern English as you believe Dr. King might have written it, reflecting his concerns about African Americans and other minorities in this country. Include a list of grievances similar to the ones concerning British rule.

3. Write a research paper about the lives and times of King and Jefferson. Compare and contrast any significant events or pertinent biographical data in their backgrounds. Argue that both men were fighting for the same (or different) things.

The Myth of the Latin Woman: I Just Met a Girl Named María

Judith Ortiz Cofer

Judith Ortiz Cofer (b. 1952) was born in Puerto Rico and immigrated to the United States in 1956. Once a bilingual teacher in Florida public schools, Cofer has written several books of poetry; plays; a novel, *The Line of the Sun* (1989); an award-winning collection of essays and poems, *Silent Dancing: A Partial Remembrance of a Puerto Rican Childhood* (1990); and a collection of short stories, *An Island Like You: Stories of the Barrio* (1995). Her more recent books include *Woman in Front of the Sun: On Becoming a Writer* (2000), *The Meaning of Consuelo* (2003), and *A Love Story Beginning in Spanish* (2005). She is a professor of English and creative writing at the University of Georgia. In the following essay, she offers both personal insight and philosophical reflection on the theme of ethnic stereotyping.

1   On a bus trip to London from Oxford University where I was earning some graduate credits one summer, a young man, obviously fresh from a pub, spotted me and as if struck by inspiration went down on his knees in the aisle. With both hands over his heart he broke into an Irish tenor's rendition of "María" from *West Side Story*. My politely amused fellow passengers gave his lovely voice the round of gentle applause it deserved. Though I was not quite as amused, I managed my version of an English smile: no show of teeth, no extreme contortions of the facial muscles—I was at this time of my life practicing reserve and cool. Oh, that British control, how I coveted it. But "María" had followed me to London, reminding me of a prime fact of my life: You can leave the island, master the English language, and travel as far as you can, but if you are a Latina, especially one like me who so obviously belongs to Rita Moreno's gene pool, the island travels with you.

2   This is sometimes a very good thing. It may win you that extra minute of someone's attention. But with some people, the same things can make *you* an island—not a tropical paradise but an Alcatraz, a place nobody wants to visit. As a Puerto Rican girl living in the United States and wanting like most children to "belong," I resented the stereotype that my Hispanic appearance called forth from many people I met.

3   Growing up in a large urban center in New Jersey during the 1960s, I suffered from what I think of as "cultural schizophrenia." Our life was designed by my parents as a microcosm of their *casas* on the island. We spoke in Spanish, ate Puerto Rican food bought at the *bodega*, and practiced strict Catholicism at a church that allotted us a one-hour slot each week for mass, performed in Spanish by a Chinese priest trained as a missionary for Latin America.

4   As a girl I was kept under strict surveillance by my parents, since my virtue and modesty were, by their cultural equation, the same as their honor. As a teenager I was lectured constantly on how to behave as a proper *senorita*. But it was a conflicting message I received, since the Puerto Rican mothers also encouraged

their daughters to look and act like women and to dress in clothes our Anglo friends and their mothers found too "mature" and flashy. The difference was, and is, cultural; yet I often felt humiliated when I appeared at an American friend's party wearing a dress more suitable to a semiformal than to a playroom birthday celebration. At Puerto Rican festivities, neither the music nor the colors we wore could be too loud.

5   I remember Career Day in our high school, when teachers told us to come dressed as if for a job interview. It quickly became obvious that to the Puerto Rican girls "dressing up" meant wearing their mother's ornate jewelry and clothing, more appropriate (by mainstream standards) for the company Christmas party than as daily office attire. That morning I had agonized in front of my closet, trying to figure out what a "career girl" would wear. I knew how to dress for school (at the Catholic school I attended, we all wore uniforms), I knew how to dress for Sunday mass, and I knew what dresses to wear for parties at my relatives' homes. Though I do not recall the precise details of my Career Day outfit, it must have been a composite of these choices. But I remember a comment my friend (an Italian American) made in later years that coalesced my impressions of that day. She said that at the business school she was attending, the Puerto Rican girls always stood out for wearing "everything at once." She meant, of course, too much jewelry, too many accessories. On that day at school we were simply made the negative models by the nuns, who were themselves not credible fashion experts to any of us. But it was painfully obvious to me that to the others, in their tailored skirts and silk blouses, we must have seemed "hopeless" and "vulgar." Though I now know that most adolescents feel out of step much of the time, I also know that for the Puerto Rican girls of my generation that sense was intensified. The way our teachers and classmates looked at us that day in school was just a taste of the cultural clash that awaited us in the real world, where prospective employers and men on the street would often misinterpret our tight skirts and jingling bracelets as a "come-on."

6   Mixed cultural signals have perpetuated certain stereotypes—for example, that of the Hispanic woman as the "hot tamale" or sexual firebrand. It is a one-dimensional view that the media have found easy to promote. In their special vocabulary, advertisers have designated "sizzling" and "smoldering" as the adjectives of choice for describing not only the foods but also the women of Latin America. From conversations in my house I recall hearing about the harassment that Puerto Rican women endured in factories where the "boss-men" talked to them as if sexual innuendo was all they understood, and worse, often gave them the choice of submitting to their advances or being fired.

7   It is custom, however, not chromosomes, that leads us to choose scarlet over pale pink. As young girls it was our mothers who influenced our decisions about clothes and colors—mothers who had grown up on a tropical island where the natural environment was a riot of primary colors, where showing your skin was one way to keep cool as well as to look sexy. Most important of all, on the island, women perhaps felt freer to dress and move more provocatively since, in most cases, they were protected by the traditions, mores, and laws of a Spanish/Catholic system of morality and machismo whose main rule was: *You may look at my sister,*

but if you touch her I will kill you. The extended family and church structure could provide a young woman with a circle of safety in her small pueblo on the island; if a man "wronged" a girl, everyone would close in to save her family honor.

8   My mother has told me about dressing in her best party clothes on Saturday nights and going to the town's plaza to promenade with her girlfriends in front of the boys they liked. The males were thus given an opportunity to admire the women and to express their admiration in the form of *piropos*: erotically charged street poems they composed on the spot. (I have myself been subjected to a few *piropos* while visiting the island, and they can be outrageous, although custom dictates that they must never cross into obscenity.) This ritual, as I understand it, also entails a show of studied indifference on the woman's part; if she is "decent," she must not acknowledge the man's impassioned words. So I do understand how things can be lost in translation. When a Puerto Rican girl dressed in her idea of what is attractive meets a man from the mainstream culture who has been trained to react to certain types of clothing as a sexual signal, a clash is likely to take place. I remember the boy who took me to my first formal dance leaning over to plant a sloppy, overeager kiss painfully on my mouth; when I didn't respond with sufficient passion, he remarked resentfully: "I thought you Latin girls were supposed to mature early," as if I were expected to *ripen* like a fruit or vegetable, not just grow into womanhood like other girls.

9   It is surprising to my professional friends that even today some people, including those who should know better, still put others "in their place." It happened to me most recently during a stay at a classy metropolitan hotel favored by young professional couples for weddings. Late one evening after the theater, as I walked toward my room with a colleague (a woman with whom I was coordinating an arts program), a middle-aged man in a tuxedo, with a young girl in satin and lace on his arm, stepped directly into our path. With his champagne glass extended toward me, he exclaimed "Evita!"

10   Our way blocked, my companion and I listened as the man half-recited, half-bellowed "Don't Cry for Me, Argentina." When he finished, the young girl said: "How about a round of applause for my daddy?" We complied, hoping this would bring the silly spectacle to a close. I was becoming aware that our little group was attracting the attention of the other guests. "Daddy" must have perceived this too, and he once more barred the way as we tried to walk past him. He began to shout-sing a ditty to the tune of "La Bamba"—except the lyrics were about a girl named María whose exploits rhymed with her name and gonorrhea. The girl kept saying "Oh, Daddy" and looking at me with pleading eyes. She wanted me to laugh along with the others. My companion and I stood silently waiting for the man to end his offensive song. When he finished, I looked not at him but at his daughter. I advised her calmly never to ask her father what he had done in the army. Then I walked between them and to my room. My friend complimented me on my cool handling of the situation, but I confessed that I had really wanted to push the jerk into the swimming pool. This same man—probably a corporate executive, well-educated, even worldly by most standards—would not have been likely to regale an Anglo woman with a dirty song in public. He might have checked his impulse by assuming that she could be somebody's wife or mother, or

at least *somebody* who might take offense. But, to him, I was just an Evita or a María: merely a character in his cartoon-populated universe.

11   Another facet of the myth of the Latin woman in the United States is the menial, the domestic—María the housemaid or countergirl. It's true that work as domestics, as waitresses, and in factories is all that's available to women with little English and few skills. But the myth of the Hispanic menial—the funny maid, mispronouncing words and cooking up a spicy storm in a shiny California kitchen—has been perpetuated by the media in the same way that "Mammy" from *Gone with the Wind* became America's idea of the black woman for generations. Since I do not wear my diplomas around my neck for all to see, I have on occasion been sent to that "kitchen" where some think I obviously belong.

12   One incident has stayed with me, though I recognize it as a minor offense. My first public poetry reading took place in Miami, at a restaurant where a luncheon was being held before the event. I was nervous and excited as I walked in with notebook in hand. An older woman motioned me to her table, and thinking (foolish me) that she wanted me to autograph a copy of my newly published slender volume of verse, I went over. She ordered a cup of coffee from me, assuming that I was the waitress. (Easy enough to mistake my poems for menus, I suppose.) I know it wasn't an intentional act of cruelty. Yet of all the good things that happened later, I remember that scene most clearly, because it reminded me of what I had to overcome before anyone would take me seriously. In retrospect I understand that my anger gave my reading fire. In fact, I have almost always taken any doubt in my abilities as a challenge, the result most often being the satisfaction of winning a convert, of seeing the cold, appraising eyes warm to my words, the body language change, the smile that indicates I have opened some avenue for communication. So that day as I read, I looked directly at that woman. Her lowered eyes told me she was embarrassed at her faux pas, and when I willed her to look up at me, she graciously allowed me to punish her with my full attention. We shook hands at the end of the reading and I never saw her again. She has probably forgotten the entire incident, but maybe not.

13   Yet I am one of the lucky ones. There are thousands of Latinas without the privilege of an education or the entrees into society that I have. For them life is a constant struggle against the misconceptions perpetuated by the myth of the Latina. My goal is to try to replace the old stereotypes with a much more interesting set of realities. Every time I give a reading, I hope the stories I tell, the dreams and fears I examine in my work, can achieve some universal truth that will get my audience past the particulars of my skin color, my accent, or my clothes.

14   I once wrote a poem in which I called all Latinas "God's brown daughters." This poem is really a prayer of sorts, offered upward, but also, through the human-to-human channel of art, outward. It is a prayer for communication and for respect. In it, Latin women pray "in Spanish to an Anglo God/with a Jewish heritage," and they are "fervently hoping/that if not omnipotent,/at least He be bilingual."

Comprehension

1. What is the thesis of the essay?

2. What does Cofer mean by the expression "cultural schizophrenia" (paragraph 3)?

3. Define the following words: *coveted* (paragraph 1), *Anglo* (paragraph 4), *coalesced* (paragraph 5), *machismo* (paragraph 7), and *entrees* (paragraph 13).

Rhetorical Analysis

4. Cofer uses many anecdotes in her discussion of stereotyping. How does this affect the tone of the essay?

5. Who is the implied audience for this essay? What aspects of the writing led you to your conclusion?

6. This essay is written in the first person, which tends to reveal a lot about the writer's personality. What adjectives come to mind when you think of the writer's singular voice?

7. Although this essay has a sociological theme, Cofer demonstrates that she has a poet's sensitivity toward language. What in the following sentence from paragraph 7 demonstrates this poetic style: "It is custom, however, not chromosomes, that leads us to choose scarlet over pale pink"? Select two other sentences from the essay that demonstrate Cofer's stylistic talent, and explain why they, too, are poetic.

8. In paragraph 8, Cofer contrasts cultural perceptions related to Hispanic and Anglo behavior. How is the paragraph structured so that this difference is demonstrated dramatically?

9. Cofer uses quotation marks to emphasize the connotation of certain words. Explain the significance of the following words: *mature* (paragraph 4), *hopeless* (paragraph 5), *hot tamale* (paragraph 6), *wronged* (paragraph 7), and *decent* (paragraph 8).

Writing

10. In a personal essay, explore whether you have experienced or observed stereotyping. How has this experience molded your perception of the world in which you live?

11. **Writing an Argument**   In an essay, write an argument about what creates cultural stereotypes, and provide suggestions on how to overcome stereotyped thinking.

A World Not Neatly Divided

Amartya Sen

Amartya Sen (b. 1933), born in Santiniketan, India, was awarded the Nobel Prize in Economics in 1988 for his groundbreaking work on welfare economics. Educated at Presidency College in Calcutta and Cambridge University (PhD, 1959), Sen has taught at Harvard University, the London School of Economics, and Oxford University; currently, he is a professor at Trinity College, Cambridge University. His major works, all of which investigate the role of poverty and inequality in the world, include *Collective Choice and Social Welfare* (1970), *On Economic Inequality* (1973), *Poverty and Famines: An Essay on Entitlement and Deprivation* (1981), *Commodities and Capabilities* (1985), *Development as Freedom* (1999), and *Identity and Violence: The Illusion of Destiny* (2006). In the following essay, which appeared in *The New York Times* in 2001, Sen suggests that generalizations about "civilization" tend to blur the realities of complex cultures.

1   When people talk about clashing civilizations, as so many politicians and academics do now, they can sometimes miss the central issue. The inadequacy of this thesis begins well before we get to the question of whether civilizations must clash. The basic weakness of the theory lies in its program of categorizing people of the world according to a unique, allegedly commanding system of classification. This is problematic because civilizational categories are crude and inconsistent and also because there are other ways of seeing people (linked to politics, language, literature, class, occupation, or other affiliations).

2   The befuddling influence of a singular classification also traps those who dispute the thesis of a clash: To talk about "the Islamic world" or "the Western world" is already to adopt an impoverished vision of humanity as unalterably divided. In fact, civilizations are hard to partition in this way, given the diversities within each society as well as the linkages among different countries and cultures. For example, describing India as a "Hindu civilization" misses the fact that India has more Muslims than any other country except Indonesia and possibly Pakistan. It is futile to try to understand Indian art, literature, music, food, or politics without seeing the extensive interactions across barriers of religious communities. These include Hindus and Muslims, Buddhists, Jains, Sikhs, Parsees, Christians (who have been in India since at least the fourth century, well before England's conversion to Christianity), Jews (present since the fall of Jerusalem), and even atheists and agnostics. Sanskrit has a larger atheistic literature than exists in any other classical language. Speaking of India as a Hindu civilization may be comforting to the Hindu fundamentalist, but it is an odd reading of India.

3   A similar coarseness can be seen in the other categories invoked, like "the Islamic world." Consider Akbar and Aurangzeb, two Muslim emperors of the

Mogul dynasty in India. Aurangzeb tried hard to convert Hindus into Muslims and instituted various policies in that direction, of which taxing the non-Muslims was only one example. In contrast, Akbar reveled in his multiethnic court and pluralist laws, and issued official proclamations insisting that no one "should be interfered with on account of religion" and that "anyone is to be allowed to go over to a religion that pleases him."

4   If a homogeneous view of Islam were to be taken, then only one of these emperors could count as a true Muslim. The Islamic fundamentalist would have no time for Akbar; Prime Minister Tony Blair, given his insistence that tolerance is a defining characteristic of Islam, would have to consider excommunicating Aurangzeb. I expect both Akbar and Aurangzeb would protest, and so would I. A similar crudity is present in the characterization of what is called "Western civilization." Tolerance and individual freedom have certainly been present in European history. But there is no dearth of diversity here, either. When Akbar was making his pronouncements on religious tolerance in Agra, in the 1590s, the Inquisitions were still going on; in 1600, Giordano Bruno was burned at the stake, for heresy, in Campo dei Fiori in Rome.

5   Dividing the world into discrete civilizations is not just crude. It propels us into the absurd belief that this partitioning is natural and necessary and must overwhelm all other ways of identifying people. That imperious view goes not only against the sentiment that "we human beings are all much the same," but also against the more plausible understanding that we are diversely different. For example, Bangladesh's split from Pakistan was not connected with religion, but with language and politics.

6   Each of us has many features in our self-conception. Our religion, important as it may be, cannot be an all-engulfing identity. Even a shared poverty can be a source of solidarity across the borders. The kind of division highlighted by, say, the so-called "antiglobalization" protesters—whose movement is, incidentally, one of the most globalized in the world—tries to unite the underdogs of the world economy and goes firmly against religious, national, or "civilizational" lines of division.

7   The main hope of harmony lies not in any imagined uniformity, but in the plurality of our identities, which cut across each other and work against sharp divisions into impenetrable civilizational camps. Political leaders who think and act in terms of sectioning off humanity into various "worlds" stand to make the world more flammable—even when their intentions are very different. They also end up, in the case of civilizations defined by religion, lending authority to religious leaders seen as spokesmen for their "worlds." In the process, other voices are muffled and other concerns silenced. The robbing of our plural identities not only reduces us; it impoverishes the world.

Comprehension

1. According to Sen, what is the "basic weakness" underlying the idea that the world is composed of "clashing civilizations" (paragraph 1)?

2. What does the writer mean by "singular classification" (paragraph 2)? According to Sen, why is classifying people in terms of their civilization "crude and inconsistent"? Why does he believe that applying singular classification to religions and other features of society is wrong?

3. What, according to Sen, is "the main hope of harmony" (paragraph 7) in the world?

Rhetorical Analysis

4. What argumentative strategy does Sen employ in the introductory paragraph? What point of view is he arguing against?

5. While arguing against a certain type of classification, Sen actually uses classification as a rhetorical strategy. How, precisely, does he employ classification to organize his argument?

6. What examples does Sen use to support his argument? Why does he use them? Why does he decide not to provide illustrations near the end of the selection?

7. What transitional devices serve to unify the essay?

8. How effective is Sen's concluding paragraph? Does it serve to confirm his claim? Why or why not?

Writing

9. Write an essay about the problems you see in your community or on campus. Explain how singular classification might explain some of these problems.

10. In an analytical essay, explain how singular classification might help explain the events of September 11, 2001.

11. **Writing an Argument** Write an essay in which you demonstrate that singular classification actually can be helpful in framing public discourse about groups, nations, or civilizations.

The Arab World

Edward T. Hall

Edward T. Hall (1914–2009) was born in Missouri and earned a master's degree at the University of Arkansas and a PhD in anthropology at Columbia University. He was a professor of anthropology at the Illinois Institute of Technology and at Northwestern University. Hall is also the author of many books on anthropology and culture, among the most famous of which are *The Silent Language* (1959), *The Hidden Dimension* (1966), *The Dance of Life* (1983), *Hidden Differences: Doing Business with the Japanese* (1987), and *Understanding Cultural Differences: Germans, French and Americans* (1990). In this selection from *The Hidden Dimension*, Hall demonstrates how such basic concepts as public and private space are perceived far differently depending on one's culture of origin.

1   In spite of over two thousand years of contact, Westerners and Arabs still do not understand each other. Proxemic research reveals some insights into this difficulty. Americans in the Middle East are immediately struck by two conflicting sensations. In public they are compressed and overwhelmed by smells, crowding, and high noise levels; in Arab homes Americans are apt to rattle around, feeling exposed and often somewhat inadequate because of too much space! (The Arab houses and apartments of the middle and upper classes which Americans stationed abroad commonly occupy are much larger than the dwellings such Americans usually inhabit.) Both the high sensory stimulation which is experienced in public places and the basic insecurity which comes from being in a dwelling that is too large provide Americans with an introduction to the sensory world of the Arab.

Behavior in Public

2   Pushing and shoving in public places is characteristic of Middle Eastern culture. Yet it is not entirely what Americans think it is (being pushy and rude) but stems from a different set of assumptions concerning not only the relations between people but how one experiences the body as well. Paradoxically, Arabs consider northern Europeans and Americans pushy, too. This was very puzzling to me when I started investigating these two views. How could Americans who stand aside and avoid touching be considered pushy? I used to ask Arabs to explain this paradox. None of my subjects was able to tell me specifically what particulars of American behavior were responsible, yet they all agreed that the impression was widespread among Arabs. After repeated unsuccessful attempts to gain insight into the cognitive world of the Arab on this particular point, I filed it away as a question that only time would answer. When the answer came, it was because of a seemingly inconsequential annoyance.

3   While waiting for a friend in a Washington, D.C., hotel lobby and wanting to be both visible and alone, I had seated myself in a solitary chair outside the

normal stream of traffic. In such a setting most Americans follow a rule, which is all the more binding because we seldom think about it, that can be stated as follows: As soon as a person stops or is seated in a public place, there balloons around him a small sphere of privacy which is considered inviolate. The size of the sphere varies with the degree of crowding, the age, sex, and the importance of the person, as well as the general surroundings. Anyone who enters this zone and stays there is intruding. In fact, a stranger who intrudes, even for a specific purpose, acknowledges the fact that he has intruded by beginning his request with "Pardon me, but can you tell me . . . ?"

4   To continue, as I waited in the deserted lobby, a stranger walked up to where I was sitting and stood close enough so that not only could I easily touch him but I could even hear him breathing. In addition, the dark mass of his body filled the peripheral field of vision on my left side. If the lobby had been crowded with people, I would have understood his behavior, but in an empty lobby his presence made me exceedingly uncomfortable. Feeling annoyed by this intrusion, I moved my body in such a way as to communicate annoyance. Strangely enough, instead of moving away, my actions seemed only to encourage him, because he moved even closer. In spite of the temptation to escape the annoyance, I put aside thoughts of abandoning my post, thinking, "To hell with it. Why should I move? I was here first and I'm not going to let this fellow drive me out even if he is a boor." Fortunately, a group of people soon arrived whom my tormentor immediately joined. Their mannerisms explained his behavior, for I knew from both speech and gestures that they were Arabs. I had not been able to make this crucial identification by looking at my subject when he was alone because he wasn't talking and he was wearing American clothes.

5   In describing the scene later to an Arab colleague, two contrasting patterns emerged. My concept and my feelings about my own circle of privacy in a "public" place immediately struck my Arab friend as strange and puzzling. He said, "After all, it's a public place, isn't it?" Pursuing this line of inquiry, I found that in Arab thought I had no rights whatsoever by virtue of occupying a given spot; neither my place nor my body was inviolate! For the Arab, there is no such thing as an intrusion in public. Public means public. With this insight, a great range of Arab behavior that had been puzzling, annoying, and sometimes even frightening began to make sense. I learned, for example, that if *A* is standing on a street corner and *B* wants his spot, *B* is within his rights if he does what he can to make *A* uncomfortable enough to move. In Beirut only the hardy sit in the last row in a movie theater, because there are usually standees who want seats and who push and shove and make such a nuisance that most people give up and leave. Seen in this light, the Arab who "intruded" on my space in the hotel lobby had apparently selected it for the very reason I had: It was a good place to watch two doors and the elevator. My show of annoyance, instead of driving him away, had only encouraged him. He thought he was about to get me to move.

6   Another silent source of friction between Americans and Arabs is in an area that Americans treat very informally—the manners and rights of the road. In general, in the United States we tend to defer to the vehicle that is bigger, more powerful, faster, and heavily laden. While a pedestrian walking along a road may

feel annoyed he will not think it unusual to step aside for a fast-moving automobile. He knows that because he is moving he does not have the right to the space around him that he has when he is standing still (as I was in the hotel lobby). It appears that the reverse is true with the Arabs who apparently *take on rights to space as they move.* For someone else to move into a space an Arab is also moving into is a violation of his rights. It is infuriating to an Arab to have someone else cut in front of him on the highway. It is the American's cavalier treatment of moving space that makes the Arab call him aggressive and pushy.

Concepts of Privacy

7   The experience described above and many others suggested to me that Arabs might actually have a wholly contrasting set of assumptions concerning the body and the rights associated with it. Certainly the Arab tendency to shove and push each other in public and to feel and pinch women in public conveyances would not be tolerated by Westerners. It appeared to me that they must not have any concept of a private zone outside the body. This proved to be precisely the case.

8   In the Western world, the person is synonymous with an individual inside a skin. And in northern Europe generally, the skin and even the clothes may be inviolate. You need permission to touch either if you are a stranger. This rule applies in some parts of France, where the mere touching of another person during an argument used to be legally defined as assault. For the Arab the location of the person in relation to the body is quite different. The person exists somewhere down inside the body. The ego is not completely hidden, however, because it can be reached very easily with an insult. It is protected from touch but not from words. The dissociation of the body and the ego may explain why the public amputation of a thief's hand is tolerated as standard punishment in Saudi Arabia. It also sheds light on why an Arab employer living in a modern apartment can provide his servant with a room that is a boxlike cubicle approximately 5 by 10 by 4 feet in size that is not only hung from the ceiling to conserve floor space but has an opening so that the servant can be spied on.

9   As one might suspect, deep orientations toward the self such as the one just described are also reflected in the language. This was brought to my attention one afternoon when an Arab colleague who is the author of an Arab-English dictionary arrived in my office and threw himself into a chair in a state of obvious exhaustion. When I asked him what had been going on, he said: "I have spent the entire afternoon trying to find the Arab equivalent of the English word 'rape.' There is no such word in Arabic. All my sources, both written and spoken, can come up with no more than an approximation, such as 'He took her against her will.' There is nothing in Arabic approaching your meaning as it is expressed in that one word."

10   Differing concepts of the placement of the ego in relation to the body are not easily grasped. Once an idea like this is accepted, however, it is possible to understand many other facets of Arab life that would otherwise be difficult to explain. One of these is the high population density of Arab cities like Cairo, Beirut, and Damascus. According to the animal studies described in the earlier chapters [of *The Hidden Dimension*], the Arabs should be living in a perpetual

behavioral sink. While it is probable that Arabs are suffering from population pressures, it is also just as possible that continued pressure from the desert has resulted in a cultural adaptation to high density which takes the form described above. Tucking the ego down inside the body shell not only would permit higher population densities but would explain why it is that Arab communications are stepped up as much as they are when compared to northern European communication patterns. Not only is the sheer noise level much higher, but the piercing look of the eyes, the touch of the hands, and the mutual bathing in the warm moist breath during conversation represent stepped up sensory inputs to a level which many Europeans find unbearably intense.

11   The Arab dream is for lots of space in the home, which unfortunately many Arabs cannot afford. Yet when he has space, it is very different from what one finds in most American homes. Arab spaces inside their upper middle-class homes are tremendous by our standards. They avoid partitions because Arabs *do not like to be alone*. The form of the home is such as to hold the family together inside a single protective shell, because Arabs are deeply involved with each other. Their personalities are intermingled and take nourishment from each other like the roots and soil. If one is not with people and actively involved in some way, one is deprived of life. An old Arab saying reflects this value: "Paradise without people should not be entered because it is Hell." Therefore, Arabs in the United States often feel socially and sensorially deprived and long to be back where there is human warmth and contact.

12   Since there is no physical privacy as we know it in the Arab family, not even a word for privacy, one could expect that the Arabs might use some other means to be alone. Their way to be alone is to stop talking. Like the English, an Arab who shuts himself off in this way is not indicating that anything is wrong or that he is withdrawing, only that he wants to be alone with his own thoughts or does not want to be intruded upon. One subject said that her father would come and go for days at a time without saying a word, and no one in the family thought anything of it. Yet for this very reason, an Arab exchange student visiting a Kansas farm failed to pick up the cue that his American hosts were mad at him when they gave him the "silent treatment." He only discovered something was wrong when they took him to town and tried forcibly to put him on a bus to Washington, D.C., the headquarters of the exchange program responsible for his presence in the U.S.

Arab Personal Distances

13   Like everyone else in the world, Arabs are unable to formulate specific rules for their informal behavior patterns. In fact, they often deny that there are any rules, and they are made anxious by suggestions that such is the case. Therefore, in order to determine how the Arab sets distances, I investigated the use of each sense separately. Gradually, definite and distinctive behavioral patterns began to emerge.

14   Olfaction occupies a prominent place in the Arab life. Not only is it one of the distance-setting mechanisms, but it is a vital part of a complex system of behavior. Arabs consistently breathe on people when they talk. However, this habit is more than a matter of different manners. To the Arab good smells are pleasing and a

way of being involved with each other. To smell one's friend is not only nice but desirable, for to deny him your breath is to act ashamed. Americans, on the other hand, trained as they are not to breathe in people's faces, automatically communicate shame in trying to be polite. Who would expect that when our highest diplomats are putting on their best manners they are also communicating shame? Yet this is what occurs constantly, because diplomacy is not only "eyeball to eyeball" but breath to breath.

15   By stressing olfaction, Arabs do not try to eliminate all the body's odors, only to enhance them and use them in building human relationships. Nor are they self-conscious about telling others when they don't like the way they smell. A man leaving his house in the morning may be told by his uncle, "Habib, your stomach is sour and your breath doesn't smell too good. Better not talk too close to people today." Smell is even considered in the choice of a mate. When couples are being matched for marriage, the man's go-between will sometimes ask to smell the girl, who may be turned down if she doesn't "smell nice." Arabs recognize that smell and disposition may be linked.

16   In a word, the olfactory boundary performs two roles in Arab life. It enfolds those who want to relate and separates those who don't. The Arab finds it essential to stay inside the olfactory zone as a means of keeping tab on changes in emotion. What is more, he may feel crowded as soon as he smells something unpleasant. While not much is known about "olfactory crowding," this may prove to be as significant as any other variable in the crowding complex because it is tied directly to the body chemistry and hence to the state of health and emotions. . . . It is not surprising, therefore, that the olfactory boundary constitutes for the Arabs an informal distance-setting mechanism in contrast to the visual mechanisms of the Westerner.

Facing and Not Facing

17   One of my earliest discoveries in the field of intercultural communication was that the position of the bodies of people in conversation varies with the culture. Even so, it used to puzzle me that a special Arab friend seemed unable to walk and talk at the same time. After years in the United States, he could not bring himself to stroll along, facing forward while talking. Our progress would be arrested while he edged ahead, cutting slightly in front of me and turning sideways so we could see each other. Once in this position, he would stop. His behavior was explained when I learned that for the Arabs to view the other person peripherally is regarded as impolite, and to sit or stand back-to-back is considered very rude. You must be involved when interacting with Arabs who are friends.

18   One mistaken American notion is that Arabs conduct all conversations at close distances. This is not the case at all. On social occasions, they may sit on opposite sides of the room and talk across the room to each other. They are, however, apt to take offense when Americans use what are to them ambiguous distances, such as the four- to seven-foot social-consultative distance. They frequently complain that Americans are cold or aloof or "don't care." This was what an elderly Arab diplomat in an American hospital thought when the American nurses used "professional" distance. He had the feeling that he was being ignored, that they

might not take good care of him. Another Arab subject remarked, referring to American behavior, "What's the matter? Do I smell bad? Or are they afraid of me?"

19   Arabs who interact with Americans report experiencing a certain flatness traceable in part to a very different use of the eyes in private and in public as well as between friends and strangers. Even though it is rude for a guest to walk around the Arab home eyeing things, Arabs look at each other in ways which seem hostile or challenging to the American. One Arab informant said that he was in constant hot water with Americans because of the way he looked at them without the slightest intention of offending. In fact, he had on several occasions barely avoided fights with American men who apparently thought their masculinity was being challenged because of the way he was looking at them. As noted earlier, Arabs look each other in the eye when talking with an intensity that makes most Americans highly uncomfortable.

Involvement

20   As the reader must gather by now, Arabs are involved with each other on many different levels simultaneously. Privacy in a public place is foreign to them. Business transactions in the bazaar, for example, are not just between buyer and seller, but are participated in by everyone. Anyone who is standing around may join in. If a grownup sees a boy breaking a window, he must stop him even if he doesn't know him. Involvement and participation are expressed in other ways as well. If two men are fighting, the crowd must intervene. On the political level, *to fail to intervene* when trouble is brewing is to take sides, which is what our State Department always seems to be doing. Given the fact that few people in the world today are even remotely aware of the cultural mold that forms their thoughts, it is normal for Arabs to view *our* behavior as though it stemmed from *their* own hidden set of assumptions.

Feelings about Enclosed Spaces

21   In the course of my interviews with Arabs the term "tomb" kept cropping up in conjunction with enclosed space. In a word, Arabs don't mind being crowded by people but hate to be hemmed in by walls. They show a much greater overt sensitivity to architectural crowding than we do. Enclosed space must meet at least three requirements that I know of if it is to satisfy the Arabs: There must be plenty of unobstructed space in which to move around (possibly as much as a thousand square feet); very high ceilings—so high in fact that they do not normally impinge on the visual field; and, in addition, there must be an unobstructed view. It was spaces such as these in which the Americans referred to earlier felt so uncomfortable. One sees the Arab's need for a view expressed in many ways, even negatively, for to cut off a neighbor's view is one of the most effective ways of spiting him. In Beirut one can see what is known locally as the "spite house." It is nothing more than a thick, four-story wall, built at the end of a long fight between neighbors, on a narrow strip of land for the express purpose of denying a view of the Mediterranean to any house built on the land behind. According to one of my informants, there is also a house on a small plot of land

between Beirut and Damascus which is completely surrounded by a neighbor's wall built high enough to cut off the view from all windows!

Boundaries

22 Proxemic patterns tell us other things about Arab culture. For example, the whole concept of the boundary as an abstraction is almost impossible to pin down. In one sense, there are no boundaries. "Edges" of towns, yes, but permanent boundaries out in the country (hidden lines), no. In the course of my work with Arab subjects I had a difficult time translating our concept of a boundary into terms which could be equated with theirs. In order to clarify the distinctions between the two very different definitions, I thought it might be helpful to pinpoint acts which constituted trespass. To date, I have been unable to discover anything even remotely resembling our own legal concept of trespass.

23 Arab behavior in regard to their own real estate is apparently an extension of, and therefore consistent with, their approach to the body. My subjects simply failed to respond whenever trespass was mentioned. They didn't seem to understand what I meant by this term. This may be explained by the fact that they organize relationships with each other according to closed social systems rather than spatially. For thousands of years Moslems, Marinites, Druses, and Jews have lived in their own villages, each with strong kin affiliations. Their hierarchy of loyalties is: first to one's self, then to kinsman, townsman, or tribesman, co-religionist and/or countryman. Anyone not in these categories is a stranger. Strangers and enemies are very closely linked, if not synonymous, in Arab thought. Trespass in this context is a matter of who you are, rather than a piece of land or a space with a boundary that can be denied to anyone and everyone, friend and foe alike.

24 In summary, proxemic patterns differ. By examining them it is possible to reveal hidden cultural frames that determine the structure of a given people's perceptual world. Perceiving the world differently leads to differential definitions of what constitutes crowded living, different interpersonal relations, and a different approach to both local and international politics.

1. This excerpt is from Hall's book *The Hidden Dimension*. What is the hidden dimension, according to the author?

2. In paragraph 10, Hall explains that "differing concepts of the placement of the ego in relation to the body are not easily grasped." What does he mean by this statement? How is it relevant to the theme of his essay?

3. The title of this essay is "The Arab World." What does the term *world* mean within the context of the essay?

4. Define the following words: *proxemic* (paragraph 1), *paradox* (paragraph 2), *inviolate* (paragraph 3), *defer* (paragraph 6), *olfaction* (paragraph 14), and *peripherally* (paragraph 17). How does understanding these words affect your understanding of Hall's essay?

Rhetorical Analysis

5. How would you characterize Hall's voice, considering his style of language and method of analysis?

6. How does Hall develop his comparison and contrast of the American versus the Arab perception of manners and driving?

7. People often favor their own perspective of life over a foreign perspective. Is Hall's comparison value-free, or does he seem to prefer one cultural system to another? Explain by making reference to his tone.

8. Who is the implied audience for this essay? Explain your view.

9. Hall makes use of personal anecdotes in explaining his theme. What other forms of support does he offer? Cite at least two others and provide an example of each.

10. Writers often have various purposes in writing—for example, to entertain, to inform, to effect change, to advise, or to persuade. What is Hall's purpose or purposes in writing this essay? Explain your view.

Writing

11. Write an essay in which you explain the use and interpretation of personal space by observing students in social situations at your college or university.

12. Write a personal anecdote about a time in your life when cultural perception caused a conflict between yourself and another person.

13. **Writing an Argument**   In a well-written essay, take a position on the importance of personal space.

The Veil

Marjane Satrapi

Marjane Satrapi (b. 1969) was born and raised in Iran in a wealthy family. She attended Tehran's Lycée Francais until leaving to study illustration in Germany and Austria. She discovered *Maus*, Art Spiegelman's graphic novel of his father's Holocaust survival. Satrapi began drawing her life in Iran after Islamic clerics seized power. She has published two autobiographical graphic novels, *Persepolis 2* (2004) and *Persepolis* (1999), which "The Veil" is from.

Comprehension

1. Comment on your experience reading Satrapi's "The Veil." Did the graphic story catch and sustain your interest? Explain.

2. What idea is conveyed through this graphic story?

3. What social, cultural, or political values are central to "The Veil"? What perspective on these values does the author take? How do you know?

Rhetorical Analysis

4. What tone is achieved through the use of black-and-white and repetition?

5. What effects are achieved with the changing perspective of close-ups; for example, the man at the podium?

6. To what extent do you think Satrapi's combination of words and pictures is effective in conveying her idea? How would the story differ if told in words only?

Writing

7. Write an essay comparing "The Veil" with a current cartoon or graphic novel. How does each author use the graphic story genre to present an idea or message?

8. **Writing a Graphic Novel** Create your own graphic novel from a short story or poem that you like. How difficult was it for you to "tell" the same story in a different medium?

Chapter Assessment

Rhetorical Analysis

Read the passage below from "The Declaration of Independence" and answer the questions that follow.

We hold these truths to be self-evident, that all men are created equal, that they are endowed by their Creator with certain unalienable Rights, that among these are Life, Liberty and the pursuit of Happiness.—That to secure these rights, Governments are instituted among Men, deriving their just powers from the consent of the governed.—That whenever any Form of Government becomes destructive of these ends, it is the Right of the People to alter or to abolish it, and to institute new Government, laying its foundation on such principles and organizing its powers in such form, as to them shall seem most likely to effect their Safety and Happiness. Prudence, indeed, will dictate that Governments long established should not be changed for light and transient causes; and accordingly all experience hath shewn that mankind are more disposed to suffer, while evils are sufferable, than to right themselves by abolishing the forms to which they are accustomed. But when a long train of abuses and usurpations, pursuing invariably the same Object evinces a design to reduce them under absolute Despotism, it is their right, it is their duty, to throw off such Government, and to provide new Guards for their future security.—Such has been the patient sufferance of these Colonies; and such is now the necessity which constrains them to alter their former Systems of Government. The history of the present King of Great Britain is a history of repeated injuries and usurpations, all having in direct object the establishment of an absolute Tyranny over these States. To prove this, let Facts be submitted to a candid world.

—From www.archives.gov/founding-docs/declaration-transcript

1. Consider the following sentence: "But when a long train of abuses and usurpations, pursuing invariably the same Object evinces a design to reduce them under absolute Despotism, it is their right, it is their duty, to throw off such Government, and to provide new Guards for their future security." Which rhetorical strategy does the writer employ?
   - A. Comparison of despotism to the abuses and usurpations of the government being established
   - B. Parallel prepositional phrases that highlight specific actions the new government must be prepared to take
   - C. Repetition by phrase to emphasize the importance of creating a more suitable government
   - D. Juxtaposition of "the same Object" to "absolute Despotism" to establish the writer's authority
   - E. Appeals to the audience's sense of duty and obligation in helping the colonists in their endeavor

Chapter Assessment

2. The main effect of the speaker's use of passive voice in the opening sentence of the passage is to
   A. Maintain the audience's focus on the rights and governing responsibilities of man for himself.
   B. Demonstrate the speaker's disbelief in God.
   C. Create a sentence that employs parallel structure.
   D. Define the nature of that which is "self-evident."
   E. Establish equality among the ideals of Life, Liberty, and the Pursuit of Happiness.

Read the passage below from the speech "I Have a Dream" and answer the questions that follow.

I have a dream that one day every valley shall be exalted, every hill and mountain shall be made low, the rough places shall be made plain, and the crooked places shall be made straight and the glory of the Lord will be revealed and all flesh shall see it together.

This is our hope. This is the faith that I go back to the South with.

—Reprinted by arrangement with The Heirs to the Estate of Martin Luther King Jr., c/o Writers House as agent for the Proprietor, New York, NY. Copyright 1963 Dr. Martin Luther King Jr.; copyright renewed 1991 Coretta Scott King.

3. In the first paragraph of the excerpt above, King uses vivid imagery primarily to
   A. Evoke a tone of optimism and idealism.
   B. Remind his audience that his dream can be realized in every location throughout the country.
   C. Allude to the Bible.
   D. Provide a pathway for the audience to follow to achieve his goals.
   E. Enable the audience to "see" his dream.

4. In the second brief paragraph, King uses repetition of the sentence opening "This is" primarily to
   A. Announce the importance of hope and faith to King's work.
   B. Establish and then expand upon a claim and that claim's connection both to King's next action and to his dream.
   C. Remind his audience of the purity of their mission and purpose.
   D. Clarify his position to his audience.
   E. Exclude non-believers from participating in his work.

Read the passage below from "The Myth of the Latin Woman: I Just Met a Girl Named Maria" and answer the questions that follow.

It is custom, however, not chromosomes, that leads us to choose scarlet over pale pink. As young girls it was our mothers who influenced our decisions about clothes and colors—mothers who had grown up on a tropical island where the natural environment was a riot of primary colors, where showing your skin was one way to keep cool as well as to look sexy. Most important of all, on the island, women perhaps felt freer to dress and move more provocatively since, in most cases, they were protected by the traditions, mores, and laws of a Spanish/Catholic system of morality and machismo whose main rule was: *You may look at my sister, but if you touch her I will kill you*. The extended family and church structure could provide a young woman with a circle of safety in her small pueblo on the island; if a man "wronged" a girl, everyone would close in to save her family honor.

5. What is the effect of including the italicized, second-person sentence?
  A. It underscores the strong familial ties that pervade the rest of the essay.
  B. It highlights the machismo evident in Latin culture.
  C. It breaks the narrative structure and includes the reader in the essay.
  D. It exemplifies the contrast between family loyalty and the violence of society.
  E. It provides a point of comparison for the color imagery in the first part of the paragraph.

6. What essential contrast does the author develop between the earlier culture of the islands and the culture of present-day Latina teenage girls?
  A. Island girls were allowed to dress provocatively while modern girls should not.
  B. Island girls were protected by their families and by a series of enculturated traditions, whereas modern girls don't necessarily have the same protections.
  C. Island girls allowed their mothers to choose their clothing for them; modern girls do not.
  D. Island girls preferred different colors than modern girls choose.
  E. Island girls convinced their mothers that they dressed "sexy" only to stay cool.

Chapter Assessment

Read the passage below from "A World Not Neatly Divided" and answer the questions that follow.

The befuddling influence of a singular classification also traps those who dispute the thesis of a clash: To talk about "the Islamic world" or "the Western world" is already to adopt an impoverished vision of humanity as unalterably divided. In fact, civilizations are hard to partition in this way, given the diversities within each society as well as the linkages among different countries and cultures. For example, describing India as a "Hindu civilization" misses the fact that India has more Muslims than any other country except Indonesia and possibly Pakistan. It is futile to try to understand Indian art, literature, music, food, or politics without seeing the extensive interactions across barriers of religious communities. These include Hindus and Muslims, Buddhists, Jains, Sikhs, Parsees, Christians (who have been in India since at least the fourth century, well before England's conversion to Christianity), Jews (present since the fall of Jerusalem), and even atheists and agnostics. Sanskrit has a larger atheistic literature than exists in any other classical language. Speaking of India as a Hindu civilization may be comforting to the Hindu fundamentalist, but it is an odd reading of India.

7. The phrase "singular classification" can best be read as referring to
   A. An impossibility because of the dichotomy expressed by the terms "Islamic world" and "Western world."
   B. A befuddling influence.
   C. The key term of the argument's central thesis.
   D. The limitation of defining a cultural phenomenon too narrowly.
   E. The simplest way to define a civilization.

8. Based on the final sentence of the paragraph, "Speaking of India as a Hindu civilization may be comforting to the Hindu fundamentalist, but it is an odd reading of India," the audience can infer that the author wishes
   A. Hindu fundamentalists would broaden their perspectives of Indian culture.
   B. India would embrace Hindu both culturally and religiously.
   C. Those from outside India would recognize the diversity of the Indian religious and cultural landscape.
   D. Authors would stop writing books about Hindu fundamentalism.
   E. More people would embrace Hindu fundamentalism.

Read the passage below from "The Arab World" and answer the questions.

One mistaken American notion is that Arabs conduct all conversations at close distances. This is not the case at all. On social occasions, they may sit on opposite sides of the room and talk across the room to each other. They are, however, apt to take offense when Americans use what are to them ambiguous distances, such as the four- to seven-foot social-consultative distance. They frequently complain that Americans are cold or aloof or "don't care." This was what an elderly Arab diplomat in an American hospital thought when the American nurses used "professional" distance. He had the feeling that he was being ignored, that they might not take good care of him. Another Arab subject remarked, referring to American behavior, "What's the matter? Do I smell bad? Or are they afraid of me?"

9. Embedding quoted material into the paragraph has which effect?
    A. Suggests the writer has interviewed subjects about their experiences
    B. Provides allusions to various experts on the topic being discussed
    C. Acknowledges that the information may be made up and cannot be trusted
    D. Establishes the ethos of the speaker as a trustworthy expert on the subject
    E. Demonstrates phrases individuals use when faced with these situations

10. The phrase "ambiguous distances" most clearly suggests which of the following?
    A. Many people discuss the proper distances at which to stand.
    B. There are cultural distinctions in social conversational space.
    C. The proper distance is always up to interpretation by experts.
    D. Ambiguity is responsible for the "don't care" attitude of non-Americans.
    E. There is a guide to proper social distances diplomats should consult.

Connections for Critical Thinking

1. Compare the Declaration of Independence with King's speech in terms of language, style, and content.

2. Write an essay exploring the topic of culture and civilization in the essays by Cofer, Hall, and Sen.

3. In an essay, describe the current position of women in our culture. Refer to any three essays in this chapter to support your main observations.

4. How does one's experience of being an outsider or stranger to a culture affect one's understanding of that culture?

5. Select the three essays you find the most compelling or the least appealing in this chapter. Discuss why you selected them.

Women's Rights

In 1920, the Nineteenth Amendment to the U.S. Constitution was ratified, giving women the right to vote in all elections. The Civil Rights Act of 1964 banned job discrimination on the basis of gender. In 1972, the Equal Employment Opportunity Act strengthened earlier laws on discrimination in hiring and firing practices, promotion, pay, and other employment actions. During the same year, Congress passed a comprehensive education law. Yet with all of these legal safeguards, some contend that the struggle for women's rights continues. Critically read and analyze the source text and images, making note of the year each appeared in print, and then answer the questions that follow.

▼ SOURCE A

A Vindication of the Rights of Woman by Mary Wollstonecraft, 1792. The following is an excerpt from British writer Mary Wollstonecraft, who drew on the political discourse of John Locke and other Enlightenment thinkers.

—From *A Vindication of the Rights of Woman: With Strictures on Political and Moral Subjects* by Mary Wollstonecraft. The Third Edition. London: J. Johnson, St. Paul's Church Yard, 1796.

To render mankind more virtuous, and happier of course, both sexes must act from the same principle; but how can that be expected when only one is allowed to see the reasonableness of it? To render also the social compact truly equitable, and in order to spread those enlightening principles, which alone can meliorate the fate of man, women must be allowed to found their virtue on knowledge, which is scarcely possible unless they be educated by the same pursuits as men. For they are now made so inferiour by ignorance and low desires, as not to deserve to be ranked with them; or, by the serpentine wrigglings of cunning they mount the tree of knowledge and only acquire sufficient to lead men astray.

▼ SOURCE B

"Woman's Wrongs" by J. Elizabeth Jones, 1850. The excerpt below is from an address Jones gave at a women's rights convention held in Salem, Ohio, in 1850. This meeting was the second major women's rights convention in the United States, after the one held in Seneca Falls, New York, in 1848.

—From *The Salem, Ohio 1850 Women's Rights Convention Proceedings,* Compiled and Edited by Robert W. Audretsch, 1976

There is not, perhaps, in the wide field of reform, any one subject so difficult to discuss as that of Woman's Rights. I use the term "Woman's Rights" because it is a technical phrase. I like not the expression. It is not Woman's *Rights* of which I design to speak, but of Woman's *Wrongs*. I shall claim nothing for ourselves because of our sex—I shall demand the recognition of no rights on the ground of our womanhood. In the contest which is now being waged in behalf of the enslaved colored man in this land, I have yet to hear the first word in favor of his rights as a colored man; the great point which is sought to be established is this, that the colored man is a human being, and as such, entitled to the free exercise of all the rights which belong to humanity. And we should demand *our* recognition as equal members of the human family. . . .

▼ SOURCE C

POLITICAL CARTOON: "That's Beautiful Tom"

Mike Peters (c) Distributed by King Features Syndicate, Inc.

▼ SOURCE D

"The Fraud of the Equal Rights Amendment" by Phyllis Schlafly. The following passage is excerpted from an article by conservative commentator Phyllis Schlafly.

Phyllis Schlafly Report Feb. 1972.

The claim that American women are downtrodden and unfairly treated is the fraud of the century. The truth is that American women never had it so good. Why should we lower ourselves to "equal rights" when we already have the status of special privilege?

This [Equal Rights] Amendment will absolutely and positively make women subject to the draft. Why any woman would support such a ridiculous and un-American proposal as this is beyond comprehension. Why any Congressman who had any regard for his wife, sister, or daughter would support such a proposition is just as hard to understand. Foxholes are bad enough for men, but they certainly are not the place for women—and we should reject any proposal which would put them there in the name of "equal rights."

Another bad effect of the Equal Rights Amendment is that it will abolish a woman's right to child support and alimony. . . .

Under present American laws, the man is always required to support his wife and each child he caused to be brought into the world. Why should women abandon these good laws. . . ?

▼ SOURCE E

Phillips* v. *Martin Marietta Corp. (U.S. Supreme Court, 1971) Mrs. Ida Phillips alleged that she had been denied employment because of her sex—that Martin Marietta Corp.'s hiring policy was different for women and men with preschool-age children. The case began in U.S. District Court, which ruled in favor of Martin Marietta Corp. The Fifth Circuit Appeals Court upheld the District Court's ruling. Phillips then took the case to the Supreme Court.

—U.S. Supreme Court, Phillips v. Martin Marietta Corp., 400 U.S. 542 (1971), http://supreme.justia.com/cases/federal/us/400/542/case.html

SYLLABUS: Under Title VII of the Civil Rights Act of 1964, an employer may not, in the absence of business necessity, refuse to hire women with pre-school-age children while hiring men with such children.

JUSTICE MARSHALL, concurring: "Certainly, an employer can require that all of his employees, both men and women, meet minimum performance standards, and he can try to insure compliance by requiring parents, both mothers and fathers, to provide for the care of their children so that job performance is not interfered with. But the [earlier] Court suggests that it would not require such uniform standards. I fear that, in this case, where the issue is not squarely before us, the Court has fallen into the trap of assuming that the [Civil Rights] Act permits ancient canards about the proper role of women to be a basis for discrimination. Congress, however, sought just the opposite result. By adding the prohibition against job discrimination based on sex to the 1964 Civil Rights Act, Congress intended to prevent employers from refusing "to hire an individual based on stereotyped characterizations of the sexes."

Women's Earnings as a Percentage of Men's Earnings by Industry.

From Bureau of Labor Statistics, "Women's Earnings and Employment by Industry, 2009," TED: The Editor's Desk (February 16, 2011).

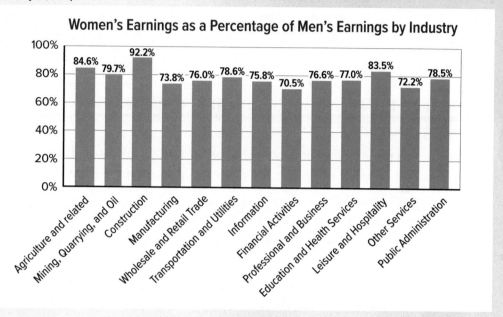

Women's Earnings as a Percentage of Men's Earnings by Industry

Applying Your Synthesis Skills

Comprehension

1. What central idea arises from each of these sources?

Rhetorical Analysis

2. Compare Sources A and B. Which source is written in the first person? Which discusses slavery? Which makes a reference to the Garden of Eden? Which seems more dramatic? Why?

3. Explain the visual and textual rhetoric in Source C.

4. What words and phrases does Schlafly use in Source D to support her argument that equal rights are wrong? What is her tone? Is her argument convincing? Defend your answer.

5. Analyze Justice Marshall's rhetoric in the Supreme Court's decision in Source E. How does his diction and syntax change from the beginning of the paragraph to the end? What is the effect or purpose of this change?

Writing an Argument

6. Why is the issue of women's rights an important issue today? Support your response using these sources as well as your own arguments.

CHAPTER 7

Business and Economics: How Do We Earn Our Keep?

As you read the essays in this chapter, consider the following questions:

- What are the significant forms of support the author uses in viewing the world of work: observation, statistics, personal experience, history, and so on?
- What assumptions does the author make about the value of work?
- Does the author discuss work in general or focus on one particular aspect of work?
- How does the writer define *work*? In what ways, if any, does she or he expand on the simple definition of work as "paid employment"?
- What issues of race, class, and gender does the author raise?
- What is the relationship of work to the changing social, political, and economic systems depicted in the author's essay?
- What tone does the writer take in his or her presentation of the work experience?
- What psychological insights does the author offer into the culture of work?
- What does the writer's style reveal about her or his attitude toward work?

Work is central to the human experience; in fact, it is work and its economic and social outcomes that provide us with the keys to an understanding of culture and civilization. Work tells us much about scarcity and abundance, poverty and affluence, the haves and have-nots in any society, as well as a nation's economic imperatives. Whether it is the rise and fall of cities, the conduct of business and corporations, or the economic policies of government, we see in the culture of work an attempt to impose order on nature. Work is our handprint on the world.

The work we perform and the careers we pursue also define us in very personal ways. "I'm a professor at Harvard" or "I work for Google" serve as identity badges. (Robert Reich, a contributor to this chapter, once worked at Harvard.) For what we do explains, at least in part, what and who we are. The very act of looking for work illuminates one's status in society, one's background, one's aspirations. Jonathan Swift, in his classic essay "A Modest Proposal," written in 1729, demonstrates how labor reveals economic and political configurations of power. (See Chapter 11.) Over 250 years later, Reich tells us the same thing in his analysis of the changing nature of work and the way these changes create an even broader gap between the rich and the poor.

Work is not merely an important human activity but an essential one for social and psychological health. You might like your work, or you might loathe it; be employed or unemployed; enjoy the reputation of a workaholic or a person who lives for leisure time; view work as a curse, as a duty, or as a joy. Regardless, it is work that occupies a central position in your relationship to society. In fact, Sigmund Freud spoke of work as the basis of one's social reality.

Whatever your perspective on work is, it is important to understand the multiple dimensions of work. In both traditional and modern societies, work prepares us for economic and social roles. It affects families, school curricula, and public policy. Ultimately, as many authors here suggest, it determines our self-esteem. Through work we come to terms with ourselves and our environment. The nature and purpose of the work we do provide us with a powerful measure of our worth.

In the era known as the Machine Age, 1918–1941, many artists, industrial designers, and architects in the United States and Europe evoked the mechanisms and images of industry in their works. During this time, the Mexican painter Diego Rivera (1886–1957) created a mural for the Detroit Institute of Arts (1932–1933), a portion of which is shown here.

Computers and robotics are used to control and run much of modern assembly lines, as shown in this photo.

Will Workers Be Completely Displaced by Machines?

Using a Critical Perspective   Diego Rivera's mural and the photograph of an automobile assembly line present industrial scenes that reveal the impact of technology on workers. What details are emphasized in each illustration? How are these two images similar and dissimilar? What, for example, is the relation of human beings to the machines that are the centerpiece of each image? Are the artist and photographer objective or subjective in the presentation of each scene? Explain.

Analyzing Visuals and Their Rhetoric

1. Compare and contrast the tone of each visual.

2. How do the perspective and visual elements of each image reveal movement?

3. What does the lack of any images of people in the assembly line photo achieve?

4. Give descriptive titles for each of the images and explain why you decided on those titles.

Does Equal Opportunity Exist?

Virginia Woolf's "Professions for Women" is ironic from the start as she readily admits she can speak expertly of only one profession, her own, which is writing. But her message is clear regarding the effect of living in a male-dominated society. Simply put, it is difficult to break the shackles of conditioning that one acquires from being told over and over again by one's culture that gender is destiny, regardless of what one aspires to. The author—through personal experience—demonstrates how this discrimination has a profound effect on the ability to see with one's own eyes and to think with one's own mind. Henry Louis Gates, Jr., presents an interesting variation on this theme. Although the outcome is the same, the premise is reversed. He demonstrates how correlating supposedly positive attributes to a group—that is, superior athletic performance and race—results in the same deadening of the sense of personal ambition and a limiting of the scope of what one can aspire to. The thoughtful reader should be able to learn valuable lessons from comparing and contrasting these essays—one of which is that misguided perception all too often can be a self-fulfilling prophecy.

Professions for Women

Virginia Woolf

Virginia Woolf (1882–1941), novelist and essayist, was the daughter of Sir Leslie Stephen, a famous critic and writer on economics. An experimental novelist, Woolf attempted to portray consciousness through a poetic, symbolic, and concrete style. Her novels include *Jacob's Room* (1922), *Mrs. Dalloway* (1925), *To the Lighthouse* (1927), and *The Waves* (1931). She was also a perceptive reader and critic; her criticism appears in *The Common Reader* (1925) and *The Second Common Reader* (1933). In the following essay, which was delivered originally as a speech to the Women's Service League in 1931, Woolf argues that women must overcome an "angel" in order to succeed in professional careers.

1   When your secretary invited me to come here, she told me that your Society is concerned with the employment of women and she suggested that I might tell you something about my own professional experiences. It is true I am a woman; it is true I am employed; but what professional experiences have I had? It is difficult to say. My profession is literature; and in that profession there are fewer experiences for women than in any other, with the exception of the stage—fewer, I mean, that are peculiar to women. For the road was cut many years ago—by Fanny Burney, by Aphra Behn, by Harriet Martineau, by Jane Austen, by George Eliot—many famous women, and many more unknown and forgotten, have been before me, making the path smooth, and regulating my

steps. Thus, when I came to write, there were very few material obstacles in my way. Writing was a reputable and harmless occupation. The family peace was not broken by the scratching of a pen. No demand was made upon the family purse. For ten and sixpence one can buy paper enough to write all the plays of Shakespeare—if one has a mind that way. Pianos and models, Paris, Vienna and Berlin, masters and mistresses, are not needed by a writer. The cheapness of writing paper is, of course, the reason why women have succeeded as writers before they have succeeded in the other professions.

2   But to tell you my story—it is a simple one. You have only got to figure to yourselves a girl in a bedroom with a pen in her hand. She had only to move that pen from left to right—from ten o'clock to one. Then it occurred to her to do what is simple and cheap enough after all—to slip a few of those pages into an envelope, fix a penny stamp in the corner, and drop the envelope into the red box at the corner. It was thus that I became a journalist; and my effort was rewarded on the first day of the following month—a very glorious day it was for me—by a letter from an editor containing a cheque for one pound ten shillings and sixpence. But to show you how little I deserve to be called a professional woman, how little I know of the struggles and difficulties of such lives, I have to admit that instead of spending that sum upon bread and butter, rent, shoes and stockings, or butcher's bills, I went out and bought a cat—a beautiful cat, a Persian cat, which very soon involved me in bitter disputes with my neighbours.

3   What could be easier than to write articles and to buy Persian cats with the profits? But wait a moment. Articles have to be about something. Mine, I seem to remember, was about a novel by a famous man. And while I was writing this review, I discovered that if I were going to review books I should need to do battle with a certain phantom. And the phantom was a woman, and when I came to know her better I called her after the heroine of a famous poem, The Angel in the House. It was she who used to come between me and my paper when I was writing reviews. It was she who bothered me and wasted my time and so tormented me that at last I killed her. You who come of a younger and happier generation may not have heard of her—you may not know what I mean by the Angel in the House. I will describe her as shortly as I can. She was intensely sympathetic. She was immensely charming. She was utterly unselfish. She excelled in the difficult arts of family life. She sacrificed herself daily. If there was chicken, she took the leg; if there was a draught she sat in it—in short she was so constituted that she never had a mind or a wish of her own, but preferred to sympathize always with the minds and wishes of others. Above all—I need not say it—she was pure. Her purity was supposed to be her chief beauty—her blushes, her great grace. In those days—the last of Queen Victoria—every house had its Angel. And when I came to write I encountered her with the very first words. The shadow of her wings fell on my page; I heard the rustling of her skirts in the room. Directly, that is to say, I took my pen in

my hand to review that novel by a famous man, she slipped behind me and whispered: "My dear, you are a young woman. You are writing about a book that has been written by a man. Be sympathetic; be tender; flatter; deceive; use all the arts and wiles of our sex. Never let anybody guess that you have a mind of your own. Above all, be pure." And she made as if to guide my pen. I now record the one act for which I take some credit to myself, though the credit rightly belongs to some excellent ancestors of mine who left me a certain sum of money—shall we say five hundred pounds a year?—so that it was not necessary for me to depend solely on charm for my living. I turned upon her and caught her by the throat. I did my best to kill her. My excuse, if I were to be had up in a court of law, would be that I acted in self-defence. Had I not killed her she would have killed me. She would have plucked the heart out of my writing. For, as I found, directly I put pen to paper, you cannot review even a novel without having a mind of your own, without expressing what you think to be the truth about human relations, morality, sex. And all these questions, according to the Angel of the House, cannot be dealt with freely and openly by women; they must charm, they must conciliate, they must—to put it bluntly— tell lies if they are to succeed. Thus, whenever I felt the shadow of her wing or the radiance of her halo upon my page, I took up the inkpot and flung it at her. She died hard. Her fictitious nature was of great assistance to her. It is far harder to kill a phantom than a reality. She was always creeping back when I thought I had despatched her. Though I flatter myself that I killed her in the end, the struggle was severe; it took much time that had better have been spent upon learning Greek grammar; or in roaming the world in search of adventures. But it was a real experience; it was an experience that was bound to befall all women writers at that time. Killing the Angel in the House was part of the occupation of a woman writer.

4   But to continue my story. The Angel was dead; what then remained? You may say that what remained was a simple and common object—a young woman in a bedroom with an inkpot. In other words, now that she had rid herself of falsehood, that young woman had only to be herself. Ah, but what is "herself"? I mean, what is a woman? I assure you, I do not know. I do not believe that you know. I do not believe that anybody can know until she has expressed herself in all the arts and professions open to human skill. That indeed is one of the reasons why I have come here out of respect for you, who are in process of showing us by your experiments what a woman is, who are in process of providing us, by your failures and successes, with that extremely important piece of information.

5   But to continue the story of my professional experiences. I made one pound ten and six by my first review; and I bought a Persian cat with the proceeds. Then I grew ambitious. A Persian cat is all very well, I said; but a Persian cat is not enough. I must have a motor car. And it was thus that I became a novelist— for it is a very strange thing that people will give you a motor car if you will tell

them a story. It is a still stranger thing that there is nothing so delightful in the world as telling stories. It is far pleasanter than writing reviews of famous novels. And yet, if I am to obey your secretary and tell you my professional experiences as a novelist, I must tell you about a very strange experience that befell me as a novelist. And to understand it you must try first to imagine a novelist's state of mind. I hope I am not giving away professional secrets if I say that a novelist's chief desire is to be as unconscious as possible. He has to induce in himself a state of perpetual lethargy. He wants life to proceed with the utmost quiet and regularity. He wants to see the same faces, to read the same books, to do the same things day after day, month after month, while he is writing, so that nothing may break the illusion in which he is living—so that nothing may disturb or disquiet the mysterious nosings about, feelings round, darts, dashes and sudden discoveries of that very shy and illusive spirit, the imagination. I suspect that this state is the same both for men and women. Be that as it may, I want you to imagine me writing a novel in a state of trance. I want you to figure to yourselves a girl sitting with a pen in her hand, which for minutes, and indeed for hours, she never dips into the inkpot. The image that comes to my mind when I think of this girl is the image of a fisherman lying sunk in dreams on the verge of a deep lake with a rod held out over the water. She was letting her imagination sweep unchecked round every rock and cranny of the world that lies submerged in the depths of our unconscious being. Now came the experience, the experience that I believe to be far commoner with women writers than with men. The line raced through the girl's fingers. Her imagination had rushed away. It had sought the pools, the depths, the dark places where the largest fish slumber. And then there was a smash. There was an explosion. There was foam and confusion. The imagination had dashed itself against something hard. The girl was roused from her dream. She was indeed in a state of the most acute and difficult distress. To speak without figure she had thought of something, something about the body, about the passions which it was unfitting for her as a woman to say. Men, her reason told her, would be shocked. The consciousness of—what men will say of a woman who speaks the truth about her passions had roused her from her artist's state of unconsciousness. She could write no more. The trance was over. Her imagination could work no longer. This I believe to be a very common experience with women writers—they are impeded by the extreme conventionality of the other sex. For though men sensibly allow themselves great freedom in these respects, I doubt that they realize or can control the extreme severity with which they condemn such freedom in women.

6   These then were two very genuine experiences of my own. These were two of the adventures of my professional life. The first—killing the Angel in the House—I think I solved. She died. But the second, telling the truth about my own experiences as a body, I do not think I solved. I doubt that any woman has

solved it yet. The obstacles against her are still immensely powerful—and yet they are very difficult to define. Outwardly, what is simpler than to write books? Outwardly, what obstacles are there for a woman rather than for a man? Inwardly, I think, the case is very different; she has still many ghosts to fight, many prejudices to overcome. Indeed it will be a long time still, I think, before a woman can sit down to write a book without finding a phantom to be slain, a rock to be dashed against. And if this is so in literature, the freest of all professions for women, how is it in the new professions which you are now for the first time entering?

7   Those are the questions that I should like, had I time, to ask you. And indeed, if I have laid stress upon these professional experiences of mine, it is because I believe that they are, though in different forms, yours also. Even when the path is nominally open—when there is nothing to prevent a woman from being a doctor, a lawyer, a civil servant—there are many phantoms and obstacles, as I believe, looming in her way. To discuss and define them is I think of great value and importance; for thus only can the labour be shared, the difficulties be solved. But besides this, it is necessary also to discuss the ends and the aims for which we are fighting, for which we are doing battle with these formidable obstacles. Those aims cannot be taken for granted; they must be perpetually questioned and examined. The whole position, as I see it—here in this hall surrounded by women practising for the first time in history I know not how many different professions—is one of extraordinary interest and importance. You have won rooms of your own in the house hitherto exclusively owned by men. You are able, though not without great labour and effort, to pay the rent. You are earning your five hundred pounds a year. But this freedom is only a beginning—the room is your own, but it is still bare. It has to be furnished; it has to be decorated; it has to be shared. How are you going to furnish it, how are you going to decorate it? With whom are you going to share it, and upon what terms? These, I think are questions of the utmost importance and interest. For the first time in history you are able to ask them; for the first time you are able to decide for yourselves what the answers should be. Willingly would I stay and discuss those questions and answers—but not to-night. My time is up; and I must cease.

Comprehension

1. This essay was presented originally as a speech. What internal evidence indicates that it was intended as a talk?

2. Who or what is the "angel" that Woolf describes in this essay? Why must she kill it? What other obstacles does a professional woman encounter?

3. Paraphrase the last two paragraphs of this essay. What is the essence of Woolf's argument?

Rhetorical Analysis

4. There is a significant amount of figurative language in the essay. Locate and explain examples. What does the figurative language contribute to the tone of the essay?

5. How do we know that Woolf is addressing an audience of women? Why does she pose so many questions, and what does this strategy contribute to the rapport she wants to establish? Explain the effect of the last two sentences.

6. How does Woolf use analogy to structure part of her argument?

7. Why does Woolf rely on personal narration? How does it affect the logic of her argument?

8. Evaluate Woolf's use of contrast to advance her argument.

9. Where does Woolf place her main proposition? How emphatic is it, and why?

Writing

10. How effectively does Woolf use her own example as a professional writer to advance a broader proposition concerning all women entering professional life? Answer this question in a brief essay.

11. Write an essay about the problems and obstacles you anticipate when you enter your chosen career.

12. **Writing an Argument**   Argue for or against the proposition that Woolf's essay has little relevance for women planning careers today.

CONTEMPORARY ▼

Delusions of Grandeur

Henry Louis Gates, Jr.

Henry Louis Gates, Jr. (b. 1950) is an educator, writer, and editor. He was born in West Virginia and educated at Yale and at Clare College in Cambridge. Gates has had a varied career, working as a general anesthetist in Tanzania and as a staff correspondent for *Time* magazine in London. His essays have appeared in such diverse publications as *Black American Literature Forum, Yale Review, New York Times Book Review,* and *Sports Illustrated*. He is also the author of *Figures in Black: Words, Signs and the Racial Self* (1987) and *The Signifying Monkey: A Theory of Afro-American Literary Criticism* (1988) and is the editor, with Nellie Y. McKey, of *The Norton Anthology of African American Literature* (1996), and, with Hollis Robbins, of *The Annotated Uncle Tom's Cabin* (2007). In this article from *Sports Illustrated,* Gates turns his attention to the limited career choices presented as viable to African American youth and to public misconceptions about blacks in sports.

Young blacks must be taught that sports are not the only avenues of opportunity.

1   Standing at the Bar of an All-Black VFW post in my hometown of Piedmont, W.Va., I offered five dollars to anyone who could tell me how many African-American professional athletes were at work today. There are 35 million African-Americans, I said.

2   "Ten million!" yelled one intrepid soul, too far into his cups.

3   "No way...more like 500,000," said another.

4   "You mean all professional sports," someone interjected, "including golf and tennis, but not counting the brothers from Puerto Rico?" Everyone laughed.

5   "Fifty thousand, minimum," was another guess.

6   Here are the facts:
There are 1,200 black professional athletes in the U.S.
There are 12 times more black lawyers than black athletes.
There are 2½ times more black dentists than black athletes.
There are 15 times more black doctors than black athletes.

7   Nobody in my local VFW believed these statistics; in fact, few people would believe them if they weren't reading them in the pages of SPORTS ILLUSTRATED. In spite of these statistics, too many African-American youngsters still believe that they have a much better chance of becoming another Magic Johnson or Michael Jordan than they do of matching the achievements of Baltimore Mayor Kurt Schmoke or neurosurgeon Dr. Benjamin Carson, both of whom, like Johnson and Jordan, are black.

8   In reality, an African-American youngster has about as much chance of becoming a professional athlete as he or she does of winning the lottery. The tragedy for our people, however, is that few of us accept that truth.

9   Let me confess that I love sports. Like most black people of my generation—I'm 40—I was raised to revere the great black athletic heroes, and I never tired of listening to the stories of triumph and defeat that, for blacks, amount to a collective epic much like those of the ancient Greeks: Joe Louis's demolition of Max Schmeling; Satchel Paige's dazzling repertoire of pitches; Jesse Owens's in-your-face performance in Hitler's 1936 Olympics; Willie Mays's over-the-shoulder basket catch; Jackie Robinson's quiet strength when assaulted by racist taunts; and a thousand other grand tales.

10   Nevertheless, the blind pursuit of attainment in sports is having a devastating effect on our people. Imbued with a belief that our principal avenue to fame and profit is through sport, and seduced by a win-at-any-cost system that corrupts even elementary school students, far too many black kids treat basketball courts and football fields as if they were classrooms in an alternative school system. "O.K., I flunked English," a young athlete will say. "But I got an A plus in slam-dunking."

11   The failure of our public schools to educate athletes is part and parcel of the schools' failure to educate almost everyone. A recent survey of the Philadelphia school system, for example, stated that "more than half of all students in the third, fifth and eighth grades cannot perform minimum math and language tasks." One in four middle school students in that city fails to pass to the next grade each year. It is a sad truth that such statistics are repeated in cities throughout the nation. Young athletes—particularly young black athletes—are especially ill-served. Many of them are functionally illiterate, yet they are passed along from year to year for the greater glory of good old Hometown High. We should not be surprised to learn, then, that only 26.6% of black athletes at the collegiate level earn their degrees. For every successful educated black professional athlete, there are thousands of dead and wounded. Yet young blacks continue to aspire to careers as athletes, and it's no wonder why; when the University of North Carolina recently commissioned a sculptor to create archetypes of its student body, guess which ethnic group was selected to represent athletes?

12   Those relatively few black athletes who do make it in the professional ranks must be prevailed upon to play a significant role in the education of all of our young people, athlete and nonathlete alike. While some have done so, many others have shirked their social obligations: to earmark small percentages of their incomes for the United Negro College Fund; to appear on television for educational purposes rather than merely to sell sneakers; to let children know the message that becoming a lawyer, a teacher or a doctor does more good for our people than winning the Super Bowl; and to form productive liaisons with educators to help forge solutions to the many ills that beset the black community. These are merely a few modest proposals.

13   A similar burden falls upon successful blacks in all walks of life. Each of us must strive to make our young people understand the realities. Tell them to cheer Bo Jackson but to emulate novelist Toni Morrison or businessman Reginald Lewis or historian John Hope Franklin or Spelman College president Johnetta Cole—the list is long.

14   Of course, society as a whole bears responsibility as well. Until colleges stop using young blacks as cannon fodder in the big-business wars of so-called nonprofessional sports, until training a young black's mind becomes as important as training his or her body, we will continue to perpetuate a system akin to that of the Roman gladiators, sacrificing a class of people for the entertainment of the mob.

Comprehension

1. What does Gates suggest is the general assumption made about African Americans in sports?

2. Why and how do American schools continue to perpetuate the myth that Gates is writing about?

3. According to Gates, what should successful African American athletes do to help guide the career choices of young African Americans?

Rhetorical Analysis

4. What is Gates's thesis? Where does it appear?

5. How does the introductory paragraph work to set up the writer's focus?

6. State Gates's purpose in using statistics in his essay.

7. What is the tone of Gates's essay? Cite specific sections where this tone seems strongest.

8. Examine the accumulation of facts in paragraph 11. How does this technique underscore Gates's point?

9. Explain Gates's allusion to Roman gladiators in his conclusion. How does it aid in emphasizing his main point?

Writing

10. Write a brief essay in which you analyze your personal reaction to Gates's statistics. Were you surprised by them? What assumptions did you have about the number of African American professional athletes? Why do you think most Americans share these assumptions?

11. Write a biographical research paper on the life and career of an African American athlete or on one of the famous African Americans mentioned in this essay.

12. **Writing an Argument**   Write an essay in which you argue for or against the proposition that sports and entertainment should (or should not) be a career choice for anyone.

Synthesizing the Classic + Contemporary Essays

1. Examine the argumentative styles of Woolf and Gates. What are their main propositions? Their minor propositions? What evidence do they provide?

2. Woolf first presented her paper as a speech before an audience of women. Gates wrote his essay as an opinion piece for *Sports Illustrated.* Write a comparative audience analysis of the two selections. Analyze the purpose, tone, style, and any other relevant aspects of these essays.

3. Gates's essay was written in 1991. Argue for or against the proposition that there has been progress in relation to barriers to employment for women, and whether the barriers are similar for African American men. Refer to the essays by Woolf and Gates to support your position.

The Death of Horatio Alger

Paul Krugman

Paul Krugman (b. 1953), who teaches at Princeton University, received the Nobel Prize for Economics in 2008 for his analysis of trade patterns and economic activity. Raised in the suburbs of New York City, Krugman attended Yale University for two years before transferring to Massachusetts Institute of Technology, where he received his PhD in economics in 1977. Krugman has published many highly specialized texts in economic theory, but also more popular works like *Peddling Prosperity* (1994), *The Accidental Theorist: And Other Dispatches from the Dismal Science* (1998), and *The Return of Depression Economics and the Crisis of 2008* (2008). A frequent contributor to such newspapers and magazines as the *New Republic, Financial Times,* and *Mother Jones,* Krugman currently is an op-ed columnist for *The New York Times.* Known for his trenchant style and oppositional viewpoints, Krugman attempts to make complex economic trends comprehensible to a broad audience. In this essay from *The Nation,* published in 2003, Krugman looks into the causes of economic inequality.

1   The other day I found myself reading a leftist rag that made outrageous claims about America. It said that we are becoming a society in which the poor tend to stay poor, no matter how hard they work; in which sons are much more likely to inherit the socioeconomic status of their father than they were a generation ago.

2   The name of the leftist rag? *Business Week,** which published an article titled "Waking Up From the American Dream." The article summarizes recent research showing that social mobility in the United States (which was never as high as legend had it) has declined considerably over the past few decades. If you put that research together with other research that shows a drastic increase in income and wealth inequality, you reach an uncomfortable conclusion: America looks more and more like a class-ridden society.

3   And guess what? Our political leaders are doing everything they can to fortify class inequality, while denouncing anyone who complains–or even points out what is happening–as a practitioner of "class warfare."

4   Let's talk first about the facts on income distribution. Thirty years ago we were a relatively middle-class nation. It had not always been thus: Gilded Age America was a highly unequal society, and it stayed that way through the 1920s. During the 1930s and '40s, however, America experienced what the economic historians Claudia Goldin and Robert Margo have dubbed the Great Compression: a drastic narrowing of income gaps, probably as a result of New Deal policies. And the new economic order persisted for more than a generation: Strong unions; taxes on inherited wealth, corporate profits and high incomes; close public scrutiny of corporate management– all helped to keep income gaps relatively small. The economy was hardly egalitarian, but a generation ago the gross inequalities of the 1920s seemed very distant.

* *Business Week* is pro-business and generally considered conservative or "right-wing."

5   Now they're back. According to estimates by the economists Thomas Piketty and Emmanuel Saez–confirmed by data from the Congressional Budget Office–between 1973 and 2000 the average real income of the bottom 90 percent of American taxpayers actually fell by 7 percent. Meanwhile, the income of the top 1 percent rose by 148 percent, the income of the top 0.1 percent rose by 343 percent and the income of the top 0.01 percent rose 599 percent. (Those numbers exclude capital gains, so they're not an artifact of the stock-market bubble.) The distribution of income in the United States has gone right back to Gilded Age levels of inequality.

6   Never mind, say the apologists, who churn out papers with titles like that of a 2001 Heritage Foundation piece, "Income Mobility and the Fallacy of Class-Warfare Arguments." America, they say, isn't a caste society–people with high incomes this year may have low incomes next year and vice versa, and the route to wealth is open to all. That's where those commies at *Business Week* come in: As they point out (and as economists and sociologists have been pointing out for some time), America actually is more of a caste society than we like to think. And the caste lines have lately become a lot more rigid.

7   The myth of income mobility has always exceeded the reality: As a general rule, once they've reached their 30s, people don't move up and down the income ladder very much. Conservatives often cite studies like a 1992 report by Glenn Hubbard, a Treasury official under the elder Bush who later became chief economic adviser to the younger Bush, that purport to show large numbers of Americans moving from low-wage to high-wage jobs during their working lives. But what these studies measure, as the economist Kevin Murphy put it, is mainly "the guy who works in the college bookstore and has a real job by his early 30s." Serious studies that exclude this sort of pseudo-mobility show that inequality in average incomes over long periods isn't much smaller than inequality in annual incomes.

8   It is true, however, that America was once a place of substantial intergenerational mobility: Sons often did much better than their fathers. A classic 1978 survey found that among adult men whose fathers were in the bottom 25 percent of the population as ranked by social and economic status, 23 percent had made it into the top 25 percent. In other words, during the first thirty years or so after World War II, the American dream of upward mobility was a real experience for many people.

9   Now for the shocker: The *Business Week* piece cites a new survey of today's adult men, which finds that this number has dropped to only 10 percent. That is, over the past generation upward mobility has fallen drastically. Very few children of the lower class are making their way to even moderate affluence. This goes along with other studies indicating that rags-to-riches stories have become vanishingly rare, and that the correlation between fathers' and sons' incomes has risen in recent decades. In modern America, it seems, you're quite likely to stay in the social and economic class into which you were born.

10   *Business Week* attributes this to the "Wal-Martization" of the economy, the proliferation of dead-end, low-wage jobs and the disappearance of jobs that provide entry to the middle class. That's surely part of the explanation. But public policy plays a role–and will, if present trends continue, play an even bigger role in the future.

11   Put it this way: Suppose that you actually liked a caste society, and you were seeking ways to use your control of the government to further entrench the advantages of the haves against the have-nots. What would you do?

12   One thing you would definitely do is get rid of the estate tax, so that large fortunes can be passed on to the next generation. More broadly, you would seek to reduce tax rates both on corporate profits and on unearned income such as dividends and capital gains, so that those with large accumulated or inherited wealth could more easily accumulate even more. You'd also try to create tax shelters mainly useful for the rich. And more broadly still, you'd try to reduce tax rates on people with high incomes, shifting the burden to the payroll tax and other revenue sources that bear most heavily on people with lower incomes.

13   Meanwhile, on the spending side, you'd cut back on healthcare for the poor, on the quality of public education and on state aid for higher education. This would make it more difficult for people with low incomes to climb out of their difficulties and acquire the education essential to upward mobility in the modern economy.

14   And just to close off as many routes to upward mobility as possible, you'd do everything possible to break the power of unions, and you'd privatize government functions so that well-paid civil servants could be replaced with poorly paid private employees.

15   It all sounds sort of familiar, doesn't it?

16   Where is this taking us? Thomas Piketty, whose work with Saez has transformed our understanding of income distribution, warns that current policies will eventually create "a class of rentiers in the U.S., whereby a small group of wealthy but untalented children controls vast segments of the US economy and penniless, talented children simply can't compete." If he's right–and I fear that he is–we will end up suffering not only from injustice, but from a vast waste of human potential.

17   Goodbye, Horatio Alger. And goodbye, American Dream.

Comprehension

1. What reasons does Krugman give for the United States becoming more of a caste society?

2. Who is Horatio Alger? Why doesn't Krugman explain who he is in his essay?

3. Krugman alludes to the "leftist rag" *Business Week*. What can you infer about the contents and political opinions of this publication?

Rhetorical Analysis

4. What is Krugman's claim, and where does he state it most clearly?

5. Comment on the types of evidence that Krugman uses to support his argument. Do you find this evidence to be sufficient and convincing? Why or why not?

6. Krugman's style is quite impersonal. Locate examples of this style, and explain the overall effect.

7. Much of this essay involves comparative analysis. What subjects and ideas does Krugman compare and contrast?

8. Krugman's conclusion is very brief. Do you find it effective? Explain.

Writing

9. Do you think your life will be better economically than that of your parents? Why or why not? Write a personal essay in response to this question.

10. Write your own analysis of class inequality in the United States or in another nation you are familiar with. Or respond to Krugman's assertion: "Our political leaders are doing everything they can to fortify class inequality, while denouncing anyone who complains—or even points out what is happening—as a practitioner of 'class warfare.'"

11. **Writing an Argument** Write a rebuttal to Krugman, arguing that the American Dream is still alive and well.

Globalization: The Super-Story*

Thomas L. Friedman

Thomas L. Friedman (b. 1953) was born in Minneapolis, Minnesota. He majored in Mediterranean studies at Brandeis University (BA 1975) and received an MA in modern Middle Eastern studies from Oxford University in 1978. As journalist, author, television commentator, and op-ed contributor to *The New York Times,* Friedman tries to provide unbiased viewpoints on cultural, political, and economic issues. From 1979 to 1984 he was the *Times* correspondent in Beirut, Lebanon, and subsequently until 1988 served as bureau chief in Jerusalem. His book recounting his 10 years in the Middle East, *From Beirut to Jerusalem* (1983), received the National Book Award for nonfiction. Friedman also has published *The Lexus and the Olive Tree: Understanding Globalization* (2000), *The World Is Flat: A Brief History of the Twenty-First Century* (2005), *Hot, Flat, and Crowded: Why We Need a Green Revolution—And How It Can Renew America* (2008), and a collection of essays, *Longitudes and Attitudes: Explaining the World after September 11* (2002), which contains the following selection.

1   I am a big believer in the idea of the super-story, the notion that we all carry around with us a big lens, a big framework, through which we look at the world, order events, and decide what is important and what is not. The events of 9/11 did not happen in a vacuum. They happened in the context of a new international system—a system that cannot explain everything but *can* explain and connect more things in more places on more days than anything else. That new international system is called globalization. It came together in the late 1980s and replaced the previous international system, the cold war system, which had reigned since the end of World War II. This new system is the lens, the super-story, through which I viewed the events of 9/11.

2   I define globalization as the inexorable integration of markets, transportation systems, and communication systems to a degree never witnessed before—in a way that is enabling corporations, countries, and individuals to reach around the world farther, faster, deeper, and cheaper than ever before, and in a way that is enabling the world to reach into corporations, countries, and individuals farther, faster, deeper, and cheaper than ever before.

3   Several important features of this globalization system differ from those of the cold war system in ways that are quite relevant for understanding the events of 9/11. I examined them in detail in my previous book, *The Lexus and the Olive Tree,* and want to simply highlight them here.

4   The cold war system was characterized by one overarching feature—and that was *division.* That world was a divided-up, chopped-up place, and whether you were a country or a company, your threats and opportunities in the cold war system tended to grow out of who you were divided from. Appropriately, this cold war system was symbolized by a single word—*wall,* the Berlin Wall.

*Titled as "Prologue: The Super Story" in *Longitudes and Attitudes.*

5   The globalization system is different. It also has one overarching feature—and that is *integration.* The world has become an increasingly interwoven place, and today, whether you are a company or a country, your threats and opportunities increasingly derive from who you are connected to. This globalization system is also characterized by a single word—*web,* the World Wide Web. So in the broadest sense we have gone from an international system built around division and walls to a system increasingly built around integration and webs. In the cold war we reached for the hotline, which was a symbol that we were divided but at least two people were in charge—the leaders of the United States and the Soviet Union. In the globalization system we reach for the Internet, which is a symbol that we are all connected and nobody is quite in charge.

6   Everyone in the world is directly or indirectly affected by this new system, but not everyone benefits from it, not by a long shot, which is why the more it becomes diffused, the more it also produces a backlash by people who feel overwhelmed by it, homogenized by it, or unable to keep pace with its demands.

7   The other key difference between the cold war system and the globalization system is how power is structured within them. The cold war system was built primarily around nation-states. You acted on the world in that system through your state. The cold war was a drama of states confronting states, balancing states, and aligning with states. And, as a system, the cold war was balanced at the center by two superstates, two superpowers: the United States and the Soviet Union.

8   The globalization system, by contrast, is built around three balances, which overlap and affect one another. The first is the traditional balance of power between nation-states. In the globalization system, the United States is now the sole and dominant superpower and all other nations are subordinate to it to one degree or another. The shifting balance of power between the United States and other states, or simply between other states, still very much matters for the stability of this system. And it can still explain a lot of the news you read on the front page of the paper, whether it is the news of China balancing Russia, Iran balancing Iraq, or India confronting Pakistan.

9   The second important power balance in the globalization system is between nation-states and global markets. These global markets are made up of millions of investors moving money around the world with the click of a mouse. I call them the Electronic Herd, and this herd gathers in key global financial centers—such as Wall Street, Hong Kong, London, and Frankfurt—which I call the Supermarkets. The attitudes and actions of the Electronic Herd and the Supermarkets can have a huge impact on nation-states today, even to the point of triggering the downfall of governments. Who ousted Suharto in Indonesia in 1998? It wasn't another state, it was the Supermarkets, by withdrawing their support for, and confidence in, the Indonesian economy. You also will not understand the front page of the newspaper today unless you bring the Supermarkets into your analysis. Because the United States can destroy you by dropping bombs, but the Supermarkets can destroy you by downgrading your bonds. In other words, the United States is the dominant player in maintaining the globalization game board, but it is hardly alone in influencing the moves on that game board.

10   The third balance that you have to pay attention to—the one that is really the newest of all and the most relevant to the events of 9/11—is the balance between individuals and nation-states. Because globalization has brought down many of the walls that limited the movement and reach of people, and because it has simultaneously wired the world into networks, it gives more power to *individuals* to influence both markets and nation-states than at any other time in history. Whether by enabling people to use the Internet to communicate instantly at almost no cost over vast distances, or by enabling them to use the Web to transfer money or obtain weapons designs that normally would have been controlled by states, or by enabling them to go into a hardware store now and buy a five-hundred-dollar global positioning device, connected to a satellite, that can direct a hijacked airplane—globalization can be an incredible force-multiplier for individuals. Individuals can increasingly act on the world stage directly, unmediated by a state.

11   So you have today not only a superpower, not only Supermarkets, but also what I call "super-empowered individuals." Some of these super-empowered individuals are quite angry, some of them quite wonderful—but all of them are now able to act much more directly and much more powerfully on the world stage.

12   Osama bin Laden declared war on the United States in the late 1990s. After he organized the bombing of two American embassies in Africa, the U.S. Air Force retaliated with a cruise missile attack on his bases in Afghanistan as though he were another nation-state. Think about that: on one day in 1998, the United States fired 75 cruise missiles at bin Laden. The United States fired 75 cruise missiles, at $1 million apiece, at a person! That was the first battle in history between a superpower and a super-empowered angry man. September 11 was just the second such battle.

13   Jody Williams won the Nobel Peace Prize in 1997 for helping to build an international coalition to bring about a treaty outlawing land mines. Although nearly 120 governments endorsed the treaty, it was opposed by Russia, China, and the United States. When Jody Williams was asked, "How did you do that? How did you organize one thousand different citizens' groups and nongovernmental organizations on five continents to forge a treaty that was opposed by the major powers?" she had a very brief answer: "E-mail." Jody Williams used e-mail and the networked world to super-empower herself.

14   Nation-states, and the American superpower in particular, are still hugely important today, but so too now are Supermarkets and super-empowered individuals. You will never understand the globalization system, or the front page of the morning paper—or 9/11—unless you see each as a complex interaction between all three of these actors: states bumping up against states, states bumping up against Supermarkets, and Supermarkets and states bumping up against super-empowered individuals—many of whom, unfortunately, are super-empowered angry men.

1. What is Friedman's "super-story"? How does he define it?

2. What are the main features of globalization? How does globalization differ from the system characterized by the cold war? Explain the "three balances" (paragraphs 8–10) that Friedman writes about.

3. What does Friedman mean by "super-empowered" individuals (paragraph 11)?

Rhetorical Analysis

4. What is Friedman's thesis or claim in this essay? Where does it appear?

5. How and why does Friedman create a personal voice as well as a colloquial style in this selection? What is the effect?

6. What definitions does Friedman establish? Are the definitions too abstract, or does he provide sufficient explanations and evidence? Explain.

7. Locate instances of classification and of comparison and contrast. Why does Friedman use these rhetorical strategies? How do the two methods complement each other?

8. Friedman uses several metaphors in this essay. What are they, and how do they function to enhance meaning?

9. Why does the writer discuss 9/11 in the final three paragraphs? What is the effect on the overall message and purpose of the essay?

Writing

10. In groups of three or four, use Friedman's essay to brainstorm about globalization. Construct a list of ideas and attributes about globalization. Using this list, write a definition essay exploring the subject of globalization. Include comparison and contrast or classification, or both, to help organize the essay.

11. Write a personal essay on how you think globalization is affecting your life.

12. **Writing an Argument**   Has globalization changed since Friedman wrote this essay in 2002? In a letter to Friedman, explain your position and support it with examples.

Nickel and Dimed

Barbara Ehrenreich

Barbara Ehrenreich (b. 1941) was born in Butte, Montana. The daughter of
working-class parents, she attended Reed College (BA 1963) and
Rockefeller University, where she received a PhD in biology in 1968. After
deciding not to pursue a career in science, Ehrenreich turned to political
causes, using her scientific training to investigate a broad range of social
issues. A prolific writer, Ehrenreich has contributed to *Time*, the *New
Republic, The Progressive*, and other magazines. She also has written
several books, including *The American Health Empire* (1970), *Complaints
and Disorders: The Sexual Politics of Sickness* (1978), *Nickel and Dimed: On
(Not) Getting By in America* (2001), *Dancing in the Streets* (2007), and a
collection of essays, *This Land Is Their Land: Reports from a Divided Nation*
(2008). In the following excerpt from *Nickel and Dimed*, Ehrenreich recounts
her experience working for a large cleaning agency.

1   I am rested and ready for anything when I arrive at The Maids' office suite
Monday at 7:30 A.M. I know nothing about cleaning services like this one, which,
according to the brochure I am given, has over three hundred franchises
nationwide, and most of what I know about domestics in general comes from
nineteenth-century British novels and *Upstairs, Downstairs*. Prophetically enough,
I caught a rerun of that very show on PBS over the weekend and was struck by
how terribly correct the servants looked in their black-and-white uniforms and
how much wiser they were than their callow, egotistical masters. We too have
uniforms, though they are more oafish than dignified—ill-fitting and in an
overloud combination of kelly-green pants and a blinding sunflower-yellow polo
shirt. And, as is explained in writing and over the next day and a half of training,
we too have a special code of decorum. No smoking anywhere, or at least not
within fifteen minutes of arrival at a house. No drinking, eating, or gum chewing
in a house. No cursing in a house, even if the owner is not present, and—perhaps
to keep us in practice—no obscenities even in the office. So this is Downstairs, is
my chirpy first thought. But I have no idea, of course, just how far down these
stairs will take me.

2   Forty minutes go by before anyone acknowledges my presence with more
than a harried nod. During this time the other employees arrive, about twenty
of them, already glowing in their uniforms, and breakfast on the free coffee,
bagels, and doughnuts The Maids kindly provides for us. All but one of the
others are female, with an average age I would guess in the late twenties,
though the range seems to go from prom-fresh to well into the Medicare years.
There is a pleasant sort of bustle as people get their breakfasts and fill plastic
buckets with rags and bottles of cleaning fluids, but surprisingly little
conversation outside of a few references to what people ate (pizza) and drank
(Jell-O shots are mentioned) over the weekend. Since the room in which we

gather contains only two folding chairs, both of them occupied, the other new girl and I sit cross-legged on the floor, silent and alert, while the regulars get sorted into teams of three or four and dispatched to the day's list of houses. One of the women explains to me that teams do not necessarily return to the same houses week after week, nor do you have any guarantee of being on the same team from one day to the next. This, I suppose, is one of the advantages of a corporate cleaning service to its customers: There are no sticky and possibly guilt-ridden relationships involved, because the customers communicate almost entirely with Tammy, the office manager, or with Ted, the franchise owner and our boss. The advantage to the cleaning person is harder to determine, since the pay compares so poorly to what an independent cleaner is likely to earn—up to $15 an hour, I've heard. While I wait in the inner room, where the phone is and Tammy has her desk, to be issued a uniform, I hear her tell a potential customer on the phone that The Maids charges $25 per person-hour. The company gets $25 and we get $6.65 for each hour we work? I think I must have misheard, but a few minutes later I hear her say the same thing to another inquirer. So the only advantage of working here as opposed to freelancing is that you don't need a clientele or even a car. You can arrive straight from welfare or, in my case, the bus station—fresh off the boat.

3   At last, after all the other employees have sped off in the company's eye-catching green-and-yellow cars, I am led into a tiny closet-sized room off the inner office to learn my trade via videotape. The manager at another maid service where I'd applied had told me she didn't like to hire people who had done cleaning before because they were resistant to learning the company's system, so I prepare to empty my mind of all prior house-cleaning experience. There are four tapes—dusting, bathrooms, kitchen, and vacuuming—each starring an attractive, possibly Hispanic young woman who moves about serenely in obedience to the male voiceover: For vacuuming, begin in the master bedroom; when dusting, begin with the room directly off the kitchen. When you enter a room, mentally divide it into sections no wider than your reach. Begin in the section to your left and, within each section, move from left to right and top to bottom. This way nothing is ever overlooked.

4   I like *Dusting* best, for its undeniable logic and a certain kind of austere beauty. When you enter a house, you spray a white rag with Windex and place it in the left pocket of your green apron. Another rag, sprayed with disinfectant, goes in the middle pocket, and a yellow rag bearing wood polish in the right-hand pocket. A dry rag, for buffing surfaces, occupies the right-hand pocket of your slacks. Shiny surfaces get Windexed, wood gets wood polish, and everything else is wiped dust-free with disinfectant. Every now and then Ted pops in to watch with me, pausing the video to underscore a particularly dramatic moment: "See how she's working around the vase? That's an accident waiting to happen." If Ted himself were in a video, it would have to be a cartoon, because the only features sketched onto his pudgy face are brown buttonlike eyes and a tiny pug nose; his belly, encased in a polo shirt, overhangs the waistline of his shorts. "You know, all this was figured out with a stopwatch," he tells me with something like pride. When the video warns against oversoaking our rags with cleaning fluids, he

pauses it to tell me there's a danger in undersoaking too, especially if it's going to slow me down. "Cleaning fluids are less expensive than your time." It's good to know that *something* is cheaper than my time, or that in the hierarchy of the company's values I rank above Windex.

5   *Vacuuming* is the most disturbing video, actually a double feature beginning with an introduction to the special backpack vacuum we are to use. Yes, the vacuum cleaner actually straps onto your back, a chubby fellow who introduces himself as its inventor explains. He suits up, pulling the straps tight across and under his chest and then says proudly into the camera: "See, I *am* the vacuum cleaner." It weighs only ten pounds, he claims, although, as I soon find out, with the attachments dangling from the strap around your waist, the total is probably more like fourteen. What about my petulant and much-pampered lower back? The inventor returns to the theme of human/machine merger: When properly strapped in, we too will be vacuum cleaners, constrained only by the cord that attaches us to an electrical outlet, and vacuum cleaners don't have backaches. Somehow all this information exhausts me, and I watch the second video, which explains the actual procedures for vacuuming, with the detached interest of a cineaste. Could the model maid be an actual maid and the model home someone's actual dwelling? And who are these people whose idea of decorating is matched pictures of mallard ducks in flight and whose house is perfectly characterless and pristine even before the model maid sets to work?

6   At first I find the videos on kitchens and bathrooms baffling, and it takes me several minutes to realize why: There is no *water*, or almost no water, involved. I was taught to clean by my mother, a compulsive housekeeper who employed water so hot you needed rubber gloves to get into it and in such Niagara-like quantities that most microbes were probably crushed by the force of it before the soap suds had a chance to rupture their cell walls. But germs are never mentioned in the videos provided by The Maids. Our antagonists exist entirely in the visible world— soap scum, dust, counter crud, dog hair, stains, and smears—and are to be attacked by damp rag or, in hard-core cases, by Dobie (the brand of plastic scouring pad we use). We scrub only to remove impurities that might be detectable to a customer by hand or by eye; otherwise our only job is to wipe. Nothing is said about the possibility of transporting bacteria, by rag or by hand, from bathroom to kitchen or even from one house to the next. It is the "cosmetic touches" that the videos emphasize and that Ted, when he wanders back into the room, continually directs my eye to. Fluff up all throw pillows and arrange them symmetrically. Brighten up stainless steel sinks with baby oil. Leave all spice jars, shampoos, etc., with their labels facing outward. Comb out the fringes of Persian carpets with a pick. Use the vacuum cleaner to create a special, fernlike pattern in the carpets. The loose ends of toilet paper and paper towel rolls have to be given a special fold (the same one you'll find in hotel bathrooms). "Messes" of loose paper, clothing, or toys are to be stacked into "neat messes." Finally, the house is to be sprayed with the cleaning service's signature floral-scented air freshener, which will signal to the owners, the moment they return home, that, yes, their house has been "cleaned."

7   After a day's training, I am judged fit to go out with a team, where I soon discover that life is nothing like the movies, at least not if the movie is *Dusting.*

For one thing, compared with our actual pace, the training videos were all in slow motion. We do not walk to the cars with our buckets full of cleaning fluids and utensils in the morning, we run, and when we pull up to a house, we run with our buckets to the door. Liza, a good-natured woman in her thirties who is my first team leader, explains that we are given only so many minutes per house, ranging from under sixty for a 1½-bathroom apartment to two hundred or more for a multibathroom "first timer." I'd like to know why anybody worries about Ted's time limits if we're being paid by the hour but hesitate to display anything that might be interpreted as attitude. As we get to each house, Liza assigns our tasks, and I cross my fingers to ward off bathrooms and vacuuming. Even dusting, though, gets aerobic under pressure, and after about an hour of it—reaching to get door tops, crawling along floors to wipe baseboards, standing on my bucket to attack the higher shelves—I wouldn't mind sitting down with a tall glass of water. But as soon as you complete your assigned task, you report to the team leader to be assigned to help someone else. Once or twice, when the normal process of evaporation is deemed too slow, I am assigned to dry a scrubbed floor by putting rags under my feet and skating around on it. Usually, by the time I get out to the car and am dumping the dirty water used on floors and wringing out rags, the rest of the team is already in the car with the motor running. Liza assures me that they've never left anyone behind at a house, not even, presumably, a very new person whom nobody knows.

8   In my interview, I had been promised a thirty-minute lunch break, but this turns out to be a five-minute pit stop at a convenience store, if that. I bring my own sandwich—the same turkey breast and cheese every day—as do a couple of the others; the rest eat convenience store fare, a bagel or doughnut salvaged from our free breakfast, or nothing at all. The two older married women I'm teamed up with eat best—sandwiches and fruit. Among the younger women, lunch consists of a slice of pizza, a "pizza pocket" (a roll of dough surrounding some pizza sauce), or a small bag of chips. Bear in mind we are not office workers, sitting around idling at the basal metabolic rate. A poster on the wall in the office cheerily displays the number of calories burned per minute at our various tasks, ranging from about 3.5 for dusting to 7 for vacuuming. If you assume an average of 5 calories per minute in a seven-hour day (eight hours minus time for travel between houses), you need to be taking in 2,100 calories in addition to the resting minimum of, say, 900 or so. I get pushy with Rosalie, who is new like me and fresh from high school in a rural northern part of the state, about the meagerness of her lunches, which consist solely of Doritos—a half-bag from the day before or a freshly purchased small-sized bag. She just didn't have anything in the house, she says (though she lives with her boyfriend and his mother), and she certainly doesn't have any money to buy lunch, as I find out when I offer to fetch her a soda from a Quik Mart and she has to admit she doesn't have eighty-nine cents. I treat her to the soda, wishing I could force her, mommylike, to take milk instead. So how does she hold up for an eight- or even nine-hour day? "Well," she concedes, "I get dizzy sometimes."

9   How poor are they, my coworkers? The fact that anyone is working this job at all can be taken as prima facie evidence of some kind of desperation or at least a

history of mistakes and disappointments, but it's not for me to ask. In the prison movies that provide me with a mental guide to comportment, the new guy doesn't go around shaking hands and asking, "Hi there, what are you in for?" So I listen, in the cars and when we're assembled in the office, and learn, first, that no one seems to be homeless. Almost everyone is embedded in extended families or families artificially extended with housemates. People talk about visiting grandparents in the hospital or sending birthday cards to a niece's husband; single mothers live with their own mothers or share apartments with a coworker or boyfriend. Pauline, the oldest of us, owns her own home, but she sleeps on the living room sofa, while her four grown children and three grandchildren fill up the bedrooms.

10   But although no one, apparently, is sleeping in a car, there are signs, even at the beginning, of real difficulty if not actual misery. Half-smoked cigarettes are returned to the pack. There are discussions about who will come up with fifty cents for a toll and whether Ted can be counted on for prompt reimbursement. One of my teammates gets frantic about a painfully impacted wisdom tooth and keeps making calls from our houses to try to locate a source of free dental care. When my—or, I should say, Liza's—team discovers there is not a single Dobie in our buckets, I suggest that we stop at a convenience store and buy one rather than drive all the way back to the office. But it turns out I haven't brought any money with me and we cannot put together $2 between the four of us.

11   The Friday of my first week at The Maids is unnaturally hot for Maine in early September—95 degrees, according to the digital time-and-temperature displays offered by banks that we pass. I'm teamed up with the sad-faced Rosalie and our leader, Maddy, whose sullenness, under the circumstances, is almost a relief after Liza's relentless good cheer. Liza, I've learned, is the highest-ranking cleaner, a sort of supervisor really, and said to be something of a snitch, but Maddy, a single mom of maybe twenty-seven or so, has worked for only three months and broods about her child care problems. Her boyfriend's sister, she tells me on the drive to our first house, watches her eighteen-month-old for $50 a week, which is a stretch on The Maids' pay, plus she doesn't entirely trust the sister, but a real day care center could be as much as $90 a week. After polishing off the first house, no problem, we grab "lunch"—Doritos for Rosalie and a bag of Pepperidge Farm Goldfish for Maddy—and head out into the exurbs for what our instruction sheet warns is a five-bathroom spread and a first-timer to boot. Still, the size of the place makes us pause for a moment, buckets in hand, before searching out an appropriately humble entrance. It sits there like a beached ocean liner, the prow cutting through swells of green turf, windows without number. "Well, well," Maddy says, reading the owner's name from our instruction sheet. "Mrs. W. and her big-ass house. I hope she's going to give us lunch."

12   Mrs. W. is not in fact happy to see us, grimacing with exasperation when the black nanny ushers us into the family room or sunroom or den or whatever kind of specialized space she is sitting in. After all, she already has the nanny, a cooklike person, and a crew of men doing some sort of finishing touches on the construction to supervise. No, she doesn't want to take us around the house, because she already explained everything to the office on the phone, but Maddy

stands there, with Rosalie and me behind her, until she relents. We are to move everything on all surfaces, she instructs during the tour, and get underneath and be sure to do every bit of the several miles, I calculate, of baseboards. And be mindful of the baby, who's napping and can't have cleaning fluids of any kind near her.

13   Then I am let loose to dust. In a situation like this, where I don't even know how to name the various kinds of rooms, The Maids' special system turns out to be a lifesaver. All I have to do is keep moving from left to right, within rooms and between rooms, trying to identify landmarks so I don't accidentally do a room or a hallway twice. Dusters get the most complete biographical overview, due to the necessity of lifting each object and tchotchke individually, and I learn that Mrs. W. is an alumna of an important women's college, now occupying herself by monitoring her investments and the baby's bowel movements. I find special charts for this latter purpose, with spaces for time of day, most recent fluid intake, consistency, and color. In the master bedroom, I dust a whole shelf of books on pregnancy, breastfeeding, the first six months, the first year, the first two years— and I wonder what the child care–deprived Maddy makes of all this. Maybe there's been some secret division of the world's women into breeders and drones, and those at the maid level are no longer supposed to be reproducing at all. Maybe this is why our office manager, Tammy, who was once a maid herself, wears inch-long fake nails and tarty little outfits—to show she's advanced to the breeder caste and can't be sent out to clean anymore.

14   It is hotter inside than out, un-air-conditioned for the benefit of the baby, I suppose, but I do all right until I encounter the banks of glass doors that line the side and back of the ground floor. Each one has to be Windexed, wiped, and buffed—inside and out, top to bottom, left to right, until it's as streakless and invisible as a material substance can be. Outside, I can see the construction guys knocking back Gatorade, but the rule is that no fluid or food item can touch a maid's lips when she's inside a house. Now, sweat, even in unseemly quantities, is nothing new to me. I live in a subtropical area where even the inactive can expect to be moist nine months out of the year. I work out, too, in my normal life and take a certain macho pride in the *V*s of sweat that form on my T-shirt after ten minutes or more on the StairMaster. But in normal life fluids lost are immediately replaced. Everyone in yuppie-land—airports, for example—looks like a nursing baby these days, inseparable from their plastic bottles of water. Here, however, I sweat without replacement or pause, not in individual drops but in continuous sheets of fluid soaking through my polo shirt, pouring down the backs of my legs. The eyeliner I put on in the morning—vain twit that I am—has long since streaked down onto my cheeks, and I could wring my braid out if I wanted to. Working my way through the living room(s), I wonder if Mrs. W. will ever have occasion to realize that every single doodad and *objet* through which she expresses her unique, individual self is, from another vantage point, only an obstacle between some thirsty person and a glass of water.

15   When I can find no more surfaces to wipe and have finally exhausted the supply of rooms, Maddy assigns me to do the kitchen floor. OK, except that Mrs. W. is *in* the kitchen, so I have to go down on my hands and knees practically at her feet.

No, we don't have sponge mops like the one I use in my own house; the hands-and-knees approach is a definite selling point for corporate cleaning services like The Maids. "We clean floors the old-fashioned way—*on our hands and knees*" (emphasis added), the brochure for a competing firm boasts. In fact, whatever advantages there may be to the hands-and-knees approach—you're closer to your work, of course, and less likely to miss a grimy patch—are undermined by the artificial drought imposed by The Maids' cleaning system. We are instructed to use less than half a small bucket of lukewarm water for a kitchen and all adjacent scrubbable floors (breakfast nooks and other dining areas), meaning that within a few minutes we are doing nothing more than redistributing the dirt evenly around the floor. There are occasional customer complaints about the cleanliness of our floors—for example, from a man who wiped up a spill on his freshly "cleaned" floor only to find the paper towel he employed for this purpose had turned gray. A mop and a full bucket of hot soapy water would not only get a floor cleaner but would be a lot more dignified for the person who does the cleaning. But it is this primal posture of submission . . . that seems to gratify the consumers of maid services.

16   I don't know, but Mrs. W.'s floor is hard—stone, I think, or at least a stonelike substance—and we have no knee pads with us today. I had thought in my middle-class innocence that knee pads were one of Monica Lewinsky's prurient fantasies, but no, they actually exist, and they're usually a standard part of our equipment. So here I am on my knees, working my way around the room like some fanatical penitent crawling through the stations of the cross, when I realize that Mrs. W. is staring at me fixedly—so fixedly that I am gripped for a moment by the wild possibility that I may have once given a lecture at her alma mater and she's trying to figure out where she's seen me before. If I were recognized, would I be fired? Would she at least be inspired to offer me a drink of water? Because I have decided that if water is actually offered, I'm taking it, rules or no rules, and if word of this infraction gets back to Ted, I'll just say I thought it would be rude to refuse. Not to worry, though. She's just watching that I don't leave out some stray square inch, and when I rise painfully to my feet again, blinking through the sweat, she says, "Could you just scrub the floor in the entryway while you're at it?"

17   I rush home to the Blue Haven at the end of the day, pull down the blinds for privacy, strip off my uniform in the kitchen—the bathroom being too small for both a person and her discarded clothes—and stand in the shower for a good ten minutes, thinking all this water is *mine*. I have paid for it, in fact, I have earned it. I have gotten through a week at The Maids without mishap, injury, or insurrection. My back feels fine, meaning I'm not feeling it at all; even my wrists, damaged by carpal tunnel syndrome years ago, are issuing no complaints. Coworkers warned me that the first time they donned the backpack vacuum they felt faint, but not me. I am strong and I am, more than that, good. Did I toss my bucket of filthy water onto Mrs. W.'s casual white summer outfit? No. Did I take the wand of my vacuum cleaner and smash someone's Chinese porcelain statues or Hummel figurines? Not once. I was at all times cheerful, energetic, helpful, and as competent as a new hire can be expected to be. If I can do one week, I can do another, and might as well, since there's never been a moment for job-hunting. The 3:30 quitting time turns out to be a myth; often we don't return to the office

until 4:30 or 5:00. And what did I think? That I was going to go out to interviews in my soaked and stinky postwork condition? I decide to reward myself with a sunset walk on Old Orchard Beach.

18   On account of the heat, there are still a few actual bathers on the beach, but I am content to sit in shorts and T-shirt and watch the ocean pummel the sand. When the sun goes down I walk back into the town to find my car and am amazed to hear a sound I associate with cities like New York and Berlin. There's a couple of Peruvian musicians playing in the little grassy island in the street near the pier, and maybe fifty people—locals and vacationers—have gathered around, offering their bland end-of-summer faces to the sound. I edge my way through the crowd and find a seat where I can see the musicians up close—the beautiful young guitarist and the taller man playing the flute. What are they doing in this rinky-dink blue-collar resort, and what does the audience make of this surprise visit from the dark-skinned South? The melody the flute lays out over the percussion is both utterly strange and completely familiar, as if it had been imprinted in the minds of my own peasant ancestors centuries ago and forgotten until this very moment. Everyone else seems to be as transfixed as I am. The musicians wink and smile at each other as they play, and I see then that they are the secret emissaries of a worldwide lower-class conspiracy to snatch joy out of degradation and filth. When the song ends, I give them a dollar, the equivalent of about ten minutes of sweat.

Comprehension

1. Why do women work for The Maids when they could earn more money as independent cleaners? How does Ehrenreich distinguish her cleaning practices from her coworkers'? Why do the maids emphasize "cosmetic touches" (paragraph 6)?

2. Describe the plight of Ehrenreich's coworkers. What "signs . . . of real difficulty if not actual misery" (paragraph 10) does she detect? What, if anything, does she do to help them?

3. Who is Mrs. W.? What is her lifestyle like, and what does she expect of the maids? How does she treat Ehrenreich?

Rhetorical Analysis

4. How does Ehrenreich structure her narrative? How much time elapses? What elements of conflict develop? What transitional devices does she employ to unify the action?

5. Where does the writer employ description, and for what purpose? What descriptive details seem most striking to you? How, for example, does Ehrenreich bring her coworkers and Mrs. W. to life?

6. Identify those instances where the writer uses process analysis and comparison and contrast to organize her essay. Why does she select these strategies? What is the effect of these strategies?

7. Explain the tone of this selection. What elements of irony and sarcasm do you detect?

8. Do you think this essay provides a straightforward account of Ehrenreich's experience working for The Maids, or does she have an argumentative point? Justify your response.

9. How does the writer conclude this selection? What elements in the last paragraph capture the main purpose behind her account?

Writing

10. Write a narrative and descriptive essay of a job you have held that involved menial labor. Establish a time frame. Describe any colleagues who worked with you. Have a thesis or an argument that you either state explicitly or permit to emerge from the account.

11. Compare and contrast a bad job you have held and a job that provided you with a degree of satisfaction.

12. **Writing an Argument** In *Nickel and Dimed,* Ehrenreich set out to find minimum-wage jobs in several parts of the United States, including a Wal-Mart in Minnesota and a restaurant in Florida. However, she knew at the outset that these jobs were temporary and that she had the luxury of going back to her comfortable life and her career as a writer and activist. Argue for or against the proposition that Ehrenreich was being unethical and exploitative in her behavior. Refer to this selection to support your position.

Why the Rich Are Getting Richer and the Poor, Poorer

Robert Reich

Robert Reich (b. 1946) is a professor of Public Policy at the University of
California at Berkeley. He served as secretary of labor in the first Clinton
administration and, before that, as a professor of economics at Harvard
University. He has written numerous books on economics and has been a
prominent lecturer for a dozen years. His books include *The Next American
Frontier* (1983) and *The Work of Nations* (1991), which takes its title from
Adam Smith's classic work on economics, *The Wealth of Nations*, written in
1776. Reich is known for his ability to see things from a unique and original
perspective. Here he warns of what exists—perhaps in front of our very
noses—but that we are too caught up in the moment to consider.

[T]he division of labour is limited by the extent of the market.
ADAM SMITH, *An Inquiry into the Nature and Causes of the Wealth of Nations* (1776)

1   Regardless of how your job is officially classified (manufacturing, service,
managerial, technical, secretarial, and so on), or the industry in which you work
(automotive, steel, computer, advertising, finance, food processing), your real
competitive position in the world economy is coming to depend on the function you
perform in it. Herein lies the basic reason why incomes are diverging. The fortunes
of routine producers are declining. In-person servers are also becoming poorer,
although their fates are less clear-cut. But symbolic analysts—who solve, identify,
and broker new problems—are, by and large, succeeding in the world economy.

2   All Americans used to be in roughly the same economic boat. Most rose or fell
together, as the corporations in which they were employed, the industries
comprising such corporations, and the national economy as a whole became more
productive—or languished. But national borders no longer define our economic
fates. We are now in different boats, one sinking rapidly, one sinking more slowly,
and the third rising steadily.

3   The boat containing routine producers is sinking rapidly. Recall that by
midcentury routine production workers in the United States were paid relatively
well. The giant pyramidlike organizations at the core of each major industry
coordinated their prices and investments—avoiding the harsh winds of competition
and thus maintaining healthy earnings. Some of these earnings, in turn, were
reinvested in new plant and equipment (yielding ever-larger-scale economies);
another portion went to top managers and investors. But a large and increasing
portion went to middle managers and production workers. Work stoppages posed
such a threat to high-volume production that organized labor was able to exact an
ever-larger premium for its cooperation. And the pattern of wages established
within the core corporations influenced the pattern throughout the national
economy. Thus the growth of a relatively affluent middle class, able to purchase all
the wondrous things produced in high volume by the core corporations.

4   But, as has been observed, the core is rapidly breaking down into global webs which earn their largest profits from clever problem-solving, -identifying, and brokering. As the costs of transporting standard things and of communicating information about them continue to drop, profit margins on high-volume, standardized production are thinning, because there are few barriers to entry. Modern factories and state-of-the-art machinery can be installed almost anywhere on the globe. Routine producers in the United States, then, are in direct competition with millions of routine producers in other nations. Twelve thousand people are added to the world's population every hour, most of whom, eventually, will happily work for a small fraction of the wages of routine producers in America.[1]

5   The consequence is clearest in older, heavy industries, where high-volume, standardized production continues its ineluctable move to where labor is cheapest and most accessible around the world. Thus, for example, the Maquiladora factories clustered along the Mexican side of the U.S. border in the sprawling shanty towns of Tijuana, Mexicali, Nogales, Agua Prieta, and Ciudad Juárez—factories owned mostly by Americans, but increasingly by Japanese—in which more than a half million routine producers assemble parts into finished goods to be shipped into the United States.

6   The same story is unfolding worldwide. Until the late 1970s, AT&T had depended on routine producers in Shreveport, Louisiana, to assemble standard telephones. It then discovered that routine producers in Singapore would perform the same tasks at a far lower cost. Facing intense competition from other global webs, AT&T's strategic brokers felt compelled to switch. So in the early 1980s they stopped hiring routine producers in Shreveport and began hiring cheaper routine producers in Singapore. But under this kind of pressure for ever lower high-volume production costs, today's Singaporean can easily end up as yesterday's Louisianan. By the late 1980s, AT&T's strategic brokers found that routine producers in Thailand were eager to assemble telephones for a small fraction of the wages of routine producers in Singapore. Thus, in 1989, AT&T stopped hiring Singaporeans to make telephones and began hiring even cheaper routine producers in Thailand.

7   The search for ever lower wages has not been confined to heavy industry. Routine data processing is equally footloose. Keypunch operators located anywhere around the world can enter data into computers, linked by satellite or transoceanic fiber-optic cable, and take it out again. As the rates charged by satellite networks continue to drop, and as more satellites and fiber-optic cables become available (reducing communication costs still further), routine data processors in the United States find themselves in ever more direct competition with their counterparts abroad, who are often eager to work for far less.

8   By 1990, keypunch operators in the United States were earning, at most, $6.50 per hour. But keypunch operators throughout the rest of the world were willing to

---

[1] The reader should note, of course, that lower wages in other areas of the world are of no particular attraction to global capital unless workers there are sufficiently productive to make the labor cost of producing *each unit* lower there than in higher-wage regions. Productivity in many low-wage areas of the world has improved due to the ease with which state-of-the-art factories and equipment can be installed there.

work for a fraction of this. Thus, many potential American data-processing jobs were disappearing, and the wages and benefits of the remaining ones were in decline. Typical was Saztec International, a $20-million-a-year data-processing firm headquartered in Kansas City, whose American strategic brokers contracted with routine data processors in Manila and with American–owned firms that needed such data-processing services. Compared with the average Philippine income of $1,700 per year, data-entry operators working for Saztec earn the princely sum of $2,650. The remainder of Saztec's employees were American problem-solvers and –identifiers, searching for ways to improve the worldwide system and find new uses to which it could be put.[2]

9   By 1990, American Airlines was employing over 1,000 data processors in Barbados and the Dominican Republic to enter names and flight numbers from used airline tickets (flown daily to Barbados from airports around the United States) into a giant computer bank located in Dallas. Chicago publisher R. R. Donnelley was sending entire manuscripts to Barbados for entry into computers in preparation for printing. The New York Life Insurance Company was dispatching insurance claims to Castleisland, Ireland, where routine producers, guided by simple directions, entered the claim and determined the amounts due, then instantly transmitted the computations back to the United States. (When the firm advertised in Ireland for twenty-five data-processing jobs, it received six hundred applications.) And McGraw-Hill was processing subscription renewal and marketing information for its magazines in nearby Galway. Indeed, literally millions of routine workers around the world were receiving information, converting it into computer-readable form, and then sending it back—at the speed of electronic impulses—whence it came.

10   The simple coding of computer software has also entered into world commerce. India, with a large English-speaking population of technicians happy to do routine programming cheaply, is proving to be particularly attractive to global webs in need of this service. By 1990, Texas Instruments maintained a software development facility in Bangalore, linking fifty Indian programmers by satellite to TI's Dallas headquarters. Spurred by this and similar ventures, the Indian government was building a teleport in Poona, intended to make it easier and less expensive for many other firms to send their routine software design specifications for coding.[3]

11   This shift of routine production jobs from advanced to developing nations is a great boon to many workers in such nations who otherwise would be jobless or working for much lower wages. These workers, in turn, now have more money with which to purchase symbolic-analytic services from advanced nations (often embedded within all sorts of complex products). The trend is also beneficial to everyone around the world who can now obtain high-volume, standardized products (including information and software) more cheaply than before.

---

[2] John Maxwell Hamilton, "A Bit Player Buys into the Computer Age," *New York Times Business World*, December 3, 1989, p. 14.
[3] Udayan Gupta, "U.S.-Indian Satellite Link Stands to Cut Software Costs," *Wall Street Journal*, March 6, 1989, p. B2.

12   But these benefits do not come without certain costs. In particular the burden is borne by those who no longer have good-paying routine production jobs within advanced economies like the United States. Many of these people used to belong to unions or at least benefited from prevailing wage rates established in collective bargaining agreements. But as the old corporate bureaucracies have flattened into global webs, bargaining leverage has been lost. Indeed, the tacit national bargain is no more.

13   Despite the growth in the number of new jobs in the United States, union membership has withered. In 1960, 35 percent of all nonagricultural workers in America belonged to a union. But by 1980 that portion had fallen to just under a quarter, and by 1989 to about 17 percent. Excluding government employees, union membership was down to 13.4 percent.[4] This was a smaller proportion even than in the early 1930s, before the National Labor Relations Act created a legally protected right to labor representation. The drop in membership has been accompanied by a growing number of collective bargaining agreements to freeze wages at current levels, reduce wage levels of entering workers, or reduce wages overall. This is an important reason why the long economic recovery that began in 1982 produced a smaller rise in unit labor costs than any of the eight recoveries since World War II—the low rate of unemployment during its course notwithstanding.

14   Routine production jobs have vanished fastest in traditional unionized industries (autos, steel, and rubber, for example), where average wages have kept up with inflation. This is because the jobs of older workers in such industries are protected by seniority; the youngest workers are the first to be laid off. Faced with a choice of cutting wages or cutting the number of jobs, a majority of union members (secure in the knowledge that there are many who are junior to them will be laid off first) often have voted for the latter.

15   Thus the decline in union membership has been most striking among young men entering the work force without a college education. In the early 1950s, more than 40 percent of this group joined unions; by the late 1980s, less than 20 percent (if public employees are excluded, less than 10 percent).[5] In steelmaking, for example, although many older workers remained employed, almost half of all routine steelmaking jobs in America vanished between 1974 and 1988 (from 480,000 to 260,000). Similarly with automobiles: During the 1980s, the United Auto Workers lost 500,000 members—one-third of their total at the start of the decade. General Motors alone cut 150,000 American production jobs during the 1980s (even as it added employment abroad). Another consequence of the same phenomenon: The gap between the average wages of unionized and nonunionized workers widened dramatically—from 14.06 percent in 1973 to 20.4 percent by the end of the 1980s.[6] The lesson is clear. If you drop out of high school or have no

[4] *Statistical Abstract of the United States* (Washington, D.C.: U.S. Government Printing Office, 1989), p. 416, table 684.
[5] Calculations from Current Population Surveys by L. Katz and A. Revenga, "Changes in the Structure of Wages: U.S. and Japan," National Bureau of Economic Research, September 1989.
[6] U.S. Department of Commerce, Bureau of Labor Statistics, "Wages of Unionized and Nonunionized Workers," various issues.

more than a high school diploma, do not expect a good routine production job to be awaiting you.

16   Also vanishing are lower- and middle-level management jobs involving routine production. Between 1981 and 1986, more than 780,000 foremen, supervisors, and section chiefs lost their jobs through plant closings and layoffs.[7] Large numbers of assistant division heads, assistant directors, assistant managers, and vice presidents also found themselves jobless. GM shed more than 40,000 white-collar employees and planned to eliminate another 25,000 by the mid-1990s.[8] As America's core pyramids metamorphosed into global webs, many middle-level routine producers were as obsolete as routine workers on the line.

17   As has been noted, foreign-owned webs are hiring some Americans to do routine production in the United States. Philips, Sony, and Toyota factories are popping up all over—to the self-congratulatory applause of the nation's governors and mayors, who have lured them with promises of tax abatements and new sewers, among other amenities. But as these ebullient politicians will soon discover, the foreign-owned factories are highly automated and will become far more so in years to come. Routine production jobs account for a small fraction of the cost of producing most items in the United States and other advanced nations, and this fraction will continue to decline sharply as computer-integrated robots take over. In 1977, it took routine producers thirty-five hours to assemble an automobile in the United States; it is estimated that by the mid-1990s, Japanese-owned factories in America will be producing finished automobiles using only eight hours of a routine producer's time.[9]

18   The productivity and resulting wages of American workers who run such robotic machinery may be relatively high, but there may not be many such jobs to go around. A case in point: In the late 1980s, Nippon Steel joined with America's ailing Inland Steel to build a new $400 million cold-rolling mill fifty miles west of Gary, Indiana. The mill was celebrated for its state-of-the-art technology, which cut the time to produce a coil of steel from twelve days to about one hour. In fact, the entire plant could be run by a small team of technicians, which became clear when Inland subsequently closed two of its old cold-rolling mills, laying off hundreds of routine workers. Governors and mayors take note: Your much-ballyhooed foreign factories may end up employing distressingly few of your constituents.

19   Overall, the decline in routine jobs has hurt men more than women. This is because the routine production jobs held by men in high-volume metal bending manufacturing industries had paid higher wages than the routine production jobs held by women in textiles and data processing. As both sets of jobs have been lost, American women in routine production have gained more equal footing with American men—equally poor footing, that is. This is a major reason why the gender gap between male and female wages began to close during the 1980s.

---

[7] U.S. Department of Labor, Bureau of Labor Statistics, "Reemployment Increases among Displaced workers," *BLS News*, USDL 86-414, October 14, 1986, table 6.

[8] *Wall Street Journal*, February 16, 1990, p. A5.

[9] Figures from the International Motor Vehicles Program, Massachusetts Institute of Technology, 1989.

20 The second of the three boats, carrying in-person servers, is sinking as well, but somewhat more slowly and unevenly. Most in-person servers are paid at or just slightly above the minimum wage and many work only part-time, with the result that their take-home pay is modest, to say the least. Nor do they typically receive all the benefits (health care, life insurance, disability, and so forth) garnered by routine producers in large manufacturing corporations or by symbolic analysts affiliated with the more affluent threads of global webs.[10] In-person servers are sheltered from the direct effects of global competition and, like everyone else, benefit from access to lower-cost products from around the world. But they are not immune to its indirect effects.

21   For one thing, in-person servers increasingly compete with former routine production workers, who, no longer able to find well-paying routine production jobs, have few alternatives but to seek in-person service jobs. The Bureau of Labor Statistics estimates that of the 2.8 million manufacturing workers who lost their jobs during the early 1980s, fully one-third were rehired in service jobs paying at least 20 percent less.[11] In-person servers must also compete with high school graduates and dropouts who years before had moved easily into routine production jobs but no longer can. And if demographic predictions about the American work force in the first decades of the twenty-first century are correct (and they are likely to be, since most of the people who will comprise the work force are already identifiable), most new entrants into the job market will be black or Hispanic men, or women—groups that in years past have possessed relatively weak technical skills. This will result in an even larger number of people crowding into in-person services. Finally, in-person servers will be competing with growing numbers of immigrants, both legal and illegal, for whom in-person services will comprise the most accessible jobs. (It is estimated that between the mid-1980s and the end of the century, about a quarter of all workers entering the American labor force will be immigrants.[12])

22   Perhaps the fiercest competition that in-person servers face comes from labor-saving machinery (much of it invented, designed, fabricated, or assembled in other nations, of course). Automated tellers, computerized cashiers, automatic car washes, robotized vending machines, self-service gasoline pumps, and all similar gadgets substitute for the human beings that customers once encountered. Even telephone operators are fast disappearing, as electronic sensors and voice simulators become capable of carrying on conversations that are reasonably intelligent and always polite. Retail sales workers—among the largest groups of in-person servers—are similarly imperiled. Through personal computers linked to television screens, tomorrow's consumers will be able to buy furniture, appliances, and all sorts of electronic toys from their living rooms—examining the merchandise from all angles, selecting whatever color, size, special features, and

[10] The growing portion of the American labor force engaged in in-person services, relative to routine production, thus helps explain why the number of Americans lacking health insurance increased by at least 6 million during the 1980s.

[11] U.S. Department of Labor, Bureau of Labor Statistics, "Reemployment Increases among Disabled Workers," October 14, 1986.

[12] Federal Immigration and Naturalization Service, *Statistical Yearbook* (Washington, D.C.: U.S. Government Printing Office, 1986, 1987).

price seem most appealing, and then transmitting the order instantly to warehouses from which the selections will be shipped directly to their homes. So, too, with financial transactions, airline and hotel reservations, rental car agreements, and similar contracts, which will be executed between consumers in their homes and computer banks somewhere else on the globe.[13]

23   Advanced economies like the United States will continue to generate sizable numbers of new in-person service jobs, of course, the automation of older ones notwithstanding. For every bank teller who loses her job to an automated teller, three new jobs open for aerobics instructors. Human beings, it seems, have an almost insatiable desire for personal attention. But the intense competition nevertheless ensures that the wages of in-person servers will remain relatively low. In-person servers—working on their own, or else dispersed widely amid many small establishments, filling all sorts of personal-care niches—cannot readily organize themselves into labor unions or create powerful lobbies to limit the impact of such competition.

24   In two respects, demographics will work in favor of in-person servers, buoying their collective boat slightly. First, as has been noted, the rate of growth of the American work force is slowing. In particular, the number of young workers is shrinking. Between 1985 and 1995, the number of the eighteen- to twenty-four-year-olds will have declined by 17.5 percent. Thus, employers will have more incentive to hire and train in-person servers whom they might previously have avoided. But this demographic relief from the competitive pressures will be only temporary. The cumulative procreative energies of the postwar baby-boomers (born between 1946 and 1964) will result in a new surge of workers by 2010 or thereabouts.[14] And immigration—both legal and illegal—shows every sign of increasing in years to come.

25   Next, by the second decade of the twenty-first century, the number of Americans aged sixty-five and over will be rising precipitously, as the baby-boomers reach retirement age and live longer. Their life expectancies will lengthen not just because fewer of them will have smoked their way to their graves and more will have eaten better than their parents, but also because they will receive all sorts of expensive drugs and therapies designed to keep them alive—barely. By 2035, twice as many Americans will be elderly as in 1988, and the number of octogenarians is expected to triple. As these decaying baby-boomers ingest all the chemicals and receive all the treatments, they will need a great deal of personal attention. Millions of deteriorating bodies will require nurses, nursing-home operators, hospital administrators, orderlies, home-care providers, hospice aides, and technicians to operate and maintain all the expensive machinery that will monitor and temporarily stave off final disintegration. There might even be a booming market for euthanasia specialists. In-person servers catering to the old and ailing will be in strong demand.[15]

---

[13] See Claudia H. Deutsch, "The Powerful Push for Self-Service," *New York Times*, April 9, 1989, section 3, p. 1.

[14] U.S. Bureau of the Census, Current Population Reports, Series P-23, no. 138, tables 2-1, 4-6. See W. Johnson, A. Packer, et al., *Workforce 2000: Work and Workers for the 21st Century* (Indianapolis: Hudson Institute, 1987).

[15] The Census Bureau estimates that by the year 2000, at least 12 million Americans will work in health services— well over 6 percent of the total work force.

26   One small problem: the decaying baby-boomers will not have enough money to pay for these services. They will have used up their personal savings years before. Their Social Security payments will, of course, have been used by the government to pay for the previous generation's retirement and to finance much of the budget deficits of the 1980s. Moreover, with relatively fewer young Americans in the population, the supply of housing will likely exceed the demand, with the result that the boomers' major investments—their homes—will be worth less (in inflation-adjusted dollars) when they retire than they planned for. In consequence, the huge cost of caring for the graying boomers will fall on many of the same people who will be paid to care for them. It will be like a great sump pump: In-person servers of the twenty-first century will have an abundance of health-care jobs, but a large portion of their earnings will be devoted to Social Security payments and income taxes, which will in turn be used to pay their salaries. The net result: No real improvement in their standard of living.

27   The standard of living of in-person servers also depends, indirectly, on the standard of living of the Americans they serve who are engaged in world commerce. To the extent that *these* Americans are richly rewarded by the rest of the world for what they contribute, they will have more money to lavish upon in-person services. Here we find the only form of "trickle-down" economics that has a basis in reality. A waitress in a town whose major factory has just been closed is unlikely to earn a high wage or enjoy much job security; in a swank resort populated by film producers and banking moguls, she is apt to do reasonably well. So, too, with nations. In-person servers in Bangladesh may spend their days performing roughly the same tasks as in-person servers in the United States, but have a far lower standard of living for their efforts. The difference comes in the value that their customers add to the world economy.

28   Unlike the boats of routine producers and in-person servers, however, the vessel containing America's symbolic analysts is rising. Worldwide demand for their insights is growing as the ease and speed of communicating them steadily increases. Not every symbolic analyst is rising as quickly or as dramatically as every other, of course; symbolic analysts at the low end are barely holding their own in the world economy. But symbolic analysts at the top are in such great demand worldwide that they have difficulty keeping track of all their earnings. Never before in history has opulence on such a scale been gained by people who have earned it, and done so legally.

29   Among symbolic analysts in the middle range are American scientists and researchers who are busily selling their discoveries to global enterprise webs. They are not limited to American customers. If the strategic brokers in General Motors' headquarters refuse to pay a high price for a new means of making high-strength ceramic engines dreamed up by a team of engineers affiliated with Carnegie Mellon University in Pittsburgh, the strategic brokers of Honda or Mercedes-Benz are likely to be more than willing.

30   So, too, with the insights of America's ubiquitous management consultants, which are being sold for large sums to eager entrepreneurs in Europe and Latin America. Also, the insights of America's energy consultants, sold for even larger sums to Arab sheikhs. American design engineers are providing insights to

Olivetti, Mazda, Siemens, and other global webs; American marketers, techniques for learning what worldwide consumers will buy; American advertisers, ploys for ensuring that they actually do. American architects are issuing designs and blueprints for opera houses, art galleries, museums, luxury hotels, and residential complexes in the world's major cities; American commercial property developers, marketing these properties to worldwide investors and purchasers.

31   Americans who specialize in the gentle art of public relations are in demand by corporations, governments, and politicians in virtually every nation. So, too, are American political consultants, some of whom, at this writing, are advising the Hungarian Socialist Party, the remnant of Hungary's ruling Communists, on how to salvage a few parliamentary seats in the nation's first free election in more than forty years. Also at this writing, a team of American agricultural consultants is advising the managers of a Soviet farm collective employing 1,700 Russians eighty miles outside Moscow. As noted, American investment bankers and lawyers specializing in financial circumnavigations are selling their insights to Asians and Europeans who are eager to discover how to make large amounts of money by moving large amounts of money.

32   Developing nations, meanwhile, are hiring American civil engineers to advise on building roads and dams. The present thaw in the Cold War will no doubt expand these opportunities. American engineers from Bechtel (a global firm notable for having employed both Caspar Weinberger and George Shultz for much larger sums than either earned in the Reagan administration) have begun helping the Soviets design and install a new generation of nuclear reactors. Nations also are hiring American bankers and lawyers to help them renegotiate the terms of their loans with global banks, and Washington lobbyists to help them with Congress, the Treasury, the World Bank, the IMF, and other politically sensitive institutions. In fits of obvious desperation, several nations emerging from communism have even hired American economists to teach them about capitalism.

33   Almost everyone around the world is buying the skills and insights of Americans who manipulate oral and visual symbols—musicians, sound engineers, film producers, makeup artists, directors, cinematographers, actors and actresses, boxers, scriptwriters, songwriters, and set designers. Among the wealthiest of symbolic analysts are Steven Spielberg, Bill Cosby, Charles Schulz, Eddie Murphy, Sylvester Stallone, Madonna, and other star directors and performers—who are almost as well known on the streets of Dresden and Tokyo as in the Back Bay of Boston. Less well rewarded but no less renowned are the unctuous anchors on Turner Broadcasting's Cable News, who appear daily, via satellite, in places ranging from Vietnam to Nigeria. Vanna White is the world's most-watched game-show hostess. Behind each of these familiar faces is a collection of American problem-solvers, -identifiers, and brokers who train, coach, advise, promote, amplify, direct, groom, represent, and otherwise add value to their talents.[16]

---

[16] In 1989, the entertainment business summoned to the United States $5.5 billion in foreign earnings—making it among the nation's largest export industries, just behind aerospace. U.S. Department of Commerce, International Trade Commission, "Composition of U.S. Exports," various issues.

34   There are also the insights of senior American executives who occupy the world headquarters of global "American" corporations and the national or regional headquarters of global "foreign" corporations. Their insights are duly exported to the rest of the world through the webs of global enterprise. IBM does not export many machines from the United States, for example. Big Blue makes machines all over the globe and services them on the spot. Its prime American exports are symbolic and analytic. From IBM's world headquarters in Armonk, New York, emanate strategic brokerage and related management services bound for the rest of the world. In return, IBM's top executives are generously rewarded.

35 The most important reason for this expanding world market and increasing global demand for the symbolic and analytic insights of Americans has been the dramatic improvement in the worldwide communication and transportation technologies. Designs, instructions, advice, and visual and audio symbols can be communicated more and more rapidly around the globe, with ever greater precision and at ever-lower cost. Madonna's voice can be transported to billions of listeners, with perfect clarity, on digital compact disks. A new invention emanating from engineers in Battelle's laboratory in Columbus, Ohio, can be sent almost anywhere via modem, in a form that will allow others to examine it in three dimensions through enhanced computer graphics. When face-to-face meetings are still required—and videoconferencing will not suffice—it is relatively easy for designers, consultants, advisers, artists, and executives to board supersonic jets and, in a matter of hours, meet directly with their worldwide clients, customers, audiences, and employees.

36   With rising demand comes rising compensation. Whether in the form of licensing fees, fees for service, salaries, or shares in final profits, the economic result is much the same. There are also nonpecuniary rewards. One of the best-kept secrets among symbolic analysts is that so many of them enjoy their work. In fact, much of it does not count as work at all, in the traditional sense. The work of routine producers and in-person servers is typically monotonous; it causes muscles to tire or weaken and involves little independence or discretion. The "work" of symbolic analysts, by contrast, often involves puzzles, experiments, games, a significant amount of chatter, and substantial discretion over what to do next. Few routine producers or in-person servers would "work" if they did not need to earn the money. Many symbolic analysts would "work" even if money were no object.

37 At mid-century, when America was a national market dominated by core pyramid-shaped corporations, there were constraints on the earnings of people at the highest rungs. First and most obviously, the market for their services was largely limited to the borders of the nation. In addition, whatever conceptual value they might contribute was small relative to the value gleaned from large scale—and it was dependent on large scale for whatever income it was to summon. Most of the problems to be identified and solved had to do with enhancing the efficiency of production and improving the flow of materials,

parts, assembly, and distribution. Inventors searched for the rare breakthrough revealing an entirely new product to be made in high volume; management consultants, executives, and engineers thereafter tried to speed and synchronize its manufacture, to better achieve scale efficiencies; advertisers and marketers sought then to whet the public's appetite for the standard item that emerged. Since white-collar earnings increased with larger scale, there was considerable incentive to expand the firm; indeed, many of America's core corporations grew far larger than scale economies would appear to have justified.

38   By the 1990s, in contrast, the earnings of symbolic analysts were limited neither by the size of the national market nor by the volume of production of the firms with which they were affiliated. The marketplace was worldwide, and conceptual value was high relative to value added from scale efficiencies.

39   There had been another constraint on high earnings, which also gave way by the 1990s. At mid-century, the compensation awarded to top executives and advisers of the largest of America's core corporations could not be grossly out of proportion to that of low-level production workers. It would be unseemly for executives who engaged in highly visible rounds of bargaining with labor unions, and who routinely responded to government requests to moderate prices, to take home wages and benefits wildly in excess of what other Americans earned. Unless white-collar executives restrained themselves, moreover, blue-collar production workers could not be expected to restrain their own demands for higher wages. Unless both groups exercised restraint, the government could not be expected to forbear from imposing direct controls and regulations.

40   At the same time, the wages of production workers could not be allowed to sink too low, lest there be insufficient purchasing power in the economy. After all, who would buy all the goods flowing out of American factories if not American workers? This, too, was part of the tacit bargain struck between American managers and their workers.

41   Recall the oft-repeated corporate platitude of the era about the chief executive's responsibility to carefully weigh and balance the interests of the corporation's disparate stakeholders. Under the stewardship of the corporate statesman, no set of stakeholders—least of all white-collar executives—was to gain a disproportionately large share of the benefits of corporate activity; nor was any stakeholder—especially the average worker—to be left with a share that was disproportionately small. Banal though it was, this idea helped to maintain the legitimacy of the core American corporation in the eyes of most Americans, and to ensure continued economic growth.

42   But by the 1990s, these informal norms were evaporating, just as (and largely because) the core American corporation was vanishing. The links between top executives and the American production worker were fading: An ever-increasing number of subordinates and contractees were foreign, and a steadily growing number of American routine producers were working for foreign-owned firms. An entire cohort of middle-level managers, who had once been deemed "white collar," had disappeared; and, increasingly, American executives were exporting their insights to global enterprise webs.

43 As the American corporation itself became a global web almost indistinguishable from any other, its stakeholders were turning into a large and diffuse group, spread over the world. Such global stakeholders were less visible, and far less noisy, than national stakeholders. And as the American corporation sold its goods and services all over the world, the purchasing power of American workers became far less relevant to its economic survival.

44 Thus have the inhibitions been removed. The salaries and benefits of America's top executives, and many of their advisers and consultants, have soared to what years before would have been unimaginable heights, even as those of other Americans have declined.

Comprehension

1. To what does the title allude? Why is this allusion significant to the meaning of the title?

2. To whom does Reich refer when he mentions "symbolic analysts"? Regardless of their occupation, what do all symbolic analysts have in common regarding the nature of their work?

3. What has traditionally been the image of and the nature of work among the white-collar workers to whom Reich alludes? Why are they now one of the groups in danger of losing employment opportunities?

Rhetorical Analysis

4. Reich uses the central metaphor of the "boat" in describing the state of economics and employment. Why? What connotations are associated with this image in regard to financial security?

5. How does Reich's introduction prepare you for the major themes he addresses in the body of his essay?

6. Examine the section breaks at the start of paragraphs 3, 11, 20, 35, and 37. How does each section relate to the theme of the essay as a whole? What transitional devices does Reich use to bridge one section to the next?

7. Paragraphs 5, 6, 9, and 16 cite specific and detailed examples of the effects of the changing global economy. How does this technique/ strategy contribute to conveying Reich's authority regarding the subject he is discussing?

8. Reich describes a dire situation for the American worker. How would you characterize the tone of this description? Is it angry, resigned, impartial, or accusatory? You may use these or any other adjectives as long as you explain your view and provide evidence.

9. Why does Reich open his essay with an epigraph from Adam Smith? What is the relationship of the quotation to the overall theme of the essay? How does the tone of the epigraph contrast with the tone of the title?

10. What is the author's purpose? Is it to inform, to explain, to warn, to enlighten, to offer solutions, or a combination of any of these? Explain your view.

Writing

11. In a classification essay, describe three areas of academic concentration that can help prepare one for a job as a symbolic analyst.

12. In an expository essay, explain whether you believe the discrepancy between high-wage and low-wage workers will increase, decrease, or remain the same. Consider changes that may have occurred since Reich wrote the essay in 1991.

13. **Writing an Argument**   In an essay, argue for or against the proposition that as long as one knows which careers command the highest salaries, it is up to the individual to decide whether he or she should pursue a job in those fields.

Rhetorical Analysis

Read the paragraph below from "Professions for Women" and answer the questions that follow.

When your secretary invited me to come here, she told me that your Society is concerned with the employment of women and she suggested that I might tell you something about my own professional experiences. It is true I am a woman; it is true I am employed; but what professional experiences have I had? It is difficult to say. My profession is literature; and in that profession there are fewer experiences for women than in any other, with the exception of the stage—fewer, I mean, that are peculiar to women. For the road was cut many years ago—by Fanny Burney, by Aphra Behn, by Harriet Martineau, by Jane Austen, by George Eliot—many famous women, and many more unknown and forgotten, have been before me, making the path smooth, and regulating my steps. Thus, when I came to write, there were very few material obstacles in my way. Writing was a reputable and harmless occupation. The family peace was not broken by the scratching of a pen. No demand was made upon the family purse. For ten and sixpence one can buy paper enough to write all the plays of Shakespeare—if one has a mind that way. Pianos and models, Paris, Vienna and Berlin, masters and mistresses, are not needed by a writer. The cheapness of writing paper is, of course, the reason why women have succeeded as writers before they have succeeded in the other professions.

1. The use of dashes throughout the passage has which of the following effects?
    A. Creates a more informal, stream-of-conscious tone.
    B. Emulates a journalistic style, in turn building the audience's trust.
    C. Presents a natural style suggesting the author did not fully plan the narrative.
    D. Emphasizes specific words and phrases.
    E. Allows the author to vary sentence length without using other punctuation.

2. Consider the sentence, "It is true I am a woman; it is true I am employed; but what professional experiences have I had?" What is the effect of the author's use of multiple semicolons in the sentence?
    A. The semicolons allow the writer to build to a climax.
    B. The semicolons incorporate repetition to strengthen the author's main point.
    C. The semicolons enable the writer to use a rhetorical question with greater significance.
    D. The semicolons indicate that the three clauses are equally weighted, inextricably linked to a single idea.
    E. The semicolons add sentence complexity and variety by linking multiple ideas.

Read the paragraph below from "Delusions of Grandeur" and answer the question.

The failure of our public schools to educate athletes is part and parcel of the schools' failure to educate almost everyone. A recent survey of the Philadelphia school system, for example, stated that "more than half of all students in the third, fifth and eighth grades cannot perform minimum math and language tasks." One in four middle school students in that city fails to pass to the next grade each year. It is a sad truth that such statistics are repeated in cities throughout the nation. Young athletes— particularly young black athletes—are especially ill-served. Many of them are functionally illiterate, yet they are passed along from year to year for the greater glory of good old Hometown High. We should not be surprised to learn, then, that only 26.6% of black athletes at the collegiate level earn their degrees. For every successful educated black professional athlete, there are thousands of dead and wounded. Yet young blacks continue to aspire to careers as athletes, and it's no wonder why; when the University of North Carolina recently commissioned a sculptor to create archetypes of its student body, guess which ethnic group was selected to represent athletes?

3. The author's rhetorical stance is developed by
   A. Providing statistics, then drawing a conclusion about these statistics based on artistic representation.
   B. Juxtaposing the athletic successes of black athletes with the discrepancy of their scholastic success rates.
   C. Using dashes to offset important clarifying information, then posing a rhetorical question.
   D. Delineating the important differences between how students are treated in middle school and how those same students fare in college.
   E. Comparing and contrasting young, black male athletes with young, white male athletes.

Read the paragraphs below from "The Death of Horatio Alger" and answer the questions that follow.

Let's talk first about the facts on income distribution. Thirty years ago we were a relatively middle-class nation. It had not always been thus: Gilded Age America was a highly unequal society, and it stayed that way through the 1920s. During the 1930s and '40s, however, America experienced what the economic historians Claudia Goldin and Robert Margo have dubbed the Great Compression: a drastic narrowing of income gaps, probably as a result of New Deal policies. And the new economic order persisted for more than a generation: Strong unions; taxes on inherited wealth, corporate profits and high incomes; close public scrutiny of corporate management– all helped to keep income gaps relatively small. The economy was hardly egalitarian, but a generation ago the gross inequalities of the 1920s seemed very distant.

Now they're back. According to estimates by the economists Thomas Piketty and Emmanuel Saez–confirmed by data from the Congressional Budget Office–between 1973 and 2000 the average real income of the bottom 90 percent of American taxpayers actually fell by 7 percent. Meanwhile, the income of the top 1 percent rose by 148 percent, the income of the top 0.1 percent rose by 343 percent and the income of the top 0.01 percent rose 599 percent. (Those numbers exclude capital gains, so they're not an artifact of the stock-market bubble.) The distribution of income in the United States has gone right back to Gilded Age levels of inequality.

4. In the first paragraph of the selection, the author is mainly concerned about doing which of the following?
   A. Informing the reader of specific national challenges that are being repeated in the modern economy.
   B. Narrowly delineating the eras that set the United States up for further income inequality.
   C. Arguing that modern income inequality is much less egregious than that of earlier eras.
   D. Establishing broad historical facts about income inequality that establish the rhetorical situation.
   E. Reminiscing for a time when Americans were more socially similar than dissimilar.

5. How does the second paragraph of the selection relate to the first paragraph of the selection?
   A. In the first paragraph, the author broadly establishes historical context for his argument, while in the second paragraph he elaborates with specific factual evidence in support of his thesis.
   B. In the first paragraph, the author develops an ethos-based argument by citing specific historical experts, while in the second paragraph he appeals to logos by quoting government statistics.
   C. He establishes an argument in the first paragraph, and then presents the counter-argument in the second paragraph.
   D. The first paragraph provides the specific argument; the second paragraph provides a more generalized basis for the argument.
   E. The first paragraph relies on the historical record, while the second paragraph points out fallacies present in the math used to define that argument.

Read the paragraph below from "Globalization: The Super-Story" and answer the question that follows.

I am a big believer in the idea of the super-story, the notion that we all carry around with us a big lens, a big framework, through which we look at the world, order events, and decide what is important and what is not. The events of 9/11 did not happen in a vacuum. They happened in the context of a new international system—a system that cannot explain everything but *can* explain and connect more things in more places on more days than anything else. That new international system is called globalization. It came together in the late 1980s and replaced the previous international system, the cold war system, which had reigned since the end of World War II. This new system is the lens, the super-story, through which I viewed the events of 9/11.

—Reprinted by permission of Farrar, Straus and Giroux: "Prologue: The Super Story" from LONGITUDES AND ATTITUDES by Thomas L. Friedman. Copyright ©2002 by Thomas L. Friedman.

6. The tone of the first sentence of the passage is described most accurately as
   A. Amazed yet sentimental.
   B. Personal and colloquial.
   C. Straightforward yet biased.
   D. Nostalgic and somber.
   E. Authoritative and sincere.

Read the paragraph below from *Nickel and Dimed* and answer the questions that follow.

Forty minutes go by before anyone acknowledges my presence with more than a harried nod. During this time the other employees arrive, about twenty of them, already glowing in their uniforms, and breakfast on the free coffee, bagels, and doughnuts The Maids kindly provides for us. All but one of the others are female, with an average age I would guess in the late twenties, though the range seems to go from prom-fresh to well into the Medicare years. There is a pleasant sort of bustle as people get their breakfasts and fill plastic buckets with rags and bottles of cleaning fluids, but surprisingly little conversation outside of a few references to what people ate (pizza) and drank (Jell-O shots are mentioned) over the weekend. Since the room in which we gather contains only two folding chairs, both of them occupied, the other new girl and I sit cross-legged on the floor, silent and alert, while the regulars get sorted into teams of three or four and dispatched to the day's list of houses. One of the women explains to me that teams do not necessarily return to the same houses week after week, nor do you have any guarantee of being on the same team from one day to the next. This, I suppose, is one of the advantages of a corporate cleaning service to its customers: There are no sticky and possibly guilt-ridden relationships involved, because the customers communicate almost entirely with Tammy, the office manager, or with Ted, the franchise owner and our boss. The advantage to the cleaning person is harder to determine, since the pay compares so poorly to what an independent cleaner is likely to earn—up to $15 an hour, I've heard. While I wait in the inner room, where the phone is and Tammy has her desk, to be issued a uniform, I hear her tell a potential customer on the phone that The Maids charges $25 per person-hour. The company gets $25 and we get $6.65 for each hour we work? I think I must have misheard, but a few minutes later I hear her say the same thing to another inquirer. So the only advantage of working here as opposed to freelancing is that you don't need a clientele or even a car. You can arrive straight from welfare or, in my case, the bus station—fresh off the boat.

—Excerpts from "Scrubbing in Maine" from the book NICKEL AND DIMED: On (Not) Getting By In America by Barbara Ehrenreich. Copyright © 2001 by Barbara Ehrenreich. Reprinted by permission of Henry Holt and Company, LLC.

7. The tone and style of the passage can most clearly be described as
   A. Sarcastic and biting.
   B. Straightforward and journalistic.
   C. Critical and demeaning.
   D. Glowing and effusive.
   E. Belligerent and enigmatic.

8. The author concludes the paragraph with the phrase "fresh off the boat," most clearly alluding to which of the following?
   A. The naiveté and even desperation of the workers employed by The Maids.
   B. The idea that many of the workers must ride a ferry in order to get to the homes they are required to clean.
   C. To the people whose houses the author and her coworkers clean as boat owners.
   D. A colloquial expression meant to convey the hominess of the situation in which these workers find themselves.
   E. A reference to the idea that many of the workers do not have legal immigration status.

Read the paragraphs below from "Why the Rich are Getting Richer and the Poor, Poorer" and answer the questions that follow.

All Americans used to be in roughly the same economic boat. Most rose or fell together, as the corporations in which they were employed, the industries comprising such corporations, and the national economy as a whole became more productive—or languished. But national borders no longer define our economic fates. We are now in different boats, one sinking rapidly, one sinking more slowly, and the third rising steadily.

The boat containing routine producers is sinking rapidly. Recall that by midcentury routine production workers in the United States were paid relatively well. The giant pyramidlike organizations at the core of each major industry coordinated their prices and investments—avoiding the harsh winds of competition and thus maintaining healthy earnings. Some of these earnings, in turn, were reinvested in new plant and equipment (yielding ever-larger-scale economies);

another portion went to top managers and investors. But a large and increasing portion went to middle managers and production workers. Work stoppages posed such a threat to high-volume production that organized labor was able to exact an ever-larger premium for its cooperation. And the pattern of wages established within the core corporations influenced the pattern throughout the national economy. Thus the growth of a relatively affluent middle class, able to purchase all the wondrous things produced in high volume by the core corporations.

9. The author most clearly uses which of the following strategies to develop his ideas in the excerpt?
   A. Anecdotal evidence from the business sector
   B. An extended metaphor likening the economic plight of Americans to a boat
   C. A direct thesis supported by specific historical examples
   D. A generalized description of the business sector
   E. Definition of terms unfamiliar to the audience

10. The second paragraph most clearly relates to the first paragraph in which of the following ways?
    A. The first paragraph establishes the topic; the second paragraph introduces the argument.
    B. The first paragraph presents a central thesis; the second paragraph elaborates on and broadens that thesis to multiple complementary arguments.
    C. The first paragraph provides a central opinion on the economy; the second paragraph provides direct evidence to support the author's assertions.
    D. The first paragraph presents a series of rhetorical situations related through a boating analogy; the second paragraph extends the boating analogy to incorporate a second allusion to pyramids to explain the author's position.
    E. The first paragraph establishes a broad central metaphor; the second paragraph describes specific examples to extend the meaning of that metaphor.

Connections for Critical Thinking

1. Using the essays of Ehrenreich and Reich, compare the effects of work on human relationships.

2. Write a definition essay titled "What Is Work?" Refer to any of the selections in this chapter to substantiate your opinions.

3. Describe the potential effect of the global marketplace as described by Reich and Friedman.

4. Compare the methods Ehrenreich and Reich use to point out the options of those on the lowest rungs of the economic system in Western society.

Online Shopping: Has It Affected Our Lives for Better or Worse?

French author Alphonse Karr (1849) observed "The more things change, the more they stay the same." Many people would argue, however, that online shopping has completely changed the way shoppers shop. The social aspects of shopping have disappeared, and companies such as Amazon have taken the place of malls, big box stores, mom-and-pop shops, and open-air markets. Has online shopping signaled the demise of retail? Critically read and analyze these sources, and answer the questions that follow.

▼ SOURCE A

Online Shopping

Georgejmclittle/Shutterstock

"6 Strange Ways Online Shopping Has Changed the World" by Mikey Rox

—Mikey Rox, WiseBread.com

If you prefer online shopping to in-store purchases, you're not alone. According to *Business Insider*, about 78% of the U.S. population age 15 and older fancies themselves a few clicks and a quick checkout when buying something new. While that's all well and good—and incredibly convenient—this new American pastime does have its downsides. Check out a few of these strange ways online shopping has changed the world—not necessarily for the better. . . .

Shopping Malls Are Becoming Ruins

Shopping malls were huge in the 1980s and '90s, so much so that they defined an entire generation. But by the 2000s, attendance at malls around the country started to dwindle. Many factors have contributed to the decline (not the least of which was that they had become locales of violence), including the rise of online shopping. Bustling hubs of commerce and social activity that once stood proud are now in ruin, relics of the past that serve as a stark reminder that American life isn't what it used to be.

"Dozens of malls have shuttered since 2010, with hundreds more on the brink," says Benjamin Glaser, features editor with *DealNews*. The few shopping centers that have been built in the last decade usually aren't traditional, enclosed malls, but larger complexes with a wider dining and entertainment options, and often open-air areas. To compete with online shopping, brick-and-mortar retailers are trying to create experiences.

This fate doesn't paint a pretty picture of what was left in the wake of the downturn or for current mall owners. Those that have already heard its final cash register cha-ching now look like sets for *The Walking Dead*, and those that still exist are being murdered by debt.

Dog Bites Have Increased

Family dogs and mail carriers have had a rocky relationship for decades, but recently our friendly canines have been acting out in droves—all because that pesky USPS employee is stopping by more often with your online packages.

According to *AdAge*, dog bites were up 14% last year, reaching a total of 6,549 incidents. The most attacks were in Houston, which had 77, while San Diego and Cleveland clocked in at 58 each.

Identity Theft Is Out of Control

Before online shopping became everybody's go-to method of buying everything from clothing to groceries, it was difficult for an identity thief to target a large amount of data. Sure, your credit card could be stolen by a single thief and charged up until the bank caught wind of suspicious activity, but the consequences pale in comparison to a million-accounts data breach that could throw your entire life out of whack. *USA Today* reports that credit-card data theft has increased 50% from 2005 to 2010, according to the U.S. Department of Justice. Likewise, because your credit card numbers can be worth hundreds of dollar a piece to resellers—the number of malicious programs written to steal your information has grown from about 1 million in 2007 to an estimated 130 million today. So basically, no one is safe, and you should take even more precautions—like not storing your credit cards with retailers online—to avoid becoming a victim.

▼ SOURCE C

Quarterly Retail E-commerce Sales

Source: U.S. Census Bureau News, U.S. Department of Commerce https://www.census.gov/retail/mrts/www/data/pdf/ec_current.pdf

Estimated Quarterly U.S. Retail Sales: Total and E-commerce[1]					
Quarter	Retail Sales (millions of dollars)		E-commerce as a Percent of Total	Percent Change From Same Quarter A Year Ago	
	Total	E-commerce		Total	E-commerce
Adjusted[2]					
1st quarter 2018	1,306,692	123,672	9.5	4.5	16.4
4th quarter 2017	1,303,931	119,012	9.1	5.7	16.9
3rd quarter 2017	1,269,763	115,303	9.1	4.3	15.4
2nd quarter 2017	1,255,530	111,369	8.9	4.1	16.0
1st quarter 2017	1,250,698	106,207	8.5	5.2	15.2

[1] E-commerce sales are sales of goods and services where the buyer places an order, or the price and terms of the sale are negotiated over an Internet, mobile device (M-commerce), extranet, Electronic Data Interchange (EDI) network, electronic mail, or other comparable online system. Payment may or may not be made online.

[2] Estimates are adjusted for seasonal variation, but not for price changes. Total sales estimates are also adjusted for trading-day differences and moving holidays.

Retail Store Closures in 2017–2018

Retail Store Closures in 2017–2018	
Store	Closures
Abercrombie & Fitch	120
American Apparel	110
American Eagle	25
Ann Taylor, Lane Bryant, and Others	667
BCBG	120
Bebe	180
Best Buy	250
Bob's Stores	21
Bon-Ton Stores	42
The Children's Place	144
Crocs	209
CVS	70
EMS	27
Family Christian	240
Foot Locker	110
Gamestop	150
Gander Mountain	30
Gap Inc.	200
Gordmans Stores	106
Guess	85
Gymboree	452

Retail Store Closures in 2017–2018	
Store	Closures
hhgregg	220
JCPenney	146
J.Crew	20
Kmart	347
The Limited	250
Macy's	79
Mattress Firm	200
Michael Kors	175
Payless	808
Radio Shack	1,430
Rue21	400
Sam's Club	63
Sears	155
Staples	70
Tailored Brands	11
Teavana	379
Toys R Us	735
Walgreens/Rite Aid	600
Wet Seal	171
Winn-Dixie, Harvey's, and Bi-Lo	94

Sources: "More than 6,400 Stores Are Shutting Down—Here's the Full List" by Dennis Green and Anaele Pelisson, September 6, 2017. "More than 3,800 Stores Will Close in 2018—Here's the Full List" by Hayley Peterson, April 7, 2018. www.businessinsider.com

▼ SOURCE E

"Why Most Shoppers Still Choose Brick-and-Mortar Stores Over e-Commerce"
by Sandy Skrovan

—Originally published in Retail Dive www.retaildive.com

Online shopping has never been easier. But the majority of American consumers want the tactile experiences offered by physical stores.

Long live the brick-and-mortar store.

Everyone knows online shopping has never been easier or more accessible. But despite the surge in e-commerce capabilities, mobile applications and other technology advancements—including voice-activated shopping and the proliferation of Amazon Dash buttons—the majority of American consumers still want the tactile experiences offered by physical stores.

The ability to see, touch and feel products as well as take items home immediately rank highest among the reasons consumers choose to shop in stores versus online, according to Retail Dive's Consumer Survey. For the first question in a six-part series looking at consumer shopping habits, we surveyed 1,425 U.S. consumers via Google Surveys about the reasons why they choose to shop in stores over online.

By a fairly wide margin, the primary motivation for shopping in stores is to see and try out products before purchasing. However, some notable differences exist among shoppers, depending on their gender, age and location. In particular, female shoppers overwhelmingly want to see, touch and feel products before buying them. Males, on the other hand, skew more toward the immediate satisfaction of taking items home with them.

Shoppers at both ends of the age spectrum—younger and older generations—want to see or try products out in stores more than their middle-aged counterparts. Young shoppers clearly convey an "I want it now" mentality versus older cohorts.

▼ SOURCE F

Amazon Distribution Centre in Staffordshire, United Kingdom

SWNS/Alamy Stock Photo

Applying Your Synthesis Skills

Comprehension

1. Summarize the stated arguments made in each source.

Rhetorical Analysis

2. Compare and contrast the tone of the images presented in Sources A and F.

3. Which sources include irony? Explain.

4. How does the use of logos in Sources C and D impact their arguments?

Writing an Argument

5. Using examples from the sources, write an essay explaining your position on whether online shopping has affected our lives for better or worse.

CHAPTER 8

Media and Pop Culture: What Is the Message?

As you read the essays in this chapter, consider the following questions:

- What is the main media form and issue on which the author focuses?
- What tone or attitude does the author take toward the subject?
- How does the author fit his or her analysis into the context of popular culture? What social, economic, psychological, or political problems or controversies are treated?
- Which areas of expertise does the author bring to bear on the subject?
- What rhetorical mode—narration and description, exposition, argument—does the writer use? If argument, what is the author's claim? What evidence does she or he provide to support this claim?
- Which essays are similar in subject, thesis, style, purpose, or method, and why?
- What have you learned about the media and popular culture from reading these essays?
- Which essays did you find the most compelling or persuasive? The least? Why?

We are surrounded today as never before by images, sounds, and texts. Radio and television programs, newspapers and websites, video games, and cell phone gadgetry increasingly mold our place in culture and society. Indeed, the power of media in our waking and subliminal lives might very well condition our understanding (or misunderstanding) of reality. Today, we can download "reality."

Today's media universe, fueled by new technology, is transforming our sense of the world. Consider the ways in which computers permit us to enter the media stream, making us willing, even compulsive, participants in and consumers of popular culture. Video games, streaming advertisements and music, newsgroups, group chats, and more—all provide data and sensation at warp computer speed. Some slow down the torrent: Bloggers question the "facts," holding newspapers and television news channels accountable for information. But if, as Marshall McLuhan declared, the medium is the message, then any medium, whether old or new, has the power to reflect or construct versions of reality.

Perhaps Americans have moved from a print-based culture to an aural/visual one, preferring electronic media for information, distraction, and entertainment. For centuries, books were the molders of popular taste and culture. Tocqueville in *Democracy in America* was amazed by the fact that in the rudest pioneer's hut could be found a copy of Shakespeare—and probably, we might add, a copy of the best seller of all time, the Bible. Today's typical household might have more media than books in a library. Of course, print media—say, a book on the ways in which major political parties manipulate the media—offer us the opportunity to scrutinize facts and sources in ways that shock jocks on radio, or talk show hosts on television, or participants in chat rooms cannot. The *medium* or *source* from which we receive sounds, images, and text—the place from which we enter the media torrent—determines the version of reality we carry with us. We can even drown in this torrent, as people who have been captured in virtual reality can attest.

The writers in this chapter invite us to enter the media torrent from a variety of places. They ask broad cultural questions about how we conduct our everyday lives and what choices we make. These questions have both local and worldwide implications, because media and their technological helpmates have created a global village permitting the instant transmission of ideas and images, as well as a subtle transfer of culture—typically American—to the remotest parts of the planet. Whether we navigate the torrent intelligently or succumb passively to the images and sounds washing over us, it is clear that the media in this century will have an increasingly significant impact on human experience.

CLASSIC ▼

CONTEMPORARY ▼

During the 1930s, the first decade of sound films, actors such as Edward G. Robinson, James Cagney, and Paul Muni created the classic portrait of the gangster as a tough-talking, violent outlaw in films such as *Little Caesar* (1931), *The Public Enemy* (1931), and *Scarface* (1932).

What Do Gangster Films Reveal About Pop Culture?

Using a Critical Perspective Gangster films and shows—like *Little Caesar, The Godfather,* and *The Sopranos* series—challenge viewers to form ethical opinions about and interpretations of the crime and the criminal character. Even if you haven't seen either the film or TV show depicted here, what do you think is happening in each frame? What details do you focus on? Do the two characters capture the essence of gangster life, and why? What aspects of film art—framing, the use of close-up or distance shots, the handling of light, shadow, and color—convey an ethical statement? More broadly, in what ways can film art serve as a commentary on American life?

HBO's award-winning series *The Sopranos* provided a more nuanced portrait of the gangster as a member of a corrupt, and corrupting, organization with shifting loyalties. For example, Tony Soprano, the character played by James Gandolfini, is a family man beset by so many problems that he must seek psychiatric help.

Analyzing Visuals and Their Rhetoric

1. How do these two visuals give a historic portrayal of the stereotypical American gangster kingpin?

2. Which visual gives a more compelling argument for the iconic gangster, and what aspects of the visual reinforce this argument as opposed to the other visual?

3. How much do you know about the gangster prototype beyond these photos? Do current movie gangsters have the same or different characteristics from these classic gangsters? Explain.

CLASSIC ▼

Are We Shaped by Characters in Pop Culture?

Gloria Steinem and Daniel Barna examine the portrayal of nontraditional "heroes" in popular culture. Steinem argues that the emergence of Wonder Woman gave girls and young women a relatable character different from the female characters who always seemed to need to be "saved" by strong males. Barna argues that a different type of male protagonist has emerged in popular culture. This new protagonist shows more sensitivity and depth with an undercurrent of independence. Essentially, both writers suggest that nontraditional heroes—women and the sensitive male—exert a powerful hold on our imagination because they represent a different yet compelling mythology of American success. Ultimately both writers urge us to go beyond our fascination with media types to examine the ethical dimensions of the world the characters inhabit.

Wonder Woman

Gloria Steinem

Gloria Steinem (b. 1934) was born and raised in Toledo, Ohio; she attended Smith College, receiving a BA in government in 1956. A noted feminist and political activist, Steinem in 1968 helped to found *New York* magazine; in 1971 she cofounded *Ms.* magazine and served as its editor. Whether campaigning for Robert Kennedy, raising money for the United Farm Workers, or championing women's reproductive rights, Steinem has been on the cutting edge of American politics and social activism for almost five decades. Her books include *The Thousand Indias* (1957), *Outrageous Acts and Everyday Rebellions* (1983), *Marilyn: Norma Jean* (1986), *Revolution from Within* (1992), *Moving Beyond Words* (1994), and *Doing Sixty and Seventy* (2006). In the following essay, Steinem explains why the comic book heroine Wonder Woman (who was on the first cover of *Ms.*) was such a formative influence during her childhood.

1   Wonder Woman is the only female super-hero to be published continuously since comic books began—indeed, she is one of the few to have existed at all or to be anything other than part of a male super-hero group—but this may strike many readers as a difference without much distinction. After all, haven't comic books always been a little disreputable? Something that would never have been assigned in school? The answer to those questions is yes, which is exactly why they are important. Comic books have power—including over the child who still lives within each of us—because they are *not* part of the "serious" grown-up world.

2   I remember hundreds of nights reading comic books under the covers with a flashlight; dozens of car trips while my parents told me I was ruining my eyes and perhaps my mind ("brain-deadeners" was what my mother called them); and countless hours spent hiding in a tree or some other inaccessible spot where I could pore over their pages in sweet freedom. Because my family's traveling meant I didn't go to school regularly until I was about twelve, comic books joined cereal boxes and ketchup labels as the primers that taught me how to read. They were even cheap enough to be the first things I bought on my own—a customer who couldn't see over the countertop but whose dignity was greatly enhanced by making a choice, counting out carefully hoarded coins, and completing a grown-up exchange.

3   I've always wondered if this seemingly innate drive toward independence in children isn't more than just "a movement toward mastery," as psychologists say. After all, each of us is the result of millennia of environment and heredity, a unique combination that could never happen before—or again. Like a seed that contains a plant, a child is already a unique person; an ancient spirit born into a body too small to express itself, or even cope with the world. I remember feeling the greatest love for my parents whenever they allowed me to express my own will, whether that meant wearing an inappropriate hat for days on end, or eating dessert before I had finished dinner.

4   Perhaps it's our memories of past competence and dreams for the future that create the need for super-heroes in the first place. Leaping skyscrapers in a single bound, seeing through walls, and forcing people to tell the truth by encircling them in a magic lasso—all would be satisfying fantasies at any age, but they may be psychological necessities when we have trouble tying our shoes, escaping a worldview composed mainly of belts and knees, and getting grown-ups to *pay attention*.

5   The problem is that the super-heroes who perform magical feats—indeed, even mortal heroes who are merely competent—are almost always men. A female child is left to believe that, even when her body is as big as her spirit, she will still be helping with minor tasks, appreciating the accomplishments of others, and waiting to be rescued. Of course, pleasure is to be found in all these experiences of helping, appreciating, and being rescued; pleasure that should be open to boys, too. Even in comic books, heroes sometimes work in groups or are called upon to protect their own kind, not just helpless females. But the truth is that a male super-hero is more likely to be vulnerable, if only to create suspense, than a female character is to be powerful or independent. For little girls, the only alternative is suppressing a crucial part of ourselves by transplanting our consciousness into a male character—which usually means a white one, thus penalizing girls of color doubly, and boys of color, too. Otherwise, choices remain limited: in the case of girls, to an "ideal" life of sitting around like a Technicolor clotheshorse, getting into jams with villains, and

saying things like, "Oh, Superman! I'll always be grateful to you"; in the case of boys of color, to identifying with villains who may be the only ethnic characters with any power; and in the case of girls of color, to making an impossible choice between parts of their identity. It hardly seems worth learning to tie our shoes.

6   I'm happy to say that I was rescued from this dependent fate at the age of seven or so; rescued (Great Hera!) by a woman. Not only did she have the wisdom of Athena and Aphrodite's power to inspire love, she was also faster than Mercury and stronger than Hercules. In her all-woman home on Paradise Island, a refuge of ancient Amazon culture protected from nosy travelers by magnetic thought-fields that created an area known to the world as the Bermuda Triangle, she had come to her many and amazing powers naturally. Together with her Amazon sisters, she had been trained in them from infancy and perfected them in Greek-style contests of dexterity, strength, and speed. The lesson was that each of us might have unknown powers within us, if we only believed and practiced them. (To me, it always seemed boring that Superman had bullet-proof skin, X-ray vision, and the ability to fly. Where was the contest?) Though definitely white, as were all her Amazon sisters, she was tall and strong, with dark hair and eyes—a relief from the weak, bosomy, blonde heroines of the 1940s.

7   Of course, this Amazon did need a few fantastic gadgets to help her once she entered a modern world governed by Ares, God of War, not Aphrodite, Goddess of Love: a magic golden lasso that compelled all within its coils to obey her command, silver bracelets that repelled bullets, and an invisible plane that carried her through time as well as space. But she still had to learn how to throw the lasso with accuracy, be agile enough to deflect bullets from her silver-encased wrists, and navigate an invisible plane.

8   Charles Moulton, whose name appeared on each episode as Wonder Woman's writer and creator, had seen straight into my heart and understood the fears of violence and humiliation hidden there. No longer did I have to pretend to like the "POW!" and "SPLAT!" of boys' comic books, from Captain Marvel to the Green Hornet. No longer did I have nightmares after looking at ghoulish images of torture and murder, bloody scenes made all the more realistic by steel-booted Nazis and fang-toothed Japanese who were caricatures of World War II enemies then marching in every newsreel. (Eventually, the sadism of boys' comic books was so extreme that it inspired Congressional hearings, and publishers were asked to limit the number of severed heads and dripping entrails—a reminder that television wasn't the first popular medium selling sadism to boys.) Best of all, I could stop pretending to enjoy the ridicule, bossing-around, and constant endangering of female characters. In these Amazon adventures, only the villains bought the idea that "masculine" meant aggression and "feminine" meant submission. Only the occasional female accomplice said things like "Girls want superior men to boss them around," and even they were usually converted to the joys of self-respect by the story's end.

9   This was an Amazon super-hero who never killed her enemies. Instead, she converted them to a belief in equality and peace, to self-reliance, and respect for the rights of others. If villains destroyed themselves, it was through their own actions or some unbloody accident. Otherwise, they might be conquered by force, but it was a force tempered by love and justice.

10   In short, she was wise, beautiful, brave, and explicitly out to change "a world torn by the hatreds and wars of men."

11   She was Wonder Woman.

12   Only much later, when I was in my thirties and modern feminism had begun to explain the political roots of women's status—instead of accepting some "natural" inferiority decreed by biology, God, or Freud—did I realize how hard Charles Moulton had tried to get an egalitarian worldview into comic book form. From Wonder Woman's birth myth as Princess Diana of Paradise Island, "that enlightened land," to her adventures in America disguised as Diana Prince, a be-spectacled army nurse and intelligence officer (a clear steal from Superman's Clark Kent), this female super-hero was devoted to democracy, peace, justice, and "liberty and freedom for all womankind."

13   One typical story centers on Prudence, a young pioneer in the days of the American Frontier, where Wonder Woman has been transported by the invisible plane that doubles as a time machine. After being rescued from a Perils of Pauline life, Prudence finally realizes her own worth, and also the worth of all women. "From now on," she says proudly to Wonder Woman, "I'll rely on myself, not on a man." Another story ends with Wonder Woman explaining her own long-running romance with Captain Steve Trevor, the American pilot whose crash-landing on Paradise Island was Aphrodite's signal that the strongest and wisest of all the Amazons must answer the call of a war-torn world. As Wonder Woman says of this colleague whom she so often rescues: "I can never love a dominant man."

14   The most consistent villain is Ares, God of War, a kind of metavillain who considers women "the natural spoils of war" and insists they stay home as the slaves of men. Otherwise, he fears women will spread their antiwar sentiments, create democracy in the world, and leave him dishonored and unemployed. That's why he keeps trying to trick Queen Hippolyte, Princess Diana's mother, into giving up her powers as Queen of the Amazons, thus allowing him to conquer Paradise Island and destroy the last refuge of ancient feminism. It is in memory of a past time when the Amazons did give in to the soldiers of Ares, and were enslaved by them, that Aphrodite requires each Amazon to wear a pair of cufflike bracelets. If captured and bound by them (as Wonder Woman sometimes is in particularly harrowing episodes), an Amazon loses all her power. Wearing them is a reminder of the fragility of female freedom.

15   In America, however, villains are marked not only by their violence, but by their prejudice and lust for money. Thomas Tighe, woman-hating industrialist, is typical. After being rescued by Wonder Woman from accidental imprisonment

in his own bank vault, he refuses to give her the promised reward of a million dollars. Though the money is needed to support Holliday College, the home of the band of college girls who aid Wonder Woman, Tighe insists that its students must first complete impossible tests of strength and daring. Only after Wonder Woman's powers allow them to meet every challenge does Tighe finally admit: "You win, Wonder Woman! . . . I am no longer a woman hater." She replies: "Then you're the real winner, Mr. Tighe! Because when one ceases to hate, he becomes stronger!"

16   Other villains are not so easily converted. Chief among them is Dr. Psycho, perhaps a parody of Sigmund Freud. An "evil genius" who "abhors women," the mad doctor's intentions are summed up in this scene-setting preface to an episode called "Battle for Womanhood": "With weird cunning and dark, forbidden knowledge of the occult, Dr. Psycho prepares to change the independent status of modern American women back to the days of the sultans and slave markets, clanking chains and abject captivity. But sly and subtle Psycho reckons without Wonder Woman!"

17   When I looked into the origins of my proto-feminist super-hero, I discovered that her pseudonymous creator had been a very non-Freudian psychologist named William Moulton Marston. Also a lawyer, businessman, prison reformer, and inventor of the lie-detector test (no doubt the inspiration for Wonder Woman's magic lasso), he had invented Wonder Woman as a heroine for little girls, and also as a conscious alternative to the violence of comic books for boys. In fact, Wonder Woman did attract some boys as readers, but the integrated world of comic book trading revealed her true status: at least three Wonder Woman comic books were necessary to trade for one of Superman. Among the many male super-heroes, only Superman and Batman were to be as long-lived as Wonder Woman, yet she was still a second-class citizen.

18   Of course, it's also true that Marston's message wasn't as feminist as it might have been. Instead of portraying the goal of full humanity for women and men, which is what feminism has in mind, he often got stuck in the subject/object, winner/loser paradigm of "masculine" versus "feminine," and came up with female superiority instead. As he wrote: "Women represent love; men represent force. Man's use of force without love brings evil and unhappiness. Wonder Woman proves that women are superior to men because they have love in addition to force." No wonder I was inspired but confused by the isolationism of Paradise Island: Did women have to live separately in order to be happy and courageous? No wonder even boys who could accept equality might have felt less than good about themselves in some of these stories: Were there *any* men who could escape the cultural instruction to be violent?

19   Wonder Woman herself sometimes got trapped in this either/or choice. As she muses to herself: "Some girls love to have a man stronger than they are to make them do things. Do I like it? I don't know, it's sort of thrilling. But isn't it more fun to make a man obey?" Even female villains weren't capable of

being evil on their own. Instead, they were hyperfeminine followers of men's commands. Consider Priscilla Rich, the upper-class antagonist who metamorphoses into the Cheetah, a dangerous she-animal. "Women have been submissive to men," wrote Marston, "and taken men's psychology [force without love] as their own."

20   In those wartime years, stories could verge on a jingoistic, even racist patriotism. Wonder Woman sometimes forgot her initial shock at America's unjust patriarchal system and confined herself to defeating a sinister foreign threat by proving that women could be just as loyal and brave as men in service of their country. Her costume was a version of the Stars and Stripes. Some of her adversaries were suspiciously short, ugly, fat, or ethnic as a symbol of "un-American" status. In spite of her preaching against violence and for democracy, the good guys were often in uniform, and no country but the United States was seen as a bastion of freedom.

21   But Marston didn't succumb to stereotypes as often as most comic book writers of the 1940s. Though Prudence, his frontier heroine, is threatened by monosyllabic Indians, Prudence's father turns out to be the true villain, who has been cheating the Indians. And the irrepressible Etta Candy, one of Wonder Woman's band of college girls, is surely one of the few fat-girl heroines in comics.

22   There are other unusual rewards. Queen Hippolyte, for instance, is a rare example of a mother who is good, powerful, and a mentor to her daughter. She founds nations, fights to protect Paradise Island, and is a source of strength to Wonder Woman as she battles the forces of evil and inequality. Mother and daughter stay in touch through a sort of telepathic TV set, and the result is a team of equals who are separated only by experience. In the flashback episode in which Queen Hippolyte succumbs to Hercules, she is even seen as a sexual being. How many girl children grew to adulthood with no such example of a strong, sensual mother—except for these slender stories? How many mothers preferred sons, or believed the patriarchal myth that competition is "natural" between mothers and daughters, or tamed their daughters instead of encouraging their wildness and strength? We are just beginning to realize the sense of anger and loss in girls whose mothers had no power to protect them, or forced them to conform out of fear for their safety, or left them to identify only with their fathers if they had any ambition at all.

23   Finally, there is Wonder Woman's ability to unleash the power of self-respect within the women around her; to help them work together and support each other. This may not seem revolutionary to male readers accustomed to stories that depict men working together, but for females who are usually seen as competing for the favors of men—especially little girls who may just be getting to the age when girlfriends betray each other for the approval of boys—this discovery of sisterhood can be exhilarating indeed. Women get a rare message of independence, of depending on themselves, not even on Wonder Woman.

"You saved yourselves," as she says in one of her inevitable morals at story's end. "I only showed you that you could."

24 Whatever the shortcomings of William Marston, his virtues became clear after his death in 1947. Looking back at the post-Marston stories I had missed the first time around—for at twelve or thirteen, I thought I had outgrown Wonder Woman and had abandoned her—I could see how little her later writers understood her spirit. She became sexier-looking and more submissive, violent episodes increased, more of her adversaries were female, and Wonder Woman herself required more help from men in order to triumph. Like so many of her real-life sisters in the postwar era of conservatism and "togetherness" of the 1950s, she had fallen on very hard times.

25 By the 1960s, Wonder Woman had given up her magic lasso, her bullet-deflecting bracelets, her invisible plane, and all her Amazonian powers. Though she still had adventures and even practiced karate, any attractive man could disarm her. She had become a kind of female James Bond, though much more boring because she was denied his sexual freedom. She was Diana Prince, a mortal who walked about in boutique, car-hop clothes and took the advice of a male mastermind named "I Ching."

26 It was in this sad state that I first rediscovered my Amazon super-hero in 1972. *Ms.* magazine had just begun, and we were looking for a cover story for its first regular issue to appear in July. Since Joanne Edgar and other of its founding editors had also been rescued by Wonder Woman in their childhoods, we decided to rescue Wonder Woman in return. Though it wasn't easy to persuade her publishers to let us put her original image on the cover of a new and unknown feminist magazine, or to reprint her 1940s Golden Age episodes inside, we finally succeeded. Wonder Woman appeared on newsstands again in all her original glory, striding through city streets like a colossus, stopping planes and bombs with one hand and rescuing buildings with the other.

27 Clearly, there were many nostalgic grown-ups and heroine-starved readers of all ages. The consensus of response seemed to be that if we had all read more about Wonder Woman and less about Dick and Jane, we might have been a lot better off. As for her publishers, they, too, were impressed. Under the direction of Dorothy Woolfolk, the first woman editor of Wonder Woman in all her long history, she was returned to her original Amazon status—golden lasso, bracelets, and all.

28 One day some months after her rebirth, I got a phone call from one of Wonder Woman's tougher male writers. "Okay," he said, "she's got all her Amazon powers back. She talks to the Amazons on Paradise Island. She even has a Black Amazon sister named Nubia. Now will you leave me alone?"

29 I said we would.

30 In the 1970s, Wonder Woman became the star of a television series. As played by Lynda Carter, she was a little blue of eye and large of breast, but she still

retained her Amazon powers, her ability to convert instead of kill, and her appeal for many young female viewers. There were some who refused to leave their TV sets on Wonder Woman night. A few young boys even began to dress up as Wonder Woman on Halloween—a true revolution.

31   In the 1980s, Wonder Woman's story line was revamped by DC Comics, which reinvented its male super-heroes Superman and Batman at about the same time. Steve Trevor became a veteran of Vietnam; he remained a friend, but was romantically involved with Etta Candy. Wonder Woman acquired a Katharine Hepburn–Spencer Tracy relationship with a street-smart Boston detective named Ed Indelicato, whose tough-guy attitude played off Wonder Woman's idealism. She also gained a friend and surrogate mother in Julia Kapatelis, a leading archaeologist and professor of Greek culture at Harvard University who can understand the ancient Greek that is Wonder Woman's native tongue, and be a model of a smart, caring, single mother for girl readers. Julia's teenage daughter, Vanessa, is the age of many readers and goes through all of their uncertainties, trials, and tribulations, but has the joy of having a powerful older sister in Wonder Woman. There is even Myndi Mayer, a slick Hollywood public relations agent who turns Wonder Woman into America's hero, and is also in constant danger of betraying Diana's idealistic spirit. In other words, there are many of the currents of society today, from single mothers to the worries of teenage daughters and a commercial culture, instead of the simpler plots of America's dangers in World War II.

32   You will see whether Wonder Woman carries her true Amazon spirit into the present. If not, let her publishers know. She belongs to you.

33 Since Wonder Woman's beginnings more than a half century ago, however, a strange thing has happened: The Amazon myth has been rethought as archaeological relics have come to light. Though Amazons had been considered figments of the imagination, perhaps the mythological evidence of man's fear of woman, there is a tentative but growing body of evidence to support the theory that some Amazon-like societies did exist. In Europe, graves once thought to contain male skeletons—because they were buried with weapons or were killed by battle wounds—have turned out to hold skeletons of females after all. In the jungles of Brazil, scientists have found caves of what appears to have been an all-female society. The caves are strikingly devoid of the usual phallic design and theme; they feature, instead, the triangular female symbol, and the only cave that does bear male designs is believed to have been the copulatorium, where Amazons mated with males from surrounding tribes, kept only the female children, and returned male infants to the tribe. Such archaeological finds have turned up not only along the Amazon River in Brazil, but at the foot of the Atlas Mountains in northwestern Africa, and on the European and Asiatic sides of the Black Sea.

34   There is still far more controversy than agreement, but a shared supposition of these myths is this: Imposing patriarchy on the gynocracy of pre-history took many centuries and great cruelty. Rather than give up freedom and worship only male gods, some bands of women resisted. They formed all-woman cultures that survived by capturing men from local tribes, mating with them, and raising their girl children to have great skills of body and mind. These bands became warriors and healers who were sometimes employed for their skills by patriarchal cultures around them. As a backlash culture, they were doomed, but they may also have lasted for centuries.

35   Perhaps that's the appeal of Wonder Woman, Paradise Island, and this comic book message. It's not only a child's need for a lost independence, but an adult's need for a lost balance between women and men, between humans and nature. As the new Wonder Woman says to Vanessa, "Remember your *power*, little sister."

36   However simplified, that is Wonder Woman's message: Remember Our Power.

"Wonder Woman" by Gloria Steinem. Reprinted by permission of Gloria Steinem, feminist activist.

Comprehension

1. According to Steinem, why are children drawn to comic books and superheroes?

2. Why did Wonder Woman appeal especially to Steinem? What distinctions does she draw between the ways boys and girls view action heroes?

3. The writer traces the development of Wonder Woman from her inception during the 1940s to the 1980s. How did Wonder Woman change over the years? How did she remain true to her creator's (William Marston) conception of her? What does Steinem think about these changes?

Rhetorical Analysis

4. What is this essay's persuasive thesis?

5. At whom is this essay aimed—lovers of comic books, or women, or a general audience? On what do you base your conclusion?

6. In part, this is a personal essay. How does Steinem create her persona or self-image? Does the personal element enhance or detract from the analysis? Explain your response.

7. Sort out the complex cause-and-effect relationships in this essay. How does the comparative method reinforce the writer's analysis?

8. What types of evidence does the writer provide? Is it sufficient to convince readers? Where, if anywhere, would more detail be helpful?

9. Steinem divides the essay into five sections. What is her purpose? How successful is she in maintaining the essay's unity by employing this method?

10. What paragraphs form the writer's conclusion? How do they recapitulate and add to the substance of the overall essay?

Writing

11. Compare and contrast the ways in which actors have portrayed action heroes. Refer to specific icons like Batman, Spiderman, and Wonder Woman to support your assessment.

12. **Writing an Argument** Think about the numerous action heroes or superheroes that young children and adolescents encounter today in various media forms. Write an essay in which you contend that exposure to such superheroes either does or does not encourage violent behavior in young people.

Today's Leading Man

Daniel Barna

Daniel Barna is a writer who has lived in Montreal and New York City and is now based in Toronto. He has a BFA in Film Studies and Art History from Concordia University and is currently part of the editorial team of the biannual arts and culture magazine *Corduroy*. The following article discusses the new type of leading man today who is not the iconic rough and tumble type of man from previous eras. The author argues that Hollywood has a new type of leading man who expands into many types of roles and situations.

Modern leading men aren't what they used to be. There are no longer the Clark Gables, Cary Grants or Humphrey Bogarts of yesteryear—and we haven't yet found another George Clooney. But we want to know: What does it mean to be a leading man today, and who is he?

1   Ryan Gosling isn't content with the status quo. After the success of *The Notebook* proved that he could open a movie and that now-iconic, rain-soaked kiss he planted on Rachel McAdams' movie-star mouth made him an instant heartthrob, Hollywood rolled out the red carpet for their newly christened matinee idol. But instead of chasing a big paycheck by donning tights and a mask in another by-the-numbers superhero flick, Gosling went all indie on us, playing deeply flawed, idiosyncratic characters in films like *Half Nelson* and *Lars and the Real Girl.* And with that, a new generation of men fed up with Hollywood's idealized version of masculinity embraced a movie star they could relate to. They had found their new leading man.

Today's Man

2   It was the summer of 2009. Johnny Depp, Denzel Washington, Tom Hanks, and Russell Crowe—once the box office equivalents of Michael Jordan with the game on the line—all released films that were underwhelming at the box office. Studios panicked, and *The New York Times* was quick to declare "the death of the movie star." The newspaper hypothesized that external forces like Twitter and the paparazzi were at play, but it was, in fact, the onset of something far more profound. It wasn't quite the death of the movie star but rather the death of a certain *type* of movie star. As increasingly self-aware men began to revolt against the cookie-cutter action figures Hollywood was constantly throwing our way (yes, Will Smith, we're talking to you), a new model of leading man began to emerge, one that boasted brains over brawn, valued quality over quantity and who was as dark as he was dapper.

3   For years, Hollywood has perpetuated a nearly unattainable version of manhood, aggressively marketing its leading men as superhuman. As a result, men often linked heroism with masculinity; there's nothing more manly than a soldier or a cowboy or a spy, right? But today's male filmgoer doesn't live in a world where the bad guy is an insane Scandinavian billionaire who dies just before the inevitable getting-of-the-girl. Today's male filmgoer lives in a world where well-paying jobs are scarcer than ever, relationships are harder to maintain and happily ever after is just a blurry myth from our childhood.

4   Nathaniel Hawthorne once wrote, "A hero cannot be a hero unless in a heroic world," an observation that's never seemed more prescient than in our web-centric culture, where global anxieties—whether they be economic, social or political—are just a Wi-Fi connection away. Today's man doesn't have the luxury of being ignorant. No matter how flawed, we are forced to confront our issues with strategic thoughtfulness or risk falling by the wayside. Suddenly, the idea of a solitary action hero taking out a legion of bad guys doesn't feel heroic; it feels idiotic. Instead, the modern male moviegoer wants to watch someone they can relate to, someone with real-world problems, someone just like them. So while Tom Cruise was out leaping from building to couch, all the way into obscurity, Ryan Gosling was playing totally unconventional, totally flawed characters trying to make sense of a complicated and overwhelming world. In other words, he was playing us.

The New Leading Man

5   Ryan Gosling's career wasn't supposed to turn out this way. After spending much of his youth belting bubblegum pop in *The All-New Mickey Mouse Club*, alongside fellow Mousketeers and future tween dreams Britney Spears, Christina Aguilera, and Justin Timberlake, Gosling seemed destined for the dreaded curse of teen idoldom (or Freddie Prinze Jr. syndrome), something Timberlake is still trying to extricate himself from. While follow-up stints on the forgettable teen soap *Breaker High* and the campy TV series *Young Hercules* wasn't exactly the work of a future generation-defining actor, it wasn't long before Gosling found the project he was looking for.

6   Ten years ago, Ryan Gosling announced himself to the world as an actor with serious chops, with his ferocious turn as a self-loathing Jewish neo-nazi in *The Believer*. It was a bravura performance by an unheralded actor in a little-seen film, but those who saw it took notice. Gosling had made a statement. While his teenage contemporaries were lining up at Hollywood's velvet-roped front door, Gosling had snuck in through the back alley. But his chilling turn in the Sundance smash wasn't exactly the stuff heartthrobs are made of, and Gosling spent the next few years ducking and dodging directors who were intent on making him Hollywood's go-to troubled teen.

7   So how did this art-house bastard child become Hollywood's new prototype for the modern leading man? Why, he starred in *The Notebook*, of course! It was that dewy, MTV-award-winning 2004 romance that introduced Gosling to mainstream audiences around the world—in particular, women—who swooned all the way to the box office and made him an instant A-lister. But instead of chasing that lucrative tentpole franchise that would have had him acting in front of a green screen for the next 10 years, Gosling used his newfound power to pursue passion projects—films that were deeply personal, films that may not have been box-office hits, but that connected with audiences on a much deeper level than any blockbuster ever could.

8   In *Half Nelson*, Gosling played a conflicted teacher with a drug problem (and earned his first Oscar nomination for Best Actor). In *Lars and the Real Girl*, he played an oddball loner in love with a blow-up doll, and in *Blue Valentine*, he shined as a tortured husband trying to preserve a fractured relationship. All three films are unique in the way in which they subvert the audience's expectation of a typical Hollywood protagonist. Gosling's characters are weird, conflicted outliers trying to keep their heads above water. His brave artistic choices reflect a generation of men no longer willing to buy into Hollywood's puffed-up take on masculinity. Gosling has won a legion of fans whose tastes are increasingly discerning and who want to be challenged when lights lower and the curtain parts. Critics, too, have fallen in line and have declared Gosling one of the most important actors of this generation.

9   Off-screen, Gosling has mastered the art of drifting just under the radar, avoiding the glare of the tabloids for the most part, and emerging only when duty calls. He can slip in and out of his broad movie-star frame with ease. He's an A-list actor by day, and one half of the experimental indie-pop duo Dead Man's Bones by night. He's even been spotted working in the kitchen at Tagine, the L.A. restaurant he co-owns, as well as spending time behind the counter at a local sandwich shop. Some might say that Gosling's revolt against the plasticity of Hollywood is a transparent attempt to live up to *US Weekly*'s claims that celebrities are "just like us." But we genuinely get the impression that movie stardom isn't the be all and end all for Gosling. He's an artist who values the work first, with fame but a pesky by-product. Unfortunately for Gosling, that fame is about to reach new heights with a slew of projects lined for 2011, including films that will see him team up with George Clooney and Sean Penn in what is shaping up to be a torch-passing of epic proportions. But like the embattled characters he plays on-screen, Gosling will cope, using the gritty charm and unassuming ease of a modern leading man.

Comprehension

1. Why have critics "fallen in line and have declared Gosling one of the most important actors of this generation" (paragraph 8)? What makes Gosling important?

2. Barna claims that Gosling has withstood the pressure to play a certain role both on and off the screen. Explain how Gosling has maintained that successful persona.

Rhetorical Analysis

3. What is Barna's thesis? Does he state or imply his main idea? Explain.

4. Identify the allusions that Barna uses in this essay. What is his purpose in referring to other characters and works?

5. Barna makes a number of assertions regarding the cultural significance of Gosling's career. What are they, and do they effectively support his thesis? Are these assertions facts or opinions? Explain your viewpoint.

6. Which paragraphs constitute what we might consider to be Barna's conclusion? Is this conclusion effective? Why or why not?

Writing

7. Watch a movie with Ryan Gosling in it, and then write your own critical response to it.

8. **Compare-Contrast Essay**   Compare Gosling to another contemporary Hollywood figure and explain how Gosling is different from that figure.

Synthesizing the Classic + Contemporary Essays

1. Steinem critiques the function and role of Wonder Woman in popular media, whereas Barna focuses on an analysis of America's new type of leading man. How do these different focuses determine the thesis of each essay?

2. Compare and contrast Steinem's and Barna's observations about American culture in their respective essays. In which of these essays do you find these cultural insights to be most convincing, and why?

3. In a well-written essay, defend, challenge, or qualify this claim: Television series like *The Sopranos* engage in negative stereotyping. State your claim, offer evidence, and structure the argument carefully in a series of key reasons in support of your claim.

The Globalization of Eating Disorders

Susan Bordo

Susan Bordo (b. 1947) was born in Newark, New Jersey, and was educated at Carleton University (BA, 1972) and the State University of New York at Stony Brook (PhD, 1982). She is the Singletary Chair in the Humanities and a professor of English and gender and women's studies at the University of Kentucky. A feminist philosopher and interdisciplinary scholar who focuses on Western culture's attitudes toward gender and the body, Bordo has written *The Flight to Objectivity: Essays on Cartesianism and Culture* (1987), *Unbearable Weight: Feminism, Western Culture, and the Body* (1993, 2004), *Twilight Zones: The Hidden Life of Cultural Images from Plato to O.J.* (1997), and *The Male Body: A New Look at Men in Public and in Private* (1999). In this selection, Bordo offers an overview of a new kind of epidemic, fueled by Western media images, that is affecting cultures around the world.

1 The young girl stands in front of the mirror. Never fat to begin with, she's been on a no-fat diet for a couple of weeks and has reached her goal weight: 115 lb., at 5'4"—exactly what she should weigh, according to her doctor's chart. But in her eyes she still looks dumpy. She can't shake her mind free of the "Lady Marmelade" video from Moulin Rouge. Christina Aguilera, Pink, L'il Kim, and Mya, each one perfect in her own way: every curve smooth and sleek, lean-sexy, nothing to spare. Self-hatred and shame start to burn in the girl, and envy tears at her stomach, enough to make her sick. She'll never look like them, no matter how much weight she loses. Look at that stomach of hers, see how it sticks out? Those thighs—they actually jiggle. Her butt is monstrous. She's fat, gross, a dough girl.

2 As you read the imaginary scenario above, whom did you picture standing in front of the mirror? If your images of girls with eating and body image problems have been shaped by *People* magazine and Lifetime movies, she's probably white, North American, and economically secure. A child whose parents have never had to worry about putting food on the family table. A girl with money to spare for fashion magazines and trendy clothing, probably college-bound. If you're familiar with the classic psychological literature on eating disorders, you may also have read that she's an extreme "perfectionist" with a hyper-demanding mother, and that she suffers from "body-image distortion syndrome" and other severe perceptual and cognitive problems that "normal" girls don't share. You probably don't picture her as Black, Asian, or Latina.

3 Read the description again, but this time imagine twenty-something Tenisha Williamson standing in front of the mirror. Tenisha is black, suffers from anorexia, and feels like a traitor to her race. "From an African-American standpoint," she writes, "we as a people are encouraged to embrace our big, voluptuous bodies. This makes me feel terrible because I don't want a big, voluptuous body! I don't ever want to be fat—ever, and I don't ever want to gain

weight. I would rather die from starvation than gain a single pound."[1] Tenisha is no longer an anomaly. Eating and body image problems are now not only crossing racial and class lines, but gender lines. They have also become a global phenomenon.

4   Fiji is a striking example. Because of their remote location, the Fiji islands did not have access to television until 1995, when a single station was introduced. It broadcasts programs from the United States, Great Britain, and Australia. Until that time, Fiji had no reported cases of eating disorders, and a study conducted by anthropologist Anne Becker showed that most Fijian girls and women, no matter how large, were comfortable with their bodies. In 1998, just three years after the station began broadcasting, 11 percent of girls reported vomiting to control weight, and 62 percent of the girls surveyed reported dieting during the previous months.[2]

5   Becker was surprised by the change; she had thought that Fijian cultural traditions, which celebrate eating and favor voluptuous bodies, would "withstand" the influence of media images. Becker hadn't yet understood that we live in an empire of images, and that there are no protective borders.

6   In Central Africa, for example, traditional cultures still celebrate voluptuous women. In some regions, brides are sent to fattening farms, to be plumped and massaged into shape for their wedding night. In a country plagued by AIDS, the skinny body has meant—as it used to among Italian, Jewish, and Black Americans—poverty, sickness, death. "An African girl must have hips," says dress designer Frank Osodi, "We have hips. We have bums. We like flesh in Africa." For years, Nigeria sent its local version of beautiful to the Miss World Competition. The contestants did very poorly. Then a savvy entrepreneur went against local ideals and entered Agbani Darego, a light-skinned, hyper-skinny beauty. (He got his inspiration from M-Net, the South African network seen across Africa on satellite television, which broadcasts mostly American movies and television shows.) Agbani Darego won the Miss World Pageant, the first Black African to do so. Now, Nigerian teenagers fast and exercise, trying to become "lepa"—a popular slang phrase for the thin "it" girls that are all the rage. Said one: "People have realized that slim is beautiful."[3]

7   How can mere images be so powerful? For one thing, they are never "just pictures," as the fashion magazines continually maintain (disingenuously) in their own defense. They speak to young people not just about how to be beautiful but also about how to become what the dominant culture admires, values, rewards. They tell them how to be cool, "get it together," overcome their shame. To girls who have been abused they may offer a fantasy of control and invulnerability, immunity from pain and hurt. For racial and ethnic groups whose bodies have been deemed "foreign," earthy, and primitive, and considered unattractive by Anglo-Saxon norms, they may cast the lure of being accepted as "normal" by the dominant culture.

8   In today's world, it is through images—much more than parents, teachers, or clergy—that we are taught how to be. And it is images, too, that teach us how to

---

[1] From the Colours of Ana website (http://coloursofana.com//ss8.asp).
[2] Reported in Nancy Snyderman, *The Girl in the Mirror* (New York: Hyperion, 2002), p. 84.
[3] Norimistsu Onishi, "Globalization of Beauty Makes Slimness Trendy," *The New York Times*, Oct. 3, 2002.

see, that educate our vision in what's a defect and what is normal, that give us the models against which our own bodies and the bodies of others are measured. Perceptual pedagogy: "How To Interpret Your Body 101." It's become a global requirement.

9   I was intrigued, for example, when my articles on eating disorders began to be translated, over the past few years, into Japanese and Chinese. Among the members of audiences at my talks, Asian women had been among the most insistent that eating and body image weren't problems for their people, and indeed, my initial research showed that eating disorders were virtually unknown in Asia. But when, this year, a Korean translation of *Unbearable Weight* was published, I felt I needed to revisit the situation. I discovered multiple reports on dramatic increases in eating disorders in China, South Korea, and Japan. "As many Asian countries become Westernized and infused with the Western aesthetic of a tall, thin, lean body, a virtual tsunami of eating disorders has swamped Asian countries," writes Eunice Park in *Asian Week* magazine. Older people can still remember when it was very different. In China, for example, where revolutionary ideals once condemned any focus on appearance and there have been several disastrous famines, "little fatty" was a term of endearment for children. Now, with fast food on every corner, childhood obesity is on the rise, and the cultural meaning of fat and thin has changed. "When I was young," says Li Xiaojing, who manages a fitness center in Beijing, "people admired and were even jealous of fat people since they thought they had a better life. . . . But now, most of us see a fat person and think 'He looks awful.'"[4]

10   Clearly, body insecurity can be exported, imported, and marketed—just like any other profitable commodity. In this respect, what's happened with men and boys is illustrative. Ten years ago men tended, if anything, to see themselves as better looking than they (perhaps) actually were. And then (as I chronicle in detail in my book *The Male Body*) the menswear manufacturers, the diet industries, and the plastic surgeons "discovered" the male body. And now, young guys are looking in their mirrors, finding themselves soft and ill defined, no matter how muscular they are. Now they are developing the eating and body image disorders that we once thought only girls had. Now they are abusing steroids, measuring their own muscularity against the oiled and perfected images of professional athletes, body-builders, and *Men's Health* models. Now the industries in body-enhancement—cosmetic surgeons, manufacturers of anti-aging creams, spas and salons—are making huge bucks off men, too.

11   What is to be done? I have no easy answers. But I do know that we need to acknowledge, finally and decisively, that we are dealing here with a cultural problem. If eating disorders were biochemical, as some claim, how can we account for their gradual "spread" across race, gender, and nationality? And with mass media culture increasingly providing the dominant "public education" in our children's lives—and those of children around the globe—how can we blame families? Families matter, of course, and so do racial and ethnic traditions. But families exist in cultural time and space—and so do racial groups. In the empire of

4 Reported in Elizabeth Rosenthal, "Beijing Journal: China's Chic Waistline: Convex to Concave," *The New York Times*, Dec. 9, 1999.

images, no one lives in a bubble of self-generated "dysfunction" or permanent immunity. The sooner we recognize that—and start paying attention to the culture around us and what it is teaching our children—the sooner we can begin developing some strategies for change.

Comprehension

1. How does Bordo define the "body-image distortion syndrome" (paragraph 2)?

2. According to the essay, why have body image and weight problems become a global phenomenon? What is the main cause of this phenomenon?

3. How, according to the author, should we deal with the globalization of eating disorders?

Rhetorical Analysis

4. How does the author establish herself as an authority on her subject? Do you think that she succeeds? Why or why not?

5. What is the writer's claim? Where does she place it, and why?

6. Bordo begins with an imaginary situation. Does this strategy enhance or detract from the validity of her argument? Justify your response.

7. How does Bordo develop this selection as a problem-solution essay? Where does the solution appear, and how effective is its placement within the essay?

Writing

8. Write a causal essay analyzing the impact of mass media on your generation's vision of the ideal body.

9. Why are women in the United States and around the world more susceptible to eating disorders than men? Answer this question in an analytical essay.

10. **Writing an Argument**   Write an essay titled "Body Images, Eating Disorders, and Cultural Imperialism." In this essay, argue for or against the proposition that American media are exporting potentially unhealthy images of the human body.

Escape From Wonderland: Disney and the Female Imagination

Deborah Ross

Deborah Ross is professor of English at Hawai'i Pacific University, where she teaches writing, literature, and humanities. She specializes in popular culture, especially from the perspective of gender. In the following research paper, published in a 2004 issue of *Marvels & Tales: Journal of Fairy-Tale Studies*, Ross analyzes a series of Disney films, all based on children's books and fairy tales; she evaluates the Disney ideology as it affects the imaginative and actual lives of girls.

1 In 1989, Disney's little mermaid first asked the musical question, "When's it my turn?" She asked it again in 1996, when her movie was re-released in theaters, and she continues to ask it, frequently, in many of our living rooms. Never has a protagonist had so many turns to demand a turn: Yet, seemingly, she remains unsatisfied. If even the heroine in a Disney "girls' movie" does not enjoy being a girl, how must the girls watching her feel about it?

2 Behind this gender question lurks a larger political one. If Ariel's feminist rhetoric is undercut by more conservative elements in her movie, so is the environmentalism of *The Lion King,* the multiculturalism of *Pocahontas,* the valuing of difference in *The Hunchback of Notre Dame*—in short, all the quasi-liberal sentiments that focus groups have no doubt caused to grace the surface of the last decade's Disney features. Ideology in Disney is a much vexed question, and I will not attempt here to untangle a knot which began forming for critics when Walt first denied having any politics back in the thirties, and which has only grown in mass and complexity since his death, as his corporation's management style has evolved to cope with a burgeoning staff of artists and technicians, changing public tastes, and changing perceptions of those tastes.

3 One generalization I do suggest, however, is that Disney the man and the corporation are known for a belief in control. The top-down management style Disney epitomizes—Auschwitz (Giroux 55), or Mouschwitz (Lewis 88), is a frequent analogy—thrives on homogeneity and rigid adherence to rules. These are features often decried in Disney production and product, both by critics of capitalism, such as Benjamin and Adorno,[1] and by far less radical proponents of individualism and open debate, from early Disney biographer Richard Schickel to educator Henry Giroux. Yet imagination, the company's major commodity, does not easily lend itself to a program of control. To encourage imagination in artists, and arouse it in viewers, is to invite unique self-expression rather than homogeneity, and spontaneity rather than predictability. Link imagination to

---

[1] Miriam Hansen discusses Benjamin's and Adorno's objections to Disney in some detail. Jack Zipes's critique of Disney also occurs within a larger argument about the "freezing" of fairy tales into myths to perpetuate bourgeois, patriarchal values (see his Introduction and Chapter 3).

the animated cartoon, an art form with roots in dada, surrealism, and radical politics, and matters could well get out of hand.[2]

4   I believe that this conflict between control and imaginative freedom is visible in the animated features that have come out of the Disney studios, from *Snow White and the Seven Dwarfs* to *Lilo and Stitch*. Of course, ambiguity is rarely viewed now as either a moral or an aesthetic flaw, and the presence of elements that contradict each other may well be preferable to consistent, monologic disapproval of imagination. Neither, however, do conflict and contradiction in themselves necessarily create a space for viewers to question values and exercise judgment. Much depends on how the elements relate to each other, or how an audience is likely to relate them. An audience even partially looking for guides to behavior along with entertainment will have to resolve apparent ambiguities into one suggested course of action. Giroux's attack on Disney rests on the contention that for children, these movies, however apparently bland, do have a didactic effect (18). For them, ambiguity at its best ultimately resolves into a connected but complex world view that embraces difference and spontaneity; at its worst, it can produce confusion and anxiety.

5   I wish to explore the overall impressions these films may give children about the value of their own imaginations, and thus about their own value as unique individuals able to envision, and eventually to enact, change. In particular, to get back to Ariel, I am concerned about what girls may learn about this potentially explosive aspect of their characters that could so easily burst the bounds of traditional femininity. To help answer this question, I have chosen to examine the way various elements of image, story, and dialogue interact to influence the valuation of imagination in three of Disney's girls' movies: *Alice in Wonderland* (1951), *The Little Mermaid* (1989), and *Beauty and the Beast* (1991, re-released 2001).

6   I have chosen these three because, although one might be called "prefeminist" and the other two "post-," all specifically concern young women who fantasize about a life more vivid and exciting than their reality. I will suggest that some of these films' discomfort with female imagination has roots far back in didactic narrative for girls by looking at Charlotte Lennox's 1759 novel, *The Female Quixote*, which concerns the fortunes of a young woman who might be considered the great-grandmother, or prototype, of the Disney heroine. Then, comparing the three Disney movies with their written fairy-tale sources, I will show how much more confusing a many-tongued message can become when it is told in pictures as well as words.

7   Girls have been learning from stories where to draw the line between fantasy and reality probably since the first story was told, but one sees this didactic purpose especially clearly beginning in the seventeenth century, when romances and literary fairy tales were first written specifically for, about, and even by women. Samuel Johnson was greatly concerned about the effects of fiction on

---

[2] Janet Wasko notes that Disney deliberately avoided the more "anarchistic and inventive" styles of animation employed at other studios (115). My own belief, on which my approach to Disney is based, is that where there is animation, anarchy can never be wholly suppressed. For discussion of the roots of animation in surrealism and dada, see Inez Hedges.

"the young, the ignorant, and the idle," and Paul Hunter has shown that there was indeed a class of new readers early in the eighteenth century who were socially displaced and looking to novels for moral and social guidance as well as entertainment (Hunter 271–72). From that time till the present, conservative authors have used romances and novels to teach girls that their dreams are dangerous and of little relevance to their daily lives. Progressive or feminist authors, on the other hand, have encouraged young women readers' belief in fantasy to help them visualize what they want, perhaps as a first step toward going after it. For example, it can be argued (as I have done elsewhere) that European women's experience with romantic fiction gradually gained them the right, first, to refuse to cooperate in arranged marriages, and eventually, to choose husbands for themselves.[3]

8   Charlotte Lennox's *The Female Quixote* illustrates both these conservative and progressive plot patterns, for it both draws upon and criticizes earlier romances, which themselves often both celebrated and punished female imagination and expressiveness.[4] Therefore, like Disney's movies today, which also use material from the romance and fairy-tale tradition, Lennox's novel can be more muddling than enlightening to young people seeking instruction on the conduct of real life. As the title suggests, the premise is that a young girl is at least as likely to have her head turned by reading romances as Cervantes's knight-errant had been over a century before. Appropriately, the romances devoured by this quixote, Arabella, are the largely female-centered French romances of d'Urfé and Scudéry, which focus more on love than on questing, and in which males are present mainly either to carry off or rescue heroines. A reader who takes too literally stories in which women wield such power, albeit of a limited kind, will not adjust well to woman's lot: being ignored, submitting always to others' convenience, like Jane Austen in her letters, perpetually waiting to be "fetched" by a male relative (Austen 9–10). Thus Arabella's reading sets her up to make many ridiculous mistakes, and ultimately to be humbled, or humiliated, when she learns her own real unimportance.

9   The novel shows its author's ambivalence about Arabella's fantasy in several ways. Overtly, she presents it as an adolescent error the heroine must grow out of in order to find happiness. Yet her very frank satire of the world to which Arabella's cure forces her to conform leaves readers wondering, along with the heroine, whether the world of romance might not be preferable. Romances also receive implicit support from the central "real" narrative's resemblance to romance: beautiful heroine, beloved by the perfect man, whom after trials and separations she marries, presumably to live happily ever after. If the novel presents a romantic story under the guise of realism, then perhaps Arabella is not so quixotic after all.

10   *The Female Quixote* thus presents contradictory impressions about the worthiness of the heroine's desires, the degree to which those desires are ultimately fulfilled

---

[3] I develop this argument in *The Excellence of Falsehood*. Marina Warner (169, 277–78) and Jack Zipes (21–23, 28) discuss the seventeenth-century *précieuses'* preoccupation with the issue of forced marriage.

[4] Warner discusses ambivalence about the old woman or "Mother Goose" figure who narrates fairy tales throughout the first half of *From the Beast to the Blonde*, and more specifically the power of the female voice in her discussion of "The Little Mermaid" (394).

or frustrated, and the amount of satisfaction with the outcome the tone directs the reader to feel. Critics of our own time naturally enjoy this ambivalence (the novel has had a comeback of sorts in the last decades and is available in paperback), which particularly lends itself to feminist approaches of the *Madwoman in the Attic,* conformist text–radical subtext variety. Yet the fact that this novel might well make a madwoman out of any young female reader looking for a framework for understanding life should also be part of our critical awareness. Critics may find it a useful model for highlighting similar constellations of ideological paradox in other stories about women's imagination, stories which also leave their audiences struggling to integrate contradictory messages.

11   Disney's female quixotes are at least as sorely beset by ambiguity as Arabella. The heroines' fantasies reveal desires for many things, including novelty, excitement, power, sex, and knowledge. Some of these desires are ridiculed, others respected; some are fulfilled, others surrendered. And the paradoxes in the plots are further complicated by words and images that seem at times to be telling stories of their own.

12   The presence of conservative elements in Disney's *Alice in Wonderland* is not surprising, considering that it was released in 1951, when "Hollywood's dark prince" was still very much alive, fighting unions, castigating the League of Women Voters, and exerting strong control over the studio's output.[5] One would perhaps not expect, though, to find an American movie of the mid-twentieth century so much more stereotypically Victorian than its nineteenth-century British source.

13   Of course, Lewis Carroll's *Alice's Adventures in Wonderland* and *Through the Looking Glass* are not typical of Victorian children's literature. In particular, most girls' stories of this era promoted humility, devotion, punctuality, and tidiness, implying that adventure (as a countess once told Lennox's Arabella) is something a nice girl would be wise to avoid (Lennox 365). The Alice stories, on the other hand, present adventure as positive: Whether wondrous or frightening, it leads the heroine in the direction of personal growth and control over her surroundings. Alice learns how to manage her size, how to talk back to a queen, and, finally, how to wear the crown of adulthood. Carroll celebrates childhood as a brief, fleeting time in which even girls may follow talking rabbits before being overtaken by the "dull reality" (115) of womanhood.

14   The Disney movie begins with the same positive message about girls' fantasies. In her opening conversation, Disney's Alice, like Carroll's, expresses the usual quixotic desires: to escape boredom (with lessons), to satisfy curiosity (about the white rabbit), and above all, to exert power. Things would be different "in my world," she notes, though her sister ridicules her ambition. Books, for one thing, would all have pictures—a remark given to Alice by Carroll in a way that almost invites someone to make an Alice movie. The first few minutes of the movie do seem to deliver what Alice wants by introducing such pictorial wonders as singing flowers and surrealistic insects.

---

[5] I refer here to the title of Marc Eliot's Disney biography. Holly Allen and Michael Denning discuss politics at the Disney studio during the 1940s. For a full discussion of Disney's rather complex politics, see Steven Watts.

15   Soon, however, the plot darkens, signaled by small but significant cuts and alterations in the original dialogue. Speaking with the Cheshire Cat, who tells her everyone in the neighborhood is mad, Alice speaks Carroll's line, "But I don't want to go among mad people" (63). The cat responds that everyone in Wonderland is mad, but he does not go on to say that Alice too is mad, so that already Disney's Alice is presented as out of her element, the lone sane and rational creature among lunatics.

16   After the mad tea party, in a section of plot invented for the movie, Disney's Alice has had enough craziness and wants to go home. Overjoyed to find what looks like a path—symbolic of her now acknowledged need for order and direction—she is reduced to helpless tears when it is erased by a fanciful broom creature. She then passively sits down to wait to be rescued, all the while lecturing herself about the importance of reason and patience, and berating herself for the curiosity that once again has led her into trouble. The movie takes a line from early in the story, "She generally gave herself very good advice (though she very seldom followed it)" (23), puts it in the first person, and makes it the center of a self-lacerating musical lament in which Alice abandons for good her fantasy of excitement and power to dwindle into a tiny, forlorn figure in the center of a large, dark frame. In the end of the movie, the defiance and assertiveness of the line, "You're only a pack of cards," are lost, as she utters it while fleeing for her life from the menacing gang of wonders she has created. She is saved, not by facing them down with dawning maturity and confidence, like the "real" Alice, but by waking up.[6]

17   British reviewers at the time of the movie's release, when the militantly innocuous Enid Blyton held sway over English children's imaginations, objected to Disney's "anarchic" alteration of what they saw as a serene and placid children's tale (Allan 137). But Carroll's story is in fact far more tolerant of anarchy, in the sense of irrationality, than the Disney version. The images used to tell the story further support this rationalist message. Despite Disney artist Claude Coats's comment that the staff had "let [them]selves go with some wild designs" (Allan 138), the visuals in fact are rather staid and restrained, mainly literal, representational renderings of the story done in the highly finished, realistic style for which the studio was famous. The fall down the rabbit hole, for example, which marks Alice's entry into the dream state, might have lent itself to surrealistic treatment like that of *Dumbo*'s "Pink Elephants on Parade" sequence, but instead it is simply a serial listing in images of the objects Carroll mentions that Alice sees on her way down.

18   Surrealism does appear, briefly, in the visual puns formed by the caterpillar's smoke (as he asks "why [k]not"), and in the wild proliferation of crockery at the tea party, the cups and saucers truly "animated" and seeming to breed like, well, rabbits. Yet the story-line ensures that just as this style reaches its climax, Alice is reaching the limits of her fear of imagination. What might have been delightful Daliesque creatures—telephone-ducks, drum-frogs—function rather to frighten the heroine at a point in the plot when she has rejected all this "nonsense" and is

---

[6] Donald Britton comments that in the Disney cartoon universe, "children don't become adults; rather, adults kill children" (120).

anxious to get home to write a book about it.[7] Writing a story, she has decided, is much safer than living one.

19   Thus all elements combine to entrap the unwary viewer: to entice her to fantasize—even to pay money for the privilege—and then to make her feel, like Alice, guilty and ashamed.

20   Contrasting Alice's defeated whining with Ariel's anthem of independence in *The Little Mermaid*, one is apt to feel girls have come a long way. Here, as Laura Sells and Marina Warner observe, the tale on which the movie is based is ostensibly more conservative than Disney's retelling (Sells 176, 177, 181; Warner 397, 403).[8] Hans Christian Andersen's story is a tragic celebration of feminine self-sacrifice. His mermaid fantasizes about becoming human partly because, like Alice, she is curious about a world she has only glimpsed (here, from below rather than from above). But that world interests her mainly because in it dwells a man who resembles a handsome statue she already adores. Her love is partly sexual, of course, since she needs to be human from the waist down to win the hero. But her ultimate desire is spiritual, for only by marrying a human can a mermaid, who normally lives three hundred years and then turns into sea foam, gain a soul and eternal life.

21   In pursuit of this desire Andersen's mermaid is willing to spend all she has: her voice, her health, and eventually her life. She buys her new legs, from which blood oozes with every agonizing step, by letting the sea witch cut out her tongue. The permanent loss of her voice means playing dumb in more ways than one, as she can only listen demurely as the prince lectures her about her own world, the sea (166).[9] Failing to bring the prince to a proposal, she could save her own life by killing him, but she chooses instead to die. Her many acts of self-torture earn her a slight reprieve as she is turned into a spirit of the air, instead of sea-foam, and given a chance to gain a soul by performing more selfless deeds. Andersen gives her this reward, not for having a dream, but for desiring martyrdom. No real authorial punishment is needed for a female quixote so intent on punishing herself.

22   Naturally in the Disney version the mutilation and blood would have to go. But much more would have to be altered to make this tragic story look and sound so convincingly like a triumph of adolescent self-will and entitlement, as befit the close of the "me decade." (Warner comments on how often, while she can speak, Ariel utters the verb "want" [403].) For example, instead of making the mermaid love the human world because she loves a human, the movie has Ariel love a human mainly because she is already curious enough about his world to have collected a cave full of human souvenirs (in Andersen's story this collection belongs to a mermaid sister). Like Alice before her initiation, Ariel imagines this other world as in a sense more her own than her actual world. She believes it to be a utopia of free movement: She dreams of legs first for "jumping" and "dancing" and "strolling," and only secondarily for marrying.

---

[7] Dali had been at the studio in 1946, and Robin Allan believes his influence was still apparent in Alice (137).

[8] See also Wasko 134.

[9] See Warner's discussion on the significance of this silence, and of the blood which in Andersen's tale connects pain with the dawning of female sexuality (387–408).

23   There is nothing masochistic about this mermaid's fantasy; nor is she willing to sacrifice herself to fulfill it, though she is willing to gamble. Her voice, for example, is not permanently lost but poured into a shell, ready to be returned to her if she succeeds, and she has every intention of succeeding. Eighties heroine that she is, she means to have it all: voice, soul, legs, and husband.

24   For the most part, the movie seems to present this female quixote's fantasy positively and reward her with her desire, as the older generation, in the person of her father, learns to abandon prejudice and let teenagers live their own lives. But there are undercurrents here, so to speak, that work against the theme of imaginative freedom. The odd thing about Ariel's quixotism—what makes the audience recognize it *as* quixotism—is that the exotic world of her fantasy is, to us, boring and commonplace. Even a two-year-old viewer knows, as the heroine does not, that forks are not used to comb hair, and that human fathers do indeed "reprimand their daughters," just like old King Triton. Thus we laugh at Ariel's naïve reveries, as Andersen's listeners must have laughed at his mermaid's amazed reaction to birds (150). In the end, it seems ludicrous that Ariel should put so much rebellious energy into becoming the girl next door.

25   The visual style of the movie makes Andersen's painful story seem oddly encouraging by comparison. Andersen shifts points of view back and forth between the mermaids, who see our world as exotic, and his own audience, who glamorize the unknown world below. He provides lavish descriptions of the shore as well as the sea in order to reawaken his listeners' sense of wonder at their own city lights, sunsets, forests, and hills (151–52). An outsider's desire to live here thus becomes quite understandable. The movie contains no such balance, for beauty and splendor are mainly found "Under the Sea," the title of the dizzying production number in which Sebastian the crab tries to convince Ariel that there's no place like home. Here creatures and objects are surrealistically combined and transformed into an underwater orchestra. Here in abundance are the magical bubbles that have signaled fun with physics in Disney movies from *Snow White* to *Dumbo* to *Cinderella*. The world of humans, in contrast, though picturesque, is static and finite. When Ariel takes a bath at Eric's palace, while mundane, gossiping laundresses wash her clothes, one is forced to notice that bubbles here just don't *do* anything. Similarly, Grimsby's pipe, which Ariel mistakes for a musical instrument, produces more soot than smoke—nothing approaching the punning puffs from the caterpillar's hookah in *Alice,* or even the smoky ink that billows about in the sea witch's cave. Clearly, Sebastian is right: It is "better down where it's wetter."

26   The images the movie uses to tell the story thus give its trendy feminism a reverse spin. Whatever Ariel might *say,* or sing, what we see her *do* is flee a world of infinite possibility to settle in the land of the banal. Her fantasy is a sort of anti-fantasy. Yes, she gets her legs, she makes her stand, she marches—but only down the aisle, to marry some guy named Eric.

27 Many fairy tales, and many more movies, end with a wedding, and for this reason they often draw censure from critics, such as Janet Wasko (116) and Elizabeth Bell (114, 155), who would like to see our daughters presented with other options.

Without question there ought to be more than one girls' story out there, relentlessly repeated with minor variations. I would also argue, however, that just as in life there are marriages and marriages, so in fiction living happily ever after is not always a euphemism for dying. When the marriage seems to grant the heroine true personal fulfillment and possibilities for further growth, the ending may actually seem like the beginning of a new life. Such is the case with *Beauty and the Beast,* a tale endowed by ancient archetypes with a feminine power that resists the attempts of individual authors, such as Madame Leprince de Beaumont in 1757, to tie its heroine down to mediocrity. With *The Little Mermaid* behind us, we might expect Disney's version to dole out a similarly dull and didactic message, clothed in mock-progressive nineties clichés of gender equality. But in Disney's *Beauty and the Beast,* thanks in part to the screenplay by Linda Woolverton (the first woman writer of a Disney animated feature), imagination flows freely in the words and the images, allowing the tale to work its magic.[10]

28   One problem with the plot that ends in marriage, of course, is its reduction of the heroine to an object of desire, and therefore a heroine actually named Beauty would not, on the face of it, seem like a good role model. In this tale, however, with its roots penetrating beyond the Cupid and Psyche tale from Apuleius's *The Golden Ass* to very old stories about beast bridegrooms (Warner 275; Zipes 24–25), the heroine is more subject than object because her quest for a desirable mate drives the plot. (Apuleius intensifies the female point of view by having the tale narrated by an old woman [Warner 275].) Of course, the whole question of the story's sexual politics hinges on whether the heroine's desire can be consciously controlled, by herself or by others; whether, as is often said in Christian wedding ceremonies, love is an act of will rather than a feeling; whether, therefore, she can make herself love the one she "ought." Conservative versions of *Beauty and the Beast* do tend to assume such schooling of the will is possible, as Jack Zipes emphasizes (29–40). Nevertheless, an important feature even in such versions is that the beast, though he may be dutifully or even cheerfully endured, cannot become a handsome prince until the heroine actively wants him, truly chooses him for reasons of her own. The young female audience is thus reassured that sex in conjunction with love is pleasant rather than frightening (Bettelheim 306; Warner 312–13); in other words, the beast of one's choice is not a beast at all.

29   At about the same time Charlotte Lennox was composing *The Female Quixote,* Madame Leprince de Beaumont, with similar concerns about young women's imaginations, was dressing this ancient tale in anti-romance, turning to her own purpose a Scudérian vocabulary of love that, to her readers, would be all too familiar. Beauty feels "esteem" for the Beast because of his "great service" to her, and eventually she comes to feel "tenderness" for him as she wants to care for him and ease his distress (Beaumont 37). Out of this tenderness comes a desire to marry him—including, one supposes, some sexual feeling. The romance code word for active sexual desire—"inclination"—never appears.[11] By telling her young readers that esteem and tenderness are the best basis for marriage, Beaumont

---

[10] See Bell 114; Murphy 133–34; Warner 313.
[11] See the Map of Tender in Scudéry's *Clelia* (1:42).

warns them not to wait for the handsome, witty lover of their fantasies; in the closing words of the rewarding fairy: "You have preferred virtue before either wit or beauty, and you deserve to find one in whom all these are united" (47). In this way, the author joins the tradition of conservative writers who urge girls to face reality and, to the very limited extent they will be permitted to choose, to choose wisely.[12] Still, while schooling the reader in what she ought to desire, Beaumont cannot avoid conveying the importance of the heroine's will, for until Beauty desires the Beast, a beast he will remain.

30   The Disney movie reaches past Beaumont to draw upon older strains of the story. For example, here, as in some older versions, including that of Beaumont's immediate predecessor, Madame de Villeneuve (Warner 290–91), it is the Beast rather than Beauty who is supposed to learn self-control. The heroine is therefore permitted—even encouraged—to fantasize to her heart's content. Where Beaumont only noted that Beauty liked to read, Disney enlarges on Belle's taste in books, which turns out to be just like Arabella's: fairy tales and romances about swordfights, magic, a prince in disguise, and above all, a "she" at the center of the action. Nor is she content just to read about "adventure in the great wide somewhere." Given the chance to tour the Beast's library—ordinarily for Belle the greatest of temptations—she chooses instead to explore the forbidden west wing of his castle, as if somehow aware that she will find there the escape from "provincial life" she has been longing and singing for. For all her quixotism, however, Belle, unlike Arabella, is seen as "rather odd" only by her neighbors, not by her audience.

31   Certainly, as several commentators observe, the movie has its share of politically correct modern touches to underscore the heroine's self-determination (Warner 316–17; Zipes 46). Interestingly, however, each apparent innovation in fact draws on the French romance tradition that Belle and Arabella revere. Most notably, the movie makes contemporary-sounding statements about gender stereotypes by introducing a new character as foil to the Beast, the hypermasculine Gaston, who boasts in a Sigmund Romberg-ish aria, "I'm especially good at expectorating," "I use antlers in all of my decorating, and "every last inch of me's covered with hair." He is the real beast, of course, an animal who sneers at the Beast for being so openly in touch with his feminine side, "the Male Chauvinist Pig [. . .] that would turn the women of any primetime talkshow audience into beasts themselves" (Jeffords 170). But Gaston is not really new. He dates back, beyond the Cocteau movie often cited as his source, to the French romance villain who loves the heroine selfishly, determined to possess her by force: by winning her in a duel, carrying her off, or scheming to get her parents to give her to him. Gaston arranges to have Belle's eccentric father locked in a madhouse unless she agrees to marry him. Then he nearly kills the Beast under the illusion that the winner gets Belle as prize. The Beast, in contrast, is the romance hero who fights the villain to win the heroine's freedom, not her hand, which he will accept only as her gift. In fact, he would rather die than oppress her. By choosing the Beast over Gaston, Belle helps this ancient story confirm the value of a woman's equal right to a will of her own.

---

[12] See Warner 292–94.

32   Gaston also helps this movie make another observation mistakenly thought of as modern: that men and women aren't nearly as different as some men would like them to be. This idea is found in women's romantic writing from the seventeenth century on,[13] and it reverberates in Belle's opening song as she wishes for someone who understands her and shares her interests. Naturally she chooses to marry the gentleman who gives her the key to his extensive library, not the "positively primeval" clod who throws her book in the mud with a warning about what happens to society when women are taught to read. And in the end, when the spell is broken and the Beast resumes his original shape, he markedly resembles Belle, unruly bangs and all. By marrying a man who can help her get what she wants, and who wants the same things, symbolically she is marrying an aspect of herself.[14]

33   The Beast's oddly familiar new face is not the only image in the movie that makes one feel the heroine's fantasy is a worthy one. Much creativity was lavished on the look of the castle that provides the atmosphere of old romance. Although for most of the movie it resembles a Gothic ruin, and Belle comes here at first as a prisoner, it is really a house of magic in which every object is alive, or "animated"— most famously the dinnerware that dances and sings "Be Our Guest." And the enchantment does not quite end with the breaking of the spell, but is rather replaced with a different kind of magic as the castle comes into its original baroque splendor with a seeming infinity of detail, something new around every corner, and always a new corner, for the eye to explore. As Belle waltzes with her Prince around that gorgeous marble hall, the title tune welling up around them, one may see as well as feel that she's getting not just a husband, but more books than she can read in a lifetime, and a home as big and beautiful as her imagination.

34   Neither age, divorce, nor parenthood has yet made me cynical enough to see the ending of this movie without a sob of satisfaction. But then Disney did begin training me to react in just that way from a very early age (the first movie I ever saw, at the age of five, was *Sleeping Beauty*). Critics have been warning the public for decades about the Disney program to bring about the complete "invasion and control of children's imaginations" (Schickel 18), as well as the silencing of fairy tales' originally female voice (Warner 416–17); no doubt I am a cipher in the company's success. How much more complete the Disney conquest will become for our children and grandchildren, with the constant replay made possible by video and DVD, is definitely cause for concern.

35   The market forces that drive Disney today are dangerous, to be sure, as is the ideology of the market-place the movies promote, as Giroux and others warn. Fortunately, however, because the overriding goal is self-promotion—because Disney will absorb and use whatever works, or whatever sells the product—the movies lack the philosophical consistency of propaganda.[15] Thus films like

---

[13] See for example the pastoral lyrics of Aphra Behn.

[14] See Clarissa Pinkola Estes for an interpretation of the Beast as an aspect of the heroine's own personality (272–73). Warner also discusses how the beast in modern versions of the tale, including Disney's, functions to help the heroine get in touch with her own inner beast, or sexuality (307–13).

[15] Giroux notes inconsistent values among elements in the films (5, 91). Wasko emphasizes consistent elements that make "classic Disney" a recognizable "brand" (3, 152), but does not explore tensions among the elements she lists as consistent, such as "work ethic" vs. "escape fantasy" (114).

Beauty and the Beast, which pays more than lip-service to the liberating potential of fantasy, can sometimes appear.

36   Nevertheless, the fact that many Disney movies implant seeds of guilt and fear to spring up along with children's developing imaginations is a serious problem. The mixed messages noticeable in *Alice* are present in earlier movies such as *Dumbo* and "The Sorcerer's Apprentice" in *Fantasia.* They continue in more recent examples such as *Hercules* and *The Hunchback of Notre Dame,* in which only evil and terrifying characters wield the transformative power that is, in essence, the animator's art; thus these movies almost identify themselves as products of black magic.[16] Some recent films seem almost to reject the notion of animation altogether, striking the eye most forcibly with stills such as the battlefield in *Mulan,* or the cathedral of Notre Dame—breathtaking, to be sure, but unlike the Beast's castle, completely static. Clearly the reluctance to embrace imagination with both arms is still present among the many and shifting ideas that make up the Disney ethos.

37   The inconsistencies found in these movies do not lighten either the parent's burden of guiding the young in their adventures with the media, or the critic's task of understanding the various manifestations of culture. On the contrary, they oblige us to do more than count the number of profane words or violent acts or exposed body parts; and also to do more than catalogue plots, count the numbers of males and females, and quantify relative levels of aggression. Instead, we must watch carefully the interplay of elements within the films and notice how many stories are going on at one time. Watching the faces of our children as they watch, we will often find that imagination, in these movies, is like Alice's garden—just beyond a little locked door, the key to which is tantalizingly, frustratingly out of reach.

Reprinted from "Escape from Wonderland: Disney and the Female Imagination" by Deborah Ross, in *Marvels & Tales: Journal of Fairy-Tale Studies* Vol.18 No.1, © 2004 Wayne State University Press, with the permission of Wayne State University Press.

Works Cited*

Alice in Wonderland. Dir. Clyde Geronimi, Hamilton Luske, and Wilfred-Jackson. Walt Disney Company, 1951.

Allan, Robin. "Alice in Disneyland." *Sight and Sound* 54 (Spring 1985): 136–38.

Allen, Holly, and Michael Denning. "The Cartoonists' Front." *South Atlantic Quarterly* 92.1 (1993): 89–117.

Andersen, Hans Christian. "The Little Mermaid." *Hans Christian Andersen: His Classic Fairy Tales.* Trans. Erik Haugaard. Garden City, NY: Doubleday, 1978. 149–70.

Apuleius. *Transformations of Lucius Otherwise Known as the Golden Ass.* Trans. Robert Graves. New York: Noonday, 1998.

Austen, Jane. *Selected Letters.* Oxford: Oxford UP, 1985.

*This Works Cited section does not follow the latest MLA style. The spacing has also been condensed.

----

[16] A notable exception is *The Emperor's New Groove,* in which magic transformative potions intended as evil by the villain turn positive and bring about both the narrative and visual climax of the movie.

Beaumont, Madame Leprince de. *Beauty and the Beast.* Trans. P. H. Muir. New York: Knopf, 1968.

Beauty and the Beast. Dir. Gary Trousdale and Kirk Wise. Walt Disney Company, 1991.

Behn, Aphra. *The Works of Aphra Behn: Poetry.* Ed. Janet Todd. Columbus: Ohio UP, 1992.

Bell, Elizabeth. "Somatexts at the Disney Shop." Bell, Haas, and Sells 107–24.

Bell, Elizabeth, Lynda Haas, and Laura Sells, eds. *From Mouse to Mermaid: The Politics of Film, Gender, and Culture.* Bloomington: Indiana UP, 1995.

Bettelheim, Bruno. *The Uses of Enchantment.* New York: Vintage, 1977.

Britton, Donald. "The Dark Side of Disneyland." *Mythomania: Fantasies, Fables, and Sheer Lies in Contemporary American Popular Art.* By Bernard Welt. Los Angeles: Art Issues, 1996. 113–26.

Carroll, Lewis. *Alice's Adventures in Wonderland and Through the Looking-Glass.* New York: New American Library, 1960.

Cinderella. Dir. Hamilton Luske and Wilfred Jackson. Walt Disney Company, 1950.

Dumbo. Dir. Ben Sharpsteen. Walt Disney Company, 1941.

Eliot, Marc. *Walt Disney: Hollywood's Dark Prince.* New York: Birch Lane, 1993.

The Emperor's New Groove. Dir. Mark Dindal. Walt Disney Company, 2000.

Estes, Clarissa Pinkola. *Women Who Run with the Wolves.* New York: Ballantine, 1992.

Fantasia. Dir. Ford Beebe and Bill Roberts. Walt Disney Company, 1942.

Gilbert, Sandra, and Susan Gubar. *The Madwoman in the Attic.* New Haven: Yale UP, 1979.

Giroux, Henry. *The Mouse That Roared: Disney and the End of Innocence.* Lanham, MD: Rowman, 1999.

Hansen, Miriam. "Of Mice and Ducks: Benjamin and Adorno on Disney." *South Atlantic Quarterly* 92.1 (1993): 27–61.

Hedges, Inez. *Languages of Revolt: Dada and Surrealist Literature and Film.* Durham: Duke UP, 1983.

Hercules. Dir. Ron Clements and John Musker. Walt Disney Company, 1997.

The Hunchback of Notre Dame. Dir. Gary Trousdale and Kirk Wise. Walt Disney Company, 1996.

Hunter, J. Paul. "'The Young, the Ignorant, and the Idle': Some Notes on Readers and the Beginnings of the English Novel." *Anticipations of the Enlightenment in England, France, and Germany.* Ed. Alan Charles Kors and Paul J. Korshin. Philadelphia: U of Pennsylvania P, 1987. 259–82.

Jefford, Susan. "The Curse of Masculinity." Bell, Haas, and Sells 161–72.

Johnson, Samuel. *The Rambler.* Ed. W. J. Bate and Albrecht B. Strauss. New Haven: Yale UP, 1969.

Lennox, Charlotte. *The Female Quixote,* 1759. Boston: Pandora, 1986.

Lewis, Jon. "Disney after Disney." *Disney Discourse: Producing the Magic Kingdom.* Ed. Eric Smoodin. New York: Routledge, 1994.

Lilo and Stitch. Dir. Dean DeBlois and Chris Sanders (III). Walt Disney Company, 2002.

The Lion King. Dir. Rob Minkoff and Roger Allers. Walt Disney Company, 1994.

The Little Mermaid. Dir. John Musker and Ron Clements. Walt Disney Company, 1989.

Mulan. Dir. Tony Bancroft and Barry Cook. Walt Disney Company, 1998.

Murphy, Patrick D. "'The Whole Wide World Was Scrubbed Clean': The Androcentric Animation of Denatured Disney." Bell, Haas, and Sells 125–36.

Pocahontas. Dir. Mike Gabriel and Eric Goldberg. Walt Disney Company, 1995.

Ross, Deborah. *The Excellence of Falsehood.* Lexington: UP of Kentucky, 1991.

Schickel, Richard. *The Disney Version.* New York: Simon, 1968.

Scudéry, Madeleine de. *Clelia.* Trans. John Davies. London: Herringman, 1678.

Sells, Laura. "'Where Do the Mermaids Stand?' Voice and Body in *The Little Mermaid.*" Bell, Haas, and Sells 175–92.

The Sleeping Beauty. Dir. Clyde Geronimi. Walt Disney Company, 1959.

Snow White and the Seven Dwarfs. Dir. David Hand. Walt Disney Company, 1938.

Warner, Marina. *From the Beast to the Blonde: On Fairy Tales and Their Tellers.* New York: Noonday, 1994.

Wasko, Janet. *Understanding Disney.* Cambridge, UK: Polity, 2001.

Watts, Steven. "Walt Disney: Art and Politics in the American Century." *Journal of American History* 82.1 (June 1995): 84–110.

Zipes, Jack. *Fairy Tale as Myth/Myth as Fairy Tale.* Lexington: UP of Kentucky, 1994.

1. How does Ross define the ideology inherent in Disney's films for girls?

2. Summarize the content of the three films that Ross discusses. What similarities and differences does Ross see among them?

3. According to the writer, what is a "female Quixote"? Where does she treat this concept directly and indirectly?

Rhetorical Analysis

4. This essay appeared in a specialized scholarly journal. What "scholarly" elements appear in the paper? How does Ross adjust her style to this specialized audience? What strategies does she use to make the essay accessible to a wider audience?

5. Where does Ross state her claim most clearly? Analyze the varieties of evidence that she uses to support her claim and the minor propositions.

6. How does the writer organize her essay? What are the main divisions, and how do they cohere?

7. Why does Ross cite other scholars and writers? How does this strategy affect the power of her argument?

8. Ross elaborates a definition of the Disney "program" or ideology. What rhetorical strategies does she use to create this extended definition?

9. How effective do you find the concluding paragraph? Justify your response.

Writing

10. Select a Disney movie other than one discussed in this essay and write an analysis of its "program"—its ethical message or ideology.

11. In a descriptive essay, explain why children's stories or fairy tales have such a hold on young people's imaginations.

12. **Writing an Argument**   Write a persuasive essay on the benefits of children's literature and film—even the films that Walt Disney produced. Present at least three extended examples to support your claim.

Plumbing the Etiquette of Baseball

George F. Will

George Frederick Will (b. 1941) is an American newspaper columnist, journalist, and author. A Pulitzer Prize winner, he is best known for his conservative commentary on politics. In 1986, the *Wall Street Journal* called him "perhaps the most powerful journalist in America," in a league with Walter Lippmann (1889–1975). Will is a fan of baseball, and has written extensively on the game, including his best-selling book *Men at Work: The Craft of Baseball.* He was one of many interview subjects for Ken Burns's PBS documentary series *Baseball.* Will serves as a member of Major League Baseball's special committee on on-field matters. Once a minority owner in the Baltimore Orioles, he is a Chicago Cubs and Chicago Bears fan. The following essay addresses the unwritten codes of baseball that actually boost its image as more principled than many other professional sports.

1   The 2006 summit that preserved the peace occurred in a laundry room in the Minneapolis Metrodome after the Twins beat the Red Sox 8-1. Twins manager Ron Gardenhire, with center fielder Torii Hunter in tow, met with Red Sox manager Terry Francona to assure him that Hunter had not intentionally sinned.

2   With the Twins seven runs ahead in the bottom of the eighth, with two outs and no one on and a 3-0 count, Hunter had swung hard at a pitch. According to baseball's common law, he should not have swung at all.

3   This episode is recounted in Jason Turbow's *The Baseball Codes* about the game's unwritten rules. Just as the common law derives from ancient precedents—judges' decisions—rather than statutes, baseball's codes are the game's distilled mores. Their unchanged purpose is to show respect for opponents and the game. ...

4   With the Red Sox down seven runs with three outs remaining, it was, according to the codes, time to "play soft." With the count 3-0, Hunter knew a fastball strike was coming from a struggling pitcher whose job was just to end the mismatch. Over 162 games, every team is going to get drubbed, so every team favors an ethic that tells when to stop stealing bases, when to not tag at third and try to score on a medium-deep fly ball, when not to bunt a runner from first to second.

5   But, Turbow notes, the codes require judgments conditioned by contingencies. Although the team on top late in a lopsided game does not stop trying to hit, it stops pressing to manufacture runs. But how big a lead is "big enough"? Well, how bad is the leading team's bullpen? Does the losing team score runs in bunches? ...

6   The codes are frequently enforced from the pitcher's mound. When a fastball hits a batter's ribs, he is reminded to stop peeking to see where—inside or outside—the catcher is preparing to receive the pitch. In 1946, Dodger Hugh Casey threw at Cardinals shortstop Marty Marion while Marion was standing out of the batter's box—but closer to it than Casey thought proper—in order to time Casey's warmup pitches.

7   Traditionally, baseball punishes preening. In a society increasingly tolerant of exhibitionism, it is splendid when a hitter is knocked down because in his last at bat he lingered at the plate to admire his home run. But it was, Turbow suggests,

proper for the Cardinals' Albert Pujols, after hitting a home run, to flip his bat high in the air to show up Pirates pitcher Oliver Perez, who earlier in the game had waved his arms to celebrate getting Pujols out.

8   The consensus was that the codes were not violated when, during Joe DiMaggio's 56-game hitting streak in 1941, with one out in the bottom of the eighth and a Yankee runner on first and DiMaggio, who was hitless, on deck, Tommy Henrich bunted just to avoid a double play and assure DiMaggio another chance to extend the streak. Which he did.

9   In the codes, as in law generally, dogmatism can be dumb. The rule is that late in a no-hitter, the first hit must not be a bunt. So the Padres' Ben Davis was denounced for his eighth-inning bunt that broke up Curt Schilling's no-hitter. But the score was 2-0; the bunt brought to the plate the potential tying run.

10   Cheating by pitchers often operates under a "don't ask, don't tell" code. When George Steinbrenner demanded during a game that Yankees manager Lou Piniella protest that Don Sutton of the Angels was scuffing the ball, Piniella said, "The guy (Tommy John) who taught Don Sutton everything he knows about cheating is the guy pitching for us tonight." When a reporter asked Gaylord Perry's 5-year-old daughter if her father threw a spitball, she replied, "It's a hard slider."

11   When the Yankees' Deion ("Neon Deion") Sanders barely moved toward first after popping up to short, White Sox catcher Carlton Fisk, 42, a keeper of the codes, screamed: "Run the (expletive) ball out, you piece of (expletive)—that's not the way we do things up here!" Were Fisk and his standards out of date? As has been said, standards are always out of date—that is why we call them standards.

Comprehension

1. What is the central thesis of the essay?

2. Give two examples of "codes" and explain the rationale behind them.

3. How was Joe DiMaggio honored by a player from his team?

Rhetorical Analysis

4. Analyze the statement "standards are always out of date—that is why we call them standards" (paragraph 11).

5. Will's essay about the codes gives a certain overall impression about baseball and its players. What is the dominant impression and how is it exemplified?

6. Analyze the tone of the opening paragraph. What is Will's purpose in opening his essay with this tone?

7. Distinguish baseball from other sports, such as football and basketball, in light of the statement "traditionally baseball punishes preening" (paragraph 7).

Writing

8. **Writing an Argument**   Write a commentary on another American sports institution and what you believe are its set of codes.

Rhetorical Analysis

Read the paragraphs below from "Wonder Woman" and answer the questions that follow.

Perhaps it's our memories of past competence and dreams for the future that create the need for super-heroes in the first place. Leaping skyscrapers in a single bound, seeing through walls, and forcing people to tell the truth by encircling them in a magic lasso—all would be satisfying fantasies at any age, but they may be psychological necessities when we have trouble tying our shoes, escaping a worldview composed mainly of belts and knees, and getting grown-ups to *pay attention.*

The problem is that the super-heroes who perform magical feats—indeed, even mortal heroes who are merely competent—are almost always men. A female child is left to believe that, even when her body is as big as her spirit, she will still be helping with minor tasks, appreciating the accomplishments of others, and waiting to be rescued. Of course, pleasure is to be found in all these experiences of helping, appreciating, and being rescued; pleasure that should be open to boys, too. Even in comic books, heroes sometimes work in groups or are called upon to protect their own kind, not just helpless females. But the truth is that a male super-hero is more likely to be vulnerable, if only to create suspense, than a female character is to be powerful or independent. For little girls, the only alternative is suppressing a crucial part of ourselves by transplanting our consciousness into a male character—which usually means a white one, thus penalizing girls of color doubly, and boys of color, too. Otherwise, choices remain limited: in the case of girls, to an "ideal" life of sitting around like a Technicolor clotheshorse, getting into jams with villains, and saying things like, "Oh, Superman! I'll always be grateful to you"; in the case of boys of color, to identifying with villains who may be the only ethnic characters with any power; and in the case of girls of color, to making an impossible choice between parts of their identity. It hardly seems worth learning to tie our shoes.

—"Wonder Woman" by Gloria Steinem. Reprinted by permission of Gloria Steinem, feminist activist.

1. In this excerpt, the author primarily argues that
    A. The majority of superheroes who are imbued with supernatural powers are male.
    B. Both girls and boys should learn at an early age that it is important to be helpful and to appreciate the help of others.
    C. It is important that comic books present more diversity in their choice of villains, so that boys of color do not find themselves always relating to an evil character.
    D. The preponderance of white, male super-heroes precludes boys of color and girls in general from being able to relate to the scenarios they present.
    E. Children learn important skills like tying shoes from comic book characters.

2. At the end of paragraph one, the words "pay attention" are italicized most likely to
   A. Draw attention to the importance of this childhood need.
   B. Emphasize a careful reading of the passage.
   C. Harken back to the skills exhibited by superheroes.
   D. Underscore the difference between children's needs and adults' wishes.
   E. Highlight the importance of "grown-ups" in the world of superheroes.

Read the paragraphs below from "Today's Leading Man" and answer the questions that follow.

For years, Hollywood has perpetuated a nearly unattainable version of manhood, aggressively marketing its leading men as superhuman. As a result, men often linked heroism with masculinity; there's nothing more manly than a soldier or a cowboy or a spy, right? But today's male filmgoer doesn't live in a world where the bad guy is an insane Scandinavian billionaire who dies just before the inevitable getting-of-the-girl. Today's male filmgoer lives in a world where well-paying jobs are scarcer than ever, relationships are harder to maintain and happily ever after is just a blurry myth from our childhood.

Nathaniel Hawthorne once wrote, "A hero cannot be a hero unless in a heroic world," an observation that's never seemed more prescient than in our web-centric culture, where global anxieties—whether they be economic, social or political—are just a Wi-Fi connection away. Today's man doesn't have the luxury of being ignorant. No matter how flawed, we are forced to confront our issues with strategic thoughtfulness or risk falling by the wayside. Suddenly, the idea of a solitary action hero taking out a legion of bad guys doesn't feel heroic; it feels idiotic. Instead, the modern male moviegoer wants to watch someone they can relate to, someone with real-world problems, someone just like them. So while Tom Cruise was out leaping from building to couch, all the way into obscurity, Ryan Gosling was playing totally unconventional, totally flawed characters trying to make sense of a complicated and overwhelming world. In other words, he was playing us.

3. Which of the following statements best summarizes the author's claim in the excerpted paragraphs?
   A. Current Hollywood villains and heroes lack the luster and gravitas of villains of the past.
   B. Movie-goers are tired of movies that feature people like them; instead, they crave action and adventure and a transcendent experience.
   C. Men today think movies about superheroes and action heroes are idiotic; therefore, these movies often do not do well at the box office.
   D. Villains of the past do not resonate with modern movie-goers; the new Hollywood hero must be someone the current movie-goer can relate to.
   E. Tom Cruise and Ryan Gosling represent the two extremes of the movie hero spectrum; it is impossible for both to appear in the same movie.

Chapter Assessment

4. The author introduces a quotation from Nathaniel Hawthorne in the second paragraph, stating "A hero cannot be a hero unless in a heroic world" primarily to

    A. Suggest that society's fascination with non-heroic protagonists is well-established and worthy of continued discussion.

    B. Establish a basis for the discussion of modern society that follows.

    C. Provide a point of juxtaposition in his discussion of "solitary action."

    D. Create a dissenting lens through which to view "global anxieties."

    E. Contrast with the "nearly unattainable version of manhood" discussed in the first paragraph.

Read the paragraph below from "The Globalization of Eating Disorders" and answer the questions that follow.

Read the description again, but this time imagine twenty-something Tenisha Williamson standing in front of the mirror. Tenisha is black, suffers from anorexia, and feels like a traitor to her race. "From an African-American standpoint," she writes, "we as a people are encouraged to embrace our big, voluptuous bodies. This makes me feel terrible because I don't want a big, voluptuous body! I don't ever want to be fat—ever, and I don't ever want to gain weight. I would rather die from starvation than gain a single pound."[1] Tenisha is no longer an anomaly. Eating and body image problems are now not only crossing racial and class lines, but gender lines. They have also become a global phenomenon.

[1] From the Colours of Ana website (http://coloursofana.com//ss8.asp).

—Copyright © Susan Bordo.

5. The author introduces "Tenisha" to the narrative primarily to

    A. Build an appeal to ethos by providing a first person account of the problem.

    B. Establish credibility by showing that the author has interviewed a variety of people who can verify the claims the author is making.

    C. Offer an example of an individual outside the expected parameters of the discussion who has indeed be affected by the topic.

    D. Provide a counter-argument to the author's own position and address this argument through concession.

    E. Show that the problem the author has identified affects a narrow subset of the population.

6. Which of the following rhetorical strategies does the author use in this paragraph?

    A. Illustration

    B. Repetition by part

    C. Classification

    D. Definition

    E. Comparison and contrast

Read the paragraph below from "Escape from Wonderland: Disney and the Female Imagination" and answer the questions that follow.

One generalization I do suggest, however, is that Disney the man and the corporation are known for a belief in control. The top-down management style Disney epitomizes—Auschwitz (Giroux 55), or Mouschwitz (Lewis 88), is a frequent analogy—thrives on homogeneity and rigid adherence to rules. These are features often decried in Disney production and product, both by critics of capitalism, such as Benjamin and Adorno,[1] and by far less radical proponents of individualism and open debate, from early Disney biographer Richard Schickel to educator Henry Giroux. Yet imagination, the company's major commodity, docs not easily lend itself to a program of control. To encourage imagination in artists, and arouse it in viewers, is to invite unique self-expression rather than homogeneity, and spontaneity rather than predictability. Link imagination to the animated cartoon, an art form with roots in dada, surrealism, and radical politics, and matters could well get out of hand.[2]

[1] Miriam Hansen discusses Benjamin's and Adorno's objections to Disney in some detail. Jack Zipes's critique of Disney also occurs within a larger argument about the "freezing" of fairy tales into myths to perpetuate bourgeois, patriarchal values (see his Introduction and Chapter 3).

[2] Janet Wasko notes that Disney deliberately avoided the more "anarchistic and inventive" styles of animation employed at other studios (115). My own belief, on which my approach to Disney is based, is that where there is animation, anarchy can never be wholly suppressed. For discussion of the roots of animation in surrealism and dada, see Inez Hedges.

—Reprinted from "Escape from Wonderland: Disney and the Female Imagination" by Deborah Ross, in *Marvels & Tales: Journal of Fairy-Tale Studies* Vol.18 No.1, © 2004 Wayne State University Press, with the permission of Wayne State University Press.

7. The main purpose of footnote 1 is to
   A. Identify conflicting opinions on the issue the author addresses and offer a concession to those viewpoints.
   B. Suggest that there is an on-going scholarly conversation on the issue by mentioning scholarly responses that support the author's perspective.
   C. Divulge a commonly held but incorrect opinion on the cultural representations the author discusses.
   D. Mention a point of view that is both outdated and recently disproven.
   E. Offer support for the author's specific argument.

8. Based on footnote 2, it is reasonable to infer that the author
   A. Frequently collaborates with Wasko.
   B. Disagrees significantly with Wasko's ideology on surrealism in animation.
   C. Considers Wasko an interesting counterpoint to her opinions on Disney, but does not fully agree with her.
   D. Believes that Hedges and Wasko share complementary theories.
   E. Espouses the view of Hedges while eschewing the musings of Wasko.

Chapter Assessment

Read the paragraph below from "Plumbing the Etiquette of Baseball" and answer the questions that follow.

Traditionally, baseball punishes preening. In a society increasingly tolerant of exhibitionism, it is splendid when a hitter is knocked down because in his last at bat he lingered at the plate to admire his home run. But it was, Turbow suggests, proper for the Cardinals' Albert Pujols, after hitting a home run, to flip his bat high in the air to show up Pirates pitcher Oliver Perez, who earlier in the game had waved his arms to celebrate getting Pujols out.

9. Based on the tone and content of the passage as a whole, the author is most likely
   A. A detractor of baseball and all professional sports.
   B. A fan of baseball.
   C. A critic who dislikes sports culture in the United States.
   D. A fan of high school sports who thinks professional sports stars are overpaid.
   E. A former coach.

10. A central irony of the passage is that
   A. While preening in baseball is frowned upon, directed celebration is acceptable.
   B. While preening in baseball is frowned upon, knocking down a player is celebrated.
   C. While knocking down a player is celebrated, society at large approves of exhibitionism.
   D. Flipping a bat high in the air is not considered exhibitionism.
   E. Players cannot be knocked down for flipping their bats high in the air.

Connections for Critical Thinking

1. Examine the role of the media in society and journalists' responsibilities or duties to humanity. Use at least three essays from this chapter to illustrate or support your thesis.

2. Define *popular culture,* using the essays of Ross and Steinem as reference points, along with any additional essays that you consider relevant.

3. Use Barna's and Ross's essays to explore media's connections to American cultural experience. What strategies do these writers use? Are their goals similar?

4. Using at least three recent films or television episodes that you have seen, write an essay in which you agree or disagree with Bordo's claim that the media are causing "eating and body image problems" for girls and women as well as for boys and men.

Social Media—Has It Empowered Us or Disenfranchised Us?

Social media could be arguably one of greatest influences on society today. Increasingly, we turn to social media to get our information. Instant information also becomes instant susceptibility to many dark Internet interferences connected to what we read and believe. Connected people have the opportunity to be empowered or disenfranchised by this form of media. Critically read and analyze the texts and images here, and then answer the questions that follow.

▼ SOURCE A

Millennials Using Social Media

Monkey Business Images/Shutterstock.com

"Social Media as Tool for Meaningful Political Activism" by Ryanne Lau.

—Ryanne Lau, Social Media as Tool for Meaningful Political Activism March 09, 2017, McGill Left Review, http://mcgillleftreview.com/article/social-media-tool-meaningful-political-activism?_sm_au_=iVVH53Q60F0kFR5Q

The advent of social media has allowed for an unprecedented ease of information distribution. The versatility of social networking sites means one can connect with broad audiences, whether it is through the low commitment of the 140-character count on Twitter, the visual-audio attraction of Instagram, or the accessibility of Facebook. The causes of organizations can be made entirely evident via 30-second videos that can be shared by millions of users. There are few members of the population that an activist is not able to speak to. The speed of information dispersal in the age of social media means reaction is close to instantaneous. The effective dissemination of information by social media has contributed to the phenomena of social media activism, where political initiatives are rapidly spread among users through the internet.

"Social media activists" may be defined in this article as anyone who uses social media to further socio-political interests. Activism was traditionally limited to those who organized in the streets or went door to door to acquire signatures for a petition. It is due to the widespread use of social media that activism is no longer restricted to organizations or prominent figures with a voice. Lobbying against companies can be done online without ever stepping outside. Activism no longer requires the extensive planning and often difficult picket-sign lobbying in its traditional form of organized protests. Due to the nature of the internet, activism is able to expand its definition to those who are continuously sharing links, petitions, and other web materials to promote their political interests. People are able to join the protests easily through hashtags or changing their profile picture. Anyone with access to the internet may become a social activist and have their voice heard.

▼ SOURCE C

"Social Media Storm: How Social Media Helped the Hurricane Harvey Victims Survive" by Eline Blaise

—"Social Media Storm - How Social Media Helped the Hurricane Harvey Victims Survive" by Eline Blaise for iRISEmedia.com, September 2017.

The power of social media has been demonstrated once again with the most recent natural disaster taking place in Houston, Texas. By now, we have all heard about Hurricane Harvey and the devastation it left behind. In times of uncertainty and desperation, tons of victims decided to turn to social media for a chance to be heard and rescued. Although 911 is still the number one emergency number, not everyone was able to get through. People turned to Facebook and Twitter as a last cry for help, stuck on roofs and waist-deep in water. #sosharvey and #helphouston were used to locate victims and dedicated accounts such as @HarveyRescue gathered information about those in need.

Countless pictures were posted on social media of Harvey victims trapped on rooftops, stuck inside buildings; Facebook even activated its safety check for users to share if they were safe, ask for help and even offer services. Being able to mark yourself safe on Facebook or check into places are not necessarily new. However, social media channels were overwhelmed with pictures of scenes of devastation that the regular media couldn't get their hands on. This is why we are calling this a never before seen "Social Media Storm." Some calls for help even went viral, attracting attention and in some cases saving lives.

A nursing home close to Houston was pushed to number one on the priority list after a picture of residents in need was posted on Twitter. In that viral picture, the residents, some in wheelchairs, were up to their chests deep in water. The owner's son-in-law posted the picture on Sunday, getting over 4,800 retweets. People were so shocked by the dramatic picture, some even thought it was a hoax. However, thanks to the countless retweets and newspaper attention, the nursing home residents were saved the same day the picture was posted.

"How Using Social Media Affects Teenagers" by Rachel Ehmke

—By Rachel Ehmke, originally published on childmind.org

The other big danger that comes from kids communicating more indirectly is that it has gotten easier to be cruel. "Kids text all sorts of things that you would never in a million years contemplate saying to anyone's face," says Dr. Donna Wick, a clinical and developmental psychologist who runs Mind to Mind Parent. She notes that this seems to be especially true of girls, who typically don't like to disagree with each other in "real life."

"You hope to teach them that they can disagree without jeopardizing the relationship, but what social media is teaching them to do is disagree in ways that are more extreme and *do* jeopardize the relationship. It's exactly what you don't want to have happen," she says.

Dr. Steiner-Adair agrees that girls are particularly at risk. "Girls are socialized more to compare themselves to other people, girls in particular, to develop their identities, so it makes them more vulnerable to the downside of all this." She warns that a lack of solid self-esteem is often to blame. "We forget that relational aggression comes from insecurity and feeling awful about yourself, and wanting to put other people down so you feel better."

Peer acceptance is a big thing for adolescents, and many of them care about their image as much as a politician running for office, and to them it can feel as serious. Add to that the fact that kids today are getting actual polling data on how much people like them or their appearance via things like "likes." It's enough to turn anyone's head. Who wouldn't want to make herself look cooler if she can? So kids can spend hours pruning their online identities, trying to project an idealized image. Teenage girls sort through hundreds of photos, agonizing over which ones to post online. Boys compete for attention by trying to out-gross one other, pushing the envelope as much as they can in the already disinhibited atmosphere online. Kids gang up on each other.

Adolescents have always been doing this, but with the advent of social media they are faced with more opportunities—and more traps—than ever before. When kids scroll through their feeds and see how great everyone seems, it only adds to the pressure. We're used to worrying about the impractical ideals that photoshopped magazine models give to our kids, but what happens with the kid next door is photoshopped, too? Even more confusing, what about when your own profile doesn't really represent the person that you feel like you are on the inside?

▼ SOURCE E

Crowdfunding. One of the newest ways for an entrepreneur to secure financing is through crowdfunding, also known as crowdsourcing: making a direct funding appeal to a "crowd" of possibly interested investors on a social networking platform. For example, if a potential entrepreneur has an idea that he or she wants to promote to an interest group, the promotion can be made for very little cost. All that is required is a good idea, a successful crowdfunding strategy, a suitable media platform, and a crowd willing to listen and, of course, contribute.

Rawpixel.com/Shutterstock

"The Pros and Cons of Social Networking" by Elise Moreau

—Elise Moreau, The Pros and Cons of Social Networking: A look at the ups and downs of being so digitally connected to people, updated April 9, 2018, Lifewire, https://www.lifewire.com/advantages-and-disadvantages-of-social-networking-3486020

. . . Online interaction substitution for offline interaction. Since people are now connected all the time and you can pull up a friend's social profile with a click of your mouse or a tap of your smartphone, it's a lot easier to use online interaction as a substitute for face-to-face interaction. Some people argue that social media actually promotes antisocial human behavior.

Distraction and procrastination. How often do you see someone look at their phone? People get distracted by all the social apps and news and messages they receive, leading to all sorts of problems like distracted driving or the lack of gaining someone's full attention during a conversation. Browsing social media can also feed procrastination habits and become something people turn to in order to avoid certain tasks or responsibilities. . . .

Applying Your Synthesis Skills

Comprehension

1. Summarize the inferred arguments made in each source.

Rhetorical Analysis

2. Explain the effectiveness of the author's use of the repeated word *activism* in Source B.

3. What is the appeal of the examples used in Source C?

4. How does Source D use ethos to highlight the pitfalls of using social media? How does it use pathos?

5. How do the visual elements and the perspective of Sources A and E reveal expressive content, or purpose?

Writing an Argument

6. Using examples from at least three of the sources, write an essay explaining your position on whether the benefits of social media outweigh its disadvantages.

CHAPTER 9

Literature and the Arts: Why Do They Matter?

As you read the essays in this chapter, consider the following questions:

- According to the author, what is the value of the art or literary form under discussion?
- What function does literature or art serve?
- Is the writer's perspective subjective or objective, and how can you tell?
- How does the author define his or her subject—whether it is poetry, fiction, art, or photography?
- Is the writer's experience of literature or art similar to or different from your own?
- In what ways do gender and race influence the writer's perspective on the subject?
- What is the main idea that the author wants to present about literature or the arts? Do you agree or disagree with this key concept?
- What have you learned about the importance of literature and the arts from reading these essays?

Imagine a world without fiction, poetry, or drama, without music, art, or other fine arts. We are so accustomed to taking the arts for granted that it is hard for us to conceive of contemporary culture without them. Our fondness for stories or paintings or any other creative form might help us understand our culture or might even move us to action. Yet the value of various artistic forms does not derive exclusively from their ability to tell us something about life. The arts can also take us into an imaginative realm offering perhaps more intense experiences than anything we encounter in the "real" world.

Think of literature and the arts as an exercise in imaginative freedom. You are free to select the books you read, the music that appeals to you, the exhibitions and concerts you attend, and the entertainment software with which you interact. Some of your decisions might be serious and consequential to your education. Other decisions, perhaps to watch a few videos on a rainy afternoon or to buy the latest bestseller, are less important. The way you view the arts—whether as a way to learn something about the temper of civilization or as a temporary escape from conventional reality—is entirely a matter of taste. Regardless of your purpose or intent, you approach literature and the arts initially for the sheer exhilaration and pleasure they provide. Art, as Plato observed, is a dream for awakened minds.

The arts awaken you to the power and intensity of the creative spirit. At the same time, you make judgments and evaluations of the nature of your creative encounter. When you assert that you like this painting or dislike that poem, you are assessing the work and the value of the artistic experience. Clearly, you develop taste and become more equipped to discern the more subtle elements of art the more you are exposed to it. Perhaps you prefer to keep your experience of literature and the other arts a pleasurable pastime or an escape from reality. Or you may wish to participate in them as a creative writer, musician, painter, or photographer. Ultimately, you may come to view literature and the arts as a transformational experience, a voyage of discovery in which you encounter diverse peoples and cultures, learn to see the world in creative terms, and begin to perceive your own creative potential in a new light.

CLASSIC AND CONTEMPORARY IMAGES

How Do We Evaluate a Work of Art?

Using a Critical Perspective Although "greatness" in art and literature might be in the mind of the beholder, it could be argued that you need certain standards of excellence or judgment to determine the quality of any work. The artist's or writer's control of the medium, the projection of a unique vision, the evidence of a superlative style—all enter into the evaluation process. As you consider these sculptures by Auguste Rodin and Jeff Koons, try to evaluate their relative worth. Which work reflects greater artistic control? What makes the sculpture appealing, and why? Which work strikes you as "new" or original, or modern? Explain your response and criteria for evaluation.

Analyzing Visuals and Their Rhetoric

1. What is the central impression created by Rodin's sculpture? How does the sculptor's technique create this impression?

2. What central impression does Koons's sculpture create? How does the sculptor's technique create this impression?

3. How did Rodin utilize line and form to "contain" *The Thinker*'s thoughts? How does the classic sculpture differ from the contemporary sculpture in the use of line and form?

4. If *The Thinker* could talk, what would he say? What would *Rabbit*'s message be?

CLASSIC ▼

What Is the Value of Literature?

Although Eudora Welty was born at the beginning of the 20th century in a small Mississippi town and Margaret Atwood several decades later in Canada, these writers share a reverence for the importance of literature in their childhood. Of course, there are understandable differences in the types of literature that formed their young minds. Welty, you will discover, grew up in a loving, middle-class household where virtually every room contained books—a treasury of English and European novels, classic fairy tales, and famous works of literature in the Western tradition. Atwood, born in Canada in 1939, was greatly influenced by George Orwell's writing—she is a poet, novelist, short-story writer, and essayist who explores the role of personal consciousness in a troubled world. Despite their disparate reading tastes, Welty and Atwood both grew up to be writers. Both attest to the value of literature. As they recount their childhoods, Welty and Atwood succeed in convincing us that whether one child reads Dickens and another reads Orwellian dystopias, ideas and insights into the world derive from the active reading of texts.

One Writer's Beginnings

Eudora Welty

Eudora Welty (1909–2001), a celebrated American writer, was born and died in Jackson, Mississippi. Raised in a close-knit bookish family, Welty attended the Mississippi State College for Women for two years and then the University of Wisconsin (BA, 1929). In the 1930s she returned to Mississippi and worked for the Works Progress Administration as a reporter and photographer, traveling the state and recording the lives of its citizens during the Depression years. She also began a career as a short-story writer and novelist. Welty's superb short fiction collections include *A Curtain of Green* (1941), *The Wide Net* (1943), and *Collected Stories* (1980), which received an American Book Award. She received the Pulitzer Prize for her novel *The Optimist's Daughter* (1972). The recipient of the President's Medal of Freedom and numerous other major awards, Welty spent virtually her entire life writing about the South but in ways that transcend her region, radiating outward to embrace universal truths. In the selection that follows, one of three lectures delivered at Harvard University in 1983 and published in her memoir *One Writer's Beginnings* (1984), Welty speaks of the value of literature and the arts in her life.

1   I learned from the age of two or three that any room in our house, at any time of day, was there to read in, or to be read to. My mother read to me. She'd read to me in the big bedroom in the mornings, when we were in her rocker together,

which ticked in rhythm as we rocked, as though we had a cricket accompanying the story. She'd read to me in the diningroom on winter afternoons in front of the coal fire, with our cuckoo clock ending the story with "Cuckoo," and at night when I'd got in my own bed. I must have given her no peace. Sometimes she read to me in the kitchen while she sat churning, and the churning sobbed along with *any* story. It was my ambition to have her read to me while *I* churned; once she granted my wish, but she read off my story before I brought her butter. She was an expressive reader. When she was reading "Puss in Boots," for instance, it was impossible not to know that she distrusted *all* cats.

2   It had been startling and disappointing to me to find out that story books had been written by *people*, that books were not natural wonders, coming up of themselves like grass. Yet regardless of where they came from, I cannot remember a time when I was not in love with them—with the books themselves, cover and binding and the paper they were printed on, with their smell and their weight and with their possession in my arms, captured and carried off to myself. Still illiterate, I was ready for them, committed to all the reading I could give them.

3   Neither of my parents had come from homes that could afford to buy many books, but though it must have been something of a strain on his salary, as the youngest officer in a young insurance company, my father was all the while carefully selecting and ordering away for what he and Mother thought we children should grow up with. They bought first for the future.

4   Besides the bookcase in the livingroom, which was always called "the library," there were the encyclopedia tables and dictionary stand under windows in our diningroom. Here to help us grow up arguing around the diningroom table were the Unabridged Webster, the Columbia Encyclopedia, Compton's Pictured Encyclopedia, the Lincoln Library of Information, and later the Book of Knowledge. And the year we moved into our new house, there was room to celebrate it with the new 1925 edition of the Britannica, which my father, his face always deliberately turned toward the future, was of course disposed to think better than any previous edition.

5   In "the library," inside the mission-style bookcase with its three diamond-latticed glass doors, with my father's Morris chair and the glass-shaded lamp on its table beside it, were books I could soon begin on—and I did, reading them all alike and as they came, straight down their rows, top shelf to bottom. There was the set of Stoddard's Lectures, in all its late nineteenth-century vocabulary and vignettes of peasant life and quaint beliefs and customs, with matching halftone illustrations: Vesuvius erupting, Venice by moonlight, gypsies glimpsed by their campfires. I didn't know then the clue they were to my father's longing to see the rest of the world. I read straight through his other love-from-afar: the Victrola Book of the Opera, with opera after opera in synopsis, with portraits in costume of Melba, Caruso, Galli-Curci, and Geraldine Farrar, some of whose voices we could listen to on our Red Seal records.

6   My mother read secondarily for information; she sank as a hedonist into novels. She read Dickens in the spirit in which she would have eloped with him. The novels of her girlhood that had stayed on in her imagination, besides those of Dickens and Scott and Robert Louis Stevenson, were *Jane Eyre, Trilby, The Woman in White, Green Mansions, King Solomon's Mines*. Marie Corelli's name would crop up but I understood she had gone out of favor with my mother, who had only kept *Ardath* out of loyalty. In time she absorbed herself in Galsworthy, Edith Wharton, above all in Thomas Mann of the *Joseph* volumes.

7   *St. Elmo* was not in our house; I saw it often in other houses. This wildly popular Southern novel is where all the Edna Earles in our population started coming from. They're all named for the heroine, who succeeded in bringing a dissolute, sinning roué and atheist of a lover (St. Elmo) to his knees. My mother was able to forgo it. But she remembered the classic advice given to rose growers on how to water their bushes long enough: "Take a chair and *St. Elmo.*"

8   To both my parents I owe my early acquaintance with a beloved Mark Twain. There was a full set of Mark Twain and a short set of Ring Lardner in our bookcase, and those were the volumes that in time united us all, parents and children.

9   Reading everything that stood before me was how I came upon a worn old book without a back that had belonged to my father as a child. It was called *Sanford and Merton*. Is there anyone left who recognizes it, I wonder? It is the famous moral tale written by Thomas Day in the 1780s, but of him no mention is made on the title page of *this* book; here it is *Sanford and Merton in Words of One Syllable* by Mary Godolphin. Here are the rich boy and the poor boy and Mr. Barlow, their teacher and interlocutor, in long discourses alternating with dramatic scenes—danger and rescue allotted to the rich and the poor respectively. It may have only words of one syllable, but one of them is "quoth." It ends with not one but two morals, both engraved on rings: "Do what you ought, come what may," and "If we would be great, we must first learn to be good."

10   This book was lacking its front cover, the back held on by strips of pasted paper, now turned golden, in several layers, and the pages stained, flecked, and tattered around the edges; its garish illustrations had come unattached but were preserved, laid in. I had the feeling even in my heedless childhood that this was the only book my father as a little boy had of his own. He had held onto it, and might have gone to sleep on its coverless face: He had lost his mother when he was seven. My father had never made any mention to his own children of the book, but he had brought it along with him from Ohio to our house and shelved it in our bookcase.

11   My mother had brought from West Virginia that set of Dickens; those books looked sad, too—they had been through fire and water before I was born, she told me, and there they were, lined up—as I later realized, waiting for *me*.

12   I was presented, from as early as I can remember, with books of my own, which appeared on my birthday and Christmas morning. Indeed, my parents could not give me books enough. They must have sacrificed to give me on my

sixth or seventh birthday—it was after I became a reader for myself—the ten-volume set of Our Wonder World. These were beautifully made, heavy books I would lie down with on the floor in front of the diningroom hearth, and more often than the rest volume 5, *Every Child's Story Book*, was under my eyes. There were the fairy tales—Grimm, Andersen, the English, the French, "Ali Baba and the Forty Thieves"; and there was Aesop and Reynard the Fox; there were the myths and legends, Robin Hood, King Arthur, and St. George and the Dragon, even the history of Joan of Arc; a whack of *Pilgrim's Progress* and a long piece of *Gulliver*. They all carried their classic illustrations. I located myself in these pages and could go straight to the stories and pictures I loved; very often "The Yellow Dwarf" was first choice, with Walter Crane's Yellow Dwarf in full color making his terrifying appearance flanked by turkeys. Now that volume is as worn and backless and hanging apart as my father's poor *Sanford and Merton*. The precious page with Edward Lear's "Jumblies" on it has been in danger of slipping out for all these years. One measure of my love for Our Wonder World was that for a long time I wondered if I would go through fire and water for it as my mother had done for Charles Dickens; and the only comfort was to think I could ask my mother to do it for me.

13   I believe I'm the only child I know of who grew up with this treasure in the house. I used to ask others, "Did you have Our Wonder World?" I'd have to tell them The Book of Knowledge could not hold a candle to it.

14   I live in gratitude to my parents for initiating me—and as early as I begged for it, without keeping me waiting—into knowledge of the word, into reading and spelling, by way of the alphabet. They taught it to me at home in time for me to begin to read before starting to school. I believe the alphabet is no longer considered an essential piece of equipment for traveling through life. In my day it was the keystone to knowledge. You learned the alphabet as you learned to count to ten, as you learned "Now I lay me" and the Lord's Prayer and your father's and mother's name and address and telephone number, all in case you were lost.

15   My love for the alphabet, which endures, grew out of reciting it but, before that, out of seeing the letters on the page. In my own story books, before I could read them for myself, I fell in love with various winding, enchanting-looking initials drawn by Walter Crane at the heads of fairy tales. In "Once upon a time," an "O" had a rabbit running it as a treadmill, his feet upon flowers. When the day came, years later, for me to see the Book of Kells, all the wizardry of letter, initial, and word swept over me a thousand times over, and the illumination, the gold, seemed a part of the word's beauty and holiness that had been there from the start.

. . .

16   Learning stamps you with its moments. Childhood's learning is made up of moments. It isn't steady. It's a pulse.

17   In a children's art class, we sat in a ring on kindergarten chairs and drew three daffodils that had just been picked out of the yard; and while I was

drawing, my sharpened pencil and the cup of the yellow daffodil gave off whiffs just alike. That the pencil doing the drawing should give off the same smell as the flower it drew seemed a part of the art lesson—as shouldn't it be? Children, like animals, use all their senses to discover the world. Then artists come along and discover it the same way, all over again. Here and there, it's the same world. Or now and then we'll hear from an artist who's never lost it.

18   In my sensory education I include my physical awareness of the *word*. Of a certain word, that is; the connection it has with what it stands for. At around age six, perhaps, I was standing by myself in our front yard waiting for supper, just at that hour in a late summer day when the sun is already below the horizon and the risen full moon in the visible sky stops being chalky and begins to take on light. There comes the moment, and I saw it then, when the moon goes from flat to round. For the first time it met my eyes as a globe. The word "moon" came into my mouth as though fed to me out of a silver spoon. Held in my mouth the moon became a word. It had the roundness of a Concord grape Grandpa took off his vine and gave me to suck out of its skin and swallow whole, in Ohio.

19   This love did not prevent me from living for years in foolish error about the moon. The new moon just appearing in the west was the rising moon to me. The new should be rising. And in early childhood the sun and moon, those opposite reigning powers, I just as easily assumed rose in east and west respectively in their opposite sides of the sky, and like partners in a reel they advanced, sun from the east, moon from the west, crossed over (when I wasn't looking) and went down on the other side. My father couldn't have known I believed that when, bending behind me and guiding my shoulder, he positioned me at our telescope in the front yard and, with careful adjustment of the focus, brought the moon close to me.

20   The night sky over my childhood Jackson was velvety black. I could see the full constellations in it and call their names; when I could read, I knew their myths. Though I was always waked for eclipses, and indeed carried to the window as an infant in arms and shown Halley's Comet in my sleep, and though I'd been taught at our diningroom table about the solar system and knew the earth revolved around the sun, and our moon around us, I never found out the moon didn't come up in the west until I was a writer and Herschel Brickell, the literary critic, told me after I misplaced it in a story. He said valuable words to me about my new profession: "Always be sure you get your moon in the right part of the sky."

      . . .

21   My mother always sang to her children. Her voice came out just a little bit in the minor key. "Wee Willie Winkie's" song was wonderfully sad when she sang the lullabies.

22   "Oh, but now there's a record. She could have her own record to listen to," my father would have said. For there came a Victrola record of "Bobby Shafftoe" and

"Rock-a-Bye Baby," all of Mother's lullabies, which could be played to take her place. Soon I was able to play her my own lullabies all day long.

23   Our Victrola stood in the diningroom. I was allowed to climb onto the seat of a diningroom chair to wind it, start the record turning, and set the needle playing. In a second I'd jumped to the floor, to spin or march around the table as the music called for—now there were all the other records I could play too. I skinned back onto the chair just in time to lift the needle at the end, stop the record and turn it over, then change the needle. That brass receptacle with a hole in the lid gave off a metallic smell like human sweat, from all the hot needles that were fed it. Winding up, dancing, being cocked to start and stop the record, was of course all in one the act of *listening*—to "Overture to *Daughter of the Regiment*," "Selections from *The Fortune Teller*," "Kiss Me Again," "Gypsy Dance from *Carmen*," "Stars and Stripes Forever," "When the Midnight Choo-Choo Leaves for Alabam," or whatever came next. Movement must be at the very heart of listening.

24   Ever since I was first read to, then started reading to myself, there has never been a line read that I didn't *hear*. As my eyes followed the sentence, a voice was saying it silently to me. It isn't my mother's voice, or the voice of any person I can identify, certainly not my own. It is human, but inward, and it is inwardly that I listen to it. It is to me the voice of the story or the poem itself. The cadence, whatever it is that asks you to believe, the feeling that resides in the printed word, reaches me through the reader-voice. I have supposed, but never found out, that this is the case with all readers—to read as listeners—and with all writers, to write as listeners. It may be part of the desire to write. The sound of what falls on the page begins the process of testing it for truth, for me. Whether I am right to trust so far I don't know. By now I don't know whether I could do either one, reading or writing, without the other.

25   My own words, when I am at work on a story, I hear too as they go, in the same voice that I hear when I read in books. When I write and the sound of it comes back to my ears, then I act to make my changes. I have always trusted this voice.

Comprehension

1. What is the significance of the essay's title? Does Welty write about one continuous "beginning" or a series of beginnings? Explain.

2. What does Welty mean when she says that her mother was a "hedonist" (paragraph 6)? Does Welty also become a hedonist? Why or why not?

3. Explain the nature of Welty's "sensory" education.

Rhetorical Analysis

4. Welty alludes to dozens of works of literature. What does she assume about her audience's knowledge of these works? How do the allusions contribute to Welty's purpose?

5. What is Welty's thesis, and how does she develop it?

6. What determines the order in which Welty organizes her essay, which she divides into three parts?

7. Welty includes several descriptive passages in this essay. Where are these passages, and what do they contribute to the overall meaning of the selection?

8. How do the last two paragraphs of the essay echo the first two paragraphs?

Writing

9. Write a description of a scene or series of events from your childhood in which you were reading (or being read to), engaged in an art project, or listening to music. In your essay, explain the impact of this memory or activity on your current life.

10. Write an essay explaining the importance of providing children with sensory stimuli involving reading, artwork, and music.

11. **Writing an Argument**   Argue for or against the proposition that children today read less than those of previous generations—and suffer the consequences.

Orwell and Me

Margaret Atwood

Margaret Atwood (b. 1939) is arguably Canada's most famous contemporary writer—a poet, novelist, short-story writer, and essayist who explores the role of personal consciousness in a troubled world. Atwood received degrees from the University of Toronto (BA, 1961) and Radcliffe College (AM, 1962). Her second collection of poetry, *The Circle Game* (1966), brought her critical recognition. Atwood is even better known as a novelist; her fiction includes *Surfacing* (1973), *Life Before Man* (1979), *The Handmaid's Tale* (1985), *Cat's Eye* (1988), *The Blind Assassin* (2000), *The Tent* (2006), and *The Year of the Flood* (2008). In the following selection, published in the Manchester *Guardian* in 2003, Atwood explains the impact of one English writer— George Orwell—on her life, as well as his relevance for the post–9/11 world.

1   I grew up with George Orwell. I was born in 1939, and *Animal Farm* was published in 1945. Thus, I was able to read it at the age of nine. It was lying around the house, and I mistook it for a book about talking animals, sort of like *Wind in the Willows*. I knew nothing about the kind of politics in the book—the child's version of politics then, just after the war, consisted of the simple notion that Hitler was bad but dead. So I gobbled up the adventures of Napoleon and Snowball, the smart, greedy, upwardly mobile pigs, and Squealer the spin-doctor, and Boxer the noble but thick-witted horse, and the easily led, slogan-chanting sheep, without making any connection with historical events.

2   To say that I was horrified by this book is an understatement. The fate of the farm animals was so grim, the pigs so mean and mendacious and treacherous, the sheep so stupid. Children have a keen sense of injustice, and this was the thing that upset me the most: the pigs were so unjust. I cried my eyes out when Boxer the horse had an accident and was carted off to be made into dog food, instead of being given the quiet corner of the pasture he'd been promised.

3   The whole experience was deeply disturbing to me, but I am forever grateful to Orwell for alerting me early to the danger flags I've tried to watch out for since. In the world of *Animal Farm*, most speechifying and public palaver is bullshit and instigated lying, and though many characters are good-hearted and mean well, they can be frightened into closing their eyes to what's really going on. The pigs browbeat the others with ideology, then twist that ideology to suit their own purposes: their language games were evident to me even at that age. As Orwell taught, it isn't the labels—Christianity, Socialism, Islam, Democracy, Two Legs Bad, Four Legs Good, the works—that are definitive, but the acts done in their name.

4   I could see, too, how easily those who have toppled an oppressive power take on its trappings and habits. Jean-Jacques Rousseau was right to warn us that

democracy is the hardest form of government to maintain; Orwell knew that to the marrow of his bones, because he had seen it in action. How quickly the precept "All Animals Are Equal" is changed into "All Animals Are Equal, but Some Are More Equal Than Others." What oily concern the pigs show for the welfare of the other animals, a concern that disguises their contempt for those they are manipulating. With what alacrity do they put on the once-despised uniforms of the tyrannous humans they have overthrown, and learn to use their whips. How self-righteously they justify their actions, helped by the verbal web-spinning of Squealer, their nimble-tongued press agent, until all power is in their trotters, pretence is no longer necessary, and they rule by naked force. A *revolution* often means only that: a revolving, a turn of the wheel of fortune, by which those who were at the bottom mount to the top, and assume the choice positions, crushing the former power-holders beneath them. We should beware of all those who plaster the landscape with large portraits of themselves, like the evil pig, Napoleon.

5   *Animal Farm* is one of the most spectacular Emperor-Has-No-Clothes books of the 20th century, and it got George Orwell into trouble. People who run counter to the current popular wisdom, who point out the uncomfortably obvious, are likely to be strenuously baa-ed at by herds of angry sheep. I didn't have all that figured out at the age of nine, of course—not in any conscious way. But we learn the patterns of stories before we learn their meanings, and *Animal Farm* has a very clear pattern.

6   Then along came *Nineteen Eighty-Four*, which was published in 1949. Thus, I read it in paperback a couple of years later, when I was in high school. Then I read it again, and again: It was right up there among my favourite books, along with *Wuthering Heights*. At the same time, I absorbed its two companions, Arthur Koestler's *Darkness At Noon* and Aldous Huxley's *Brave New World*. I was keen on all three of them, but I understood *Darkness At Noon* to be a tragedy about events that had already happened, and *Brave New World* to be a satirical comedy, with events that were unlikely to unfold in exactly that way. (Orgy-Porgy, indeed.) *Nineteen Eighty-Four* struck me as more realistic, probably because Winston Smith was more like me—a skinny person who got tired a lot and was subjected to physical education under chilly conditions (this was a feature of my school)—and who was silently at odds with the ideas and the manner of life proposed for him. (This may be one of the reasons *Nineteen Eighty-Four* is best read when you are an adolescent: most adolescents feel like that.) I sympathised particularly with Winston's desire to write his forbidden thoughts down in a deliciously tempting, secret blank book: I had not yet started to write, but I could see the attractions of it. I could also see the dangers, because it's this scribbling of his—along with illicit sex, another item with considerable allure for a teenager of the 50s—that gets Winston into such a mess.

7   *Animal Farm* charts the progress of an idealistic movement of liberation towards a totalitarian dictatorship headed by a despotic tyrant; *Nineteen Eighty-Four* describes what it's like to live entirely within such a system. Its hero,

Winston, has only fragmentary memories of what life was like before the present dreadful regime set in: he's an orphan, a child of the collectivity. His father died in the war that has ushered in the repression, and his mother has disappeared, leaving him with only the reproachful glance she gave him as he betrayed her over a chocolate bar—a small betrayal that acts both as the key to Winston's character and as a precursor to the many other betrayals in the book.

8   The government of Airstrip One, Winston's "country," is brutal. The constant surveillance, the impossibility of speaking frankly to anyone, the looming, ominous figure of Big Brother, the regime's need for enemies and wars—fictitious though both may be—which are used to terrify the people and unite them in hatred, the mind-numbing slogans, the distortions of language, the destruction of what has really happened by stuffing any record of it down the Memory Hole—these made a deep impression on me. Let me re-state that: they frightened the stuffing out of me. Orwell was writing a satire about Stalin's Soviet Union, a place about which I knew very little at the age of 14, but he did it so well that I could imagine such things happening anywhere.

9   There is no love interest in *Animal Farm*, but there is in *Nineteen Eighty-Four*. Winston finds a soulmate in Julia; outwardly a devoted Party fanatic, secretly a girl who enjoys sex and makeup and other spots of decadence. But the two lovers are discovered, and Winston is tortured for thought-crime—inner disloyalty to the regime. He feels that if he can only remain faithful in his heart to Julia, his soul will be saved—a romantic concept, though one we are likely to endorse. But like all absolutist governments and religions, the Party demands that every personal loyalty be sacrificed to it, and replaced with an absolute loyalty to Big Brother. Confronted with his worst fear in the dreaded Room 101, where a nasty device involving a cage-full of starving rats can be fitted to the eyes, Winston breaks: "Don't do it to me," he pleads, "do it to Julia." (This sentence has become shorthand in our household for the avoidance of onerous duties. Poor Julia—how hard we would make her life if she actually existed. She'd have to be on a lot of panel discussions, for instance.)

10   After his betrayal of Julia, Winston becomes a handful of malleable goo. He truly believes that two and two make five, and that he loves Big Brother. Our last glimpse of him is sitting drink-sodden at an outdoor cafe, knowing he's a dead man walking and having learned that Julia has betrayed him, too, while he listens to a popular refrain: "Under the spreading chestnut tree / I sold you and you sold me. . ."

11   Orwell has been accused of bitterness and pessimism—of leaving us with a vision of the future in which the individual has no chance, and where the brutal, totalitarian boot of the all-controlling Party will grind into the human face, for ever. But this view of Orwell is contradicted by the last chapter in the book, an essay on Newspeak—the doublethink language concocted by the regime. By expurgating all words that might be troublesome—"bad" is no longer permitted, but becomes "double-plus-ungood"—and by making other words

mean the opposite of what they used to mean—the place where people get tortured is the Ministry of Love, the building where the past is destroyed is the Ministry of Information—the rulers of Airstrip One wish to make it literally impossible for people to think straight. However, the essay on Newspeak is written in standard English, in the third person, and in the past tense, which can only mean that the regime has fallen, and that language and individuality have survived. For whoever has written the essay on Newspeak, the world of *Nineteen Eighty-Four* is over. Thus, it's my view that Orwell had much more faith in the resilience of the human spirit than he's usually been given credit for.

12   Orwell became a direct model for me much later in my life—in the real 1984, the year in which I began writing a somewhat different dystopia, *The Handmaid's Tale*. By that time I was 44, and I had learned enough about real despotisms—through the reading of history, travel, and my membership of Amnesty International—so that I didn't need to rely on Orwell alone.

13   The majority of dystopias—Orwell's included—have been written by men, and the point of view has been male. When women have appeared in them, they have been either sexless automatons or rebels who have defied the sex rules of the regime. They have acted as the temptresses of the male protagonists, however welcome this temptation may be to the men themselves. Thus Julia; thus the cami-knicker-wearing, orgy-porgy seducer of the Savage in *Brave New World*; thus the subversive femme fatale of Yevgeny Zamyatin's 1924 seminal classic, *We*. I wanted to try a dystopia from the female point of view—the world according to Julia, as it were. However, this does not make *The Handmaid's Tale* a "feminist dystopia," except insofar as giving a woman a voice and an inner life will always be considered "feminist" by those who think women ought not to have these things.

14   The 20th century could be seen as a race between two versions of man-made hell—the jackbooted state totalitarianism of Orwell's *Nineteen Eighty-Four* and the hedonistic ersatz paradise of *Brave New World*, where absolutely everything is a consumer good and human beings are engineered to be happy. With the fall of the Berlin Wall in 1989, it seemed for a time that *Brave New World* had won—from henceforth, state control would be minimal, and all we would have to do was go shopping and smile a lot, and wallow in pleasures, popping a pill or two when depression set in.

15   But with 9/11, all that changed. Now it appears we face the prospect of two contradictory dystopias at once—open markets, closed minds—because state surveillance is back again with a vengeance. The torturer's dreaded Room 101 has been with us for millennia. The dungeons of Rome, the Inquisition, the Star Chamber, the Bastille, the proceedings of General Pinochet and of the junta in Argentina—all have depended on secrecy and on the abuse of power. Lots of countries have had their versions of it—their ways of silencing troublesome dissent. Democracies have traditionally defined themselves by, among other things, openness and the rule of law. But now it seems that we

in the west are tacitly legitimising the methods of the darker human past, upgraded technologically and sanctified to our own uses, of course. For the sake of freedom, freedom must be renounced. To move us towards the improved world—the utopia we're promised—dystopia must first hold sway. It's a concept worthy of doublethink. It's also, in its ordering of events, strangely Marxist. First the dictatorship of the proletariat, in which lots of heads must roll; then the pie-in-the-sky classless society, which oddly enough never materialises. Instead, we just get pigs with whips.

16   I often ask myself: what would George Orwell have to say about it?

17   Quite a lot.

Comprehension

1. This article is an edited extract of a talk that Atwood gave on BBC Radio. Why do you think her talk would be of interest to a radio audience?

2. Summarize what you learn from Atwood's essay about George Orwell and his novels *Animal Farm* and *Nineteen Eighty-Four*.

3. What does Atwood learn from Orwell? What does she think all of us should learn from him today in our "post–9/11 world"?

Rhetorical Analysis

4. Why does Atwood begin on a personal note: "I grew up with George Orwell"? What is the effect of beginning the essay this way?

5. What is Atwood's main claim? What premises or warrants does she establish, and how sound is the logic? Justify your response.

6. Consider the appeal of ethos. Atwood seems to speak from a position of authority. How does she establish this sense of authority in the essay?

7. Why does Atwood summarize Orwell's two novels at considerable length? How does she use comparison and contrast to frame her discussion of the novels?

8. What causes and effects does Atwood analyze in this essay? In each, what is her purpose?

9. How does Atwood conclude her discussion of Orwell? How successful do you find the ending, and why?

Writing

10. Read *Animal Farm* or view the film version. Then write your own analysis of Orwell's work.

11. **Writing an Argument**   Atwood raises the question of whether writers and artists should warn us about dangers confronting society. Write a persuasive essay in which you take a clear stand on this issue. Provide examples drawn from literature, art, and the media.

Synthesizing the Classic + Contemporary Essays

1. Summarize and critique these two writers' purposes, explaining where their ideas overlap and where they diverge.

2. According to both writers, reading in childhood is important. How do Welty and Atwood support this claim? What types of evidence do they present?

3. Compare and contrast the style of each essay. Which essay seems more accessible to you, and why?

Moving Along

John Updike

John Updike (1932–2009), a major American novelist, short-story writer, poet, and critic, was born in Shillington, Pennsylvania. He graduated from Harvard University (AB, 1954) and attended the Ruskin School of Drawing and Fine Art at Oxford University. Associated for decades with *The New Yorker*, where his short fiction, poetry, reviews, and criticism frequently appeared, Updike carved for himself a rare reputation as a master of several literary genres. He published more than 40 books during his career. Focusing in his fiction on suburban middle-class life, Updike received two Pulitzer Prizes and many other major awards, including a National Book Award for his novel *The Centaur* (1963). His fiction includes the much-admired "Rabbit" quintet, five novels that track one central character, first introduced in *Rabbit, Run* (1960), through the passages in his life. Updike's poetry collections include *The Carpentered Hen and Other Tame Creatures* (1958) and *Americana: And Other Poems* (2001). Updike included the following essay in *Just Looking* (1981), a collection of his art criticism.

1   In dreams, one is frequently travelling, and the more hallucinatory moments of our waking life, many of them, are spent in cars, trains, and airplanes. For millennia, Man has walked or run to where he wanted to go; the first naked ape who had the mad idea of mounting a horse (or was it a *Camelops*?) launched a series of subtle internal dislocations of which jet lag is a vivid modern form. When men come to fly through space at near the speed of light, they will return to earth a century later but only a few years older. Now, driving (say) from Boston to Pittsburgh in a day, we arrive feeling greatly aged by the engine's innumerable explosive heartbeats, by the monotony of the highway surface and the constant windy press of unnatural speed. Beside the highway, a clamorous parasitic life signals for attention and halt; localities where generations have lived, bred, labored, and died are flung through the windshield and out through the rearview mirror. Men on the move brutalize themselves and render the world they arrow through phantasmal.

2   Our two artists, separated by two centuries, capture well the eeriness of travel. In the Punjab Hills painting, Baz Bahadur, prince of Malwa, has eloped with the lovely Rupmati; in order to keep him faithful to her, the legend goes, she takes him riding by moonlight. The moon appears to exist not only in the sky but behind a grove of trees. Deer almost blend into the mauve-gray hills. A little citadel basks in starlight on a hilltop. In this soft night, nothing is brighter than the scarlet pasterns of the horses. Baz Bahadur's steed bears on his hide a paler version of the starry sky, and in his violet genitals carries a hint of this nocturnal ride's sexual undercurrent. To judge from the delicacy of their gestures and glances, the riders are being borne along as smoothly as on a merry-go-round.

Though these lovers and their panoply are formalized to static perfection, if we cover them, a surprising depth appears in the top third of the painting, and carries the eye away.

Artist unknown, *Baz Bahadur and Rupmati Riding by Moonlight,* c. 1780. Pahari miniature in Kangra style, 8 ¾ x 6 ¼". The British Museum, Department of Oriental Antiquities, London.

3   The riders in Roy de Forest's contemporary painting move through a forest as crowded, garish, and menacing as the neon-lit main drag of a city. A throng of sinister bystanders, one built of brick and another with eyes that are paste gems, witness the passage of this *Canoe of Fate,* which with the coarseness of its stitching and the bulk of its passengers would make slow headway even on a less crowded canvas. Beyond the mountains, heavenly medallions and balloons of stippled color pre-empt space. Only the gesture of the black brave, echoing that of George

Washington in another fabulous American crossing, gives a sense of direction and promises to open a path. Two exotic birds, a slavering wolf, and what may be a fair captive (gazing backward toward settlements where other red-haired bluefaces mourn her) freight the canoe with a suggestion of allegory, of myths to which we have lost the key. The personnel of the aboriginal New World, at any rate, are here deep-dyed but not extinguished by the glitter and jazz of an urban-feeling wilderness.

Roy De Forest, *Canoe of Fate*, 1974. Polymer on canvas, 66 ¾ x 90 ¼". Philadelphia Museum of Art

4   In both representations, the movement is from right to left, like that of writing in the Semitic languages, like the motion of a mother when she instinctively shifts her baby to her left arm, to hold it closer to her heart. It feels natural, this direction, and slightly uphill. We gaze at these dreamlike tapestries of travel confident that no progress will be made—we will awaken in our beds.

1. According to Updike, why does the idea of travel have such a hold on the collective imagination? What is the relationship of the travel motif to art?

2. Describe the two paintings that Updike analyzes in this essay. What other famous painting does he allude to in paragraph 3?

3. Why does Updike emphasize the "eeriness" of the two paintings? What is he saying about the human psyche?

Rhetorical Analysis

4. How does Updike design his introductory paragraph? What is his purpose?

5. What is Updike's thesis? Does he state or imply it? Explain.

6. Identify specific passages that highlight Updike's descriptive style. What types of figurative language does he employ?

7. Explain Updike's comparative method. What do the reproductions of the two paintings contribute to the overall comparative effect? Would this brief essay be as effective without these images? Why or why not?

8. Why is Updike's concluding paragraph relatively brief when compared with the preceding paragraphs? Is this end paragraph effective? Justify your response.

Writing

9. Consider the two paintings that Updike reproduces, and write your own comparative essay based on them.

10. **Writing an Argument** Argue for or against the proposition that when viewing a work of art, it is not necessary to relate it—as Updike does—to human behavior.

Finding Neverland

David Gates

David Gates (b. 1947) is an American journalist and fiction writer. Gates attended Bard College and the University of Connecticut in the mid-1960s, subsequently working as a cab driver and in other capacities while refining his literary craft. His first novel, *Jernigan* (1991), was nominated for a Pulitzer Prize. Both his second novel, *Preston Falls* (1998), and the collection *The Wonders of the Invisible World: Stories* (1999), were finalists for the National Book Critics Circle Award. Gates is a senior editor and writer at *Newsweek*, covering books and popular music. He also teaches in the graduate writing programs at Bennington College and New School University. In this essay from the July 13, 2009, issue of *Newsweek*, Gates surveys the life, death, and career of music legend Michael Jackson.

1   True, for a while he was the king of pop—a term apparently originated by his friend Elizabeth Taylor—and he's the last we're ever likely to have. Before Michael Jackson came Frank Sinatra, Elvis Presley, and the Beatles; after him has come absolutely no one, however brilliant or however popular, who couldn't be ignored by vast segments of an ever-more-fragmented audience. Not Kurt Cobain, not Puffy, not Mariah Carey, not Céline Dion, not Beyoncé, not Radiohead—not even Madonna, his closest competitor. When the news of his death broke, the traffic on Twitter caused the site to crash, even though he hadn't had a hit song for years. But starting long before and continuing long after he lorded over the world of entertainment in the 1980s—his 1982 *Thriller* remains the bestselling album of all time—Jackson was the Prince of Artifice. As the prepubescent frontboy of the Jackson 5, he sang in a cherubic mezzo-soprano of sexual longing he could not yet have fully felt. As a young man, however accomplished and even impassioned his singing was, he never had the sexual credibility of a James Brown or a Wilson Pickett, in part because of his still-high-pitched voice, in part because he seemed never to fully inhabit himself—whoever that self was. In middle age, he consciously took on the role of Peter Pan, with his Neverland Ranch and its amusement-park rides, with his lost-boy "friends" and with what he seemed to believe was an ageless, androgynous physical appearance—let's hope he believed it—thanks to straightened hair and plastic surgery. (No one—least of all Jackson himself—would have wanted to see the Dorian Gray portrait in his attic.) He did his best to construct an alternate reality on top of what must have been an initially miserable life: Imagine *Gypsy* with—as Jackson claimed in interviews—a physically abusive father in place of Mama Rose, set among Jehovah's Witnesses. Which was the more imaginative creation: his music or his persona?

2   In retrospect, so much of what Jackson achieved seems baldly symbolic. This was the black kid from Gary, Ind., who ended up marrying Elvis's daughter, setting up Neverland in place of Graceland, and buying the Beatles' song catalog—bold acts of appropriation and mastery, if not outright aggression. (Of course,

Elvis and the Beatles had come out of obscurity, too, but that was a long, long time ago, in a galaxy far away.) He made trademarks of the very emblems of his remoteness: his moonwalk and robot dances and his jeweled glove—*noli me tangere*, and vice versa. He morphed relentlessly from the most adorable of kiddie performers (his 1972 movie-soundtrack hit, "Ben," was a love song to a pet rat) to the most sinister of superstars: not by adopting a campy persona, like those of his older contemporaries Alice Cooper or Ozzy Osbourne, but in real life, dodging accusations of child molestation, one of which led to a trial and acquittal in 2005. (One shrink concluded at the time that he was not a pedophile, but merely a case of arrested development.) The 2002 episode in which he briefly dangled his son Prince Michael II (a.k.a. Blanket) over a balcony in Berlin, above horrified, fascinated fans, seemed like a ritualized attempt to dispose of his own younger self. And eventually his several facial surgeries, a skin ailment, serious weight loss, and God knows what else made him look like both a vampire and a mummy—Peter Pan's undead evil twins. That is, like the skeletal, pale-faced zombies he danced with in Jon Landis's 14-minute "Thriller" video. When you watch it today, it appears to be a whole stage full of Michael Jacksons, the real one now the least familiar-looking, the most unreal of all.

3   But whatever strictly personal traumas Jackson may have reenacted and transcended—and then re-reenacted—he performed his dance of death as a central figure in America's long racial horror show. He was, quintessentially, one of those "pure products of America," who, as William Carlos Williams wrote in 1923, "go crazy." To take the uplifting view, enunciated after his death by the likes of the Rev. Al Sharpton, he was a transracial icon, a black person whom white Americans took to their hearts and whose blackness came to seem incidental— along with Nat (King) Cole, Sammy Davis Jr., Sidney Poitier, Harry Belafonte, Sam Cooke, Jimi Hendrix, Arthur Ashe, Michael Jordan, Oprah Winfrey, Tiger Woods, and, inevitably, Barack Obama. As a singer-dancer, he clearly belongs not just in the tradition of Jackie Wilson, James Brown, and the Temptations—who seem to have been among his immediate inspirations—but also in the tradition of such dancing entertainers as Fred Astaire and Gene Kelly, who, in turn, drew from such black performers as Bill (Bojangles) Robinson. In the 1978 film version of *The Wiz*, Jackson even appropriated and reinvented Ray Bolger's old role as the Scarecrow in *The Wizard of Oz*. And as a messianic global superstar, he resembles no one so much as his father-in-law, Elvis Presley (who died long before Jackson married his daughter), a transracial figure from the other side of the color line. When Presley's first records were played on the radio in Memphis, DJs made a point of noting that he graduated from the city's all-white Humes High School, lest listeners mistake him for black. Given the ubiquity of television, nobody mistook the wispy-voiced young Michael Jackson for white, but it seemed, superficially, not to matter.

4   Yet Jackson, always the artificer, surely knew that part of his own appeal to white audiences—who contributed substantially to the $50 million to $75 million a year he earned in his prime—lay initially in his precocious cuteness, and when he was a grown man, in his apparent lack of adult sexuality. He was energetic, charismatic, and supremely gifted, but sexually unassertive—unlike swaggeringly

heterosexual black male performers from Big Joe Turner ("Shake, Rattle, and Roll") to Jay-Z ("Big Pimpin'"). He neutered himself racially, too: his hair went from kinky to straight, his lips from full to thin, his nose from broad to pinched, his skin from dark to a ghastly pallor. You can't miss the connection between these forms of neutering if you know the history of white America's atavistic dread of black male sexuality; the 1955 murder of 14-year-old Emmett Till, for supposedly flirting with a white woman, is just one *locus classicus*. That happened only three years before Jackson was born; when he was 13, he was singing "Ben." No wonder Jackson chose—with whatever degree of calculation—to remake himself as an American Dream of innocence and belovedness.

5   No wonder, either, that the artifice eventually turned scary, and the face of the icon came to look more and more corpselike. Readers of Toni Morrison's latest novel, *A Mercy*, might recall the passage in which an African woman tells about her first sight of white slavers: "There we see men we believe are ill or dead. We soon learn they are neither. Their skin is confusing." That's the middle-aged Michael Jackson to a T. Jackson arguably looked his "blackest" on the original cover of 1979's *Off the Wall*; by *Thriller*, the transformation had begun. *Off the Wall* was his declaration of manhood: It came out the year he turned 21, and it was his greatest purely musical moment. Why did he feel so deeply uncomfortable with himself? The hopeless task of sculpting and bleaching yourself into a simulacrum of a white man suggests a profound loathing of blackness. If Michael Jackson couldn't be denounced as a race traitor, who could? Somehow, though, black America overlooked it, and continued to buy his records, perhaps because some African-Americans, with their hair relaxers and skin-lightening creams, understood why Jackson was remaking himself, even if they couldn't condone it.

6   As with Ernest Hemingway—another case of deeply confused identity and (who knew?) androgynous sexuality—we need to look past the deliberate creation of an image and a persona to appreciate the artistry. A more masterly entertainer never took the stage. In 1988, the *New York Times* dance critic Anna Kisselgoff called him "a virtuoso . . . who uses movement for its own sake. Yes, Michael Jackson is an avant-garde dancer, and his dances could be called abstract. Like Merce Cunningham, he shows us that movement has a value of its own." Better yet, Astaire himself once called Jackson to offer his compliments. As a singer, Jackson was too much of a chameleon—from the tenderness of "I'll Be There" to the rawness of "The Way You Make Me Feel" to the silken sorrow of "She's Out of My Life"—to stamp every song with his distinct personality, as Sinatra did, or Ray Charles, or Hank Williams. But these are demigods—Jackson was merely a giant. (And how'd you like *their* dancing?) As a musical conceptualizer, probably only James Brown has had a comparable influence: Jackson and his visionary producer, Quincy Jones, fused disco, soul, and pop in a manner that can still be heard every hour of every day on every top-40 radio station—only not as well. Tommy Mottola, former head of Sony Music, called Jackson "the corner-stone to the entire music business." The best recordings by Jackson and Jones—"Don't Stop 'Til You Get Enough," "Billie Jean"— belong identifiably to their time, as do Sinatra's 1950s recordings with the arranger Nelson Riddle. Yet like Sinatra's "I've Got the World on a String" or "In the Wee

Small Hours of the Morning," they're so perfect of their kind that they'll never sound dated.

7   The night before he died, Jackson was rehearsing at the Staples Center in Los Angeles for an epic comeback—a series of 50 concerts, beginning in July, at London's O2 Arena. If that sounds impossibly grandiose, consider that all 50 shows had already sold out. People around him had been wondering if he was really up to it, and the opening had already been put off by a week. He was 50 years old, after all: long in the tooth for a *puer aeternus*—eight years older than Elvis when he left the building, and a quarter century past his peak. Jackson had had health problems for years. Drug problems, too, apparently: In 2007, according to the Associated Press, an L.A. pharmacy sued him, claiming he owed $100,000 for two years' worth of prescription meds. And money problems: In 2008, the ranch nearly went into foreclosure—he defaulted on a $24.5 million debt—and even the $50 million he stood to realize from his potentially grueling London concerts might have seemed like chump change after the glory years. And of course, just problems: His very existence—as a son, as a black man—was problematic. In his last days, did the prospect of a comeback, of remythologizing himself one more time, excite him as much as it excited his fans? Did his magical moments in performance have an incandescent density that outweighed what must often have been burdensome hours and days? Ask him sometime, if you see him. Whatever his life felt like from inside, from outside it was manifestly a work of genius, whether you want to call it a triumph or a freak show—those are just words. We'd never seen anyone like this before, either in his artistic inventiveness or his equally artistic self-invention, and we won't forget him—until the big Neverland swallows us all.

1. Summarize Gates's perception of Michael Jackson. How do you interpret the title? Why does Gates call Jackson an "artificer"? What does Gates mean by Jackson's "androgynous sexuality"?

2. Gates alludes to many stars from the world of music, dance, literature, and the arts. What is Gates's purpose in listing so many of them?

3. What, in Gates's opinion, is Michael Jackson's legacy?

Rhetorical Analysis

4. Does this essay have an explicitly stated thesis? If so, where is it? If the thesis is implied, paraphrase it.

5. The first paragraph of this essay is quite long. What is Gates's strategy and purpose here? Does this lengthy opening paragraph weaken or strengthen the body of the essay? Explain.

6. Identify and comment on Gates's use of figurative language in this essay. How does figurative language—and Gates's overall style—influence the essay's tone?

7. What comparative points does Gates make about Jackson and other artists? How does the comparative method serve to organize the essay?

8. Explain the effect of the last paragraph, which resembles the introductory paragraph in length. Do you think this resemblance was intentional? Why or why not?

Writing

9. Write your own evaluation of Michael Jackson or another celebrity from the world of music, explaining why you think this artist's achievement is important.

10. Write a comparative essay in which you discuss two artists from the world of music, film, or television.

11. **Writing an Argument**   Argue for or against the proposition that the media makes too much of the deaths or lives of prominent celebrities.

Theme for English B

Langston Hughes

James Langston Hughes (1902–1967), poet, playwright, fiction writer, biographer, and essayist, was for more than 50 years one of the most productive and significant American authors. In *The Weary Blues* (1926), *The Ways of White Folks* (1934), *Simple Speaks His Mind* (1950), *Selected Poems* (1959), and dozens of other books, he strove, in his own words, "to explain the Negro condition in America." Hughes wrote "Theme for English B" in 1949.

The instructor said,
   Go home and write
   a page tonight.
   And let that page come out of you—
5   *Then, it will be true.*

I wonder if it's that simple?
I am twenty-two, colored, born in Winston-Salem.
I went to school there, then Durham, then here
to this college on the hill above Harlem.
10 I am the only colored student in my class.
The steps from the hill lead down into Harlem,
through a park, then I cross St. Nicholas,
Eighth Avenue, Seventh, and I come to the Y,
the Harlem Branch Y, where I take the elevator
15 up to my room, sit down, and write this page:

It's not easy to know what is true for you or me
at twenty-two, my age. But I guess I'm what
I feel and see and hear, Harlem, I hear you.
hear you, hear me—we two—you, me, talk on this page.
20 (I hear New York, too.) Me—who?
Well, I like to eat, sleep, drink, and be in love.
I like to work, read, learn, and understand life.
I like a pipe for a Christmas present,
or records—Bessie, bop, or Bach.
25 I guess being colored doesn't make me not like
the same things other folks like who are other races.
So will my page be colored that I write?
Being me, it will not be white.
But it will be
30 a part of you, instructor.
You are white—
yet a part of me, as I am a part of you.
That's American.

Sometimes perhaps you don't want to be a part of me.
35 Nor do I often want to be a part of you.
But we are, that's true!
As I learn from you,
I guess you learn from me—
although you're older—and white—
40 and somewhat more free.

This is my page for English B.

Comprehension

1. The writer experiences an inner struggle as he tries to respond to the instructor's directive. What is the crux of his internal struggle?

2. Carefully looking at each word, explain what the title of the poem implies.

3. In line 27, when the writer asks "will my page be colored that I write?", what is he really asking of his white instructor?

Rhetorical Analysis

4. Lines 38–40 before the last declaration "This is my page for English B" deliberately slows down the pace of the poem through the use of dashes. Why do the words become more deliberate and slow? What are the purpose and effect of the use of dashes in lines 38–40?

5. An apparently complicated connection exists between Harlem, the area of New York City where the writer feels most comfortable, and New York City itself. How does he personalize this connection?

6. What is the desired effect of the rhetorical question in line 6, "I wonder if it's that simple"? Examine the diction used in the question and Hughes's responses to the question.

Writing

7. Describe an assignment that you have written in an extremely truthful manner. What caused you to be honest with yourself and others?

8. **Writing an Argument**   Argue for or against separating students into different levels of classes at school (gifted, regular, basic).

The Raven & The Philosophy of Composition

Edgar Allan Poe

Edgar Allan Poe (1809–1849) was well known for his bleak and often morbid short stories and poems. Although he achieved some fame while he lived, it was in death that he became one of the most popular American writers of all time. His writings are a staple in most American literature books. In "The Philosophy of Composition" (1846), Poe discusses how he created "The Raven" (1845).

The Raven

Once upon a midnight dreary, while I pondered, weak and weary,
Over many a quaint and curious volume of forgotten lore—
While I nodded, nearly napping, suddenly there came a tapping,
As of some one gently rapping, rapping at my chamber door—
5 " 'Tis some visiter," I muttered, "tapping at my chamber door—
　　Only this and nothing more."

Ah, distinctly I remember it was in the bleak December;
And each separate dying ember wrought its ghost upon the floor.
Eagerly I wished the morrow;—vainly I had sought to borrow
10 From my books surcease of sorrow—sorrow for the lost Lenore—
For the rare and radiant maiden whom the angels name Lenore—
　　Nameless *here* for evermore.

And the silken sad uncertain rustling of each purple curtain
Thrilled me—filled me with fantastic terrors never felt before;
15 So that now, to still the beating of my heart, I stood repeating
　　" 'Tis some visiter entreating entrance at my chamber door—
Some late visiter entreating entrance at my chamber door;—
　　This it is and nothing more."

Presently my soul grew stronger; hesitating then no longer,
20 "Sir," said I, "or Madam, truly your forgiveness I implore;
But the fact is I was napping, and so gently you came rapping,
And so faintly you came tapping, tapping at my chamber door,
　　That I scarce was sure I heard you"—here I opened wide the door;—
　　Darkness there and nothing more.

25 Deep into that darkness peering, long I stood there wondering, fearing,
Doubting, dreaming dreams no mortals ever dared to dream before;
But the silence was unbroken, and the stillness gave no token,
And the only word there spoken was the whispered word, "Lenore!"
This I whispered, and an echo murmured back the word, "Lenore!"
30 　　Merely this and nothing more.

Back into the chamber turning, all my soul within me burning,
Soon again I heard a tapping something louder than before.
"Surely," said I, "surely that is something at my window lattice;
Let me see, then, what thereat is and this mystery explore—
35 Let my heart be still a moment and this mystery explore;—
        'Tis the wind and nothing more."

Open here I flung the shutter, when, with many a flirt and flutter,
In there stepped a stately Raven of the saintly days of yore;
Not the least obeisance made he; not a minute stopped or stayed he;
40 But, with mien of lord or lady, perched above my chamber door—
Perched upon a bust of Pallas just above my chamber door—
        Perched, and sat, and nothing more.

Then the ebony bird beguiling my sad fancy into smiling,
By the grave and stern decorum of the countenance it wore,
45 "Though thy crest be shorn and shaven, thou," I said, "art sure no craven,
Ghastly grim and ancient Raven wandering from the Nightly shore—
Tell me what thy lordly name is on the Night's Plutonian shore!"
        Quoth the Raven "Nevermore."

Much I marvelled this ungainly fowl to hear discourse so plainly,
50 Though its answer little meaning—little relevancy bore;
For we cannot help agreeing that no living human being
Ever yet was blessed with seeing bird above his chamber door—
Bird or beast upon the sculptured bust above his chamber door,
        With such name as "Nevermore."

55 But the Raven, sitting lonely on that placid bust, spoke only
That one word, as if its soul in that one word he did outpour.
Nothing farther then he uttered—not a feather then he fluttered—
Till I scarcely more than muttered "Other friends have flown before—
On the morrow he will leave me, as my Hopes have flown before."
60   Then the bird said "Nevermore."

Startled at the stillness broken by reply so aptly spoken,
"Doubtless," said I, "what it utters is its only stock and store
Caught from some unhappy master whom unmerciful Disaster
Followed fast and followed faster till his songs one burden bore—
65 Till the dirges of his Hope that melancholy burden bore
        Of 'Never—nevermore.'"

But the Raven still beguiling all my sad soul into smiling,
Straight I wheeled a cushioned seat in front of bird and bust and door;
Then, upon the velvet sinking, I betook myself to linking
70 Fancy unto fancy, thinking what this ominous bird of yore—
What this grim, ungainly, ghastly, gaunt, and ominous bird of yore
        Meant in croaking "Nevermore."

Thus I sat engaged in guessing, but no syllable expressing
To the fowl whose fiery eyes now burned into my bosom's core;
75 This and more I sat divining, with my head at ease reclining
On the cushion's velvet lining that the lamp-light gloated o'er,
But whose velvet-violet lining with the lamp-light gloating o'er,
    She shall press, ah, nevermore!

Then, methought, the air grew denser, perfumed from an unseen censer
80 Swung by Seraphim whose foot-falls tinkled on the tufted floor.
"Wretch," I cried, "thy God hath lent thee—by these angels he hath sent thee
Respite—respite and nepenthe from thy memories of Lenore;
Quaff, oh quaff this kind nepenthe and forget this lost Lenore!"
    Quoth the Raven, "Nevermore."

85 "Prophet!" said I, "thing of evil!—prophet still, if bird or devil!—
Whether Tempter sent, or whether tempest tossed thee here ashore,
Desolate yet all undaunted, on this desert land enchanted—
On this home by Horror haunted—tell me truly, I implore—
Is there—is there balm in Gilead?—tell me—tell me, I implore!"
90   Quoth the Raven, "Nevermore."

"Prophet!" said I, "thing of evil!—prophet still, if bird or devil!
By that Heaven that bends above us—by that God we both adore—
Tell this soul with sorrow laden if, within the distant Aidenn,
It shall clasp a sainted maiden whom the angels name Lenore—
95 Clasp a rare and radiant maiden whom the angels name Lenore."
    Quoth the Raven, "Nevermore."

"Be that word our sign of parting, bird or fiend!" I shrieked, upstarting—
"Get thee back into the tempest and the Night's Plutonian shore!
Leave no black plume as a token of that lie thy soul hath spoken!
100 Leave my loneliness unbroken!—quit the bust above my door!
Take thy beak from out my heart, and take thy form from off my door!"
    Quoth the Raven, "Nevermore."

And the Raven, never flitting, still is sitting, still is sitting
On the pallid bust of Pallas just above my chamber door;
105 And his eyes have all the seeming of a demon's that is dreaming,
And the lamp-light o'er him streaming throws his shadow on the floor;
And my soul from out that shadow that lies floating on the floor
    Shall be lifted—nevermore!

The Philosophy of Composition

1   CHARLES DICKENS, in a note now lying before me, alluding to an examination I once made of the mechanism of *Barnaby Rudge*, says—"By the way, are you aware that Godwin wrote his *Caleb Williams* backwards? He first involved his hero in a web of difficulties, forming the second volume, and then, for the first, cast about him for some mode of accounting for what had been done."

2   I cannot think this the *precise* mode of procedure on the part of Godwin—and indeed what he himself acknowledges, is not altogether in accordance with Mr. Dickens' idea—but the author of *Caleb Williams* was too good an artist not to perceive the advantage derivable from at least a somewhat similar process. Nothing is more clear than that every plot, worth the name, must be elaborated to its *dénouement* before anything be attempted with the pen. It is only with the *dénouement* constantly in view that we can give a plot its indispensable air of consequence, or causation, by making the incidents, and especially the tone at all points, tend to the development of the intention.

3   There is a radical error, I think, in the usual mode of constructing a story. Either history affords a thesis—or one is suggested by an incident of the day—or, at best, the author sets himself to work in the combination of striking events to form merely the basis of his narrative—designing, generally, to fill in with description, dialogue, or autorial comment, whatever crevices of fact, or action, may, from page to page, render themselves apparent.

4   I prefer commencing with the consideration of an *effect*. Keeping originality *always* in view—for he is false to himself who ventures to dispense with so obvious and so easily attainable a source of interest—I say to myself, in the first place, "Of the innumerable effects, or impressions, of which the heart, the intellect, or (more generally) the soul is susceptible, what one shall I, on the present occasion, select?" Having chosen a novel, first, and secondly a vivid effect, I consider whether it can be best wrought by incident or tone—whether by ordinary incidents and peculiar tone, or the converse, or by peculiarity both of incident and tone—afterward looking about me (or rather within) for such combinations of event, or tone, as shall best aid me in the construction of the effect.

5   I have often thought how interesting a magazine paper might be written by any author who would—that is to say, who could—detail, step by step, the processes by which any one of his compositions attained its ultimate point of completion. Why such a paper has never been given to the world, I am much at a loss to say—but, perhaps, the autorial vanity has had more to do with the omission than any one other cause. Most writers—poets in especial—prefer having it understood that they compose by a species of fine frenzy—an ecstatic intuition—and would positively shudder at letting the public take a peep behind the scenes, at the elaborate and vacillating crudities of thought—at the true purposes seized only at the last moment—at the innumerable glimpses of idea that arrived not at the maturity of full view—at the fully matured fancies discarded in despair as unmanageable—at the cautious selections and rejections—at the painful erasures and interpolations—in a word, at the wheels and pinions—the tackle for scene-shifting—the step-ladders and demon-traps—the cock's

feathers, the red paint and the black patches, which, in ninety-nine cases out of the hundred, constitute the properties of the literary *histrio*.

6   I am aware, on the other hand, that the case is by no means common, in which an author is at all in condition to retrace the steps by which his conclusions have been attained. In general, suggestions, having arisen pell-mell, are pursued and forgotten in a similar manner.

7   For my own part, I have neither sympathy with the repugnance alluded to, nor, at any time, the least difficulty in recalling to mind the progressive steps of any of my compositions; and, since the interest of an analysis, or reconstruction, such as I have considered a *desideratum*, is quite independent of any real or fancied interest in the thing analyzed, it will not be regarded as a breach of decorum on my part to show the *modus operandi* by which some one of my own works was put together. I select "The Raven," as the most generally known. It is my design to render it manifest that no one point in its composition is referable either to accident or intuition—that the work proceeded, step by step, to its completion with the precision and rigid consequence of a mathematical problem.

8   Let us dismiss, as irrelevant to the poem, *per se*, the circumstance—or say the necessity—which, in the first place, gave rise to the intention of composing *a* poem that should suit at once the popular and the critical taste.

9   We commence, then, with this intention.

10   The initial consideration was that of extent. If any literary work is too long to be read at one sitting, we must be content to dispense with the immensely important effect derivable from unity of impression—for, if two sittings be required, the affairs of the world interfere, and everything like totality is at once destroyed. But since, *ceteris paribus*, no poet can afford to dispense with *anything* that may advance his design, it but remains to be seen whether there is, in extent, any advantage to counterbalance the loss of unity which attends it. Here I say no, at once. What we term a long poem is, in fact, merely a succession of brief ones—that is to say, of brief poetical effects. It is needless to demonstrate that a poem is such, only inasmuch as it intensely excites, by elevating, the soul; and all intense excitements are, through a psychal necessity, brief. For this reason, at least one-half of the *Paradise Lost* is essentially prose—a succession of poetical excitements interspersed, *inevitably*, with corresponding depressions—the whole being deprived, through the extremeness of its length, of the vastly important artistic element, totality, or unity, of effect.

11   It appears evident, then, that there is a distinct limit, as regards length, to all works of literary art—the limit of a single sitting—and that, although in certain classes of prose composition, such as "Robinson Crusoe" (demanding no unity), this limit may be advantageously overpassed, it can never properly be overpassed in a poem. Within this limit, the extent of a poem may be made to bear mathematical relation to its merit—in other words, to the excitement or elevation—again, in other words, to the degree of the true poetical effect which it is capable of inducing; for it is clear that the brevity must be in direct ratio of the intensity of the intended effect—this, with one proviso—that a certain degree of duration is absolutely requisite for the production of any effect at all.

12   Holding in view these considerations, as well as that degree of excitement which I deemed not above the popular, while not below the critical taste, I

reached at once what I conceived the proper length for my intended poem—a length of about one hundred lines. It is, in fact, a hundred and eight.

13   My next thought concerned the choice of an impression, or effect, to be conveyed: and here I may as well observe that throughout the construction, I kept steadily in view the design of rendering the work universally appreciable. I should be carried too far out of my immediate topic were I to demonstrate a point upon which I have repeatedly insisted, and which, with the poetical, stands not in the slightest need of demonstration—the point, I mean, that Beauty is the sole legitimate province of the poem. A few words, however, in elucidation of my real meaning, which some of my friends have evinced a disposition to misrepresent. That pleasure which is at once the most intense, the most elevating, and the most pure is, I believe, found in the contemplation of the beautiful. When, indeed, men speak of Beauty, they mean, precisely, not a quality, as is supposed, but an effect—they refer, in short, just to that intense and pure elevation of soul—not of intellect, or of heart—upon which I have commented, and which is experienced in consequence of contemplating the "beautiful." Now I designate Beauty as the province of the poem, merely because it is an obvious rule of Art that effects should be made to spring from direct causes—that objects should be attained through means best adapted for their attainment—no one as yet having been weak enough to deny that the peculiar elevation alluded to is most readily attained in the poem. Now the object Truth, or the satisfaction of the intellect, and the object Passion, or the excitement of the heart, are, although attainable to a certain extent in poetry, far more readily attainable in prose. Truth, in fact, demands a precision, and Passion, a homeliness (the truly passionate will comprehend me), which are absolutely antagonistic to that Beauty which, I maintain, is the excitement or pleasurable elevation of the soul. It by no means follows, from anything here said, that passion, or even truth, may not be introduced, and even profitably introduced, into a poem for they may serve in elucidation, or aid the general effect, as do discords in music, by contrast—but the true artist will always contrive, first, to tone them into proper subservience to the predominant aim, and, secondly, to enveil them, as far as possible, in that Beauty which is the atmosphere and the essence of the poem.

14   Regarding, then, Beauty as my province, my next question referred to the tone of its highest manifestation—and all experience has shown that this tone is one of sadness. Beauty of whatever kind in its supreme development invariably excites the sensitive soul to tears. Melancholy is thus the most legitimate of all the poetical tones.

15   The length, the province, and the tone, being thus determined, I betook myself to ordinary induction, with the view of obtaining some artistic piquancy which might serve me as a key-note in the construction of the poem—some pivot upon which the whole structure might turn. In carefully thinking over all the usual artistic effects—or more properly points, in the theatrical sense—I did not fail to perceive immediately that no one had been so universally employed as that of the refrain. The universality of its employment sufficed to assure me of its intrinsic value, and spared me the necessity of submitting it to analysis. I considered it, however, with regard to its susceptibility of improvement, and soon saw it to be in a

primitive condition. As commonly used, the refrain, or burden, not only is limited to lyric verse, but depends for its impression upon the force of monotone—both in sound and thought. The pleasure is deduced solely from the sense of identity—of repetition. I resolved to diversify, and so heighten the effect, by adhering in general to the monotone of sound, while I continually varied that of thought: that is to say, I determined to produce continuously novel effects, by the variation of the application of the refrain—the refrain itself remaining for the most part, unvaried.

16 These points being settled, I next bethought me of the nature of my refrain. Since its application was to be repeatedly varied it was clear that the refrain itself must be brief, for there would have been an insurmountable difficulty in frequent variations of application in any sentence of length. In proportion to the brevity of the sentence would, of course, be the facility of the variation. This led me at once to a single word as the best refrain.

17 The question now arose as to the character of the word. Having made up my mind to a refrain, the division of the poem into stanzas was of course a corollary, the refrain forming the close to each stanza. That such a close, to have force, must be sonorous and susceptible of protracted emphasis, admitted no doubt, and these considerations inevitably led me to the long o as the most sonorous vowel in connection with r as the most producible consonant.

18 The sound of the refrain being thus determined, it became necessary to select a word embodying this sound, and at the same time in the fullest possible keeping with that melancholy which I had pre-determined as the tone of the poem. In such a search it would have been absolutely impossible to overlook the word "Nevermore." In fact it was the very first which presented itself.

19 The next desideratum was a pretext for the continuous use of the one word "nevermore." In observing the difficulty which I had at once found in inventing a sufficiently plausible reason for its continuous repetition, I did not fail to perceive that this difficulty arose solely from the preassumption that the word was to be so continuously or monotonously spoken by a human being—I did not fail to perceive, in short, that the difficulty lay in the reconciliation of this monotony with the exercise of reason on the part of the creature repeating the word. Here, then, immediately arose the idea of a non-reasoning creature capable of speech, and very naturally, a parrot, in the first instance, suggested itself, but was superseded forthwith by a Raven as equally capable of speech, and infinitely more in keeping with the intended tone.

20 I had now gone so far as the conception of a Raven, the bird of ill-omen, monotonously repeating the one word "Nevermore" at the conclusion of each stanza in a poem of melancholy tone, and in length about one hundred lines. Now, never losing sight of the object—supremeness or perfection at all points, I asked myself—"Of all melancholy topics what, according to the universal understanding of mankind, is the most melancholy?" Death, was the obvious reply. "And when," I said, "is this most melancholy of topics most poetical?" From what I have already explained at some length the answer here also is obvious—"When it most closely allies itself to Beauty: the death then of a beautiful woman is unquestionably the most poetical topic in the world, and equally is it beyond doubt that the lips best suited for such topic are those of a bereaved lover."

21   I had now to combine the two ideas of a lover lamenting his deceased mistress and a Raven continuously repeating the word "Nevermore." I had to combine these, bearing in mind my design of varying at every turn the application of the word repeated, but the only intelligible mode of such combination is that of imagining the Raven employing the word in answer to the queries of the lover. And here it was that I saw at once the opportunity afforded for the effect on which I had been depending, that is to say, the effect of the variation of application. I saw that I could make the first query propounded by the lover—the first query to which the Raven should reply "Nevermore"—that I could make this first query a commonplace one, the second less so, the third still less, and so on, until at length the lover, startled from his original nonchalance by the melancholy character of the word itself, by its frequent repetition, and by a consideration of the ominous reputation of the fowl that uttered it, is at length excited to superstition, and wildly propounds queries of a far different character—queries whose solution he has passionately at heart—propounds them half in superstition and half in that species of despair which delights in self-torture—propounds them not altogether because he believes in the prophetic or demoniac character of the bird (which reason assures him is merely repeating a lesson learned by rote), but because he experiences a frenzied pleasure in so modelling his questions as to receive from the expected "Nevermore" the most delicious because the most intolerable of sorrows. Perceiving the opportunity thus afforded me, or, more strictly, thus forced upon me in the progress of the construction, I first established in my mind the climax or concluding query—that query to which "Nevermore" should be in the last place an answer—that query in reply to which this word "Nevermore" should involve the utmost conceivable amount of sorrow and despair.

22   Here then the poem may be said to have had its beginning—at the end where all works of art should begin—for it was here at this point of my preconsiderations that I first put pen to paper in the composition of the stanza:

> "Prophet!" said I, "thing of evil! prophet still if bird or devil!
> By that Heaven that bends above us—by that God we both adore,
> Tell this soul with sorrow laden, if, within the distant Aidenn,
> It shall clasp a sainted maiden whom the angels name Lenore—
> Clasp a rare and radiant maiden whom the angels name Lenore."
> Quoth the Raven—"Nevermore."

23   I composed this stanza, at this point, first that, by establishing the climax, I might the better vary and graduate, as regards seriousness and importance, the preceding queries of the lover, and secondly, that I might definitely settle the rhythm, the metre, and the length and general arrangement of the stanza, as well as graduate the stanzas which were to precede, so that none of them might surpass this in rhythmical effect. Had I been able in the subsequent composition to construct more vigorous stanzas I should without scruple have purposely enfeebled them so as not to interfere with the climacteric effect.

24   And here I may as well say a few words of the versification. My first object (as usual) was originality. The extent to which this has been neglected in versification is one of the most unaccountable things in the world. Admitting that there is little

possibility of variety in mere rhythm, it is still clear that the possible varieties of metre and stanza are absolutely infinite, and yet, for centuries, no man, in verse, has ever done, or ever seemed to think of doing, an original thing. The fact is that originality (unless in minds of very unusual force) is by no means a matter, as some suppose, of impulse or intuition. In general, to be found, it must be elaborately sought, and although a positive merit of the highest class, demands in its attainment less of invention than negation.

25   Of course I pretend to no originality in either the rhythm or metre of the "Raven." The former is trochaic—the latter is octametre acatalectic, alternating with heptametre catalectic repeated in the refrain of the fifth verse, and terminating with tetrametre catalectic. Less pedantically the feet employed throughout (trochees) consist of a long syllable followed by a short, the first line of the stanza consists of eight of these feet, the second of seven and a half (in effect two-thirds), the third of eight, the fourth of seven and a half, the fifth the same, the sixth three and a half. Now, each of these lines taken individually has been employed before, and what originality the "Raven" has, is in their combination into stanza; nothing even remotely approaching this has ever been attempted. The effect of this originality of combination is aided by other unusual and some altogether novel effects, arising from an extension of the application of the principles of rhyme and alliteration.

26   The next point to be considered was the mode of bringing together the lover and the Raven—and the first branch of this consideration was the locale. For this the most natural suggestion might seem to be a forest, or the fields—but it has always appeared to me that a close circumscription of space is absolutely necessary to the effect of insulated incident—it has the force of a frame to a picture. It has an indisputable moral power in keeping concentrated the attention, and, of course, must not be confounded with mere unity of place.

27   I determined, then, to place the lover in his chamber—in a chamber rendered sacred to him by memories of her who had frequented it. The room is represented as richly furnished—this in mere pursuance of the ideas I have already explained on the subject of Beauty, as the sole true poetical thesis.

28   The locale being thus determined, I had now to introduce the bird—and the thought of introducing him through the window was inevitable. The idea of making the lover suppose, in the first instance, that the flapping of the wings of the bird against the shutter, is a "tapping" at the door, originated in a wish to increase, by prolonging, the reader's curiosity, and in a desire to admit the incidental effect arising from the lover's throwing open the door, finding all dark, and thence adopting the half-fancy that it was the spirit of his mistress that knocked.

29   I made the night tempestuous, first to account for the Raven's seeking admission, and secondly, for the effect of contrast with the (physical) serenity within the chamber.

30   I made the bird alight on the bust of Pallas, also for the effect of contrast between the marble and the plumage—it being understood that the bust was absolutely suggested by the bird—the bust of Pallas being chosen, first, as most in keeping with the scholarship of the lover, and secondly, for the sonorousness of the word, Pallas, itself.

31   About the middle of the poem, also, I have availed myself of the force of contrast, with a view of deepening the ultimate impression. For example, an air of

the fantastic—approaching as nearly to the ludicrous as was admissible—is given to the Raven's entrance. He comes in "with many a flirt and flutter."

Not the least obeisance made he—not a moment stopped or stayed he,
But with mien of lord or lady, perched above my chamber door.

32   In the two stanzas which follow, the design is more obviously carried out:—

Then this ebony bird, beguiling my sad fancy into smiling
By the grave and stern decorum of the countenance it wore,
"Though thy crest be shorn and shaven, thou," I said, "art sure no craven,
Ghastly grim and ancient Raven wandering from the Nightly shore—
Tell me what thy lordly name is on the Night's Plutonian shore?"
        Quoth the Raven—"Nevermore."

Much I marvelled this ungainly fowl to hear discourse so plainly,
Though its answer little meaning—little relevancy bore;
For we cannot help agreeing that no living human being
Ever yet was blessed with seeing bird above his chamber door—
Bird or beast upon the sculptured bust above his chamber door,
        With such name as "Nevermore."

33   The effect of the *denouement* being thus provided for, I immediately drop the fantastic for a tone of the most profound seriousness—this tone commencing in the stanza directly following the one last quoted, with the line,

        But the Raven, sitting lonely on that placid bust, spoke only, etc.

34   From this epoch the lover no longer jests—no longer sees anything even of the fantastic in the Raven's demeanour. He speaks of him as a "grim, ungainly, ghastly, gaunt, and ominous bird of yore," and feels the "fiery eyes" burning into his "bosom's core." This revolution of thought, or fancy, on the lover's part, is intended to induce a similar one on the part of the reader—to bring the mind into a proper frame for the *denouement*—which is now brought about as rapidly and as directly as possible.

35   With the *denouement* proper—with the Raven's reply, "Nevermore," to the lover's final demand if he shall meet his mistress in another world—the poem, in its obvious phase, that of a simple narrative, may be said to have its completion. So far, everything is within the limits of the accountable—of the real. A raven, having learned by rote the single word "Nevermore," and having escaped from the custody of its owner, is driven at midnight, through the violence of a storm, to seek admission at a window from which a light still gleams—the chamber-window of a student, occupied half in poring over a volume, half in dreaming of a beloved mistress deceased. The casement being thrown open at the fluttering of the bird's wings, the bird itself perches on the most convenient seat out of the immediate reach of the student, who amused by the incident and the oddity of the visitor's demeanour, demands of it, in jest and without looking for a reply, its name. The raven addressed, answers with its customary word, "Nevermore"—a word which finds immediate echo in the melancholy heart of the student, who, giving utterance aloud to certain thoughts suggested by the occasion, is again startled by

the fowl's repetition of "Nevermore." The student now guesses the state of the case, but is impelled, as I have before explained, by the human thirst for self-torture, and in part by superstition, to propound such queries to the bird as will bring him, the lover, the most of the luxury of sorrow, through the anticipated answer, "Nevermore." With the indulgence, to the extreme, of this self-torture, the narration, in what I have termed its first or obvious phase, has a natural termination, and so far there has been no overstepping of the limits of the real.

36   But in subjects so handled, however skillfully, or with however vivid an array of incident, there is always a certain hardness or nakedness which repels the artistical eye. Two things are invariably required—first, some amount of complexity, or more properly, adaptation; and, secondly, some amount of suggestiveness—some under-current, however indefinite, of meaning. It is this latter, in especial, which imparts to a work of art so much of that richness (to borrow from colloquy a forcible term), which we are too fond of confounding with the ideal. It is the excess of the suggested meaning—it is the rendering this the upper instead of the under-current of the theme—which turns into prose (and that of the very flattest kind), the so-called poetry of the so-called transcendentalists.

37   Holding these opinions, I added the two concluding stanzas of the poem—their suggestiveness being thus made to pervade all the narrative which has preceded them. The under-current of meaning is rendered first apparent in the line—
"Take thy beak from out my heart, and take thy form from off my door!"
        Quoth the Raven "Nevermore!"

38   It will be observed that the words, "from out my heart," involve the first metaphorical expression in the poem. They, with the answer, "Nevermore," dispose the mind to seek a moral in all that has been previously narrated. The reader begins now to regard the Raven as emblematical—but it is not until the very last line of the very last stanza that the intention of making him emblematical of *Mournful and never-ending Remembrance* is permitted distinctly to be seen:
And the Raven, never flitting, still is sitting, still is sitting,
On the pallid bust of Pallas just above my chamber door;
And his eyes have all the seeming of a demon that is dreaming,
And the lamplight o'er him streaming throws his shadow on the floor;
And my soul from out that shadow that lies floating on the floor
        Shall be lifted—nevermore!

The *Poetical Works of Edgar Allen Poe, Together With His Essay on the Philosophy of Composition*, with introduction and notes by M.A Eaton, B.A. Copyrighted by Educational Publishing Company, 1906.

Comprehension

1. In his essay "The Philosophy of Composition," what does Poe stress about reading a poem? How does this belief affect the length of "The Raven"?

2. What factors influenced Poe to choose a raven as the messenger in the chamber?

3. Explain the circumstances that lead the raven to arrive at the dwelling.

4. Knowing that Pallas is the goddess of wisdom, discuss how Pallas affects the speaker's interpretation of the raven's response.

Rhetorical Analysis

5. One of the rhetorical hallmarks of "The Raven" is the effect of its diction, repetition, and alliteration. Explain the connotation of the words that lend themselves to this effect.

6. People often ask rhetorical questions, never truly seeking the answer. Explain how the speaker's questions in the poem allow him to fall into deeper despair.

7. In paragraph 38 of "The Philosophy of Composition," Poe explains that "It will be observed that the words, 'from out my heart,' involve the first metaphorical expression in the poem." Why does he include this observation in his essay?

Writing

8. Writing either poetry or prose, imitate Poe's method by beginning with the climactic event and then building from there.

9. **Writing a Narration**   Write about a life event that altered your way of thinking about something.

Chapter Assessment

Rhetorical Analysis

Read the passage below from *One Writer's Beginnings* and answer the questions that follow.

I live in gratitude to my parents for initiating me—and as early as I begged for it, without keeping me waiting—into knowledge of the word, into reading and spelling, by way of the alphabet. They taught it to me at home in time for me to begin to read before starting to school. I believe the alphabet is no longer considered an essential piece of equipment for traveling through life. In my day it was the keystone to knowledge. You learned the alphabet as you learned to count to ten, as you learned "Now I lay me" and the Lord's Prayer and your father's and mother's name and address and telephone number, all in case you were lost.

—ONE WRITER'S BEGINNINGS by Eudora Welty, Cambridge, Mass.: Harvard University Press, Copyright © 1983, 1984 by Eudora Welty. Reprinted by the permission of Russell & Volkening as agents for the author. Copyright © 1983, 1984 by Eudora Welty.

1. Which statement best describes the main idea of the excerpt?
   A. Children should listen to their parents' early instruction in both religion and life lessons.
   B. Children become better readers if they learn to read at home before beginning school.
   C. Parents offer children an undeniable gift when they provide them with early access to literacy.
   D. In order to successfully learn math skills, the alphabet must be learned at a young age.
   E. Parents are more important than school in terms of a child's early education.

2. The effect of shifting from first person pronouns to second person pronouns is primarily that
   A. The readers feel invited to complicity with the author in considering their own early experiences with language.
   B. The author shifts the burden of literacy from the parents to the reader.
   C. The tone changes from being sentimental to accusatory.
   D. The shift unbalances the audience, evoking an appeal to pathos as an emotional response to the author's description of childhood.
   E. The movement creates a disconnect between the evocative memories of the speaker and the remembered telling of the narrative.

Read the passage below from "Orwell and Me" and answer the questions that follow.

Orwell has been accused of bitterness and pessimism—of leaving us with a vision of the future in which the individual has no chance, and where the brutal, totalitarian boot of the all-controlling Party will grind into the human face, for ever. But this view of Orwell is contradicted by the last chapter in the book, an essay on Newspeak—the doublethink language concocted by the regime. By expurgating all words that might be troublesome—"bad" is no longer permitted, but becomes "double-plus-ungood"—and by making other words mean the opposite of what they used to mean—the place where people get tortured is the Ministry of Love, the building where the past is destroyed is the Ministry of Information—the rulers of Airstrip One wish to make it literally impossible for people to think straight. However, the essay on Newspeak is written in standard English, in the third person, and in the past tense, which can only mean that the regime has fallen, and that language and individuality have survived. For whoever has written the essay on Newspeak, the world of *Nineteen Eighty-Four* is over. Thus, it's my view that Orwell had much more faith in the resilience of the human spirit than he's usually been given credit for.

3. Which statement best sums up the central argument of the excerpt?
   A. Orwell's writing has traditionally been viewed as acrimonious, and this reading can be supported by close analysis of his essay on Newspeak.
   B. Although many have seen Orwell as essentially cynical, the final chapter of *Nineteen Eighty-Four* in fact proves his optimism for humanity.
   C. Newspeak provides a better, more accurate representation of language, and Orwell should have fully committed to its use.
   D. Language reflects the governmental institutions of the writer's day.
   E. Orwell is not given enough credit for creating Newspeak.

4. The author's extensive use of dashes primarily does which of the following?
   A. Emphasizes key points in the author's argument, allowing the author to accentuate certain ideas
   B. Brings to light elements of the discussion that have hitherto been ignored by critics
   C. Explains archaic concepts that will likely be foreign to the reader
   D. Summarizes elements of Orwell's book that might not be familiar to the audience
   E. Suggests that the complexity of the topic cannot be explained in simplistic terms and requires elaboration at multiple points by the author

Chapter Assessment

Read the passage below from "Moving Along" and answer the questions that follow.

In dreams, one is frequently travelling, and the more hallucinatory moments of our waking life, many of them, are spent in cars, trains, and airplanes. For millennia, Man has walked or run to where he wanted to go; the first naked ape who had the mad idea of mounting a horse (or was it a *Camelops*?) launched a series of subtle internal dislocations of which jet lag is a vivid modern form. When men come to fly through space at near the speed of light, they will return to earth a century later but only a few years older. Now, driving (say) from Boston to Pittsburgh in a day, we arrive feeling greatly aged by the engine's innumerable explosive heartbeats, by the monotony of the highway surface and the constant windy press of unnatural speed. Beside the highway, a clamorous parasitic life signals for attention and halt; localities where generations have lived, bred, labored, and died are flung through the windshield and out through the rearview mirror. Men on the move brutalize themselves and render the world they arrow through phantasmal.

—"Moving Along" from JUST LOOKING: ESSAYS ON ART by John Updike, copyright © 1989 by John Updike. Used by permission of Alfred A. Knopf, an imprint of the Knopf Doubleday Publishing Group, a division of Penguin Random House LLC. All rights reserved.

5. Words such as *dislocations* and *brutalize* imply which of the following about the author?
   - **A.** He views modern locomotion as a troubling and trying concept that prevents humanity from recognizing the multiple realities that surround us.
   - **B.** He is critical of those who believe we should invest in space travel and movement at unnatural speeds.
   - **C.** He believes that the dreamlike state of traveling is as valid and important as the state of wakened traveling.
   - **D.** He wishes that people would return to traveling by horse.
   - **E.** He mourns the necessity of travel in the modern world.

6. The author juxtaposes the occurrence of travel in dreams and in reality in order to
   - **A.** Exaggerate the problem of modern travel.
   - **B.** Suggest that dreams of travel lead to actual waking travel.
   - **C.** Convey the idea that obsession with movement indicates an unsettled mental state.
   - **D.** Reinforce the idea that modern society is obsessed with faster and faster travel.
   - **E.** Imply that travel has contributed to the breakdown of the American family.

Read the passage below from "Finding Neverland" and answer the questions that follow.

But whatever strictly personal traumas Jackson may have reenacted and transcended—and then re-reenacted—he performed his dance of death as a central figure in America's long racial horror show. He was, quintessentially, one of those "pure products of America," who, as William Carlos Williams wrote in 1923, "go crazy." To take the uplifting view, enunciated after his death by the likes of the Rev. Al Sharpton, he was a transracial icon, a black person whom white Americans took to their hearts and whose blackness came to seem incidental—along with Nat (King) Cole, Sammy Davis Jr., Sidney Poitier, Harry Belafonte, Sam Cooke, Jimi Hendrix, Arthur Ashe, Michael Jordan, Oprah Winfrey, Tiger Woods, and, inevitably, Barack Obama. As a singer-dancer, he clearly belongs not just in the tradition of Jackie Wilson, James Brown, and the Temptations—who seem to have been among his immediate inspirations—but also in the tradition of such dancing entertainers as Fred Astaire and Gene Kelly, who, in turn, drew from such black performers as Bill (Bojangles) Robinson. In the 1978 film version of *The Wiz*, Jackson even appropriated and reinvented Ray Bolger's old role as the Scarecrow in *The Wizard of Oz*. And as a messianic global superstar, he resembles no one so much as his father-in-law, Elvis Presley (who died long before Jackson married his daughter), a transracial figure from the other side of the color line. When Presley's first records were played on the radio in Memphis, DJs made a point of noting that he graduated from the city's all-white Humes High School, lest listeners mistake him for black. Given the ubiquity of television, nobody mistook the wispy-voiced young Michael Jackson for white, but it seemed, superficially, not to matter.

7. A central irony of the passage is that the author
   A. Offers Jackson as a member of an elite listing of non-singing performers who are famous, ignoring the fact that he was a "dancing entertainer."
   B. Allows that Jackson was as famous as only one other entertainer—his father-in-law, Elvis Presley.
   C. Compares Michael Jackson to poet William Carlos Williams, who was neither a singer nor a dancer.
   D. Suggests that Jackson's success was predicted in 1923.
   E. Presents Jackson as a "transracial icon," while eventually concluding that due to the "ubiquity of television" Jackson's race was clear to viewers.

Chapter Assessment

8. The author uses exemplification and listing in order to
    A. Place Jackson within a continuum of other celebrities, all of whom transcended race-related identification.
    B. Compare Jackson to other financially successful entertainers.
    C. Clarify Jackson's place within the chronological appearance of celebrities recognized for transcending the color line.
    D. Defend the importance of celebrities who came along after the death of Jackson's father-in-law, Elvis Presley.
    E. Substantiate the earlier claim that Jackson "re-enacted" his own personal trauma.

Read the passage below from "The Philosophy of Composition" and answer the questions that follow.

I have often thought how interesting a magazine paper might be written by any author who would—that is to say, who could—detail, step by step, the processes by which any one of his compositions attained its ultimate point of completion. Why such a paper has never been given to the world, I am much at a loss to say—but, perhaps, the autorial vanity has had more to do with the omission than any one other cause. Most writers—poets in especial—prefer having it understood that they compose by a species of fine frenzy—an ecstatic intuition—and would positively shudder at letting the public take a peep behind the scenes, at the elaborate and vacillating crudities of thought—at the true purposes seized only at the last moment—at the innumerable glimpses of idea that arrived not at the maturity of full view—at the fully matured fancies discarded in despair as unmanageable—at the cautious selections and rejections—at the painful erasures and interpolations—in a word, at the wheels and pinions—the tackle for scene-shifting—the step-ladders and demon-traps—the cock's feathers, the red paint and the black patches, which, in ninety-nine cases out of the hundred, constitute the properties of the literary *histrio*.

—*The Poetical Works of Edgar Allen Poe, Together With His Essay on the Philosophy of Composition*, with introduction and notes by M.A Eaton, B.A. Copyrighted by Educational Publishing Company, 1906.

9. In the passage, terms such as *processes*, *discarded*, and *rejections* emphasize which of the following?
    A. The editorial procedures undertaken by all major magazines.
    B. The importance of process analysis to rhetoric.
    C. The drudgery that accompanies the creation of the *histrio*.
    D. The iterative process a writer employs in creating any substantial work.
    E. The isolation experienced by the writer during the writing process.

10. The author employs the metaphor of the *histrio* in order to compare writing to

    A. The documentation of fact through historical interpretation.

    B. The artistic representations of multimedia.

    C. The gears of machinery.

    D. The creation of a character in theater.

    E. The items necessary, but seldom mentioned, used in running a successful farm.

Connections for Critical Thinking

1. Write an essay comparing and contrasting literature and any other art form. What merits or limitations does each form have? Which do you find more satisfying? Which form is more accessible? Use at least three essays in this chapter to illustrate or support your thesis.

2. Write an essay exploring the importance of role models in art and literature. Refer to the essays by Welty and Gates to address the issue.

3. Use the essays by Welty, Updike, and Gates to explore the question of excellence in the arts. Answer this question: How do you know the work of art is good?

4. Examine the role of the artist in society and the artist's purpose in or duty to society. How would the writers in this chapter address this issue?

Living and Dying in Poetry and Art

All humans experience the common bonds of life and death. So it is no surprise that life and death are the subject of many poets' and artists' works. Critically read and analyze the poems and images, and then answer the questions that follow.

▼ SOURCE A

"Janet Waking" by John Crowe Ransom (1888–1974)

Beautifully Janet slept
Till it was deeply morning. She woke then
And thought about her dainty-feathered hen,
To see how it had kept.

One kiss she gave her mother,
Only a small one gave she to her daddy
Who would have kissed each curl of his shining baby;
No kiss at all for her brother.

"Old Chucky, Old Chucky!" she cried,
Running across the world upon the grass
To Chucky's house, and listening. But alas,
Her Chucky had died.

It was a transmogrifying bee
Came droning down on Chucky's old bald head
And sat and put the poison. It scarcely bled,
But how exceedingly

And purply did the knot
Swell with the venom and communicate
Its rigour! Now the poor comb stood up straight
But Chucky did not.

So there was Janet
Kneeling on the wet grass, crying her brown hen
(Translated far beyond the daughters of men)
To rise and walk upon it.

And weeping fast as she had breath
Janet implored us, "Wake her from her sleep!"
And would not be instructed in how deep
Was the forgetful kingdom of death.

"Picnic, Lightning" by Billy Collins (b. 1941)

—"Picnic, Lightning" from *Picnic, Lightning*, by Billy Collins, © 1998. Reprinted by permission of the University of Pittsburgh Press.

"My very photogenic mother died in a freak accident (picnic, lightning) when I was three." Lolita

It is possible to be struck by a meteor
or a single-engine plane
while reading in a chair at home.
Safes drop from rooftops
and flatten the odd pedestrian
mostly within the panels of the comics,
but still, we know it is possible,
as well as the flash of summer lightning,
the thermos toppling over,
spilling out onto the grass.
And we know the message
can be delivered from within.
The heart, no valentine,
decides to quit after lunch,
the power shut off like a switch,
or a tiny dark ship is unmoored
into the flow of the body's rivers,
the brain a monastery,
defenseless on the shore.
This is what I think about
when I shovel compost
into a wheelbarrow,
and when I fill the long flower boxes,
then press into rows
the limp roots of red impatiens--
the instant hand of Death
always ready to burst forth
from the sleeve of his voluminous cloak.
Then the soil is full of marvels,
bits of leaf like flakes off a fresco,
red-brown pine needles, a beetle quick
to burrow back under the loam.
Then the wheelbarrow is a wilder blue,
the clouds a brighter white,
and all I hear is the rasp of the steel edge
against a round stone,
the small plants singing
with lifted faces, and the click
of the sundial
as one hour sweeps into the next.

▼ SOURCE C

"The Scream" by Edvard Munch (1863–1944)

Mariano Garcia/Alamy Stock Photo

"Dreamwood" by Adrienne Rich (1929–2012)

In the old, scratched, cheap wood of the typing stand
there is a landscape, veined, which only a child can see
or the child's older self,
a woman dreaming when she should be typing
the last report of the day.   If this were a map,
she thinks, a map laid down to memorize
because she might be walking it, it shows
ridge upon ridge fading into hazed desert,
here and there a sign of aquifers
and one possible watering-hole.   If this were a map
it would be the map of the last age of her life,
not a map of choices but a map of variations
on the one great choice. It would be the map by which
she could see the end of touristic choices,
of distances blued and purpled by romance,
by which she would recognize that poetry
isn't revolution but a way of knowing
why it must come.   If this cheap, massproduced
wooden stand from the Brooklyn Union Gas Co.,
massproduced yet durable, being here now,
is what it is yet a dream-map
so obdurate, so plain,
she thinks, the material and the dream can join
and that is the poem and that is the late report.

▼ SOURCE E

"The Gulf Stream" by Winslow Homer (1836–1910)

The Metropolitan Museum of Art, New York, Catharine Lorillard Wolfe Collection, Wolfe Fund, 1906

"O Me! O Life!" by Walt Whitman (1819–1892)

—From *Leaves of Grass* by Walt Whitman. Copyright 1881 by Walt Whitman. Philadelphia: Rees Welsh & Co., 1882.

O ME! O life! of the questions of these recurring,
Of the endless trains of the faithless, of cities fill'd with the foolish,
Of myself forever reproaching myself, (for who more foolish than I, and who more faithless?)
Of eyes that vainly crave the light, of the objects mean, of the struggle ever renew'd;
Of the poor results of all, of the plodding and sordid crowds I see around me,
Of the empty and useless years of the rest, with the rest me intertwined,
The question, O me! so sad, recurring—What good amid these, O me, O life?

Answer.

That you are here—that life exists and identity,
That the powerful play goes on, and you may contribute a verse.

Applying Your Synthesis Skills

Comprehension

1. Which of the sources address death, and what is the main message of each?

2. Which of the sources address life, and what is the main message of each?

Rhetorical Analysis

3. Compare and contrast Munch's *The Scream* to Homer's *The Gulf Stream*. Address style, appeals, and purpose in your comparison.

4. Many of the sources address life as a journey. Elaborate on ways the journey metaphor weaves itself into at least three of the sources here.

Writing an Argument

5. Using examples from at least three of these sources, write an essay answering these questions: What is the biggest challenge you face? Why is it the biggest challenge?

CHAPTER 10

Nature and the Environment: How Do We Relate to the Natural World?

As you read the essays in this chapter, consider the following questions:

- According to the author, what should our relationship to the natural world be?
- What claims or arguments does the author make about the importance of nature? Do you agree or disagree with these claims and arguments?
- What specific ecological problem does the author investigate?
- How does the author think that nature influences human behavior?
- What cultural factors are involved in our approach to the environment?
- Is the writer's tone optimistic, pessimistic, or neutral in the assessment of our ability to conserve nature?
- Do you find that the author is too idealistic or sentimental in the depiction of nature? Why?
- Based on the author's essay, how does he or she qualify as a nature writer?
- What rhetorical strategies do the authors employ?
- How have you been challenged or changed by the essays in this chapter?

We are at a point in the history of civilization where consciousness of our fragile relationship with nature and the environment is high. Even as you spend an hour reading a few of the essays in this chapter, it is estimated that we are losing 3,000 acres of rain forest around the world and four species of plants or animals. From pollution, to the population explosion, to the depletion of the ozone layer, to global climate change, we seem to be confronted with ecological catastrophe. Nevertheless, as Rachel Carson reminds us, we have "an obligation to endure," to survive potential natural catastrophes by understanding and managing our relationship with the natural world.

Ecology, or the study of nature and the environment, as many of the essayists in this chapter attest, involves us in the conservation of the earth. It moves us to suppress our rapacious destruction of the planet. Clearly, the biological stability of the planet is increasingly precarious. More plants, insects, birds, and animals became extinct in the 20th century than in any era since the Cretaceous catastrophe more than 65 million years ago that led to the extinction of the dinosaurs. Within this ecological context, writers like Carson become our literary conscience, reminding us of how easily natural processes can break down unless we insist on a degree of ecological economy.

Of course, any modification of human behavior in an effort to conserve nature is a complex matter. To save the spotted owl in the Pacific Northwest, we must sacrifice the jobs of people in the timber industry. To reduce pollution, we must forsake gas and oil for alternate energy sources that are costly to develop. To reduce the waste stream, we must shift from a consumption to a conservation ethos. The ecological debate is complicated, but it is clear that the preservation of the myriad life cycles on earth is crucial, for we, too, could become an endangered species.

The language of nature is as enigmatic as the sounds of dolphins and whales communicating with their respective species. Writers like Barry Lopez and Rachel Carson help us decipher the language of our environment. These writers encourage us to converse with nature, learn from it, and even revere it. All of us are guests on this planet; the natural world is our host. If we do not protect the earth, how can we guarantee the survival of civilization?

CLASSIC **AND CONTEMPORARY** IMAGES

CLASSIC ▼

Smithsonian American Art Museum – Washington – DC/Art Resource - NY

CONTEMPORARY ▼

Damian Dovarganes/AP Images

The painters of the Hudson River School such as John Frederick Kensett (1816–1872) celebrated American landscapes in their art, painting breathtaking scenes in meticulous detail. In *Along the Hudson* (1852), the beauty of the river is unspoiled.

Are We Destroying Our Natural World?

Using a Critical Perspective Imagine yourself to be part of each of the scenes depicted in these two images. How do you feel, and why? Now examine the purpose of each image. What details do the artist and photographer emphasize to convey their feelings about our relationship to the natural world? What images do the artist and photographer create to capture your attention and direct your viewing and thinking toward a specific, dominant impression?

Analyzing Visuals and Their Rhetoric

1. Why is it fitting that California is acting on the vehicle emission problem in that state? Why does Los Angeles epitomize the problem?

Vehicles travel on the 405 Freeway where it intersects with the 10 West Freeway in Los Angeles. California could take the lead in the international effort to reduce global warming after the state's Air Resources Board gave approval to a package of regulations that would cut vehicle emissions by as much as 25 percent.

2. What intentional effect does *Along the Hudson* have on the person who views this painting?

3. How is "pace" exemplified in both images?

4. What do these visuals "say" about time and progress?

How Should We View Nature?

The reflections of Charles Eastman regarding the natural world are complemented by the meditations, nearly a century later, of naturalist and writer Barry Lopez. Charles Eastman urges people to see themselves in harmony with nature or, more specifically, as inseparable from it. Barry Lopez has a similar message. He speaks of "a sense of responsibility toward children," and urges adults to both teach and learn from children about the wonders of nature and how the natural world can inform us about our human condition. With a personal touch, Lopez recounts key encounters with children and nature, finding evidence of that union with nature that Charles Eastman speaks of. Although Charles Eastman and Barry Lopez speak in different levels of discourse, they share an awe of nature and a desire to inform their respective audiences of the sacredness of all life.

What Can the Out-of-Doors Do for Our Children?

Charles A. Eastman

Dr. Charles A. Eastman (Ohiyesa) (1858–1939), a Santee Sioux, was born in Minnesota but fled with his grandmother and uncle to Canada after a Sioux uprising in 1862. He became acculturated into white society at age 15 when his father came for him and they returned to the Dakota Territory, but he did not forsake his Native American heritage. Eastman received a BS degree at Dartmouth College in 1887. After earning his MD from Boston University in 1890, he was appointed physician at the Pine Ridge Agency in South Dakota, where he witnessed and treated survivors of the Wounded Knee massacre. He later became a government field agent and inspector who worked to improve reservation life and protect Native Americans' rights. He also helped establish YMCAs on reservations, and was long associated with the Boy Scouts of America and Camp Fire Girls. Eastman published many articles, short stories, and eleven books on Native American culture, and he lectured throughout the country and in London. His first book, *Indian Boyhood* (1902), was autobiographical and extremely popular—and one of the first books published by a Native American about Native Americans. *Indian Heroes and Great Chieftains* (1918), his last book, includes biographies of Native American leaders, some of whom Eastman interviewed personally. In the excerpt below from one of his articles, Eastman discusses the importance of "outside."

1   It was not long ago that I sat with an old, old chief in Washington, and translated to him a few things that were in the Congressional Record. I came to the words, "raw material," and he said, "What do you mean by that?" I said, "Earth, and trees, and stones, uncut, unpolished, unground. That is what the white man calls raw material." He shook his head and he said: "There is only one raw material, and that is fresh air coming through rich sunshine. All things live on that; all things come from that, the animate and the inanimate—and inanimate things are animated by it."

2   Another one not long ago said to me: "We came from Nature, and we must return to Nature; between times we must replenish our bodies with that Nature. When we do not do it we suffer." . . .

3   I shall never forget how an old Indian rebuked the young Indians for buying bright little trinkets. He said to the young people who wore them, "What do you call those?" "Those are jewels—diamonds, and so on," they said. The old fellow shook his head and replied: "We used to walk over those. There is only one jewel, and that is the dewdrop on the blade of grass. And when the sun shines on it, we can see it twinkle—God's jewel; and when it drops down, everybody is prancing and dancing; and then the jewels come down in the brooklets and then into the mighty rivers, and then to the ocean. They cut mountains in two, and only to be born again in the mid-sky, when God's sun kisses the ocean—and they will go on and on, being born again and again. It is the only jewel the Indian had, and he washes in it morning and evening; and when there is no lake, the Indian washes on the grass. There he gets his magnetism, there he is revived, and the Indian sees God in every phase of His creation." Some of the old Indians have a little philosophy—elementary philosophy, and it is clear as crystal. And there is something in the Indian's philosophy that we can use. There is no race that can discard sunshine and fresh air and live long. There is no race that can be godly if it discards sunshine and fresh air. We must put our children out-of-doors. Let the teachers be trained in the fresh air. They cannot give anything in the line of knowledge that will stick unless they have fresh air. That is the only place where you can find the true leaders again—out-of-doors. And they will be agile, supple, not only in physical action, but in mind and in soul, because they are saturated with fresh air and God's sunshine. They are flexible. They fit anywhere. They are magnetic.

From *Education: A Monthly Magazine*, Volume XLI, September, 1920-June, 1921. Frank Herbert Palmer, Editor. Boston: The Palmer Company. © 1921

Comprehension

1. How does Eastman serve as a knowledgeable intermediary between Native American and white cultures?

2. What is the main point of Eastman's text?

Rhetorical Analysis

3. How does parallel structure empower this excerpt? Use an example from the text.

4. Analyze the difference in syntax, or sentence structure, between Eastman's writing and the excerpts from the "old Indians" Eastman interviews. What does this difference in syntax suggest?

5. What is ironic about the response of the "old, old chief" to Eastman's description of "raw material"?

6. Identify a metaphorical example of Native Americans' reverence for nature.

Writing

7. Write a 250-word essay in which you analyze the wisdom of Eastman's excerpt.

8. **Writing an Argument**   Argue for or against the view that teaching and learning should occur only "out-of-doors."

Children in the Woods

Barry Lopez

Barry Lopez (b. 1945) was born in New York City but grew up in southern California's San Fernando Valley, which at the time was still largely rural. He attended the University of Notre Dame (BA, 1966) and the University of Oregon (MA, 1968), and he pursued additional graduate work before starting a career as a full-time writer. Lopez's early essays in such periodicals as *National Geographic, Wilderness, Science*, and *Harper's* established him as an authoritative voice in the environmental movement. His first major nonfiction work, *Of Wolves and Men* (1978), brought him national acclaim, an American Book Award nomination, and the John Burroughs medal for nature writing. His venture into fiction with *River Notes: The Dance of Herons* (1979) and *Winter Count* (1980) were also well received. Among Lopez's other books are *Arctic Dreams: Imagination and Desire in a Northern Landscape* (1986), *Crossing Open Ground* (1988), *The Rediscovery of North America* (1991), *Crow and Weasel* (1999), the autobiography *About This Life* (1999), and a short-story collection, *Resistance* (2004). Lopez sees himself as a storyteller, someone who has the responsibility to create an atmosphere in which the wisdom of the work can reveal itself and, as he has written, "make the reader feel part of something." In this essay from his collection *Crossing Open Ground*, Lopez sets himself and other children in the natural world in order to discover their own part of something.

1   When I was a child growing up in the San Fernando Valley in California, a trip into Los Angeles was special. The sensation of movement from a rural area into an urban one was sharp. On one of these charged occasions, walking down a sidewalk with my mother, I stopped suddenly, caught by a pattern of sunlight trapped in a spiraling imperfection in a windowpane. A stranger, an elderly woman in a cloth coat and a dark hat, spoke out spontaneously, saying how remarkable it is that children notice these things.

2   I have never forgotten the texture of this incident. Whenever I recall it I am moved not so much by any sense of my young self but by a sense of responsibility toward children, knowing how acutely I was affected in that moment by that woman's words. The effect, for all I know, has lasted a lifetime.

3   Now, years later, I live in a rain forest in western Oregon, on the banks of a mountain river in relatively undisturbed country, surrounded by 150-foot-tall Douglas firs, delicate deer-head orchids, and clearings where wild berries grow. White-footed mice and mule deer, mink and coyote move through here. My wife and I do not have children, but children we know, or children whose parents we are close to, are often here. They always want to go into the woods. And I wonder what to tell them.

4   In the beginning, years ago, I think I said too much. I spoke with an encyclopedic knowledge of the names of plants or the names of birds passing through in season. Gradually I came to say less. After a while the only words I spoke, beyond answering a question or calling attention quickly to the slight difference between a sprig of red cedar and a sprig of incense cedar, were to elucidate single objects.

5   I remember once finding a fragment of a raccoon's jaw in an alder thicket. I sat down alongside the two children with me and encouraged them to find out who this was—with only the three teeth still intact in a piece of the animal's maxilla to guide them. The teeth told by their shape and placement what this animal ate. By a kind of visual extrapolation its size became clear. There were other clues, immediately present, which told, with what I could add of climate and terrain, how this animal lived, how its broken jaw came to be lying here. Raccoon, they surmised. And tiny tooth marks along the bone's broken edge told of a mouse's hunger for calcium.

6   We set the jaw back and went on.

7   If I had known more about raccoons, finer points of osteology, we might have guessed more: say, whether it was male or female. But what we deduced was all we needed. Hours later, the maxilla, lost behind us in the detritus of the forest floor, continued to effervesce. It was tied faintly to all else we spoke of that afternoon.

8   In speaking with children who might one day take a permanent interest in natural history—as writers, as scientists, as filmmakers, as anthropologists—I have sensed that an extrapolation from a single fragment of the whole is the most invigorating experience I can share with them. I think children know that nearly anyone can learn the names of things; the impression made on them at this level is fleeting. What takes a lifetime to learn, they comprehend, is the existence and substance of myriad relationships: It is these relationships, not the things themselves, that ultimately hold the human imagination.

9   The brightest children, it has often struck me, are fascinated by metaphor—with what is shown in the set of relationships bearing on the raccoon, for example, to lie quite beyond the raccoon. In the end, you are trying to make clear to them that everything found at the edge of one's senses—the high note of the winter wren, the thick perfume of propolis that drifts downwind from spring willows, the brightness of wood chips scattered by beaver—that all this fits together. The indestructibility of these associations conveys a sense of permanence that nurtures the heart, that cripples one of the most insidious of human anxieties, the one that says, you do not belong here, you are unnecessary.

10 Whenever I walk with a child, I think how much I have seen disappear in my own life. What will there be for this person when he is my age? If he senses something ineffable in the landscape, will I know enough to encourage it?—to somehow show him that, yes, when people talk about violent death, spiritual exhilaration, compassion, futility, final causes, they are drawing on forty thousand years of human meditation on *this*—as we embrace Douglas firs, or stand by a river across whose undulating back we skip stones, or dig out a camas bulb, biting down into a taste so much wilder than last night's potatoes.

11 The most moving look I ever saw from a child in the woods was on a mud bar by the footprints of a heron. We were on our knees, making handprints beside the footprints. You could feel the creek vibrating in the silt and sand. The sun beat down heavily on our hair. Our shoes were soaking wet. The look said: I did not know until now that I needed someone much older to confirm this, the feeling I have of life here. I can now grow older, knowing it need never be lost.

12 The quickest door to open in the woods for a child is the one that leads to the smallest room, by knowing the name each thing is called. The door that leads to the cathedral is marked by a hesitancy to speak at all, rather to encourage by example a sharpness of the senses. If one speaks it should only be to say, as well as one can, how wonderfully all this fits together, to indicate what a long, fierce peace can derive from this knowledge.

Comprehension

1. What is Lopez's primary purpose in this essay? How does the title relate to the purpose?

2. Does Lopez assume his audience has the same value position as he does? Why or why not?

3. What, ultimately, does Lopez want children to learn about the natural world? How does he teach them?

Rhetorical Analysis

4. Does Lopez state his thesis or imply it? Justify your response.

5. Why does Lopez use a personal tone or voice at the start of this essay? How does his opening paragraph connect to the body of the essay?

6. Cite instances where Lopez moves from vivid description to response and reflection.

7. Where does Lopez employ the comparative method, and toward what objective?

8. What extended metaphor does Lopez establish in the final paragraph? Is this an appropriate and effective metaphor to end the essay? Why or why not?

Writing

9. Write a narrative and descriptive essay in which you recount a childhood experience that taught you something about the natural world.

10. How would you speak to children if you were taking them on a nature walk? Write a reflective essay addressing this question.

11. **Writing an Argument**   Argue for or against the proposition that you can learn profound truths about yourself and the world by immersing yourself in nature.

Synthesizing the Classic + Contemporary Essays

1. Charles Eastman and Barry Lopez consider nature as a physical and spiritual presence. In what ways are their stakes in nature the same? In what ways are they different? Does either writer have the power to effect a transformation in our attitude toward nature? Explain.

2. It has often been said that intellectual knowledge changes one's relationship with the world environment. Do Lopez's essay and Eastman's excerpt confirm that statement? Use examples from the pieces to support your argument.

3. Public service announcements, or PSAs, are advertisements designed to raise awareness about issues, not sell products or services. Draft a PSA that informs or educates the public about an environmental issue. Include an excerpt from both Eastman's and Lopez's essays as illustrative support for your PSA.

Why I Hunt

Rick Bass

Rick Bass (b. 1958) was born in Fort Worth, Texas, and grew up in the Texas hill country where his grandfather taught him how to hunt. His collection of essays, *The Deer Pasture* (1985), recounts his Texas years, the ethos of hunting, and the allure of the outdoors. Bass studied at Utah State University (BS, 1979) and worked as an oil and gas geologist in Mississippi for eight years. His time working in the oil fields of the South is documented in *Oil Notes* (1979). Bass has written more than a dozen works of nonfiction and fiction, many of them reflecting environmental issues and people's search for balance in the natural world. An environmental advocate and land conservationist, Bass lives in the remote Yaak Valley on the Montana–Canada border, a region depicted in his books such as *Winter: Notes from Montana* (1991), *Brown Dog of the Yaak: Essays on Art and Activism* (1999), and *The Roadless Yaak: Reflections and Observations about One of Our Last Great Wild Places* (2002). His most recent book of fiction is *Nashville Chrome* (2010). Bass wrote this vivid and provocative essay on the allure of the hunt for *Sierra* magazine in 2001.

1   I was a hunter before I came far up into northwest Montana, but not to the degree I am now. It astounds me sometimes to step back particularly at the end of autumn, the end of the hunting season, and take both mental and physical inventory of all that was hunted and all that was gathered from this life in the mountains. The woodshed groaning tight, full of firewood. The fruits and herbs and vegetables from the garden, canned or dried or frozen; the wild mushrooms, huckleberries, thimbleberries, and strawberries. And most precious of all, the flesh of the wild things that share with us these mountains and the plains to the east—the elk, the whitetail and mule deer; the ducks and geese, grouse and pheasant and Hungarian partridge and dove and chukar and wild turkey; the trout and whitefish. Each year the cumulative bounty seems unbelievable. What heaven is this into which we've fallen?

2   How my wife and I got to this valley—the Yaak—15 years ago is a mystery, a move that I've only recently come to accept as having been inevitable. We got in the truck one day feeling strangely restless in Mississippi, and we drove. What did I know? Only that I missed the West's terrain of space. Young and healthy, and not coincidentally new-in-love, we hit that huge and rugged landscape in full stride. We drove north until we ran out of country—until the road ended, and we reached Canada's thick blue woods—and then we turned west and traveled until we ran almost out of mountains: the backside of the Rockies, to the wet, west-slope rainforest.

3   We came over a little mountain pass—it was August and winter was already fast approaching—and looked down on the soft hills, the dense purples of the spruce and fir forests, the ivory crests of the ice-capped peaks, and the slender ribbons of

gray thread rising from the chimneys of the few cabins nudged close to the winding river below, and we fell in love with the Yaak Valley and the hard-logged Kootenai National Forest—the way people in movies fall with each other, star and starlet, as if a trap door has been pulled out from beneath them: tumbling through the air, arms windmilling furiously, and suddenly no other world but each other, no other world but this one and eyes for no one, or no place, else.

4   Right from the beginning, I could see that there was extraordinary bounty in this low-elevation forest, resting as it does in a magical seam between the Pacific Northwest and the northern Rockies. Some landscapes these days have been reduced to nothing but dandelions and fire ants, knapweed and thistle, where the only remaining wildlife are sparrows, squirrels, and starlings. In the blessed Yaak, however, not a single mammal has gone extinct since the end of the Ice Age. This forest sustains more types of hunters—carnivores—than any valley in North America. It is a predator's showcase, home not just to wolves and grizzlies, but wolverines, lynx, bobcat, marten, fisher, black bear, mountain lion, golden eagle, bald eagle, coyote, fox, weasel. In the Yaak, everything is in motion, either seeking its quarry, or seeking to avoid becoming quarry.

5   The people who have chosen to live in this remote valley—few phones, very little electricity, and long, dark winters—possess a hardness and a dreaminess both. They—we—can live a life of deprivation, and yet are willing to enter the comfort of daydreams and imagination. There is something mysterious happening here between the landscape and the people, a thing that stimulates our imagination, and causes many of us to set off deep into the woods in search of the unknown, and sustenance—not just metaphorical or spiritual sustenance, but the real thing.

6   Only about 5 percent of the nation and 15 to 20 percent of Montanans are hunters. But in this one valley, almost everyone is a hunter. It is not the peer pressure of the local culture that recruits us into hunting, nor even necessarily the economic boon of a few hundred pounds of meat in a cash-poor society. Rather, it is the terrain itself, and one's gradual integration into it, that summons the hunter. Nearly everyone who has lived here for any length of time has ended up— sometimes almost against one's conscious wishes—becoming a hunter. This wild and powerful landscape sculpts us like clay. I don't find such sculpting an affront to the human spirit, but instead, wonderful testimony to our pliability, our ability to adapt to a place.

7 I myself love to hunt the deer, the elk, and the grouse—to follow them into the mouth of the forest, to disappear in their pursuit—to get lost following their snowy tracks up one mountain and down the next. One sets out after one's quarry with senses fully engaged, wildly alert: entranced, nearly hypnotized. The tiniest of factors can possess the largest significance—the crack of a twig, the shift of a breeze, a single stray hair caught on a piece of bark, a fresh-bent blade of grass.

8   Each year during such pursuits, I am struck more and more by the conceit that people in a hunter-gatherer culture might have richer imaginations than those who dwell more fully in an agricultural or even post-agricultural environment. What else is the hunt but a stirring of the imagination, with the quarry, or goal, or treasure

lying just around the corner or over the next rise? A hunter's imagination has no choice but to become deeply engaged, for it is never the hunter who is in control, but always the hunted, in that the prey directs the predator's movements.

9   The hunted shapes the hunter; the pursuit and evasion of predator and prey are but shadows of the same desire. The thrush wants to remain a thrush. The goshawk wants to consume the thrush and in doing so, partly become the thrush—to take its flesh into its flesh. They weave through the tangled branches of the forest, zigging and zagging, the goshawk right on the thrush's tail, like a shadow. Or perhaps it is the thrush that is the shadow thrown by the light of the goshawk's fiery desire.

10   Either way, the escape maneuvers of the thrush help carve and shape and direct the muscles of the goshawk. Even when you are walking through the woods seeing nothing but trees, you can feel the unseen passage of pursuits that might have occurred earlier that morning, precisely where you are standing—pursuits that will doubtless, after you are gone, sweep right back across that same spot again and again.

11   As does the goshawk, so too do human hunters imagine where their prey might be, or where it might go. They follow tracks hinting at not only distance and direction traveled, but also pace and gait and the general state of mind of the animal that is evading them. They plead to the mountain to deliver to them a deer, an elk. They imagine and hope that they are moving toward their goal of obtaining game.

12   When you plant a row of corn, there is not so much unknown. You can be fairly sure that, if the rains come, the corn is going to sprout. The corn is not seeking to elude you. But when you step into the woods, looking for a deer—well, there's nothing in your mind, or in your blood, or in the world, but imagination.

13   Most Americans neither hunt nor gather nor even grow their own food, nor make, with their own hands, any of their other necessities. In this post-agricultural society, too often we confuse anticipation with imagination. When we wander down the aisle of the supermarket searching for a chunk of frozen chicken, or cruise into Dillard's department store looking for a sweater, we can be fairly confident that grayish wad of chicken or that sweater is going to be there, thanks to the vigor and efficiency of a supply-and-demand marketplace. The imagination never quite hits second gear. Does the imagination atrophy, from such chronic inactivity? I suspect that it does.

14   All I know is that hunting—beyond being a thing I like to do—helps keep my imagination vital. I would hope never to be so blind as to offer it as prescription; I offer it only as testimony to my love of the landscape where I live—a place that is still, against all odds, its own place, quite unlike any other. I don't think I would be able to sustain myself as a dreamer in this strange landscape if I did not take off three months each year to wander the mountains in search of game; to hunt, stretching and exercising not just my imagination, but my spirit. And to wander the mountains, too, in all the other seasons. And to be nourished by the river of spirit that flows, shifting and winding, between me and the land.

Comprehension

1. Why did Bass and his wife fall in love with the Yaak Valley? What does this fondness for wild places tell us about his character and interests?

2. Explain the relationship between the people residing in the Yaak Valley and their fondness for hunting.

3. Does Bass apologize for his fondness for hunting? Explain your response.

Rhetorical Analysis

4. Bass wrote this essay for the official magazine of the Sierra Club, of which he is an active member. Why would an organization whose goal is the preservation of wilderness and wildlife agree to publish an article expressing love for hunting? How does Bass anticipate objections to his argument?

5. What is Bass's claim and where does he state it? Does he rely on logical, ethical, or emotional appeal—or a combination—to advance his argument, and why?

6. What causal connection does Bass establish between landscape and human behavior? Where does he use comparison and contrast to distinguish this place and its people from other places and other Americans?

7. Cite examples of Bass's descriptive skills and his use of figurative language. How does description and figurative language enhance the appeal of the writer's argument?

8. What is the dominant impression that Bass creates of the Yaak Valley region?

9. Evaluate Bass's conclusion. How does it serve as a writer's justification for hunting?

Writing

10. Select a natural landscape that you know well and, including description as one rhetorical strategy, explain how this site might affect the behavior of people and/or their values.

11. **Writing an Argument**   What is the difference between killing the game that you consume and buying meat in a grocery store or supermarket? Is one act more ethical than the other? Compose an argumentative essay dealing with this issue.

The Environmental Issue from Hell

Bill McKibben

Bill McKibben (b. 1960) was born in Palo Alto, California. After receiving a BA from Harvard University (1982), McKibben became a staff writer for *The New Yorker*. McKibben's chief concern is the impact of humans on the environment and the ways in which consumerism affects the global ecosystem. A prominent writer for the environmental movement, he has published several books, among them *The End of Nature* (1989), *The Age of Missing Information* (1992), *Long Distance: A Year of Living Strenuously* (2000), *Enough: Staying Human in an Engineered Age* (2003), and *The Bill McKibben Reader: Pieces from an Active Life* (2009). In the essay that follows, a longer version of which was published in *In These Times* in 2001, McKibben argues for a new approach to global warming.

1   When global warming first emerged as a potential crisis in the late 1980s, one academic analyst called it "the public policy problem from hell." The years since have only proven him more astute: Fifteen years into our understanding of climate change, we have yet to figure out how we're going to tackle it. And environmentalists are just as clueless as anyone else: Do we need to work on lifestyle or on lobbying, on photovoltaics or on politics? And is there a difference? How well we handle global warming will determine what kind of century we inhabit—and indeed what kind of planet we leave behind. The issue cuts close to home and also floats off easily into the abstract. So far it has been the ultimate "can't get there from here" problem, but the time has come to draw a road map— one that may help us deal with the handful of other issues on the list of real, world-shattering problems.

2   Typically, when you're mounting a campaign, you look for self-interest, you scare people by saying what will happen to us if we don't do something: All the birds will die, the canyon will disappear beneath a reservoir, we will choke to death on smog. But in the case of global warming, that doesn't exactly do the trick, at least in the time frame we're discussing. In temperate latitudes, climate change will creep up on us. Severe storms already have grown more frequent and more damaging. The progression of seasons is less steady. Some agriculture is less reliable. But face it: Our economy is so enormous that it takes those changes in stride. Economists who work on this stuff talk about how it will shave a percentage or two off the GNP over the next few decades. And most of us live lives so divorced from the natural world that we hardly notice the changes anyway. Hotter? Turn up the air-conditioning. Stormier? Well, an enormous percentage of Americans commute from remote-controlled garage to office parking garage—it may have been some time since they got good and wet in a rainstorm. By the time the magnitude of the change is truly in our faces, it will be too late to do much about it: There's such a lag time to increased levels of carbon dioxide in the atmosphere that we need to be making the switch to solar and

wind and hydrogen power right now to prevent disaster decades away. Yesterday, in fact.

3   So maybe we should think of global warming in a different way—as the great moral crisis of our time, the equivalent of the civil rights movement of the 1960s.

4   Why a moral question? In the first place, no one's ever figured out a more effective way to screw the marginalized and poor of this planet than climate change. Having taken their dignity, their resources, and their freedom under a variety of other schemes, we now are taking the very physical stability on which their already difficult lives depend.

5   Our economy can absorb these changes for a while, but consider Bangladesh for a moment. In 1998 the sea level in the Bay of Bengal was higher than normal, just the sort of thing we can expect to become more frequent and severe. The waters sweeping down the Ganges and the Brahmaputra rivers from the Himalayas could not drain easily into the ocean—they backed up across the country, forcing most of its inhabitants to spend three months in thigh-deep water. The fall rice crop didn't get planted. We've seen this same kind of disaster over the past few years in Mozambique and Honduras and Venezuela and other places.

6   And global warming is a moral crisis, too, if you place any value on the rest of creation. Coral reef researchers indicate that these spectacularly intricate ecosystems are also spectacularly vulnerable. Rising water temperatures are likely to bleach them to extinction by mid-century. In the Arctic, polar bears are 20 percent scrawnier than they were a decade ago: As pack ice melts, so does the opportunity for hunting seals. All in all, the 21st century seems poised to see extinctions at a rate not observed since the last big asteroid slammed into the planet. But this time the asteroid is us.

7   It's a moral question, finally, if you think we owe any debt to the future. No one ever has figured out a more thoroughgoing way to strip-mine the present and degrade what comes after—all the people who will ever be related to you. Ever. No generation yet to come will ever forget us—we are the ones present at the moment when the temperature starts to spike, and so far we have not reacted. If it had been done to us, we would loathe the generation that did it, precisely as we will one day be loathed.

8   But trying to launch a moral campaign is no easy task. In most moral crises, there is a villain—some person or class or institution that must be overcome. Once the villain is identified, the battle can commence. But you can't really get angry at carbon dioxide, and the people responsible for its production are, well, us. So perhaps we need some symbols to get us started, some places to sharpen the debate and rally ourselves to action. There are plenty to choose from: our taste for ever bigger houses and the heating and cooling bills that come with them, our penchant for jumping on airplanes at the drop of a hat. But if you wanted one glaring example of our lack of balance, you could do worse than point the finger at sport utility vehicles.

9   SUVs are more than mere symbols. They are a major part of the problem—we emit so much more carbon dioxide now than we did a decade ago in part because our fleet of cars and trucks actually has gotten steadily less fuel efficient for the past 10 years. If you switched today from the average American car to a big SUV,

and drove it for just one year, the difference in carbon dioxide that you produced would be the equivalent of opening your refrigerator door and then forgetting to close it for six years. SUVs essentially are machines for burning fossil fuel that just happen to also move you and your stuff around.

10   But what makes them such a perfect symbol is the brute fact that they are simply unnecessary. Go to the parking lot of the nearest suburban supermarket and look around: The only conclusion you can draw is that to reach the grocery, people must drive through three or four raging rivers and up the side of a canyon. These are semi-military machines, armored trucks on a slight diet. While they do not keep their occupants appreciably safer, they do wreck whatever they plow into, making them the perfect metaphor for a heedless, supersized society.

11   That's why we need a much broader politics than the Washington lobbying that's occupied the big environmental groups for the past decade. We need to take all the brilliant and energetic strategies of local grassroots groups fighting dumps and cleaning up rivers and apply those tactics in the national and international arenas. That's why some pastors are starting to talk with their congregations about what cars to buy, and why some college seniors are passing around petitions pledging to stay away from the Ford Explorers and Excursions, and why some auto dealers have begun to notice informational picketers outside their showrooms on Saturday mornings urging customers to think about gas mileage when they look at cars.

12   The point is not that such actions by themselves—any individual actions—will make any real dent in the levels of carbon dioxide pouring into our atmosphere. Even if you got 10 percent of Americans really committed to changing their energy use, their solar homes wouldn't make much of a difference in our national totals. But 10 percent would be enough to change the politics around the issue, enough to pressure politicians to pass laws that would cause us all to shift our habits. And so we need to begin to take an issue that is now the province of technicians and turn it into a political issue, just as bus boycotts began to make public the issue of race, forcing the system to respond. That response is likely to be ugly—there are huge companies with a lot to lose, and many people so tied in to their current ways of life that advocating change smacks of subversion. But this has to become a political issue—and fast. The only way that may happen, short of a hideous drought or monster flood, is if it becomes a personal issue first.

"The Environmental Issue from Hell" by Bill McKibben. This article originally appeared in *In These Times* magazine (April 30, 2001).

Comprehension

1. According to McKibben, what are the causes of global warming?

2. What instances of ecological disaster does the writer say will occur if we do not change our habits?

3. Why is a new approach to the problem of global warming needed? What approach does McKibben suggest?

Rhetorical Analysis

4. How does McKibben's title capture the tone of the essay? What is his purpose in writing the essay? Does he see his readers as hostile or sympathetic to his position? How do you know?

5. How does McKibben develop his introduction? Why does he pose questions? Where does he state his claim?

6. Does McKibben make his argument through appeals to reason, emotion, ethics—or a combination of these elements? Justify your response.

7. How does the writer contend with possible objections to his position on global warming?

8. Explain the pattern of cause and effect that McKibben uses to structure his essay.

9. What varieties of evidence does the writer present to support his claim? What extended illustration does he provide? How effective is it, and why?

10. In the concluding paragraph, McKibben issues a call to action. How does the body of the essay prepare the reader for this persuasive appeal?

Writing

11. Research and write an essay in which you explain your own understanding of the causes and effects of global warming.

12. Research your state's policy concerning global warming. Present your findings in a summary essay.

13. **Writing an Argument** McKibben argues that SUVs are a primary cause of wastefulness and global warming and that both moral persuasion and political activism are required to change consumers' habits. Do you agree or disagree with his assertions? Write an argumentative essay responding to this issue.

The Obligation to Endure

Rachel Carson

Rachel Carson (1907–1964) was a seminal figure in the environmental movement. Born in Pennsylvania, she awakened public consciousness to environmental issues through her writing. Her style was both literary and scientific as she described nature's riches in such books as *The Sea Around Us* (1951) and *The Edge of the Sea* (1954). Her last book, *Silent Spring* (1962), aroused controversy and concern with its indictment of insecticides. In the following excerpt from that important book, Carson provides compelling evidence of the damage caused by indiscriminate use of insecticides and the danger of disturbing the earth's delicate balance.

1 The history of life on earth has been a history of interaction between living things and their surroundings. To a large extent, the physical form and the habits of the earth's vegetation and its animal life have been molded by the environment. Considering the whole span of earthly time, the opposite effect, in which life actually modifies its surroundings, has been relatively slight. Only within the moment of time represented by the present century has one species—man—acquired significant power to alter the nature of his world.

2 During the past quarter century this power has not only increased to one of disturbing magnitude but it has changed in character. The most alarming of all man's assaults upon the environment is the contamination of air, earth, rivers, and sea with dangerous and even lethal materials. This pollution is for the most part irrecoverable; the chain of evil it initiates not only in the world that must support life but in living tissues is for the most part irreversible. In this now universal contamination of the environment, chemicals are the sinister and little-recognized partners of radiation in changing the very nature of the world—the very nature of its life. Strontium 90, released through nuclear explosions into the air, comes to earth in rain or drifts down as fallout, lodges in soil, enters into the grass or corn or wheat grown there, and in time takes up its abode in the bones of a human being, there to remain until his death. Similarly, chemicals sprayed on croplands or forests or gardens lie long in soil, entering into living organisms, passing from one to another in a chain of poisoning and death. Or they pass mysteriously by underground streams until they emerge and, through the alchemy of air and sunlight, combine into new forms that kill vegetation, sicken cattle, and work unknown harm on those who drink from once pure wells. As Albert Schweitzer has said, "Man can hardly even recognize the devils of his own creation."

3 It took hundreds of millions of years to produce the life that now inhabits the earth—eons of time in which that developing and evolving and diversifying life reached a state of adjustment and balance with its surroundings. The environment, rigorously shaping and directing the life it supported, contained elements that were hostile as well as supporting. Certain rocks gave out dangerous radiation; even within the light of the sun, from which all life draws

its energy, there were shortwave radiations with power to injure. Given time—time not in years but in millennia—life adjusts, and a balance has been reached. For time is the essential ingredient; but in the modern world there is no time.

4   The rapidity of change and the speed with which new situations are created follow the impetuous and heedless pace of man rather than the deliberate pace of nature. Radiation is no longer merely the background radiation of rocks, the bombardment of cosmic rays, the ultraviolet of the sun that have existed before there was any life on earth; radiation is now the unnatural creation of man's tampering with the atom. The chemicals to which life is asked to make its adjustment are no longer merely the calcium and silica and copper and all the rest of the minerals washed out of the rocks and carried in rivers to the sea; they are the synthetic creations of man's inventive mind, brewed in his laboratories, and having no counterparts in nature.

5   To adjust to these chemicals would require time on the scale that is nature's; it would require not merely the years of a man's life but the life of generations. And even this, were it by some miracle possible, would be futile, for the new chemicals come from our laboratories in an endless stream; almost five hundred annually find their way into actual use in the United States alone. The figure is staggering and its implications are not easily grasped—500 new chemicals to which the bodies of men and animals are required somehow to adapt each year, chemicals totally outside the limits of biologic experience.

6   Among them are many that are used in man's war against nature. Since the mid-1940s over 200 basic chemicals have been created for use in killing insects, weeds, rodents, and other organisms described in the modern vernacular as "pests"; and they are sold under several thousand different brand names.

7   These sprays, dusts, and aerosols are now applied almost universally to farms, gardens, forests, and homes—nonselective chemicals that have the power to kill every insect, the "good" and the "bad," to still the song of birds and the leaping of fish in the streams, to coat the leaves with a deadly film, and to linger on in soil—all this though the intended target may be only a few weeds or insects. Can anyone believe it is possible to lay down such a barrage of poisons on the surface of the earth without making it unfit for all life? They should not be called "insecticides," but "biocides."

8   The whole process of spraying seems caught up in an endless spiral. Since DDT was released for civilian use, a process of escalation has been going on in which ever more toxic materials must be found. This has happened because insects, in a triumphant vindication of Darwin's principle of the survival of the fittest, have evolved super races immune to the particular insecticide used, hence a deadlier one has always to be developed—and then a deadlier one than that. It has happened also because, for reasons to be described later, destructive insects often undergo a "flareback," or resurgence, after spraying in numbers greater than before. Thus the chemical war is never won, and all life is caught in its violent crossfire.

9   Along with the possibility of the extinction of mankind by nuclear war, the central problem of our age has therefore become the contamination of man's total environment with such substances of incredible potential for harm—substances

that accumulate in the tissues of plants and animals and even penetrate the germ cells to shatter or alter the very material of heredity upon which the shape of the future depends.

10   Some would-be architects of our future look toward a time when it will be possible to alter the human germ plasm by design. But we may easily be doing so now by inadvertence, for many chemicals, like radiation, bring about gene mutations. It is ironic to think that man might determine his own future by something so seemingly trivial as the choice of an insect spray.

11   All this has been risked—for what? Future historians may well be amazed by our distorted sense of proportion. How could intelligent beings seek to control a few unwanted species by a method that contaminated the entire environment and brought the threat of disease and death even to their own kind? Yet this is precisely what we have done. We have done it, moreover, for reasons that collapse the moment we examine them. We are told that the enormous and expanding use of pesticides is necessary to maintain farm production. Yet is our real problem not one of *overproduction*? Our farms, despite measures to remove acreages from production and to pay farmers *not* to produce, have yielded such a staggering excess of crops that the American taxpayer in 1962 is paying out more than one billion dollars a year as the total carrying cost of the surplus-food storage program. And is the situation helped when one branch of the Agriculture Department tries to reduce production while another states, as it did in 1958, "It is believed generally that reduction of crop acreages under provisions of the Soil Bank will stimulate interest in use of chemicals to obtain maximum production on the land retained in crops."

12   All this is not to say there is no insect problem and no need of control. I am saying, rather, that control must be geared to realities, not to mythical situations, and that the methods employed must be such that they do not destroy us along with the insects.

13 The problem whose attempted solution has brought such a train of disaster in its wake is an accompaniment of our modern way of life. Long before the age of man, insects inhabited the earth—a group of extraordinarily varied and adaptable beings. Over the course of time since man's advent, a small percentage of the more than half a million species of insects have come into conflict with human welfare in two principal ways: as competitors for the food supply and as carriers of human disease.

14   Disease-carrying insects become important where human beings are crowded together, especially under conditions where sanitation is poor, as in times of natural disaster or war or in situations of extreme poverty and deprivation. Then control of some sort becomes necessary. It is a sobering fact, however, as we shall presently see, that the method of massive chemical control has had only limited success, and also threatens to worsen the very conditions it is intended to curb.

15   Under primitive agricultural conditions the farmer had few insect problems. These arose with the intensification of agriculture—the devotion of immense acreages to a single crop. Such a system set the stage for explosive increases in specific insect populations. Single-crop farming does not take advantage of the principles by which nature works; it is agriculture as an engineer might conceive

it to be. Nature has introduced great variety into the landscape, but man has displayed a passion for simplifying it. Thus he undoes the built-in checks and balances by which nature holds the species within bounds. One important natural check is a limit on the amount of suitable habitat for each species. Obviously then, an insect that lives on wheat can build up its population to much higher levels on a farm devoted to wheat than on one in which wheat is intermingled with other crops to which the insect is not adapted.

16   The same thing happens in other situations. A generation or more ago, the towns of large areas of the United States lined their streets with the noble elm tree. Now the beauty they hopefully created is threatened with complete destruction as disease sweeps through the elms, carried by a beetle that would have only limited chance to build up large populations and to spread from tree to tree if the elms were only occasional trees in a richly diversified planting.

17   Another factor in the modern insect problem is one that must be viewed against a background of geologic and human history: the spreading of thousands of different kinds of organisms from their native homes to invade new territories. This worldwide migration has been studied and graphically described by the British ecologist Charles Elton in his recent book *The Ecology of Invasions*. During the Cretaceous Period, some hundred million years ago, flooding seas cut many land bridges between continents and living things found themselves confined in what Elton calls "colossal separate nature reserves." There, isolated from others of their kind, they developed many new species. When some of the land masses were joined again, about 15 million years ago, these species began to move out into new territories—a movement that is not only still in progress but is now receiving considerable assistance from man.

18   The importation of plants is the primary agent in the modern spread of species, for animals have almost invariably gone along with the plants, quarantine being a comparatively recent and not completely effective innovation. The United States Office of Plant Introduction alone has introduced almost 200,000 species and varieties of plants from all over the world. Nearly half of the 180 or so major insect enemies of plants in the United States are accidental imports from abroad, and most of them have come as hitchhikers on plants.

19   In new territory, out of reach of the restraining hand of the natural enemies that kept down its numbers in its native land, an invading plant or animal is able to become enormously abundant. Thus it is no accident that our most troublesome insects are introduced species.

20   These invasions, both the naturally occurring and those dependent on human assistance, are likely to continue indefinitely. Quarantine and massive chemical campaigns are only extremely expensive ways of buying time. We are faced, according to Dr. Elton, "with a life-and-death need not just to find new technological means of suppressing this plant or that animal"; instead we need the basic knowledge of animal populations and their relations to their surroundings that will "promote an even balance and damp down the explosive power of outbreaks and new invasions."

21   Much of the necessary knowledge is now available but we do not use it. We train ecologists in our universities and even employ them in our governmental

agencies but we seldom take their advice. We allow the chemical death rain to fall as though there were no alternative, whereas in fact there are many, and our ingenuity could soon discover many more if given opportunity.

22   Have we fallen into a mesmerized state that makes us accept as inevitable that which is inferior or detrimental, as though having lost the will or the vision to demand that which is good? Such thinking, in the words of the ecologist Paul Shepard, "idealizes life with only its head out of water, inches above the limits of toleration of the corruption of its own environment. . . . Why should we tolerate a diet of weak poisons, a home in insipid surroundings, a circle of acquaintances who are not quite our enemies, the noise of motors with just enough relief to prevent insanity? Who would want to live in a world which is just not quite fatal?"

23   Yet such a world is pressed upon us. The crusade to create a chemically sterile, insect-free world seems to have engendered a fanatic zeal on the part of many specialists and most of the so-called control agencies. On every hand there is evidence that those engaged in spraying operations exercise a ruthless power. "The regulatory entomologists . . . function as prosecutor, judge and jury, tax assessor and collector and sheriff to enforce their own orders," said Connecticut entomologist Neely Turner. The most flagrant abuses go unchecked in both state and federal agencies.

24   It is not my contention that chemical insecticides must never be used. I do contend that we have put poisonous and biologically potent chemicals indiscriminately into the hands of persons largely or wholly ignorant of their potentials for harm. We have subjected enormous numbers of people to contact with these poisons, without their consent and often without their knowledge. If the Bill of Rights contains no guarantee that a citizen shall be secure against lethal poisons distributed either by private individuals or by public officials, it is surely only because our forefathers, despite their considerable wisdom and foresight, could conceive of no such problem.

25   I contend, furthermore, that we have allowed these chemicals to be used with little or no advance investigation of their effect on soil, water, wildlife, and man himself. Future generations are unlikely to condone our lack of prudent concern for the integrity of the natural world that supports all life.

26   There is still very limited awareness of the nature of the threat. This is an era of specialists, each of whom sees his own problem and is unaware of or intolerant of the larger frame into which it fits. It is also an era dominated by industry, in which the right to make a dollar at whatever cost is seldom challenged. When the public protests, confronted with some obvious evidence of damaging results of pesticide applications, it is fed little tranquilizing pills of half truth. We urgently need an end to these false assurances, to the sugar coating of unpalatable facts. It is the public that is being asked to assume the risks that the insect controllers calculate. The public must decide whether it wishes to continue on the present road, and it can do so only when in full possession of the facts. In the words of Jean Rostand, "The obligation to endure gives us the right to know."

Comprehension

1. What does Carson mean by "the obligation to endure"?

2. What reasons does the author cite for the overpopulation of insects?

3. What remedies does Carson propose?

Rhetorical Analysis

4. What tone does Carson use in her essay? Does she seem to be a subjective or an objective writer? Give specific support for your response.

5. How does the use of words such as *dangerous, evil, irrevocable,* and *sinister* help shape the reader's reaction to the piece? What emotional and ethical appeals do such words indicate?

6. Examine the ordering of ideas in paragraph 4, and consider how such an order serves to reinforce Carson's argument.

7. Paragraph 9 consists of only one (long) sentence. What is its function in the essay's scheme?

8. Examine Carson's use of expert testimony. How does it help strengthen her thesis?

9. How effectively does the essay's conclusion help tie up Carson's points? What is the writer's intent in this final paragraph? How does she accomplish this aim?

Writing

10. Write an essay in which you suggest solutions to the problems brought up in Carson's piece. You may want to suggest measures that the average citizen can take to eliminate the casual use of insecticides to control the insect population.

11. Write a biographical research paper on Carson that focuses on her involvement with nature and environmental issues.

12. **Writing an Argument** Write an essay titled "Insects Are Not the Problem; Humanity Is." In this essay, argue that it is humanity's greed that has caused such an imbalance in nature as to threaten the planet's survival.

Am I Blue?

Alice Walker

Alice Walker (b. 1941) was born in Eatonton, Georgia, and now lives in San Francisco and Mendocino County, California. She attended Spelman College and graduated from Sarah Lawrence College. A celebrated and prolific novelist, short-story writer, poet, and essayist, she has also been active in the civil rights movement. Walker often draws on both her personal experience and historical records to reflect on the African American experience. Her books include *The Color Purple* (1976), which won the American Book Award and the Pulitzer Prize; *You Can't Keep a Good Woman Down* (1981); *Living in the World: Selected Essays, 1973–1987* (1987); *The Temple of My Familiar* (1989); *By the Light of My Father's Smile* (1999); *The Way Forward Is with a Broken Heart* (2001); *Why War Is Never a Good Idea* (2007), and *Devil's My Enemy* (2008). In the following essay from *Living in the World*, Walker questions the distinctions commonly made between human and animal.

1   For about three years my companion and I rented a small house in the country that stood on the edge of a large meadow that appeared to run from the end of our deck straight into the mountains. The mountains, however, were quite far away, and between us and them there was, in fact, a town. It was one of the many pleasant aspects of the house that you never really were aware of this.

2   It was a house of many windows, low, wide, nearly floor to ceiling in the living room, which faced the meadow, and it was from one of these that I first saw our closest neighbor, a large white horse, cropping grass, flipping its mane, and ambling about—not over the entire meadow, which stretched well out of sight of the house, but over the five or so fenced-in acres that were next to the twenty-odd that we had rented. I soon learned that the horse, whose name was Blue, belonged to a man who lived in another town, but was boarded by our neighbors next door. Occasionally, one of the children, usually a stocky teenager, but sometimes a much younger girl or boy, could be seen riding Blue. They would appear in the meadow, climb up on his back, ride furiously for ten or fifteen minutes, then get off, slap Blue on the flanks, and not be seen again for a month or more.

3   There were many apple trees in our yard, and one by the fence that Blue could almost reach. We were soon in the habit of feeding him apples, which he relished, especially because by the middle of summer the meadow grasses—so green and succulent since January—had dried out from lack of rain, and Blue stumbled about munching the dried stalks half-heartedly. Sometimes he would stand very still just by the apple tree, and when one of us came out he would whinny, snort loudly, or stamp the ground. This meant, of course: I want an apple.

4   It was quite wonderful to pick a few apples, or collect those that had fallen to the ground overnight, and patiently hold them, one by one, up to his large, toothy

mouth. I remained as thrilled as a child by his flexible dark lips, huge, cubelike teeth that crunched the apples, core and all, with such finality, and his high, broad-breasted *enormity*; beside which, I felt small indeed. When I was a child, I used to ride horses, and was especially friendly with one named Nan until the day I was riding and my brother deliberately spooked her and I was thrown, head first, against the trunk of a tree. When I came to, I was in bed and my mother was bending worriedly over me; we silently agreed that perhaps horseback riding was not the safest sport for me. Since then I have walked, and prefer walking to horseback riding—but I had forgotten the depth of feeling one could see in horses' eyes.

5   I was therefore unprepared for the expression in Blue's. Blue was lonely. Blue was horribly lonely and bored. I was not shocked that this should be the case; five acres to tramp by yourself, endlessly, even in the most beautiful of meadows—and his was—cannot provide many interesting events, and once the rainy season turned to dry that was about it. No, I was shocked that I had forgotten that human animals and nonhuman animals can communicate quite well; if we are brought up around animals as children we take this for granted. By the time we are adults we no longer remember. However, the animals have not changed. They are in fact *completed* creations (at least they seem to be, so much more than we) who are not likely *to* change; it is their nature to express themselves. What else are they going to express? And they do. And, generally speaking, they are ignored.

6   After giving Blue the apples, I would wander back to the house, aware that he was observing me. Were more apples not forthcoming then? Was that to be his sole entertainment for the day? My partner's small son had decided he wanted to learn how to piece a quilt; we worked in silence on our respective squares as I thought . . .

7   Well, about slavery: about white children, who were raised by black people, who knew their first all-accepting love from black women, and then, when they were twelve or so, were told they must "forget" the deep levels of communication between themselves and "mammy" that they knew. Later they would be able to relate quite calmly, "My old mammy was sold to another good family." "My old mammy was _____." Fill in the blank. Many more years later a white woman would say: "I can't understand these Negroes, these blacks. What do they want? They're so different from us."

8   And about the Indians, considered to be "like animals" by the "settlers" (a very benign euphemism for what they actually were), who did not understand their description as a compliment.

9   And about the thousands of American men who marry Japanese, Korean, Filipina, and other non-English-speaking women and of how happy they report they are, *"blissfully,"* until their brides learn to speak English, at which point the marriages tend to fall apart. What then did the men see, when they looked into the eyes of the women they married, before they could speak English? Apparently only their own reflections.

10   I thought of society's impatience with the young. "Why are they playing the music so loud?" Perhaps the children have listened to much of the music of

oppressed people their parents danced to before they were born, with its passionate but soft cries for acceptance and love, and they have wondered why their parents failed to hear.

11   I do not know how long Blue had inhabited his five beautiful, boring acres before we moved into our house; a year after we had arrived—and had also traveled to other valleys, other cities, other worlds—he was still there.

12   But then, in our second year at the house, something happened in Blue's life. One morning, looking out the window at the fog that lay like a ribbon over the meadow, I saw another horse, a brown one, at the other end of Blue's field. Blue appeared to be afraid of it, and for several days made no attempt to go near. We went away for a week. When we returned, Blue had decided to make friends and the two horses ambled or galloped along together, and Blue did not come nearly as often to the fence underneath the apple tree.

13   When he did, bringing his new friend with him, there was a different look in his eyes. A look of independence, of self-possession, of inalienable *horse*ness. His friend eventually became pregnant. For months and months there was, it seemed to me, a mutual feeling between me and the horses of justice, of peace. I fed apples to them both. The look in Blue's eyes was one of unabashed "this is *it*ness."

14   It did not, however, last forever. One day, after a visit to the city, I went out to give Blue some apples. He stood waiting, or so I thought, though not beneath the tree. When I shook the tree and jumped back from the shower of apples, he made no move. I carried some over to him. He managed to half-crunch one. The rest he let fall to the ground. I dreaded looking into his eyes—because I had of course noticed that Brown, his partner, had gone—but I did look. If I had been born into slavery, and my partner had been sold or killed, my eyes would have looked like that. The children next door explained that Blue's partner had been "put with him" (the same expression that old people used, I had noticed, when speaking of an ancestor during slavery who had been impregnated by her owner) so that they could mate and she conceive. Since that was accomplished, she had been taken back by her owner, who lived somewhere else.

15   Will she be back? I asked.

16   They didn't know.

17   Blue was like a crazed person. Blue *was*, to me, a crazed person. He galloped furiously, as if he were being ridden, around and around his five beautiful acres. He whinnied until he couldn't. He tore at the ground with his hooves. He butted himself against his single shade tree. He looked always and always toward the road down which his partner had gone. And then, occasionally, when he came up for apples, or I took apples to him, he looked at me. It was a look so piercing, so full of grief, a look so *human*, I almost laughed (I felt too sad to cry) to think there are people who do not know that animals suffer. People like me who have forgotten, and daily forget, all that animals try to tell us. "Everything you do to us will happen to you; we are your teachers, as you are ours. We are one lesson" is essentially it, I think. There are those who never once have even considered animals' rights: those who have been taught that animals actually want to be used and abused by us, as small children "love" to be frightened, or women "love" to be mutilated and raped. . . . They are the great-grandchildren of those who honestly

thought, because someone taught them this: "Woman can't think" and "niggers can't faint." But most disturbing of all, in Blue's large brown eyes was a new look, more painful than the look of despair: the look of disgust with human beings, with life; the look of hatred. And it was odd what the look of hatred did. It gave him, for the first time, the look of a beast. And what that meant was that he had put up a barrier within to protect himself from further violence; all the apples in the world wouldn't change that fact.

18   And so Blue remained, a beautiful part of our landscape, very peaceful to look at from the window, white against the grass. Once a friend came to visit and said, looking out on the soothing view: "And it *would* have to be a *white* horse; the very image of freedom." And I thought, yes, the animals are forced to become for us merely "images" of what they once so beautifully expressed. And we are used to drinking milk from containers showing "contented" cows, whose real lives we want to hear nothing about, eating eggs and drumsticks from "happy" hens, and munching hamburgers advertised by bulls of integrity who seem to command their fate.

19   As we talked of freedom and justice one day for all, we sat down to steaks. I am eating misery, I thought, as I took the first bite. And spit it out.

Comprehension

1. What is the major thesis of the essay? Is it stated explicitly in the text, or does one have to infer it? Explain.

2. In paragraph 5, Walker states that animals are "*completed* creations (at least they seem to be, so much more than we) who are not likely *to* change." What does she mean by making this distinction between animals and humans?

3. What is the significance of the title of the essay? Does it have more than one meaning? Explain your answer.

Rhetorical Analysis

4. In paragraph 4, Walker creates a vivid description of Blue. How does she achieve this?

5. In paragraph 7, Walker makes a cognitive association between the relationship between humans and animals and the relationship between whites and blacks during slavery. Does this transition seem too abrupt, or is there a rhetorical reason for the immediate comparison? Explain.

6. Explore the other analogies Walker makes in paragraphs 8 and 9. Are they pertinent? What is the rhetorical effect of juxtaposing seemingly different realms to convey one central idea?

7. Walker often breaks the conventions of "college English." For example, paragraphs 8 and 9 both begin with the coordinating conjunction *and*. Paragraph 12 begins with the coordinating conjunction *but*. Paragraphs 15 and 16 are only one short sentence each. Explain the effect of each of these rhetorical devices. Find three other unusual rhetorical strategies—either on the paragraph or sentence level—and explain their effects.

8. In paragraphs 17 and 18, Walker speeds up the tempo of her writing by beginning many of the sentences with the conjunction *and*. What is the purpose and rhetorical effect of this strategy, and how does it mimic—in linguistic terms—Blue's altered emotional state?

9. Walker seems to have a profound empathy for animals, yet it is only at the end that she is repulsed by the thought of eating meat. What rhetorical strategy is she employing in the conclusion that helps bring closure to her meditation on Blue? Does it matter whether the culminating event actually occurred in her experience, or is it all right for an essayist to use poetic license for stylistic purposes?

Writing

10. Write a personal essay in which you describe your relationship with a favorite pet. Include your observations of, responses to, and attitude toward your pet. Compare and contrast this relationship to those you have with humans.

11. Some writers have argued that it matters little if certain "nonessential" endangered species become extinct if they interfere with "human progress." Argue for or against this proposition.

12. **Writing an Argument** Argue for or against one of the following practices: (**a**) hunting for the sake of the hunt, (**b**) eating meat, or (**c**) keeping animals in zoos.

Two Views of the Mississippi

Mark Twain

Samuel Langhorne Clemens (1835–1910) better known by his pen name **Mark Twain**, was an American author and humorist. He is most noted for his novel *The Adventures of Tom Sawyer* (1876) and its sequel, *Adventures of Huckleberry Finn* (1885), the latter often called "the Great American Novel." Twain grew up in Hannibal, Missouri, which would later provide the setting for Huckleberry Finn and Tom Sawyer. He began his career as a printer and typesetter, which allowed him to contribute articles to his older brother's newspaper. He eventually left the printing business and became a master riverboat pilot on the Mississippi River, although he eventually joined his brother Orion out West. These experiences resulted in many famous publications, including *Roughing It* (1872). His wit and satire gained him the respect of critics and peers throughout the world. "Two Views of the Mississippi" addresses his years as a riverboat pilot.

1   Now when I had mastered the language of this water and had come to know every trifling feature that bordered the great river as familiarly as I knew the letters of the alphabet, I had made a valuable acquisition. But I had lost something, too. I had lost something which could never be restored to me while I lived. All the grace, the beauty, the poetry, had gone out of the majestic river! I still kept in mind a certain wonderful sunset which I witnessed when steamboating was new to me. A broad expanse of the river was turned to blood; in the middle distance the red hue brightened into gold, through which a solitary log came floating, black and conspicuous; one place a long, slanting mark lay sparkling upon the water; in another the surface was broken by boiling, tumbling rings, that were as many-tinted as an opal; where the ruddy flush was faintest, was a smooth spot that was covered with graceful circles and radiating lines, ever so delicately traced; the shore on our left was densely wooded, and the sombre shadow that fell from this forest was broken in one place by a long, ruffled trail that shone like silver; and high above the forest wall a clean-stemmed dead tree waved a single leafy bough that glowed like a flame in the unobstructed splendor that was flowing from the sun. There were graceful curves, reflected images, woody heights, soft distances; and over the whole scene, far and near, the dissolving lights drifted steadily, enriching it every passing moment with new marvels of coloring.

2   I stood like one bewitched. I drank it in, in a speechless rapture. The world was new to me, and I had never seen any thing like this at home. But as I have said, a day came when I began to cease from noting the glories and the charms which the moon and the sun and the twilight wrought upon the river's face; another day came when I ceased altogether to note them. Then, if that sunset scene had been repeated, I should have looked upon it without rapture, and should have commented upon it, inwardly, after this fashion: "This sun means that we are going to have wind to-morrow; that floating log means that the river is rising, small thanks to it; that slanting mark on the water refers to a bluff reef which is going to kill somebody's steamboat one of these nights, if it keeps on stretching out like that; those tumbling 'boils' show a dissolving bar and a changing channel there; the lines and circles in the slick water over yonder are a warning that that troublesome place is shoaling up dangerously; that silver streak in the shadow of the forest is the 'break' from a new snag, and he has located himself in the very best place he could have found to fish for steamboats; that tall dead tree, with a single living branch, is not going to last long, and then how is a body ever going to get through this blind place at night without the friendly old landmark?"

3   No, the romance and the beauty were all gone from the river. All the value any feature of it had for me now was the amount of usefulness it could furnish toward compassing the safe piloting of a steamboat. Since those days, I have pitied doctors from my heart. What does the lovely flush in a beauty's cheek mean to a doctor but a "break" that ripples above some deadly disease? Are not all her visible charms sown thick with what are to him the signs and symbols of hidden decay? Does he ever see her beauty at all, or doesn't he simply view her professionally, and comment upon her unwholesome condition all to himself? And doesn't he sometimes wonder whether he has gained most or lost most by learning his trade?

From *Life on the Mississippi* by Mark Twain. Harper & Brothers Publishers, 1901. Copyright 1874 and 1875 by H.O. Houghton and Company. Copyright 1883 by Samuel L. Clemens. All rights reserved.

Comprehension

1. Twain's experiences on the Mississippi River made him think about another profession, and Twain pities the members of that profession. Discuss what the people in this profession lose.

2. What does Twain "lose" as a result of his profession as a steamboat pilot?

3. What is Twain's strongest desire concerning his views on the world of the river?

Rhetorical Analysis

4. What is the thesis of this essay?

5. How does the river become Twain's enemy/nemesis?

6. What does Twain mean when he declares that he has "mastered the language of the river"?

7. What images does Twain use to point out the beauty of the river and its surrounding area? Discuss the effect of these images.

8. What function does the "tall dead tree" serve, and what saddens Twain about this tree?

Writing

9. Write a paragraph about the thrill of a new discovery you made.

10. Explain a lesson that you have learned from nature.

11. **Writing an Argument** Argue for or against the idea that once people understand how something works, they lose their appreciation of it. Give specific examples that back up the argument.

The Last Americans: Environmental Collapse and the End of Civilization

Jared Diamond

Jared Diamond (b. 1937), who was born in Boston, is a physiologist, ecologist, and prolific writer who has published hundreds of popular and scientific articles. He has a BA from Harvard University (1958) and a PhD from Cambridge University (1961). Currently a professor of geography at UCLA and formerly professor of physiology at UCLA's School of Medicine, Diamond has conducted research in ecology and evolutionary biology in New Guinea and other southwest Pacific islands. As a field researcher and director of the World Wildlife Fund, Diamond helped to establish New Guinea's national park system. He received the Pulitzer Prize for *Guns, Germs, and Steel: The Fates of Human Societies* (1997). Another well-received book of Diamond's is *Collapse: How Societies Choose to Fail or Succeed* (2004). In the following essay, which appeared in the June 2003 issue of *Harper's*, Diamond examines the environmental crises and failures of previous societies and civilizations, and how we might be able to learn lessons from these lost worlds.

I met a traveler from an antique land
Who said: Two vast and trunkless legs of stone
Stand in the desert. . . . Near them, on the sand,
Half sunk, a shattered visage lies, whose frown,
And wrinkled lip, and sneer of cold command,
Tell that its sculptor well those passions read
Which yet survive, stamped on these lifeless things,
The hand that mocked them, and the heart that fed:
And on the pedestal these words appear:
"My name is Ozymandias, king of kings:
Look on my works, ye Mighty, and despair!"
Nothing beside remains. Round the decay
Of that colossal wreck, boundless and bare
The lone and level sands stretch far away.

—*"Ozymandias," Percy Bysshe Shelley*

1   One of the disturbing facts of history is that so many civilizations collapse. Few people, however, least of all our politicians, realize that a primary cause of the collapse of those societies has been the destruction of the environmental resources on which they depended. Fewer still appreciate that many of those civilizations share a sharp curve of decline. Indeed, a society's demise may begin only a decade or two after it reaches its peak population, wealth, and power.

2   Recent archaeological discoveries have revealed similar courses of collapse in such otherwise dissimilar ancient societies as the Maya in the Yucatán, the

Anasazi in the American Southwest, the Cahokia mound builders outside St. Louis, the Greenland Norse, the statue builders of Easter Island, ancient Mesopotamia in the Fertile Crescent, Great Zimbabwe in Africa, and Angkor Wat in Cambodia. These civilizations, and many others, succumbed to various combinations of environmental degradation and climate change, aggression from enemies taking advantage of their resulting weakness, and declining trade with neighbors who faced their own environmental problems. Because peak population, wealth, resource consumption, and waste production are accompanied by peak environmental impact—approaching the limit at which impact outstrips resources—we can now understand why declines of societies tend to follow swiftly on their peaks.

3   These combinations of undermining factors were compounded by cultural attitudes preventing those in power from perceiving or resolving the crisis. That's a familiar problem today. Some of us are inclined to dismiss the importance of a healthy environment, or at least to suggest that it's just one of many problems facing us—an "issue." That dismissal is based on three dangerous misconceptions.

4   Foremost among these misconceptions is that we must balance the environment against human needs. That reasoning is exactly upside-down. Human needs and a healthy environment are not opposing claims that must be balanced; instead, they are inexorably linked by chains of cause and effect. We need a healthy environment because we need clean water, clean air, wood, and food from the ocean, plus soil and sunlight to grow crops. We need functioning natural ecosystems, with their native species of earthworms, bees, plants, and microbes, to generate and aerate our soils, pollinate our crops, decompose our wastes, and produce our oxygen. We need to prevent toxic substances from accumulating in our water and air and soil. We need to prevent weeds, germs, and other pest species from becoming established in places where they aren't native and where they cause economic damage. Our strongest arguments for a healthy environment are selfish: We want it for ourselves, not for threatened species like snail darters, spotted owls, and Furbish louseworts.

5   Another popular misconception is that we can trust in technology to solve our problems. Whatever environmental problem you name, you can also name some hoped-for technological solution under discussion. Some of us have faith that we shall solve our dependence on fossil fuels by developing new technologies for hydrogen engines, wind energy, or solar energy. Some of us have faith that we shall solve our food problems with new or soon-to-be-developed genetically modified crops. Some of us have faith that new technologies will succeed in cleaning up the toxic materials in our air, water, soil, and foods without the horrendous cleanup expenses that we now incur.

6   Those with such faith assume that the new technologies will ultimately succeed, but in fact some of them may succeed and others may not. They assume that the new technologies will succeed quickly enough to make a big difference soon, but all of these major technological changes will actually take five to thirty years to develop and implement—if they catch on at all. Most of all, those with faith assume that new technology won't cause any new problems. In fact, technology merely constitutes increased power, which produces changes that can be either for the

better or for the worse. All of our current environmental problems are unanticipated harmful consequences of our existing technology. There is no basis for believing that technology will miraculously stop causing new and unanticipated problems while it is solving the problems that it previously produced.

7   The final misconception holds that environmentalists are fear-mongering, overreacting extremists whose predictions of impending disaster have been proved wrong before and will be proved wrong again. Behold, say the optimists: Water still flows from our faucets, the grass is still green, and the supermarkets are full of food. We are more prosperous than ever before, and that's the final proof that our system works.

8   Well, for a few billion of the world's people who are causing us increasing trouble, there isn't any clean water, there is less and less green grass, and there are no supermarkets full of food. To appreciate what the environmental problems of those billions of people mean for us Americans, compare the following two lists of countries. First ask some ivory-tower academic ecologist who knows a lot about the environment but never reads a newspaper and has no interest in politics to list the overseas countries facing some of the worst problems of environmental stress, overpopulation, or both. The ecologist would answer, "That's a no-brainer, it's obvious. Your list of environmentally stressed or overpopulated countries should surely include Afghanistan, Bangladesh, Burundi, Haiti, Indonesia, Iraq, Nepal, Pakistan, the Philippines, Rwanda, the Solomon Islands, and Somalia, plus others." Then ask a First World politician who knows nothing, and cares less, about the environment and population problems to list the world's worst trouble spots: countries where state government has already been overwhelmed and has collapsed, or is now at risk of collapsing, or has been wracked by recent civil wars; and countries that, as a result of their problems, are also creating problems for us rich First World countries, which may be deluged by illegal immigrants, or have to provide foreign aid to those countries, or may decide to provide them with military assistance to deal with rebellions and terrorists, or may even (God forbid) have to send in our own troops. The politician would answer, "That's a no-brainer, it's obvious. Your list of political trouble spots should surely include Afghanistan, Bangladesh, Burundi, Haiti, Indonesia, Iraq, Nepal, Pakistan, the Philippines, Rwanda, the Solomon Islands, and Somalia, plus others."

9   The connection between the two lists is transparent. Today, just as in the past, countries that are environmentally stressed, overpopulated or both are at risk of becoming politically stressed, and of seeing their governments collapse. When people are desperate and undernourished, they blame their government, which they see as responsible for failing to solve their problems. They try to emigrate at any cost. They start civil wars. They kill one another. They figure that they have nothing to lose, so they become terrorists, or they support or tolerate terrorism. The results are genocides such as the ones that already have exploded in Burundi, Indonesia, and Rwanda; civil wars, as in Afghanistan, Indonesia, Nepal, the Philippines, and the Solomon Islands; calls for the dispatch of First World troops, as to Afghanistan, Indonesia, Iraq, the Philippines, Rwanda, the Solomon Islands, and Somalia; the collapse of central government, as has already happened in Somalia; and overwhelming poverty, as in all of the countries on these lists.

10   But what about the United States? Some might argue that the environmental collapse of ancient societies is relevant to the modern decline of weak, far-off, overpopulated Rwanda and environmentally devastated Somalia, but isn't it ridiculous to suggest any possible relevance to the fate of our own society? After all, we might reason, those ancients didn't enjoy the wonders of modern environment-friendly technologies. Those ancients had the misfortune to suffer from the effects of climate change. They behaved stupidly and ruined their own environment by doing obviously dumb things, like cutting down their forests, watching their topsoil erode, and building cities in dry areas likely to run short of water. They had foolish leaders who didn't have books and so couldn't learn from history, and who embroiled them in destabilizing wars and didn't pay attention to problems at home. They were overwhelmed by desperate immigrants, as one society after another collapsed, sending floods of economic refugees to tax the resources of the societies that weren't collapsing. In all those respects, we modern Americans are fundamentally different from those primitive ancients, and there is nothing that we could learn from them.

11   Or so the argument goes. It's an argument so ingrained both in our subconscious and in public discourse that it has assumed the status of objective reality. We think we are different. In fact, of course, all of those powerful societies of the past thought that they too were unique, right up to the moment of their collapse. It's sobering to consider the swift decline of the ancient Maya, who 1,200 years ago were themselves the most advanced society in the Western Hemisphere, and who, like us now, were then at the apex of their own power and numbers. Two excellent recent books, David Webster's *The Fall of the Ancient Maya* and Richardson Gill's *The Great Maya Droughts,* help bring the trajectory of Maya civilization back to life for us. Their studies illustrate how even sophisticated societies like that of the Maya (and ours) can be undermined by details of rainfall, farming methods, and motives of leaders.

12   By now, millions of modern Americans have visited Maya ruins. To do so, one need only take a direct flight from the United States to the Yucatán capital of Mérida, jump into a rental car or minibus, and drive an hour on a paved highway. Most Maya ruins, with their great temples and monuments, lie surrounded by jungles (seasonal tropical forests), far from current human settlement. They are "pure" archaeological sites. That is, their locations became depopulated, so they were not covered up by later buildings as were so many other ancient cities, like the Aztec capital of Tenochtitlán—now buried under modern Mexico City—and Rome.

13   One of the reasons few people live there now is that the Maya homeland poses serious environmental challenges to would-be farmers. Although it has a somewhat unpredictable rainy season from May to October, it also has a dry season from January through April. Indeed, if one focuses on the dry months, one could describe the Yucatán as a "seasonal desert."

14   Complicating things, from a farmer's perspective, is that the part of the Yucatán with the most rain, the south, is also the part at the highest elevation above the water table. Most of the Yucatán consists of karst—a porous, spongelike, limestone

terrain—and so rain runs straight into the ground, leaving little or no surface water. The Maya in the lower-elevation regions of the north were able to reach the water table by way of deep sinkholes called cenotes, and the Maya in low coastal areas without sinkholes could reach it by digging wells up to 75 feet deep. Most Maya, however, lived in the south. How did they deal with their resulting water problem?

15 Technology provided an answer. The Maya plugged up leaks on karst promontories by plastering the bottoms of depressions to create reservoirs, which collected rain and stored it for use in the dry season. The reservoirs at the Maya city of Tikal, for example, held enough water to meet the needs of about 10,000 people for eighteen months. If a drought lasted longer than that, though, the inhabitants of Tikal were in deep trouble.

16 Maya farmers grew mostly corn, which constituted the astonishingly high proportion of about 70 percent of their diet, as deduced from isotope analyses of ancient Maya skeletons. They grew corn by means of a modified version of swidden slash-and-burn agriculture, in which forest is cleared, crops are grown in the resulting clearing for a few years until the soil is exhausted, and then the field is abandoned for fifteen to twenty years until regrowth of wild vegetation restores the soil's fertility. Because most of the land under a swidden agricultural system is fallow at any given time, it can support only modest population densities. Thus, it was a surprise for archaeologists to discover that ancient Maya population densities, judging from numbers of stone foundations of farmhouses, were often far higher than what unmodified swidden agriculture could support: often 250 to 750 people per square mile. The Maya probably achieved those high populations by such means as shortening the fallow period and tilling the soil to restore soil fertility, or omitting the fallow period entirely and growing crops every year, or, in especially moist areas, growing two crops per year.

17 Socially stratified societies, ours included, consist of farmers who produce food, plus nonfarmers such as bureaucrats and soldiers who do not produce food and are in effect parasites on farmers. The farmers must grow enough food to meet not only their own needs but also those of everybody else. The number of nonproducing consumers who can be supported depends on the society's agricultural productivity. In the United States today, with its highly efficient agriculture, farmers make up only 2 percent of our population, and each farmer can feed, on the average, 129 other people. Ancient Egyptian agriculture was efficient enough for an Egyptian peasant to produce five times the food required for himself and his family. But a Maya peasant could produce only twice the needs of himself and his family.

18 Fully 80 percent of Maya society consisted of peasants. Their inability to support many nonfarmers resulted from several limitations of their agriculture. It produced little protein, because corn has much lower protein content than wheat, and because the few edible domestic animals kept by the Maya (turkeys, ducks, and dogs) included no large animals like our cows and sheep. There was little use of terracing or irrigation to increase production. In the Maya area's humid climate, stored corn would rot or become infested after a year, so the Maya couldn't get through a longer drought by eating surplus corn accumulated in good years. And

unlike Old World peoples with their horses, oxen, donkeys, and camels, the Maya had no animal-powered transport. Indeed, the Maya lacked not only pack animals and animal-drawn plows but also metal tools, wheels, and boats with sails. All of those great Maya temples were built by stone and wooden tools and human muscle power alone, and all overland transport went on the backs of human porters.

19   Those limitations on food supply and food transport may in part explain why Maya society remained politically organized in small kingdoms that were perpetually at war with one another and that never became unified into large empires like the Aztec empire of the Valley of Mexico (fed by highly productive agriculture) or the Inca empire of the Andes (fed by diverse crops carried on llamas). Maya armies were small and unable to mount lengthy campaigns over long distances. The typical Maya kingdom held a population of only up to 50,000 people, within a radius of two or three days' walk from the king's palace. From the top of the temple of some Maya kingdoms, one could see the tops of the temples of other kingdoms.

20   Presiding over the temple was the king himself, who functioned both as head priest and as political leader. It was his responsibility to pray to the gods, to perform astronomical and calendrical rituals, to ensure the timely arrival of the rains on which agriculture depended, and thereby to bring prosperity. The king claimed to have the supernatural power to deliver those good things because of his asserted family relationship to the gods. Of course, that exposed him to the risk that his subjects would become disillusioned if he couldn't fulfill his boast of being able to deliver rains and prosperity.

21   Those are the basic outlines of Classic Maya society, which for all its limitations lasted more than 500 years. Indeed, the Maya themselves believed that it had lasted for much longer. Their remarkable Long Count calendar had its starting date (analogous to January 1, A.D. 1 of our calendar) backdated into the remote preliterate past, at August 11, 3114 B.C. The first physical evidence of civilization within the Maya area, in the form of villagers and pottery, appeared around 1400 B.C., substantial buildings around 500 B.C., and writing around 400 B.C. The so-called Classic period of Maya history arose around A.D. 250, when evidence for the first kings and dynasties emerged. From then, the Maya population increased almost exponentially, to reach peak numbers in the eighth century A.D. The largest monuments were erected toward the end of that century. All the indicators of a complex society declined throughout the ninth century, until the last date on any monument was A.D. 909. This decline of Maya population and architecture constitutes what is known as the Classic Maya collapse.

22   What happened? Let's consider in more detail a city whose ruins now lie in western Honduras at the world-famous site of Copán. The most fertile ground in the Copán area consists of five pockets of flat land along a river valley with a total area of only one square mile; the largest of those five pockets, known as the Copán pocket, has an area of half a square mile. Much of the land around Copán consists of steep hills with poor soil. Today, corn yields from valley-bottom fields are two or three times those of fields on hill slopes, which suffer rapid erosion and lose most of their productivity within a decade of farming.

23   To judge by the number of house sites, population growth in the Copán valley rose steeply from the fifth century up to a peak estimated at around 27,000 people between A.D. 750 and 900. Construction of royal monuments glorifying kings became especially massive from A.D. 650 onward. After A.D. 700, nobles other than kings got into the act and began erecting their own palaces, increasing the burden that the king and his own court already imposed on the peasants. The last big buildings at Copán were put up around A.D. 800; the last date on an incomplete altar possibly bearing a king's name is A.D. 822.

24   Archaeological surveys of different types of habitats in the Copán valley show that they were occupied in a regular sequence. The first area farmed was the large Copán pocket of bottomland, followed by occupation of the other four bottomland pockets. During that time the human population was growing, but the hills remained uninhabited. Hence that increased population must have been accommodated by intensifying production in the bottomland pockets: probably some combination of shorter fallow periods and double-cropping. By A.D. 500, people had started to settle the hill slopes, but those sites were occupied only briefly. The percentage of Copán's total population that was in the hills, rather than in the valleys, peaked in the year 575 and then declined, as the population again became concentrated in the pockets.

25   What caused that pullback of population from the hills? From excavation of building foundations on the valley floor we know that they became covered with sediment during the eighth century, meaning that the hill slopes were becoming eroded and probably also leached of nutrients. The acidic hill soils being carried down into the valley would have reduced agricultural yields. The reason for that erosion of the hillsides is clear: the forests that formerly covered them and protected their soil were being cut down. Dated pollen samples show that the pine forests originally covering the hilltops were eventually all cleared, to be burned for fuel. Besides causing sediment accumulation in the valleys and depriving valley inhabitants of wood supplies, that deforestation may have begun to cause a "man-made drought" in the valley bottom, because forests play a major role in water cycling, such that massive deforestation tends to result in lowered rainfall.

26   Hundreds of skeletons recovered from Copán archaeological sites have been studied for signs of disease and poor nutrition, such as porous bones and stress lines in the teeth. Those skeletal signs show that the health of Copán's inhabitants deteriorated from A.D. 650 to 850, among both the elite and commoners, though the health of commoners was worse.

27   Recall that Copán's population was growing rapidly while the hills were being occupied. The subsequent abandonment of all of those hill fields meant that the burden of feeding the extra population formerly dependent on the hills now fell increasingly on the valley floor, and that more and more people were competing for the food grown on that one square mile of bottomland. That would have led to fighting among the farmers themselves for the best land, or for any land, just as in modern Rwanda. Because the king was failing to deliver on his promises of rain and prosperity, he would have been the scapegoat for this agricultural failure, which explains why the last that we hear of any king is A.D. 822, and why the royal palace was burned around A.D. 850.

28   Datable pieces of obsidian, the sharp rock from which the Maya made their stone tools, suggest that Copán's total population decreased more gradually than did its signs of kings and nobles. The estimated population in the year A.D. 950 was still around 15,000, or 55 percent of the peak population of 27,000. That population continued to dwindle, until there are few signs of anyone in the Copán valley after around A.D. 1235. The reappearance of pollen from forest trees thereafter provides independent evidence that the valley became virtually empty of people.

29 The Maya history that I have just related, and Copán's history in particular, illustrate why we talk about "the Maya collapse." But the story grows more complicated, for at least five reasons. There was not only that enormous Classic collapse but also at least two smaller pre-Classic collapses, around A.D. 150 and 600, as well as some post-Classic collapses. The Classic collapse was obviously not complete, because hundreds of thousands of Maya survived, in areas with stable water supplies, to meet and fight the Spaniards. The collapse of population (as gauged by numbers of house sites and of obsidian tools) was in some cases much slower than the decline in numbers of Long Count dates. Many apparent collapses of cities were nothing more than "power cycling"; i.e., particular cities becoming more powerful at the expense of neighboring cities, then declining or getting conquered by neighbors, without changes in the whole population. Finally, cities in different parts of the Maya area rose and fell on different trajectories.

30   Some archaeologists focus on these complications and don't want to recognize a Classic Maya collapse at all. But this overlooks the obvious fact that cries out for explanation: the disappearance of between 90 and 99 percent of the Maya population after A.D. 800, and of the institution of the kingship, Long Count calendars, and other complex political and cultural institutions. Before we can understand those disappearances, however, we need first to understand the roles of warfare and of drought.

31   Archaeologists for a long time believed the ancient Maya to be gentle and peaceful people. We now know that Maya warfare was intense, chronic, and unresolvable, because limitations of food supply and transportation made it impossible for any Maya principality to unite the whole region in an empire. The archaeological record shows that wars became more intense and frequent toward the time of the Classic collapse. That evidence comes from discoveries of several types since the Second World War: archaeological excavations of massive fortifications surrounding many Maya sites; vivid depictions of warfare and captives on stone monuments and on the famous painted murals discovered in 1946 at Bonampak; and the decipherment of Maya writing, much of which proved to consist of royal inscriptions boasting of conquests. Maya kings fought to capture and torture one another; an unfortunate loser was a Copán king with the to us unforgettable name of King 18 Rabbit.

32   Maya warfare involved well-documented types of violence: wars among separate kingdoms; attempts of cities within a kingdom to secede by revolting against the capital; and civil wars resulting from frequent violent attempts by

would-be kings to usurp the throne. All of these events were described or depicted on monuments, because they involved kings and nobles. Not considered worthy of description, but probably even more frequent, were fights between commoners over land, as overpopulation became excessive and land became scarce.

33   The other phenomenon important to understanding all of these collapses is the repeated occurrence of droughts, as inferred by climatologists from evidence of lake evaporation preserved in lake sediments, and as summarized by Gill in *The Great Maya Droughts.* The rise of Maya civilization may have been facilitated by a rainy period beginning around 250 B.C., until a temporary drought after A.D. 125 was associated with a pre-Classic collapse at some sites. That collapse was followed by the resumption of rainy conditions and the buildup of Classic Maya cities, briefly interrupted by another drought around 600 corresponding to a decline at Tikal and some other sites. Finally, around A.D. 750 there began the worst drought in the past 7,000 years, peaking around the year A.D. 800, and suspiciously associated with the Classic collapse.

34   The area most affected by the Classic collapse was the southern highlands, probably for the two reasons already mentioned: It was the area with the densest population, and it also had the most severe water problems because it lay too high above the water table for cenotes or wells to provide water. The southern highlands lost more than 99 percent of its population in the course of the Classic collapse. When Cortés and his Spanish army marched in 1524 and 1525 through an area formerly inhabited by millions of Maya, he nearly starved because he encountered so few villagers from whom to acquire corn. The Spaniards passed within only a few miles of the abandoned ruins of the great Classic cities of Tikal and Palenque, but still they heard or saw nothing of them.

35 We can identify increasingly familiar strands in the Classic Maya collapse. One consisted of population growth outstripping available resources: the dilemma foreseen by Thomas Malthus in 1798. As Webster succinctly puts it in *The Fall of the Ancient Maya,* "Too many farmers grew too many crops on too much of the landscape." While population was increasing, the area of usable farmland paradoxically was decreasing from the effects of deforestation and hillside erosion.

36   The next strand consisted of increased fighting as more and more people fought over fewer resources. Maya warfare, already endemic, peaked just before the collapse. That is not surprising when one reflects that at least 5 million people, most of them farmers, were crammed into an area smaller than the state of Colorado. That's a high population by the standards of ancient farming societies, even if it wouldn't strike modern Manhattan-dwellers as crowded.

37   Bringing matters to a head was a drought that, although not the first one the Maya had been through, was the most severe. At the time of previous droughts, there were still uninhabited parts of the Maya landscape, and people in a drought area or dust bowl could save themselves by moving to another site. By the time of the Classic collapse, however, there was no useful unoccupied land in the vicinity on which to begin anew, and the whole population could not be accommodated in the few areas that continued to have reliable water supplies.

38   The final strand is political. Why did the kings and nobles not recognize and solve these problems? A major reason was that their attention was evidently focused on the short-term concerns of enriching themselves, waging wars, erecting monuments, competing with one another, and extracting enough food from the peasants to support all those activities. Like most leaders throughout human history, the Maya kings and nobles did not have the leisure to focus on long-term problems, insofar as they perceived them.

39   What about those same strands today? The United States is also at the peak of its power, and it is also suffering from many environmental problems. Most of us have become aware of more crowding and stress. Most of us living in large American cities are encountering increased commuting delays, because the number of people and hence of cars is increasing faster than the number of freeway lanes. I know plenty of people who in the abstract doubt that the world has a population problem, but almost all of those same people complain to me about crowding, space issues, and traffic experienced in their personal lives.

40   Many parts of the United States face locally severe problems of water restriction (especially southern California, Arizona, the Everglades, and, increasingly, the Northeast); forest fires resulting from logging and forest-management practices throughout the intermontane West; and losses of farmlands to salinization, drought, and climate change in the northern Great Plains. Many of us frequently experience problems of air quality, and some of us also experience problems of water quality and taste. We are losing economically valuable natural resources. We have already lost American chestnut trees, the Grand Banks cod fishery, and the Monterey sardine fishery; we are in the process of losing swordfish and tuna and Chesapeake Bay oysters and elm trees; and we are losing topsoil.

41   The list goes on: All of us are experiencing personal consequences of our national dependence on imported energy, which affects us not only through higher gas prices but also through the current contraction of the national economy, itself the partial result of political problems associated with our oil dependence. We are saddled with expensive toxic cleanups at many locations, most notoriously near Montana mines, on the Hudson River, and in the Chesapeake Bay. We also face expensive eradication problems resulting from hundreds of introduced pest species—including zebra mussels, Mediterranean fruit flies, Asian longhorn beetles, water hyacinth, and spotted knapweed—that now affect our agriculture, forests, waterways, and pastures.

42   These particular environmental problems, and many others, are enormously expensive in terms of resources lost, cleanup and restoration costs, and the cost of finding substitutes for lost resources: a billion dollars here, 10 billion there, in dozens and dozens of cases. Some of the problems, especially those of air quality and toxic substances, also exact health costs that are large, whether measured in dollars or in lost years or in quality of life. The cost of our home-grown environmental problems adds up to a large fraction of our gross national product, even without mentioning the costs that we incur from environmental problems overseas, such as the military operations that they inspire. Even the

mildest of bad scenarios for our future include a gradual economic decline, as happened to the Roman and British empires. Actually, in case you didn't notice it, our economic decline is already well under way. Just check the numbers for our national debt, yearly government budget deficit, unemployment statistics, and the value of your investment and pension funds.

43 The environmental problems of the United States are still modest compared with those of the rest of the world. But the problems of environmentally devastated, overpopulated, distant countries are now our problems as well. We are accustomed to thinking of globalization in terms of us rich, advanced First Worlders sending our good things, such as the Internet and Coca-Cola, to those poor backward Third Worlders. Globalization, however, means nothing more than improved worldwide communication and transportation, which can convey many things in either direction; it is not restricted to good things carried only from the First to the Third World. They in the Third World can now, intentionally or unintentionally, send us their bad things: terrorists; diseases such as AIDS, SARS, cholera, and West Nile fever, carried inadvertently by passengers on transcontinental airplanes; unstoppable numbers of immigrants, both legal and illegal, arriving by boat, truck, train, plane, and on foot; and other consequences of their Third World problems. We in the United States are no longer the isolated Fortress America to which some of us aspired in the 1930s; instead, we are tightly and irreversibly connected to overseas countries. The United States is the world's leading importer, and it is also the world's leading exporter. Our own society opted long ago to become interlocked with the rest of the world.

44   That's why political stability anywhere in the world now affects us, our trade routes, and our overseas markets and suppliers. We are so dependent on the rest of the world that if a decade ago you had asked a politician to name the countries most geopolitically irrelevant to U.S. interests because of their being so remote, poor, and weak, the list would have begun with Afghanistan and Somalia, yet these countries were subsequently considered important enough to warrant our dispatching U.S. troops. The Maya were "globalized" only within the Yucatán: the southern Yucatán Maya affected the northern Yucatán Maya and may have had some effects on the Valley of Mexico, but they had no contact with Somalia. That's because Maya transportation was slow, short-distance, on foot or else in canoes, and had low cargo capacity. Our transport today is much more rapid and has much higher cargo capacity. The Maya lived in a globalized Yucatán; we live in a globalized world.

45 If all of this reasoning seems straightforward when expressed so bluntly, one has to wonder: Why don't those in power today get the message? Why didn't the leaders of the Maya, Anasazi, and those other societies also recognize and solve their problems? What were the Maya thinking while they watched loggers clearing the last pine forests on the hills above Copán? Here, the past really is a useful guide to the present. It turns out that there are at least a dozen reasons why past societies failed to *anticipate* some problems before they developed, or failed to *perceive* problems that had already developed, or failed even to try to

solve problems that they did perceive. All of those dozen reasons still can be seen operating today. Let me mention just three of them.

46   First, it's difficult to recognize a slow trend in some quantity that fluctuates widely up and down anyway, such as seasonal temperature, annual rainfall, or economic indicators. That's surely why the Maya didn't recognize the oncoming drought until it was too late, given that rainfall in the Yucatán varies several-fold from year to year. Natural fluctuations also explain why it's only within the last few years that all climatologists have become convinced of the reality of climate change, and why our president still isn't convinced but thinks that we need more research to test for it.

47   Second, when a problem *is* recognized, those in power may not attempt to solve it because of a clash between their short-term interests and the interests of the rest of us. Pumping that oil, cutting down those trees, and catching those fish may benefit the elite by bringing them money or prestige and yet be bad for society as a whole (including the children of the elite) in the long run. Maya kings were consumed by immediate concerns for their prestige (requiring more and bigger temples) and their success in the next war (requiring more followers), rather than for the happiness of commoners or of the next generation. Those people with the greatest power to make decisions in our own society today regularly make money from activities that may be bad for society as a whole and for their own children; those decision-makers include Enron executives, many land developers, and advocates of tax cuts for the rich.

48   Finally, it's difficult for us to acknowledge the wisdom of policies that clash with strongly held values. For example, a belief in individual freedom and a distrust of big government are deeply ingrained in Americans, and they make sense under some circumstances and up to a certain point. But they also make it hard for us to accept big government's legitimate role in ensuring that each individual's freedom to maximize the value of his or her land holdings doesn't decrease the value of the collective land of all Americans.

49 Not all societies make fatal mistakes. There are parts of the world where societies have unfolded for thousands of years without any collapse, such as Java, Tonga, and (until 1945) Japan. Today, Germany and Japan are successfully managing their forests, which are even expanding in area rather than shrinking. The Alaskan salmon fishery and the Australian lobster fishery are being managed sustainably. The Dominican Republic, hardly a rich country, nevertheless has set aside a comprehensive system of protected areas encompassing most of the country's natural habitats.

50   Is there any secret to explain why some societies acquire good environmental sense while others don't? Naturally, part of the answer depends on accidents of individual leaders' wisdom (or lack thereof). But part also depends upon whether a society is organized so as to minimize built-in clashes of interest between its decision-making elites and its masses. Given how our society is organized, the executives of Enron, Tyco, and Adelphi correctly calculated that their own interests would be best promoted by looting the company coffers, and that they would probably get away with most of their loot. A good example of a

society that minimizes such clashes of interest is the Netherlands, whose citizens have perhaps the world's highest level of environmental awareness and of membership in environmental organizations. I never understood why, until on a recent trip to the Netherlands I posed the question to three of my Dutch friends while driving through their countryside.

51   Just look around you, they said. All of this farmland that you see lies below sea level. One fifth of the total area of the Netherlands is below sea level, as much as 22 feet below, because it used to be shallow bays, and we reclaimed it from the sea by surrounding the bays with dikes and then gradually pumping out the water. We call these reclaimed lands "polders." We began draining our polders nearly a thousand years ago. Today, we still have to keep pumping out the water that gradually seeps in. That's what our windmills used to be for, to drive the pumps to pump out the polders. Now we use steam, diesel, and electric pumps instead. In each polder there are lines of them, starting with those farthest from the sea, pumping the water in sequence until the last pump finally deposits it into a river or the ocean. And all of us, rich or poor, live down in the polders. It's not the case that rich people live safely up on top of the dikes while poor people live in the polder bottoms below sea level. If the dikes and pumps fail, we'll all drown together.

52   Throughout human history, all peoples have been connected to some other peoples, living together in virtual polders. For the ancient Maya, their polder consisted of most of the Yucatán and neighboring areas. When the Classic Maya cities collapsed in the southern Yucatán, refugees may have reached the northern Yucatán, but probably not the Valley of Mexico, and certainly not Florida. Today, our whole world has become one polder, such that events in even Afghanistan and Somalia affect Americans. We do indeed differ from the Maya, but not in ways we might like: We have a much larger population, we have more potent destructive technology, and we face the risk of a worldwide rather than a local decline. Fortunately, we also differ from the Maya in that we know their fate, and they did not. Perhaps we can learn.

Comprehension

1. Explain the significance of Shelley's poem "Ozymandias" for Diamond's essay.

2. What are the "three dangerous misconceptions" (paragraph 3) about the environment that Diamond discusses?

3. List all the civilizations that Diamond mentions in this essay. Which civilization does he emphasize? According to Diamond, why did previous civilizations fail, and how do these collapses provide guides to the state of contemporary American civilization?

Rhetorical Analysis

4. State Diamond's argument or major proposition. Where does his claim appear most clearly? What minor propositions does he develop? How does he deal with opposing viewpoints?

5. What types of evidence does the writer provide to support his claim?

6. Why does Diamond divide his essay into so many sections? What relationships do you detect between and among these sections?

7. Where does Diamond use comparison and contrast and causal analysis to organize parts of his essay? What is the significance or effect of these two techniques?

8. How does classification operate as a rhetorical element in this article?

9. Assess the relative effectiveness of Diamond's conclusion. How does the ending serve as a coda for the entire essay?

Writing

10. Write an essay focusing on a local environmental problem. Analyze the ways in which this environmental problem affects the lives of nearby residents.

11. Select one civilization that Diamond mentions. Conduct research on this civilization, and then write a report on the environmental factors that led to the decline of that society.

12. **Writing an Argument**   Write a persuasive essay in which you warn readers about three environmental dangers confronting the United States today.

Chapter Assessment

Rhetorical Analysis

Read the paragraph below from "What Can the Out-of-Doors Do for Our Children?" and answer the questions that follow.

It was not long ago that I sat with an old, old chief in Washington, and translated to him a few things that were in the Congressional Record. I came to the words, "raw material," and he said, "What do you mean by that?" I said, "Earth, and trees, and stones, uncut, unpolished, unground. That is what the white man calls raw material." He shook his head and he said: "There is only one raw material, and that is fresh air coming through rich sunshine. All things live on that; all things come from that, the animate and the inanimate—and inanimate things are animated by it."

From *Education: A Monthly Magazine*, Volume XLI, September, 1920-June, 1921. Frank Herbert Palmer, Editor. Boston: The Palmer Company. © 1921

1. In the passage's first sentence, the author
   A. Implies that government documents must be delivered in a manner that is understandable by all people—including those for whom English is not a native language.
   B. Suggests that his job in Washington was mainly as a translator.
   C. Establishes himself as familiar to the chief, and capable of fully speaking the chief's native language, thereby establishing his credibility.
   D. Provides an important example of the ongoing breakdown in communication between the national government and Native American governing bodies.
   E. Argues that national government does not take into consideration the wishes of indigenous people.

2. The chief claims, "There is only one raw material, and that is fresh air coming through rich sunshine. All things live on that; all things come from that, the animate and the inanimate—and inanimate things are animated by it." This can best be described rhetorically as which of the following?
   A. Metaphor
   B. Direct comparison
   C. Antithesis
   D. Allusion
   E. Paradox

Read the paragraphs below from "Children in the Woods" and answer the questions that follow.

When I was a child growing up in the San Fernando Valley in California, a trip into Los Angeles was special. The sensation of movement from a rural area into an urban one was sharp. On one of these charged occasions, walking down a sidewalk with my mother, I stopped suddenly, caught by a pattern of sunlight trapped in a spiraling imperfection in a windowpane. A stranger, an elderly woman in a cloth coat and a dark hat, spoke out spontaneously, saying how remarkable it is that children notice these things.

I have never forgotten the texture of this incident. Whenever I recall it I am moved not so much by any sense of my young self but by a sense of responsibility toward children, knowing how acutely I was affected in that moment by that woman's words. The effect, for all I know, has lasted a lifetime.

Reprinted by permission of SLL/Sterling Lord Literistic, Inc. Copyright by Barry Lopez.

3. In the context in which it appears, the word *texture* in the first line of the second paragraph most nearly means which of the following?
    A. Character
    B. Coarseness
    C. Balance
    D. Touch
    E. Roughness

4. Words such as *responsibility* and *affected* in the final paragraph imply which of the following about the author?
    A. He maintains a sense of obligation to care for all children around him and treating them with compassion and empathy.
    B. He has carried with him an abiding recognition for the role even small incidents play in shaping the life and self-image of a child.
    C. He has avoided interaction with children during his adult life in order to avoid negatively impacting them in an accidental way.
    D. He continues to distrust older women when they address him directly.
    E. He has a keen memory for minutiae.

Read the paragraphs below from "Why I Hunt" and answer the question that follows.

The people who have chosen to live in this remote valley—few phones, very little electricity, and long, dark winters—possess a hardness and a dreaminess both. They—we—can live a life of deprivation, and yet are willing to enter the comfort of daydreams and imagination. There is something mysterious happening here between the landscape and the people, a thing that stimulates our imagination, and causes many of us to set off deep into the woods in search of the unknown, and sustenance—not just metaphorical or spiritual sustenance, but the real thing.

Only about 5 percent of the nation and 15 to 20 percent of Montanans are hunters. But in this one valley, almost everyone is a hunter. It is not the peer pressure of the local culture that recruits us into hunting, nor even necessarily the economic boon of a few hundred pounds of meat in a cash-poor society. Rather, it is the terrain itself, and one's gradual integration into it, that summons the hunter. Nearly everyone who has lived here for any length of time has ended up—sometimes almost against one's conscious wishes—becoming a hunter. This wild and powerful landscape sculpts us like clay. I don't find such sculpting an affront to the human spirit, but instead, wonderful testimony to our pliability, our ability to adapt to a place.

Copyright © Rick Bass.

5. In context of this passage, *sustenance* most clearly suggests which of the following?
   A. Livelihood
   B. Subsistence
   C. Nourishment
   D. Game
   E. Maintenance

Read the paragraph below from "The Environmental Issue from Hell" and answer the question that follows.

When global warming first emerged as a potential crisis in the late 1980s, one academic analyst called it "the public policy problem from hell." The years since have only proven him more astute: Fifteen years into our understanding of climate change, we have yet to figure out how we're going to tackle it. And environmentalists are just as clueless as anyone else: Do we need to work on lifestyle or on lobbying, on photovoltaics or on politics? And is there a difference? How well we handle global warming will determine what kind of century we inhabit—and indeed what kind of planet we leave behind. The issue cuts close to home and also floats off easily into the abstract. So far it has been the ultimate "can't get there from here" problem, but the time has come to draw a road map—one that may help us deal with the handful of other issues on the list of real, world-shattering problems.

"The Environmental Issue from Hell" by Bill McKibben. This article originally appeared in *In These Times* magazine (April 30, 2001).

6. What is the effect of the multiple questions in the passage?
   A. Expands on the earlier claim that "we have yet to figure out how we're going to tackle it" by specifying questions that need to be answered
   B. Asks a series of rhetorical questions to instill a mood of hopelessness and frustration in the reader when faced with unanswerable questions
   C. Provides the reader with an agenda of potential topics to consider in finding an answer to the "public policy issue from hell"
   D. Demonstrates that not much improvement has occurred since the "crisis in the late 1980s"
   E. Highlights the logical and chronological issues associated with environmental policy

Read the paragraph below from "The Obligation to Endure" and answer the question that follows.

Another factor in the modern insect problem is one that must be viewed against a background of geologic and human history: the spreading of thousands of different kinds of organisms from their native homes to invade new territories. This worldwide migration has been studied and graphically described by the British ecologist Charles Elton in his recent book *The Ecology of Invasions*. During the Cretaceous Period, some hundred million years ago, flooding seas cut many land bridges between continents and living things found themselves confined in what Elton calls "colossal separate nature reserves." There, isolated from others of their kind, they developed many new species. When some of the land masses were joined again, about 15 million years ago, these species began to move out into new territories—a movement that is not only still in progress but is now receiving considerable assistance from man.

7. The author uses which of the following to develop ideas in the passage?
   A. An allusion to a literary work that provides a metaphorical connection between ideas
   B. An anecdote that relates key ideas through imagery
   C. An assertion followed by a series of counterarguments
   D. A claim that is supported by a series of facts cited by a noted expert
   E. A generalization that is narrowed by specific examples of that generalization

Chapter Assessment

Read the paragraphs below from "Am I Blue?" and answer the question that follows.

For about three years my companion and I rented a small house in the country that stood on the edge of a large meadow that appeared to run from the end of our deck straight into the mountains. The mountains, however, were quite far away, and between us and them there was, in fact, a town. It was one of the many pleasant aspects of the house that you never really were aware of this.

It was a house of many windows, low, wide, nearly floor to ceiling in the living room, which faced the meadow, and it was from one of these that I first saw our closest neighbor, a large white horse, cropping grass, flipping its mane, and ambling about—not over the entire meadow, which stretched well out of sight of the house, but over the five or so fenced-in acres that were next to the twenty-odd that we had rented. I soon learned that the horse, whose name was Blue, belonged to a man who lived in another town, but was boarded by our neighbors next door. Occasionally, one of the children, usually a stocky teenager, but sometimes a much younger girl or boy, could be seen riding Blue. They would appear in the meadow, climb up on his back, ride furiously for ten or fifteen minutes, then get off, slap Blue on the flanks, and not be seen again for a month or more.

8. The idea that the house is isolated is suggested by the author's suggestion of all of the following EXCEPT
    A. "Blue" is the "closest neighbor."
    B. "There was, in fact, a town."
    C. The horse is seen frequently without a human present.
    D. The meadow "stretched well out of sight of the house."
    E. "Blue" has access to both "the five or so fenced-in acres that were next to the twenty-odd that we had rented."

Read the paragraph below from "Two Views of the Mississippi" and answer the question that follows.

I stood like one bewitched. I drank it in, in a speechless rapture. The world was new to me, and I had never seen anything like this at home. But as I have said, a day came when I began to cease from noting the glories and the charms which the moon and the sun and the twilight wrought upon the river's face; another day came when I ceased altogether to note them. Then, if that sunset scene had been repeated, I should have looked upon it without rapture, and should have commented upon it, inwardly, after this fashion: "This sun means that we are going to have wind tomorrow; that floating log means that the river is rising, small thanks to it; that slanting mark on the water refers to a bluff reef which is going to kill somebody's steamboat one of these nights, if it keeps on stretching out like that; those tumbling 'boils' show a dissolving bar and a changing channel there; the lines and circles in the slick water over yonder are a warning that that troublesome place is shoaling up dangerously; that silver streak in the shadow of the forest is the 'break' from a new snag, and he has located himself in the very best place he could have found to fish for steamboats; that tall dead tree, with a single living branch, is not going to last long, and then how is a body ever going to get through this blind place at night without the friendly old landmark?"

From *Life on the Mississippi* by Mark Twain. Harper & Brothers Publishers, 1901.Copyright 1874 and 1875 by H.O. Houghton and Company.Copyright 1883 by Samuel L. Clemens. All rights reserved.

9. Words and phrases such as "bewitched" and "speechless rapture" suggest which of the following about the author's relationship with the river?
    A. He is essentially narcissistic in his relationship with the river.
    B. He is focused on his own internal reaction to the river and ignores those around him.
    C. The river is so loud that he is unable to speak above its roar.
    D. He finds it intimidating and even scary, which he indicates by invoking the idea of witchcraft.
    E. Initially, he is awed by the newfound beauty of the river.

Read the paragraph below from "The Last Americans: Environmental Collapse and the End of Civilization" and answer the question that follows.

Foremost among these misconceptions is that we must balance the environment against human needs. That reasoning is exactly upside-down. Human needs and a healthy environment are not opposing claims that must be balanced; instead, they are inexorably linked by chains of cause and effect. We need a healthy environment because we need clean water, clean air, wood, and food from the ocean, plus soil and sunlight to grow crops. We need functioning natural ecosystems, with their native species of earthworms, bees, plants, and microbes, to generate and aerate our soils, pollinate our crops, decompose our wastes, and produce our oxygen. We need to prevent toxic substances from accumulating in our water and air and soil. We need to prevent weeds, germs, and other pest species from becoming established in places where they aren't native and where they cause economic damage. Our strongest arguments for a healthy environment are selfish: We want it for ourselves, not for threatened species like snail darters, spotted owls, and Furbish louseworts.

10. In the paragraph, the author uses all of the following rhetorical strategies EXCEPT

    A. Paradoxical conclusion that ends in a different way than the reader would suggest.

    B. Parallel logical constructions.

    C. Repetition of a phrase.

    D. Anecdotal examples.

    E. Causal analysis.

Connections for Critical Thinking

1. Using support from the works of Eastman, Lopez, Carson, and others, write a causal-analysis essay tracing our relationship to the land. To what extent have history, greed, and fear helped shape our attitude? Can this attitude be changed? How?

2. Consider the empathy and sensitivity Walker has toward animals. How do her attitude and perceptions coincide with the views expressed by Bass and Eastman concerning the natural world?

3. Write a letter to the op-ed page of a newspaper objecting to a governmental ruling harmful to the environment. State the nature of the policy, its possible dangers, and your reasons for opposing it. Use support from McKibben, Diamond, and any other writers in this chapter. Extra reading or research may be necessary.

4. Consider why we fear nature. Why do we consider it an enemy, an alien, something to be destroyed? How would Walker, Lopez, and Eastman respond to this question? Do you agree or disagree with them?

5. Both Lopez and Diamond use narration and description to explore our relationship to the land. How do they approach their subject in terms of language, attitude, and style?

6. Choose an author in this chapter whose essay, in your opinion, romanticizes nature. Compare his or her attitude with that of a writer with a more pragmatic approach to the subject. Compare the two views, and specify the elements in their writing that contribute to the overall strength of their arguments.

7. Write an essay titled "Nature's Revenge" in which you examine the consequences of environmental abuse. Consider the short- as well as the long-term effects on the quality of life. Use support from any three writers in this chapter to defend your opinion.

8. Write specifically about our relationship to other living creatures on our planet. Is it one of exploitation, cooperation, or tyranny? How does this relationship influence how we treat each other? Explore the answers to these questions in an essay. Use the works of Eastman, Lopez, and Walker to support your thesis.

GMOs—Are They Good for the World or Not?

Genetically modified organisms (GMOs) are a hotly debated topic with strong opinions from those for and against the use of them. Are GMOs the safe answer for our world hunger problem, or are they just another politicized issue that benefits a select few? Critically read and analyze these sources, and answer the questions that follow.

▼ SOURCE A

"What Are the Benefits of Agricultural Biotechnology?"

—From U.S. Department of Agriculture, www.usda.gov

The application of biotechnology in agriculture has resulted in benefits to farmers, producers, and consumers. Biotechnology has helped to make both insect pest control and weed management safer and easier while safeguarding crops against disease. For example, genetically engineered insect-resistant cotton has allowed for a significant reduction in the use of persistent, synthetic pesticides that may contaminate groundwater and the environment.

In terms of improved weed control, herbicide-tolerant soybeans, cotton, and corn enable the use of reduced-risk herbicides that break down more quickly in soil and are non-toxic to wildlife and humans. Herbicide-tolerant crops are particularly compatible with no-till or reduced tillage agriculture systems that help preserve topsoil from erosion.

Agricultural biotechnology has been used to protect crops from devastating diseases. The papaya ringspot virus threatened to derail the Hawaiian papaya industry until papayas resistant to the disease were developed through genetic engineering. This saved the U.S. papaya industry. Research on potatoes, squash, tomatoes, and other crops continues in a similar manner to provide resistance to viral diseases that otherwise are very difficult to control. . . .

Biotech crops may provide enhanced quality traits such as increased levels of beta-carotene in rice to aid in reducing vitamin A deficiencies and improved oil compositions in canola, soybean, and corn. Crops with the ability to grow in salty soils or better withstand drought conditions are also in the works and the first such products are just entering the marketplace. Such innovations may be increasingly important in adapting to or in some cases helping to mitigate the effects of climate change.

The tools of agricultural biotechnology have been invaluable for researchers in helping to understand the basic biology of living organisms. For example, scientists have identified the complete genetic structure of several strains of Listeria and Campylobacter, the bacteria often responsible for major outbreaks of food-borne illness in people. This genetic information is providing a wealth of opportunities that help researchers improve the safety of our food supply. The tools of biotechnology have "unlocked doors" and are also helping in the development of improved animal and plant varieties, both those produced by conventional means as well as those produced through genetic engineering.

"Genetic Engineers Document Why GM Foods Are Dangerous" by Ken Roseboro

—Ken Roseboro, Editor, The Organic & Non-GMO Report

A new report, "GMO Myths and Truths," presents a large body of peer-reviewed scientific and other authoritative evidence of the hazards to health and the environment posed by genetically engineered crops and organisms.

Importantly, the initiative for the report came from two genetic engineers who believe there are good scientific reasons to be wary of GM foods and crops.

One of the report's authors, Dr. Michael Antoniou of King's College London School of Medicine in the UK, uses genetic engineering for medical applications but warns against its use in developing crops for human food and animal feed.

Dr. Antoniou said: "GM crops are promoted on the basis of ambitious claims—that they are safe to eat, environmentally beneficial, increase yields, reduce reliance on pesticides, and can help solve world hunger.

"Research studies show that genetically modified crops have harmful effects on laboratory animals in feeding trials and on the environment during cultivation. They have increased the use of pesticides and have failed to increase yields. Our report concludes that there are safer and more effective alternatives to meeting the world's food needs."

Another author of the report, Dr. John Fagan, is a former genetic engineer who in 1994 returned $614,000 in grant money to the National Institutes of Health due to concerns about the safety and ethics of the technology. He subsequently founded a GMO testing company.

Dr. Fagan said: "Crop genetic engineering as practiced today is a crude, imprecise, and outmoded technology. It can create unexpected toxins or allergens in foods and affect their nutritional value. Recent advances point to better ways of using our knowledge of genomics to improve food crops that do not involve GM.

"Over 75% of all GM crops are engineered to tolerate being sprayed with herbicide. This has led to the spread of herbicide-resistant superweeds and has resulted in massively increased exposure of farmers and communities to these toxic chemicals. Epidemiological studies suggest a link between herbicide use and birth defects and cancer."

▼ SOURCE C

Adoption of Genetically Engineered Crops in the United States, 1996–2017

—From "Recent Trends in GE Adoption." Economic Research Service, United States Department of Agriculture. https://www.ers.usda.gov/data-products/adoption-of-genetically-engineered-crops-in-the-us/recent-trends-in-ge-adoption/

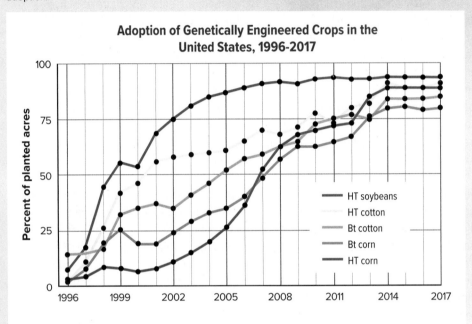

Note: Bt crops have insect-resistant traits; HT crops have herbicide-tolerance traits. Data for each crop category include varieties with both HT and Bt (stacked) traits.

Sources: USDA, Economic Research Service using data from Fernandez-Cornejo and McBride (2002) for the years 1996-99 and USDA, National Agricultural Statistics Service, *June Agricultural Survey* for the years 2000-17.

Herbicide-tolerant (HT) crops, which tolerate potent herbicides (such as glyphosate or glufosinate), provide farmers with a broad variety of options for effective weed control. Based on USDA survey data, the percent of domestic soybean acres planted with HT seeds rose from 17 percent in 1997 to 68 percent in 2001, before plateauing at 94 percent in 2014. HT cotton acreage expanded from approximately 10 percent in 1997 to 56 percent in 2001, before reaching a high of 91 percent in 2014. Adoption rates for HT corn grew relatively slowly immediately following the commercialization of GE seeds. However, adoption rates increased following the turn of the century. Currently, approximately 89 percent of domestic corn acres are produced with HT seeds.

Insect-resistant crops, which contain genes from the soil bacterium Bt (Bacillus thuringiensis) and produce insecticidal proteins, have been available for corn and cotton since 1996. Domestic Bt corn acreage grew from approximately 8 percent in 1997 to 19 percent in 2000, before climbing to 81 percent in 2015. Bt cotton acreage also expanded rapidly, from 15 percent of U.S. cotton acreage in 1997 to 37 percent in 2001. Currently, 85 percent of U.S. cotton acres are planted with genetically engineered, insect-resistant seeds.

"Avoiding GMOs Isn't Just Anti-Science. It's Immoral." by Mitch Daniels

Of the several claims of "anti-science" that clutter our national debates these days, none can be more flagrantly clear than the campaign against modern agricultural technology, most specifically the use of molecular techniques to create genetically modified organisms (GMOs). Here, there are no credibly conflicting studies, no arguments about the validity of computer models, no disruption of an ecosystem nor any adverse human health or even digestive problems, after 5 billion acres have been cultivated cumulatively and trillions of meals consumed.

And yet a concerted, deep-pockets campaign, as relentless as it is baseless, has persuaded a high percentage of Americans and Europeans to avoid GMO products, and to pay premium prices for "non-GMO" or "organic" foods that may in some cases be less safe and less nutritious. Thank goodness the toothpaste makers of the past weren't cowed so easily; the tubes would have said "No fluoride inside!" and we'd all have many more cavities.

This is the kind of foolishness that rich societies can afford to indulge. But when they attempt to inflict their superstitions on the poor and hungry peoples of the planet, the cost shifts from affordable to dangerous and the debate from scientific to moral.

. . . It's time to move the argument to a new plane. For the rich and well-fed to deny Africans, Asians or South Americans the benefits of modern technology is not merely anti-scientific. It's cruel, it's heartless, it's inhumane—and it ought to be confronted on moral grounds that ordinary citizens, including those who have been conned into preferring non-GMO Cheerios, can understand.

Travel to Africa with any of Purdue University's three recent World Food Prize winners, and you won't find the conversation dominated by anti-GMO protesters. There, where more than half of the coming population increase will occur, consumers and farmers alike are eager to share in the life-saving and life-enhancing advances that modern science alone can bring. Efforts to persuade them otherwise, or simply block their access to the next round of breakthroughs, are worse than anti-scientific. They're immoral.

▼ SOURCE E

"Genetic Roulette: The Documented Health Risks of Genetically Engineered Foods" by Jeffrey M. Smith

Lab animals tests with GM foods had stunted growth, impaired immune systems, bleeding stomachs, abnormal and potentially precancerous cell growth in the intestines, impaired blood cell development, misshapen cell structures in the liver, pancreas, and testicles, altered gene expression and cell metabolism, liver and kidney lesions, partially atrophied livers, inflamed kidneys, less developed brains and testicles, enlarged livers, pancreases, and intestines, reduced digestive enzymes, higher blood sugar, inflamed lung tissue, increased death rates, and higher offspring mortality. About two dozen farmers report that GM corn varieties caused their pigs or cows to become sterile, 71 shepherds say that 25% of their sheep died from grazing on Bt [from *Bacillus thuringiensis*] cotton plants, and others say that cows, water buffaloes, chickens, and horses also died from eating GM crops. Filipinos in at least five villages fell sick when nearby *Bt* corn was pollinating and hundreds of laborers in India report allergic reactions from handling *Bt* cotton. Soy allergies skyrocketed by 50% in the United Kingdom, soon after genetically engineered soy was introduced; and one human subject out of the few tested showed a skin prick allergic-type reaction to GM soy, but not to natural soy. In the 1980s, a GM food supplement killed about one hundred Americans and caused sickness and disability in another five to ten thousand people.

How do biotech companies deal with adverse reactions to their products? A cursory look at how Monsanto responded to adverse reactions from its toxic chemical PCBs (polychlorinated biphenyls) gives us some insight. In communication with the US Public Health Service, Monsanto claimed their experience "has been singularly free of difficulties." Their internal files obtained from a lawsuit, however, reveal that this was part of a cover-up and denial that lasted decades. Company memos referred to liver disease, skin problems, and even deaths in workers associated with exposure. Monsanto's medical department wanted to prohibit employees from eating at the factory because research showed that PCBs "were quite toxic materials by ingestion or inhalation." The US Navy refused the produce because in their safety study, all exposed animals died.

Genetically Modified Tomatoes

Jack Dykinga/USDA

Applying Your Synthesis Skills

Comprehension

1. Briefly summarize the stated or inferred arguments made in each source.

Rhetorical Analysis

2. Identify the emotion-laden diction in the titles of the sources. How do the titles create tone?

3. Compare the number of positive and negative words in Sources A, B, and E. How do the words support the purpose of each source?

4. Which sources use logos to support their arguments? Which sources use pathos? Provide examples.

5. Describe the visual rhetoric in Source F.

Writing an Argument

6. Using examples from at least three of the sources, write an essay explaining who—in your opinion—benefits the most from the production of GMO plants.

PART

3

AP FAVORITES

CHAPTERS AT A GLANCE

CHAPTER **11**

Favorite Essays

In a survey of several hundred AP teachers across the nation, leaders in their field were asked what their five favorite pieces to teach in class were. The most popular responses were the group of selections here. The vast majority of teachers listed these offerings, stating that these selections best represent the AP program. These pieces range across time periods, geographical areas, and genres—and highlight the art of voice.

Contents

Graduation

Maya Angelou

Maya Angelou (1928–2014) was a celebrated poet, speaker, and writer. Born Marguerite Johnson in St. Louis, Missouri, Angelou spent much of her childhood in rural, racially segregated Stamps, Arkansas. She wrote eloquently about this and other periods of her life in a series of autobiographical books. Angelou had many careers before discovering her niche as an author and a poet, including four years living and working in Ghana—a country on the west coast of Africa. She gave an inspirational reading of her poem "On the Pulse of Morning" at President Bill Clinton's first inauguration in January 1993. Angelou's "Graduation," the twenty-third chapter in her renowned book *I Know Why the Caged Bird Sings*, discusses her 8th grade graduation in Stamps, Arkansas. Angelou came a long way from the little girl in the segregationist South, innocently and eagerly awaiting that 8th grade graduation.

1   The children in Stamps trembled visibly with anticipation. Some adults were excited too, but to be certain the whole young population had come down with graduation epidemic. Large classes were graduating from both the grammar school and the high school. Even those who were years removed from their own day of glorious release were anxious to help with preparations as a kind of dry run. The junior students who were moving into the vacating classes' chairs were tradition-bound to show their talents for leadership and management. They strutted through the school and around the campus exerting pressure on the lower grades. Their authority was so new that occasionally if they pressed a little too hard it had to be overlooked. After all, next term was coming, and it never hurt a sixth grader to have a play sister in the eighth grade, or a tenth-year student to be able to call a twelfth grader Bubba. So all was endured in a spirit of shared understanding. But the graduating classes themselves were the nobility. Like travelers with exotic destinations on their minds, the graduates were remarkably forgetful. They came to school without their books, or tablets or even pencils. Volunteers fell over themselves to secure replacements for the missing equipment. When accepted, the willing workers might or might not be thanked, and it was of no importance to the pregraduation rites. Even teachers were respectful of the now quiet and aging seniors, and tended to speak to them, if not as equals, as beings only slightly lower than themselves. After tests were returned and grades given, the student body, which acted like an extended family, knew who did well, who excelled, and what piteous ones had failed.

2   Unlike the white high school, Lafayette County Training School distinguished itself by having neither lawn, nor hedges, nor tennis court, nor climbing ivy. Its two buildings (main classrooms, the grade school and home economics) were set on a dirt hill with no fence to limit either its boundaries or those of bordering farms. There was a large expanse to the left of the school which was used

alternately as a baseball diamond or basketball court. Rusty hoops on swaying poles represented the permanent recreational equipment, although bats and balls could be borrowed from the P.E. teacher if the borrower was qualified and if the diamond wasn't occupied.

3   Over this rocky area relieved by a few shady tall persimmon trees the graduating class walked. The girls often held hands and no longer bothered to speak to the lower students. There was a sadness about them, as if this old world was not their home and they were bound for higher ground. The boys, on the other hand, had become more friendly, more outgoing. A decided change from the closed attitude they projected while studying for finals. Now they seemed not ready to give up the old school, the familiar paths and classrooms. Only a small percentage would be continuing on to college—one of the South's A & M (agricultural and mechanical) schools, which trained Negro youths to be carpenters, farmers, handymen, masons, maids, cooks and baby nurses. Their future rode heavily on their shoulders, and blinded them to the collective joy that had pervaded the lives of the boys and girls in the grammar school graduating class.

4   Parents who could afford it had ordered new shoes and readymade clothes for themselves from Sears and Roebuck or Montgomery Ward. They also engaged the best seamstresses to make the floating graduating dresses and to cut down secondhand pants which would be pressed to a military slickness for the important event.

5   Oh, it was important, all right. Whitefolks would attend the ceremony, and two or three would speak of God and home, and the Southern way of life, and Mrs. Parsons, the principal's wife, would play the graduation march while the lower grade graduates paraded down the aisles and took their seats below the platform. The high school seniors would wait in empty classrooms to make their dramatic entrance.

6   In the Store I was the person of the moment. The birthday girl. The center. Bailey had graduated the year before, although to do so he had had to forfeit all pleasures to make up for his time lost in Baton Rouge.

7   My class was wearing butter-yellow piqué dresses, and Momma launched out on mine. She smocked the yoke into tiny crisscrossing puckers, then shirred the rest of the bodice. Her dark fingers ducked in and out of the lemony cloth as she embroidered raised daisies around the hem. Before she considered herself finished she had added a crocheted cuff on the puff sleeves, and a pointy crocheted collar.

8   I was going to be lovely. A walking model of all the various styles of fine hand sewing and it didn't worry me that I was only twelve years old and merely graduating from the eighth grade. Besides, many teachers in Arkansas Negro schools had only that diploma and were licensed to impart wisdom.

9   The days had become longer and more noticeable. The faded beige of former times had been replaced with strong and sure colors. I began to see my classmates' clothes, their skin tones, and the dust that waved off pussy willows. Clouds that lazed across the sky were objects of great concern to me. Their shiftier shapes might have held a message that in my new happiness and with a little bit of time I'd soon decipher. During that period I looked at the arch of

heaven so religiously my neck kept a steady ache. I had taken to smiling more often, and my jaws hurt from the unaccustomed activity. Between the two physical sore spots, I suppose I could have been uncomfortable, but that was not the case. As a member of the winning team (the graduating class of 1940) I had outdistanced unpleasant sensations by miles. I was headed for the freedom of open fields.

10   Youth and social approval allied themselves with me and we trammeled memories of slights and insults. The wind of our swift passage remodeled my features. Lost tears were pounded to mud and then to dust. Years of withdrawal were brushed aside and left behind, as hanging ropes of parasitic moss.

11   My work alone had awarded me a top place and I was going to be one of the first called in the graduating ceremonies. On the classroom blackboard, as well as on the bulletin board in the auditorium, there were blue stars and white stars and red stars. No absences, no tardinesses, and my academic work was among the best of the year. I could say the preamble to the Constitution even faster than Bailey. We timed ourselves often: "WethepeopleoftheUnitedStatesinordertoformamoreperfectunion . . ." I had memorized the Presidents of the United States from Washington to Roosevelt in chronological as well as alphabetical order.

12   My hair pleased me too. Gradually the black mass had lengthened and thickened, so that it kept at last to its braided pattern, and I didn't have to yank my scalp off when I tried to comb it.

13   Louise and I had rehearsed the exercises until we tired out ourselves. Henry Reed was class valedictorian. He was a small, very black boy with hooded eyes, a long, broad nose and an oddly shaped head. I had admired him for years because each term he and I vied for the best grades in our class. Most often he bested me, but instead of being disappointed I was pleased that we shared top places between us. Like many Southern Black children, he lived with his grandmother, who was as strict as Momma and as kind as she knew how to be. He was courteous, respectful and softspoken to elders, but on the playground he chose to play the roughest games. I admired him. Anyone, I reckoned, sufficiently afraid or sufficiently dull could be polite. But to be able to operate at a top level with both adults and children was admirable.

14   His valedictory speech was entitled "To Be or Not to Be." The rigid tenth-grade teacher had helped him write it. He'd been working on the dramatic stresses for months.

15   The weeks until graduation were filled with heady activities. A group of small children were to be presented in a play about buttercups and daisies and bunny rabbits. They could be heard throughout the building practicing their hops and their little songs that sounded like silver bells. The older girls (nongraduates, of course) were assigned the task of making refreshments for the night's festivities. A tangy scent of ginger, cinnamon, nutmeg and chocolate wafted around the home economics building as the budding cooks made samples for themselves and their teachers.

16   In every corner of the workshop, axes and saws split fresh timber as the woodshop boys made sets and stage scenery. Only the graduates were left out of

the general bustle. We were free to sit in the library at the back of the building or look in quite detachedly, naturally, on the measures being taken for our event.

17   Even the minister preached on graduation the Sunday before. His subject was, "Let your light so shine that men will see your good works and praise your Father, Who is in Heaven." Although the sermon was purported to be addressed to us, he used the occasion to speak to backsliders, gamblers and general ne'er-do-wells. But since he had called our names at the beginning of the service we were mollified.

18   Among Negroes the tradition was to give presents to children going only from one grade to another. How much more important this was when the person was graduating at the top of the class. Uncle Willie and Momma had sent away for a Mickey Mouse watch like Bailey's. Louise gave me four embroidered handkerchiefs. (I gave her crocheted doilies.) Mrs. Sneed, the minister's wife, made me an undershirt to wear for graduation, and nearly every customer gave me a nickel or maybe even a dime with the instruction "Keep on moving to higher ground," or some such encouragement.

19   Amazingly the great day finally dawned and I was out of bed before I knew it. I threw open the back door to see it more clearly, but Momma said, "Sister, come away from that door and put your robe on."

20   I hoped the memory of that morning would never leave me. Sunlight was itself young, and the day had none of the insistence maturity would bring it in a few hours. In my robe and barefoot in the backyard, under cover of going to see about my new beans, I gave myself up to the gentle warmth and thanked God that no matter what evil I had done in my life He had allowed me to live to see this day. Somewhere in my fatalism I had expected to die, accidentally, and never have the chance to walk up the stairs in the auditorium and gracefully receive my hard-earned diploma. Out of God's merciful bosom I had won reprieve.

21   Bailey came out in his robe and gave me a box wrapped in Christmas paper. He said he had saved his money for months to pay for it. It felt like a box of chocolates, but I knew Bailey wouldn't save money to buy candy when we had all we could want under our noses.

22   He was as proud of the gift as I. It was a soft-leather-bound copy of a collection of poems by Edgar Allan Poe, or, as Bailey and I called him, "Eap." I turned to "Annabel Lee" and we walked up and down the garden rows, the cool dirt between our toes, reciting the beautifully sad lines.

23   Momma made a Sunday breakfast although it was only Friday. After we finished the blessing, I opened my eyes to find the watch on my plate. It was a dream of a day. Everything went smoothly and to my credit, I didn't have to be reminded or scolded for anything. Near evening I was too jittery to attend to chores, so Bailey volunteered to do all before his bath.

24   Days before, we had made a sign for the Store, and as we turned out the lights Momma hung the cardboard over the doorknob. It read clearly: CLOSED. GRADUATION.

25   My dress fitted perfectly and everyone said that I looked like a sunbeam in it. On the hill, going toward the school, Bailey walked behind with Uncle Willie, who muttered, "Go on, Ju." He wanted him to walk ahead with us because it

embarrassed him to have to walk so slowly. Bailey said he'd let the ladies walk together, and the men would bring up the rear. We all laughed, nicely.

26   Little children dashed by out of the dark like fireflies. Their crepe-paper dresses and butterfly wings were not made for running and we heard more than one rip, dryly, and the regretful "uh uh" that followed.

27   The school blazed without gaiety. The windows seemed cold and unfriendly from the lower hill. A sense of ill-fated timing crept over me, and if Momma hadn't reached for my hand I would have drifted back to Bailey and Uncle Willie, and possibly beyond. She made a few slow jokes about my feet getting cold, and tugged me along to the now-strange building.

28   Around the front steps, assurance came back. There were my fellow "greats," the graduating class. Hair brushed back, legs oiled, new dresses and pressed pleats, fresh pocket handkerchiefs and little handbags, all homesewn. Oh, we were up to snuff, all right. I joined my comrades and didn't even see my family go in to find seats in the crowded auditorium.

29   The school band struck up a march and all classes filed in as had been rehearsed. We stood in front of our seats, as assigned, and on a signal from the choir director, we sat. No sooner had this been accomplished than the band started to play the national anthem. We rose again and sang the song, after which we recited the pledge of allegiance. We remained standing for a brief minute before the choir director and principal signaled to us, rather desperately I thought, to take our seats. The command was so unusual that our carefully rehearsed and smooth-running machine was thrown off. For a full minute we fumbled for our chairs and bumped into each other awkwardly. Habits change or solidify under pressure, so in our state of nervous tension we had been ready to follow our usual assembly pattern: the American national anthem, then the pledge of allegiance, then the song every Black person I knew called the Negro National Anthem. All done in the same key, with the same passion and most often standing on the same foot.

30   Finding my seat at last, I was overcome with a presentiment of worse things to come. Something unrehearsed, unplanned, was going to happen, and we were going to be made to look bad. I distinctly remember being explicit in the choice of pronoun. It was "we," the graduating class, the unit, that concerned me then.

31   The principal welcomed "parents and friends" and asked the Baptist minister to lead us in prayer. His invocation was brief and punchy, and for a second I thought we were getting on the high road to right action. When the principal came back to the dais, however, his voice had changed. Sounds always affected me profoundly and the principal's voice was one of my favorites. During assembly it melted and lowed weakly into the audience. It had not been in my plan to listen to him, but my curiosity was piqued and I straightened up to give him my attention.

32   He was talking about Booker T. Washington, our "late great leader," who said we can be as close as the fingers on the hand, etc. . . . . Then he said a few vague things about friendship and the friendship of kindly people to those less fortunate than themselves. With that his voice nearly faded, thin, away. Like a river diminishing to a stream and then to a trickle. But he cleared his throat and said, "Our speaker tonight, who is also our friend, came from Texarkana to deliver the

commencement address, but due to the irregularity of the train schedule, he's going to, as they say, 'speak and run.'" He said that we understood and wanted the man to know that we were most grateful for the time he was able to give us and then something about how we were willing always to adjust to another's program, and without more ado—"I give you Mr. Edward Donleavy."

33   Not one but two white men came through the door off-stage. The shorter one walked to the speaker's platform, and the tall one moved to the center seat and sat down. But that was our principal's seat, and already occupied. The dislodged gentleman bounced around for a long breath or two before the Baptist minister gave him his chair, then with more dignity than the situation deserved, the minister walked off the stage.

34   Donleavy looked at the audience once (on reflection, I'm sure that he wanted only to reassure himself that we were really there), adjusted his glasses and began to read from a sheaf of papers.

35   He was glad "to be here and to see the work going on just as it was in the other schools."

36   At the first "Amen" from the audience I willed the offender to immediate death by choking on the word. But Amens and Yes sir's began to fall around the room like rain through a ragged umbrella.

37   He told us of the wonderful changes we children in Stamps had in store. The Central School (naturally, the white school was Central) had already been granted improvements that would be in use in the fall. A well-known artist was coming from Little Rock to teach art to them. They were going to have the newest microscopes and chemistry equipment for their laboratory. Mr. Donleavy didn't leave us long in the dark over who made these improvements available to Central High. Nor were we to be ignored in the general betterment scheme he had in mind.

38   He said that he had pointed out to people at a very high level that one of the first-line football tacklers at Arkansas Agricultural and Mechanical College had graduated from good old Lafayette County Training School. Here fewer Amen's were heard. Those few that did break through lay dully in the air with the heaviness of habit.

39   He went on to praise us. He went on to say how he had bragged that "one of the best basketball players at Fisk sank his first ball right here at Lafayette County Training School."

40   The white kids were going to have a chance to become Galileos and Madame Curies and Edisons and Gauguins, and our boys (the girls weren't even in on it) would try to be Jesse Owenses and Joe Louises.

41   Owens and the Brown Bomber were great heroes in our world, but what school official in the white-goddom of Little Rock had the right to decide that those two men must be our only heroes? Who decided that for Henry Reed to become a scientist he had to work like George Washington Carver, as a bootblack, to buy a lousy microscope? Bailey was obviously always going to be too small to be an athlete, so which concrete angel glued to what country seat had decided that if my brother wanted to become a lawyer he had to first pay penance for his skin by picking cotton and hoeing corn and studying correspondence books at night for twenty years?

42   The man's dead words fell like bricks around the auditorium and too many settled in my belly. Constrained by hard-learned manners I couldn't look behind me, but to my left and right the proud graduating class of 1940 had dropped their heads. Every girl in my row had found something new to do with her handkerchief. Some folded the tiny squares into love knots, some into triangles, but most were wadding them, then pressing them flat on their yellow laps.

43   On the dais, the ancient tragedy was being replayed. Professor Parsons sat, a sculptor's reject, rigid. His large, heavy body seemed devoid of will or willingness, and his eyes said he was no longer with us. The other teachers examined the flag (which was draped stage right) or their notes, or the windows which opened on our now-famous playing diamond.

44   Graduation, the hush-hush magic time of frills and fits and congratulations and diplomas, was finished for me before my name was called. The accomplishment was nothing. The meticulous maps, drawn in three colors of ink, learning and spelling decasyllabic words, memorizing the whole of *The Rape of Lucrece*—it was for nothing. Donleavy had exposed us.

45   We were maids and farmers, handymen and washerwomen, and anything higher that we aspired to was farcical and presumptuous.

46   Then I wished that Gabriel Prosser and Nat Turner had killed all whitefolks in their beds and that Abraham Lincoln had been assassinated before the signing of the Emancipation Proclamation, and that Harriet Tubman had been killed by that blow on her head and Christopher Columbus had drowned in the *Santa Maria*.

47   It was awful to be a Negro and have no control over my life. It was brutal to be young and already trained to sit quietly and listen to charges brought against my color with no chance of defense. We should all be dead. I thought I should like to see us all dead, one on top of the other. A pyramid of flesh with the whitefolks on the bottom, as the broad base, then the Indians with their silly tomahawks and teepees and wigwams and treaties, the Negroes with the mops and recipes and cotton sacks and spirituals sticking out of their mouths. The Dutch children should all stumble in their wooden shoes and break their necks. The French should choke to death on the Louisiana Purchase (1803) while silkworms ate all the Chinese with their stupid pigtails. As a species, we were an abomination. All of us.

48   Donleavy was running for election, and assured our parents that if he won we could count on having the only colored paved playing field in that part of Arkansas. Also—he never looked up to acknowledge the grunts of acceptance— also, we were bound to get some new equipment for the home economics building and the workshop.

49   He finished, and since there was no need to give any more than the most perfunctory thank-you's, he nodded to the men on the stage, and the tall white man who was never introduced joined him at the door. They left with the attitude that now they were off to something really important. (The graduation ceremonies at Lafayette County Training School had been a mere preliminary.)

50   The ugliness they left was palpable. An uninvited guest who wouldn't leave. The choir was summoned and sang a modern arrangement of "Onward, Christian Soldiers," with new words pertaining to graduates seeking their place in the world. But it didn't work. Elouise, the daughter of the Baptist minister, recited

"Invictus," and I could have cried at the impertinence of "I am the master of my fate, I am the captain of my soul."

51   My name had lost its ring of familiarity and I had to be nudged to go and receive my diploma. All my preparations had fled. I neither marched up to the stage like a conquering Amazon, nor did I look in the audience for Bailey's nod of approval. Marguerite Johnson, I heard the name again, my honors were read, there were noises in the audience of appreciation, and I took my place on the stage as rehearsed.

52   I thought about colors I hated: ecru, puce, lavender, beige and black.

53   There was shuffling and rustling around me, then Henry Reed was giving his valedictory address, "To Be or Not to Be." Hadn't he heard the whitefolks? We couldn't *be*, so the question was a waste of time. Henry's voice came out clear and strong. I feared to look at him. Hadn't he got the message? There was no "nobler in the mind" for Negroes because the world didn't think we had minds, and they let us know it. "Outrageous fortune?" Now, that was a joke. When the ceremony was over I had to tell Henry Reed some things. That is, if I still cared. Not "rub," Henry, "erase.'" "Ah, there's the erase.'" Us.

54   Henry had been a good student in elocution. His voice rose on tides of promise and fell on waves of warnings. The English teacher had helped him to create a sermon winging through Hamlet's soliloquy. To be a man, a doer, a builder, a leader, or to be a tool, an unfunny joke, a crusher of funky toadstools. I marveled that Henry could go through with the speech as if we had a choice.

55   I had been listening and silently rebutting each sentence with my eyes closed; then there was a hush, which in an audience warns that something unplanned is happening. I looked up and saw Henry Reed, the conservative, the proper, the A student, turn his back to the audience and turn to us (the proud graduating class of 1940) and sing, nearly speaking,

"Lift ev'ry voice and sing
Till earth and heaven ring
Ring with the harmonies of Liberty . . ."

56   It was the poem written by James Weldon Johnson. It was the music composed by J. Rosamond Johnson. It was the Negro national anthem. Out of habit we were singing it.

57   Our mothers and fathers stood in the dark hall and joined the hymn of encouragement. A kindergarten teacher led the small children onto the stage and the buttercups and daisies and bunny rabbits marked time and tried to follow:

"Stony the road we trod
Bitter the chastening rod
Felt in the days when hope, unborn, had died.
Yet with a steady beat
Have not our weary feet
Come to the place for which our fathers sighed?"

58   Each child I knew had learned that song with his ABC's and along with "Jesus Loves Me This I Know." But I personally had never heard it before. Never heard the words, despite the thousands of times I had sung them. Never thought they had anything to do with me.

59   On the other hand, the words of Patrick Henry had made such an impression on me that I had been able to stretch myself tall and trembling and say, "I know not what course others may take, but as for me, give me liberty or give me death."

60   And now I heard, really for the first time:

"We have come over a way that with tears
has been watered,
We have come, treading our path through
The blood of the slaughtered."

61   While echoes of the song shivered in their air, Henry Reed bowed his head, said "Thank you," and returned to his place in the line. The tears that slipped down many faces were not wiped away in shame.

62   We were on top again. As always, again. We survived. The depths had been icy and dark, but now a bright sun spoke to our souls. I was no longer simply a member of the proud graduating class of 1940; I was a proud member of the wonderful, beautiful Negro race.

63   Oh, Black known and unknown poets, how often have your auctioned pains sustained us? Who will compute the lonely nights made less lonely by your songs, or the empty pots made less tragic by your tales?

64   If we were a people much given to revealing secrets, we might raise monuments and sacrifice to the memories of our poets, but slavery cured us of that weakness. It may be enough, however, to have it said that we survive in exact relationship to the dedication of our poets (include preachers, musicians and blues singers).

1. What is the significance of the title?

2. The graduation speaker, Mr. Edward Donleavy, praises recent graduates for their achievements. How do these achievements differ from the narrator's hopes for herself and her classmates?

3. Why does the narrator initially admire Henry Reed? How does he come through for the community at the end?

Rhetorical Analysis

4. Look at the images in paragraph 47 and describe their effect on the narrator's feelings at the moment.

5. What are some of the details concerning dress in "Graduation" that give it a culturally historical feel? How does dress show Angelou's family's community status?

6. Explain the significance of the last two paragraphs on the overall effect of the essay.

7. What is the purpose of intertwining objective and subjective narration in this essay? How does it change the effect of the essay?

8. What effects foreshadow Mr. Donleavy's speech?

9. Why was the graduation's response to the speaker, described in paragraph 36, like "rain through a ragged umbrella"?

Writing

10. Describe a time when an anticipated event did not turn out as planned. Express the emotions connected with the anticipated and actual event.

11. Do a Google search of Stamps, Arkansas, along with additional research, then compare and contrast its current circumstances with the circumstances of Angelou's day.

12. **Writing an Argument**   Write a response to Mr. Donleavy about his speech from the perspective of Henry Reed.

Of Revenge

Francis Bacon

Francis Bacon (1561–1626), an English statesman and philosopher, is also known as a founder of a new scientific method. Bacon was afforded a fine academic career due to his family's economic and political standing. He entered Trinity College at Cambridge at age 12, completing his studies there in December 1575. He then enrolled in a law program at the Honourable Society of Gray's Inn. Through the following years, Bacon worked his way up in politics, law, and the royal court. In 1618 he was named Lord Chancellor—the highest honor in the British legal profession—and took the title Viscount St. Albans. Yet in 1621 Bacon was convicted of taking bribes to support his extravagant lifestyle. After resigning in disgrace, he pursued his scholarly interests. Bacon contributed to such fields as philosophy, biology, physics, chemistry, and architecture. He wrote a digest of British laws, a history of Great Britain, and biographies of Tudor monarchs. As one of the developers of the modern scientific method, Bacon introduced many concepts and methods used today, such as observation, hypothesis, and inductive reasoning. "Of Revenge" and "Of Studies" come from a book of ten essays published in 1597, the first such book to become popular in England. In his essays, Bacon offered advice about how to get ahead in life.

Revenge is a kind of wild justice, which the more man's nature runs to, the more ought law to weed it out; for as for the first wrong, it doth but offend the law, but the revenge of that wrong, putteth the law out of office. Certainly, in taking revenge, a man is but even with his enemy, but in passing it over, he is
5   superior; for it is a prince's part to pardon; and Solomon, I am sure, saith, "It is the glory of a man to pass by an offence." That which is past is gone and irrevocable, and wise men have enough to do with things present and to come; therefore they do but trifle with themselves that labor in past matters. There is no man doth a wrong for the wrong's sake, but thereby to purchase himself profit, or
10 pleasure, or honor, or the like; therefore, why should I be angry with a man for loving himself better than me? And if any man should do wrong merely out of ill-nature, why, yet it is but like the thorn or briar, which prick and scratch, because they can do no other. The most tolerable sort of revenge is for those wrongs which there is no law to remedy; but then, let a man take heed the revenge be such as
15 there is no law to punish, else a man's enemy is still beforehand, and it is two for one. Some, when they take revenge, are desirous the party should know whence it cometh. This is the more generous; for the delight seemeth to be not so much in doing the hurt as in making the party repent; but base and crafty cowards are like the arrow that flieth in the dark. Cosmus, Duke of Florence[1], had a desperate

---

[1] He alludes to Cosmo de Medici, or Cosmo I., chief of the Republic of Florence, the encourager of literature and the fine arts.

20 saying against perfidious or neglecting friends, as if those wrongs were unpardonable. "You shall read," saith he, "that we are commanded to forgive our enemies; but you never read that we are commanded to forgive our friends." But yet the spirit of Job was in a better tune: "Shall we," saith he, "take good at God's hands, and not be content to take evil also?"[2] and so of friends in a proportion.

25 This is certain, that a man that studieth revenge keeps his own wounds green, which otherwise would heal and do well. Public revenges[3] are for the most part fortunate; as that for the death of Cæsar;[4] for the death of Pertinax; for the death of Henry the Third of France;[5] and many more. But in private revenges it is not so; nay, rather, vindictive persons live the life of witches, who, as they are 30 mischievous, so end they unfortunate.

"Of Revenge" by Francis Bacon, 1625. From *Bacon's Essays and Wisdom of the Ancients*. Cambridge, Mass: The University Press. Copyright © 1884 by Little, Brown, and Company.

---

[2] Job ii. 10.—"Shall we receive good at the hand of God, and shall we not receive evil?"

[3] By "public revenges," he means punishment awarded by the state with the sanction of the laws.

[4] He alludes to the retribution dealt by Augustus and Anthony to the murderers of Julius Cæsar. It is related by ancient historians, as a singular fact, that not one of them died a natural death.

[5] Henry III. of France was assassinated in 1599, by Jacques Clement, a Jacobin monk, in the frenzy of fanaticism. Although Clement justly suffered punishment, the end of this bloodthirsty and bigoted tyrant may be justly deemed a retribution dealt by the hand of an offended Providence.

Comprehension

1. What is the primary theme of "Of Revenge"?

2. According to Bacon, who and what get hurt when one takes revenge?

Rhetorical Analysis

3. Identify the logos in Bacon's essay.

4. Explain the metaphor in the opening statement, "Revenge is a kind of wild justice, which the more man's nature runs to, the more ought law to weed it out."

5. How does Bacon make use of pathos in his argument?

6. Explain the purpose of the imagery used in the following line: "But base and crafty cowards are like the arrow that flieth in the dark."

Writing

7. Write a paragraph expanding on Bacon's notion that a man who "studieth revenge keeps his own wounds green." Give examples that fit this description.

8. **Writing an Argument**   Is it possible to let go of revenge? Using your examples from the writing assignment above, take a stand on this issue, clarify, and build upon it.

Of Studies

Francis Bacon

Studies serve for delight, for ornament, and for ability. Their chief use for delight, is in privateness and retiring; for ornament, is in discourse; and for ability, is in the judgment and disposition of business; for expert men can execute, and perhaps judge of particulars one by one; but the general counsels,

5 and the plots and marshalling of affairs, come best from those that are learned. To spend too much time in studies, is sloth; to use them too much for ornament, is affectation; to make judgment wholly by their rules, is the humor of a scholar. They perfect nature, and are perfected by experience; for natural abilities are like natural plants, that need pruning by study; and studies

10 themselves do give forth directions too much at large, except they be bounded in by experience. Crafty men contemn studies, simple men admire them, and wise men use them; for they teach not their own use; but that is a wisdom without them and above them, won by observation. Read not to contradict and confute, nor to believe and take for granted, nor to find talk and discourse, but

15 to weigh and consider. Some books are to be tasted, others to be swallowed, and some few to be chewed and digested; that is, some books are to be read only in parts; others to be read, but not curiously;[1] and some few to be read wholly, and with diligence and attention. Some books also may be read by deputy, and extracts made of them by others; but that would be only in the less

20 important arguments and the meaner sort of books; else distilled books are, like common distilled waters, flashy[2] things. Reading maketh a full man; conference a ready man; and writing an exact man; and, therefore, if a man write little, he had need have a great memory; if he confer little, he had need have a present wit; and if he read little, he had need have much cunning, to

25 seem to know that he doth not. Histories make men wise; poets, witty; the mathematics, subtile; natural philosophy, deep; moral, grave; logic and rhetoric, able to contend: "*Abeunt studia in mores;*"[3] nay, there is no stand or impediment in the wit, but may be wrought out by fit studies. Like as diseases of the body may have appropriate exercises, bowling is good for the stone and reins,[4]

30 shooting for the lungs and breast, gentle walking for the stomach, riding for the head and the like; so, if a man's wit be wandering, let him study the mathematics; for in demonstrations, if his wit be called away never so little, he must begin again; if his wit be not apt to distinguish or find difference, let him study the schoolmen,[5] for they are "*Cymini sectores.*"[6] If he be not apt to beat

---

[1] Attentively.

[2] Vapid: without taste or spirit.

[3] "Studies become habits" or "Studies affect people's character."

[4] Kidney stones and other kidney disorders

[5] Medieval philosophers

[6] "Splitters of cummin-seeds;" or, as we now say, "splitters of straws," or "hairsplitters."

[35] over matters, and to call up one thing to prove and illustrate another, let him study the lawyers' cases; so every defect of the mind may have a special receipt.[7]

"Of Studies" by Francis Bacon, 1625. From *Bacon's Essays and Wisdom of the Ancients*. Cambridge, Mass: The University Press. Copyright © 1884 by Little, Brown, and Company.

---

[7] Remedy

Comprehension

1. According to Bacon, what are the three main benefits of study? In Bacon's opinion, what danger can result from each benefit?

2. What is the proper attitude and purpose Bacon advises readers to take toward their books? What does this advice tell you about Bacon's attitude toward learning?

Rhetorical Analysis

3. What analogy does Bacon make between different kinds of study and different kinds of physical exercise?

4. Find three examples of parallelism in "Of Studies." How does Bacon's use of parallelism help emphasize his ideas?

5. Examine Bacon's diction in listing the benefits of studying history, poetry, mathematics, philosophy, logic, and rhetoric. How do his word choices affect the tone of the list?

Writing

6. Bacon states, "Some books are to be tasted, others to be swallowed, and some few to be chewed and digested." Write an essay describing one book you merely "tasted," or read parts of; one you "swallowed," or read quickly; and one you "chewed," or read carefully and thought about.

7. **Writing an Argument** Write an essay agreeing or disagreeing with Bacon's belief that spending "too much time in studies, is sloth."

I Want a Wife

Judy Brady

Judy Brady (1937–2017) wrote "I Want a Wife" when she was known as Judy Syfers, and she read her essay in San Francisco in 1970 when people were assembled to celebrate the 50th anniversary of the passing of the Nineteenth Amendment. This essay went on to be celebrated in the first issue of *Ms. Magazine* in 1971. Brady was an activist for social justice and feminist rights.

1   I belong to that classification of people known as wives. I am A Wife. And, not altogether incidentally, I am a mother.

2   Not too long ago a male friend of mine appeared on the scene fresh from a recent divorce. He had one child, who is, of course, with his ex-wife. He is looking for another wife. As I thought about him while I was ironing one evening, it suddenly occurred to me that I, too, would like to have a wife. Why do I want a wife?

3   I would like to go back to school so that I can become economically independent, support myself, and, if need be, support those dependent upon me. I want a wife who will work and send me to school. And while I am going to school I want a wife to take care of my children. I want a wife to keep track of the children's doctor and dentist appointments. And to keep track of mine, too. I want a wife to make sure my children eat properly and are kept clean. I want a wife who will wash the children's clothes and keep them mended. I want a wife who is a good nurturant attendant to my children, who arranges for their school, makes sure that they have an adequate social life with their peers, takes them to the park, the zoo, etc. I want a wife who takes care of the children when they are sick, a wife who arranges to be around when the children need special care, because, of course, I cannot miss classes at school. My wife must arrange to lose time at work and not lose the job. It may mean a small cut in my wife's income from time to time, but I guess I can tolerate that. Needless to say, my wife will arrange and pay for the care of the children while my wife is working.

4   I want a wife who will take care of *my* physical needs. I want a wife who will keep my house clean. A wife who will pick up after my children, a wife who will pick up after me. I want a wife who will keep my clothes clean, ironed, mended, replaced when need be, and who will see to it that my personal things are kept in their proper place so that I can find what I need the minute I need it. I want a wife who cooks the meals, a wife who is a *good* cook. I want a wife who will plan the menus, do the necessary grocery shopping, prepare the meals, serve them pleasantly, and then do the cleaning up while I do my studying. I want a wife who will care for me when I am sick and sympathize with my pain and loss of time from school. I want a wife to go along when our family takes a vacation so that someone can continue to care for me and my children when I need a rest and change of scene.

5   I want a wife who will not bother me with rambling complaints about a wife's duties. But I want a wife who will listen to me when I feel the need to explain a rather difficult point I have come across in my course of studies. And I want a wife who will type my papers for me when I have written them.

6   I want a wife who will take care of the details of my social life. When my wife and I are invited out by my friends, I want a wife who will take care of the babysitting arrangements. When I meet people at school that I like and want to entertain, I want a wife who will have the house clean, will prepare a special meal, serve it to me and my friends, and not interrupt when I talk about things that interest me and my friends. I want a wife who will have arranged that the children do not bother us. I want a wife who takes care of the needs of my guests so that they feel comfortable, who makes sure that they have an ashtray, that they are passed the hors d/oeuvres, that they are offered a second helping of the food, that their wine glasses are replenished when necessary, that the coffee is served to them as they like it. And I want a wife who knows that sometimes I need a night out by myself.

7   I want a wife who is sensitive to my sexual needs, a wife who makes love passionately and eagerly when I feel like it, a wife who makes sure that I am satisfied. And, of course, I want a wife who will not demand sexual attention when I am not in the mood for it. I want a wife who assumes the complete responsibility for birth control, because I do not want more children. I want a wife who will remain sexually faithful to me so that I do not have to clutter up my intellectual life with jealousies. And I want a wife who understands that *my* sexual needs may entail more than strict adherence to monogamy. I must, after all, be able to relate to people as fully as possible.

8   If, by chance, I find another person more suitable as a wife than the wife I already have, I want the liberty to replace my present wife with another one. Naturally, I will expect a fresh, new life; my wife will take the children and be solely responsible for them so that I am left free.

9   When I am through with school and have a job, I want my wife to quit working and remain at home so that my wife can more fully and completely take care of a wife's duties.

10   My God, who *wouldn't* want a wife?

Judith E. Brady (Formerly Judith Syfers).

Comprehension

1. Make a list of the wife's general expected duties.

2. Were you surprised when you read this essay? Why or why not?

Rhetorical Analysis

3. What is the tone of the essay? Point out the irony in the essay.

4. Explain the use of the rhetorical device anaphora in this essay.

5. How does the author get the reader emotionally involved (pathos)?

Writing

6. Write a parody of this essay using another occupation to replace "wife."

7. **Writing an Argument**   Explain why this essay is or is not outdated.

Marrying Absurd

Joan Didion

Joan Didion (b. 1934) has published an immense number of writings, ranging from screen plays to books of essays. Didion was married to literary figure John Gregory Dunne, who died of a heart attack in 2003. She also suffered through the lingering illness and eventual death of their daughter Quintana. Her experiences with both losses were told in *The Year of Magical Thinking*, which received the National Book Award for Nonfiction in 2005. She followed that book with a 2011 memoir *Blue Nights*, which speaks to the feminine journey through life. She maintains a high profile connected to women's issues, especially when they are connected to social manifestations. In "Marrying Absurd" (1967), Didion's sardonic viewpoint about Las Vegas weddings displays an ironic sense about America's fascination with a fast-food mentality.

1   To be married in Las Vegas, Clark County's Nevada, a bride must swear that she is eighteen or has parental permission and a bridegroom that he is twenty-one or has parental permission. Someone must put up five dollars for the license. (Sundays and holidays, fifteen dollars. The Clark County Courthouse issues marriage licenses at any time of the day or night except between noon and one in the afternoon, between eight and nine in the evening, and between four and five in the morning.) Nothing else is required. The State of Nevada, alone among the United States, demands neither a premarital blood test nor a waiting period before or after the issuance of a marriage license. Driving in across the Mojave from Los Angeles, one sees the signs way out on the desert, looming up from that moonscape of rattlesnakes and mesquite, even before the Las Vegas lights appear like a mirage on the horizon: "GETTING MARRIED? Free License Information First Strip Exit." Perhaps the Las Vegas wedding industry achieved its peak operational efficiency between 9:00 P.M. and midnight of August 26, 1965, an otherwise unremarkable Thursday which happened to be, by Presidential order, the last day on which anyone could improve his draft status merely by getting married. One hundred and seventy-one couples were pronounced man and wife in the name of Clark County and the State of Nevada that night, sixty-seven of them by a single justice of the peace, Mr. James A. Brennan. Mr. Brennan did one wedding at the Dunes and the other sixty-six in his office, and charged each couple eight dollars. One bride lent her veil to six others. "I got it down from five to three minutes," Mr. Brennan said later of his feat. "I could've married them *en masse*, but they're people, not cattle. People expect more when they get married."

2   What people who get married in Las Vegas actually do expect—what, in the largest sense, their "expectations" are—strikes one as a curious and self-contradictory business. Las Vegas is the most extreme and allegorical of American settlements, bizarre and beautiful in its venality and in its devotion to immediate gratification, a place the tone of which is set by mobsters and call girls and ladies' room attendants with amyl nitrite poppers in their uniform pockets. Almost everyone notes that there is no "time" in Las Vegas, no night and no day and no past and no future (no Las Vegas casino, however, has taken the obliteration of the ordinary time sense quite so far as Harold's Club in Reno, which for a while issued, at odd intervals in the day and night, mimeographed "bulletins" carrying news from the world outside); neither is there any logical sense of where one is. One is standing on a highway in the middle of a vast hostile desert looking at an eighty-foot sign which blinks "STARDUST" or "CAESAR'S PALACE." Yes, but what does that explain? This geographical implausibility reinforces the sense that what happens there has no connection with "real" life; Nevada cities like Reno and Carson are ranch towns, Western towns, places behind which there is some historical imperative. But Las Vegas seems to exist only in the eye of beholder. All of which makes it an extraordinary and interesting place, but an odd one in which to want to wear a candlelight satin Priscilla of Boston wedding dress with Chantilly lace insets, tapered sleeves and a detachable modified train.

3   And yet the Las Vegas wedding business seems to appeal to precisely that impulse. "Sincere and Dignified Since 1954," one wedding chapel advertises. There are nineteen such wedding chapels in Las Vegas, intensely competitive, each offering better, faster, and, by implication, more sincere services than the next: Our Photos Best Anywhere, Your Wedding on A Phonograph Record, Candlelight with Your Ceremony, Honeymoon Accommodations, Free Transportation from Your Motel to Courthouse to Chapel and Return to Motel, Religious or Civil Ceremonies, Dressing Rooms, Flowers, Rings, Announcements, Witnesses Available, and Ample Parking. All of these services, like most others in Las Vegas (sauna baths, payroll-check cashing, chinchilla coats for sale or rent) are offered twenty-four hours a day, seven days a week, presumably on the premise that marriage, like craps, is a game to be played when the table seems hot.

4   But what strikes one most about the Strip chapels, with their wishing wells and stained-glass paper windows and their artificial bouvardia, is that so much of their business is by no means a matter of simple convenience, of late-night liaisons between show girls and baby Crosbys. Of course there is some of that. (One night about eleven o'clock in Las Vegas I watched a bride in an orange minidress and masses of flame-colored hair stumble from a Strip chapel on the arm of her bridegroom, who looked the part of the expendable nephew in movies like *Miami Syndicate*. "I gotta get the kids," the bride whimpered. "I gotta pick up the sitter, I gotta get to the midnight show." "What you gotta get," the bridegroom

said, opening the door of a Cadillac Coupe de Ville and watching her crumple on the seat, "is sober.") But Las Vegas seems to offer something other than "convenience"; it is merchandising "niceness," the facsimile of proper ritual, to children who do not know how else to find it, how to make the arrangements, how to do it "right." All day and evening long on the Strip, one sees actual wedding parties, waiting under the harsh lights at a crosswalk, standing uneasily in the parking lot of the Frontier while the photographer hired by The Little Church of the West ("Wedding Place of the Stars") certifies the occasion, takes the picture: the bride in a veil and white satin pumps, the bridegroom usually a white dinner jacket, and even an attendant or two, a sister or best friend in hot-pink *peau de soie,* a flirtation veil, a carnation nosegay. "When I Fall in Love It Will Be Forever," the organist plays, and then a few bars of Lohengrin. The mother cries; the stepfather, awkward in his role, invites the chapel hostess to join them for a drink at the Sands. The hostess declines with a professional smile; she has already transferred her interest to the group waiting outside. One bride out, another in, and again the sign goes up on the chapel door: "One moment please—Wedding."

5   I sat next to one such wedding party in a Strip restaurant last time I was in Las Vegas. The marriage had just taken place; the bride still wore her dress, the mother her corsage. A bored waiter poured out a few swallows of pink champagne ("on the house") for everyone but the bride, who was too young to be served. "You'll need something with more kick than that," the bride's father said with heavy jocularity to his new son-in-law; the ritual jokes about the wedding night had a certain Panglossian character, since the bride was clearly several months pregnant. Another round of pink champagne, this time not on the house, and the bride began to cry, "It was just as nice," she sobbed, "as I hoped and dreamed it would be."

Reprinted by permission of Farrar, Straus and Giroux: "Marrying Absurd" from SLOUCHING TOWARDS BETHLEHEM by Joan Didion, Copyright© 1966, 1968, renewed 1996 by Joan Didion.

1. Explain how the title relates to the essay.

2. Didion views Vegas weddings to be "the facsimile of proper ritual, to children who do not know how else to find it." Who are these "children" she mentions in paragraph 4?

3. What attracts people to the Las Vegas setting in order to get married?

Rhetorical Analysis

4. Why is the last line in the essay so ironic?

5. Explain Didion's attitude about Las Vegas weddings and the people who participate in them. Give at least two specific examples to back up that attitude.

6. "Marrying Absurd" conveys more than Joan Didion's criticism of Las Vegas marriages. It also suggests something of Didion's attitude toward a larger world problem of what she describes in paragraph 2 as "venality" and "a devotion to immediate gratification." Explain what she means by this.

7. How does the craps metaphor in paragraph 3 add to this essay?

8. In making her argument about Vegas weddings, Didion appeals to the reader's ethos (sense of character). She achieves this by making what points?

Writing

9. Would Didion's take on Las Vegas weddings be different if it were written from a removed, male point of view? Using first person, give a description of how these types of weddings would appear from a man's outlook.

10. **Writing an Argument**   Much has been made about the loss of traditions. Many argue that marriage itself is a tradition that people increasingly choose not to follow. Is the tradition of marriage on its way out in our culture?

Meditation (No Man Is an Island)

John Donne

John Donne (1572–1631) was born into an affluent Roman Catholic family in 1572, a time when anti-Catholic sentiment ran high in England. After attending Oxford and Cambridge universities, he studied law in London. Perhaps to prove his patriotism and pave the way for a government career, Donne joined the Earl of Essex on two daring military expeditions against Spain. On his return to England in 1597, Donne secured the position of secretary to Sir Thomas Egerton. By this time, Donne had abandoned Catholicism and joined the Church of England. His career flourished until 1601, when he eloped with Egerton's seventeen-year-old niece, Anne More. Anne's father, furious, responded by having Donne fired from his post and thrown briefly into jail. Donne lost all hope of a government career, Anne lost her dowry, and, without funds, the couple was forced to move to a cottage and live on the charity of Anne's cousin. Over the next 14 years, Donne supported his growing family with odd jobs and writing. His friends, moved by the power of his religious poems, urged him to enter the Anglican ministry. At age 43, he did just that, and he soon became chaplain to King James I. Two years later, Donne's wife died shortly after giving birth to their twelfth child. Grief-stricken, Donne poured himself into preaching with passionate intensity. The force and eloquence of his sermons helped lead to his appointment, at age 49, to the deanship of London's St. Paul's Cathedral in 1621. Donne preached not only to huge crowds but also to the royal court, where he became a favorite of Kings James I and Charles I. In 1624, he wrote "Devotions Upon Emergent Occasions," from which "Meditation" is an excerpt. By the time Donne died, he was considered the greatest preacher in England.

Now, this bell tolling softly for another, says to me, thou must die.

Perchance he for whom this bell tolls, may be so ill, as that he knows not it tolls for him. And perchance I may think myself so much better than I am, as that they who are about me, and see my state, may have caused it to toll for me, and I know not that. The church is catholic,[1] universal, so are all her actions; all that she does,
5 belongs to all. When she baptizes a child, that action concerns me; for that child is thereby connected to that head,[2] which is my head too, and ingraffed into that body,[3] whereof I am a member. And when she buries a man, that action concerns me; all mankind is of one author, and is one volume; when one man dies, one chapter is not torn out of the book, but translated into a better language; and
10 every chapter must be so translated; God employs several translators; some pieces are translated by age, some by sickness, some by war, some by justice; but God's

---

[1] When Donne says the church is *catholic,* he means that it embraces all humankind.

[2] *Head* stands for Christ, the head of the church.

[3] *Body* stands for the church.

hand is in every translation; and his hand shall bind up all our scattered leaves[4] again, for that library where every book shall lie open to one another; as therefore the bell that rings to a sermon, calls not upon the preacher only, but upon the

15 congregation to come; so this bell calls us all; but how much more me, who am brought so near the door by this sickness. There was a contention as far as a suit[5] (in which, both piety and dignity, religion and estimation, were mingled) which of the religious orders should ring to prayers first in the morning; and it was determined, that they should ring first that rose earliest. If we understand aright

20 the dignity of this bell, that tolls for our evening prayer, we would be glad to make it ours, by rising early, in that application, that it might be ours, as well as his, whose indeed it is. The bell doth toll for him, that thinks it doth; and though it intermit again, yet from that minute, that that occasion wrought upon him, he is united to God. Who casts not up his eye to the sun when it rises? But who takes

25 off his eye from a comet, when that breaks out? who bends not his ear to any bell, which upon any occasion rings? But who can remove it from that bell, which is passing a piece of himself out of this world? No man is an island, entire of itself; every man is a piece of the continent, a part of the main;[6] if a clod be washed away by the sea, Europe is the less, as well as if a promontory were, as well as if a

30 manor of thy friend's or of thine own were; any man's death diminishes me, because I am involved in mankind, and therefore never send to know for whom the bells tolls; it tolls for thee. Neither can we call this a begging of misery, or a borrowing of misery, as though we were not miserable enough of ourselves, but must fetch in more from the next house, in taking upon us the misery of our

35 neighbours. Truly it were an excusable covetousness, if we did; for affliction is a treasure, and scarce any man hath enough of it. No man hath affliction enough, that is not matured, and ripened by it, and made fit for God by that affliction. If a man carry treasure in bullion or in a wedge of gold, and have none coined into current moneys, his treasure will not defray[7] him as he travels. Tribulation[8] is

40 treasure in the nature of it, but it is not current money in the use of it, except we get nearer and nearer our home, heaven, by it. Another may be sick too, and sick to death, and this affliction may lie in his bowels, as gold in a mine, and be of no use to him; but this bell that tells me of his affliction, digs out, and applies that gold to me: if by this consideration of another's danger, I take mine own into

45 contemplation, and so secure myself, by making my recourse[9] to my God, who is our only security.

"Meditation" by John Donne, 1624. From "Devotions Upon Emergent Occasions" in *The Works of John Donne*, Vol. III. London: John W. Parker, West Strand. 1839.

---

[4] *Leaves*, in this context, are pages.

[5] Dispute or controversy that resulted in a lawsuit

[6] Short for *mainland*

[7] Reimburse

[8] Misery or suffering

[9] Appeal for help or protection

Comprehension

1. In your opinion, what is Donne's message in lines 1-4?

2. In the last few lines, what does Donne think he will gain from "consideration of another's danger"?

3. What purpose does the tolling bell serve?

4. According to Donne, what act would be "an excusable covetousness"? Why?

Rhetorical Analysis

5. What are some points of comparison Donne makes between humankind and "one volume" by "one author"? Is the comparison effective?

6. According to Donne, in what ways are people like a "piece of the continent"?

7. Explain Donne's metaphor when he states that when a man dies he is "translated into a better language."

8. Find several examples of alliteration in the essay. How do the examples affect the tone of the essay?

Writing

9. In a short essay, explain ways that Donne's statement "no man is an island" applies to you.

10. **Writing an Argument**   Write a short essay arguing for or against Donne's assertion that "affliction is a treasure."

Sinners in the Hands of an Angry God

Jonathan Edwards

Jonathan Edwards (1703–1758), a fiery preacher, is credited with helping to shape the Great Awakening—a religious revival that swept New England in the 1740s—and strengthening the Protestant Covenant. Edwards entered Yale before the age of 13 and graduated first in his class. The son and grandson of Puritan ministers, he was ordained a minister at the age of 23. He soon became known for his "preaching of terror," which grew out of his belief that God was all powerful, and humans had no free will. Edwards preached strict Calvinism, which stressed predestination, or the belief that only a select few chosen by God would be saved and go to heaven. By 1750 some members of his congregation in Northampton, a village in the Massachusetts Bay Colony, were no longer comfortable with his extreme teachings and dismissed Edwards. He moved his family to the frontier village of Stockbridge and worked as a missionary with Native Americans. During this time, he wrote important theological works, including *The Nature of True Virtue* and *Freedom of Will.* He died shortly after becoming president of what is now Princeton University. Calvinist ideas are reflected in his most famous sermon, "Sinners in the Hands of an Angry God."

Deuteronomy xxxii.35.—Their foot shall slide in due time.

1 In this verse is threatened the vengeance of God on the wicked unbelieving Israelites, that were God's visible people, and lived under means of grace; and that notwithstanding all God's wonderful works that he had wrought towards that people, yet remained, as is expressed, verse 28, void of counsel, having no understanding in them; and that, under all the cultivations of heaven, brought forth bitter and poisonous fruit; as in the two verses next preceding the text.

2   The expression that I have chosen for my text, *their foot shall slide in due time,* seems to imply the following things relating to the punishment and destruction that these wicked Israelites were exposed to.

3   1. That they were *always* exposed to destruction; as one that stands or walks in slippery places is always exposed to fall. This is implied in the manner of their destruction's coming upon them, being represented by their foot's sliding. The same is expressed, Psalm lxxiii. 18: "Surely thou didst set them in slippery places; thou castedst them down into destruction."

4   2. It implies that they were always exposed to *sudden,* unexpected destruction; as he that walks in slippery places is every moment liable to fall, he can't foresee one moment whether he shall stand or fall the next; and when he does fall, he falls at once, without warning, which is also expressed in that Psalm lxxiii. 18, 19: "Surely thou didst set them in slippery places: thou castedst them down into destruction. How are they brought into desolation, as *in a moment!*"

⁵   3. Another thing implied is, that they are liable to fall of *themselves*, without being thrown down by the hand of another; as he that stands or walks on slippery ground needs nothing but his own weight to throw him down.

⁶   4. That the reason why they are not fallen already, and don't fall now, is only that God's appointed time is not come. For it is said that when that due time, or appointed time comes, *their foot shall slide*. Then they shall be left to fall, as they are inclined by their own weight. God won't hold them up in these slippery places any longer, but will let them go; and then, at that very instant, they shall fall to destruction; as he that stands in such slippery declining ground on the edge of a pit that he can't stand alone, when he is let go he immediately falls and is lost.

⁷   The observation from the words that I would now insist upon is this,

There is nothing that keeps wicked men at any one moment out of hell, but the mere pleasure of God.

⁸   By the mere pleasure of God, I mean his sovereign pleasure, his arbitrary will, restrained by no obligation, hindered by no manner of difficulty, any more than if nothing else but God's mere will had in the least degree or in any respect whatsoever any hand in the preservation of wicked men one moment.

⁹   The truth of this observation may appear by the following considerations.

¹⁰   1. There is no want of *power* in God to cast wicked men into hell at any moment. Men's hands can't be strong when God rises up: the strongest have no power to resist him, nor can any deliver out of his hands.

¹¹   He is not only able to cast wicked men into hell, but he can most easily do it. Sometimes an earthly prince meets with a great deal of difficulty to subdue a rebel that has found means to fortify himself, and has made himself strong by the number of his followers. But it is not so with God. There is no fortress that is any defence against the power of God. Though hand join in hand, and vast multitudes of God's enemies combine and associate themselves, they are easily broken in pieces: they are as great heaps of light chaff before the whirlwind; or large quantities of dry stubble before devouring flames. We find it easy to tread on and crush a worm that we see crawling on the earth; so 'tis easy for us to cut or singe a slender thread that any thing hangs by; thus easy is it for God, when he pleases, to cast his enemies down to hell. What are we, that we should think to stand before him, at whose rebuke the earth trembles, and before whom the rocks are thrown down!

¹²   2. They *deserve* to be cast into hell; so that divine justice never stands in the way, it makes no objection against God's using his power at any moment to destroy them. Yea, on the contrary, justice calls aloud for an infinite punishment of their sins. Divine justice says of the tree that brings forth such grapes of Sodom, "Cut it down; why cumbereth it the ground?" Luke xiii. 7. The sword of divine justice is every moment brandished over their heads, and 'tis nothing but the hand of arbitrary mercy, and God's mere will, that holds it back.

¹³   3. They are *already* under a sentence of condemnation to hell. They don't only justly deserve to be cast down thither, but the sentence of the law of God, that eternal and immutable rule of righteousness that God has fixed between him and

mankind, is gone out against them, and stands against them; so that they are bound over already to hell: John iii. 18, "He that believeth not is condemned already." So that every unconverted man properly belongs to hell; that is his place; from thence he is: John viii. 23, "Ye are from beneath:" and thither he is bound; 'tis the place that justice, and God's word, and the sentence of his unchangeable law, assigns to him.

14   4. They are now the objects of that very *same* anger and wrath of God, that is expressed in the torments of hell: and the reason why they don't go down to hell at each moment is not because God, in whose power they are, is not then very angry with them; as angry as he is with many of those miserable creatures that he is now tormenting in hell, and do there feel and bear the fierceness of his wrath. Yea, God is a great deal more angry with great numbers that are now on earth, yea, doubtless, with many that are now in this congregation, that, it may be, are at ease and quiet, than he is with many of those that are now in the flames of hell.

15   So that it is not because God is unmindful of their wickedness, and don't resent it, that he don't let loose his hand and cut them off. God is not altogether such a one as themselves, though they may imagine him to be so. The wrath of God burns against them; their damnation don't slumber; the pit is prepared; the fire is made ready; the furnace is now hot, ready to receive them; the flames do now rage and glow. The glittering sword is whet, and held over them, and the pit hath opened her mouth under them.

16   5. The *devil* stands ready to fall upon them, and seize them as his own, at what moment God shall permit him. They belong to him; he has their souls in his possession, and under his dominion. The Scripture represents them as his *goods*, Luke xi. 21. The devils watch them; they are ever by them, at their right hand; they stand waiting for them, like greedy hungry lions that see their prey, and expect to have it, but are for the present kept back; if God should withdraw his hand by which they are restrained, they would in one moment fly upon their poor souls. The old serpent is gaping for them; hell opens its mouth wide to receive them; and if God should permit it, they would be hastily swallowed up and lost.

17   6. There are in the souls of wicked men those hellish *principles* reigning, that would presently kindle and flame out into hell-fire, if it were not for God's restraints. There is laid in the very nature of carnal men a foundation for the torments of hell: there are those corrupt principles, in reigning power in them, and in full possession of them, that are seeds of hell-fire. These principles are active and powerful, exceeding violent in their nature, and if it were not for the restraining hand of God upon them, they would soon break out, they would flame out after the same manner as the same corruptions, the same enmity does in the heart of damned souls, and would beget the same torments in 'em as they do in them. The souls of the wicked are in Scripture compared to the troubled sea, Isaiah lvii. 20. For the present God restrains their wickedness by his mighty power, as he does the raging waves of the troubled sea, saying, "Hitherto shalt thou come, and no further;" but if God should withdraw that restraining power, it would soon carry all afore it. Sin is the ruin and misery of the soul; it is destructive in its nature; and if God should leave it without restraint, there would need nothing else to make the soul perfectly miserable. The corruption of the

heart of man is a thing that is immoderate and boundless in its fury; and while wicked men live here, it is like fire pent up by God's restraints, whenas if it were let loose, it would set on fire the course of nature; and as the heart is now a sink of sin, so, if sin was not restrained, it would immediately turn the soul into a fiery oven, or a furnace of fire and brimstone.

18   7. It is no security to wicked men for one moment, that there are no *visible means of death* at hand. 'Tis no security to a natural man, that he is now in health, and that he don't see which way he should now immediately go out of the world by any accident, and that there is no visible danger in any respect in his circumstances. The manifold and continual experience of the world in all ages shows that this is no evidence that a man is not on the very brink of eternity, and that the next step won't be into another world. The unseen, unthought of ways and means of persons going suddenly out of the world are innumerable and inconceivable. Unconverted men walk over the pit of hell on a rotten covering, and there are innumerable places in this covering so weak that they won't bear their weight, and these places are not seen. The arrows of death fly unseen at noonday; the sharpest sight can't discern them. God has so many different, unsearchable ways of taking wicked men out of the world and sending 'em to hell, that there is nothing to make it appear that God had need to be at the expense of a miracle, or go out of the ordinary course of his providence, to destroy any wicked man, at any moment. All the means that there are of sinners' going out of the world are so in God's hands, and so absolutely subject to his power and determination, that it don't depend at all less on the mere will of God, whether sinners shall at any moment go to hell, than if means were never made use of, or at all concerned in the case.

19   8. Natural men's *prudence* and *care* to preserve their own *lives*, or the care of others to preserve them, don't secure 'em a moment. This, divine providence and universal experience does also bear testimony to. There is this clear evidence that men's own wisdom is no security to them from death; that if it were otherwise we should see some difference between the wise and politic men of the world, and others, with regard to their liableness to early and unexpected death; but how is it in fact? Eccles. ii. 16, "How dieth the wise man? As the fool."

20   9. All wicked men's *pains* and *contrivance* they use to escape *hell*, while they continue to reject Christ, and so remain wicked men, don't secure 'em from hell one moment. Almost every natural man that hears of hell flatters himself that he shall escape it; he depends upon himself for his own security, he flatters himself in what he has done, in what he is now doing, or what he intends to do; every one lays out matters in his own mind how he shall avoid damnation, and flatters himself that he contrives well for himself, and that his schemes won't fail. They hear indeed that there are but few saved, and that the bigger part of men that have died heretofore are gone to hell; but each one imagines that he lays out matters better for his own escape than others have done: he don't intend to come to that place of torment; he says within himself, that he intends to take care that shall be effectual, and to order matters so for himself as not to fail.

21   But the foolish children of men do miserably delude themselves in their own schemes, and in their confidence in their own strength and wisdom; they trust to

nothing but a shadow. The bigger part of those that heretofore have lived under the same means of grace, and are now dead, are undoubtedly gone to hell; and it was not because they were not as wise as those that are now alive; it was not because they did not lay out matters as well for themselves to secure their own escape. If it were so that we could come to speak with them, and could inquire of them, one by one, whether they expected, when alive, and when they used to hear about hell, ever to be subjects of that misery, we, doubtless, should hear one and another reply, "No, I never intended to come here: I had laid out matters otherwise in my mind; I thought I should contrive well for myself: I thought my scheme good: I intended to take effectual care; but it came upon me unexpected; I did not look for it at that time, and in that manner; it came as a thief: death outwitted me: God's wrath was too quick for me. O my cursed foolishness! I was flattering myself, and pleasing myself with vain dreams of what I would do hereafter; and when I was saying peace and safety, then sudden destruction came upon me."

22   10. God has laid himself under *no obligation,* by any promise, to keep any natural man out of hell one moment. God certainly has made no promises either of eternal life, or of any deliverance or preservation from eternal death, but what are contained in the covenant of grace, the promises that are given in Christ, in whom all the promises are yea and amen. But surely they have no interest in the promises of the covenant of grace that are not the children of the covenant, and that do not believe in any of the promises of the covenant, and have no interest in the Mediator of the covenant.

23   So that, whatever some have imagined and pretended about promises made to natural men's earnest seeking and knocking, 'tis plain and manifest, that whatever pains a natural man takes in religion, whatever prayers he makes, till he believes in Christ, God is under no manner of obligation to keep him a moment from eternal destruction.

24   So that thus it is, that natural men are held in the hand of God over the pit of hell; they have deserved the fiery pit, and are already sentenced to it; and God is dreadfully provoked, his anger is as great towards them as to those that are actually suffering the executions of the fierceness of his wrath in hell, and they have done nothing in the least to appease or abate that anger, neither is God in the least bound by any promise to hold 'em up one moment; the devil is waiting for them, hell is gaping for them, the flames gather and flash about them, and would fain lay hold on them and swallow them up; the fire pent up in their own hearts is struggling to break out; and they have no interest in any Mediator, there are no means within reach that can be any security to them. In short they have no refuge, nothing to take hold of; all that preserves them every moment is the mere arbitrary will, and uncovenanted, unobliged forbearance of an incensed God.

APPLICATION

25   The use may be of *awakening* to unconverted persons in this congregation. This that you have heard is the case of every one of you that are out of Christ. That world of misery, that lake of burning brimstone, is extended abroad under you. *There* is the dreadful pit of the glowing flames of the wrath of God; there is hell's wide gaping mouth open; and you have nothing to stand upon, nor any

thing to take hold of. There is nothing between you and hell but the air; 'tis only the power and mere pleasure of God that holds you up.

26   You probably are not sensible of this; you find you are kept out of hell, but don't see the hand of God in it, but look at other things, as the good state of your bodily constitution, your care of your own life, and the means you use for your own preservation. But indeed these things are nothing; if God should withdraw his hand, they would avail no more to keep you from falling than the thin air to hold up a person that is suspended in it.

27   Your wickedness makes you as it were heavy as lead, and to tend downwards with great weight and pressure towards hell; and if God should let you go, you would immediately sink and swiftly descend and plunge into the bottomless gulf, and your healthy constitution, and your own care and prudence, and best contrivance, and all your righteousness, would have no more influence to uphold you and keep you out of hell than a spider's web would have to stop a falling rock. Were it not that so is the sovereign pleasure of God, the earth would not bear you one moment; for you are a burden to it; the creation groans with you; the creature is made subject to the bondage of your corruption, not willingly; the sun don't willingly shine upon you to give you light to serve sin and Satan; the earth don't willingly yield her increase to satisfy your lusts; nor is it willingly a stage for your wickedness to be acted upon; the air don't willingly serve you for breath to maintain the flame of life in your vitals, while you spend your life in the service of God's enemies. God's creatures are good, and were made for men to serve God with, and don't willingly subserve to any other purpose, and groan when they are abused to purposes so directly contrary to their nature and end. And the world would spew you out, were it not for the sovereign hand of him who hath subjected it in hope. There are the black clouds of God's wrath now hanging directly over your heads, full of the dreadful storm, and big with thunder; and were it not for the restraining hand of God, it would immediately burst forth upon you. The sovereign pleasure of God, for the present, stays his rough wind; otherwise it would come with fury, and your destruction would come like a whirlwind, and you would be like the chaff of the summer threshing floor.

28   The wrath of God is like great waters that are dammed for the present; they increase more and more, and rise higher and higher, till an outlet is given; and the longer the stream is stopped, the more rapid and mighty is its course, when once it is let loose. 'Tis true, that judgment against your evil work has not been executed hitherto; the floods of God's vengeance have been withheld; but your guilt in the mean time is constantly increasing, and you are every day treasuring up more wrath; the waters are continually rising, and waxing more and more mighty; and there is nothing but the mere pleasure of God that holds the waters back, that are unwilling to be stopped, and press hard to go forward. If God should only withdraw his hand from the floodgate, it would immediately fly open, and the fiery floods of the fierceness and wrath of God would rush forth with inconceivable fury, and would come upon you with omnipotent power; and if your strength were ten thousand times greater than it is, yea, ten thousand times greater than the strength of the stoutest, sturdiest devil in hell, it would be nothing to withstand or endure it.

29   The bow of God's wrath is bent, and the arrow made ready on the string, and justice bends the arrow at your heart, and strains the bow, and it is nothing but the mere pleasure of God, and that of an angry God, without any promise or obligation at all, that keeps the arrow one moment from being made drunk with your blood.

30   Thus are all you that never passed under a great change of heart by the mighty power of the Spirit of God upon your souls; all that were never born again, and made new creatures, and raised from being dead in sin to a state of new and before altogether unexperienced light and life, (however you may have reformed your life in many things, and may have had religious affections, and may keep up a form of religion in your families and closets, and in the house of God, and may be strict in it), you are thus in the hands of an angry God; 'tis nothing but his mere pleasure that keeps you from being this moment swallowed up in everlasting destruction.

31   However unconvinced you may now be of the truth of what you hear, by and by you will be fully convinced of it. Those that are gone from being in the like circumstances with you see that it was so with them; for destruction came suddenly upon most of them; when they expected nothing of it, and while they were saying, Peace and safety: now they see, that those things that they depended on for peace and safety were nothing but thin air and empty shadows.

32   The God that holds you over the pit of hell, much as one holds a spider or some loathsome insect over the fire, abhors you, and is dreadfully provoked; his wrath towards you burns like fire; he looks upon you as worthy of nothing else, but to be cast into the fire; he is of purer eyes than to bear to have you in his sight; you are ten thousand times so abominable in his eyes, as the most hateful and venomous serpent is in ours. You have offended him infinitely more than ever a stubborn rebel did his prince: and yet it is nothing but his hand that holds you from falling into the fire every moment. 'Tis ascribed to nothing else, that you did not go to hell the last night; that you was suffered to awake again in this world after you closed your eyes to sleep; and there is no other reason to be given why you have not dropped into hell since you arose in the morning, but that God's hand has held you up. There is no other reason to be given why you han't gone to hell since you have sat here in the house of God, provoking his pure eyes by your sinful wicked manner of attending his solemn worship. Yea, there is nothing else that is to be given as a reason why you don't this very moment drop down into hell.

33   O sinner! consider the fearful danger you are in. 'Tis a great furnace of wrath, a wide and bottomless pit, full of the fire of wrath, that you are held over in the hand of that God whose wrath is provoked and incensed as much against you as against many of the damned in hell. You hang by a slender thread, with the flames of divine wrath flashing about it, and ready every moment to singe it and burn it asunder; and you have no interest in any Mediator, and nothing to lay hold of to save yourself, nothing to keep off the flames of wrath, nothing of your own, nothing that you ever have done, nothing that you can do, to induce God to spare you one moment.

34   And consider here more particularly several things concerning that wrath that you are in such danger of.

35   1. *Whose* wrath it is. It is the wrath of the infinite God. If it were only the wrath of man, though it were of the most potent prince, it would be comparatively little to be regarded. The wrath of kings is very much dreaded, especially of absolute monarchs, that have the possessions and lives of their subjects wholly in their power, to be disposed of at their mere will. Prov. xx. 2, "The fear of a king is as the roaring of a lion: whoso provoketh him to anger sinneth against his own soul." The subject that very much enrages an arbitrary prince is liable to suffer the most extreme torments that human art can invent, or human power can inflict. But the greatest earthly potentates, in their greatest majesty and strength, and when clothed in their greatest terrors, are but feeble, despicable worms of the dust, in comparison of the great and almighty Creator and King of heaven and earth: it is but little that they can do when most enraged, and when they have exerted the utmost of their fury. All the kings of the earth before God are as grasshoppers; they are nothing, and less than nothing: both their love and their hatred is to be despised. The wrath of the great King of kings is as much more terrible than theirs, as his majesty is greater. Luke xii. 4, 5, "And I say unto you my friends, Be not afraid of them that kill the body, and after that have no more that they can do. But I will forewarn you whom ye shall fear: Fear him, which after he hath killed hath power to cast into hell; yea, I say unto you, Fear him."

36   2. 'Tis the *fierceness* of his wrath that you are exposed to. We often read of the *fury* of God; as in Isaiah lix. 18: "According to their deeds, accordingly he will repay fury to his adversaries." So Isaiah lxvi. 15, "For, behold, the Lord will come with fire, and with his chariots like a whirlwind, to render his anger with fury, and his rebukes with flames of fire." And so in many other places. So we read of God's *fierceness*. Rev. xix. 15. There we read of "the wine-press of the fierceness and wrath of Almighty God." The words are exceeding terrible: if it had only been said, "the wrath of God," the words would have implied that which is infinitely dreadful: but 'tis not only said so, but "the fierceness and wrath of God." The fury of God! The fierceness of Jehovah! Oh, how dreadful must that be! Who can utter or conceive what such expressions carry in them! But it is not only said so, but "the fierceness and wrath of Almighty God." As though there would be a very great manifestation of his almighty power in what the fierceness of his wrath should inflict, as though omnipotence should be as it were enraged, and exerted, as men are wont to exert their strength in the fierceness of their wrath. Oh! then, what will be the consequence! What will become of the poor worm that shall suffer it! Whose hands can be strong! And whose heart endure! To what a dreadful, inexpressible, inconceivable depth of misery must the poor creature be sunk who shall be the subject of this!

37   Consider this, you that are here present, that yet remain in an unregenerate state. That God will execute the fierceness of his anger implies that he will inflict wrath without any pity. When God beholds the ineffable extremity of your case, and sees your torment so vastly disproportioned to your strength, and sees how your poor soul is crushed, and sinks down, as it were, into an infinite gloom; he will have no compassion upon you, he will not forbear the executions of his wrath, or in the least lighten his hand; there shall be no moderation or mercy, nor

will God then at all stay his rough wind; he will have no regard to your welfare, nor be at all careful lest you should suffer too much in any other sense, than only that you should not suffer beyond what strict justice requires: nothing shall be withheld because it is so hard for you to bear. Ezek. viii. 18, "Therefore will I also deal in fury: mine eye shall not spare, neither will I have pity: and though they cry in mine ears with a loud voice, yet will I not hear them." Now God stands ready to pity you; this is a day of mercy; you may cry now with some encouragement of obtaining mercy: but when once the day of mercy is past, your most lamentable and dolorous cries and shrieks will be in vain; you will be wholly lost and thrown away of God, as to any regard to your welfare; God will have no other use to put you to, but only to suffer misery; you shall be continued in being to no other end; for you will be a vessel of wrath fitted to destruction; and there will be no other use of this vessel, but only to be filled full of wrath: God will be so far from pitying you when you cry to him, that 'tis said he will only "laugh and mock," Prov. i. 25, 26, &c.

38   How awful are those words, Isaiah lxiii. 3, which are the words of the great God: "I will tread them in mine anger, and will trample them in my fury; and their blood shall be sprinkled upon my garments, and I will stain all my raiment." 'Tis perhaps impossible to conceive of words that carry in them greater manifestations of these three things, viz., contempt and hatred and fierceness of indignation. If you cry to God to pity you, he will be so far from pitying you in your doleful case, or showing you the least regard or favor, that instead of that he'll only tread you under foot: and though he will know that you can't bear the weight of omnipotence treading upon you, yet he won't regard that, but he will crush you under his feet without mercy; he'll crush out your blood, and make it fly, and it shall be sprinkled on his garments, so as to stain all his raiment. He will not only hate you, but he will have you in the utmost contempt; no place shall be thought fit for you but under his feet, to be trodden down as the mire of the streets.

39   3. The misery you are exposed to is that which God will inflict to that end, that he might *show* what that *wrath* of *Jehovah* is. God hath had it on his heart to show to angels and men, both how excellent his love is, and also how terrible his wrath is. Sometimes earthly kings have a mind to show how terrible their wrath is, by the extreme punishments they would execute on those that provoke 'em. Nebuchadnezzar, that mighty and haughty monarch of the Chaldean empire, was willing to show his wrath when enraged with Shadrach, Meshech, and Abednego; and accordingly gave order that the burning fiery furnace should be heated seven times hotter than it was before; doubtless, it was raised to the utmost degree of fierceness that human art could raise it; but the great God is also willing to show his wrath, and magnify his awful Majesty and mighty power in the extreme sufferings of his enemies. Rom. ix. 22, "What if God, willing to show his wrath, and to make his power known, endured with much long-suffering the vessels of wrath fitted to destruction?" And seeing this is his design, and what he has determined, to show how terrible the unmixed, unrestrained wrath, the fury and fierceness of Jehovah is, he will do it to effect. There will be something accomplished and brought to pass that will be dreadful with a witness. When the great and angry

God hath risen up and executed his awful vengeance on the poor sinner, and the wretch is actually suffering the infinite weight and power of his indignation, then will God call upon the whole universe to behold that awful majesty and mighty power that is to be seen in it. Isa. xxxiii. 12, 13, 14, "And the people shall be as the burnings of lime, as thorns cut up shall they be burnt in the fire. Hear, ye that are far off, what I have done; and ye that are near, acknowledge my might. The sinners in Zion are afraid; fearfulness hath surprised the hypocrites," &c.

40   Thus it will be with you that are in an unconverted state, if you continue in it; the infinite might, and majesty, and terribleness, of the Omnipotent God shall be magnified upon you in the ineffable strength of your torments. You shall be tormented in the presence of the holy angels, and in the presence of the Lamb; and when you shall be in this state of suffering, the glorious inhabitants of heaven shall go forth and look on the awful spectacle, that they may see what the wrath and fierceness of the Almighty is; and when they have seen it, they will fall down and adore that great power and majesty. Isa. lxvi. 23, 24, "And it shall come to pass, that from one new moon to another, and from one sabbath to another, shall all flesh come to worship before me, saith the Lord. And they shall go forth, and look upon the carcasses of the men that have transgressed against me: for their worm shall not die, neither shall their fire be quenched; and they shall be an abhorring unto all flesh."

41   4. It is *everlasting* wrath. It would be dreadful to suffer this fierceness and wrath of Almighty God one moment; but you must suffer it to all eternity: there will be no end to this exquisite, horrible misery. When you look forward, you shall see a long forever, a boundless duration before you, which will swallow up your thoughts, and amaze your soul; and you will absolutely despair of ever having any deliverance, any end, any mitigation, any rest at all; you will know certainly that you must wear out long ages, millions of millions of ages, in wrestling and conflicting with this almighty, merciless vengeance; and then when you have so done, when so many ages have actually been spent by you in this manner, you will know that all is but a point to what remains. So that your punishment will indeed be infinite. Oh, who can express what the state of a soul in such circumstances is! All that we can possibly say about it gives but a very feeble, faint representation of it; it is inexpressible and inconceivable: for "who knows the power of God's anger?"

42   How dreadful is the state of those that are daily and hourly in danger of this great wrath and infinite misery! But this is the dismal case of every soul in this congregation that has not been born again, however moral and strict, sober and religious, they may otherwise be. Oh, that you would consider it, whether you be young or old! There is reason to think that there are many in this congregation now hearing this discourse, that will actually be the subjects of this very misery to all eternity. We know not who they are, or in what seats they sit, or what thoughts they now have. It may be they are now at ease, and hear all these things without much disturbance, and are now flattering themselves that they are not the persons, promising themselves that they shall escape. If we knew that there was one person, and but one, in the whole congregation, that was to be the subject of this misery, what an awful thing it would be to think of! If we knew

who it was, what an awful sight would it be to see such a person! How might all the rest of the congregation lift up a lamentable and bitter cry over him! But alas! instead of one, how many is it likely will remember this discourse in hell! And it would be a wonder, if some that are now present should not be in hell in a very short time, before this year is out. And it would be no wonder if some persons that now sit here in some seats of this meeting-house in health, and quiet and secure, should be there before to-morrow morning. Those of you that finally continue in a natural condition, that shall keep out of hell longest, will be there in a little time! Your damnation don't slumber; it will come swiftly and, in all probability, very suddenly upon many of you. You have reason to wonder that you are not already in hell. 'Tis doubtless the case of some that heretofore you have seen and known, that never deserved hell more than you and that heretofore appeared as likely to have been now alive as you. Their case is past all hope; they are crying in extreme misery and perfect despair. But here you are in the land of the living and in the house of God, and have an opportunity to obtain salvation. What would not those poor, damned, hopeless souls give for one day's such opportunity as you now enjoy!

43 And now you have an extraordinary opportunity, a day wherein Christ has flung the door of mercy wide open, and stands in the door calling and crying with a loud voice to poor sinners; a day wherein many are flocking to him and pressing into the Kingdom of God. Many are daily coming from the east, west, north and south; many that were very likely in the same miserable condition that you are in are in now a happy state, with their hearts filled with love to him that has loved them and washed them from their sins in his own blood, and rejoicing in hope of the glory of God. How awful is it to be left behind at such a day! To see so many others feasting, while you are pining and perishing! To see so many rejoicing and singing for joy of heart, while you have cause to mourn for sorrow of heart and howl for vexation of spirit! How can you rest one moment in such a condition? Are not your souls as precious as the souls of the people at Suffield, [the next neighbor town] where they are flocking from day to day to Christ?

44 Are there not many here that have lived long in the world that are not to this day born again, and so are aliens from the commonwealth of Israel and have done nothing ever since they have lived but treasure up wrath against the day of wrath? Oh, sirs, your case in an especial manner is extremely dangerous; your guilt and hardness of heart is extremely great. Don't you see how generally persons of your years are passed over and left in the present remarkable and wonderful dispensation of God's mercy? You had need to consider yourselves and wake thoroughly out of sleep; you cannot bear the fierceness and the wrath of the infinite God.

45 And you that are young men and young women, will you neglect this precious season that you now enjoy, when so many others of your age are renouncing all youthful vanities and flocking to Christ? You especially have now an extraordinary opportunity; but if you neglect it, it will soon be with you as it is with those persons that spent away all the precious days of youth in sin and are now come to such a dreadful pass in blindness and hardness.

46   And you children that are unconverted, don't you know that you are going down to hell to bear the dreadful wrath of that God that is now angry with you every day, and every night? Will you be content to be the children of the devil, when so many other children in the land are converted and are become the holy and happy children of the King of kings?

47   And let every one that is yet out of Christ and hanging over the pit of hell, whether they be old men and women or middle-aged or young people or little children, now hearken to the loud calls of God's word and providence. This acceptable year of the Lord that is a day of such great favor to some will doubtless be a day of as remarkable vengeance to others. Men's hearts harden and their guilt increases apace at such a day as this, if they neglect their souls. And never was there so great danger of such persons being given up to hardness of heart and blindness of mind. God seems now to be hastily gathering in his elect in all parts of the land; and probably the bigger part of adult persons that ever shall be saved will be brought in now in a little time, and that it will be as it was on that great outpouring of the Spirit upon the Jews in the Apostles' days, the election will obtain and the rest will be blinded. If this should be the case with you, you will eternally curse this day, and will curse the day that ever you was born to see such a season of the pouring out of God's Spirit, and will wish that you had died and gone to hell before you had seen it. Now undoubtedly it is as it was in the days of John the Baptist, the axe is in an extraordinary manner laid at the root of the trees, that every tree that bringeth not forth good fruit may be hewn down and cast into the fire.

48   Therefore let every one that is out of Christ now awake and fly from the wrath to come. The wrath of Almighty God is now undoubtedly hanging over great part of this congregation. Let every one fly out of Sodom. *"Haste and escape for your lives, look not behind you, escape to the mountain, lest ye be consumed."*

"Sinners in the Hands of an Angry God" by Jonathan Edwards, 1741. From *Selected Sermons of Jonathan Edwards*, *Edited with Introduction and Notes* by H. Norman Gardiner. New York: The Macmillan Company and London: Macmillan & Co., Ltd. 1904.

Comprehension

1. What is the central idea Edwards delivers in this sermon?

2. Edwards plays on a certain emotion from the congregation as he delivers this sermon. What emotion does he hope to draw from the congregation?

3. Why does Edwards choose to use a variety of simple images that personify land and water?

4. Why does Edwards open his sermon with the Biblical text from Deuteronomy 32:35, "Their foot shall slide in due time"?

Rhetorical Analysis

5. What image of a great storm does Edwards use to describe the power of God, and why is it effective?

6. Edwards's rhetorical use of repetition is also effective. Give examples of this repetition and explain the intent of the repetition.

7. How do the Biblical references help the argument?

8. Edwards references fruit and the bearing of fruit twice. He views sin as a "bitter and poisonous fruit" and sees it to be like the "grapes of Sodom." What is the desired effect of these metaphors?

9. What is the effect of the metaphor of God holding the souls of men over Hell "much as one holds a spider or some loathsome insect over the fire"?

10. What sensory details does Edwards include in paragraph 4? What effect does this imagery have on the reader?

Writing

11. Write an extended definition of your concept of the term "religious freedom."

12. Write an essay analyzing Edwards's rhetorical strategy, considering his use of such strategies as figurative language, diction, details, and repetition.

13. **Writing an Argument** Knowing that the congregation was comprised of people whose Puritan families had left England in order to obtain religious freedom, a reader can safely see the effect this sermon would have on such moral and pious people. Would this sermon be as successful in most congregations today? Would it depend on the particular religion or congregation? Qualify your argument with specific examples.

The Golden Speech

Queen Elizabeth I

Queen Elizabeth I (1533–1603), in what would be her last speech to members of Parliament, addressed trade monopolies (grants) in England that had negatively affected the price of certain commodities. Facing a discontented audience (a Parliament of men) on November 30, 1601, she delivered a rousing speech that was so successful it became known as the Golden Speech because it was noted in a pamphlet that "this speech ought to be set in letters of gold."

1 Mr. Speaker, we have heard your declaration, and perceive your care of our state, by falling into the consideration of a grateful acknowledgment of such benefits as you have received; and that your coming is to present thanks unto us, which I accept with no less joy than your loves can have desire to offer such a present.

2 I do assure you, that there is no prince that loveth his subjects better, or whose love can countervail our love. There is no jewel, be it of never so rich a price, which I prefer before this jewel, I mean your love: for I do more esteem it than of any treasure or riches; for that we know how to prize, but love and thanks I count inestimable.

3 And though God hath raised me high, yet this I count the glory of my crown, that I have reigned with your loves. This makes me that I do not so much rejoice, that God hath made me to be a queen, as to be a queen over so thankful a people.

4 Therefore, I have cause to wish nothing more than to content the subject, and that is a duty which I owe. Neither do I desire to live longer days, than that I may see your prosperity, and that is my only desire.

5 And as I am that person that still, yet under God, hath delivered you; so I trust, by the Almighty power of God, that I still shall be his instrument to preserve you from envy, peril, dishonor, shame, tyranny and oppression, partly by means of your intended helps, which we take very acceptably, because it manifesteth the largeness of your loves and loyalties unto your sovereign.

6 Of myself, I must say this, I was never any greedy, scraping grasper, nor a strait fast-holding prince, nor yet a waster; my heart was never set on worldly goods, but only for my subjects good. What you do bestow on me, I will not hoard it up, but receive it to bestow on you again. Yea, mine own proprieties I count yours, to be expended for your good.

7 Therefore render unto them from me, I beseech you, Mr. Speaker, such thanks as you imagine my heart yieldeth, but my tongue cannot express.

All this while they kneeled. Whereupon her maj. said,

8 Mr. Speaker, I would wish you and the rest to stand up, for I shall yet trouble you with longer speech.

So they all stood up, and she went on in her speech.

9   Mr. Speaker, you give me thanks, but I doubt me, I have more cause to thank you all, than you me: and I charge you to thank them of the house of commons from me: for had I not received a knowledge from you, I might have fallen into the lap of an error, only for lack of true information.

10   Since I was queen, yet never did I put my pen to any grant, but that upon pretext and semblance made unto me, that it was both good and beneficial to the subjects in general, though a private profit to some of my ancient servants who had deserved well: but the contrary being found by experience, I am exceedingly beholding to such subjects as would move the same at first. And I am not so simple to suppose, but that there be some of the lower house whom these grievances never touched; and for them I think they speak out of zeal to their countries, and not out of spleen or malevolent affection, as being parties grieved; and I take it exceeding grateful from them, because it gives us to know that no respects or interests had moved them, other than the minds they bear to suffer no diminution of our honor, and our subjects love unto us. The zeal of which affection, tending to ease my people and knit their hearts unto me, I embrace with a princely care; for above all earthly treasure I esteem my people's love, more than which I desire not to merit.

11   That my grants should be grievous to my people, and oppressions to be privileged under colour of our patents, our kingly dignity shall not suffer it; yea, when I heard it, I could give no rest to my thoughts until I had reformed it.

12   Shall they think to escape unpunished, that have thus oppressed you, and have been respectless of their duty, and regardless of our honour? No. Mr. Speaker, I assure you, it is more for conscience-sake, than for any glory or increase of love, that I desire these errors, troubles, vexations and oppressions done by these varlets and lewd persons, not worthy the name of subjects, should not escape without condign punishment.

13   But I perceive they dealt with me like physicians, who ministering a drug make it more acceptable by giving it a good aromatical savour, or when they give pills do gild them all over.

14   I have ever used to set the last judgment day before mine eyes, and so to rule as I shall be judged to answer before a higher judge. To whose judgment seat I do appeal, that never thought was cherished in my heart that tended not to my people's good. And now if my kingly bounty hath been abused, and my grants turned to the hurt of my people, contrary to my will and meaning; or if any in authority under me, have neglected or perverted what I have committed to them, I hope God will not lay their culps and offences to my charge; and though there were danger in repealing our grants, yet what danger would not I rather incur for your good, than I would suffer them still to continue?

15   I know the title of a king is a glorious title; but assure yourself, that the shining glory of princely authority hath not so dazzled the eyes of our understanding, but that we well know and remember, that we also are to yield an account of our actions before the great judge.

16   To be a king and wear a crown is more glorious to them that see it, than it is pleasure to them that bear it. For myself, I was never so much enticed with the glorious name of a king, or royal authority of a queen, as delighted that God hath

made me his instrument to maintain his truth and glory, and to defend this kingdom (as I said) from peril, dishonor, tyranny and oppression.

17   There will never queen sit in my seat with more zeal to my country, or care to my subjects, and that will sooner, with willingness, yield and venture her life for your good and safety than myself. And though you have had, and may have, many princes more mighty and wise, sitting in this seat; yet you never had, or shall have, any that will be more careful and loving.

18   Should I ascribe any thing to myself and my sexly weakness, I were not worthy to live then, and of all most unworthy of the mercies I have had from God, who hath ever yet given me a heart which never yet feared foreign or home enemies. I speak it to give God the praise as a testimony before you, and not to attribute any thing unto myself, for I, O Lord, what am I, whom practices and perils past should not fear! O what can I do (these she spake with a great emphasis)

19   that I should speak for any glory! God forbid.

20   This, Mr. Speaker, I pray you deliver unto the house, to whom heartily recommend me.

21   And so I commit you all to your best fortunes, and further councils. And I pray you, Mr. Comptroller, Mr. Secretary, and you of my council, that before these gentlemen depart into their countries, you bring them all to kiss my hand.

"The Golden Speech" by Queen Elizabeth I, 1601. From *Cobbett's Parliamentary History of England.* Vol. I. London: Printed by T. Curson Hansard, Peterborough-Court, Fleet-Street. 1806.

Comprehension

1. What was Elizabeth I's greatest challenge delivering this speech?

2. Summarize what Elizabeth I is stating in paragraph 16.

3. How does she use her gender, in her role as Queen, in a strongly affirmative manner?

Rhetorical Analysis

4. Considering that many connotations exist for the word *gold,* list other ways that Elizabeth and her speech could be considered "golden."

5. What tone does Elizabeth establish in the first 3 paragraphs of her speech?

6. What persuasive strategies does Elizabeth use in her speech?

7. Analyze Elizabeth I's rhetoric of death in paragraphs 4 and 14.

Writing

8. Compare and contrast Elizabeth I's "Golden Speech" to her speech to the troops at Tilbury in 1588.

9. **Writing an Argument** Agree or disagree with the following statement, and provide supporting details and examples: Queen Elizabeth I has been the world's greatest leader since the eleventh century.

Education

Ralph Waldo Emerson

Ralph Waldo Emerson (1803–1882), a philosopher, poet, essayist, and public speaker, was one of the most quoted men of his time. Emerson was born in Boston, where his father was a Unitarian minister. When Emerson was 14, he received a scholarship to attend Harvard College, and in 1825 he entered Harvard Divinity College. A brilliant writer and speaker, Emerson had become a successful Boston minister by 1829. Two years later, his life took a new path. His wife died, and he grieved for her tremendously. Also, he had long been developing his own beliefs. He maintained that each person contained a spark of divinity and that people should search for truths in nature and within themselves—the basis of the philosophical movement known as transcendentalism. In 1833 he settled in Concord, Massachusetts. For a century, many schoolchildren knew of Emerson from his poem "Concord Hymn," which includes the famous line about the American Revolution: "the shot heard round the world." Emerson's essay "Nature" (1836) earned him accolades, and his lectures on philosophy attracted wide audiences. He, along with Henry David Thoreau, Susan B. Anthony, Frederick Douglass, and Nathaniel Hawthorne, traveled throughout the Northeast and Midwest discussing issues such as abolition, universal suffrage, and individualism. In "Education," Emerson points out that students must take an active role in their education. He argues that for one to be educated, one has to remain alive and focused on all aspects of growth.

1   I believe that our own experience instructs us that the secret of Education lies in respecting the pupil. It is not for you to choose what he shall know, what he shall do. It is chosen and foreordained, and he only holds the key to his own secret. By your tampering and thwarting and too much governing he may be hindered from his end and kept out of his own. Respect the child. Wait and see the new product of Nature. Nature loves analogies, but not repetitions. Respect the child. Be not too much his parent. Trespass not on his solitude.

2   But I hear the outcry which replies to this suggestion:—Would you verily throw up the reins of public and private discipline; would you leave the young child to the mad career of his own passions and whimsies, and call this anarchy a respect for the child's nature? I answer,—Respect the child, respect him to the end, but also respect yourself. Be the companion of his thought, the friend of his friendship, the lover of his virtue,—but no kinsman of his sin. Let him find you so true to yourself that you are the irreconcilable hater of his vice and imperturbable slighter of his trifling.

3   The two points in a boy's training are, to keep his *naturel* and train off all but that:—to keep his *naturel*, but stop off his uproar, fooling and horse-play;—keep his nature and arm it with knowledge in the very direction in which it points. Here are the two capital facts, Genius and Drill. The first is the inspiration in the

well-born healthy child, the new perception he has of nature. Somewhat he sees in forms or hears in music or apprehends in mathematics, or believes practicable in mechanics or possible in political society, which no one else sees or hears or believes. This is the perpetual romance of new life, the invasion of God into the old dead world, when he sends into quiet houses a young soul with a thought which is not met, looking for something which is not there, but which ought to be there: the thought is dim but it is sure, and he casts about restless for means and masters to verify it; he makes wild attempts to explain himself and invoke the aid and consent of the bystanders. Baffled for want of language and methods to convey his meaning, not yet clear to himself, he conceives that though not in this house or town, yet in some other house or town is the wise master who can put him in possession of the rules and instruments to execute his will. Happy this child with a bias, with a thought which entrances him, leads him, now into deserts now into cities, the fool of an idea. Let him follow it in good and in evil report, in good or bad company; it will justify itself; it will lead him at last into the illustrious society of the lovers of truth.

4   In London, in a private company, I became acquainted with a gentleman, Sir Charles Fellowes, who, being at Xanthus, in the Ægean Sea, had seen a Turk point with his staff to some carved work on the corner of a stone almost buried in the soil. Fellowes scraped away the dirt, was struck with the beauty of the sculptured ornaments, and, looking about him, observed more blocks and fragments like this. He returned to the spot, procured laborers and uncovered many blocks. He went back to England, bought a Greek grammar and learned the language; he read history and studied ancient art to explain his stones; he interested Gibson the sculptor; he invoked the assistance of the English Government; he called in the succor of Sir Humphry Davy to analyze the pigments; of experts in coins, of scholars and connoisseurs; and at last in his third visit brought home to England such statues and marble reliefs and such careful plans that he was able to reconstruct, in the British Museum where it now stands, the perfect model of the Ionic trophy-monument, fifty years older than the Parthenon of Athens, and which had been destroyed by earthquakes, then by iconoclast Christians, then by savage Turks. But mark that in the task he had achieved an excellent education, and become associated with distinguished scholars whom he had interested in his pursuit; in short, had formed a college for himself; the enthusiast had found the master, the masters, whom he sought. Always genius seeks genius, desires nothing so much as to be a pupil and to find those who can lend it aid to perfect itself.

5   Nor are the two elements, enthusiasm and drill, incompatible. Accuracy is essential to beauty. The very definition of the intellect is Aristotle's: "that by which we know terms or boundaries." Give a boy accurate perceptions. Teach him the difference between the similar and the same. Make him call things by their right names. Pardon in him no blunder. Then he will give you solid satisfaction as long as he lives. It is better to teach the child arithmetic and Latin grammar than rhetoric or moral philosophy, because they require exactitude of performance; it is made certain that the lesson is mastered, and that power of performance is worth more than the knowledge. He can learn anything which is important to him now

that the power to learn is secured: as mechanics say, when one has learned the use of tools, it is easy to work at a new craft.

6   Letter by letter, syllable by syllable, the child learns to read, and in good time can convey to all the domestic circle the sense of Shakespeare. By many steps each just as short, the stammering boy and the hesitating collegian, in the school debate, in college clubs, in mock court, comes at last to full, secure, triumphant unfolding of his thought in the popular assembly, with a fullness of power that makes all the steps forgotten.

7   But this function of opening and feeding the human mind is not to be fulfilled by any mechanical or military method; is not to be trusted to any skill less large than Nature itself. You must not neglect the form, but you must secure the essentials. It is curious how perverse and intermeddling we are, and what vast pains and cost we incur to do wrong. Whilst we all know in our own experience and apply natural methods in our own business,—in education our common sense fails us, and we are continually trying costly machinery against nature, in patent schools and academies and in great colleges and universities.

8   The natural method forever confutes our experiments, and we must still come back to it. The whole theory of the school is on the nurse's or mother's knee. The child is as hot to learn as the mother is to impart. There is mutual delight. The joy of our childhood in hearing beautiful stories from some skilful aunt who loves to tell them, must be repeated in youth. The boy wishes to learn to skate, to coast, to catch a fish in the brook, to hit a mark with a snowball or a stone; and a boy a little older is just as well pleased to teach him these sciences. Not less delightful is the mutual pleasure of teaching and learning the secret of algebra, or of chemistry, or of good reading and good recitation of poetry or of prose, or of chosen facts in history or in biography.

9   Nature provided for the communication of thought, by planting with it in the receiving mind a fury to impart it. 'Tis so in every art, in every science. One burns to tell the new fact, the other burns to hear it. See how far a young doctor will ride or walk to witness a new surgical operation. I have seen a carriage-maker's shop emptied of all its workmen into the street, to scrutinize a new pattern from New York. So in literature, the young man who has taste for poetry, for fine images, for noble thoughts, is insatiable for this nourishment, and forgets all the world for the more learned friend,—who finds equal joy in dealing out his treasures.

10   Happy the natural college thus self-instituted around every natural teacher; the young men of Athens around Socrates; of Alexandria around Plotinus; of Paris around Abelard; of Germany around Fichte, or Niebuhr, or Goethe: in short the natural sphere of every leading mind. But the moment this is organized, difficulties begin. The college was to be the nurse and home of genius; but, though every young man is born with some determination in his nature, and is a potential genius; is at last to be one; it is, in the most, obstructed and delayed, and, whatever they may hereafter be, their senses are now opened in advance of their minds. They are more sensual than intellectual. Appetite and indolence they have, but no enthusiasm. These come in numbers to the college: few geniuses: and the teaching comes to be arranged for these many, and not for those few.

Hence the instruction seems to require skilful tutors, of accurate and systematic mind, rather than ardent and inventive masters. Besides, the youth of genius are eccentric, won't drill, are irritable, uncertain, explosive, solitary, not men of the world, not good for every-day association. You have to work for huge classes instead of individuals; you must lower your flag and reef your sails to wait for the dull sailors; you grow departmental, routinary, military almost with your discipline and college police. But what doth such a school to form a great and heroic character? What abiding Hope can it inspire? What Reformer will it nurse? What poet will it breed to sing to the human race? What discoverer of Nature's laws will it prompt to enrich us by disclosing in the mind the statute which all matter must obey? What fiery soul will it send out to warm a nation with his charity? What tranquil mind will it have fortified to walk with meekness in private and obscure duties, to wait and to suffer? Is it not manifest that our academic institutions should have a wider scope; that they should not be timid and keep the ruts of the last generation, but that wise men thinking for themselves and heartily seeking the good of mankind, and counting the cost of innovation, should dare to arouse the young to a just and heroic life; that the moral nature should he addressed in the school-room, and children should be treated as the high-born candidates of truth and virtue?

[11] So to regard the young child, the young man, requires, no doubt, rare patience: a patience that nothing but faith in the remedial forces of the soul can give. You see his sensualism; you see his want of those tastes and perceptions which make the power and safety of your character. Very likely. But he has something else. If he has his own vice, he has its correlative virtue. Every mind should be allowed to make its own statement in action, and its balance will appear. In these judgments one needs that foresight which was attributed to an eminent reformer, of whom it was said "his patience could see in the bud of the aloe the blossom at the end of a hundred years." Alas for the cripple Practice when it seeks to come up with the bird Theory, which flies before it. Try your design on the best school. The scholars are of all ages and temperaments and capacities. It is difficult to class them, some are too young, some are slow, some perverse. Each requires so much consideration, that the morning hope of the teacher, of a day of love and progress, is often closed at evening by despair. Each single case, the more it is considered, shows more to be done; and the strict conditions of the hours, on one side, and the number of tasks, on the other. Whatever becomes of our method, the conditions stand fast, – six hours, and thirty, fifty, or a hundred and fifty pupils. Something must be done, and done speedily, and in this distress the wisest are tempted to adopt violent means, to proclaim martial law, corporal punishment, mechanical arrangement, bribes, spies, wrath, main strength and ignorance, in lieu of that wise genial providential influence they had hoped, and yet hope at some future day to adopt. Of course the devotion to details reacts injuriously on the teacher. He cannot indulge his genius, he cannot delight in personal relations with young friends, when his eye is always on the clock, and twenty classes are to be dealt with before the day is done. Besides, how can he please himself with genius, and foster modest virtue? A sure proportion of rogue and dunce finds its way into every school and requires a cruel share of time, and the gentle teacher, who wished to be a Providence to youth, is

grown a martinet, sore with suspicions; knows as much vice as the judge of a police court, and his love of learning is lost in the routine of grammars and books of elements.

12   A rule is so easy that it does not need a man to apply it; an automaton, a machine, can be made to keep a school so. It facilitates labor and thought so much that there is always the temptation in large schools to omit the endless task of meeting the wants of each single mind, and to govern by steam. But it is at frightful cost. Our modes of Education aim to expedite, to save labor; to do for masses what cannot be done for masses, what must be done reverently, one by one: say rather, the whole world is needed for the tuition of each pupil. The advantages of this system of emulation and display are so prompt and obvious, it is such a time-saver, it is so energetic on slow and on bad natures, and is of so easy application, needing no sage or poet, but any tutor or schoolmaster in his first term can apply it,—that it is not strange that this calomel of culture should be a popular medicine. On the other hand, total abstinence from this drug, and the adoption of simple discipline and the following of nature, involves at once immense claims on the time, the thoughts, on the life of the teacher. It requires time, use, insight, event, all the great lessons and assistances of God; and only to think of using it implies character and profoundness; to enter on this course of discipline is to be good and great. It is precisely analogous to the difference between the use of corporal punishment and the methods of love. It is so easy to bestow on a bad boy a blow, overpower him, and get obedience without words, that in this world of hurry and distraction, who can wait for the returns of reason and the conquest of self; in the uncertainty too whether that will ever come? And yet the familiar observation of the universal compensations might suggest the fear that so summary a stop of a bad humor was more jeopardous than its continuance.

13   Now the correction of this quack practice is to import into Education the wisdom of life. Leave this military hurry and adopt the pace of Nature. Her secret is patience. Do you know how the naturalist learns all the secrets of the forest, of plants, of birds, of beasts, of reptiles, of fishes, of the rivers and the sea? When he goes into the woods the birds fly before him and he finds none; when he goes to the river bank, the fish and the reptile swim away and leave him alone. His secret is patience; he sits down, and sits still; he is a statue; he is a log. These creatures have no value for their time, and he must put as low a rate on his. By dint of obstinate sitting still, reptile, fish, bird and beast, which all wish to return to their haunts, begin to return. He sits still; if they approach, he remains passive as the stone he sits upon. They lose their fear. They have curiosity too about him. By and by the curiosity masters the fear, and they come swimming, creeping and flying towards him; and as he is still immovable, they not only resume their haunts and their ordinary labors and manners, show themselves to him in their work-day trim, but also volunteer some degree of advances towards fellowship and good understanding with a biped who behaves so civilly and well. Can you not baffle the impatience and passion of the child by your tranquillity? Can you not wait for him, as Nature and Providence do? Can you not keep for his mind and ways, for his secret, the same curiosity you give to the squirrel, snake, rabbit, and the sheldrake and the deer? He has a secret; wonderful methods in him; he is,—every

child,—a new style of man; give him time and opportunity. Talk of Columbus and Newton! I tell you the child just born in yonder hovel is the beginning of a revolution as great as theirs. But you must have the believing and prophetic eye. Have the self-command you wish to inspire. Your teaching and discipline must have the reserve and taciturnity of Nature. Teach them to hold their tongues by holding your own. Say little; do not snarl; do not chide; but govern by the eye. See what they need, and that the right thing is done.

14 I confess myself utterly at a loss in suggesting particular reforms in our ways of teaching. No discretion that can be lodged with a school-committee, with the overseers or visitors of an academy, of a college, can at all avail to reach these difficulties and perplexities, but they solve themselves when we leave institutions and address individuals. The will, the male power, organizes, imposes its own thought and wish on others, and makes that military eye which controls boys as it controls men; admirable in its results, a fortune to him who has it, and only dangerous when it leads the workman to overvalue and overuse it and precludes him from finer means. Sympathy, the female force,—which they must use who have not the first,—deficient in instant control and the breaking down of resistance, is more subtle and lasting and creative. I advise teachers to cherish mother-wit. I assume that you will keep the grammar, reading, writing and arithmetic in order; 'tis easy and of course you will. But smuggle in a little contraband wit, fancy, imagination, thought. If you have a taste which you have suppressed because it is not shared by those about you, tell them that. Set this law up, whatever becomes of the rules of the school: they must not whisper, much less talk; but if one of the young people says a wise thing, greet it, and let all the children clap their hands. They shall have no book but school-books in the room; but if one has brought in a Plutarch or Shakespeare or Don Quixote or Goldsmith or any other good book, and understands what he reads, put him at once at the head of the class. Nobody shall be disorderly, or leave his desk without permission, but if a boy runs from his bench, or a girl, because the fire falls, or to check some injury that a little dastard is inflicting behind his desk on some helpless sufferer, take away the medal from the head of the class and give it on the instant to the brave rescuer. If a child happens to show that he knows any fact about astronomy, or plants, or birds, or rocks, or history, that interests him and you, hush all the classes and encourage him to tell it so that all may hear. Then you have made your school-room like the world. Of course you will insist on modesty in the children, and respect to their teachers, but if the boy stops you in your speech, cries out that you are wrong and sets you right, hug him!

15 To whatsoever upright mind, to whatsoever beating heart I speak, to you it is committed to educate men. By simple living, by an illimitable soul, you inspire, you correct, you instruct, you raise, you embellish all. By your own act you teach the beholder how to do the practicable. According to the depth from which you draw your life, such is the depth not only of your strenuous effort, but of your manners and presence.

16 The beautiful nature of the world has here blended your happiness with your power. Work straight on in absolute duty, and you lend an arm and an encouragement to all the youth of the universe. Consent yourself to be an organ

of your highest thought, and lo! suddenly you put all men in your debt, and are the fountain of an energy that goes pulsing on with waves of benefit to the borders of society, to the circumference of things.

"Education" from *Lectures and Biographical Sketches* by Ralph Waldo Emerson. Boston: Houghton, Mifflin and Company, 1884

Comprehension

1. Why, in paragraph 5, does Emerson believe "[i]t is better to teach the child arithmetic and Latin than rhetoric or moral philosophy"?

2. What are Emerson's defining characteristics of an ideal education?

3. In paragraph 10, why does Emerson criticize schools as bureaucratic institutions?

Rhetorical Analysis

4. How would you describe the overall tone of this essay?

5. Emerson uses the rhetorical strategy of extended example in paragraph 4. What purpose does this example achieve?

6. Explain the paradoxical relationship between "Genius and Drill" in paragraph 3.

7. What is Emerson's point when he says "Nature loves analogies, but not repetitions"?

Writing

8. Write a response to Emerson's assertion that it is important when working with boys "to keep his *naturel* and train off all but that:—to keep his *naturel*, but stop off his uproar, fooling and horse-play."

9. **Writing an Argument**   Write an essay in which you support or discourage the idea that certain educational practices have a direct effect on national tests.

Leviathan

Thomas Hobbes

Thomas Hobbes (1588–1679), an English philosopher, is considered one
of the founders of modern political philosophy. His book *Leviathan* (1651)
argued the points associated with the individual's rights over state's rights
and sovereignty. A believer that the government should be a true
representative of those it serves, Hobbes continued to work on those ideas
that legitimized the social contract theory. What follows are Chapters IV and V
from *Leviathan*.

CHAPTER IV: OF SPEECH.

1　The Invention of *Printing*, though ingenious, compared with the invention of
Letters, is no great matter. But who was the first that found the use of Letters, is
not known. He that first brought them into *Greece*, men say was *Cadmus*, the
sonne of *Agenor*, King of Phoenicia. A profitable Invention for continuing the
memory of time past, and the conjunction of mankind, dispersed into so many,
and distant regions of the Earth; and with all difficult, as proceeding from a
watchfull observation of the divers motions of the Tongue, Palat, Lips, and other
organs of Speech; whereby to make as many differences of characters, to
remember them. But the most noble and profitable invention of all other, was that
of SPEECH, consisting of *Names* or *Appellations*, and their Connexion; whereby
men register their Thoughts; recall them when they are past; and also declare
them one to another for mutuall utility and conversation; without which, there
had been amongst men, neither Common-wealth, nor Society, nor Contract, nor
Peace, no more than amongst Lyons, Bears, and Wolves. The first author of
Speech was *God* himself, that instructed *Adam* how to name such creatures as he
presented to his sight; For the Scripture goeth no further in this matter. But this
was sufficient to direct him to adde more names, as the experience and use of the
creatures should give him occasion; and to joyn them in such manner by degrees,
as to make himself understood; and so by succession of time, so much language
might be gotten, as he had found use for; though not so copious, as an Orator or
Philosopher has need of. For I do not find any thing in the Scripture, out of
which, directly or by consequence can be gathered, that *Adam* was taught the
names of all Figures, Numbers, Measures, Colours, Sounds, Fancies, Relations;
much less the names of Words and Speech, as *Generall, Speciall, Affirmative,
Negative, Interrogative, Optative*[1]*, Infinitive*, all which are usefull; and least of all, of
Entity, Intentionality, Quiddity[2], and other insignificant words of the School.

2　　But all this language gotten, and augmented by *Adam* and his posterity, was
again lost at the tower of *Babel*, when by the hand of God, every man was stricken
for his rebellion, with an oblivion of his former language. And being hereby

---

[1] Expressing a wish or hope
[2] A trifling point

forced to disperse themselves into severall parts of the world, it must needs be, that the diversity of Tongues that now is, proceeded by degrees from them, in such manner, as need (the mother of all inventions) taught them; and in tract of time grew every where more copious.

3   The generall use of Speech, is to transferre our Mentall Discourse, into Verbal; or the Trayne of our Thoughts, into a Trayne of Words; and that for two commodities; whereof one is the Registring of the Consequences of our Thoughts; which being apt to slip out of our memory, and put us to a new labour, may again be recalled, by such words as they were marked by. So that the first use of names, is to serve for *Markes*, or *Notes* of remembrance. Another is, when many use the same words, to signifie (by their connexion and order,) one to another, what they conceive, or think of each matter; and also what they desire, feare, or have any other passion for. And for this use they are called *Signes*. Speciall uses of Speech are these; First, to Register, what by cogitation, wee find to be the cause of any thing, present or past; and what we find things present or past may produce, or effect: which in summe, is acquiring of Arts. Secondly, to shew to others that knowledge which we have attained; which is, to Counsell, and Teach one another. Thirdly, to make known to others our wills, and purposes, that we may have the mutuall help of one another. Fourthly, to please and delight our selves, and others, by playing with our words, for pleasure or ornament, innocently.

4   To these Uses, there are also foure correspondent Abuses. First, when men register their thoughts wrong, by the inconstancy of the signification of their words; by which they register for their conceptions, that which they never conceived; and so deceive themselves. Secondly, when they use words metaphorically; that is, in other sense than that they are ordained for; and thereby deceive others. Thirdly, when by words they declare that to be their will, which is not. Fourthly, when they use them to grieve one another: for seeing nature hath armed living creatures, some with teeth, some with horns, and some with hands, to grieve an enemy, it is but an abuse of Speech, to grieve him with the tongue, unlesse it be one whom wee are obliged to govern; and then it is not to grieve, but to correct, and amend.

5   The manner how Speech serveth to the remembrance of the consequence of causes and effects, consisteth in the imposing of *Names*, and the *Connexion* of them.

6   Of Names, some are *Proper*, and singular to one onely[3] thing; as *Peter, John, This man, this Tree*: and some are *Common* to many things; as *Man, Horse, Tree*; every of which though but one Name, is nevertheless the name of divers particular things; in respect of all which together, it is called an *Universall*; there being nothing in the world Universall but Names; for the things named, are every one of them Individuall and Singular.

7   One Universall name is imposed on many things, for their similitude in some quality, or other accident: And wheras a Proper Name bringeth to mind one thing onely; Universals recall any one of those many.

8   And of Names Universall, some are of more, and some of lesse extent; the larger comprehending the lesse large: and some again of equall extent, comprehending each other reciprocally. As for example, the Name *Body* is of

---

[3] only

larger signification than the word *Man*, and comprehendeth it; and the names *Man* and *Rationall*, are of equall extent, comprehending mutually one another. But here wee must take notice, that by a Name is not alwayes understood, as in Grammar, one onely Word; but sometimes by circumlocution many words together. For all these words, *Hee that in his actions observeth the Lawes of his Country*, make but one Name, equivalent to this one word, *Just*.

9   By this imposition of Names, some of larger, some of stricter signification, we turn the reckoning of the consequences of things imagined in the mind, into a reckoning of the consequences of Appellations. For example, a man that hath no use of Speech at all, (such, as is born and remains perfectly deafe and dumb,) if he set before his eyes a triangle, and by it two right angles, (such as are the corners of a square figure,) he may by meditation compare and find, that the three angles of that triangle, are equall to those two right angles that stand by it. But if another triangle be shewn him different in shape from the former, he cannot know without a new labour, whether the three angles of that also be equall to the same. But he that hath the use of words, when he observes, that such equality was consequent[4], not to the length of the sides, nor to any other particular thing in his triangle; but onely to this, that the sides were straight, and the angles three; and that that was all, for which he named it a Triangle; will boldly conclude Universally, that such equality of angles is in all triangles whatsoever; and register his invention in these generall termes, *Every triangle hath its three angles equall to two right angles.* And thus the consequence found in one particular, comes to be registred and remembered as an Universall rule; and discharges our mentall reckoning, of time and place; and delivers us from all labour of the mind, saving the first; and makes that which was found true *here*, and *now*, to be true in *all times* and *places*.

10   But the use of words in registring our thoughts, is in nothing so evident as in Numbring. A naturall foole that could never learn by heart the order of numerall words, as *one, two,* and *three,* may observe every stroak of the Clock, and nod to it, or say one, one, one; but can never know what houre it strikes. And it seems, there was a time when those names of number were not in use; and men were fayn[5] to apply their fingers of one or both hands, to those things they desired to keep account of; and that thence it proceeded, that now our numerall words are but ten, in any Nation, and in some but five, and then they begin again. And he that can tell ten, if he recite them out of order, will lose himselfe, and not know when he has done: Much lesse will he be able to adde, and substract, and performe all other operations of Arithmetique. So that without words there is no possibility of reckoning of Numbers; much lesse of Magnitudes, of Swiftnesse, of Force, and other things, the reckonings whereof are necessary to the being, or well-being of man-kind.

11   When two Names are joyned together into a Consequence, or Affirmation; as thus, *A man is a living creature*; or thus, *if he be a man, he is a living creature,* If the later name *Living creature,* signifie all that the former name *Man* signifieth, then the affirmation, or consequence is *true*; otherwise *false.* For *True* and *False* are attributes

---

[4] As a result of
[5] Compelled

of Speech, not of Things. And where Speech is not, there is neither *Truth* nor *Falshood*. *Errour* there may be, as when wee expect that which shall not be; or suspect what has not been: but in neither case can a man be charged with Untruth.

12   Seeing then that *truth* consisteth in the right ordering of names in our affirmations, a man that seeketh precise *truth*, had need to remember what every name he uses stands for; and to place it accordingly; or else he will find himselfe entangled in words, as a bird in lime-twiggs[6]; the more he struggles, the more belimed. And therefore in Geometry, (which is the onely Science that it hath pleased God hitherto to bestow on mankind,) men begin at settling the significations of their words; which settling of significations, they call *Definitions*; and place them in the beginning of their reckoning.

13   By this it appears how necessary it is for any man that aspires to true Knowledge, to examine the Definitions of former Authors; and either to correct them, where they are negligently set down; or to make them himselfe. For the errours of Definitions multiply themselves, according as the reckoning proceeds; and lead men into absurdities, which at last they see, but cannot avoyd, without reckoning anew from the beginning; in which lyes the foundation of their errours. From whence it happens, that they which trust to books, do as they that cast up many little summs into a greater, without considering whether those little summes were rightly cast up or not; and at last finding the errour visible, and not mistrusting their first grounds, know not which way to cleere themselves; but spend time in fluttering over their bookes; as birds that entring by the chimney, and finding themselves inclosed in a chamber, flutter at the false light of a glasse window, for want of wit to consider which way they came in. So that in the right Definition of Names, lyes the first use of Speech; which is the Acquisition of Science: And in wrong, or no Definitions, lyes the first abuse; from which proceed all false and senslesse Tenets; which make those men that take their instruction from the authority of books, and not from their own meditation, to be as much below the condition of ignorant men, as men endued with true Science are above it. For between true Science, and erroneous Doctrines, Ignorance is in the middle. Naturall sense and imagination, are not subject to absurdity. Nature it selfe cannot erre: and as men abound in copiousnesse of language; so they become more wise, or more mad than ordinary. Nor is it possible without Letters for any man to become either excellently wise, or (unless his memory be hurt by disease, or ill constitution of organs) excellently foolish. For words are wise mens counters, they do but reckon by them: but they are the mony[7] of fooles, that value them by the authority of an *Aristotle*, a *Cicero*, or a *Thomas*, or any other Doctor whatsoever, if but a man.

14   *Subject to Names*, is whatsoever can enter into, or be considered in an account; and be added one to another to make a summe; or substracted one from another, and leave a remainder. The Latines called Accounts of mony *Rationes*, and accounting, *Ratiocinatio*: and that which we in bills or books of account call *Items*, they called *Nomina*; that is, *Names*: and thence it seems to proceed, that they extended the word *Ratio*, to the faculty of Reckoning in all other things. The Greeks

---

[6] Twigs covered in a sticky substance to catch small birds
[7] Money

have but one word [*logos*], for both *Speech* and *Reason*; not that they thought there was no Speech without Reason; but no Reasoning without Speech: And the act of reasoning they called *Syllogisme*; which signifieth summing up of the consequences of one saying to another. And because the same things may enter into account for divers accidents; their names are (to shew that diversity) diversly wrested, and diversified. This diversity of names may be reduced to foure generall heads.

15   First, a thing may enter into account for *Matter*, or *Body*; as *living, sensible, rationall, hot, cold, moved, quiet*; with all which names the word *Matter*, or *Body* is understood; all such, being names of Matter.

16   Secondly, it may enter into account, or be considered, for some accident or quality, which we conceive to be in it; as for *being moved*, for *being so long*, for *being hot*, &c; and then, of the name of the thing it selfe, by a little change or wresting, wee make a name for that accident, which we consider; and for *living* put into the account *life*; for *moved*, *motion*; for *hot*, *heat*; for *long*, *length*, and the like: And all such Names, are the names of the accidents and properties, by which one Matter, and Body is distinguished from another. These are called *names Abstract*; because severed[8] (not from Matter, but) from the account of Matter.

17   Thirdly, we bring into account, the Properties of our own bodies, whereby we make such distinction: as when any thing is *Seen* by us, we reckon not the thing it selfe; but the *sight*, the *Colour*, the *Idea* of it in the fancy: and when any thing is *heard*, wee reckon it not; but the *hearing*, or *sound* onely, which is our fancy or conception of it by the Eare: and such are names of fancies.

18   Fourthly, we bring into account, consider, and give names, to *Names* themselves, and to *Speeches*: For, *generall, universall, speciall, equivocall*, are names of Names. And *Affirmation, Interrogation, Commandement, Narration, Syllogisme, Sermon, Oration*, and many other such, are names of Speeches. And this is all the variety of Names *Positive*; which are put to mark somewhat which is in Nature, or may be feigned by the mind of man, as Bodies that are, or may be conceived to be; or of bodies, the Properties that are, or may be feigned to be; or Words and Speech.

19   There be also other Names, called *Negative*; which are notes to signifie that a word is not the name of the thing in question; as these words: *Nothing, no man, infinite, indocible*[9], *three want foure*, and the like; which are nevertheless of use in reckoning, or in correcting of reckoning; and call to mind our past cogitations, though they be not names of any thing; because they make us refuse to admit of Names not rightly used.

20   All other Names, are but insignificant sounds; and those of two sorts. One, when they are new, and yet their meaning not explained by Definition; whereof there have been aboundance coyned by Schoole-men, and pusled[10] Philosophers.

21   Another, when men make a name of two Names, whose significations are contradictory and inconsistent; as this name, an *incorporeall body*, or (which is all one) an *incorporeall substance*, and a great number more. For whensoever any affirmation is false, the two names of which it is composed, put together and made one, signifie nothing at all. For example, if it be a false affirmation to say *a*

---

[8] Separate
[9] Unteachable
[10] Puzzled

quadrangle is round, the word *round quadrangle* signifies nothing; but is a meere sound. So likewise if it be false, to say that vertue can be powred, or blown up and down; the words *In-powred vertue, In-blown vertue*, are as absurd and insignificant, as a *round quadrangle*. And therefore you shall hardly meet with a senslesse and insignificant word, that is not made up of some Latin or Greek names. A Frenchman seldome hears our Saviour called by the name of *Parole*, but by the name of *Verbe* often; yet *Verbe* and *Parole* differ no more, but that one is Latin, the other French.

22   When a man, upon the hearing of any Speech, hath those thoughts which the words of that Speech, and their connexion, were ordained and constituted to signifie; Then he is said to understand it: *Understanding* being nothing else, but conception caused by Speech. And therefore if Speech be peculiar to man (as for ought I know it is,) then is Understanding peculiar to him also. And therefore of absurd and false affirmations, in case they be universall, there can be no Understanding; though many think they understand, then, when they do but repeat the words softly, or con them in their mind.

23   What kinds of Speeches signifie the Appetites, Aversions, and Passions of mans mind; and of their use and abuse, I shall speak when I have spoken of the Passions.

24   The names of such things as affect us, that is, which please, and displease us, because all men be not alike affected with the same thing, nor the same man at all times, are in the common discourses of men, of *inconstant* signification. For seeing all names are imposed to signifie our conceptions; and all our affections are but conceptions; when we conceive the same things differently, we can hardly avoyd different naming of them. For though the nature of that we conceive, be the same; yet the diversity of our reception of it, in respect of different constitutions of body, and prejudices of opinion, gives every thing a tincture of our different passions. And therefore in reasoning, a man must take heed of words; which, besides the signification of what we imagine of their nature, have a signification also of the nature, disposition, and interest of the speaker; such as are the names of Vertues and Vices; For one man calleth *Wisdome*, what another calleth *feare*; and one *cruelty*, what another *justice*; one *prodigality*, what another *magnanimity*; and one *gravity*, what another *stupidicy*, &c. And therefore such names can never be true grounds of any ratiocination.[11] No more can Metaphors, and Tropes of speech: but these are less dangerous, because they profess their inconstancy; which the other do not.

Chapter V: Of Reason, and Science.

25 When a man *Reasoneth*, hee does nothing else but conceive a summe totall, from *Addition* of parcels; or conceive a Remainder, from *Substraction* of one summe from another: which (if it be done by Words,) is conceiving of the consequence of the names of all the parts, to the name of the whole; or from the names of the whole and one part, to the name of the other part. And though in some things, (as in numbers,) besides *Adding* and *Substracting*, men name other operations, as *Multiplying* and *Dividing*; yet they are the same; for Multiplication, is but Adding

---

[11] Reasoning

together of things equall; and Division, but Substracting of one thing, as often as we can. These operations are not incident to Numbers onely, but to all manner of things that can be added together, and taken one out of another. For as Arithmeticians teach to adde and substract in *numbers*; so the Geometricians teach the same in *lines, figures* (solid and superficiall,), *angles, proportions, times,* degrees of *swiftnesse, force, power,* and the like; The Logicians teach the same in *Conseque[n]ces of words*; adding together *two Names*, to make an *Affirmation*; and *two Affirmations*, to make a *Syllogisme*; and *many Syllogismes* to make a *Demonstration*; and from the *summe*, or *Conclusion* of a *Syllogisme*, they substract one *Proposition*, to finde the other. Writers of Politiques, adde together *Pactions*[12] to find mens *duties*; and Lawyers, *Lawes,* and *facts*, to find what is *right* and *wrong* in the actions of private men. In summe, in what matter soever there is place for *addition* and *substraction*, there also is place for *Reason*; and where these have no place, there *Reason* has nothing at all to do.

26   Out of all which we may define, (that is to say determine,) what that is, which is meant by this word *Reason*, when wee reckon it amongst the Faculties of the mind. For REASON, in this sense, is nothing but *Reckoning* (that is, Adding and Substracting) of the Consequences of generall names agreed upon, for the *marking* and *signifying* of our thoughts; I say *marking* them, when we reckon by our selves; and *signifying*, when we demonstrate, or approve our reckonings to other men.

27   And as in Arithmetique, unpractised men must, and Professors themselves may often erre, and cast up false; so also in any other subject of Reasoning, the ablest, most attentive, and most practised men, may deceive themselves, and inferre false Conclusions; Not but that Reason it selfe is alwayes Right Reason, as well as Arithmetique is a certain and infallible Art: But no one mans Reason, nor the Reason of any one number of men, makes the certaintie; no more than an account is therefore well cast up, because a great many men have unanimously approved it. And therfore, as when there is a controversy in an account, the parties must by their own accord, set up for right Reason, the Reason of some Arbitrator, or Judge, to whose sentence they will both stand, or their controversie must either come to blowes, or be undecided, for want of a right Reason constituted by Nature; so is it also in all debates of what kind soever: And when men that think themselves wiser than all others, clamor and demand right Reason for judge; yet seek no more, but that things should be determined, by no other mens reason but their own, it is as intolerable in the society of men, as it is in play after t[r]ump is turned, to use for trump on every occasion, that suite whereof they have most in their hand. For they do nothing els[13], that will have every of their passions, as it comes to bear sway in them, to be taken for right Reason, and that in their own controversies: bewraying[14] their want of right Reason, by the claym they lay to it.

28   The Use and End of Reason, is not the finding of the summe, and truth of one, or a few consequences, remote from the first definitions, and settled significations of names; but to begin at these; and proceed from one consequence to another.

---

[12] Agreements; contracts
[13] Else
[14] Betraying

For there can be no certainty of the last Conclusion, without a certainty of all those Affirmations and Negations, on which it was grounded, and inferred. As when a master of a family, in taking an account, casteth up the summs of all the bills of expence, into one sum; and not regarding how each bill is summed up, by those that give them in account; nor what it is he payes for; he advantages himself no more, than if he allowed the account in grosse, trusting to every of the accountants skill and honesty: so also in Reasoning of all other things, he that takes up conclusions on the trust of Authors, and doth not fetch them from the first Items in every Reckoning, (which are the significations of names settled by definitions), loses his labour; and does not know any thing; but onely beleeveth[15].

29   When a man reckons without the use of words, which may be done in particular things, (as when upon the sight of any one thing, wee conjecture what was likely to have preceded, or is likely to follow upon it;) if that which he thought likely to follow, followes not; or that which he thought likely to have preceded it, hath not preceded it, this is called ERROR; to which even the most prudent men are subject. But when we Reason in Words of generall signification, and fall upon a generall inference which is false; though it be commonly called *Error*, it is indeed an ABSURDITY, or senslesse Speech. For Error is but a deception, in presuming that somewhat is past, or to come; of which, though it were not past, or not to come; yet there was no impossibility discoverable. But when we make a generall assertion, unlesse it be a true one, the possibility of it is unconceivable. And words whereby we conceive nothing but the sound, are those we call *Absurd*, *Insignificant*, and *Nonsense*. And therefore if a man should talk to me of a *round Quadrangle*; or *accidents of Bread in Cheese*; or *Immateriall Substances*; or of *A free Subject*; *A free-Will*; or any *Free*, but free from being hindred by opposition, I should not say he were in an Errour; but that his words were without meaning; that is to say, Absurd.

30   I have said before, (in the second chapter,) that a Man did excell all other Animals in this faculty, that when he conceived any thing whatsoever, he was apt to enquire the consequences of it, and what effects he could do with it. And now I adde this other degree of the same excellence, that he can by words reduce the consequences he findes to generall Rules, called *Theoremes*, or *Aphorismes*; that is, he can Reason, or reckon, not onely in number, but in all other things, whereof one may be added unto, or substracted from another.

31   But this priv[il]edge, is allayed by another; and that is, by the priviledge of Absurdity; to which no living creature is subject, but men onely. And of men, those are of all most subject to it, that professe Philosophy. For it is most true that *Cicero* sayth of them somewhere; that there can be nothing so absurd, but may be found in the books of Philosophers. And the reason is manifest. For there is not one of them that begins his ratiocination from the Definitions, or Explications of the names they are to use; which is a method that hath been used onely in Geometry; whose Conclusions have thereby been made indisputable.

32   1. The first cause of Absurd conclusions I ascribe to the want of Method; in that they begin not their Ratiocination from Definitions; that is, from settled significations of their words: as if they could cast account, without knowing the value of the numerall words, *one*, *two*, and *three*.

---

[15] Only believes

33   And whereas all bodies enter into account upon divers considerations, (which I
have mentioned in the precedent chapter;) these considerations being diversely
named, divers absurdities proceed from the confusion, and unfit connexion of
their names into assertions. And therefore

34   2. The second cause of Absurd assertions, I ascribe to the giving of names of
bodies, to *accidents*; or of *accidents*, to *bodies*; As they do, that say, *Faith is infused*, or
inspired; when nothing can be *powred*, or *breathed* into any thing, but body; and
that, *extension is body*; that *phantasmes* are *spirits*, &c.

35   3. The third I ascribe to the giving of the names of the *accidents of bodies without
us*, to the *accidents* of our *own bodies*; as they do that say, the *colour is in the body*;
the sound is in the ayre, &c.

36   4. The fourth, to the giving of the names of *bodies*, to *names*, or *speeches*; as they
do that say, that *there be things universall*; that *a living creature is Genus*, or *a generall
thing*, &c.

37   5. The fifth, to the giving of the names of *accidents*, to *names* and *speeches*; as
they do that say, *the nature of a thing is its definition*; *a mans command is his will*; and
the like.

38   6. The sixth, to the use of Metaphors, Tropes, and other Rhetoricall figures, in
stead of words proper. For though it be lawfull to say, (for example) in common
speech, *the way goeth, or leadeth hither, or thither, The Proverb sayes this or that*
(whereas wayes cannot go, nor Proverbs speak;) yet in reckoning, and seeking of
truth, such speeches are not to be admitted.

39   7. The seventh, to names that signifie nothing; but are taken up, and learned
by rote from the Schooles, as *hypostatical, transubstantiate, consubstantiate, eternal-
Now*, and the like canting of Schoolemen.

40   To him that can avoyd these things, it is not easie to fall into any absurdity,
unlesse it be by the length of an account; wherein he may perhaps forget what
went before. For all men by nature reason alike, and well, when they have good
principles. For who is so stupid, as both to mistake in Geometry, and also to
persist in it, when another detects his error to him?

41   By this it appears that Reason is not as Sense, and Memory, borne with us; nor
gotten by Experience onely, as Prudence is; but attayned by Industry; first in apt
imposing of Names; and secondly by getting a good and orderly Method in
proceeding from the Elements, which are Names, to Assertions made by
Connexion of one of them to another; and so to Syllogismes, which are the
Connexions of one Assertion to another, till we come to a knowledge of all the
Consequences of names appertaining to the subject in hand; and that is it, men
call SCIENCE. And whereas Sense and Memory are but knowledge of Fact, which
is a thing past, and irrevocable; *Science* is the knowledge of Consequences, and
dependance of one fact upon another; by which, out of that we can presently do,
we know how to do something else when we will, or the like, another time:
Because when we see how any thing comes about, upon what causes, and by what
manner; when the like causes come into our power, wee see how to make it
produce the like effects.

42   Children therefore are not endued with Reason at all, till they have attained the
use of Speech: but are called Reasonable Creatures, for the possibility apparent of

having the use of Reason in time to come. And the most part of men, though they have the use of Reasoning a little way, as in numbring to some degree; yet it serves them to little use in common life; in which they govern themselves, some better, some worse, according to their differences of experience, quicknesse of memory, and inclinations to severall ends; but specially according to good or evill fortune, and the errors of one another. For as for *Science*, or certain rules of their actions, they are so farre from it, that they know not what it is. Geometry they have thought Conjuring: But for other Sciences, they who have not been taught the beginnings, and some progresse in them, that they may see how they be acquired and generated, are in this point like children, that having no thought of generation, are made believe by the women, that their brothers and sisters are not born, but found in the garden.

43   But yet they that have no *Science*, are in better, and nobler condition with their naturall Prudence; than men, that by mis-reasoning, or by trusting them that reason wrong, fall upon false and absurd generall rules. For ignorance of causes, and of rules, does not set men so farre out of their way, as relying on false rules, and taking for causes of what they aspire to, those that are not so, but rather causes of the contrary.

44   To conclude, The Light of humane minds is Perspicuous[16] Words, but by exact definitions first snuffed, and purged from ambiguity; *Reason* is the *pace*; Encrease of *Science*, the *way*; and the Benefit of man-kind, the *end*. And on the contrary, Metaphors, and senslesse and ambiguous words, are like *ignes fatui*;[17] and reasoning upon them, is wandering amongst innumerable absurdities; and their end, contention, and sedition, or contempt.

45   As, much Experience, is *Prudence*; so, is much Science, *Sapience*. For though wee usually have one name of Wisedome for them both; yet the Latines did always distinguish between *Prudentia* and *Sapientia*; ascribing the former to Experience, the later to Science. But to make their difference appeare more cleerly, let us suppose one man endued with an excellent naturall use, and dexterity in handling his armes; and another to have added to that dexterity, an acquired Science, of where he can offend, or be offended by his adversarie, in every possible posture, or guard: The ability of the former, would be to the ability of the later, as Prudence to Sapience; both usefull; but the later infallible. But they that trusting onely to the authority of books, follow the blind blindly, are like him that trusting to the false rules of a master of Fence, ventures praesumptuously upon an adversary, that either kills, or disgraces him.

46   The signes of Science, are some, certain and infallible; some, uncertain. Certain, when he that pretendeth the Science of any thing, can teach the same; that is to say, demonstrate the truth thereof perspicuously to another: Uncertain, when only some particular events answer to his pretence, and upon many occasions prove so as he sayes they must. Signes of prudence are all uncertain; because to observe by experience, and remember all circumstances that may alter the successe, is impossible. But in any businesse, whereof a man has not infallible Science to proceed by; to forsake his own naturall judgement, and be guided by

---

[16] Precise; clear
[17] Phosphorescent light seen over marshy ground at night

generall sentences read in Authors, and subject to many exceptions, is a signe of folly, and generally scorned by the name of Pedantry. And even of those men themselves, that in Councells of the Common-wealth, love to shew their reading of Politiques and History, very few do it in their domestique affaires, where their particular interest is concerned; having Prudence enough for their private affaires: but in publique they study more the reputation of their owne wit, than the success of anothers businesse.

Leviathan by Thomas Hobbes, 1651. From *Thomas Hobbes Leviathan, Or the Matter, Forme & Power of a Commonwealth, Ecclesiasticall and Civill.* Edited by A.R. Waller. London: C. J. Clay and Sons, Cambridge University Press. 1904.

Comprehension

1. What, ultimately, is Hobbes's attitude about science?

2. Hobbes uses the word *absurd* several times throughout this essay. Explain his definition of *absurd*.

Rhetorical Analysis

3. Explain what one could consider the irony in the last few sentences of paragraph 24.

4. What rhetorical skill does Hobbes use to dispute his sixth point in paragraph 38?

5. How does Hobbes further the arithmetic metaphor in paragraph 27?

6. Explain how using an anecdote in paragraph 28 furthers Hobbes's argument.

7. What purpose does language serve, according to Hobbes? How does the language in the following statement fortify his belief: "To conclude, The Light of humane minds is Perspicuous Words, but by exact definitions first snuffed, and purged from ambiguity; *Reason* is the *pace*; Encrease of *Science*, the *way*; and the Benefit of man-kind, the *end*. And on the contrary, Metaphors, and senslesse and ambiguous words, are like *ignes fatui*; and reasoning upon them, is wandering amongst innumerable absurdities; and their end, contention, and sedition, or contempt."

8. What is the overall tone of the passage?

Writing

9. Write a paragraph in which you, as the persona of Ralph Waldo Emerson, respond to Hobbes's major assertions.

10. **Writing an Argument** Write an essay agreeing or disagreeing with Hobbes's assertion that the world is essentially a complex machine that can only be governed by logic and fact.

Inaugural Address

John F. Kennedy

John F. Kennedy (1917–1963) took the oath of office for president on January 20, 1961. He had just finished competing in a highly charged race with close results and was entering the presidency as the youngest person—and first Catholic—to be elected. His political life had already given him the reputation of one who was tough on domestic and global strife. He was facing the real chill of the Cold War and the real threat of Cuba and communism. Yet, under these circumstances his address reigns as one of the most significant addresses in current American history. Eloquent, to the point, and filled with positive imagery, Kennedy succeeded in uniting a torn country and set the tone for a return to service as being the greatest gift citizens could give their country.

1   Vice President Johnson, Mr. Speaker, Mr. Chief Justice, President Eisenhower, Vice President Nixon, President Truman, reverend clergy, fellow citizens: We observe today not a victory of party, but a celebration of freedom—symbolizing an end, as well as a beginning—signifying renewal, as well as change. For I have sworn before you and Almighty God the same solemn oath our forebears prescribed nearly a century and three-quarters ago.

2   The world is very different now. For man holds in his mortal hands the power to abolish all forms of human poverty and all forms of human life. And yet the same revolutionary beliefs for which our forebears fought are still at issue around the globe—the belief that the rights of man come not from the generosity of the state, but from the hand of God.

3   We dare not forget today that we are the heirs of that first revolution. Let the word go forth from this time and place, to friend and foe alike, that the torch has been passed to a new generation of Americans—born in this century, tempered by war, disciplined by a hard and bitter peace, proud of our ancient heritage—and unwilling to witness or permit the slow undoing of those human rights to which this Nation has always been committed, and to which we are committed today at home and around the world.

4   Let every nation know, whether it wishes us well or ill, that we shall pay any price, bear any burden, meet any hardship, support any friend, oppose any foe, in order to assure the survival and the success of liberty.

5   This much we pledge—and more.

6   To those old allies whose cultural and spiritual origins we share, we pledge the loyalty of faithful friends. United, there is little we cannot do in a host of cooperative ventures. Divided, there is little we can do—for we dare not meet a powerful challenge at odds and split asunder.

7   To those new States whom we welcome to the ranks of the free, we pledge our word that one form of colonial control shall not have passed away merely to be replaced by a far more iron tyranny. We shall not always expect to find them

supporting our view. But we shall always hope to find them strongly supporting their own freedom—and to remember that, in the past, those who foolishly sought power by riding the back of the tiger ended up inside.

8   To those peoples in the huts and villages across the globe struggling to break the bonds of mass misery, we pledge our best efforts to help them help themselves, for whatever period is required—not because the Communists may be doing it, not because we seek their votes, but because it is right. If a free society cannot help the many who are poor, it cannot save the few who are rich.

9   To our sister republics south of our border, we offer a special pledge—to convert our good words into good deeds—in a new alliance for progress—to assist free men and free governments in casting off the chains of poverty. But this peaceful revolution of hope cannot become the prey of hostile powers. Let all our neighbors know that we shall join with them to oppose aggression or subversion anywhere in the Americas. And let every other power know that this Hemisphere intends to remain the master of its own house.

10   To that world assembly of sovereign states, the United Nations, our last best hope in an age where the instruments of war have far outpaced the instruments of peace, we renew our pledge of support—to prevent it from becoming merely a forum for invective—to strengthen its shield of the new and the weak—and to enlarge the area in which its writ may run.

11   Finally, to those nations who would make themselves our adversary, we offer not a pledge but a request: that both sides begin anew the quest for peace, before the dark powers of destruction unleashed by science engulf all humanity in planned or accidental self-destruction.

12   We dare not tempt them with weakness. For only when our arms are sufficient beyond doubt can we be certain beyond doubt that they will never be employed.

13   But neither can two great and powerful groups of nations take comfort from our present course—both sides overburdened by the cost of modern weapons, both rightly alarmed by the steady spread of the deadly atom, yet both racing to alter that uncertain balance of terror that stays the hand of mankind's final war.

14   So let us begin anew—remembering on both sides that civility is not a sign of weakness, and sincerity is always subject to proof. Let us never negotiate out of fear. But let us never fear to negotiate.

15   Let both sides explore what problems unite us instead of belaboring those problems which divide us.

16   Let both sides, for the first time, formulate serious and precise proposals for the inspection and control of arms—and bring the absolute power to destroy other nations under the absolute control of all nations.

17   Let both sides seek to invoke the wonders of science instead of its terrors. Together let us explore the stars, conquer the deserts, eradicate disease, tap the ocean depths, and encourage the arts and commerce.

18   Let both sides unite to heed in all corners of the earth the command of Isaiah—to "undo the heavy burdens . . . (and) let the oppressed go free."

19   And if a beachhead of cooperation may push back the jungle of suspicion, let both sides join in creating a new endeavor, not a new balance of power, but a new world of law, where the strong are just and the weak secure and the peace preserved.

20   All this will not be finished in the first 100 days. Nor will it be finished in the first 1,000 days, nor in the life of this Administration, nor even perhaps in our lifetime on this planet. But let us begin.

21   In your hands, my fellow citizens, more than in mine, will rest the final success or failure of our course. Since this country was founded, each generation of Americans has been summoned to give testimony to its national loyalty. The graves of young Americans who answered the call to service surround the globe.

22   Now the trumpet summons us again—not as a call to bear arms, though arms we need; not as a call to battle, though embattled we are—but a call to bear the burden of a long twilight struggle, year in and year out, "rejoicing in hope, patient in tribulation"—a struggle against the common enemies of man: tyranny, poverty, disease and war itself.

23   Can we forge against these enemies a grand and global alliance, North and South, East and West, that can assure a more fruitful life for all mankind? Will you join in that historic effort?

24   In the long history of the world, only a few generations have been granted the role of defending freedom in its hour of maximum danger. I do not shrink from this responsibility—I welcome it. I do not believe that any of us would exchange places with any other people or any other generation. The energy, the faith, the devotion which we bring to this endeavor will light our country and all who serve it—and the glow from that fire can truly light the world.

25   And so, my fellow Americans: ask not what your country can do for you—ask what you can do for your country.

26   My fellow citizens of the world: ask not what America will do for you, but what together we can do for the freedom of man.

27   Finally, whether you are citizens of America or citizens of the world, ask of us the same high standards of strength and sacrifice which we ask of you. With a good conscience our only sure reward, with history the final judge of our deeds, let us go forth to lead the land we love, asking His blessing and His help, but knowing that here on earth God's work must truly be our own.

Inaugural Address of John F. Kennedy. Transcription courtesy of the John F. Kennedy Presidential Library and Museum. www.ourdocuments.gov

Comprehension

1. What foreign political experience is Kennedy addressing in paragraphs 8–11? How does his language affect his message?

2. Paraphrase the following two famous statements: "And so, my fellow Americans: ask not what your country can do for you—ask what you can do for your country. My fellow citizens of the world: ask not what America will do for you, but what together we can do for the freedom of man."

3. What are Kennedy's goals, as articulated in this speech? How does he believe they can best be achieved?

4. Who did Kennedy consider to be the audience of this speech?

5. What rhetorical strategies are used in the opening paragraph of this speech?

6. This speech lasted approximately nine minutes. One of Kennedy's directives to Ted Sorenson, who helped him with this speech, was to eliminate the word "I" as much as possible. The word "we" is used approximately 33 times. What effect did Kennedy hope to achieve by this?

7. Explain the paradox in the statement, "Only when our arms are sufficient beyond doubt can we be certain beyond doubt that they will never be employed."

8. What is the effect of the extended metaphor "Now the trumpet summons us again—not as a call to bear arms, though arms we need; not as a call to battle, though embattled we are—but a call to bear the burden of a long twilight struggle, year in and year out, 'rejoicing in hope, patient in tribulation'—a struggle against the common enemies of man: tyranny, poverty, disease, and war itself"?

9. How does Kennedy use juxtaposition to assure his audience "that the torch has been passed to a new generation of Americans—born in this century, tempered by war, disciplined by a hard and bitter peace"; further pointing out that "we observe today not a victory of party, but a celebration of freedom—symbolizing an end, as well as a beginning— signifying renewal, as well as change"?

Writing

10. Write an essay analyzing Kennedy's rhetorical strategy. Consider his appeals to logos, pathos, and ethos. Be sure to address parallel structure, juxtaposition, and historical references.

11. Read Abraham Lincoln's Second Inaugural Address, and then write a paragraph describing what advice you think Lincoln would give Kennedy to improve Kennedy's Inaugural Address.

12. **Writing an Argument**   Using historical and political examples, agree or disagree with the following premise: Historically speaking, presidential inaugural addresses do not fulfill the expectations of a growing number of political skeptics.

Letter From Birmingham Jail

Martin Luther King, Jr.

Martin Luther King, Jr. (1929–1968) was a leader of the Civil Rights Movement, figuring prominently in it in the 1950s and 1960s. An advocate of nonviolent protest against unjust laws and behaviors, King led the people of the South through marches, sit-ins, and demonstrations such as the one that landed him in the Birmingham jail in the spring of 1963. Dismayed by the police brutality that occurred outside and inside the jail—and the reaction of both black and white clergy who criticized him for the potential endangerment of those who attended the demonstration—King was compelled to write what is now known as one of the most famous letters in American history. In this letter, he movingly expounds on his beliefs that waiting for some type of civil resolution will never occur if people continue to ignore the very problems affecting human rights.

Birmingham City Jail
April 16, 1963
My dear Fellow Clergymen,

1   While confined here in the Birmingham City Jail, I came across your recent statement calling our present activities "unwise and untimely." Seldom, if ever, do I pause to answer criticism of my work and ideas. If I sought to answer all the criticisms that cross my desk, my secretaries would be engaged in little else in the course of the day and I would have no time for constructive work. But since I feel that you are men of genuine goodwill and your criticisms are sincerely set forth, I would like to answer your statement in what I hope will be patient and reasonable terms.

2   I think I should give the reason for my being in Birmingham, since you have been influenced by the argument of "outsiders coming in." I have the honor of serving as president of the Southern Christian Leadership Conference, an organization operating in every Southern state with headquarters in Atlanta, Georgia. We have some eighty-five affiliate organizations all across the South—one being the Alabama Christian Movement for Human Rights. Whenever necessary and possible we share staff, educational, and financial resources with our affiliates. Several months ago our local affiliate here in Birmingham invited us to be on call to engage in a nonviolent direct action program if such were deemed necessary. We readily consented and when the hour came we lived up to our promises. So I am here, along with several members of my staff, because we were invited here. I am here because I have basic organizational ties here. Beyond this, I am in Birmingham because injustice is here. Just as the eighth century prophets left their little villages and carried their "thus saith the Lord" far beyond the boundaries of their home town, and just as the Apostle Paul left his little village of Tarsus and carried the gospel of Jesus Christ to practically every hamlet and city of the Graeco-Roman world, I too am compelled to carry the gospel of freedom beyond my particular home town. Like Paul, I must constantly respond to the Macedonian call for aid.

3   Moreover, I am cognizant of the interrelatedness of all communities and states. I cannot sit idly by in Atlanta and not be concerned about what happens in Birmingham. Injustice anywhere is a threat to justice everywhere. We are caught in an inescapable network of mutuality tied in a single garment of destiny. Whatever affects one directly affects all indirectly. Never again can we afford to live with the narrow, provincial "outside agitator" idea. Anyone who lives inside the United States can never be considered an outsider anywhere in this country.

4   You deplore the demonstrations that are presently taking place in Birmingham. But I am sorry that your statement did not express a similar concern for the conditions that brought the demonstrations into being. I am sure that each of you would want to go beyond the superficial social analyst who looks merely at effects, and does not grapple with underlying causes. I would not hesitate to say that it is unfortunate that so-called demonstrations are taking place in Birmingham at this time, but I would say in more emphatic terms that it is even more unfortunate that the white power structure of this city left the Negro community with no other alternative.

5   In any nonviolent campaign there are four basic steps: (1) Collection of the facts to determine whether injustices are alive; (2) Negotiation; (3) Self-purification; and (4) Direct action. We have gone through all of these steps in Birmingham. There can be no gainsaying of the fact that racial injustice engulfs this community. Birmingham is probably the most thoroughly segregated city in the United States. Its ugly record of police brutality is known in every section of this country. Its unjust treatment of Negroes in the courts is a notorious reality. There have been more unsolved bombings of Negro homes and churches in Birmingham than any city in this nation. These are the hard, brutal, and unbelievable facts. On the basis of these conditions Negro leaders sought to negotiate with the city fathers. But the political leaders consistently refused to engage in good faith negotiation.

6   Then came the opportunity last September to talk with some of the leaders of the economic community. In these negotiating sessions certain promises were made by the merchants—such as the promise to remove the humiliating racial signs from the stores. On the basis of these promises Rev. Shuttlesworth and the leaders of the Alabama Christian Movement for Human Rights agreed to call a moratorium on any type of demonstrations. As the weeks and months unfolded we realized that we were the victims of a broken promise. The signs remained. As in so many experiences of the past we were confronted with blasted hopes, and the dark shadow of a deep disappointment settled upon us. So we had no alternative except that of preparing for direct action, whereby we would present our very bodies as a means of laying our case before the conscience of the local and national community. We were not unmindful of the difficulties involved. So we decided to go through a process of self-purification. We started having workshops on nonviolence and repeatedly asked ourselves the questions, "Are you able to accept blows without retaliating?" "Are you able to endure the ordeals of jail?"

7   We decided to set our direct-action program around the Easter season, realizing that with the exception of Christmas, this was the largest shopping period of the year. Knowing that a strong economic withdrawal program would be the by-product of direct action, we felt that this was the best time to bring

pressure on the merchants for the needed changes. Then it occurred to us that the March election was ahead, and so we speedily decided to postpone action until after election day. When we discovered that Mr. Connor was in the run-off, we decided again to postpone action so that the demonstrations could not be used to cloud the issues. At this time we agreed to begin our nonviolent witness the day after the run-off.

8   This reveals that we did not move irresponsibly into direct action. We too wanted to see Mr. Connor defeated; so we went through postponement after postponement to aid in this community need. After this we felt that direct action could be delayed no longer.

9   You may well ask, Why direct action? Why sit-ins, marches, etc.? Isn't negotiation a better path?" You are exactly right in your call for negotiation. Indeed, this is the purpose of direct action. Nonviolent direct action seeks to create such a crisis and establish such creative tension that a community that has constantly refused to negotiate is forced to confront the issue. It seeks so to dramatize the issue that it can no longer be ignored. I just referred to the creation of tension as a part of the work of the nonviolent resister. This may sound rather shocking. But I must confess that I am not afraid of the word tension. I have earnestly worked and preached against violent tension, but there is a type of constructive nonviolent tension that is necessary for growth. Just as Socrates felt that it was necessary to create a tension in the mind so that individuals could rise from the bondage of myths and half-truths to the unfettered realm of creative analysis and objective appraisal, we must see the need of having nonviolent gadflies to create the kind of tension in society that will help men rise from the dark depths of prejudice and racism to the majestic heights of understanding and brotherhood. So the purpose of the direct action is to create a situation so crisis-packed that it will inevitably open the door to negotiation. We, therefore, concur with you in your call for negotiation. Too long has our beloved Southland been bogged down in the tragic attempt to live in monologue rather than dialogue.

10   One of the basic points in your statement is that our acts are untimely. Some have asked, "Why didn't you give the new administration time to act?" The only answer that I can give to this inquiry is that the new administration must be prodded about as much as the outgoing one before it acts. We will be sadly mistaken if we feel that the election of Mr. Boutwell will bring the millennium to Birmingham. While Mr. Boutwell is much more articulate and gentle than Mr. Connor, they are both segregationists dedicated to the task of maintaining the status quo. The hope I see in Mr. Boutwell is that he will be reasonable enough to see the futility of massive resistance to desegregation. But he will not see this without pressure from the devotees of civil rights. My friends, I must say to you that we have not made a single gain in civil rights without determined legal and nonviolent pressure. History is the long and tragic story of the fact that privileged groups seldom give up their privileges voluntarily. Individuals may see the moral light and voluntarily give up their unjust posture; but as Reinhold Niebuhr has reminded us, groups are more immoral than individuals.

11   We know through painful experience that freedom is never voluntarily given by the oppressor; it must be demanded by the oppressed. Frankly I have never yet

engaged in a direct action movement that was "well timed," according to the timetable of those who have not suffered unduly from the disease of segregation. For years now I have heard the word "Wait!" It rings in the ear of every Negro with a piercing familiarity. This "wait" has almost always meant "never." It has been a tranquilizing thalidomide, relieving the emotional stress for a moment, only to give birth to an ill-formed infant of frustration. We must come to see with the distinguished jurist of yesterday that "justice too long delayed is justice denied." We have waited for more than three hundred and forty years for our constitutional and God-given rights. The nations of Asia and Africa are moving with jet-like speed toward the goal of political independence, and we still creep at horse and buggy pace toward the gaining of a cup of coffee at a lunch counter.

12   I guess it is easy for those who have never felt the stinging darts of segregation to say wait. But when you have seen vicious mobs lynch your mothers and fathers at will and drown your sisters and brothers at whim; when you have seen hate filled policemen curse, kick, brutalize, and even kill your black brothers and sisters with impunity; when you see the vast majority of your twenty million Negro brothers smothering in an air-tight cage of poverty in the midst of an affluent society; when you suddenly find your tongue twisted and your speech stammering as you seek to explain to your six-year-old daughter why she can't go to the public amusement park that has just been advertised on television, and see tears welling up in her little eyes when she is told that Funtown is closed to colored children, and see the depressing clouds of inferiority begin to form in her little mental sky, and see her begin to distort her little personality by unconsciously developing a bitterness toward white people; when you have to concoct an answer for a five-year-old son asking in agonizing pathos: "Daddy, why do white people treat colored people so mean?"; when you take a cross-country drive and find it necessary to sleep night after night in the uncomfortable corners of your automobile because no motel will accept you; when you are humiliated day in and day out by nagging signs reading "white" men and "colored"; when your first name becomes "nigger" and your middle name becomes "boy" (however old you are) and your last name becomes "John," and when your wife and mother are never given the respected title "Mrs."; when you are harried by day and haunted by night by the fact that you are a Negro, living constantly at tip-toe stance never quite knowing what to expect next, and plagued with inner fears and outer resentments; when you are forever fighting a degenerating sense of "nobodiness"—then you will understand why we find it difficult to wait. There comes a time when the cup of endurance runs over, and men are no longer willing to be plunged into an abyss of injustice where they experience the bleakness of corroding despair. I hope, sirs, you can understand our legitimate and unavoidable impatience.

13   You express a great deal of anxiety over our willingness to break laws. This is certainly a legitimate concern. Since we so diligently urge people to obey the Supreme Court's decision of 1954 outlawing segregation in the public schools, it is rather strange and paradoxical to find us consciously breaking laws. One may well ask: "How can you advocate breaking some laws and obeying others?" The answer is found in the fact that there are two types of laws: There are just laws and there are unjust laws. I would be the first to advocate obeying just laws. One

has not only a legal but moral responsibility to obey just laws. Conversely, one has a moral responsibility to disobey unjust laws. I would agree with Saint Augustine that "An unjust law is no law at all."

14   Now what is the difference between the two? How does one determine when a law is just or unjust? A just law is a man-made code that squares with the moral law or the law of God. An unjust law is a code that is out of harmony with the moral law. To put it in the terms of Saint Thomas Aquinas, an unjust law is a human law that is not rooted in eternal and natural law. Any law that uplifts human personality is just. Any law that degrades human personality is unjust. All segregation statutes are unjust because segregation distorts the soul and damages the personality. It gives the segregator a false sense of superiority and the segregated a false sense of inferiority. To use the words of Martin Buber, the great Jewish philosopher, segregation substitutes an "I-it" relationship for an "I-thou" relationship, and ends up relegating persons to the status of things. So segregation is not only politically, economically, and sociologically unsound, but it is morally wrong and sinful. Paul Tillich has said that sin is separation. Isn't segregation an existential expression of man's tragic separation, an expression of his awful estrangement, his terrible sinfulness? So I can urge men to obey the 1954 decision of the Supreme Court because it is morally right, and I can urge them to disobey segregation ordinances because they are morally wrong.

15   Let us turn to a more concrete example of just and unjust laws. An unjust law is a code that a majority inflicts on a minority that is not binding on itself. This is difference made legal. On the other hand a just law is a code that a majority compels a minority to follow that it is willing to follow itself. This is sameness made legal.

16   Let me give another explanation. An unjust law is a code inflicted upon a minority which that minority had no part in enacting or creating because they did not have the unhampered right to vote. Who can say that the legislature of Alabama which set up the segregation laws was democratically elected? Throughout the state of Alabama all types of conniving methods are used to prevent Negroes from becoming registered voters and there are some counties without a single Negro registered to vote despite the fact that the Negro constitutes a majority of the population. Can any law set up in such a state be considered democratically structured?

17   These are just a few examples of unjust and just laws. There are some instances when a law is just on its face but unjust in its application. For instance, I was arrested Friday on a charge of parading without a permit. Now there is nothing wrong with an ordinance which requires a permit for a parade, but when the ordinance is used to preserve segregation and to deny citizens the First Amendment privilege of peaceful assembly and peaceful protest, then it becomes unjust.

18   I hope you can see the distinction I am trying to point out. In no sense do I advocate evading or defying the law as the rabid segregationist would do. This would lead to anarchy. One who breaks an unjust law must do it openly, lovingly (not hatefully as the white mothers did in New Orleans when they were seen on television screaming "nigger, nigger, nigger") and with a willingness to accept the penalty. I submit that an individual who breaks a law that conscience tells him is

unjust, and willingly accepts the penalty by staying in jail to arouse the conscience of the community over its injustice, is in reality expressing the very highest respect for law.

19   Of course there is nothing new about this kind of civil disobedience. It was seen sublimely in the refusal of Shadrach, Meshach, and Abednego to obey the laws of Nebuchadnezzar because a higher moral law was involved. It was practiced superbly by the early Christians who were willing to face hungry lions and the excruciating pain of chopping blocks, before submitting to certain unjust laws of the Roman Empire. To a degree academic freedom is a reality today because Socrates practiced civil disobedience.

20   We can never forget that everything Hitler did in Germany was "legal" and everything the Hungarian freedom fighters did in Hungary was "illegal." It was "illegal" to aid and comfort a Jew in Hitler's Germany. But I am sure that, if I had lived in Germany during that time, I would have aided and comforted my Jewish brothers even though it was illegal. If I lived in a communist country today where certain principles dear to the Christian faith are suppressed, I believe I would openly advocate disobeying these anti-religious laws.

21   I must make two honest confessions to you, my Christian and Jewish brothers. First, I must confess that over the last few years I have been gravely disappointed with the white moderate. I have almost reached the regrettable conclusion that the Negroes' great stumbling block in the stride toward freedom is not the White Citizen's "Counciler" or the Ku Klux Klanner, but the white moderate who is more devoted to "order" than to justice; who prefers a negative peace which is the absence of tension to a positive peace which is the presence of justice; who constantly says "I agree with you in the goal you seek, but I can't agree with your methods of direct action"; who paternalistically feels that he can set the timetable for another man's freedom; who lives by the myth of time and who constantly advises the Negro to wait until a "more convenient season." Shallow understanding from people of good will is more frustrating than absolute misunderstanding from people of ill will. Lukewarm acceptance is much more bewildering than outright rejection.

22   I had hoped that the white moderate would understand that law and order exist for the purpose of establishing justice, and that when they fail to do this they become dangerously structured dams that block the flow of social progress. I had hoped that the white moderate would understand that the present tension in the South is merely a necessary phase of the transition from an obnoxious negative peace, where the Negro passively accepted his unjust plight, to a substance-filled positive peace, where all men will respect the dignity and worth of human personality. Actually, we who engage in nonviolent direct action are not the creators of tension. We merely bring to the surface the hidden tension that is already alive. We bring it out in the open where it can be seen and dealt with. Like a boil that can never be cured as long as it is covered up but must be opened with all its pus-flowing ugliness to the natural medicines of air and light, injustice must likewise be exposed, with all of the tension its exposing creates, to the light of human conscience and the air of national opinion before it can be cured.

23   In your statement you asserted that our actions, even though peaceful, must be condemned because they precipitate violence. But can this assertion be logically

made? Isn't this like condemning the robbed man because his possession of money precipitated the evil act of robbery? Isn't this like condemning Socrates because his unswerving commitment to truth and his philosophical delvings precipitated the misguided popular mind to make him drink the hemlock? Isn't this like condemning Jesus because His unique God consciousness and never-ceasing devotion to His will precipitated the evil act of crucifixion? We must come to see, as federal courts have consistently affirmed, that it is immoral to urge an individual to withdraw his efforts to gain his basic constitutional rights because the quest precipitates violence. Society must protect the robbed and punish the robber.

24   I had also hoped that the white moderate would reject the myth of time. I received a letter this morning from a white brother in Texas which said: "All Christians know that the colored people will receive equal rights eventually, but is it possible that you are in too great of a religious hurry? It has taken Christianity almost 2,000 years to accomplish what it has. The teachings of Christ take time to come to earth." All that is said here grows out of a tragic misconception of time. It is the strangely irrational notion that there is something in the very flow of time that will inevitably cure all ills. Actually time is neutral. It can be used either destructively or constructively. I am coming to feel that the people of ill will have used time much more effectively than the people of good will. We will have to repent in this generation not merely for the vitriolic words and actions of the bad people, but for the appalling silence of the good people. We must come to see that human progress never rolls in on wheels of inevitability. It comes through the tireless efforts and persistent work of men willing to be co-workers with God, and without this hard work time itself becomes an ally of the forces of social stagnation.

25   We must use time creatively, and forever realize that the time is always ripe to do right. Now is the time to make real the promise of democracy, and transform our pending national elegy into a creative psalm of brotherhood. Now is the time to lift our national policy from the quicksand of racial injustice to the solid rock of human dignity.

26   You spoke of our activity in Birmingham as extreme. At first I was rather disappointed that fellow clergymen would see my nonviolent efforts as those of the extremist. I started thinking about the fact that I stand in the middle of two opposing forces in the Negro community. One is a force of complacency made up of Negroes who, as a result of long years of oppression, have been so completely drained of self-respect and a sense of "somebodiness" that they have adjusted to segregation, and of a few Negroes in the middle class who, because of a degree of academic and economic security, and because at points they profit by segregation, have unconsciously become insensitive to the problems of the masses. The other force is one of bitterness and hatred and comes perilously close to advocating violence. It is expressed in the various black nationalist groups that are springing up over the nation, the largest and best known being Elijah Muhammad's Muslim movement. This movement is nourished by the contemporary frustration over the continued existence of racial discrimination. It is made up of people who have lost faith in America, who have absolutely repudiated Christianity, and who have concluded that the white man is an incurable "devil." I have tried to stand between these two forces saying that we need not follow the "do-nothingism" of

the complacent or the hatred and despair of the black nationalist. There is the more excellent way of love and nonviolent protest. I'm grateful to God that, through the Negro church, the dimension of nonviolence entered our struggle. If this philosophy had not emerged I am convinced that by now many streets of the South would be flowing with floods of blood. And I am further convinced that if our white brothers dismiss us as "rabble rousers" and "outside agitators"—those of us who are working through the channels of nonviolent direct action—and refuse to support our nonviolent efforts, millions of Negroes, out of frustration and despair, will seek solace and security in black-nationalist ideologies, a development that will lead inevitably to a frightening racial nightmare.

27   Oppressed people cannot remain oppressed forever. The urge for freedom will eventually come. This is what has happened to the American Negro. Something within has reminded him of his birthright of freedom; something without has reminded him that he can gain it. Consciously and unconsciously, he has been swept in by what the Germans call the Zeitgeist, and with his black brothers of Africa, and his brown and yellow brothers of Asia, South America, and the Caribbean, he is moving with a sense of cosmic urgency toward the promised land of racial justice. Recognizing this vital urge that has engulfed the Negro community, one should readily understand public demonstrations. The Negro has many pent-up resentments and latent frustrations. He has to get them out. So let him march sometime; let him have his prayer pilgrimages to the city hall; understand why he must have sit-ins and freedom rides. If his repressed emotions do not come out in these nonviolent ways, they will come out in ominous expressions of violence. This is not a threat; it is a fact of history. So I have not said to my people, "Get rid of your discontent." But I have tried to say that this normal and healthy discontent can be channeled through the creative outlet of nonviolent direct action. Now this approach is being dismissed as extremist. I must admit that I was initially disappointed in being so categorized.

28   But as I continued to think about the matter I gradually gained a bit of satisfaction from being considered an extremist. Was not Jesus an extremist in love? "Love your enemies, bless them that curse you, pray for them that despitefully use you." Was not Amos an extremist for justice—"Let justice roll down like waters and righteousness like a mighty stream." Was not Paul an extremist for the gospel of Jesus Christ—"I bear in my body the marks of the Lord Jesus." Was not Martin Luther an extremist—"Here I stand; I can do none other so help me God." Was not John Bunyan an extremist—"I will stay in jail to the end of my days before I make a butchery of my conscience." Was not Abraham Lincoln an extremist—"This nation cannot survive half slave and half free." Was not Thomas Jefferson an extremist—"We hold these truths to be self-evident, that all men are created equal." So the question is not whether we will be extremist but what kind of extremist will we be. Will we be extremists for hate or will we be extremists for love? Will we be extremists for the preservation of injustice—or will we be extremists for the cause of justice? In that dramatic scene on Calvary's hill three men were crucified. We must never forget that all three were crucified for the same crime—the crime of extremism. Two were extremists for immorality, and thus fell below their environment. The other, Jesus Christ, was an extremist for

love, truth, and goodness, and thereby rose above His environment. So, after all, maybe the South, the nation, and the world are in dire need of creative extremists.

29 I had hoped that the white moderate would see this. Maybe I was too optimistic. Maybe I expected too much. I guess I should have realized that few members of a race that has oppressed another race can understand or appreciate the deep groans and passionate yearnings of those that have been oppressed, and still fewer have the vision to see that injustice must be rooted out by strong, persistent, and determined action. I am thankful, however, that some of our white brothers have grasped the meaning of this social revolution and committed themselves to it. They are still all too small in quantity, but they are big in quality. Some like Ralph McGill, Lillian Smith, Harry Golden, and James Dabbs have written about our struggle in eloquent, prophetic, and understanding terms. Others have marched with us down nameless streets of the South. They have languished in filthy, roach-infested jails, suffering the abuse and brutality of angry policemen who see them as "dirty nigger lovers." They, unlike so many of their moderate brothers and sisters, have recognized the urgency of the moment and sensed the need for powerful "action" antidotes to combat the disease of segregation.

30 Let me rush on to mention my other disappointment. I have been so greatly disappointed with the white Church and its leadership. Of course there are some notable exceptions. I am not unmindful of the fact that each of you has taken some significant stands on this issue. I commend you, Rev. Stallings, for your Christian stand on this past Sunday, in welcoming Negroes to your worship service on a non-segregated basis. I commend the Catholic leaders of this state for integrating Spring Hill College several years ago.

31 But despite these notable exceptions I must honestly reiterate that I have been disappointed with the Church. I do not say that as one of those negative critics who can always find something wrong with the Church. I say it as a minister of the gospel, who loves the Church; who was nurtured in its bosom; who has been sustained by its spiritual blessings and who will remain true to it as long as the cord of life shall lengthen.

32 I had the strange feeling when I was suddenly catapulted into the leadership of the bus protest in Montgomery several years ago that we would have the support of the white Church. I felt that the white ministers, priests, and rabbis of the South would be some of our strongest allies. Instead, some have been outright opponents, refusing to understand the freedom movement and misrepresenting its leaders; all too many others have been more cautious than courageous and have remained silent behind the anesthetizing security of the stained glass windows.

33 In spite of my shattered dreams of the past, I came to Birmingham with the hope that the white religious leadership of this community would see the justice of our cause and with deep moral concern, serve as the channel through which our just grievances could get to the power structure. I had hoped that each of you would understand. But again I have been disappointed.

34 I have heard numerous religious leaders of the South call upon their worshippers to comply with a desegregation decision because it is the law, but I have longed to hear white ministers say follow this decree because integration is morally right and the Negro is your brother. In the midst of blatant injustices

inflicted upon the Negro, I have watched white churches stand on the sideline and merely mouth pious irrelevancies and sanctimonious trivialities. In the midst of a mighty struggle to rid our nation of racial and economic injustice, I have heard so many ministers say, "Those are social issues with which the gospel has no real concern," and I have watched so many churches commit themselves to a completely other-worldly religion which made a strange distinction between body and soul, the sacred and the secular.

35 So here we are moving toward the exit of the twentieth century with a religious community largely adjusted to the status quo, standing as a tail-light behind other community agencies rather than a headlight leading men to higher levels of justice.

36 I have travelled the length and breadth of Alabama, Mississippi and all the other southern states. On sweltering summer days and crisp autumn mornings I have looked at her beautiful churches with their spires pointing heavenward. I have beheld the impressive outlay of her massive religious education buildings. Over and over again I have found myself asking: "Who worships here? Who is their God? Where were their voices when the lips of Governor Barnett dripped with words of interposition and nullification? Where were they when Governor Wallace gave the clarion call for defiance and hatred? Where were their voices of support when tired, bruised, and weary Negro men and women decided to rise from the dark dungeons of complacency to the bright hills of creative protest?"

37 Yes, these questions are still in my mind. In deep disappointment, I have wept over the laxity of the church. But be assured that my tears have been tears of love. There can be no deep disappointment where there is not deep love. Yes, I love the Church; I love her sacred walls. How could I do otherwise? I am in the rather unique position of being the son, the grandson, and the great-grandson of preachers. Yes, I see the Church as the body of Christ. But, oh! How we have blemished and scarred that body through social neglect and fear of being nonconformist.

38 There was a time when the Church was very powerful. It was during that period when the early Christians rejoiced when they were deemed worthy to suffer for what they believed. In those days the Church was not merely a thermometer that recorded the ideas and principles of popular opinion; it was a thermostat that transformed the mores of society. Wherever the early Christians entered a town the power structure got disturbed and immediately sought to convict them for being "disturbers of the peace" and "outside agitators." But they went on with the conviction that they were "a colony of heaven" and had to obey God rather than man. They were small in number but big in commitment. They were too God-intoxicated to be "astronomically intimidated." They brought an end to such ancient evils as infanticide and gladiatorial contest.

39 Things are different now. The contemporary Church is so often a weak, ineffectual voice with an uncertain sound. It is so often the arch-supporter of the status quo. Far from being disturbed by the presence of the Church, the power structure of the average community is consoled by the Church's silent and often vocal sanction of things as they are.

40 But the judgment of God is upon the Church as never before. If the Church of today does not recapture the sacrificial spirit of the early Church, it will lose its authentic ring, forfeit the loyalty of millions, and be dismissed as an irrelevant

social club with no meaning for the twentieth century. I am meeting young people every day whose disappointment with the Church has risen to outright disgust.

41   Maybe again I have been too optimistic. Is organized religion too inextricably bound to the status quo to save our nation and the world? Maybe I must turn my faith to the inner spiritual Church, the church within the Church, as the true ecclesia and the hope of the world. But again I am thankful to God that some noble souls from the ranks of organized religion have broken loose from the paralyzing chains of conformity and joined us as active partners in the struggle for freedom. They have left their secure congregations and walked the streets of Albany, Georgia, with us. They have gone through the highways of the South on torturous rides for freedom. Yes, they have gone to jail with us. Some have been kicked out of their churches and lost the support of their bishops and fellow ministers. But they have gone with the faith that right defeated is stronger than evil triumphant. These men have been the leaven in the lump of the race. Their witness has been the spiritual salt that has preserved the true meaning of the Gospel in these troubled times. They have carved a tunnel of hope through the dark mountain of disappointment.

42   I hope the Church as a whole will meet the challenge of this decisive hour. But even if the Church does not come to the aid of justice, I have no despair about the future. I have no fear about the outcome of our struggle in Birmingham, even if our motives are presently misunderstood. We will reach the goal of freedom in Birmingham and all over the nation, because the goal of America is freedom. Abused and scorned though we may be, our destiny is tied up with the destiny of America. Before the pilgrims landed at Plymouth, we were here. Before the pen of Jefferson etched across the pages of history the majestic words of the Declaration of Independence, we were here. For more than two centuries our foreparents labored in this country without wages; they made cotton "king"; and they built the homes of their masters in the midst of brutal injustice and shameful humiliation—and yet out of a bottomless vitality they continued to thrive and develop. If the inexpressible cruelties of slavery could not stop us, the opposition we now face will surely fail. We will win our freedom because the sacred heritage of our nation and the eternal will of God are embodied in our echoing demands.

43   I must close now. But before closing I am impelled to mention one other point in your statement that troubled me profoundly. You warmly commend the Birmingham police force for keeping "order" and "preventing violence." I don't believe you would have so warmly commended the police force if you had seen its angry violent dogs literally biting six unarmed, nonviolent Negroes. I don't believe you would so quickly commend the policemen if you would observe their ugly and inhuman treatment of Negroes here in the city jail; if you would watch them push and curse old Negro women and young Negro girls; if you would see them slap and kick old Negro men and young Negro boys; if you will observe them, as they did on two occasions, refuse to give us food because we wanted to sing our grace together. I'm sorry that I can't join you in your praise for the police department.

44   It is true that they have been rather disciplined in their public handling of the demonstrators. In this sense they have been rather publicly "nonviolent." But for what purpose? To preserve the evil system of segregation. Over the last few years

I have consistently preached that nonviolence demands the means we use must be as pure as the ends we seek. So I have tried to make it clear that it is wrong to use immoral means to attain moral ends. But now I must affirm that it is just as wrong or even more so to use moral means to preserve immoral ends. Maybe Mr. Connor and his policemen have been rather publicly nonviolent, as Chief Pritchett was in Albany, Georgia, but they have used the moral means of nonviolence to maintain the immoral end of flagrant injustice. T. S. Eliot has said that there is no greater treason than to do the right deed for the wrong reason.

45   I wish you had commended the Negro sit-inners and demonstrators of Birmingham for their sublime courage, their willingness to suffer, and their amazing discipline in the midst of the most inhuman provocation. One day the South will recognize its real heroes. They will be the James Merediths, courageously and with a majestic sense of purpose, facing jeering and hostile mobs and the agonizing loneliness that characterizes the life of the pioneer. They will be old, oppressed, battered Negro women, symbolized in a seventy-two year old woman of Montgomery, Alabama, who rose up with a sense of dignity and with her people decided not to ride the segregated buses, and responded to one who inquired about her tiredness with ungrammatical profundity: "My feets is tired, but my soul is rested." They will be the young high school and college students, young ministers of the gospel and a host of their elders courageously and nonviolently sitting-in at lunch counters and willingly going to jail for conscience sake. One day the South will know that when these disinherited children of God sat down at lunch counters they were in reality standing up for the best in the American dream and the most sacred values in our Judaeo-Christian heritage, and thus carrying our whole nation back to great wells of democracy which were dug deep by the founding fathers in the formulation of the Constitution and the Declaration of Independence.

46   Never before have I written a letter this long (or should I say a book?). I'm afraid it is much too long to take your precious time. I can assure you that it would have been much shorter if I had been writing from a comfortable desk, but what else is there to do when you are alone for days in the dull monotony of a narrow jail cell other than write long letters, think strange thoughts, and pray long prayers?

47   If I have said anything in this letter that is an overstatement of the truth and is indicative of an unreasonable impatience, I beg you to forgive me. If I have said anything in this letter that is an understatement of the truth and is indicative of my having a patience that makes me patient with anything less than brotherhood, I beg God to forgive me.

48   I hope this letter finds you strong in the faith. I also hope that circumstances will soon make it possible for me to meet each of you, not as an integrationist or a civil rights leader, but as a fellow clergyman and a Christian brother. Let us all hope that the dark clouds of racial prejudice will soon pass away and the deep fog of misunderstanding will be lifted from our fear-drenched communities and in some not too distant tomorrow the radiant stars of love and brotherhood will shine over our great nation with all their scintillating beauty.

Yours for the cause of Peace and Brotherhood, Martin Luther King, Jr.

1. King begins this letter by addressing the eight clergymen who protested his actions in Birmingham as "unwise and untimely." How does his initial approach referring to common spiritual shared beliefs help to dissolve the clergymen's words?

2. How does King address the clergymen's argument that he is basically an outsider?

3. King eloquently pays respect to two unsung heroes in this time of civil unrest. He gives these examples to achieve what purpose?

4. How does King appeal to an academic audience who have turned deaf ears to the plight of black Americans?

Rhetorical Analysis

5. In the last paragraph, King uses figurative language associated with how one views the sky and discrimination. Analyze the effectiveness of this metaphor.

6. Biblical allusions abound in his text. Explain the effectiveness of these allusions.

7. Explain King's rhetorical goals when he genderizes the South of the 1960s by stating: "I have travelled the length and breadth of Alabama, Mississippi and all the other southern states. On sweltering summer days and crisp autumn mornings I have looked at her beautiful churches with their spires pointing heavenward. I have beheld the impressive outlay of her massive religious education buildings. Over and over again I have found myself asking: "Who worships here? Who is their God? Where were their voices when the lips of Governor Barnett dripped with words of interposition and nullification? Where were they when Governor Wallace gave the clarion call for defiance and hatred? Where were their voices of support when tired, bruised, and weary Negro men and women decided to rise from the dark dungeons of complacency to the bright hills of creative protest?"

8. In paragraph 26, King uses interesting terms such as "somebodiness" and "donothingism." Explain why he chose these colloquial terms.

9. What purpose separates King's distinction between "just" and "unjust"?

10. Identify a paragraph in this letter where King successfully uses repetition (and parallel structure) to his advantage.

11. The length of this letter is a stark contrast to the brevity of two presidential inaugural addresses included in this book. Compare the strategy of embellishment versus succinctness in these three rhetorical iconic addresses. What did each hope to achieve?

12. **Writing an Argument** Argue the principles that surrounded your, or another family or friend's decision, to respond through an act of civil disobedience. Would King approve?

Second Inaugural Address

Abraham Lincoln

Abraham Lincoln (1809–1865) delivered his Second Inaugural Address on the Capitol steps on March 4, 1865, under gloomy circumstances. The Civil War was drawing to an end, and the nation continued to be divided. He needed to mend the past and unite citizens toward the future. In a mere 702 words, Lincoln delivers what many believe to be one of the best speeches in American history and certainly one of the most inspiring inaugural addresses ever given.

1   Fellow Countrymen: At this second appearing to take the oath of the Presidential office there is less occasion for an extended address than there was at the first. Then a statement somewhat in detail of a course to be pursued seemed fitting and proper. Now, at the expiration of four years, during which public declarations have been constantly called forth on every point and phase of the great contest which still absorbs the attention and engrosses the energies of the nation, little that is new could be presented. The progress of our arms, upon which all else chiefly depends, is as well known to the public as to myself, and it is, I trust, reasonably satisfactory and encouraging to all. With high hope for the future, no prediction in regard to it is ventured.

2   On the occasion corresponding to this four years ago all thoughts were anxiously directed to an impending civil war. All dreaded it—all sought to avert it. While the inaugural address was being delivered from this place, devoted altogether to saving the Union without war, insurgent agents were in the city seeking to destroy it without war—seeking to dissolve the Union and divide effects by negotiation. Both parties deprecated war, but one of them would make war rather than let the nation survive, and the other would accept war rather than let it perish, and the war came.

3   One-eighth of the whole population were colored slaves, not distributed generally over the Union, but localized in the Southern part of it. These slaves constituted a peculiar and powerful interest. All knew that this interest was somehow the cause of the war. To strengthen, perpetuate, and extend this interest was the object for which the insurgents would rend the Union even by war, while the Government claimed no right to do more than to restrict the territorial enlargement of it. Neither party expected for the war the magnitude or the duration which it has already attained. Neither anticipated that the <u>cause</u> of the conflict might cease with or even before the conflict itself should cease. Each looked for an easier triumph, and a result less fundamental and astounding. Both read the same Bible and pray to the same God, and each invokes His aid against the other.

4   It may seem strange that any men should dare to ask a just God's assistance in wringing their bread from the sweat of other men's faces, but let us judge not, that we be not judged. The prayers of both could not be answered. That of neither has been answered fully. The Almighty has His own purposes. "Woe unto the world because of offenses; for it must needs be that offenses come, but woe to that man by whom the offense cometh."

5   If we shall suppose that American slavery is one of those offenses which, in the providence of God, must needs come, but which, having continued through His appointed time, He now wills to remove, and that He gives to both North and South this terrible war as the woe due to those by whom the offense came, shall we discern therein any departure from those divine attributes which the believers in a living God always ascribe to Him? Fondly do we hope—fervently do we pray—that this mighty scourge of war may speedily pass away. Yet, if God wills that it continue until all the wealth piled by the bondsman's two hundred and fifty years of unrequited toil shall be sunk, and until every drop of blood drawn with the lash shall be paid by another drawn with the sword, as was said three thousand years ago, so still it must be said "the judgments of the Lord are true and righteous altogether."

6   With malice toward none, with charity for all, with firmness in the right as God gives us to see the right, let us strive on to finish the work we are in, to bind up the nation's wounds, to care for him who shall have borne the battle and for his widow and his orphan—to do all which may achieve and cherish a just and lasting peace among ourselves, and with all nations.

Second Inaugural Address of Abraham Lincoln. www.ourdocuments.gov

Comprehension

1. Knowing that Lincoln, in his Second Inaugural Address, reasoned with a country much different than that of his First Inaugural Address, explain the main points that had to dominate this particular inaugural speech.

2. The overall theme of Lincoln's references are Biblical. Why does Lincoln choose an evangelical theme?

3. Lincoln aptly does not place the blame for this war totally on the South. He brings up some historical realities that push forward the idea that everyone is to blame. What historical reality does he refer to?

Rhetorical Analysis

4. What rhetorical impact does paragraph 6 display?

5. What does Lincoln hope to gain by using this statement: "let us judge not, that we be not judged"?

6. Explain the rhetorical genius behind Lincoln's brevity of response.

Writing

7. Would the outcome of Lincoln's Second Inaugural Address have been different if he had not been assassinated soon after this address? Historically we know that his successor, Andrew Johnson, did not make a positive impact on the government or nation at the time. Write a paragraph predicting what would have happened if Lincoln could have enjoyed a full second term.

8. **Writing an Argument** Compare and contrast Kennedy's Inaugural Address and Lincoln's Second Inaugural Address.

The Prince

Machiavelli

Niccolò Machiavelli (1469–1527), the educated son of a Florentine legal official, began a career in government service in 1494. He was, in many ways, intricately involved with the downfall and rise of the powerful Medici family. His most famous work, *The Prince*, written in 1513 and posthumously published (1532; trans. 1640), focuses on the deviously cunning practices a prince must acquire in order to stay in power. Machiavelli asserted that a ruler could be successful only through unethical means. To gain and maintain power, the rules are those of the ruler alone. Controversy followed this book, basically because of its imitations of the Medici family, and it was condemned by Pope Clement VIII. Here are excerpts from one of *The Prince*'s most famous chapters.

CHAPTER XVII — CONCERNING CRUELTY AND CLEMENCY, AND WHETHER IT IS BETTER TO BE LOVED THAN FEARED

1   Coming now to the other qualities mentioned above, I say that every prince ought to desire to be considered clement and not cruel. Nevertheless he ought to take care not to misuse this clemency. Cesare Borgia was considered cruel; notwithstanding, his cruelty reconciled the Romagna, unified it, and restored it to peace and loyalty. And if this be rightly considered, he will be seen to have been much more merciful than the Florentine people, who, to avoid a reputation for cruelty, permitted Pistoia to be destroyed. Therefore a prince, so long as he keeps his subjects united and loyal, ought not to mind the reproach of cruelty; because with a few examples he will be more merciful than those who, through too much mercy, allow disorders to arise, from which follow murder or robbery; for these are wont to injure the whole people, whilst those executions which originate with a prince offend the individual only.

2   And of all princes, it is impossible for the new prince to avoid the imputation of cruelty, owing to new states being full of dangers. Hence Virgil, through the mouth of Dido, excuses the inhumanity of her reign owing to its being new, saying:

"Res dura, et regni novitas me talia cogunt
Moliri, et late fines custode tueri."*

---

*. . . against my will, my fate,
A throne unsettled, and an infant state,
Bid me defend my realms with all my pow'rs,
And guard with these severities my shores. —Christopher Pitt

3   Nevertheless he ought to be slow to believe and to act, nor should he himself show fear, but proceed in a temperate manner with prudence and humanity, so that too much confidence may not make him incautious and too much distrust render him intolerable.

4   Upon this a question arises: whether it be better to be loved than feared or feared than loved? It may be answered that one should wish to be both, but, because it is difficult to unite them in one person, it is much safer to be feared than loved, when, of the two, either must be dispensed with. Because this is to be asserted in general of men, that they are ungrateful, fickle, false, cowards, covetous, and as long as you succeed they are yours entirely; they will offer you their blood, property, life, and children, as is said above, when the need is far distant; but when it approaches they turn against you. And that prince who, relying entirely on their promises, has neglected other precautions, is ruined; because friendships that are obtained by payments, and not by greatness or nobility of mind, may indeed be earned, but they are not secured, and in time of need cannot be relied upon; and men have less scruple in offending one who is beloved than one who is feared, for love is preserved by the link of obligation which, owing to the baseness of men, is broken at every opportunity for their advantage; but fear preserves you by a dread of punishment which never fails.

5   Nevertheless a prince ought to inspire fear in such a way that, if he does not win love, he avoids hatred; because he can endure very well being feared whilst he is not hated, which will always be as long as he abstains from the property of his citizens and subjects and from their women. But when it is necessary for him to proceed against the life of some one, he must do it on proper justification and for manifest cause, but above all things he must keep his hands off the property of others, because men more quickly forget the death of their father than the loss of their patrimony. Besides, pretexts for taking away the property are never wanting; for he who has once begun to live by robbery will always find pretexts for seizing what belongs to others; but reasons for taking life, on the contrary, are more difficult to find and sooner lapse. But when a prince is with his army, and has under control a multitude of soldiers, then it is quite necessary for him to disregard the reputation of cruelty, for without it he would never hold his army united or disposed to its duties.

6   Among the wonderful deeds of Hannibal this one is enumerated: that having led an enormous army, composed of many various races of men, to fight in foreign lands, no dissensions arose either among them or against the prince, whether in his bad or in his good fortune. This arose from nothing else than his inhuman cruelty, which, with his boundless valour, made him revered and terrible in the sight of his soldiers, but without that cruelty, his other virtues were not sufficient to produce this effect. And short-sighted writers admire his deeds from one point of view and from another condemn the principal cause of them. That it is true his other virtues would not have been sufficient for him may be proved by the case of Scipio, that most excellent man, not only of his own times but within the memory of man, against whom, nevertheless, his army rebelled in Spain; this arose from nothing but his too great forbearance, which gave his soldiers more licence than is consistent with military discipline. For this he was upbraided in the Senate by Fabius Maximus, and called the corruptor of the

Roman soldiery. The Locrians were laid waste by a legate of Scipio, yet they were not avenged by him, nor was the insolence of the legate punished, owing entirely to his easy nature. Insomuch that some one in the Senate, wishing to excuse him, said there were many men who knew much better how not to err than to correct the errors of others. This disposition, if he had been continued in the command, would have destroyed in time the fame and glory of Scipio; but, he being under the control of the Senate, this injurious characteristic not only concealed itself, but contributed to his glory.

7   Returning to the question of being feared or loved, I come to the conclusion that, men loving according to their own will and fearing according to that of the prince, a wise prince should establish himself on that which is in his own control and not in that of others; he must endeavour only to avoid hatred, as is noted.

The Prince by Nicolo Machiavelli. Translated by W.K. Marriott, F.R. Hist. S. From *Everyman's Library*, Edited by Ernest Rhys. London: J.M. Dent & Sons, Ltd. New York: E.P. Dutton & Co. 1908.

Comprehension

1. What is Machiavelli's main contention concerning respect?

2. Machiavelli gives historical reference as to why fear, love, and hatred have not worked. What are some of his major points given at the beginning of this passage?

3. Machiavelli points out an innate nature of man that one should never discount. What is that innate nature?

Rhetorical Analysis

4. Why does Machiavelli consider many writers of Hannibal's famed acclaim to be "short-sighted"?

5. How might females respond to Machiavelli's points of argument if he had been less gender-biased?

6. Discuss the irony of Machiavelli equally considering clemency and cruelty in terms of maintaining power.

7. Machiavelli argues that "men more quickly forget the death of their father than the loss of their patrimony." What does this observation signify?

Writing

8. Argue whether Machiavelli is a proponent of civil disobedience. Support your arguments with historical, socio-cultural and/or personal examples.

9. Write a paragraph explaining that Machiavelli's notions do or do not ring true with the current state of politics.

10. **Writing an Argument**   In a carefully worded essay referencing Machiavelli and some other contemporaries in this book, defend or argue the point that it is better to be feared than loved.

On Being a Cripple

Nancy Mairs

Nancy Mairs (1943–2016) wrote significant and substantial essays that delve into religion studies, feminism, and her experiences with multiple sclerosis. She received numerous writing awards, including the 1984 Western States Book Award in poetry for *In All the Rooms of the Yellow House* (1984) and a National Endowment for the Arts Fellowship in 1991. In addition, she wrote many texts, including the memoir *Remembering the Bone House*, and the spiritual autobiography *Ordinary Time: Cycles in Marriage, Faith, and Renewal*. Many agree that she wrote from her heart with a healthy twist of humor, as is evidenced in her essay "On Being a Cripple."

To escape is nothing. Not to escape is nothing. —Louise Bogan

1   The other day I was thinking of writing an essay on being a cripple. I was thinking hard in one of the stalls of the women's room in my office building, as I was shoving my shirt into my jeans and tugging up my zipper. Preoccupied, I flushed, picked up my book bag, took my cane down from the hook, and unlatched the door. So many movements unbalanced me, and as I pulled the door open I fell over backward, landing fully clothed on the toilet seat with my legs splayed in front of me: the old beetle-on-its-back routine. Saturday afternoon, the building deserted, I was free to laugh aloud as I wriggled back to my feet, my voice bouncing off the yellowish tiles from all directions. Had anyone been there with me, I'd have been still and faint and hot with chagrin. I decided that it was high time to write the essay.

2   First, the matter of semantics. I am a cripple. I choose this word to name me. I choose from among several possibilities, the most common of which are "handicapped" and "disabled." I made the choice a number of years ago, without thinking, unaware of my motives for doing so. Even now, I'm not sure what those motives are, but I recognize that they are complex and not entirely flattering. People—crippled or not—wince at the word "cripple," as they do not at "handicapped" or "disabled." Perhaps I want them to wince. I want them to see me as a tough customer, one to whom the fates / gods / viruses have not been kind, but who can face the brutal truth of her existence squarely. As a cripple, I swagger.

3   But, to be fair to myself, a certain amount of honesty underlies my choice. "Cripple" seems to me a clean word, straightforward and precise. It has an honorable history, having made its first appearance in the Lindisfarne Gospel in the tenth century. As a lover of words, I like the accuracy with which it describes my condition: I have lost the full use of my limbs. "Disabled," by contrast, suggests any incapacity, physical or mental. And I certainly don't like "handicapped," which implies that I have deliberately been put at a disadvantage, by whom I can't imagine (my God is not a Handicapper General), in order to equalize chances in the great race of life. These words seem to me to be moving away from my

condition, to be widening the gap between word and reality. Most remote is the recently coined euphemism "differently abled," which partakes of the same semantic hopefulness that transformed countries from "undeveloped" to "underdeveloped," then to "less developed," and finally to "developing" nations. People have continued to starve in those countries during the shift. Some realities do not obey the dictates of language.

4   Mine is one of them. Whatever you call me, I remain crippled. But I don't care what you call me, so long as it isn't "differently abled," which strikes me as pure verbal garbage designed, by its ability to describe anyone, to describe no one. I subscribe to George Orwell's thesis that "the slovenliness of our language makes it easier for us to have foolish thoughts." And I refuse to participate in the degeneration of the language to the extent that I deny that I have lost anything in the course of this calamitous disease; I refuse to pretend that the only differences between you and me are the various ordinary ones that distinguish any one person from another. But call me "disabled" or "handicapped" if you like. I have long since grown accustomed to them; and if they are vague, at least they hint at the truth. Moreover, I use them myself. Society is no readier to accept crippledness than to accept death, war, sex, sweat, or wrinkles. I would never refer to another person as a cripple. It is the word I use to name only myself.

5   I haven't always been crippled, a fact for which I am soundly grateful. To be whole of limb is, I know from experience, infinitely more pleasant and useful than to be crippled; and if that knowledge leaves me open to bitterness at MY loss, the physical soundness I once enjoyed (though I did not enjoy it half enough) is well worth the occasional stab of regret. Though never any good at sports, I was a normally active child and young adult. I climbed trees, played hopscotch, jumped rope, skated, swam, rode my bicycle, sailed. I despised team sports, spending some of the wretchedest afternoons of my life, sweaty and humiliated, behind a field-hockey stick and under a basketball hoop. I tramped alone for miles along the bridle paths that webbed the woods behind the house I grew up in. I swayed through countless dim hours in the arms of one man or another under the scattered shot of light from mirrored balls, and gyrated through countless more as Tab Hunter and Johnny Mathis gave way to the Rolling Stones, Creedence Clearwater Revival, Cream. I walked down the aisle. I pushed baby carriages, changed tires in the rain, marched for peace.

6   When I was twenty-eight I started to trip and drop things. What at first seemed my natural clumsiness soon became too pronounced to shrug off. I consulted a neurologist, who told me that I had a brain tumor. A battery of tests, increasingly disagreeable, revealed no tumor. About a year and a half later I developed a blurred spot in one eye. I had, at last, the episodes "disseminated in space and time" requisite for a diagnosis: multiple sclerosis. I have never been sorry for the doctor's initial misdiagnosis, however. For almost a week, until the negative results of the tests were in, I thought that I was going to die right away. Every day for the past nearly ten years, then, has been a kind of gift. I accept all gifts.

7   Multiple sclerosis is a chronic degenerative disease of the central nervous system, in which the myelin that sheathes the nerves is somehow eaten away and scar tissue forms in its place, interrupting the nerves' signals. During its course,

which is unpredictable and uncontrollable, one may lose vision, hearing, speech, the ability to walk, control of bladder and/or bowels, strength in any or all extremities, sensitivity to touch, vibration, and/or pain, potency, coordination of movements—the list of possibilities is lengthy and, yes, horrifying. One may also lose one's sense of humor. That's the easiest to lose and the hardest to survive without.

8   In the past ten years, I have sustained some of these losses. Characteristic of MS are sudden attacks, called exacerbations, followed by remissions, and these I have not had. Instead, my disease has been slowly progressive. My left leg is now so weak that I walk with the aid of a brace and a cane; and for distances I use an Amigo, a variation on the electric wheelchair that looks rather like an electrified kiddie car. I no longer have much use of my left hand. Now my right side is weakening as well. I still have the blurred spot in my right eye. Overall, though, I've been lucky so far. My world has, of necessity, been circumscribed by my losses, but the terrain left me has been ample enough for me to continue many of the activities that absorb me: writing, teaching, raising children and cats and plants and snakes, reading, speaking publicly about MS and depression, even playing bridge with people patient and honorable enough to let me scatter cards every which way without sneaking a peek.

9   Lest I begin to sound like Pollyanna, however, let me say that I don't like having MS. I hate it. My life holds realities—harsh ones, some of them—that no right-minded human being ought to accept without grumbling. One of them is fatigue. I know of no one with MS who does not complain of bone-weariness; in a disease that presents an astonishing variety of symptoms, fatigue seems to be a common factor. I wake up in the morning feeling the way most people do at the end of a bad day, and I take it from there. As a result, I spend a lot of time in extremis and, impatient with limitation, I tend to ignore my fatigue until my body breaks down in some way and forces rest. Then I miss picnics, dinner parties, poetry readings, the brief visits of old friends from out of town. The offspring of a puritanical tradition of exceptional venerability, I cannot view these lapses without shame. My life often seems a series of small failures to do as I ought.

10   I lead, on the whole, an ordinary life, probably rather like the one I would have led had I not had MS. I am lucky that my predilections were already solitary, sedentary, and bookish—unlike the world-famous French cellist I have read about, or the young woman I talked with one long afternoon who wanted only to be a jockey. I had just begun graduate school when I found out something was wrong with me, and I have remained, interminably, a graduate student. Perhaps I would not have if I'd thought I had the stamina to return to a full-time job as a technical editor; but I've enjoyed my studies.

11   In addition to studying, I teach writing courses. I also teach medical students how to give neurological examinations. I pick up freelance editing jobs here and there. I have raised a foster son and sent him into the world, where he has made me two grandbabies, and I am still escorting my daughter and son through adolescence. I go to Mass every Saturday. I am a superb, if messy, cook. I am also an enthusiastic laundress, capable of sorting a hamper full of clothes into five subtly differentiated piles, but a terrible housekeeper. I can do italic writing and, in an emergency, bathe an oil-soaked cat. I play a fiendish game of Scrabble.

When I have the time and the money, I like to sit on my front steps with my husband, drinking Amaretto and smoking a cigar, as we imagine our counterparts in Leningrad and make sure that the sun gets down once more behind the sharp childish scrawl of the Tucson Mountains.

12   This lively plenty has its bleak complement, of course, in all the things I can no longer do. I will never run again, except in dreams, and one day I may have to write that I will never walk again. I like to go camping, but I can't follow George and the children along the trails that wander out of a campsite through the desert or into the mountains. In fact, even on the level I've learned never to check the weather or try to hold a coherent conversation: I need all my attention for my wayward feet. Of late, I have begun to catch myself wondering how people can propel themselves without canes. With only one usable hand, I have to select my clothing with care not so much for style as for ease of ingress and egress, and even so, dressing can be laborious. I can no longer do fine stitchery, pick up babies, play the piano, braid my hair. I am immobilized by acute attacks of depression, which may or may not be physiologically related to MS but are certainly its logical concomitant.

13   These two elements, the plenty and the privation, are never pure, nor are the delight and wretchedness that accompany them. Almost every pickle that I get into as a result of my weakness and clumsiness—and I get into plenty—is funny as well as maddening and sometimes painful. I recall one May afternoon when a friend and I were going out for a drink after finishing up at school. As we were climbing into opposite sides of my car, chatting, I tripped and fell, flat and hard, onto the asphalt parking lot, my abrupt departure interrupting him in mid-sentence. "Where'd you go?" he called as he came around the back of the car to find me hauling myself up by the door frame. "Are you all right?" Yes, I told him, I was fine, just a bit rattly, and we drove off to find a shady patio and some beer. When I got home an hour or so later, my daughter greeted me with "What have you done to yourself?" I looked down. One elbow of my white turtleneck with the green froggies, one knee of my white trousers, one white kneesock were blood-soaked. We peeled off the clothes and inspected the damage, which was nasty enough but not alarming. That part wasn't funny: The abrasions took a long time to heal, and one got a little infected. Even so, when I think of my friend talking earnestly, suddenly, to the hot thin air while I dropped from his view as though through a trap door, I find the image as silly as something from a Marx Brothers movie.

14   I may find it easier than other cripples to amuse myself because I live propped by the acceptance and the assistance and, sometimes, the amusement of those around me. Grocery clerks tear my checks out of my checkbook for me, and sales clerks find chairs to put into dressing rooms when I want to try on clothes. The people I work with make sure I teach at times when I am least likely to be fatigued, in places I can get to, with the materials I need. My students, with one anonymous exception (in an end-of-the-semester evaluation), have been unperturbed by my disability. Some even like it. One was immensely cheered by the information that I paint my own fingernails; she decided, she told me, that if I could go to such trouble over fine details, she could keep on writing essays. I suppose I became some sort of bright-fingered muse. She wrote good essays, too.

15   The most important struts in the framework of my existence, of course, are my husband and children. Dismayingly few marriages survive the MS test, and why should they? Most twenty-two- and nineteen-year-olds, like George and me, can vow in clear conscience, after a childhood of chicken pox and summer colds, to keep one another in sickness and in health so long as they both shall live. Not many are equipped for catastrophe: the dismay, the depression, the extra work, the boredom that a degenerative disease can insinuate into a relationship. And our society, with its emphasis on fun and its association of fun with physical performance, offers little encouragement for a whole spouse to stay with a crippled partner. Children experience similar stresses when faced with a crippled parent, and they are more helpless, since parents and children can't usually get divorced. They hate, of course, to be different from their peers, and the child whose mother is tacking down the aisle of a school auditorium packed with proud parents like a Cape Cod dinghy in a stiff breeze jolly well stands out in a crowd. Deprived of legal divorce, the child can at least deny the mother's disability, even her existence, forgetting to tell her about recitals and PTA meetings, refusing to accompany her to stores or church or the movies, never inviting friends to the house. Many do.

16   But I've been limping along for ten years now, and so far George and the children are still at my left elbow, holding tight. Anne and Matthew vacuum floors and dust furniture and haul trash and rake up dog droppings and button my cuffs and bake lasagna and Toll House cookies with just enough grumbling so I know that they don't have brain fever. And far from hiding me, they're forever dragging me by racks of fancy clothes or through teeming school corridors, or welcoming gaggles of friends while I'm wandering through the house in Anne's filmy pink babydoll pajamas. George generally calls before he brings someone home, but he does just as many dumb thankless chores as the children. And they all yell at me, laugh at some of my jokes, write me funny letters when we're apart—in short, treat me as an ordinary human being for whom they have some use. I think they like me. Unless they're faking. . . .

17   Faking. There's the rub. Tugging at the fringes of my consciousness always is the terror that people are kind to me only because I'm a cripple. My mother almost shattered me once, with that instinct mothers have—blind, I think, in this case, but unerring nonetheless—for striking blows along the fault-lines of their children's hearts, by telling me, in an attack on my selfishness, "We all have to make allowances for you, of course, because of the way you are." From the distance of a couple of years, I have to admit that I haven't any idea just what she meant, and I'm not sure that she knew either. She was awfully angry. But at the time, as the words thudded home, I felt my worst fear, suddenly realized. I could bear being called selfish: I am. But I couldn't bear the corroboration that those around me were doing in fact what I'd always suspected them of doing, professing fondness while silently putting up with me because of the way I am. A cripple. I've been a little cracked ever since.

18   Along with this fear that people are secretly accepting shoddy goods comes a relentless pressure to please—to prove myself worth the burdens I impose, I guess, or to build a substantial account of goodwill against which I may write drafts in

times of need. Part of the pressure arises from social expectations. In our society, anyone who deviates from the norm had better find some way to compensate. Like fat people, who are expected to be jolly, cripples must bear their lot meekly and cheerfully. A grumpy cripple isn't playing by the rules. And much of the pressure is self-generated. Early on I vowed that, if I had to have MS, by God I was going to do it well. This is a class act, ladies and gentlemen. No tears, no recriminations, no faint-heartedness.

19   One way and another, then, I wind up feeling like Tiny Tim, peering over the edge of the table at the Christmas goose, waving my crutch, piping down God's blessing on us all. Only sometimes I don't want to play Tiny Tim. I'd rather be Caliban, a most scurvy monster. Fortunately, at home no one much cares whether I'm a good cripple or a bad cripple as long as I make vichyssoise with fair regularity. One evening several years ago, Anne was reading at the dining-room table while I cooked dinner. As I opened a can of tomatoes, the can slipped in my left hand and juice spattered me and the counter with bloody spots. Fatigued and infuriated, I bellowed, "I'm so sick of being crippled!" Anne glanced at me over the top of her book. "There now," she said, "do you feel better?" "Yes," I said, "yes, I do." She went back to her reading. I felt better. That's about all the attention my scurviness ever gets.

20   Because I hate being crippled, I sometimes hate myself for being a cripple. Over the years I have come to expect—even accept—attacks of violent self-loathing. Luckily, in general our society no longer connects deformity and disease directly with evil (though a charismatic once told me that I have MS because a devil is in me) and so I'm allowed to move largely at will, even among small children. But I'm not sure that this revision of attitude has been particularly helpful. Physical imperfection, even freed of moral disapprobation, still defies and violates the ideal, especially for women, whose confinement in their bodies as objects of desire is far from over. Each age, of course, has its ideal, and I doubt that ours is any better or worse than any other. Today's ideal woman, who lives on the glossy pages of dozens of magazines, seems to be between the ages of eighteen and twenty-five; her hair has body, her teeth flash white, her breath smells minty, her underarms are dry; she has a career but is still a fabulous cook, especially of meals that take less than twenty minutes to prepare; she does not ordinarily appear to have a husband or children; she is trim and deeply tanned; she jogs, swims, plays tennis, rides a bicycle, sails, but does not bowl; she travels widely, even to out-of-the-way places like Finland and Samoa, always in the company of the ideal man, who possesses a nearly identical set of characteristics. There are a few exceptions. Though usually white and often blonde, she may be black, Hispanic, Asian, or Native American, so long as she is unusually sleek. She may be old, provided she is selling a laxative or is Lauren Bacall. If she is selling a detergent, she may be married and have a flock of strikingly messy children. But she is never a cripple.

21   Like many women I know, I have always had an uneasy relationship with my body. I was not a popular child, largely, I think now, because I was peculiar: intelligent, intense, moody, shy, given to unexpected actions and inexplicable notions and emotions. But as I entered adolescence, I believed myself unpopular because I was homely: my breasts too flat, my mouth too wide, my hips too

narrow, my clothing never quite right in fit or style. I was not, in fact, particularly ugly, old photographs inform me, though I was well off the ideal; but I carried this sense of self-alienation with me into adulthood, where it regenerated in response to the depredations of MS. Even with my brace I walk with a limp so pronounced that, seeing myself on the videotape of a television program on the disabled, I couldn't believe that anything but an inchworm could make progress humping along like that. My shoulders droop and my pelvis thrusts forward as I try to balance myself upright, throwing my frame into a bony S. As a result of contractures, one shoulder is higher than the other and I carry one arm bent in front of me, the fingers curled into a claw. My left arm and leg have wasted into pipe-stems, and I try always to keep them covered. When I think about how my body must look to others, especially to men, to whom I have been trained to display myself, I feel ludicrous, even loathsome.

22   At my age, however, I don't spend much time thinking about my appearance. The burning egocentricity of adolescence, which assures one that all the world is looking all the time, has passed, thank God, and I'm generally too caught up in what I'm doing to step back, as I used to, and watch myself as though upon a stage. I'm also too old to believe in the accuracy of self-image. I know that I'm not a hideous crone, that in fact, when I'm rested, well dressed, and well made up, I look fine. The self-loathing I feel is neither physically nor intellectually substantial. What I hate is not me but a disease.

23   I am not a disease.

24   And a disease is not—at least not single-handedly—going to determine who I am, though at first it seemed to be going to. Adjusting to a chronic incurable illness, I have moved through a process similar to that outlined by Elizabeth Kubler-Ross in *On Death and Dying*. The major difference—and it is far more significant than most people recognize—is that I can't be sure of the outcome, as the terminally ill cancer patient can. Research studies indicate that, with proper medical care, I may achieve a "normal" life span. And in our society, with its vision of death as the ultimate evil, worse even than decrepitude, the response to such news is, "Oh well, at least you're not going to die." Are there worse things than dying? I think that there may be.

25   I think of two women I know, both with MS, both enough older than I to have served me as models. One took to her bed several years ago and has been there ever since. Although she can sit in a high-backed wheelchair, because she is incontinent she refuses to go out at all, even though incontinence pants, which are readily available at any pharmacy, could protect her from embarrassment. Instead, she stays at home and insists that her husband, a small quiet man, a retired civil servant, stay there with her except for a quick weekly foray to the supermarket. The other woman, whose illness was diagnosed when she was eighteen, a nursing student engaged to a young doctor, finished her training, married her doctor, accompanied him to Germany when he was in the service, bore three sons and a daughter, now grown and gone. When she can, she travels with her husband; she plays bridge, embroiders, swims regularly; she works, like me, as a symptomatic-patient instructor of medical students in neurology. Guess which woman I hope to be.

26   At the beginning, I thought about having MS almost incessantly. And because of the unpredictable course of the disease, my thoughts were always terrified. Each night I'd get into bed wondering whether I'd get out again the next morning, whether I'd be able to see, to speak, to hold a pen between my fingers. Knowing that the day might come when I'd be physically incapable of killing myself, I thought perhaps I ought to do so right away, while I still had the strength. Gradually I came to understand that the Nancy who might one day lie inert under a bedsheet, arms and legs paralyzed, unable to feed or bathe herself, unable to reach out for a gun, a bottle of pills, was not the Nancy I was at present, and that I could not presume to make decisions for that future Nancy, who might well not want in the least to die. Now the only provision I've made for the future Nancy is that when the time comes—and it is likely to come in the form of pneumonia, friend to the weak and the old—I am not to be treated with machines and medications. If she is unable to communicate by then, I hope she will be satisfied with these terms.

27   Thinking all the time about having MS grew tiresome and intrusive, especially in the large and tragic mode in which I was accustomed to considering my plight. Months and even years went by without catastrophe (at least without one related to MS), and really I was awfully busy, what with George and children and snakes and students and poems, and I hadn't the time, let alone the inclination, to devote myself to being a disease. Too, the richer my life became, the funnier it seemed, as though there were some connection between largesse and laughter, and so my tragic stance began to waver until, even with the aid of a brace and a cane, I couldn't hold it for very long at a time.

28   After several years I was satisfied with my adjustment. I had suffered my grief and fury and terror, I thought, but now I was at ease with my lot. Then one summer day I set out with George and the children across the desert for a vacation in California. Part way to Yuma I became aware that my right leg felt funny. "I think I've had an exacerbation," I told George. "What shall we do?" he asked. "I think we'd better get the hell to California," I said, "because I don't know whether I'll ever make it again." So we went on to San Diego and then to Orange, up the Pacific Coast Highway to Santa Cruz, across to Yosemite, down to Sequoia and Joshua Tree, and so back over the desert to home. It was a fine two-week trip, filled with friends and fair weather, and I wouldn't have missed it for the world, though I did in fact make it back to California two years later. Nor would there have been any point in missing it, since in MS, once the symptoms have appeared, the neurological damage has been done, and there's no way to predict or prevent that damage.

29   The incident spoiled my self-satisfaction, however. It renewed my grief and fury and terror, and I learned that one never finishes adjusting to MS. I don't know now why I thought one would. One does not, after all, finish adjusting to life, and MS is simply a fact of my life—not my favorite fact, of course—but as ordinary as my nose and my tropical fish and my yellow Mazda station wagon. It may at any time get worse, but no amount of worry or anticipation can prepare me for a new loss. My life is a lesson in losses. I learn one at a time.

30   And I had best be patient in the learning, since I'll have to do it like it or not. As any rock fan knows, you can't always get what you want. Particularly when you have MS. You can't, for example, get cured. In recent years researchers and

the organizations that fund research have started to pay MS some attention even though it isn't fatal; perhaps they have begun to see that life is something other than a quantitative phenomenon, that one may be very much alive for a very long time in a life that isn't worth living. The researchers have made some progress toward understanding the mechanism of the disease: It may well be an autoimmune reaction triggered by a slow-acting virus. But they are nowhere near its prevention, control, or cure. And most of us want to be cured. Some, unable to accept incurability, grasp at one treatment after another; no matter how bizarre: megavitamin therapy, gluten-free diet, injections of cobra venom, hypothermal suits, lymphocytopharesis, hyperbaric chambers. Many treatments are probably harmless enough, but none are curative.

31   The absence of a cure often makes MS patients bitter toward their doctors. Doctors are, after all, the priests of modern society, the new shamans, whose business is to heal, and many an MS patient roves from one to another, searching for the "good" doctor who will make him well. Doctors too think of themselves as healers, and for this reason many have trouble dealing with MS patients, whose disease in its intransigence defeats their aims and mocks their skills. Too few doctors, it is true, treat their patients as whole human beings, but the reverse is also true. I have always tried to be gentle with my doctors, who often have more at stake in terms of ego than I do. I may be frustrated, maddened, depressed by the incurability of my disease, but I am not diminished by it, and they are. When I push myself up from my seat in the waiting room and stumble toward them, I incarnate the limitation of their powers. The least I can do is refuse to press on their tenderest spots.

32   This gentleness is part of the reason that I'm not sorry to be a cripple. I didn't have it before. Perhaps I'd have developed it anyway—how could I know such a thing?—and I wish I had more of it, but I'm glad of what I have. It has opened and enriched my life enormously. This sense that my frailty and need must be mirrored in others, that in searching for and shaping a stable core in a life wrenched by change and loss, change and loss, I must recognize the same process, under individual conditions, in the lives around me. I do not deprecate such knowledge, however I've come by it.

33   All the same, if a cure were found, would I take it? In a minute. I may be a cripple, but I'm only occasionally a loony and never a saint. Anyway, in my brand of theology God doesn't give bonus points for a limp. I'd take a cure; I just don't need one. A friend who also has MS startled me once by asking, "Do you ever say to yourself, 'Why me, Lord?'" "No, Michael, I don't," I told him, "because whenever I try, the only response I can think of is 'Why not?'" If I could make a cosmic deal, whom would I put in my place? What in my life would I give up in exchange for sound limbs and a thrilling rush of energy? No one. Nothing. I might as well do the job myself. Now that I'm getting the hang of it.

From *Plaintext* by Nancy Mairs. © 1992 The Arizona Board of Regents. Reprinted by permission of the University of Arizona Press.

Comprehension

1. Mairs adamantly defends the viewpoint that she will define herself as a "cripple." Why does she use this specific term and not some other, more gentle term?

2. Explain how the opening bathroom anecdote of Mairs's situates the rest of the tone of the essay.

3. List some areas of her life where Mairs considers herself fortunate.

Rhetorical Analysis

4. Mairs's reference to several pop culture icons serves what purpose?

5. Mairs's definition of herself as a "cripple" goes far beyond the word itself. What type of person does Mairs really want to show herself to be?

6. Explain the irony in her observation that "as a cripple, I swagger."

7. Mairs shows a finesse for conveying sarcastic humor while making valid points. Look at paragraph 3 and discuss how this humor is expressed in her use of figurative language.

Writing

8. Based on Mairs's narrative, how does she successfully argue that it is better to get busy living, rather than to get busy dying?

9. Analyze points in this essay where Mairs might unintentionally be revealing her vulnerability.

10. **Writing an Argument**   Giving examples from history and current events, including your own personal experiences, argue that a disability does not stand in the way of a person living a full life.

The Things They Carried

Tim O'Brien

Tim O'Brien (b. 1946) was born in Austin, Minnesota, and was educated at Macalester College and Harvard University. Drafted into the army right after college in 1968, O'Brien became a sergeant in Vietnam and earned a Purple Heart, an award given to U.S. soldiers wounded or killed in battle. His first book, *If I Die in a Combat Zone* (1973) was a memoir of his tour of duty. His novel *Going After Cacciato* won the National Book Award for fiction in 1979. "The Things They Carried," first published in 1986, joined a series of other interlocking stories, including one titled "How to Tell a True War Story." He builds a picture of soldiers' daily lives by compiling masses of sensory details. Besides writing novels and short stories, O'Brien has worked as a national affairs reporter for the *Washington Post* and as a writing teacher.

1   First Lieutenant Jimmy Cross carried letters from a girl named Martha, a junior at Mount Sebastian College in New Jersey. They were not love letters, but Lieutenant Cross was hoping, so he kept them folded in plastic at the bottom of his rucksack. In the late afternoon, after a day's march, he would dig his foxhole, wash his hands under a canteen, unwrap the letters, hold them with the tips of his fingers, and spend the last hour of light pretending. He would imagine romantic camping trips into the White Mountains in New Hampshire. He would sometimes taste the envelope flaps, knowing her tongue had been there. More than anything, he wanted Martha to love him as he loved her, but the letters were mostly chatty, elusive on the matter of love. She was a virgin, he was almost sure. She was an English major at Mount Sebastian, and she wrote beautifully about her professors and roommates and midterm exams, about her respect for Chaucer and her great affection for Virginia Woolf. She often quoted lines of poetry; she never mentioned the war, except to say, Jimmy, take care of yourself. The letters weighed ten ounces. They were signed "Love, Martha," but Lieutenant Cross understood that "Love" was only a way of signing and did not mean what he sometimes pretended it meant. At dusk, he would carefully return the letters to his rucksack. Slowly, a bit distracted, he would get up and move among his men, checking the perimeter, then at full dark he would return to his hole and watch the night and wonder if Martha was a virgin.

2   The things they carried were largely determined by necessity. Among the necessities or near necessities were P-38 can openers, pocket knives, heat tabs, wrist watches, dog tags, mosquito repellant, chewing gum, candy, cigarettes, salt tablets, packets of Kool-Aid, lighters, matches, sewing kits, Military Payment Certificates, C rations, and two or three canteens of water. Together, these items weighed between fifteen and twenty pounds, depending upon a man's habits or rate of metabolism. Henry Dobbins, who was a big man, carried extra rations; he was especially fond of canned peaches in heavy syrup over pound cake. Dave Jensen, who practiced field hygiene, carried a toothbrush, dental floss, and

several hotel-size bars of soap he'd stolen on R&R in Sydney, Australia. Ted Lavender, who was scared, carried tranquilizers until he was shot in the head outside the village of Than Khe in mid-April. By necessity, and because it was SOP[1], they all carried steel helmets that weighed five pounds including the liner and camouflage cover. They carried the standard fatigue jackets and trousers. Very few carried underwear. On their feet they carried jungle boots—2.1 pounds— and Dave Jensen carried three pairs of socks and a can of Dr. Scholl's foot powder as a precaution against trench foot. Until he was shot, Ted Lavender carried six or seven ounces of premium dope, which for him was a necessity. Mitchell Sanders, the RTO[2], carried condoms. Norman Bowker carried a diary. Rat Kiley carried comic books. Kiowa, a devout Baptist, carried an illustrated New Testament that had been presented to him by his father, who taught Sunday school in Oklahoma City, Oklahoma. As a hedge against bad times, however, Kiowa also carried his grandmother's distrust of the white man, his grandfather's old hunting hatchet. Necessity dictated. Because the land was mined and booby-trapped, it was SOP for each man to carry a steel-centered, nylon-covered flak jacket, which weighed 7.6 pounds, but which on hot days seemed much heavier. Because you could die so quickly, each man carried at least one large compress bandage, usually in the helmet band for easy access. Because the nights were cold, and because the monsoons were wet, each carried a green plastic poncho that could be used as a raincoat or ground sheet or makeshift tent. With its quilted liner, the poncho weighed almost two pounds, but it was worth every ounce. In April, for instance, when Ted Lavender was shot, they used his poncho to wrap him up, then to carry him across the paddy, then to lift him into the chopper that took him away.

3   They were called legs or grunts.

4   To carry something was to "hump" it, as when Lieutenant Jimmy Cross humped his love for Martha up the hills and through the swamps. In its intransitive form, "to hump" meant "to walk," or "to march," but it implied burdens far beyond the intransitive.

5   Almost everyone humped photographs. In his wallet, Lieutenant Cross carried two photographs of Martha. The first was a Kodachrome snapshot signed "Love," though he knew better. She stood against a brick wall. Her eyes were gray and neutral, her lips slightly open as she stared straight-on at the camera. At night, sometimes, Lieutenant Cross wondered who had taken the picture, because he knew she had boyfriends, because he loved her so much, and because he could see the shadow of the picture taker spreading out against the brick wall. The second photograph had been clipped from the 1968 Mount Sebastian yearbook. It was an action shot—women's volleyball—and Martha was bent horizontal to the floor, reaching, the palms of her hands in sharp focus, the tongue taut, the expression frank and competitive. There was no visible seat. She wore white gym shorts. Her legs, he thought, were almost certainly the legs of a virgin, dry and without hair, the left knee cocked and carrying her entire weight, which was just over one hundred pounds. Lieutenant Cross remembered touching that left knee.

---

[1] SOP standard operating procedure
[2] RTO radiotelephone operator

A dark theater, he remembered, and the move was *Bonnie and Clyde,* and Martha wore a tweed skirt, and during the final scene, when he touched her knee, she turned and looked at him in a sad, sober way that made him pull his hand back, but he would always remember the feel of the tweed skirt and the knee beneath it and the sound of the gunfire that killed Bonnie and Clyde, how embarrassing it was, how slow and oppressive. He remembered kissing her good night at the dorm door. Right then, he thought, he should've done something brave. He should've carried her up the stairs to her room and tied her to the bed and touched that left knee all night long. He should've risked it. Whenever he looked at the photographs, he thought of new things he should've done.

6 What they carried was partly a function of rank, partly of field specialty.

7   As a first lieutenant and platoon leader, Jimmy Cross carried a compass, maps, code books, binoculars, and a .45-caliber pistol that weighed 2.9 pounds fully loaded. He carried a strobe light and the responsibilities for the lives of his men.

8   As an RTO, Mitchell Sanders carried the PR C-25 radio, a killer, twenty-six pounds with its battery.

9   As a medic, Rat Kiley carried a canvas satchel filled with morphine and plasma and malaria tablets and surgical tape and comic books and all the things a medic must carry, including M&M's for especially bad wounds, for a total weight of nearly twenty pounds.

10   As a big man, therefore a machine gunner, Henry Dobbins carried the M-60, which weighed twenty-three pounds unloaded, but which was almost always loaded. In addition, Dobbins carried between ten and fifteen pounds of ammunition draped in belts across his chest and shoulder.

11   As PFCs or Spec 4s, most of them were common grunts and carried the standard M-16 gas-operated assault rifle. The weapon weighed 7.6 pounds unloaded, 8.2 pounds with its full twenty-round magazine. Depending on numerous factors, such as topography and psychology, the riflemen carried anywhere from twelve to twenty magazines, usually in cloth bandoliers, adding on another 8.4 pounds at minimum, fourteen pounds at maximum. When it was available, they also carried M-16 maintenance gear—rods and steel brushes and swabs and tubes of LSA oil—all of which weighed about a pound. Among the grunts, some carried the M-79 grenade launcher, 5.9 pounds unloaded, a reasonably light weapon except for the ammunition, which was heavy. A single round weighed ten ounces. The typical load was twenty-five rounds. But Ted Lavender, who was scared, carried thirty-four rounds when he was shot and killed outside Than Khe, and he went down under an exceptional burden, more than twenty pounds of ammunition, plus the flak jacket and helmet and rations and water and toilet paper and tranquilizers and all the rest, plus the unweighed fear. He was dead weight. There was no twitching or flopping. Kiowa, who saw it happen, said it was like watching a rock fall, or a big sandbag or something—just boom, then down—not like the movies where the dead guy rolls around and does fancy spins and goes ass over teakettle—not like that, Kiowa said, the poor bastard just flat-fuck fell. Boom. Down. Nothing else. It was a bright morning in mid-April. Lieutenant Cross felt the pain. He blamed himself. They stripped off Lavender's canteens and ammo, all the heavy things, and

Rat Kiley said the obvious, the guy's dead, and Mitchell Sanders used his radio to report one U.S. KIA[3] and to request a chopper. Then they wrapped Lavender in his poncho. They carried him out to a dry paddy, established security, and sat smoking the dead man's dope until the chopper came. Lieutenant Cross kept to himself. He pictured Martha's smooth young face, thinking he loved her more than anything, more than his men, and now Ted Lavender was dead because he loved her so much and could not stop thinking about her. When the dust-off arrived, they carried Lavender aboard. Afterward they burned Than Khe. They marched until dusk, then dug their holes, and that night Kiowa kept explaining how you had to be there, how fast it was, how the poor guy just dropped like so much concrete. Boom-down, he said. Like cement.

12   In addition to the three standard weapons—the M-60, M-16, and M-79—they carried whatever presented itself, or whatever seemed appropriate as a means of killing or staying alive. They carried catch-as-catch-can. At various times, in various situations, they carried M-14s and CAR-15s and Swedish Ks and grease guns and captured AK-47s and Chi-Coms and RPGs and Simonov carbines and black-market Uzis and .38-caliber Smith & Wesson handguns and 66 mm LAWs and shotguns and silencers and black-jacks and bayonets and C-4 plastic explosives. Lee Strunk carried a slingshot; a weapon of last resort, he called it. Mitchell Sanders carried brass knuckles. Kiowa carried his grandfather's feathered hatchet. Every third or fourth man carried a Claymore antipersonnel mine—3.5 pounds with its firing device. They all carried fragmentation grenades— fourteen ounces each. They all carried at least one M-18 colored smoke grenade— twenty-four ounces. Some carried CS or tear-gas grenades. Some carried white-phosphorus grenades. They carried all they could bear, and then some, including a silent awe for the terrible power of the things they carried.

13   In the first week of April, before Lavender died, Lieutenant Jimmy Cross received a good-luck charm from Martha. It was a simple pebble, an ounce at most. Smooth to the touch, it was a milky-white color with flecks of orange and violet, oval-shaped, like a miniature egg. In the accompanying letter, Martha wrote that she had found the pebble on the Jersey shoreline, precisely where the land touched water at high tide, where things came together but also separated. It was this separate-but-together quality, she wrote, that had inspired her to pick up the pebble and to carry it in her breast pocket for several days, where it seemed weightless, and then to send it through the mail, by air, as a token of her truest feelings for him. Lieutenant Cross found this romantic. But he wondered what her truest feelings were, exactly, and what she meant by separate-but-together. He wondered how the tides and waves had come into play on that afternoon along the Jersey shoreline when Martha saw the pebble and bent down to rescue it from geology. He imagined bare feet. Martha was a poet, with the poet's sensibilities, and her feet would be brown and bare, the toenails unpainted, the eyes chilly and somber like the ocean in March, and though it was painful, he wondered who had been with her that afternoon. He imagined a pair of shadows moving along the strip of sand where things came together but also separated. It was phantom

---

[3] KIA killed in action

jealousy, he knew, but he couldn't help himself. He loved her so much. On the march, through the hot days of early April, he carried the pebble in his mouth, turning it with his tongue, tasting sea salt and moisture. His mind wandered. He had difficulty keeping his attention on the war. On occasion he would yell at his men to spread out the column, to keep their eyes open, but then he would slip away into daydreams, just pretending, walking barefoot along the Jersey shore, with Martha, carrying nothing. He would feel himself rising. Sun and waves and gentle winds, all love and lightness.

14 What they carried varied by mission.

15   When a mission took them to the mountains, they carried mosquito netting, machetes, canvas tarps, and extra bug juice.

16   If a mission seemed especially hazardous, or if it involved a place they knew to be bad, they carried everything they could. In certain heavily mined AOs[4], where the land was dense with Toe Poppers and Bouncing Betties, they took turns humping a twenty-eight-pound mine detector. With its headphones and big sensing plate, the equipment was a stress on the lower back and shoulders, awkward to handle, often useless because of the shrapnel in the earth, but they carried it anyway, partly for safety, partly for the illusion of safety.

17   On ambush, or other night missions, they carried peculiar little odds and ends. Kiowa always took along his New Testament and a pair of moccasins for silence. Dave Jensen carried night-sight vitamins high in carotene. Lee Strunk carried his slingshot; ammo, he claimed, would never be a problem. Rat Kiley carried brandy and M&M's candy. Until he was shot, Ted Lavender carried the starlight scope, which weighed 6.3 pounds with its aluminum carrying case. Henry Dobbins carried his girlfriend's pantyhose wrapped around his neck as a comforter. They all carried ghosts. When dark came, they would move out single file across the meadows and paddies to their ambush coordinates, where they would quietly set up the Claymores and lie down and spend the night waiting.

18   Other missions were more complicated and required special equipment. In mid-April, it was their mission to search out and destroy the elaborate tunnel complexes in the Than Khe area south of Chu Lai. To blow the tunnels, they carried one-pound blocks of pentrite high explosives, four blocks to a man, sixty-eight pounds in all. They carried wiring, detonators, and battery-powered clackers. Dave Jensen carried earplugs. Most often, before blowing the tunnels, they were ordered by higher command to search them, which was considered bad news, but by and large they just shrugged and carried out orders. Because he was a big man, Henry Dobbins was excused from tunnel duty. The others would draw numbers. Before Lavender died there were seventeen men in the platoon, and whoever drew the number seventeen would strip off his gear and crawl in head first with a flashlight and Lieutenant Cross's .45-caliber pistol. The rest of them would fan out as security. They would sit down or kneel, not facing the hole, listening to the ground beneath them, imagining cobwebs and ghosts, whatever was down there—the tunnel walls squeezing—how the flashlight seemed impossibly heavy in the hand and how it was tunnel vision in the very strictest

---

[4] AOs areas of operations

sense, compression in all ways, even time, and how you had to wiggle in—ass and elbows—a swallowed-up feeling—and how you found yourself worrying about odd things—will your flashlight go dead? Do rats carry rabies? If you screamed, how far would sound carry? Would your buddies hear it? Would they have the courage to drag you out? In some respects, though not many, the waiting was worse than the tunnel itself. Imagination was a killer.

19   On April 16, when Lee Strunk drew the number seventeen, he laughed and muttered something and went down quickly. The morning was hot and very still. Not good, Kiowa said. He looked at the tunnel opening, then out across a dry paddy toward the village of Than Khe. Nothing moved. No clouds or birds or people. As they waited the men smoked and drank Kool-Aid, not talking much, feeling sympathy for Lee Strunk but also feeling the luck of the draw. You win some, you lose some, said Mitchell Sanders, and sometimes you settle for a rain check. It was a tired line and no one laughed.

20   Henry Dobbins ate a tropical chocolate bar. Ted Lavender popped a tranquilizer and went off to pee.

21   After five minutes, Lieutenant Jimmy Cross moved to the tunnel, leaned down, and examined the darkness. Trouble, he thought—a cave-in maybe. And then suddenly, without willing it, he was thinking about Martha. The stresses and fractures, the quick collapse, the two of them buried alive under all that weight. Dense, crushing love. Kneeling, watching the hole, he tried to concentrate on Lee Strunk and the war, all the dangers, but his love was too much for him, he felt paralyzed, he wanted to sleep inside her lungs and breathe her blood and be smothered. He wanted her to be a virgin and not a virgin, all at once. He wanted to know her. Intimate secrets—why poetry? Why so sad? Why the grayness in her eyes? Why so alone? Not lonely, just alone—riding her bike across campus or sitting off by herself in the cafeteria. Even dancing, she danced alone—and it was the aloneness that filled him with love. He remembered telling her that one evening. How she nodded and looked away. And how, later, when he kissed her, she received the kiss without returning it, her eyes wide open, not afraid, not a virgin's eyes, just flat and uninvolved.

22   Lieutenant Cross gazed at the tunnel. But he was not there. He was buried with Martha under the white sand at the Jersey shore. They were pressed together, and the pebble in his mouth was her tongue. He was smiling. Vaguely, he was aware of how quiet the day was, the sullen paddies, yet he could not bring himself to worry about matters of security. He was beyond that. He was just a kid at war, in love. He was twenty-two years old. He couldn't help it.

23   A few moments later Lee Strunk crawled out of the tunnel. He came up grinning, filthy but alive. Lieutenant Cross nodded and closed his eyes while the others clapped Strunk on the back and made jokes about rising from the dead.

24   Worms, Rat Kiley said. Right out of the grave. Fuckin' zombie.

25   The men laughed. They all felt great relief.

26   Spook City, said Mitchell Sanders.

27   Lee Strunk made a funny ghost sound, a kind of moaning, yet very happy, and right then, when Strunk made that high happy moaning sound, when he went *Ahhooooo*, right then Ted Lavender was shot in the head on his way back from

peeing. He lay with his mouth open. The teeth were broken. There was a swollen black bruise under his left eye. The cheekbone was gone. Oh shit, Rat Kiley said, the guy's dead. The guy's dead, he kept saying, which seemed profound—the guy's dead. I mean really.

28   The things they carried were determined to some extent by superstition. Lieutenant Cross carried his good-luck pebble. Dave Jensen carried a rabbit's foot. Norman Bowker, otherwise a very gentle person, carried a thumb that had been presented to him as a gift by Mitchell Sanders. The thumb was dark brown, rubbery to the touch, and weighed four ounces at most. It had been cut from a VC corpse, a boy of fifteen or sixteen. They'd found him at the bottom of an irrigation ditch, badly burned, flies in his mouth and eyes. The boy wore black shorts and sandals. At the time of his death he had been carrying a pouch of rice, a rifle, and three magazines of ammunition.

29   You want my opinion, Mitchell Sanders, said there's a definite moral here.

30   He put his hand on the dead boy's wrist. He was quiet for a time, as if counting a pulse, then he patted the stomach, almost affectionately, and used Kiowa's hunting hatchet to remove the thumb.

31   Henry Dobbins asked what the moral was.

32   Moral?

33   You know. *Moral.*

34   Sanders wrapped the thumb in toilet paper and handed it across to Norman Bowker. There was no blood. Smiling, he kicked the boy's head, watched the flies scatter, and said, It's like with that old TV show—Paladin. Have gun, will travel.

35   Henry Dobbins thought about it.

36   Yeah, well, he finally said. I don't see no moral.

37   There it is, man.

38   Fuck off.

39   They carried USO stationery and pencils and pens. They carried Sterno, safety pins, trip flares, signal flares, spools of wire, razor blades, chewing tobacco, liberated joss sticks and statuettes of the smiling Buddha, candles, grease pencils, *The Stars and Stripes,* fingernail clippers, Psy Ops[5] leaflets, bush hats, bolos, and much more. Twice a week, when the resupply choppers came in, they carried hot chow in green Mermite cans and large canvas bags filled iced beer and soda pop. They carried plastic water containers, each with a two-gallon capacity. Mitchell Sanders carried a set of starched tiger fatigues for special occasions. Henry Dobbins carried Black Flag insecticide. Dave Jensen carried empty sandbags that could be filled at night for added protection. Lee Strunk carried tanning lotion. Some things they carried in common. Taking turns, they carried the big PRC-77 scrambler radio, which weighed thirty pounds with its battery. They shared the weight of memory. They took up what others could no longer bear. Often, they carried each other, the wounded or weak. They carried infections. They carried chess sets, basketballs, Vietnamese-English dictionaries, insignia of rank, Bronze Stars and Purple Hearts, plastic cards imprinted with the Code of Conduct. They carried diseases, among

---

[5] Psy Ops psychological operations

them malaria and dysentery. They carried lice and ringworm and leeches and paddy algae and various rots and molds. They carried the land itself—Vietnam, the place, the soil—a powdery orange-red dust that covered their boots and fatigues and faces. They carried the sky. The whole atmosphere, they carried it, the humidity, the monsoons, the stink of fungus and decay, all of it, they carried gravity. They moved like mules. By daylight they took sniper fire, at night they were mortared, but it was not battle, it was just the endless march, village to village, without purpose, nothing won or lost. They marched for the sake of the march. They plodded along slowly, dumbly, leaning forward against the heat, unthinking, all blood and bone, simple grunts, soldiering with their legs, toiling up the hills and down into the paddies and across the rivers and up again and down, just humping, one step and then the next and then another, but no volition, no will, because it was automatic, it was anatomy, and the war was entirely a matter of posture and carriage, the hump was everything, a kind of inertia, a kind of emptiness, a dullness of desire and intellect and conscience and hope and human sensibility. Their principles were in their feet. Their calculations were biological. They had no sense of strategy or mission. They searched the villages without knowing what to look for, not caring, kicking over jars of rice, frisking children and old men, blowing tunnels, sometimes setting fires and sometimes not, then forming up and moving on to the next village, then other villages, where it would always be the same. They carried their own lies. The pressures were enormous. In the heat of early afternoon, they would remove their helmets and flak jackets, walking bare, which was dangerous but which helped ease the strain. They would often discard things along the route of march. Purely for comfort, they would throw away rations, blow their Claymores and grenades, no matter, because by nightfall the resupply choppers would arrive with more of the same, then a day or two later still more, fresh watermelons and crates of ammunition and sunglasses and woolen sweaters—the resources were stunning—sparklers for the Fourth of July, colored eggs for Easter. It was the great American war chest—the fruits of science, the smokestacks, the canneries, the arsenals at Hartford, the Minnesota forests, the machine shops, the vast fields of corn and wheat—they carried like freight trains; they carried it on their backs and shoulders—and for all the ambiguities of Vietnam, all the mysteries and unknowns, there was at least the single abiding certainty that they would never be at a loss for things to carry.

40 After the chopper took Lavender away, Lieutenant Jimmy Cross led his men into the village of Than Khe. They burned everything. They shot chickens and dogs, they trashed the village well, they called in artillery and watched the wreckage, then they marched for several hours through the hot afternoon, and then at dusk, while Kiowa explained how Lavender died, Lieutenant Cross found himself trembling.

41   He tried not to cry. With his entrenching tool, which weighed five pounds, he began digging a hole in the earth.

42   He felt shame. He hated himself. He had loved Martha more than his men, and as a consequence Lavender was now dead, and this was something he would have to carry like a stone in his stomach for the rest of the war.

43   All he could do was dig. He used his entrenching tool like an ax, slashing, feeling both love and hate, and then later, when it was full dark, he sat at the bottom of his foxhole and wept. It went on for a long while. In part, he was grieving for Ted Lavender, but mostly it was for Martha, and for himself, because she belonged to another world, which was not quite real, and because she was a junior at Mount Sebastian College in New Jersey, a poet and a virgin and uninvolved, and because he realized she did not love him and never would.

44   Like cement, Kiowa whispered in the dark. I swear to God—boom-down. Not a word.

45   I've heard this, said Norman Bowker.

46   A pisser, you know? Still zipping himself up. Zapped while zipping.

47   All right, fine. That's enough.

48   Yeah, but you had to see it, the guy just—

49   I *heard*, man. Cement. So why not shut the fuck up?

50   Kiowa shook his head sadly and glanced over at the hole where Lieutenant Jimmy Cross sat watching the night. The air was thick and wet. A warm, dense fog had settled over the paddies and there was the stillness that precedes rain.

51   After a time Kiowa sighed.

52   One thing for sure, he said. The Lieutenant's in some deep hurt. I mean that crying jag—the way he was carrying on—it wasn't fake or anything, it was real heavy-duty hurt. The man cares.

53   Sure, Norman Bowker said.

54   Say what you want, the man does care.

55   We all got problems.

56   Not Lavender.

57   No, I guess not, Bowker said. Do me a favor, though.

58   Shut up?

59   That's a smart Indian. Shut up.

60   Shrugging, Kiowa pulled off his boots. He wanted to say more, just to lighten up his sleep, but instead he opened his New Testament and arranged it beneath his head as a pillow. The fog made things seem hollow and unattached. He tried not to think about Ted Lavender, but then he was thinking how fast it was, no drama, down and dead, and how it was hard to feel anything except surprise. It seemed un-Christian. He wished he could find some great sadness, or even anger, but the emotion wasn't there and he couldn't make it happen. Mostly he felt pleased to be alive. He liked the smell of the New Testament under his cheek, the leather and ink and paper and glue, whatever the chemicals were. He liked hearing the sounds of night. Even his fatigue, it felt fine, the stiff muscles and the prickly awareness of his own body, a floating feeling. He enjoyed not being dead. Lying there, Kiowa admired Lieutenant Jimmy Cross's capacity for grief. He wanted to share the man's pain, he wanted to care as Jimmy Cross cared. And yet when he closed his eyes, all he could think was Boom-down, and all he could feel was the pleasure of having his boots off and the fog curling in around him and the damp soil and the Bible smells and the plush comfort of night.

61   After a moment Norman Bowker sat up in the dark.

62   What the hell, he said. You want to talk, *talk*. Tell it to me.

63   Forget it.

64   No, man, go on. One thing I hate, it's a silent Indian.

65 For the most part they carried themselves with poise, a kind of dignity. Now and then, however, there were times of panic, when they squealed or wanted to squeal but couldn't, when they twitched and made moaning sounds and covered their heads and said Dear Jesus and flopped around on the earth and fired their weapons blindly and cringed and sobbed and begged for the noise to stop and went wild and made stupid promises to themselves and to God and to their mothers and fathers, hoping not to die. In different ways, it happened to all of them. Afterward, when the firing ended, they would blink and peek up. They would touch their bodies, feeling shame, then quickly hiding it. They would force themselves to stand. As if in slow motion, frame by frame, the world would take on the old logic—absolute silence, then the wind, then sunlight, then voices. It was the burden of being alive. Awkwardly, the men would reassemble themselves, first in private, then in groups, becoming soldiers again. They would repair the leaks in their eyes. They would check for casualties, call in dust-offs, light cigarettes, try to smile, clear their throats and spit and begin cleaning their weapons. After a time someone would shake his head and say, No lie, I almost shit my pants, and someone else would laugh, which meant it was bad, yes, but the guy had obviously not shit his pants, it wasn't that bad, and in any case nobody would ever do such a thing and then go ahead and talk about it. They would squint into the dense, oppressive sunlight. For a few moments, perhaps, they would fall silent, lighting a joint and tracing its passage from man to man, inhaling, holding in the humiliation. Scary stuff, one of them might say. But then someone else would grin or flick his eyebrows and say, Roger-dodger, almost cut me a new asshole, *almost.*

66   There were numerous such poses. Some carried themselves with a sort of wistful resignation, others with pride or stiff soldierly discipline or good humor or macho zeal. They were afraid of dying but they were even more afraid to show it.

67   They found jokes to tell.

68   They used a hard vocabulary to contain the terrible softness. *Greased,* they'd say. *Offed, lit up, zapped while zipping.* It wasn't cruelty, just stage presence. They were actors and the war came at them in 3-D. When someone died, it wasn't quite dying, because in a curious way it seemed scripted, and because they had their line mostly memorized, irony mixed with tragedy, and because they called it by other names, as if to encyst and destroy the reality of death itself. They kicked corpses. They cut off thumbs. They talked grunt lingo. They told stories about Ted Lavender's supply of tranquilizers, how the poor guy didn't feel a thing, how incredibly tranquil he was.

69   There's a moral here, said Mitchell Sanders.

70   They were waiting for Lavender's chopper, smoking the dead man's dope.

71   The moral's pretty obvious, Sanders said, and winked. Stay away from drugs. No joke, they'll ruin your day every time.

72   Cute, said Henry Dobbins.

73   Mind-blower, get it? Talk about wiggy—nothing left, just blood and brains.

74   They made themselves laugh.

75   There it is, they'd say, over and over, as if the repetition itself were an act of poise, a balance between crazy and almost crazy, knowing without going. There it is, which meant be cool, let it ride, because oh yeah, man, you can't change what can't be changed, there it is, there it absolutely and positively and fucking well is.

76   They were tough.

77   They carried all the emotional baggage of men who might die. Grief, terror, love, longing—these were intangibles, but the intangibles had their own mass and specific gravity, they had tangible weight. They carried shameful memories. They carried the common secret of cowardice barely restrained, the instinct to run or freeze or hide, and in many respects this was the heaviest burden of all, for it could never be put down, it required perfect balance and perfect posture. They carried their reputations. They carried the soldier's greatest fear, which was the fear of blushing. Men killed, and died, because they were embarrassed not to. It was what had brought them to the war in the first place, nothing positive, no dreams of glory or honor, just to avoid the blush of dishonor. They died so as not to die of embarrassment. They crawled into tunnels and walked point and advanced under fire. Each morning, despite the unknowns, they made their legs move. They endured. They kept humping. They did not submit to the obvious alternative, which was simply to close the eyes and fall. So easy, really. Go limp and tumble to the ground and let the muscles unwind and not speak, and not budge until your buddies picked you up and lifted you into the chopper that would roar and dip its nose and carry you off to the world. A mere matter of falling, yet no one ever fell. It was not courage, exactly; the object was not valor. Rather, they were too frightened to be cowards.

78   By and large they carried these things inside, maintaining the masks of composure. They sneered at sick call. They spoke bitterly about guys who had found release by shooting off their own toes or fingers. Pussies, they'd say. Candyasses. It was fierce, mocking talk, with only a trace of envy or awe, but even so, the image played itself out behind their eyes.

79   They imagined the muzzle against flesh. They imagined the quick, sweet pain, then the evacuation to Japan, then a hospital with warm beds and cute geisha nurses.

80   They dreamed of freedom birds.

81   At night, on guard, staring into the dark, they were carried away by jumbo jets. They felt the rush of takeoff. *Gone!* They yelled. And then velocity, wings and engines, a smiling stewardess—but it was more than a plane, it was a real bird, a big sleek silver bird with feathers and talons and high screeching. They were flying. The weights fell off, there was nothing to bear. They laughed and held on tight, feeling the cold slap of wind and altitude, soaring, thinking *It's over, I'm gone!*—they were naked, they were light and free—it was all lightness, bright and fast and buoyant, light as light, a helium buzz in the brain, a giddy bubbling in the lungs as they were taken up over the clouds and the war, beyond duty, beyond gravity and mortification and global entanglements—*Sin loi!*[6] They yelled,

---

[6] *Sin loi* Sorry about that

I'm sorry, motherfuckers, but I'm out of it, I'm goofed, I'm on a space cruise, I'm gone!—and it was a restful, disencumbered sensation, just riding the light waves, sailing that big silver freedom bird over the mountains and oceans, over America, over the farms and great sleeping cities and cemeteries and highways and the golden arches of McDonald's. It was flight, a kind of fleeing, a kind of falling, falling higher and higher, spinning off the edge of the earth and beyond the sun and through the vast, silent vacuum where there were no burdens and where everything weighed exactly nothing. *Gone!* They screamed, *I'm sorry but I'm gone!* And so at night, not quite dreaming, they gave themselves over to lightness, they were carried, they were purely borne.

82 On the morning after Ted Lavender died, First Lieutenant Jimmy Cross crouched at the bottom of his foxhole and burned Martha's letters. Then he burned the two photographs. There was a steady rain falling, which made it difficult, but he used heat tabs and Sterno to build a small fire, screening it with his body, holding the photographs over the tight blue flame with the tips of his fingers.

83   He realized it was only a gesture. Stupid, he thought. Sentimental, too, but mostly just stupid.

84   Lavender was dead. You couldn't burn the blame.

85   Besides, the letters were in his head. And even now, without photographs, Lieutenant Cross could see Martha playing volleyball in her white gym shorts and yellow T-shirt. He could see her moving in the rain.

86   When the fire died out, Lieutenant Cross pulled his poncho over his shoulders and ate breakfast from a can.

87   There was no great mystery, he decided.

88   In those burned letters Martha had never mentioned the war, except to say, Jimmy, take care of yourself. She wasn't involved. She signed the letters "Love," but it wasn't love, and all the fine lines and technicalities did not matter.

89   The morning came up wet and blurry. Everything seemed part of everything else, the fog and Martha and the deepening rain.

90   It was a war, after all.

91 Half smiling, Lieutenant Jimmy Cross took out his maps. He shook his head hard, as it to clear it, then bent forward and began planning the day's march. In ten minutes, or maybe twenty, he would rouse the men and they would pack up and head west, where the maps showed the country to be green and inviting. They would do what they had always done. The rain might add some weight, but otherwise it would be one more day layered upon all the other days.

92   He was realistic about it. There was that new hardness in his stomach.

93   No more fantasies, he told himself.

94   Henceforth, when he thought about Martha, it would be only to think that she belonged elsewhere. He would shut down the daydreams. This was not Mount Sebastian, it was another world, where there were no pretty poems or midterm exams, a place where men died because of carelessness and gross stupidity. Kiowa was right. Boom-down, and you were dead, never partly dead.

95   Briefly, in the rain, Lieutenant Cross saw Martha's gray eyes gazing back at him.

96   He understood.

97   It was very sad, he thought. The things men carried inside. The things men did or felt they had to do.

98   He almost nodded at her, but didn't.

99   Instead he went back to his maps. He was now determined to perform his duties firmly and without negligence. It wouldn't help Lavender, he knew that, but from this point on he would comport himself as a soldier. He would dispose of his good-luck pebble. Swallow it, maybe, or use Lee Strunk's slingshot, or just drop it along the trail. On the march he would impose strict field discipline. He would be careful to send out flank security, to prevent straggling or bunching up, to keep his troops moving at the proper pace and at the proper interval. He would insist on clean weapons. He would confiscate the remainder of Lavender's dope. Later in the day, perhaps, he would call the men together and speak to them plainly. He would accept the blame for what had happened to Ted Lavender. He would be a man about it. He would look them in the eyes, keeping his chin level, and he would issue the new SOPs in a calm, impersonal tone of voice, an officer's voice, leaving no room for argument or discussion. Commencing immediately, he'd tell them, they would no longer abandon equipment along the route of march. They would police up their acts. They would get their shit together, and keep it together, and maintain it neatly and in good working order.

100   He would not tolerate laxity. He would show strength, distancing himself.

101   Among the men there would be grumbling, of course, and maybe worse, because their days would seem longer and their loads heavier, but Lieutenant Cross reminded himself that his obligation was not to be loved but to lead. He would dispense with love; it was not now a factor. And if anyone quarreled or complained, he would simply tighten his lips and arrange his shoulders in the correct command posture. He might give a curt little nod. Or he might not. He might just shrug and say Carry on, then they would saddle up and form into a column and move out toward the villages west of Than Khe.

Comprehension

1. What are your impressions of war after reading this story? Do you think this story is more about the physical or psychological realities of war?

2. In addition to the "necessities," what other tangible things do individual soldiers carry? Reread the second paragraph. What do these additional "things" reveal about the soldiers who carry them?

3. What intangible things do the men carry?

4. How do the soldiers keep from being overwhelmed by the threat and reality of death?

Rhetorical Analysis

5. What irony does O'Brien reveal with the "moral" that Mitchell Sanders finds in the dead Vietcong boy in the irrigation ditch?

6. What is incongruous about "the great American war chest," which includes "sparklers for the Fourth of July [and] colored eggs for Easter"? Is there any bitterness in the narrative at this point? If so, at whom or what is it directed?

7. What is the effect of O'Brien interrupting the essay with deliberate line spaces?

8. Point out an example of repetition O'Brien uses to add "weight" to the soldiers.

Writing

9. Do you think Lieutenant Cross was responsible for Lavender's death? Why does he burn Martha's letters and photographs? Use excerpts from the piece to support your answer in a paragraph.

10. **Writing a Description**   Write an essay in a manner similar to O'Brien's in which you describe what you carry to school.

Shooting an Elephant

George Orwell

George Orwell (1903–1950) was the pseudonym of Eric Arthur Blair, an English novelist, essayist, and journalist. Orwell fought in the Spanish Civil War and acquired from his experience a disdain of totalitarian and imperialistic systems. This attitude is reflected in the satiric fable *Animal Farm* (1945) and in the bleak, futuristic novel *1984* (1949). He also served with the Indian Imperial Police from 1922 to 1927 in Burma. This essay discusses an incident where he had to carry out a repugnant act to keep order with the Burman people.

1   In Moulmein, in Lower Burma, I was hated by large numbers of people—the only time in my life that I have been important enough for this to happen to me. I was sub-divisional police officer of the town, and in an aimless, petty kind of way anti-European feeling was very bitter. No one had the guts to raise a riot, but if a European woman went through the bazaars alone somebody would probably spit betel juice over her dress. As a police officer I was an obvious target and was baited whenever it seemed safe to do so. When a nimble Burman tripped me up on the football field and the referee (another Burman) looked the other way, the crowd yelled with hideous laughter. This happened more than once. In the end the sneering yellow faces of young men that met me everywhere, the insults hooted after me when I was at a safe distance, got badly on my nerves. The young Buddhist priests were the worst of all. There were several thousands of them in the town and none of them seemed to have anything to do except stand on street corners and jeer at Europeans.

2   All this was perplexing and upsetting. For at that time I had already made up my mind that imperialism was an evil thing and the sooner I chucked up my job and got out of it the better. Theoretically—and secretly, of course—I was all for the Burmese and all against their oppressors, the British. As for the job I was doing, I hated it more bitterly than I can perhaps make clear. In a job like that you see the dirty work of Empire at close quarters. The wretched prisoners huddling in the stinking cages of the lock-ups, the grey, cowed faces of the long-term convicts, the scarred buttocks of the men who had been flogged with bamboos—all these oppressed me with an intolerable sense of guilt. But I could get nothing into perspective. I was young and ill-educated and I had had to think out my problems in the utter silence that is imposed on every Englishman in the East. I did not even know that the British Empire is dying, still less did I know that it is a great deal better than the younger empires that are going to supplant it. All I knew was that I was stuck between my hatred of the empire I served and my rage against the evil-spirited little beasts who tried to make my job impossible. With one part of my mind I thought of the British Raj as an unbreakable tyranny, as something clamped down, in *saecula saeculorum,* upon the will of prostrate peoples; with another part I thought that the greatest joy in the world would be to drive a

bayonet into a Buddhist priest's guts. Feelings like these are the normal by-products of imperialism; ask any Anglo-Indian official, if you can catch him off duty.

3   One day something happened which in a roundabout way was enlightening. It was a tiny incident in itself, but it gave me a better glimpse than I had had before of the real nature of imperialism—the real motives for which despotic governments act. Early one morning the sub-inspector at a police station the other end of the town rang me up on the phone and said that an elephant was ravaging the bazaar. Would I please come and do something about it? I did not know what I could do, but I wanted to see what was happening and I got on to a pony and started out. I took my rifle, an old .44 Winchester and much too small to kill an elephant, but I thought the noise might be useful *in terrorem*. Various Burmans stopped me on the way and told me about the elephant's doings. It was not, of course, a wild elephant, but a tame one which had gone 'must'. It had been chained up, as tame elephants always are when their attack of 'must' is due, but on the previous night it had broken its chain and escaped. Its mahout, the only person who could manage it when it was in that state, had set out in pursuit, but had taken the wrong direction and was now twelve hours' journey away, and in the morning the elephant had suddenly reappeared in the town. The Burmese population had no weapons and were quite helpless against it. It had already destroyed somebody's bamboo hut, killed a cow and raided some fruit-stalls and devoured the stock; also it had met the municipal rubbish van and, when the driver jumped out and took to his heels, had turned the van over and inflicted violences upon it.

4   The Burmese sub-inspector and some Indian constables were waiting for me in the quarter where the elephant had been seen. It was a very poor quarter, a labyrinth of squalid bamboo huts, thatched with palmleaf, winding all over a steep hillside. I remember that it was a cloudy, stuffy morning at the beginning of the rains. We began questioning the people as to where the elephant had gone and, as usual, failed to get any definite information. That is invariably the case in the East; a story always sounds clear enough at a distance, but the nearer you get to the scene of events the vaguer it becomes. Some of the people said that the elephant had gone in one direction, some said that he had gone in another, some professed not even to have heard of any elephant. I had almost made up my mind that the whole story was a pack of lies, when we heard yells a little distance away. There was a loud, scandalized cry of 'Go away, child! Go away this instant!' and an old woman with a switch in her hand came round the corner of a hut, violently shooing away a crowd of naked children. Some more women followed, clicking their tongues and exclaiming; evidently there was something that the children ought not to have seen. I rounded the hut and saw a man's dead body sprawling in the mud. He was an Indian, a black Dravidian coolie, almost naked, and he could not have been dead many minutes. The people said that the elephant had come suddenly upon him round the corner of the hut, caught him with its trunk, put its foot on his back and ground him into the earth. This was the rainy season and the ground was soft, and his face had scored a trench a foot deep and a couple of yards long. He was lying on his belly with arms crucified and head sharply twisted to one side. His face was coated with mud, the eyes wide open, the teeth bared

and grinning with an expression of unendurable agony. (Never tell me, by the way, that the dead look peaceful. Most of the corpses I have seen looked devilish.) The friction of the great beast's foot had stripped the skin from his back as neatly as one skins a rabbit. As soon as I saw the dead man I sent an orderly to a friend's house nearby to borrow an elephant rifle. I had already sent back the pony, not wanting it to go mad with fright and throw me if it smelt the elephant.

5   The orderly came back in a few minutes with a rifle and five cartridges, and meanwhile some Burmans had arrived and told us that the elephant was in the paddy fields below, only a few hundred yards away. As I started forward practically the whole population of the quarter flocked out of the houses and followed me. They had seen the rifle and were all shouting excitedly that I was going to shoot the elephant. They had not shown much interest in the elephant when he was merely ravaging their homes, but it was different now that he was going to be shot. It was a bit of fun to them, as it would be to an English crowd; besides they wanted the meat. It made me vaguely uneasy. I had no intention of shooting the elephant—I had merely sent for the rifle to defend myself if necessary—and it is always unnerving to have a crowd following you. I marched down the hill, looking and feeling a fool, with the rifle over my shoulder and an ever-growing army of people jostling at my heels. At the bottom, when you got away from the huts, there was a metalled road and beyond that a miry waste of paddy fields a thousand yards across, not yet ploughed but soggy from the first rains and dotted with coarse grass. The elephant was standing eight yards from the road, his left side towards us. He took not the slightest notice of the crowd's approach. He was tearing up bunches of grass, beating them against his knees to clean them and stuffing them into his mouth.

6   I had halted on the road. As soon as I saw the elephant I knew with perfect certainty that I ought not to shoot him. It is a serious matter to shoot a working elephant—it is comparable to destroying a huge and costly piece of machinery—and obviously one ought not to do it if it can possibly be avoided. And at that distance, peacefully eating, the elephant looked no more dangerous than a cow. I thought then and I think now that his attack of 'must' was already passing off; in which case he would merely wander harmlessly about until the mahout came back and caught him. Moreover, I did not in the least want to shoot him. I decided that I would watch him for a little while to make sure that he did not turn savage again, and then go home.

7   But at that moment I glanced round at the crowd that had followed me. It was an immense crowd, two thousand at the least and growing every minute. It blocked the road for a long distance on either side. I looked at the sea of yellow faces above the garish clothes—faces all happy and excited over this bit of fun, all certain that the elephant was going to be shot. They were watching me as they would watch a conjurer about to perform a trick. They did not like me, but with the magical rifle in my hands I was momentarily worth watching. And suddenly I realized that I should have to shoot the elephant after all. The people expected it of me and I had got to do it; I could feel their two thousand wills pressing me forward, irresistibly. And it was at this moment, as I stood there with the rifle in my hands, that I first grasped the hollowness, the futility of the white man's

dominion in the East. Here was I, the white man with his gun, standing in front of the unarmed native crowd—seemingly the leading actor of the piece; but in reality I was only an absurd puppet pushed to and fro by the will of those yellow faces behind. I perceived in this moment that when the white man turns tyrant it is his own freedom that he destroys. He becomes a sort of hollow, posing dummy, the conventionalized figure of a sahib. For it is the condition of his rule that he shall spend his life in trying to impress the 'natives', and so in every crisis he has got to do what the 'natives' expect of him. He wears a mask, and his face grows to fit it. I had got to shoot the elephant. I had committed myself to doing it when I sent for the rifle. A sahib has got to act like a sahib; he has got to appear resolute, to know his own mind and do definite things. To come all that way, rifle in hand, with two thousand people marching at my heels, and then to trail feebly away, having done nothing—no, that was impossible. The crowd would laugh at me. And my whole life, every white man's life in the East, was one long struggle not to be laughed at.

8   But I did not want to shoot the elephant. I watched him beating his bunch of grass against his knees, with that preoccupied grandmotherly air that elephants have. It seemed to me that it would be murder to shoot him. At that age I was not squeamish about killing animals, but I had never shot an elephant and never wanted to. (Somehow it always seems worse to kill a *large* animal.) Besides, there was the beast's owner to be considered. Alive, the elephant was worth at least a hundred pounds; dead, he would only be worth the value of his tusks, five pounds, possibly. But I had got to act quickly. I turned to some experienced-looking Burmans who had been there when we arrived, and asked them how the elephant had been behaving. They all said the same thing: he took no notice of you if you left him alone, but he might charge if you went too close to him.

9   It was perfectly clear to me what I ought to do. I ought to walk up to within, say, twenty-five yards of the elephant and test his behavior. If he charged, I could shoot; if he took no notice of me, it would be safe to leave him until the mahout came back. But also I knew that I was going to do no such thing. I was a poor shot with a rifle and the ground was soft mud into which one would sink at every step. If the elephant charged and I missed him, I should have about as much chance as a toad under a steam-roller. But even then I was not thinking particularly of my own skin, only of the watchful yellow faces behind. For at that moment, with the crowd watching me, I was not afraid in the ordinary sense, as I would have been if I had been alone. A white man mustn't be frightened in front of 'natives'; and so, in general, he isn't frightened. The sole thought in my mind was that if anything went wrong those two thousand Burmans would see me pursued, caught, trampled on and reduced to a grinning corpse like that Indian up the hill. And if that happened it was quite probable that some of them would laugh. That would never do.

10   There was only one alternative. I shoved the cartridges into the magazine and lay down on the road to get a better aim. The crowd grew very still, and a deep, low, happy sigh, as of people who see the theatre curtain go up at last, breathed from innumerable throats. They were going to have their bit of fun after all. The rifle was a beautiful German thing with cross-hair sights. I did not then know that in shooting an elephant one would shoot to cut an imaginary bar running from ear-hole to ear-hole. I ought, therefore, as the elephant was sideways on, to have

aimed straight at his ear-hole, actually I aimed several inches in front of this, thinking the brain would be further forward.

11   When I pulled the trigger I did not hear the bang or feel the kick—one never does when a shot goes home—but I heard the devilish roar of glee that went up from the crowd. In that instant, in too short a time, one would have thought, even for the bullet to get there, a mysterious, terrible change had come over the elephant. He neither stirred nor fell, but every line of his body had altered. He looked suddenly stricken, shrunken, immensely old, as though the frightful impact of the bullet had paralysed him without knocking him down. At last, after what seemed a long time—it might have been five seconds, I dare say—he sagged flabbily to his knees. His mouth slobbered. An enormous senility seemed to have settled upon him. One could have imagined him thousands of years old. I fired again into the same spot. At the second shot he did not collapse but climbed with desperate slowness to his feet and stood weakly upright, with legs sagging and head drooping. I fired a third time. That was the shot that did for him. You could see the agony of it jolt his whole body and knock the last remnant of strength from his legs. But in falling he seemed for a moment to rise, for as his hind legs collapsed beneath him he seemed to tower upward like a huge rock toppling, his trunk reaching skyward like a tree. He trumpeted, for the first and only time. And then down he came, his belly towards me, with a crash that seemed to shake the ground even where I lay.

12   I got up. The Burmans were already racing past me across the mud. It was obvious that the elephant would never rise again, but he was not dead. He was breathing very rhythmically with long rattling gasps, his great mound of a side painfully rising and falling. His mouth was wide open—I could see far down into caverns of pale pink throat. I waited a long time for him to die, but his breathing did not weaken. Finally I fired my two remaining shots into the spot where I thought his heart must be. The thick blood welled out of him like red velvet, but still he did not die. His body did not even jerk when the shots hit him, the tortured breathing continued without a pause. He was dying, very slowly and in great agony, but in some world remote from me where not even a bullet could damage him further. I felt that I had got to put an end to that dreadful noise. It seemed dreadful to see the great beast lying there, powerless to move and yet powerless to die, and not even to be able to finish him. I sent back for my small rifle and poured shot after shot into his heart and down his throat. They seemed to make no impression. The tortured gasps continued as steadily as the ticking of a clock.

13   In the end I could not stand it any longer and went away. I heard later that it took him half an hour to die. Burmans were bringing dash and baskets even before I left, and I was told they had stripped his body almost to the bones by the afternoon.

14   Afterwards, of course, there were endless discussions about the shooting of the elephant. The owner was furious, but he was only an Indian and could do nothing. Besides, legally I had done the right thing, for a mad elephant has to be killed, like a mad dog, if its owner fails to control it. Among the Europeans opinion was divided. The older men said I was right, the younger men said it was

a damn shame to shoot an elephant for killing a coolie, because an elephant was worth more than any damn Coringhee coolie. And afterwards I was very glad that the coolie had been killed; it put me legally in the right and it gave me a sufficient pretext for shooting the elephant. I often wondered whether any of the others grasped that I had done it solely to avoid looking a fool.

Comprehension

1. Briefly summarize the events that take place in the essay.

2. How does Orwell reconcile that his actions were correct?

3. In paragraph 8, Orwell gives several logical reasons for not killing the elephant. What are they, and are they believable?

4. What forces Orwell to carry out his duty?

Rhetorical Analysis

5. Orwell confesses that he is anti-Imperialist and emphasizes the damage done, through Imperialism, to both the conquered and the conqueror. How does the language in the last paragraph of this essay emphasize this belief?

6. In paragraph 12, how does Orwell use language to give dignity to the elephant's death?

7. Explain the paradox presented with Orwell's views of the "beasts" in this essay.

8 Orwell sets the tone of this essay at the beginning by describing the setting as a "cloudy, stuffy morning at the beginning of the rains." How does this setting expand into the overall mood of what occurs?

9. Describe rhetorical examples and assumptions in paragraph 7, using a short quote and analysis, that exemplify how Orwell views himself both as a magician and puppet of the people he supposedly controls.

Writing

10. Rewrite the title "Shooting an Elephant" to reveal its true message.

11. What would Martin Luther King, Jr., have to say about George Orwell's act of shooting the elephant? How does the larger sense of democratic freedom work into this response?

12. **Writing an Argument**   Is it better to uphold the laws, rather than buck against the system if the law seems wrong?

Allegory of the Cave

Plato

Plato (428/427–348/347 B.C.E.), pupil and friend of Socrates, was one of the greatest philosophers of the ancient world. Plato's surviving works are all dialogues and epistles, many of the dialogues purporting to be conversations of Socrates and his disciples. Two key aspects of his philosophy are the dialectical method—represented by the questioning and probing of the particular event to reveal the general truth—and the existence of Forms. Plato's best-known works include the *Phaedo, Symposium, Phaedrus,* and *Timaeus.* The following selection, from *The Republic,* is an early description of the nature of learning. Plato's allegory is one of the most famous passages in literature. In this passage, Socrates is talking to a friend named Glaucon. Presented as a conversation, the myth dramatically builds in tension until the final revelation: This allegory symbolizes our lives.

1   And now, I said, let me show in a figure how far our nature is enlightened or unenlightened: Behold! human beings living in a underground den, which has a mouth open towards the light and reaching all along the den; here they have been from their childhood, and have their legs and necks chained so that they cannot move, and can only see before them, being prevented by the chains from turning round their heads. Above and behind them a fire is blazing at a distance, and between the fire and the prisoners there is a raised way; and you will see, if you look, a low wall built along the way, like the screen which marionette players have in front of them, over which they show the puppets.

2   I see.

3   And do you see, I said, men passing along the wall carrying all sorts of vessels, and statues and figures of animals made of wood and stone and various materials, which appear over the wall? Some of them are talking, others silent.

4   You have shown me a strange image, and they are strange prisoners.

5   Like ourselves, I replied; and they see only their own shadows, or the shadows of one another, which the fire throws on the opposite wall of the cave?

6   True, he said; how could they see anything but the shadows if they were never allowed to move their heads?

7   And of the objects which are being carried in like manner they would only see the shadows?

8   Yes, he said.

9   And if they were able to converse with one another, would they not suppose that they were naming what was actually before them?

10   Very true.

11   And suppose further that the prison had an echo which came from the other side, would they not be sure to fancy when one of the passers-by spoke that the voice which they heard came from the passing shadow?

12   No question, he replied.

13   To them, I said, the truth would be literally nothing but the shadows of the images.

14   That is certain.

15   And now look again, and see what will naturally follow if the prisoners are released and disabused of their error. At first, when any of them is liberated and compelled suddenly to stand up and turn his neck round and walk and look towards the light, he will suffer sharp pains; the glare will distress him, and he will be unable to see the realities of which in his former state he had seen the shadows; and then conceive some one saying to him, that what he saw before was an illusion, but that now, when he is approaching nearer to being and his eye is turned towards more real existence, he has a clearer vision,—what will be his reply? And you may further imagine that his instructor is pointing to the objects as they pass and requiring him to name them,—will he not be perplexed? Will he not fancy that the shadows which he formerly saw are truer than the objects which are now shown to him?

16   Far truer.

17   And if he is compelled to look straight at the light, will he not have a pain in his eyes which will make him turn away to take refuge in the objects of vision which he can see, and which he will conceive to be in reality clearer than the things which are now being shown to him?

18   True, he said.

19   And suppose once more, that he is reluctantly dragged up a steep and rugged ascent, and held fast until he is forced into the presence of the sun himself, is he not likely to be pained and irritated? When he approaches the light his eyes will be dazzled, and he will not be able to see anything at all of what are now called realities.

20   Not all in a moment, he said.

21   He will require to grow accustomed to the sight of the upper world. And first he will see the shadows best, next the reflections of men and other objects in the water, and then the objects themselves; then he will gaze upon the light of the moon and the stars and the spangled heaven; and he will see the sky and the stars by night better than the sun or the light of the sun by day?

22   Certainly.

23   Last of all he will be able to see the sun, and not mere reflections of him in the water, but he will see him in his own proper place, and not in another; and he will contemplate him as he is.

24   Certainly.

25   He will then proceed to argue that this is he who gives the season and the years, and is the guardian of all that is in the visible world, and in a certain way the cause of all things which he and his fellows have been accustomed to behold?

26   Clearly, he said, he would first see the sun and then reason about him.

27   And when he remembered his old habitation, and the wisdom of the den and his fellow-prisoners, do you not suppose that he would felicitate himself on the change, and pity them?

28   Certainly, he would.

29   And if they were in the habit of conferring honors among themselves on those who were quickest to observe the passing shadows and to remark which of them went before, and which followed after, and which were together; and who were therefore best able to draw conclusions as to the future, do you think that he would care for such honors and glories, or envy the possessors of them? Would he not say with Homer,

"Better to be the poor servant of a poor master,"
and to endure anything, rather than think as they do and live after their manner?

30　　Yes, he said, I think that he would rather suffer anything than entertain these false notions and live in this miserable manner.

31　　Imagine once more, I said, such an one coming suddenly out of the sun to be replaced in his old situation; would he not be certain to have his eyes full of darkness?

32　　To be sure, he said.

33　　And if there were a contest, and he had to compete in measuring the shadows with the prisoners who had never moved out of the den, while his sight was still weak, and before his eyes had become steady (and the time which would be needed to acquire this new habit of sight might be very considerable), would he not be ridiculous? Men would say of him that up he went and down he came without his eyes; and that it was better not even to think of ascending; and if any one tried to loose another and lead him up to the light, let them only catch the offender, and they would put him to death.

34　　No question, he said.

35　　This entire allegory, I said, you may now append, dear Glaucon, to the previous argument; the prison-house is the world of sight, the light of the fire is the sun, and you will not misapprehend me if you interpret the journey upwards to be the ascent of the soul into the intellectual world according to my poor belief, which, at your desire, I have expressed--whether rightly or wrongly God knows. But, whether true or false, my opinion is that in the world of knowledge the idea of good appears last of all, and is seen only with an effort; and, when seen, is also inferred to be the universal author of all things beautiful and right, parent of light and of the lord of light in this visible world, and the immediate source of reason and truth in the intellectual; and that this is the power upon which he who would act rationally either in public or private life must have his eye fixed.

36　　I agree, he said, as far as I am able to understand you.

37　　Moreover, I said, you must not wonder that those who attain to this beatific vision are unwilling to descend to human affairs; for their souls are ever hastening into the upper world where they desire to dwell; which desire of theirs is very natural, if our allegory may be trusted.

38　　Yes, very natural.

39　　And is there anything surprising in one who passes from divine contemplations to the evil state of man, misbehaving himself in a ridiculous manner; if, while his eyes are blinking and before he has become accustomed to the surrounding darkness, he is compelled to fight in courts of law, or in other places, about the images or the shadows of images of justice, and is endeavoring to meet the conceptions of those who have never yet seen absolute justice?

40　　Anything but surprising, he replied.

41　　Anyone who has common-sense will remember that the bewilderments of the eyes are of two kinds, and arise from two causes, either from coming out of the light or from going into the light, which is true of the mind's eye, quite as much as of the bodily eye; and he who remembers this when he sees any one whose vision is perplexed and weak, will not be too ready to laugh; he will first ask whether that soul of man has come out of the brighter life, and is unable to see because unaccustomed to the dark, or having turned from darkness to the day is dazzled by excess of light. And he will count the one happy in his condition and state of being, and he will pity the other; or, if he have a mind to laugh at the soul which comes from below into the light, there will be more reason in this than in the laugh which greets him who returns from above out of the light into the den.

42   That, he said, is a very just distinction.

Comprehension

1. What does Plato hope to convey to readers of his allegory?

2. According to Plato, do human beings typically perceive reality? To what does he compare the world?

3. According to Plato, what often happens to people who develop a true idea of reality? How well do they compete with others? Who is usually considered superior? Why?

Rhetorical Analysis

4. Is the conversation portrayed here realistic? How effective is this conversational style at conveying information?

5. How do you interpret such details of this allegory as the chains, the cave, and the fire? What connotations do such symbols have?

6. How does Plato use conversation to develop his argument? What is Glaucon's role in the conversation?

7. Note examples of transition words that mark contrasts between the real and the shadow world. How does Plato use contrast to develop his idea of the true real world?

8. Plato uses syllogistic reasoning to derive human behavior from his allegory. Trace his line of reasoning, noting transitional devices and the development of ideas in paragraphs 5–14. Find and describe a similar line of reasoning.

9. In what paragraph does Plato explain his allegory? Why do you think he locates his explanation where he does?

Writing

10. Are Plato's ideas still influencing contemporary society? How do his ideas affect our evaluation of materialism, sensuality, sex, and love?

11. Write an allegory based on a sport, business, or space flight to explain how we act in the world.

12. **Writing an Argument**   In an extended essay, try to convince your audience that *The Matrix* films are based on Plato's essay.

Me Talk Pretty One Day

David Sedaris

David Sedaris (b. 1956), who was born in Johnson City, New York, and grew up in Raleigh, North Carolina, is a well-known humorist, essayist, diarist, short-story writer, and radio commentator. After graduating from the Art Institute of Chicago in 1987, Sedaris held several temporary jobs, ranging from a cleaner of apartments to an elf in SantaLand at Macy's. His stint on National Public Radio's *Morning Edition* established Sedaris as a popular if quirky humorist and led to his first collection of essays, *Barrel Fever* (2000). Termed by *Entertainment Weekly* "a crackpot in the best sense of the word," Sedaris has also written *Naked* (1997), *Me Talk Pretty One Day* (2000), *Dress Your Family in Corduroy and Denim* (2004), and other works. In this essay, Sedaris humorously explains what happens when he tries to learn French.

1 At the age of forty-one, I am returning to school and have to think of myself as what my French textbook calls "a true debutant." After paying my tuition, I was issued a student ID, which allows me a discounted entry fee at movie theaters, puppet shows, and Festyland, a far-flung amusement park that advertises with billboards picturing a cartoon stegosaurus sitting in a canoe and eating what appears to be a ham sandwich.

2 I've moved to Paris with hopes of learning the language. My school is an easy ten-minute walk from my apartment, and on the first day of class I arrived early, watching as the returning students greeted one another in the school lobby. Vacations were recounted, and questions were raised concerning mutual friends with names like Kang and Vlatnya. Regardless of their nationalities, everyone spoke what sounded to me like excellent French. Some accents were better than others, but the students exhibited an ease and confidence that I found intimidating. As an added discomfort, they were all young, attractive, and well-dressed, causing me to feel not unlike Pa Kettle trapped backstage after a fashion show.

3 The first day of class was nerve-racking because I knew I'd be expected to perform. That's the way they do it here—it's everybody into the language pool, sink or swim. The teacher marched in, deeply tanned from a recent vacation, and proceeded to rattle off a series of administrative announcements. I've spent quite a few summers in Normandy, and I took a monthlong French class before leaving New York. I'm not completely in the dark, yet I understood only half of what this woman was saying.

4 "If you have not meimslsxp or lgpdmurct by this time, then you should not be in this room. Has everyone apzkiubjxow? Everyone? Good, we shall begin." She spread out her lesson plan and sighed, saying, "All right, then, who knows the alphabet?"

5 It was startling because (a) I hadn't been asked that question in a while and (b) I realized, while laughing, that I myself did not know the alphabet. They're the same letters, but in France they're pronounced differently. I know the shape of the alphabet but had no idea what it actually sounded like.

6 "Ahh." The teacher went to the board and sketched the letter a. "Do we have anyone in the room whose first name commences with an ahh?"

7   Two Polish Annas raised their hands, and the teacher instructed them to present themselves by stating their names, nationalities, occupations, and a brief list of things they liked and disliked in this world. The first Anna hailed from an industrial town outside of Warsaw and had front teeth the size of tombstones. She worked as a seamstress, enjoyed quiet times with friends, and hated the mosquito.

8   "Oh, really," the teacher said. "How very interesting. I thought that everyone loved the mosquito, but here, in front of all the world, you claim to detest him. How is it that we've been blessed with someone as unique and original as you? Tell us, please."

9   The seamstress did not understand what was being said but knew that this was an occasion for shame. Her rabbity mouth huffed for breath, and she stared down at her lap as though the appropriate comeback were stitched somewhere alongside the zipper of her slacks.

10   The second Anna learned from the first and claimed to love sunshine and detest lies. It sounded like a translation of one of those Playmate of the Month data sheets, the answers always written in the same loopy handwriting: "Turn-ons: Mom's famous fivealarm chili! Turn offs: insecurity and guys who come on too strong!!!!"

11   The two Polish Annas surely had clear notions of what they loved and hated, but like the rest of us, they were limited in terms of vocabulary, and this made them appear less than sophisticated. The teacher forged on, and we learned that Carlos, the Argentine bandonion player, loved wine, music, and, in his words, "making sex with the womans of the world." Next came a beautiful young Yugoslav who identified herself as an optimist, saying that she loved everything that life had to offer.

12   The teacher licked her lips, revealing a hint of the saucebox we would later come to know. She crouched low for her attack, placed her hands on the young woman's desk, and leaned close, saying, "Oh yeah? And do you love your little war?"

13   While the optimist struggled to defend herself, I scrambled to think of an answer to what had obviously become a trick question. How often is one asked what he loves in this world? More to the point, how often is one asked and then publicly ridiculed for his answer? I recalled my mother, flushed with wine, pounding the table top one night, saying, "Love? I love a good steak cooked rare. I love my cat, and I love . . ." My sisters and I leaned forward, waiting to hear our names. "Tums," our mother said. "I love Tums."

14   The teacher killed some time accusing the Yugoslavian girl of masterminding a program of genocide, and I jotted frantic notes in the margins of my pad. While I can honestly say that I love leafing through medical textbooks devoted to severe dermatological conditions, the hobby is beyond the reach of my French vocabulary, and acting it out would only have invited controversy.

15   When called upon, I delivered an effortless list of things that I detest: blood sausage, intestinal pates, brain pudding. I'd learned these words the hard way. Having given it some thought, I then declared my love for IBM typewriters, the French word for bruise, and my electric floor waxer. It was a short list, but still I managed to mispronounce IBM and assign the wrong gender to both the floor waxer and the typewriter. The teacher's reaction led me to believe that these mistakes were capital crimes in the country of France.

16   "Were you always this palicmkrexis?" she asked. "Even a fiuscrzsa ticiwelmun knows that a typewriter is feminine."

17   I absorbed as much of her abuse as I could understand, thinking—but not saying—that I find it ridiculous to assign a gender to an inanimate object which is incapable of disrobing and making an occasional fool of itself. Why refer to Lady Crack Pipe or Good Sir Dishrag when these things could never live up to all that their sex implied?

18   The teacher proceeded to belittle everyone from German Eva, who hated laziness, to Japanese Yukari, who loved paintbrushes and soap. Italian, Thai, Dutch, Korean, and Chinese—we all left class foolishly believing that the worst was over. She'd shaken us up a little, but surely that was just an act designed to weed out the deadweight. We didn't know it then, but the coming months would teach us what it was like to spend time in the presence of a wild animal, something completely unpredictable. Her temperament was not based on a series of good and bad days but, rather, good and bad moments. We soon learned to dodge chalk and protect our heads and stomachs whenever she approached us with a question. She hadn't yet punched anyone, but it seemed wise to protect ourselves against the inevitable.

19   Though we were forbidden to speak anything but French, the teacher would occasionally use us to practice any of her five fluent languages.

20   "I hate you," she said to me one afternoon. Her English was flawless. "I really, really hate you." Call me sensitive, but I couldn't help but take it personally.

21   After being singled out as a lazy kfdtinvfm, I took to spending four hours a night on my homework, putting in even more time whenever we were assigned an essay. I suppose I could have gotten by with less, but I was determined to create some sort of identity for myself: David, the hardworker, David the cut-up. We'd have one of those "complete this sentence" exercises, and I'd fool with the thing for hours, invariably settling on something like, "A quick run around the lake? I'd love to! Just give me a moment while I strap on my wooden leg." The teacher, through word and action, conveyed the message that if this was my idea of an identity, she wanted nothing to do with it.

22   My fear and discomfort crept beyond the borders of the classroom and accompanied me out onto the wide boulevards. Stopping for a coffee, asking directions, depositing money in my bank account: these things were out of the question, as they involved having to speak. Before beginning school, there'd been no shutting me up, but now I was convinced that everything I said was wrong. When the phone rang, I ignored it. If someone asked me a question, I pretended to be deaf. I knew my fear was getting the best of me when I started wondering why they don't sell cuts of meat in vending machines.

23   My only comfort was the knowledge that I was not alone. Huddled in the hallways and making the most of our pathetic French, my fellow students and I engaged in the sort of conversation commonly overhead in refugee camps.

24   "Sometimes me cry alone at night."

25   "That be common for I, also, but be more strong, you. Much work and someday you talk pretty. People start love you soon. Maybe tomorrow, okay."

26   Unlike the French class I had taken in New York, here there was no sense of competition. When the teacher poked a shy Korean in the eyelid with a freshly sharpened pencil, we took no comfort in the fact that, unlike Hyeyoon Cho, we

all knew the irregular past tense of the verb to defeat. In all fairness, the teacher hadn't meant to stab the girl, but neither did she spend much time apologizing, saying only, "Well, you should have been vkkdyo more kdeynfulh."

27   Over time it became impossible to believe that any of us would ever improve. Fall arrived and it rained every day, meaning we would now be scolded for the water dripping from our coats and umbrellas. It was mid-October when the teacher singled me out, saying, "Every day spent with you is like having a cesarean section." And it struck me that, for the first time since arriving in France, I could understand every word that someone was saying.

28   Understanding doesn't mean that you can suddenly speak the language. Far from it. It's a small step, nothing more, yet its rewards are intoxicating and deceptive. The teacher continued her diatribe and I settled back, bathing in the subtle beauty of each new curse and insult.

29   "You exhaust me with your foolishness and reward my efforts with nothing but pain, do you understand me?"

30   The world opened up, and it was with great joy that I responded, "I know the thing that you speak exact now. Talk me more, you, plus, please, plus."

Comprehension

1. Why does Sedaris use words that are unfamiliar to the vast majority of readers? What point is he trying to make?

2. In paragraph 28, Sedaris notes that, "Understanding doesn't mean that you can suddenly speak the language." What does he mean by this statement?

Rhetorical Analysis

3. What makes this essay immediately appealing to the reader?

4. What is significant about the title, and how does it successfully introduce the point of the essay?

5. Sedaris compares his French class to a refugee camp in paragraphs 23–24. Why does his analogy seem realistic?

6. Describe how paragraphs 26–27 highlight the gloomily amusing situation of this French class.

Writing

7. Describe an incident where you were the victim of some misunderstanding. Explain the absurdity of the situation.

8. **Writing an Argument**   Learning a new language is difficult. Argue what attitudes aid in understanding how to acclimate to a new language.

Black Men and Public Space

Brent Staples

Brent Staples (b. 1951) was born in Chester, Pennsylvania, and obtained a PhD in psychology from the University of Chicago in 1982. He is an essayist, author, journalist, scholar, and columnist for *The New York Times*. In 1986, he wrote "Just Walk On By" for *Ms. Magazine*. The piece, revised and renamed "Black Men and Public Space," appeared the following year in *Harper's*. Staples's many publications have focused on themes of culture, growing up, education, finding one's identity, and politics.

1 My first victim was a woman—white, well dressed, probably in her late twenties. I came upon her late one evening on a deserted street in Hyde Park, a relatively affluent neighborhood in an otherwise mean, impoverished section of Chicago. As I swung onto the avenue behind her, there seemed to be a discreet, uninflammatory distance between us. Not so. She cast back a worried glance. To her, the youngish black man—a broad six feet two inches with a beard and billowing hair, both hands shoved into the pockets of a bulky military jacket—seemed menacingly close. After a few more quick glimpses, she picked up her pace and was soon running in earnest. Within seconds she disappeared into a cross street.

2 That was more than a decade ago, I was twenty-two years old, a graduate student newly arrived at the University of Chicago. It was in the echo of that terrified woman's footfalls that I first began to know the unwieldy inheritance I'd come into—the ability to alter public space in ugly ways. It was clear that she thought herself the quarry of a mugger, a rapist, or worse. Suffering a bout of insomnia, however, I was stalking sleep, not defenseless wayfarers. As a softy who is scarcely able to take a knife to a raw chicken—let alone hold one to a person's throat—I was surprised, embarrassed, and dismayed all at once. Her flight made me feel like an accomplice in tyranny. It also made it clear that I was indistinguishable from the muggers who occasionally seeped into the area from the surrounding ghetto. That first encounter, and those that followed, signified that a vast, unnerving gulf lay between nighttime pedestrians—particularly women—and me. And I soon gathered that being perceived as dangerous is a hazard in itself. I only needed to turn a corner into a dicey situation, or crowd some frightened, armed person in a foyer somewhere, or make an errant move after being pulled over by a policeman. Where fear and weapons meet—and they often do in urban America—there is always the possibility of death.

3 In that first year, my first away from my hometown, I was to become thoroughly familiar with the language of fear. At dark, shadowy intersections, I could cross in front of a car stopped at a traffic light and elicit the thunk, thunk, thunk of the driver—black, white, male, or female—hammering down the door locks. On less traveled streets after dark, I grew accustomed to but never comfortable with people crossing to the other side of the street rather than pass me. Then there were the standard unpleasantries with policemen, doormen,

bouncers, cabdrivers, and others whose business it is to screen out troublesome individuals before there is any nastiness.

4   I moved to New York nearly two years ago and I have remained an avid night walker. In central Manhattan, the near-constant crowd cover minimizes tense one-on-one street encounters. Elsewhere—in SoHo, for example, where sidewalks are narrow and tightly spaced buildings shut out the sky—things can get very taut indeed.

5   After dark, on the warrenlike streets of Brooklyn where I live, I often see women who fear the worst from me. They seem to have set their faces on neutral, and with their purse straps strung across their chests bandolier-style, they forge ahead as though bracing themselves against being tackled. I understand, of course, that the danger they perceive is not a hallucination. Women are particularly vulnerable to street violence, and young black males are drastically overrepresented among the perpetrators of that violence. Yet these truths are no solace against the kind of alienation that comes of being ever the suspect, a fearsome entity with whom pedestrians avoid making eye contact.

6   It is not altogether clear to me how I reached the ripe old age of twenty-two without being conscious of the lethality nighttime pedestrians attributed to me. Perhaps it was because in Chester, Pennsylvania, the small, angry industrial town where I came of age in the 1960s, I was scarcely noticeable against a backdrop of gang warfare, street knifings, and murders. I grew up one of the good boys, had perhaps a half-dozen fistfights. In retrospect, my shyness of combat has clear sources.

7   As a boy, I saw countless tough guys locked away; I have since buried several, too. They were babies, really—a teenage cousin, a brother of twenty-two, a childhood friend in his mid-twenties—all gone down in episodes of bravado played out in the streets. I came to doubt the virtues of intimidation early on. I chose, perhaps unconsciously, to remain a shadow—timid, but a survivor.

8   The fearsomeness mistakenly attributed to me in public places often has a perilous flavor. The most frightening of these confusions occurred in the late 1970s and early 1980s, when I worked as a journalist in Chicago. One day, rushing into the office of a magazine I was writing for with a deadline story in hand, I was mistaken for a burglar. The office manager called security and, with an ad hoc posse, pursued me through the labyrinthine halls, nearly to my editor's door. I had no way of proving who I was. I could only move briskly toward the company of someone who knew me.

9   Another time I was on assignment for a local paper and killing time before an interview. I entered a jewelry store on the city's affluent Near North Side. The proprietor excused herself and returned with an enormous red Doberman pinscher straining at the end of a leash. She stood, the dog extended toward me, silent to my questions, her eyes bulging nearly out of her head. I took a cursory look around, nodded, and bade her good night.

10   Relatively speaking, however, I never fared as badly as another black male journalist. He went to nearby Waukegan, Illinois, a couple of summers ago to work on a story about a murderer who was born there. Mistaking the reporter for the killer, police officers hauled him from his car at gunpoint and but for his press

credentials would probably have tried to book him. Such episodes are not uncommon. Black men trade tales like this all the time.

11   Over the years, I learned to smother the rage I felt at so often being taken for a criminal. Not to do so would surely have led to madness. I now take precautions to make myself less threatening. I move about with care, particularly late in the evening. I give a wide berth to nervous people on subway platforms during the wee hours, particularly when I have exchanged business clothes for jeans. If I happen to be entering a building behind some people who appear skittish, I may walk by, letting them clear the lobby before I return, so as not to seem to be following them. I have been calm and extremely congenial on those rare occasions when I've been pulled over by the police.

12   And on late-evening constitutionals I employ what has proved to be an excellent tension-reducing measure: I whistle melodies from Beethoven and Vivaldi and the more popular classical composers. Even steely New Yorkers hunching toward nighttime destinations seem to relax, and occasionally they even join in the tune. Virtually everybody seems to sense that a mugger wouldn't be warbling bright, sunny selections from Vivaldi's *Four Seasons*. It is my equivalent of the cowbell that hikers wear when they know they are in bear country.

Brent Staples writes editorials on politics and culture for *The New York Times* and is author of "Parallel Time," a memoir.

Comprehension

1. What was your reaction to the title of this essay?

2. Staples determined (as related in paragraph 12) that whistling Beethoven and Vivaldi along with more "popular classical composers" was a therapeutic gesture. Elaborate on the intended purpose of that gesture.

3. What is Staples's main purpose in writing this essay?

Rhetoric Analysis

4. What image does the word *victim* conjure up in Staples's opening sentence?

5. What images and sounds does Staples use to describe the "language of fear" that had entered his awareness?

6. Explain the irony of Staples's situation.

7. Describe the alliterative effect used in some of Staples's sentences.

Writing

8. Write about an experience where you felt victimized. Was it justified? How did you feel? Why has it continued to stay with you?

9. **Writing an Argument**   Is a person's appearance as important as a person's actions? Using popular culture icons as well as recent current events, take a side and argue for or against this importance.

A Modest Proposal

Preventing the Children of Poor People in Ireland from Being a Burden to
Their Parents or Country, and for Making Them Beneficial to the Public

Jonathan Swift

Jonathan Swift (1667–1745) is best known as the author of three satires: *A
Tale of a Tub* (1704), *Gulliver's Travels* (1726), and *A Modest Proposal* (1729).
In these satires, Swift pricks the balloon of many of his contemporaries' and
our own most cherished prejudices, pomposities, and delusions. He was
also a famous poet, political journalist, and cleric (dean of St. Patrick's
Cathedral in Dublin), and an eloquent spokesperson for Irish rights. The
following selection, perhaps the most famous satiric essay in the English
language, offers modest advice to a nation suffering from poverty,
overpopulation, and political injustice.

1   It is a melancholy object to those, who walk through this great town, or travel in
the country, when they see the streets, the roads, and cabbin-doors crowded with
beggars of the female sex, followed by three, four, or six children, all in rags, and
importuning every passenger for an alms. These mothers instead of being able to
work for their honest livelihood, are forced to employ all their time in stroling to
beg sustenance for their helpless infants who, as they grow up, either turn thieves
for want of work, or leave their dear native country, to fight for the Pretender in
Spain, or sell themselves to the Barbadoes.

2   I think it is agreed by all parties, that this prodigious number of children in the
arms, or on the backs, or at the heels of their mothers, and frequently of their fathers,
is in the present deplorable state of the kingdom, a very great additional grievance;
and therefore whoever could find out a fair, cheap, and easy method of making these
children sound and useful members of the commonwealth, would deserve so well of
the publick, as to have his statue set up for a preserver of the nation.

3   But my intention is very far from being confined to provide only for the
children of professed beggars; it is of a much greater extent, and shall take in the
whole number of infants at a certain age, who are born of parents in effect as little
able to support them, as those who demand our charity in the streets.

4   As to my own part, having turned my thoughts for many years, upon this
important subject, and maturely weighed the several schemes of other projectors,
I have always found them grossly mistaken in the computation. It is true, a child
just dropt from its dam, may be supported by her milk, for a solar year, with little
other nourishment: at most not above the value of two shillings, which the
mother may certainly get, or the value in scraps, by her lawful occupation of
begging; and it is exactly at one year old that I propose to provide for them in
such a manner, as, instead of being a charge upon their parents, or the parish, or
wanting food and raiment for the rest of their lives, they shall, on the contrary,
contribute to the feeding, and partly to the cloathing, of many thousands.

5   There is likewise another great advantage in my scheme, that it will prevent those voluntary abortions, and that horrid practice of women murdering their bastard children, alas! too frequent among us, sacrificing the poor innocent babes, I doubt, more to avoid the expence than the shame, which would move tears and pity in the most savage and inhuman breast.

6   The number of souls in this kingdom being usually reckoned one million and a half, of these I calculate there may be about two hundred thousand couple whose wives are breeders; from which number I subtract thirty thousand couple, who are able to maintain their own children, (although I apprehend there cannot be so many, under the present distresses of the kingdom) but this being granted, there will remain an hundred and seventy thousand breeders. I again subtract fifty thousand, for those women who miscarry, or whose children die by accident or disease within the year. There only remain an hundred and twenty thousand children of poor parents annually born. The question therefore is, How this number shall be reared, and provided for? which, as I have already said, under the present situation of affairs, is utterly impossible by all the methods hitherto proposed. For we can neither employ them in handicraft or agriculture; they neither build houses, (I mean in the country) nor cultivate land: they can very seldom pick up a livelihood by stealing till they arrive at six years old; except where they are of towardly parts, although I confess they learn the rudiments much earlier; during which time they can however be properly looked upon only as probationers: As I have been informed by a principal gentleman in the county of Cavan, who protested to me, that he never knew above one or two instances under the age of six, even in a part of the kingdom so renowned for the quickest proficiency in that art.

7   I am assured by our merchants, that a boy or a girl before twelve years old, is no saleable commodity, and even when they come to this age, they will not yield above three pounds, or three pounds and half a crown at most, on the exchange; which cannot turn to account either to the parents or kingdom, the charge of nutriments and rags having been at least four times that value.

8   I shall now therefore humbly propose my own thoughts, which I hope will not be liable to the least objection.

9   I have been assured by a very knowing American of my acquaintance in London, that a young healthy child well nursed, is, at a year old, a most delicious nourishing and wholesome food, whether stewed, roasted, baked, or boiled; and I make no doubt that it will equally serve in a fricasie, or a ragoust.

10   I do therefore humbly offer it to publick consideration, that of the hundred and twenty thousand children, already computed, twenty thousand may be reserved for breed, whereof only one fourth part to be males; which is more than we allow to sheep, black cattle, or swine, and my reason is, that these children are seldom the fruits of marriage, a circumstance not much regarded by our savages, therefore, one male will be sufficient to serve four females. That the remaining hundred thousand may, at a year old, be offered in sale to the persons of quality and fortune, through the kingdom, always advising the mother to let them suck plentifully in the last month, so as to render them plump, and fat for a good table. A child will make two dishes at an entertainment for friends, and when the family dines alone,

the fore or hind quarter will make a reasonable dish, and seasoned with a little pepper or salt, will be very good boiled on the fourth day, especially in winter.

11   I have reckoned upon a medium, that a child just born will weigh 12 pounds, and in a solar year, if tolerably nursed, encreaseth to 28 pounds.

12   I grant this food will be somewhat dear, and therefore very proper for landlords, who, as they have already devoured most of the parents, seem to have the best title to the children.

13   Infant's flesh will be in season throughout the year, but more plentiful in March, and a little before and after; for we are told by a grave author, an eminent French physician, that fish being a prolifick dyet, there are more children born in Roman Catholick countries about nine months after Lent, the markets will be more glutted than usual, because the number of Popish infants, is at least three to one in this kingdom, and therefore it will have one other collateral advantage, by lessening the number of Papists among us.

14   I have already computed the charge of nursing a beggar's child (in which list I reckon all cottagers, labourers, and four-fifths of the farmers) to be about two shillings per annum, rags included; and I believe no gentleman would repine to give ten shillings for the carcass of a good fat child, which, as I have said, will make four dishes of excellent nutritive meat, when he hath only some particular friend, or his own family to dine with him. Thus the squire will learn to be a good landlord, and grow popular among his tenants, the mother will have eight shillings neat profit, and be fit for work till she produces another child.

15   Those who are more thrifty (as I must confess the times require) may flea the carcass; the skin of which, artificially dressed, will make admirable gloves for ladies, and summer boots for fine gentlemen.

16   As to our City of Dublin, shambles may be appointed for this purpose, in the most convenient parts of it, and butchers we may be assured will not be wanting; although I rather recommend buying the children alive, and dressing them hot from the knife, as we do roasting pigs.

17   A very worthy person, a true lover of his country, and whose virtues I highly esteem, was lately pleased, in discoursing on this matter, to offer a refinement upon my scheme. He said, that many gentlemen of this kingdom, having of late destroyed their deer, he conceived that the want of venison might be well supply'd by the bodies of young lads and maidens, not exceeding fourteen years of age, nor under twelve; so great a number of both sexes in every country being now ready to starve for want of work and service: And these to be disposed of by their parents if alive, or otherwise by their nearest relations. But with due deference to so excellent a friend, and so deserving a patriot, I cannot be altogether in his sentiments; for as to the males, my American acquaintance assured me from frequent experience, that their flesh was generally tough and lean, like that of our school-boys, by continual exercise, and their taste disagreeable, and to fatten them would not answer the charge. Then as to the females, it would, I think, with humble submission, be a loss to the publick, because they soon would become breeders themselves: And besides, it is not improbable that some scrupulous people might be apt to censure such a practice, (although indeed very unjustly) as a little bordering upon cruelty, which, I confess, hath always been with me the strongest objection against any project, how well soever intended.

18   But in order to justify my friend, he confessed, that this expedient was put into his head by the famous Salmanaazor, a native of the island Formosa, who came from thence to London, above twenty years ago, and in conversation told my friend, that in his country, when any young person happened to be put to death, the executioner sold the carcass to persons of quality, as a prime dainty; and that, in his time, the body of a plump girl of fifteen, who was crucified for an attempt to poison the Emperor, was sold to his imperial majesty's prime minister of state, and other great mandarins of the court in joints from the gibbet, at four hundred crowns. Neither indeed can I deny, that if the same use were made of several plump young girls in this town, who without one single groat to their fortunes, cannot stir abroad without a chair, and appear at a play-house and assemblies in foreign fineries which they never will pay for; the kingdom would not be the worse.

19   Some persons of a desponding spirit are in great concern about that vast number of poor people, who are aged, diseased, or maimed; and I have been desired to employ my thoughts what course may be taken, to ease the nation of so grievous an incumbrance. But I am not in the least pain upon that matter, because it is very well known, that they are every day dying, and rotting, by cold and famine, and filth, and vermin, as fast as can be reasonably expected. And as to the young labourers, they are now in almost as hopeful a condition. They cannot get work, and consequently pine away from want of nourishment, to a degree, that if at any time they are accidentally hired to common labour, they have not strength to perform it, and thus the country and themselves are happily delivered from the evils to come.

20   I have too long digressed, and therefore shall return to my subject. I think the advantages by the proposal which I have made are obvious and many, as well as of the highest importance.

21   For first, as I have already observed, it would greatly lessen the number of Papists, with whom we are yearly over-run, being the principal breeders of the nation, as well as our most dangerous enemies, and who stay at home on purpose with a design to deliver the kingdom to the Pretender, hoping to take their advantage by the absence of so many good Protestants, who have chosen rather to leave their country, than stay at home and pay tithes against their conscience to an episcopal curate.

22   Secondly, The poorer tenants will have something valuable of their own, which by law may be made liable to a distress, and help to pay their landlord's rent, their corn and cattle being already seized, and money a thing unknown.

23   Thirdly, Whereas the maintanance of an hundred thousand children, from two years old, and upwards, cannot be computed at less than ten shillings a piece per annum, the nation's stock will be thereby encreased fifty thousand pounds per annum, besides the profit of a new dish, introduced to the tables of all gentlemen of fortune in the kingdom, who have any refinement in taste. And the money will circulate among our selves, the goods being entirely of our own growth and manufacture.

24   Fourthly, The constant breeders, besides the gain of eight shillings sterling per annum by the sale of their children, will be rid of the charge of maintaining them after the first year.

25   Fifthly, This food would likewise bring great custom to taverns, where the vintners will certainly be so prudent as to procure the best receipts for dressing it to perfection; and consequently have their houses frequented by all the fine gentlemen, who justly value themselves upon their knowledge in good eating; and a skilful cook, who understands how to oblige his guests, will contrive to make it as expensive as they please.

26   Sixthly, This would be a great inducement to marriage, which all wise nations have either encouraged by rewards, or enforced by laws and penalties. It would encrease the care and tenderness of mothers towards their children, when they were sure of a settlement for life to the poor babes, provided in some sort by the publick, to their annual profit instead of expence. We should soon see an honest emulation among the married women, which of them could bring the fattest child to the market. Men would become as fond of their wives, during the time of their pregnancy, as they are now of their mares in foal, their cows in calf, or sow when they are ready to farrow; nor offer to beat or kick them (as is too frequent a practice) for fear of a miscarriage.

27   Many other advantages might be enumerated. For instance, the addition of some thousand carcasses in our exportation of barrel'd beef: the propagation of swine's flesh, and improvement in the art of making good bacon, so much wanted among us by the great destruction of pigs, too frequent at our tables; which are no way comparable in taste or magnificence to a well grown, fat yearly child, which roasted whole will make a considerable figure at a Lord Mayor's feast, or any other publick entertainment. But this, and many others, I omit, being studious of brevity.

28   Supposing that one thousand families in this city, would be constant customers for infants flesh, besides others who might have it at merry meetings, particularly at weddings and christenings, I compute that Dublin would take off annually about twenty thousand carcasses; and the rest of the kingdom (where probably they will be sold somewhat cheaper) the remaining eighty thousand.

29   I can think of no one objection, that will possibly be raised against this proposal, unless it should be urged, that the number of people will be thereby much lessened in the kingdom. This I freely own, and 'twas indeed one principal design in offering it to the world. I desire the reader will observe, that I calculate my remedy for this one individual Kingdom of Ireland, and for no other that ever was, is, or, I think, ever can be upon Earth. Therefore let no man talk to me of other expedients: Of taxing our absentees at five shillings a pound: Of using neither cloaths, nor houshold furniture, except what is of our own growth and manufacture: Of utterly rejecting the materials and instruments that promote foreign luxury: Of curing the expensiveness of pride, vanity, idleness, and gaming in our women: Of introducing a vein of parsimony, prudence and temperance: Of learning to love our country, wherein we differ even from Laplanders, and the inhabitants of Topinamboo: Of quitting our animosities and factions, nor acting any longer like the Jews, who were murdering one another at the very moment their city was taken: Of being a little cautious not to sell our country and consciences for nothing: Of teaching landlords to have at least one degree of mercy towards their tenants. Lastly, of putting a spirit of honesty, industry, and

skill into our shop-keepers, who, if a resolution could now be taken to buy only our native goods, would immediately unite to cheat and exact upon us in the price, the measure, and the goodness, nor could ever yet be brought to make one fair proposal of just dealing, though often and earnestly invited to it.

30   Therefore I repeat, let no man talk to me of these and the like expedients, 'till he hath at least some glympse of hope, that there will ever be some hearty and sincere attempt to put them into practice.

31   But, as to my self, having been wearied out for many years with offering vain, idle, visionary thoughts, and at length utterly despairing of success, I fortunately fell upon this proposal, which, as it is wholly new, so it hath something solid and real, of no expence and little trouble, full in our own power, and whereby we can incur no danger in disobliging England. For this kind of commodity will not bear exportation, and flesh being of too tender a consistence, to admit a long continuance in salt, although perhaps I could name a country, which would be glad to eat up our whole nation without it.

32   After all, I am not so violently bent upon my own opinion, as to reject any offer, proposed by wise men, which shall be found equally innocent, cheap, easy, and effectual. But before something of that kind shall be advanced in contradiction to my scheme, and offering a better, I desire the author or authors will be pleased maturely to consider two points. First, As things now stand, how they will be able to find food and raiment for a hundred thousand useless mouths and backs. And secondly, There being a round million of creatures in humane figure throughout this kingdom, whose whole subsistence put into a common stock, would leave them in debt two million of pounds sterling, adding those who are beggars by profession, to the bulk of farmers, cottagers and labourers, with their wives and children, who are beggars in effect; I desire those politicians who dislike my overture, and may perhaps be so bold to attempt an answer, that they will first ask the parents of these mortals, whether they would not at this day think it a great happiness to have been sold for food at a year old, in the manner I prescribe, and thereby have avoided such a perpetual scene of misfortunes, as they have since gone through, by the oppression of landlords, the impossibility of paying rent without money or trade, the want of common sustenance, with neither house nor cloaths to cover them from the inclemencies of the weather, and the most inevitable prospect of intailing the like, or greater miseries, upon their breed for ever.

33   I profess, in the sincerity of my heart, that I have not the least personal interest in endeavouring to promote this necessary work, having no other motive than the publick good of my country, by advancing our trade, providing for infants, relieving the poor, and giving some pleasure to the rich. I have no children, by which I can propose to get a single penny; the youngest being nine years old, and my wife past child-bearing.

"A Modest Proposal" by Dr. Jonathan Swift, 1729. http://www.gutenberg.org/files/1080/1080-h/1080-h.htm

Comprehension

1. Who is Swift's audience for this essay? Defend your answer.

2. Describe the persona in this essay. How is the unusual narrative personality (as distinguished from Swift's personality) revealed by the author in degrees? How can we tell that the speaker's opinions are not shared by Swift?

3. What are the major propositions behind Swift's modest proposal? What are the minor propositions?

Rhetorical Analysis

4. Explain the importance of the word *modest* in the title. What stylistic devices does this "modesty" contrast with?

5. What is the effect of Swift's persistent reference to people as "breeders," "dams," "carcass," and the like? Why does he define *children* in economic terms? Find other words that contribute to this motif.

6. Analyze the purpose of the relatively long introduction, consisting of paragraphs 1–7. How does Swift establish his ironic-satiric tone in this initial section?

7. What contrasts and discrepancies are at the heart of Swift's ironic statement in paragraphs 9 and 10? Explain both the subtlety and savagery of the satire in paragraph 12.

8. Paragraphs 13–20 develop six advantages of Swift's proposal, while paragraphs 21–26 list them in enumerative manner. Analyze the progression of these propositions. What is the effect of the listing? Why is Swift parodying argumentative techniques?

9. How does the author both sustain and suspend the irony in paragraph 29? How is the strategy repeated in paragraph 32? How does the concluding paragraph cap his satiric commentary on human nature?

Writing

10. Discuss Swift's social, political, religious, and economic views as they are revealed in the essay.

11. Write a comprehensive critique of America's failure to address the needs of its poor.

12. **Writing an Argument**   Write a modest proposal on how to change an issue in society, advancing an absurd proposition through various argumentative techniques.

On the Duty of Civil Disobedience

Henry David Thoreau

Henry David Thoreau (1817–1862)—writer, transcendentalist, abolitionist—is best known as the author of *Walden* (1854) and *On the Duty of Civil Disobedience* (1849). Ralph Waldo Emerson, Thoreau's neighbor and friend in Concord, Massachusetts, wrote *Nature*, which ultimately led Thoreau, at the age of 28, to live at Walden Pond and record in his famous book his experiment of living by nature's terms. *Walden* was not embraced by the public, so Thoreau spent the next nine years rewriting it while continuing to work as a surveyor and pencil maker. He railed against injustice, whether social or economic or political. He first published *Civil Disobedience* (originally titled *Resistance to Civil Government*) in 1849. Already a well-known transcendentalist, Thoreau in this essay takes issue with American citizens' seemingly lackadaisical contentment with unjust laws. He questions why people simply go along with antiquated laws that should be removed. This disgust had much to do with his views on taxes being earmarked for questionable wars, and the inhumanity of slavery. Thoreau died of tuberculosis at the age of 44.

1   I heartily accept the motto,—"That government is best which governs least"; and I should like to see it acted up to more rapidly and systematically. Carried out, it finally amounts to this, which also I believe,—"That government is best which governs not at all"; and when men are prepared for it, that will be the kind of government which they will have. Government is at best but an expedient; but most governments are usually, and all governments are sometimes, inexpedient. The objections which have been brought against a standing army, and they are many and weighty, and deserve to prevail, may also at last be brought against a standing government. The standing army is only an arm of the standing government. The government itself, which is only the mode which the people have chosen to execute their will, is equally liable to be abused and perverted before the people can act through it. Witness the present Mexican war, the work of comparatively a few individuals using the standing government as their tool; for, in the outset, the people would not have consented to this measure.

2   This American government,—what is it but a tradition, though a recent one, endeavoring to transmit itself unimpaired to posterity, but each instant losing some of its integrity? It has not the vitality and force of a single living man; for a single man can bend it to his will. It is a sort of wooden gun to the people themselves. But it is not the less necessary for this; for the people must have some complicated machinery or other, and hear its din, to satisfy that idea of government which they have. Governments show thus how successfully men can be imposed on, even impose on themselves, for their own advantage. It is excellent, we must all allow. Yet this government never of itself furthered any enterprise, but by the alacrity with which it got out of its way. *It* does not keep the country free. *It* does not settle

the West. *It* does not educate. The character inherent in the American people has done all that has been accomplished; and it would have done somewhat more, if the government had not sometimes got in its way. For government is an expedient by which men would fain succeed in letting one another alone; and, as has been said, when it is most expedient, the governed are most let alone by it. Trade and commerce, if they were not made of india-rubber, would never manage to bounce over obstacles which legislators are continually putting in their way; and, if one were to judge these men wholly by the effects of their actions and not partly by their intentions, they would deserve to be classed and punished with those mischievous persons who put obstructions on the railroads.

3   But, to speak practically and as a citizen, unlike those who call themselves no-government men, I ask for, not at once no government, but *at once* a better government. Let every man make known what kind of government would command his respect, and that will be one step toward obtaining it.

4   After all, the practical reason why, when the power is once in the hands of the people, a majority are permitted, and for a long period continue, to rule is not because they are most likely to be in the right, nor because this seems fairest to the minority, but because they are physically the strongest. But a government in which the majority rule in all cases cannot be based on justice, even as far as men understand it. Can there not be a government in which majorities do not virtually decide right and wrong, but conscience?—in which majorities decide only those questions to which the rule of expediency is applicable? Must the citizen ever for a moment, or in the least degree, resign his conscience to the legislator? Why has every man a conscience, then? I think that we should be men first, and subjects afterward. It is not desirable to cultivate a respect for the law, so much as for the right. The only obligation which I have a right to assume is to do at any time what I think right. It is truly enough said, that a corporation has no conscience; but a corporation of conscientious men is a corporation *with* a conscience. Law never made men a whit more just; and, by means of their respect for it, even the well-disposed are daily made the agents of injustice. A common and natural result of an undue respect for law is, that you may see a file of soldiers, colonel, captain, corporal, privates, powder-monkeys, and all, marching in admirable order over hill and dale to the wars, against their wills, ay, against their common sense and consciences, which makes it very steep marching indeed, and produces a palpitation of the heart. They have no doubt that it is a damnable business in which they are concerned; they are all peaceably inclined. Now, what are they? Men at all? or small movable forts and magazines, at the service of some unscrupulous man in power? Visit the Navy-yard, and behold a marine, such a man as an American government can make, or such as it can make a man with its black arts,—a mere shadow and reminiscence of humanity, a man laid out alive and standing, and already, as one may say, buried under arms with funeral accompaniments, though it may be,—

5   "Not a drum was heard, not a funeral note,
    As his corse to the rampart we hurried;
    Not a soldier discharged his farewell shot
    O'er the grave where our hero was buried."

6   The mass of men serve the State thus, not as men mainly, but as machines, with their bodies. They are the standing army, and the militia, jailers, constables, posse comitatus, etc. In most cases there is no free exercise whatever of the judgment or of the moral sense; but they put themselves on a level with wood and earth and stones; and wooden men can perhaps be manufactured that will serve the purpose as well. Such command no more respect than men of straw or a lump of dirt. They have the same sort of worth only as horses and dogs. Yet such as these even are commonly esteemed good citizens. Others—as most legislators, politicians, lawyers, ministers, and office-holders—serve the State chiefly with their heads; and, as they rarely make any moral distinctions, they are as likely to serve the Devil, without *intending* it, as God. A very few, as heroes, patriots, martyrs, reformers in the great sense, and *men*, serve the State with their consciences also, and so necessarily resist it for the most part; and they are commonly treated as enemies by it. A wise man will only be useful as a man, and will not submit to be "clay," and "stop a hole to keep the wind away," but leave that office to his dust at least:—

7   "I am too high-born to be propertied,
     To be a secondary at control,
     Or useful serving-man and instrument
     To any sovereign state throughout the world."

8   He who gives himself entirely to his fellow-men appears to them useless and selfish; but he who gives himself partially to them is pronounced a benefactor and philanthropist.

9   How does it become a man to behave toward this American government to-day? I answer, that he cannot without disgrace be associated with it. I cannot for an instant recognize that political organization as *my* government which is the *slave's* government also.

10   All men recognize the right of revolution; that is, the right to refuse allegiance to, and to resist, the government, when its tyranny or its inefficiency are great and unendurable. But almost all say that such is not the case now. But such was the case, they think, in the Revolution of '75. If one were to tell me that this was a bad government because it taxed certain foreign commodities brought to its ports, it is most probable that I should not make an ado about it, for I can do without them. All machines have their friction; and possibly this does enough good to counterbalance the evil. At any rate, it is a great evil to make a stir about it. But when the friction comes to have its machine, and oppression and robbery are organized, I say, let us not have such a machine any longer. In other words, when a sixth of the population of a nation which has undertaken to be the refuge of liberty are slaves, and a whole country is unjustly overrun and conquered by a foreign army, and subjected to military law, I think that it is not too soon for honest men to rebel and revolutionize. What makes this duty the more urgent is the fact that the country so overrun is not our own, but ours is the invading army.

11   Paley, a common authority with many on moral questions, in his chapter on the "Duty of Submission to Civil Government," resolves all civil obligation into expediency; and he proceeds to say, "that so long as the interest of the whole society requires it, that is, so long as the established government cannot be

resisted or changed without public inconveniency, it is the will of God that the established government be obeyed, and no longer. . . . This principle being admitted, the justice of every particular case of resistance is reduced to a computation of the quantity of the danger and grievance on the one side, and of the probability and expense of redressing it on the other." Of this, he says, every man shall judge for himself. But Paley appears never to have contemplated those cases to which the rule of expediency does not apply, in which a people, as well as an individual, must do justice, cost what it may. If I have unjustly wrested a plank from a drowning man, I must restore it to him though I drown myself. This, according to Paley, would be inconvenient. But he that would save his life, in such a case, shall lose it. This people must cease to hold slaves, and to make war on Mexico, though it cost them their existence as a people.

12   In their practice, nations agree with Paley; but does any one think that Massachusetts does exactly what is right at the present crisis?

13   "A drab of state, a cloth-o'-silver slut,
      To have her train borne up, and her soul trail in the dirt."

14   Practically speaking, the opponents to a reform in Massachusetts are not a hundred thousand politicians at the South, but a hundred thousand merchants and farmers here, who are more interested in commerce and agriculture than they are in humanity, and are not prepared to do justice to the slave and to Mexico, *cost what it may*. I quarrel not with far-off foes, but with those who, near at home, co-operate with, and do the bidding of, those far away, and without whom the latter would be harmless. We are accustomed to say that the mass of men are unprepared; but improvement is slow, because the few are not materially wiser or better than the many. It is not so important that many should be as good as you, as that there be some absolute goodness somewhere; for that will leaven the whole lump. There are thousands who are *in opinion* opposed to slavery and to the war, who yet in effect do nothing to put an end to them; who, esteeming themselves children of Washington and Franklin, sit down with their hands in their pockets, and say that they know not what to do, and do nothing; who even postpone the question of freedom to the question of free-trade, and quietly read the prices-current along with the latest advices from Mexico, after dinner, and, it may be, fall asleep over them both. What is the price-current of an honest man and patriot to-day? They hesitate, and they regret, and sometimes they petition; but they do nothing in earnest and with effect. They will wait, well disposed, for others to remedy the evil, that they may no longer have it to regret. At most, they give only a cheap vote, and a feeble countenance and God-speed, to the right, as it goes by them. There are nine hundred and ninety-nine patrons of virtue to one virtuous man. But it is easier to deal with the real possessor of a thing than with the temporary guardian of it.

15   All voting is a sort of gaming, like checkers or backgammon, with a slight moral tinge to it, a playing with right and wrong, with moral questions; and betting naturally accompanies it. The character of the voters is not staked. I cast my vote, perchance, as I think right; but I am not vitally concerned that that right should prevail. I am willing to leave it to the majority. Its obligation, therefore, never exceeds that of expediency. Even voting *for the right* is *doing* nothing for it. It is only expressing to men feebly your desire that it should prevail. A wise man

will not leave the right to the mercy of chance, nor wish it to prevail through the power of the majority. There is but little virtue in the action of masses of men. When the majority shall at length vote for the abolition of slavery, it will be because they are indifferent to slavery, or because there is but little slavery left to be abolished by their vote. *They* will then be the only slaves. Only *his* vote can hasten the abolition of slavery who asserts his own freedom by his vote.

16   I hear of a convention to be held at Baltimore, or elsewhere, for the selection of a candidate for the Presidency, made up chiefly of editors, and men who are politicians by profession; but I think, what is it to any independent, intelligent, and respectable man what decision they may come to? Shall we not have the advantage of his wisdom and honesty, nevertheless? Can we not count upon some independent votes? Are there not many individuals in the country who do not attend conventions? But no: I find that the respectable man, so called, has immediately drifted from his position, and despairs of his country, when his country has more reason to despair of him. He forthwith adopts one of the candidates thus selected as the only *available* one, thus proving that he is himself *available* for any purposes of the demagogue. His vote is of no more worth than that of any unprincipled foreigner or hireling native, who may have been bought. O for a man who is a *man*, and, as my neighbor says, has a bone in his back which you cannot pass your hand through! Our statistics are at fault: the population has been returned too large. How many *men* are there to a square thousand miles in the country? Hardly one. Does not America offer any inducement for men to settle here? The American has dwindled into an Odd Fellow,—one who may be known by the development of his organ of gregariousness, and a manifest lack of intellect and cheerful self-reliance; whose first and chief concern, on coming into the world, is to see that the Almshouses are in good repair; and, before yet he has lawfully donned the virile garb, to collect a fund for the support of the widows and orphans that may be; who, in short, ventures to live only by the aid of the Mutual Insurance company, which has promised to bury him decently.

17   It is not a man's duty, as a matter of course, to devote himself to the eradication of any, even the most enormous wrong; he may still properly have other concerns to engage him; but it is his duty, at least, to wash his hands of it, and, if he gives it no thought longer, not to give it practically his support. If I devote myself to other pursuits and contemplations, I must first see, at least, that I do not pursue them sitting upon another man's shoulders. I must get off him first, that he may pursue his contemplations too. See what gross inconsistency is tolerated. I have heard some of my townsmen say, "I should like to have them order me out to help put down an insurrection of the slaves, or to march to Mexico;—see if I would go"; and yet these very men have each, directly by their allegiance, and so indirectly, at least, by their money, furnished a substitute. The soldier is applauded who refuses to serve in an unjust war by those who do not refuse to sustain the unjust government which makes the war; is applauded by those whose own act and authority he disregards and sets at naught; as if the State were penitent to that degree that it hired one to scourge it while it sinned, but not to that degree that it left off sinning for a moment. Thus, under the name of Order and Civil Government, we are all made at last to pay homage to and support our own meanness. After the first blush

of sin comes its indifference; and from immoral it becomes, as it were, *un*moral, and not quite unnecessary to that life which we have made.

18   The broadest and most prevalent error requires the most disinterested virtue to sustain it. The slight reproach to which the virtue of patriotism is commonly liable, the noble are most likely to incur. Those who, while they disapprove of the character and measures of a government, yield to it their allegiance and support are undoubtedly its most conscientious supporters, and so frequently the most serious obstacles to reform. Some are petitioning the State to dissolve the Union, to disregard the requisitions of the President. Why do they not dissolve it themselves,—the union between themselves and the State,—and refuse to pay their quota into its treasury? Do not they stand in same relation to the State that the State does to the Union? And have not the same reasons prevented the State from resisting the Union which have prevented them from resisting the State?

19   How can a man be satisfied to entertain an opinion merely and enjoy *it*? Is there any enjoyment in it, if his opinion is that he is aggrieved? If you are cheated out of a single dollar by your neighbor, you do not rest satisfied with knowing you are cheated, or with saying that you are cheated, or even with petitioning him to pay you your due; but you take effectual steps at once to obtain the full amount, and see that you are never cheated again. Action from principle, the perception and the performance of right, changes things and relations; it is essentially revolutionary, and does not consist wholly with anything which was. It not only divides states and churches, it divides families; ay, it divides the *individual*, separating the diabolical in him from the divine.

20   Unjust laws exist: shall we be content to obey them, or shall we endeavor to amend them, and obey them until we have succeeded, or shall we transgress them at once? Men generally, under such a government as this, think that they ought to wait until they have persuaded the majority to alter them. They think that, if they should resist, the remedy would be worse than the evil. But it is the fault of the government itself that the remedy *is* worse than the evil. *It* makes it worse. Why is it not more apt to anticipate and provide for reform? Why does it not cherish its wide minority? Why does it cry and resist before it is hurt? Why does it not encourage its citizens to be on the alert to point out its faults, and *do* better than it would have them? Why does it always crucify Christ, and excommunicate Copernicus and Luther, and pronounce Washington and Franklin rebels?

21   One would think, that a deliberate and practical denial of its authority was the only offense never contemplated by government; else, why has it not assigned its definite, its suitable and proportionate penalty? If a man who has no property refuses but once to earn nine shillings for the State, he is put in prison for a period unlimited by any law that I know, and determined only by the discretion of those who placed him there; but if he should steal ninety times nine shillings from the State, he is soon permitted to go at large again.

22   If the injustice is part of the necessary friction of the machine of government, let it go, let it go: perchance it will wear smooth,—certainly the machine will wear out. If the injustice has a spring, or a pulley, or a rope, or a crank, exclusively for itself, then perhaps you may consider whether the remedy will not be worse than

the evil; but if it is of such a nature that it requires you to be the agent of injustice to another, then, I say, break the law. Let your life be a counter-friction to stop the machine. What I have to do is to see, at any rate, that I do not lend myself to the wrong which I condemn.

23   As for adopting the ways which the State has provided for remedying the evil, I know not of such ways. They take too much time, and a man's life will be gone. I have other affairs to attend to. I came into this world, not chiefly to make this a good place to live in, but to live in it, be it good or bad. A man has not everything to do, but something; and because he cannot do *everything*, it is not necessary that he should do *something* wrong. It is not my business to be petitioning the Governor or the Legislature any more than it is theirs to petition me; and if they should not hear my petition, what should I do then? But in this case the State has provided no way: its very Constitution is the evil. This may seem to be harsh and stubborn and unconciliatory; but it is to treat with the utmost kindness and consideration the only spirit that can appreciate or deserves it. So is all change for the better, like birth and death, which convulse the body.

24   I do not hesitate to say, that those who call themselves Abolitionists should at once effectually withdraw their support, both in person and property, from the government of Massachusetts, and not wait till they constitute a majority of one, before they suffer the right to prevail through them. I think that it is enough if they have God on their side, without waiting for that other one. Moreover, any man more right than his neighbors constitutes a majority of one already.

25   I meet this American government, or its representative, the state government, directly, and face to face, once a year—no more—in the person of its tax-gatherer; this is the only mode in which a man situated as I am necessarily meets it; and it then says distinctly, Recognize me; and the simplest, the most effectual, and, in the present posture of affairs, the indispensablest mode of treating with it on this head, of expressing your little satisfaction with and love for it, is to deny it then. My civil neighbor, the tax-gatherer, is the very man I have to deal with,—for it is, after all, with men and not with parchment that I quarrel,—and he has voluntarily chosen to be an agent of the government. How shall he ever know well what he is and does as an officer of the government, or as a man, until he is obliged to consider whether he shall treat me, his neighbor, for whom he has respect, as a neighbor and well-disposed man, or as a maniac and disturber of the peace, and see if he can get over this obstruction to his neighborliness without a ruder and more impetuous thought or speech corresponding with his action. I know this well, that if one thousand, if one hundred, if ten men whom I could name—if ten *honest* men only—ay, if *one* HONEST man, in this State of Massachusetts, *ceasing to hold slaves*, were actually to withdraw from this co-partnership, and be locked up in the county jail therefor, it would be the abolition of slavery in America. For it matters not how small the beginning may seem to be: what is once well done is done forever. But we love better to talk about it: that we say is our mission. Reform keeps many scores of newspapers in its service, but not one man. If my esteemed neighbor, the State's ambassador, who will devote his days to the settlement of the question of human rights in the Council Chamber, instead of being threatened with the prisons of Carolina, were to sit down the prisoner of

Massachusetts, that State which is so anxious to foist the sin of slavery upon her sister,—though at present she can discover only an act of inhospitality to be the ground of a quarrel with her,—the Legislature would not wholly waive the subject the following winter.

26   Under a government which imprisons any unjustly, the true place for a just man is also a prison. The proper place to-day, the only place which Massachusetts has provided for her freer and less desponding spirits, is in her prisons, to be put out and locked out of the State by her own act, as they have already put themselves out by their principles. It is there that the fugitive slave, and the Mexican prisoner on parole, and the Indian come to plead the wrongs of his race, should find them; on that separate, but more free and honorable ground, where the State places those who are not *with* her, but *against* her,—the only house in a slave State in which a free man can abide with honor. If any think that their influence would be lost there, and their voices no longer afflict the ear of the State, that they would not be as an enemy within its walls, they do not know by how much truth is stronger than error, nor how much more eloquently and effectively he can combat injustice who has experienced a little in his own person. Cast your whole vote, not a strip of paper merely, but your whole influence. A minority is powerless while it conforms to the majority; it is not even a minority then; but it is irresistible when it clogs by its whole weight. If the alternative is to keep all just men in prison, or give up war and slavery, the State will not hesitate which to choose. If a thousand men were not to pay their tax-bills this year, that would not be a violent and bloody measure, as it would be to pay them, and enable the State to commit violence and shed innocent blood. This is, in fact, the definition of a peaceful revolution, if any such is possible. If the tax-gatherer, or any other public officer, asks me, as one has done, "But what shall I do?" my answer is, "If you really wish to do anything, resign your office." When the subject has refused allegiance, and the officer has resigned his office, then the revolution is accomplished. But even suppose blood should flow. Is there not a sort of blood shed when the conscience is wounded? Through this wound a man's real manhood and immortality flow out, and he bleeds to an everlasting death. I see this blood flowing now.

27   I have contemplated the imprisonment of the offender, rather than the seizure of his goods,—though both will serve the same purpose,—because they who assert the purest right, and consequently are most dangerous to a corrupt State, commonly have not spent much time in accumulating property. To such the State renders comparatively small service, and a slight tax is wont to appear exorbitant, particularly if they are obliged to earn it by special labor with their hands. If there were one who lived wholly without the use of money, the State itself would hesitate to demand it of him. But the rich man—not to make any invidious comparison—is always sold to the institution which makes him rich. Absolutely speaking, the more money the less virtue; for money comes between a man and his objects, and obtains them for him; it was certainly no great virtue to obtain it. It puts to rest many questions which he would otherwise be taxed to answer; while the only new question which it puts is the hard but superfluous one, how to spend it. Thus his moral ground is taken from under his feet. The opportunities of living are diminished in proportion as that are called the "means" are increased.

The best thing a man can do for his culture when he is rich is to endeavor to carry out those schemes which he entertained when he was poor. Christ answered the Herodians according to their condition. "Show me the tribute-money," said he;—and one took a penny out of his pocket;—if you use money which has the image of Caesar on it, and which he has made current and valuable, that is, *if you are men of the State*, and gladly enjoy the advantages of Caesar's government, then pay him back some of his own when he demands it. "Render therefore to Caesar that which is Caesar's, and to God those things which are God's,"—leaving them no wiser than before as to which was which; for they did not wish to know.

28   When I converse with the freest of my neighbors, I perceive that, whatever they may say about the magnitude and seriousness of the question, and their regard for the public tranquillity, the long and the short of the matter is, that they cannot spare the protection of the existing government, and they dread the consequences to their property and families of disobedience to it. For my own part, I should not like to think that I ever rely on the protection of the State. But, if I deny the authority of the State when it presents its tax-bill, it will soon take and waste all my property, and so harass me and my children without end. This is hard. This makes it impossible for a man to live honestly, and at the same time comfortably, in outward respects. It will not be worth the while to accumulate property; that would be sure to go again. You must hire or squat somewhere, and raise but a small crop, and eat that soon. You must live within yourself, and depend upon yourself always tucked up and ready for a start, and not have many affairs. A man may grow rich in Turkey even, if he will be in all respects a good subject of the Turkish government. Confucius said: "If a state is governed by the principles of reason, poverty and misery are subjects of shame; if a state is not governed by the principles of reason, riches and honors are the subjects of shame." No: until I want the protection of Massachusetts to be extended to me in some distant Southern port, where my liberty is endangered, or until I am bent solely on building up an estate at home by peaceful enterprise, I can afford to refuse allegiance to Massachusetts, and her right to my property and life. It costs me less in every sense to incur the penalty of disobedience to the State than it would to obey. I should feel as if I were worth less in that case.

29   Some years ago the State met me in behalf of the Church, and commanded me to pay a certain sum toward the support of a clergyman whose preaching my father attended, but never I myself. "Pay," it said, "or be locked up in the jail." I declined to pay. But, unfortunately, another man saw fit to pay it. I did not see why the schoolmaster should be taxed to support the priest, and not the priest the schoolmaster; for I was not the State's schoolmaster, but I supported myself by voluntary subscriptions. I did not see why the lyceum should not present its tax-bill, and have the State to back its demand, as well as the Church. However, at the request of the selectmen, I condescended to make some such statement as this in writing:— "Know all men by these presents, that I, Henry Thoreau, do not wish to be regarded as a member of any incorporated society which I have not joined." This I gave to the town clerk; and he has it. The State, having thus learned that I did not wish to be regarded as a member of that church, has never made a like

demand on me since; though it said that it must adhere to its original presumption that time. If I had known how to name them, I should then have signed off in detail from all the societies which I never signed on to; but I did not know where to find a complete list.

30   I have paid no poll-tax for six years. I was put into a jail once on this account, for one night; and, as I stood considering the walls of solid stone, two or three feet thick, the door of wood and iron, a foot thick, and the iron grating which strained the light, I could not help being struck with the foolishness of that institution which treated me as if I were mere flesh and blood and bones, to be locked up. I wondered that it should have concluded at length that this was the best use it could put me to, and had never thought to avail itself of my services in some way. I saw that, if there was a wall of stone between me and my townsmen, there was a still more difficult one to climb or break through before they could get to be as free as I was. I did not for a moment feel confined, and the walls seemed a great waste of stone and mortar. I felt as if I alone of all my townsmen had paid my tax. They plainly did not know how to treat me, but behaved like persons who are underbred. In every threat and in every compliment there was a blunder; for they thought that my chief desire was to stand the other side of that stone wall. I could not but smile to see how industriously they locked the door on my meditations, which followed them out again without let or hindrance, and *they* were really all that was dangerous. As they could not reach me, they had resolved to punish my body; just as boys, if they cannot come at some person against whom they have a spite, will abuse his dog. I saw that the State was half-witted, that it was timid as a lone woman with her silver spoons, and that it did not know its friends from its foes, and I lost all my remaining respect for it, and pitied it.

31   Thus the State never intentionally confronts a man's sense, intellectual or moral, but only his body, his senses. It is not armed with superior wit or honesty, but with superior physical strength. I was not born to be forced. I will breathe after my own fashion. Let us see who is the strongest. What force has a multitude? They only can force me who obey a higher law than I. They force me to become like themselves. I do not hear of *men* being *forced* to live this way or that by masses of men. What sort of life were that to live? When I meet a government which says to me, "Your money or your life," why should I be in haste to give it my money? It may be in a great strait, and not know what to do: I cannot help that. It must help itself; do as I do. It is not worth the while to snivel about it. I am not responsible for the successful working of the machinery of society. I am not the son of the engineer. I perceive that, when an acorn and a chestnut fall side by side, the one does not remain inert to make way for the other, but both obey their own laws, and spring and grow and flourish as best they can, till one, perchance, overshadows and destroys the other. If a plant cannot live according to its nature, it dies; and so a man.

· · · · · · · · · · · · · ·

32   I have never declined paying the highway tax, because I am as desirous of being a good neighbor as I am of being a bad subject; and as for supporting schools, I am doing my part to educate my fellow-countrymen now. It is for no particular item in the tax-bill that I refuse to pay it. I simply wish to refuse

allegiance to the State, to withdraw and stand aloof from it effectually. I do not care to trace the course of my dollar, if I could, till it buys a man or a musket to shoot one with,—the dollar is innocent, but I am concerned to trace the effects of my allegiance. In fact, I quietly declare war with the State, after my fashion, though I will still make what use and get what advantage of her I can, as is usual in such cases.

33   If others pay the tax which is demanded of me, from a sympathy with the State, they do but what they have already done in their own case, or rather they abet injustice to a greater extent than the State requires. If they pay the tax from a mistaken interest in the individual taxed, to save his property, or prevent his going to jail, it is because they have not considered wisely how far they let their private feelings interfere with the public good.

34   This, then, is my position at present. But one cannot be too much on his guard in such a case, lest his action be biased by obstinacy or an undue regard for the opinions of men. Let him see that he does only what belongs to himself and to the hour.

35   I think sometimes, Why, this people mean well, they are only ignorant; they would do better if they knew how: why give your neighbors this pain to treat you as they are not inclined to? But I think again, This is no reason why I should do as they do, or permit others to suffer much greater pain of a different kind. Again, I sometimes say to myself, When many millions of men, without heat, without ill-will, without personal feeling of any kind, demand of you a few shillings only, without possibility, such is their constitution, of retracing or altering their present demand, and without the possibility, on your side, of appeal to any other millions, why expose yourself to this overwhelming brute force? You do not resist cold and hunger, the winds and the waves, thus obstinately; you quietly submit to a thousand similar necessities. You do not put your head into the fire. But just in proportion as I regard this as not wholly a brute force, but partly a human force, and consider that I have relations to those millions as to so many millions of men, and not of mere brute or inanimate things, I see that appeal is possible, first and instantaneously, from them to the Maker of them, and, secondly, from them to themselves. But if I put my head deliberately into the fire, there is no appeal to fire or to the Maker of fire, and I have only myself to blame. If I could convince myself that I have any right to be satisfied with men as they are, and to treat them accordingly, and not according, in some respects, to my requisitions and expectations of what they and I ought to be, then, like a good Mussulman [Muslim] and fatalist, I should endeavor to be satisfied with things as they are, and say it is the will of God. And, above all, there is this difference between resisting this and a purely brute or natural force, that I can resist this with some effect; but I cannot expect, like Orpheus, to change the nature of the rocks and trees and beasts.

36   I do not wish to quarrel with any man or nation. I do not wish to split hairs, to make fine distinctions, or set myself up as better than my neighbors. I seek rather, I may say, even an excuse for conforming to the laws of the land. I am but too ready to conform to them. Indeed, I have reason to suspect myself on this head; and each year, as the tax-gatherer comes round, I find myself disposed to review

the acts and position of the general and State governments, and the spirit of the people, to discover a pretext for conformity.

37   "We must affect our country as our parents,
    And if at any time we alienate
    Out love or industry from doing it honor,
    We must respect effects and teach the soul
    Matter of conscience and religion,
    And not desire of rule or benefit."

38   I believe that the State will soon be able to take all my work of this sort out of my hands, and then I shall be no better a patriot than my fellow-countrymen. Seen from a lower point of view, the Constitution, with all its faults, is very good; the law and the courts are very respectable; even this State and this American government are, in many respects, very admirable, and rare things, to be thankful for, such as a great many have described them; but seen from a point of view a little higher, they are what I have described them; seen from a higher still, and the highest, who shall say what they are, or that they are worth looking at or thinking of at all?

39   However, the government does not concern me much, and I shall bestow the fewest possible thoughts on it. It is not many moments that I live under a government, even in this world. If a man is thought-free, fancy-free, imagination-free, that which *is not* never for a long time appearing *to be* to him, unwise rulers or reformers cannot fatally interrupt him.

40   I know that most men think differently from myself; but those whose lives are by profession devoted to the study of these or kindred subjects content me as little as any. Statesmen and legislators, standing so completely within the institution, never distinctly and nakedly behold it. They speak of moving society, but have no resting-place without it. They may be men of a certain experience and discrimination, and have no doubt invented ingenious and even useful systems, for which we sincerely thank them; but all their wit and usefulness lie within certain not very wide limits. They are wont to forget that the world is not governed by policy and expediency. . . . The lawyer's truth is not Truth, but consistency or a consistent expediency. Truth is always in harmony with herself, and is not concerned chiefly to reveal the justice that may consist with wrong-doing. . . .

41   They who know of no purer sources of truth, who have traced up its stream no higher, stand, and wisely stand, by the Bible and the Constitution, and drink at it there with reverence and humility; but they who behold where it comes trickling into this lake or that pool, gird up their loins once more, and continue their pilgrimage toward its fountain-head. . . . For eighteen hundred years, though perchance I have no right to say it, the New Testament has been written; yet where is the legislator who has wisdom and practical talent enough to avail himself of the light which it sheds on the science of legislation?

42   The authority of government, even such as I am willing to submit to,—for I will cheerfully obey those who know and can do better than I, and in many things even those who neither know nor can do so well,—is still an impure one: to be strictly just, it must have the sanction and consent of the governed. It can have no

pure right over my person and property but what I concede to it. The progress from an absolute to a limited monarchy, from a limited monarchy to a democracy, is a progress toward a true respect for the individual. Even the Chinese philosopher was wise enough to regard the individual as the basis of the empire. Is a democracy, such as we know it, the last improvement possible in government? Is it not possible to take a step further towards recognizing and organizing the rights of man? There will never be a really free and enlightened State until the State comes to recognize the individual as a higher and independent power, from which all its own power and authority are derived, and treats him accordingly. I please myself with imagining a State at last which can afford to be just to all men, and to treat the individual with respect as a neighbor; which even would not think it inconsistent with its own repose if a few were to live aloof from it, not meddling with it, nor embraced by it, who fulfilled all the duties of neighbors and fellow-men. A State which bore this kind of fruit, and suffered it to drop off as fast as it ripened, would prepare the way for a still more perfect and glorious State, which also I have imagined, but not yet anywhere seen.

"On the Duty of Civil Disobedience" by Henry David Thoreau, 1849. From *Man or the State? A Group of Essays by Famous Writers.* Compiled and Edited by Waldo R. Browne. New York: B.W. Huebsch, 1919.

Comprehension

1. What issue grounds Thoreau's justification for civil disobedience?

2. How would you define "civil disobedience" and how does it affect your own life? Give examples that better define your own term of civil disobedience.

3. What does Thoreau think about the word *eloquence*?

Rhetorical Analysis

4. One successful technique Thoreau employs is first person narration. How does this essay benefit from this point of view?

5. Another technique Thoreau uses is his repetition of terms to further emphasize his belief that it is a citizen's duty to question the government and the humans who comprise it. Thoreau writes, "*It* does not keep the country free. *It* does not settle the West. *It* does not educate." How does the repetition help make the point?

Writing

6. Write a cause and effect essay relaying the events that led up to Thoreau spending the night in jail. What reasons did Thoreau give for his actions?

7. Expand on Thoreau's acceptance of the motto "That government is best which governs least." Is the motto really possible in today's world? Explain.

8. **Writing an Argument**   Discuss a law that ought to be repealed. Present both sides of the argument, but clearly give your reasons for why it is an unjust law. This may be a national, state, or local law.

A Room of One's Own

Virginia Woolf

Virginia Woolf (1882–1941) was one of the most influential writers of the twentieth century. Woolf was born in London and grew up in a literary family, which gave her an advantage when she began her writing career. Despite her literary success, Woolf struggled with what is now believed to be bipolar disorder until her suicide in 1941. Today, Woolf is known for her essays, and for her advocating of women. In 1928, Woolf delivered a series of talks titled "Women and Fiction" to the women's colleges at Cambridge. These lectures were later edited and published in 1929 under the title *A Room of One's Own*. This text argues for the promotion of women writers.

1   My aunt, Mary Beton, I must tell you, died by a fall from her horse when she was riding out to take the air in Bombay. The news of my legacy reached me one night about the same time that the act was passed that gave votes to women. A solicitor's letter fell into the post-box and when I opened it I found that she had left me five hundred pounds a year for ever. Of the two—the vote and the money—the money, I own, seemed infinitely the more important. Before that I had made my living by cadging odd jobs from newspapers, by reporting a donkey show here or a wedding there; I had earned a few pounds by addressing envelopes, reading to old ladies, making artificial flowers, teaching the alphabet to small children in a kindergarten. Such were the chief occupations that were open to women before 1918. I need not, I am afraid, describe in any detail the hardness of the work, for you know perhaps women who have done it; nor the difficulty of living on the money when it was earned, for you may have tried. But what still remains with me as a worse infliction than either was the poison of fear and bitterness which those days bred in me. To begin with, always to be doing work that one did not wish to do, and to do it like a slave, flattering and fawning, not always necessarily perhaps, but it seemed necessary and the stakes were too great to run risks; and then the thought of that one gift which it was death to hide—a small one but dear to the possessor—perishing and with it myself, my soul,—all this became like a rust eating away the bloom of the spring, destroying the tree at its heart. However, as I say, my aunt died; and whenever I change a ten-shilling note a little of that rust and corrosion is rubbed off, fear and bitterness go. Indeed, I thought, slipping the silver into my purse, it is remarkable, remembering the bitterness of those days, what a change of temper a fixed income will bring about. No force in the world can take from me my five hundred pounds. Food, house and clothing are mine forever. Therefore not merely do effort and labour cease, but also hatred and bitterness. I need not hate any man; he cannot hurt me. I need not flatter any man; he has nothing to give me. So imperceptibly I found myself adopting a new attitude towards the other half of the human race. It was absurd to blame any class or any sex, as a whole. Great bodies of people are never responsible for what they do. They are driven by instincts which are not within their control. They too, the

patriarchs, the professors, had endless difficulties, terrible drawbacks to contend with. Their education had been in some ways as faulty as my own. It had bred in them defects as great. True, they had money and power, but only at the cost of harbouring in their breasts an eagle, a vulture, forever tearing the liver out and plucking at the lungs—the instinct for possession, the rage for acquisition which drives them to desire other people's fields and goods perpetually; to make frontiers and flags; battleships and poison gas; to offer up their own lives and their children's lives. Walk through the Admiralty Arch (I had reached that monument), or any other avenue given up to trophies and cannon, and reflect upon the kind of glory celebrated there. Or watch in the spring sunshine the stockbroker and the great barrister going indoors to make money and more money and more money when it is a fact that five hundred pounds a year will keep one alive in the sunshine. These are unpleasant instincts to harbour, I reflected. They are bred of the conditions of life; of the lack of civilization, I thought, looking at the statue of the Duke of Cambridge, and in particular at the feathers in his cocked hat, with a fixity that they have scarcely ever received before. And, as I realized these drawbacks, by degrees fear and bitterness modified themselves into pity and toleration; and then in a year or two, pity and toleration went, and the greatest release of all came, which is freedom to think of things in themselves. That building, for example, do I like it or not? Is that picture beautiful or not? Is that in my opinion a good book or a bad? Indeed my aunt's legacy unveiled the sky to me, and substituted for the large and imposing figure of a gentleman, which Milton recommended for my perpetual adoration, a view of the open sky.

2   So thinking, so speculating I found my way back to my house by the river. Lamps were being lit and an indescribable change had come over London since the morning hour. It was as if the great machine after labouring all day had made with our help a few yards of something very exciting and beautiful—a fiery fabric flashing with red eyes, a tawny monster roaring with hot breath. Even the wind seemed flung like a flag as it lashed the houses and rattled the hoardings.

3   In my little street, however, domesticity prevailed. The house painter was descending his ladder; the nursemaid was wheeling the perambulator carefully in and out back to nursery tea; the coal-heaver was folding his empty sacks on top of each other; the woman who keeps the green grocer's shop was adding up the day's takings with her hands in red mittens. But so engrossed was I with the problem you have laid upon my shoulders that I could not see even these usual sights without referring them to one centre. I thought how much harder it is now than it must have been even a century ago to say which of these employments is the higher, the more necessary. Is it better to be a coal-heaver or a nursemaid; is the charwoman who has brought up eight children of less value to the world than, the barrister who has made a hundred thousand pounds? it is useless to ask such questions; for nobody can answer them. Not only do the comparative values of charwomen and lawyers rise and fall from decade to decade, but we have no rods with which to measure them even as they are at the moment. I had been foolish to ask my professor to furnish me with 'indisputable proofs' of this or that in his argument about women. Even if one could state the value of any one gift at the moment, those values will change; in a century's time very possibly they will

have changed completely. Moreover, in a hundred years, I thought, reaching my own doorstep, women will have ceased to be the protected sex. Logically they will take part in all the activities and exertions that were once denied them. The nursemaid will heave coal. The shopwoman will drive an engine. All assumptions founded on the facts observed when women were the protected sex will have disappeared—as, for example (here a squad of soldiers marched down the street), that women and clergymen and gardeners live longer than other people. Remove that protection, expose them to the same exertions and activities, make them soldiers and sailors and engine-drivers and dock labourers, and will not women die off so much younger, so much quicker, than men that one will say, 'I saw a woman to-day', as one used to say, 'I saw an aeroplane'. Anything may happen when womanhood has ceased to be a protected occupation, I thought, opening the door. But what bearing has all this upon the subject of my paper, Women and Fiction? I asked, going indoors.

4   It was disappointing not to have brought back in the evening some important statement, some authentic fact. Women are poorer than men because—this or that. Perhaps now it would be better to give up seeking for the truth, and receiving on one's head an avalanche of opinion hot as lava, discoloured as dish-water. It would be better to draw the curtains; to shut out distractions; to light the lamp; to narrow the enquiry and to ask the historian, who records not opinions but facts, to describe under what conditions women lived, not throughout the ages, but in England, say, in the time of Elizabeth.

5   For it is a perennial puzzle why no woman wrote a word of that extraordinary literature when every other man, it seemed, was capable of song or sonnet. What were the conditions in which women lived? I asked myself; for fiction, imaginative work that is, is not dropped like a pebble upon the ground, as science may be; fiction is like a spider's web, attached ever so lightly perhaps, but still attached to life at all four corners. Often the attachment is scarcely perceptible; Shakespeare's plays, for instance, seem to hang there complete by themselves. But when the web is pulled askew, hooked up at the edge, torn in the middle, one remembers that these webs are not spun in mid-air by incorporeal creatures, but are the work of suffering human beings, and are attached to grossly material things, like health and money and the houses we live in.

6   I went, therefore, to the shelf where the histories stand and took down one of the latest, Professor Trevelyan's HISTORY OF ENGLAND. Once more I looked up Women, found 'position of' and turned to the pages indicated. 'Wife-beating', I read, 'was a recognized right of man, and was practised without shame by high as well as low. . . . Similarly,' the historian goes on, 'the daughter who refused to marry the gentleman of her parents' choice was liable to be locked up, beaten and flung about the room, without any shock being inflicted on public opinion. Marriage was not an affair of personal affection, but of family avarice, particularly in the "chivalrous" upper classes. . . . Betrothal often took place while one or both of the parties was in the cradle, and marriage when they were scarcely out of the nurses' charge.' That was about 1470, soon after Chaucer's time. The next reference to the position of women is some two hundred years later, in the time of the Stuarts. 'It was still the exception for women of the upper and middle class to

choose their own husbands, and when the husband had been assigned, he was lord and master, so far at least as law and custom could make him. Yet even so,' Professor Trevelyan concludes, 'neither Shakespeare's women nor those of authentic seventeenth-century memoirs, like the Verneys and the Hutchinsons, seem wanting in personality and character.' Certainly, if we consider it, Cleopatra must have had a way with her; Lady Macbeth, one would suppose, had a will of her own; Rosalind, one might conclude, was an attractive girl. Professor Trevelyan is speaking no more than the truth when he remarks that Shakespeare's women do not seem wanting in personality and character. Not being a historian, one might go even further and say that women have burnt like beacons in all the works of all the poets from the beginning of time—Clytemnestra, Antigone, Cleopatra, Lady Macbeth, Phedre, Cressida, Rosalind, Desdemona, the Duchess of Malfi, among the dramatists; then among the prose writers: Millamant, Clarissa, Becky Sharp, Anna Karenina, Emma Bovary, Madame de Guermantes—the names flock to mind, nor do they recall women 'lacking in personality and character.' Indeed, if woman had no existence save in the fiction written by men, one would imagine her a person of the utmost importance; very various; heroic and mean; splendid and sordid; infinitely beautiful and hideous in the extreme; as great as a man, some think even greater.[1] But this is woman in fiction. In fact, as Professor Trevelyan points out, she was locked up, beaten and flung about the room.

7   A very queer, composite being thus emerges. Imaginatively she is of the highest importance; practically she is completely insignificant. She pervades poetry from cover to cover; she is all but absent from history. She dominates the lives of kings and conquerors in fiction; in fact she was the slave of any boy whose parents forced a ring upon her finger. Some of the most inspired words, some of the most profound thoughts in literature fall from her lips; in real life she could hardly read, could scarcely spell, and was the property of her husband.

8   It was certainly an odd monster that one made up by reading the historians first and the poets afterwards—a worm winged like an eagle; the spirit of life and beauty in a kitchen chopping up suet. But these monsters, however amusing to the imagination, have no existence in fact. What one must do to bring her to life was to think poetically and prosaically at one and the same moment, thus keeping in touch with fact—that she is Mrs. Martin, aged thirty-six, dressed in blue, wearing a black hat and brown shoes; but not losing sight of fiction either— that she is a vessel in which all sorts of spirits and forces are coursing and flashing perpetually. The moment, however, that one tries this method with the Elizabethan woman, one branch of illumination fails; one is held up by the

---

[1] 'It remains a strange and almost inexplicable fact that in Athena's city, where women were kept in almost Oriental suppression as odalisques or drudges, the stage should yet have produced figures like Clytemnestra and Cassandra Atossa and Antigone, Phedre and Medea, and all the other heroines who dominate play after play of the "misogynist" Euripides. But the paradox of this world where in real life a respectable woman could hardly show her face alone in the street, and yet on the stage woman equals or surpasses man, has never been satisfactorily explained. In modern tragedy the same predominance exists. At all events, a very cursory survey of Shakespeare's work (similarly with Webster, though not with Marlowe or Jonson) suffices to reveal how this dominance, this initiative of women, persists from Rosalind to Lady Macbeth. So too in Racine; six of his tragedies bear their heroines' names; and what male characters of his shall we set against Hermione and Andromaque, Berenice and Roxane, Phedre and Athalie? So again with Ibsen; what men shall we match with Solveig and Nora, Heda and Hilda Wangel and Rebecca West?'—F. L. LUCAS, TRAGEDY, pp. 114–15.

scarcity of facts. One knows nothing detailed, nothing perfectly true and substantial about her. History scarcely mentions her. And I turned to Professor Trevelyan again to see what history meant to him. I found by looking at his chapter headings that it meant—

9   'The Manor Court and the Methods of Open-field Agriculture . . . The Cistercians and Sheep-farming . . . The Crusades . . . The University . . . The House of Commons . . . The Hundred Years' War . . . The Wars of the Roses . . . The Renaissance Scholars . . . The Dissolution of the Monasteries . . . Agrarian and Religious Strife . . . The Origin of English Sea-power . . . The Armada . . .' and so on. Occasionally an individual woman is mentioned, an Elizabeth, or a Mary; a queen or a great lady. But by no possible means could middle-class women with nothing but brains and character at their command have taken part in any one of the great movements which, brought together, constitute the historian's view of the past. Nor shall we find her in collection of anecdotes. Aubrey hardly mentions her. She never writes her own life and scarcely keeps a diary; there are only a handful of her letters in existence. She left no plays or poems by which we can judge her. What one wants, I thought—and why does not some brilliant student at Newnham or Girton supply it?—is a mass of information; at what age did she marry; how many children had she as a rule; what was her house like, had she a room to herself; did she do the cooking; would she be likely to have a servant? All these facts lie somewhere, presumably, in parish registers and account books; the life of the average Elizabethan woman must be scattered about somewhere, could one collect it and make a book of it. It would be ambitious beyond my daring, I thought, looking about the shelves for books that were not there, to suggest to the students of those famous colleges that they should rewrite history, though I own that it often seems a little queer as it is, unreal, lop-sided; but why should they not add a supplement to history, calling it, of course, by some inconspicuous name so that women might figure there without impropriety? For one often catches a glimpse of them in the lives of the great, whisking away into the back ground, concealing, I sometimes think, a wink, a laugh, perhaps a tear. And, after all, we have lives enough of Jane Austen; it scarcely seems necessary to consider again the influence of the tragedies of Joanna Baillie upon the poetry of Edgar Allan Poe; as for myself, I should not mind if the homes and haunts of Mary Russell Mitford were closed to the public for a century at least. But what I find deplorable, I continued, looking about the bookshelves again, is that nothing is known about women before the eighteenth century. I have no model in my mind to turn about this way and that. Here am I asking why women did not write poetry in the Elizabethan age, and I am not sure how they were educated; whether they were taught to write; whether they had sitting-rooms to themselves; how many women had children before they were twenty-one; what, in short, they did from eight in the morning till eight at night. They had no money evidently; according to Professor Trevelyan they were married whether they liked it or not before they were out of the nursery, at fifteen or sixteen very likely. It would have been extremely odd, even upon this showing, had one of them suddenly written the plays of Shakespeare, I concluded, and I thought of that old gentleman, who is dead now, but was a bishop, I think, who declared that it was impossible for any woman, past, present, or to come, to have the genius of

Shakespeare. He wrote to the papers about it. He also told a lady who applied to him for information that cats do not as a matter of fact go to heaven, though they have, he added, souls of a sort. How much thinking those old gentlemen used to save one! How the borders of ignorance shrank back at their approach! Cats do not go to heaven. Women cannot write the plays of Shakespeare.

10   Be that as it may, I could not help thinking, as I looked at the works of Shakespeare on the shelf, that the bishop was right at least in this; it would have been impossible, completely and entirely, for any woman to have written the plays of Shakespeare in the age of Shakespeare. Let me imagine, since facts are so hard to come by, what would have happened had Shakespeare had a wonderfully gifted sister, called Judith, let us say. Shakespeare himself went, very probably,—his mother was an heiress—to the grammar school, where he may have learnt Latin— Ovid, Virgil and Horace—and the elements of grammar and logic. He was, it is well known, a wild boy who poached rabbits, perhaps shot a deer, and had, rather sooner than he should have done, to marry a woman in the neighbourhood, who bore him a child rather quicker than was right. That escapade sent him to seek his fortune in London. He had, it seemed, a taste for the theatre; he began by holding horses at the stage door. Very soon he got work in the theatre, became a successful actor, and lived at the hub of the universe, meeting everybody, knowing everybody, practising his art on the boards, exercising his wits in the streets, and even getting access to the palace of the queen. Meanwhile his extraordinarily gifted sister, let us suppose, remained at home. She was as adventurous, as imaginative, as agog to see the world as he was. But she was not sent to school. She had no chance of learning grammar and logic, let alone of reading Horace and Virgil. She picked up a book now and then, one of her brother's perhaps, and read a few pages. But then her parents came in and told her to mend the stockings or mind the stew and not moon about with books and papers. They would have spoken sharply but kindly, for they were substantial people who knew the conditions of life for a woman and loved their daughter—indeed, more likely than not she was the apple of her father's eye. Perhaps she scribbled some pages up in an apple loft on the sly but was careful to hide them or set fire to them. Soon, however, before she was out of her teens, she was to be betrothed to the son of a neighbouring wool-stapler. She cried out that marriage was hateful to her, and for that she was severely beaten by her father. Then he ceased to scold her. He begged her instead not to hurt him, not to shame him in this matter of her marriage. He would give her a chain of beads or a fine petticoat, he said; and there were tears in his eyes. How could she disobey him? How could she break his heart? The force of her own gift alone drove her to it. She made up a small parcel of her belongings, let herself down by a rope one summer's night and took the road to London. She was not seventeen. The birds that sang in the hedge were not more musical than she was. She had the quickest fancy, a gift like her brother's, for the tune of words. Like him, she had a taste for the theatre. She stood at the stage door; she wanted to act, she said. Men laughed in her face. The manager—a fat, loose-lipped man—guffawed. He bellowed something about poodles dancing and women acting—no woman, he said, could possibly be an actress. He hinted—you can imagine what. She could get no training in her craft. Could she even seek her

dinner in a tavern or roam the streets at midnight? Yet her genius was for fiction and lusted to feed abundantly upon the lives of men and women and the study of their ways. At last—for she was very young, oddly like Shakespeare the poet in her face, with the same grey eyes and rounded brows—at last Nick Greene the actor-manager took pity on her; she found herself with child by that gentleman and so—who shall measure the heat and violence of the poet's heart when caught and tangled in a woman's body?—killed herself one winter's night and lies buried at some cross-roads where the omnibuses now stop outside the Elephant and Castle.

11   That, more or less, is how the story would run, I think, if a woman in Shakespeare's day had had Shakespeare's genius. But for my part, I agree with the deceased bishop, if such he was—it is unthinkable that any woman in Shakespeare's day should have had Shakespeare's genius. For genius like Shakespeare's is not born among labouring, uneducated, servile people. It was not born in England among the Saxons and the Britons. It is not born today among the working classes. How, then, could it have been born among women whose work began, according to Professor Trevelyan, almost before they were out of the nursery, who were forced to it by their parents and held to it by all the power of law and custom? Yet genius of a sort must have existed among women as it must have existed among the working classes. Now and again an Emily Brontë or a Robert Burns blazes out and proves its presence. But certainly it never got itself on to paper. When, however, one reads of a witch being ducked, of a woman possessed by devils, of a wise woman selling herbs, or even of a very remarkable man who had a mother, then I think we are on the track of a lost novelist, a suppressed poet, of some mute and inglorious Jane Austen, some Emily Brontë who dashed her brains out on the moor or mopped and mowed about the highways crazed with the torture that her gift had put her to. Indeed, I would venture to guess that Anon, who wrote so many poems without singing them, was often a woman. It was a woman Edward Fitzgerald, I think, suggested who made the ballads and the folk-songs, crooning them to her children, beguiling her spinning with them, or the length of the winter's night.

12   This may be true or it may be false—who can say? —but what is true in it, so it seemed to me, reviewing the story of Shakespeare's sister as I had made it, is that any woman born with a great gift in the sixteenth century would certainly have gone crazed, shot herself, or ended her days in some lonely cottage outside the village, half witch, half wizard, feared and mocked at. For it needs little skill in psychology to be sure that a highly gifted girl who had tried to use her gift for poetry would have been so thwarted and hindered by other people, so tortured and pulled asunder by her own contrary instincts, that she must have lost her health and sanity to a certainty. No girl could have walked to London and stood at a stage door and forced her way into the presence of actor-managers without doing herself a violence and suffering an anguish which may have been irrational—for chastity may be a fetish invented by certain societies for unknown reasons—but were none the less inevitable. Chastity had then, it has even now, a religious importance in a woman's life, and has so wrapped itself round with nerves and instincts that to cut it free and bring it to the light of day demands courage of the rarest. To have lived a free life in London in the sixteenth century

would have meant for a woman who was poet and playwright a nervous stress and dilemma which might well have killed her. Had she survived, whatever she had written would have been twisted and deformed, issuing from a strained and morbid imagination. And undoubtedly, I thought, looking at the shelf where there are no plays by women, her work would have gone unsigned. That refuge she would have sought certainly. It was the relic of the sense of chastity that dictated anonymity to women even so late as the nineteenth century. Currer Bell, George Eliot, George Sand, all the victims of inner strife as their writings prove, sought ineffectively to veil themselves by using the name of a man. Thus they did homage to the convention, which if not implanted by the other sex was liberally encouraged by them (the chief glory of a woman is not to be talked of, said Pericles, himself a much-talked-of man) that publicity in women is detestable. Anonymity runs in their blood. The desire to be veiled still possesses them.

.   .   .   .

13   I told you in the course of this paper that Shakespeare had a sister; but do not look for her in Sir Sidney Lee's life of the poet. She died young—alas, she never wrote a word. She lies buried where the omnibuses now stop, opposite the Elephant and Castle. Now my belief is that this poet who never wrote a word and was buried at the cross-roads still lives. She lives in you and in me, and in many other women who are not here to-night, for they are washing up the dishes and putting the children to bed. But she lives; for great poets do not die; they are continuing presences; they need only the opportunity to walk among us in the flesh. This opportunity, as I think, it is now coming within your power to give her. For my belief is that if we live another century or so—I am talking of the common life which is the real life and not of the little separate lives which we live as individuals—and have five hundred a year each of us and rooms of our own; if we have the habit of freedom and the courage to write exactly what we think; if we escape a little from the common sitting-room and see human beings not always in their relation to each other but in relation to reality; and the sky too, and the trees or whatever it may be in themselves; if we look past Milton's bogey, for no human being should shut out the view; if we face the fact, for it is a fact, that there is no arm to cling to, but that we go alone and that our relation is to the world of reality and not only to the world of men and women, then the opportunity will come and the dead poet who was Shakespeare's sister will put on the body which she has so often laid down. Drawing her life from the lives of the unknown who were her forerunners, as her brother did before her, she will be born. As for her coming without that preparation, without that effort on our part, without that determination that when she is born again she shall find it possible to live and write her poetry, that we cannot expect, for that would be impossible. But I maintain that she would come if we worked for her, and that so to work, even in poverty and obscurity, is worth while.

1. One of the most important points Woolf makes is why women have been limited by their lack of ways of making money. How does she make the argument that by lacking rooms of their own, women have been prevented from making money and being more of a literary force?

2. What do Woolf's musings about Shakespeare's sister and "Judith's" belief that she would not have been considered a genius, even if she shared the same mental capacities of her brother, prove in aiding Woolf's thesis?

3. What makes the one major character in this essay so uncanny?

4. What is the effect of the repetition of the word *without* when describing what life might be like today for Shakespeare's sister in the closing paragraph?

5. What does Woolf's rhetoric suggest about the literature women did write at the time, and its connection to men?

6. "A Room of One's Own," by the words alone, is a metaphor for independent and respected living. Come up with some other metaphors that have similar meanings.

7. Explain the irony presented in paragraph 7.

8. Write an analytic essay in which you analyze Woolf's attitude about the role of money. Use the text to support your analysis.

9. Woolf says, "Of the two—the vote and the money—the money, I own, seemed infinitely the more important." In a comparison essay, compare and contrast the benefits and drawbacks of choosing money over the right to vote.

10. **Writing an Argument**   Woolf argues that, "Great bodies of people are never responsible for what they do. They are driven by instincts which are not within their control." Do you agree with this statement? Write an argumentative essay defending your position.

CHAPTER 12

Sample Student Essays

What can you expect to see on the AP Language and Composition Exam from the College Board? The exam consists of two sections. The first section includes 45 multiple-choice questions. The second section includes 3 essay prompts.

Multiple-Choice Questions

The multiple-choice section of the exam counts for 45 percent of the total score. You will have 60 minutes to answer the multiple-choice questions. About half the questions are tied to two nonfiction passages and require you to examine both the style and meaning of the passages. Three "draft" passages have composition questions that require you to consider revisions. Answer all of the questions, even the ones you do not know. Points are not taken off for wrong answers. You can see what the multiple-choice section looks like on the **AP Language and Composition Practice Exam** in Part 5 of this textbook.

Free-Response Questions

After you have completed the multiple-choice section, you will write 3 essays in section two of the exam, which includes the free-response questions (FRQs). This part of the exam counts for 55 percent of the total score. You have 135 minutes for section two, with 15 minutes of this time suggested for reading the sources for the Synthesis essay. This results in 40 minutes to write each essay. You can see what the FRQ section looks like in the AP Language and Composition Practice Exam in Part 5.

The three types of essays you will write are:
Q1 Synthesis
Q2 Rhetorical Analysis
Q3 Argument

The **Synthesis** FRQ presents you with an argument and asks you to respond. The Synthesis question provides you with source material that you must incorporate into your argument. Evidence you use in this essay lies in a combination of your own general knowledge and experience as well as the series of sources related to the essay's topic. (Refer to Chapter 3 to review additional information about the Synthesis and Argument questions on the AP Language and Composition Exam.)

The **Rhetorical Analysis** FRQ gives you a nonfiction passage—typically an excerpt from a speech, a letter, or a book—and asks you to examine the choices the author makes in crafting the passage, as well as the effects of those choices on the audience. The evidence you add to your essay lies in the author's rhetorical techniques. How does he or she create meaning?

The **Argument** FRQ presents you with a statement or a very short passage and asks you to determine its argument or claim. Your task is then to take a position in response to that argument. You will make a claim and then develop convincing evidence to support your position. Unlike the Synthesis FRQ, you are not given sources from which to pull evidence.

All three essays require you to use wide-ranging vocabulary, a variety of sentence structures, logical organization, and a balance of generalization and illustrative details. In other words, use good writing as you support your claims. The table below summarizes the task of each FRQ, and identifies where you will obtain the evidence to support the claim you make in each essay's thesis statement.

Q1 Synthesis	Q2 Analysis	Q3 Argument
Your task is to build an original response to a question after analyzing a variety of sources.	Your task is to analyze a passage for HOW the writer crafts a message to affect the audience.	Your task is to develop a position in response to a given topic.
Evidence lies in a combination of your own general knowledge and experience AND a series of sources related to the essay's topic.	Evidence lies in the rhetorical choices the author makes in his or her passage: What is the writer saying? How is he saying it? What is his purpose in writing? How does he move his audience?	Evidence lies in your own general knowledge and experience.

Student Essays

The following pages of this chapter show three student essays—Synthesis, Analysis, and Argument—that received high scores. Read the introduction to each essay, which provides the general prompt the students responded to. You can find the full prompts and sources at the College Board website.

Sample Student Synthesis Essay

By Ariel Carter
White Bear Lake High School South Campus
White Bear Lake, Minnesota

Responding to Question 1 from the 2009 Released Exam, this essay offers
a documented opinion on the considerations the United States government
should take in funding space exploration.

When it comes to making decisions regarding space exploration,
financial issues should be considered above all others. Money and
government's allocation of that money leads to additional discussion of
resources, determines the quality of life for regular citizens.

Since the beginning of space exploration, people have looked to the stars
in wonder, asking what could be out there, but also questioning whether or
not space exploration is the best use of tax payer money—especially since
there has been little found. According to Source E, the United States spent
17 billion dollars in 2006 alone on space exploration. This may be an obvious
statement, but that's a lot of money, and one has to ask, what else could that
money have gone to? 2006 was two years before the Great Recession, and
that same 17 billion dollars could have been used to support American
citizens in more direct ways. See, space exploration does not financially help
many people. Yes, it helps engineers and those directly involved in space
exploration, but it does little for everyone else besides take money away
from roads, schools, and other public institutions, such as the National
Institutes of Health (Source D). As seen in the source, in 1975, several years
following the rise of space exploration, money was siphoned away from
space exploration and into medical research, ostensibly benefitting many.
Considering this example, government needs to consider finances above all
else—including the applicability and benefit of financing scientific research—
when considering space exploration or any other type of exploration. It is
simply unethical to take resources away from those who need support in
preference for national pride.

Space exploration started as a way to show the world, but mostly the
Soviet Union, that the United States was an intelligent and well-defended
country. By getting a man to the moon before the Soviets were able to do
so, Americans felt a surge of national pride swell through themselves,
believing this scientific achievement proved that as a nation we were
moving forward. However, some feel spending taxpayer money on space
exploration is no longer needed, which is voiced in Source H's spare, yet
artful declaration that we are better served leaving "the money here on
earth." Now, United States citizens are begging for the money to stay on

Earth, not float around where they can't reach it. Now, every head of every country wants to show that their country and their people can do the unthinkable and are willing to spend the money to show that. But both citizens and leaders need to ask themselves whether or not their people, their citizens, benefit from spending their money exploring space.

Many people would say that finances don't matter as much as ethics when it comes to space exploration. They may say that by exploring space, the nations are coming closer as they discuss how to show Earth as the model planet for the galaxy, dissolving the lines between themselves in a common pursuit. However, money buys resources, and resources help people to better themselves and their lives, often eliminating what could accumulate into ethical concerns. Finances matter more than the potential ethical boon of improved international relations because alleviating poverty and addressing critical needs can change those ethical discussions, possibly fixing or at least improving the world. Peace and prosperity and a lack of poverty will allow the people of the world to grow closer.

Sample Student Rhetorical Analysis Essay

By Arianna Kholanjani
New Century Technology High School
Huntsville, Alabama

Written as a response to Question 2 from the 2017 Released Exam, this essay analyzes the choices made by Clare Boothe Luce in the introduction to her speech to a consortium of female journalists.

In Luce's speech to journalists at the Women's National Press Club, she sets up her argument that the American press sacrifices integrity for sensationalist stories in order to convince her audience to write truthfully.

Luce's use of repetition in her speech successfully establishes the base for her argument by ingraining key words into the minds of her audience which will remind the audience of Luce's stance when she makes her argument. In paragraph 1, Luce repeats "you" throughout the paragraph. In this context, "you" is directly addressing the journalists' wrongdoings. By repeating and emphasizing "you," Luce emphasizes the wrongdoings of the journalists and establishes that the problem with the American press starts with the members of the audience. Addressing the audience in this manner immediately lets the audience know that Luce is about to argue that they are the problem, which sets a foundation for Luce's argument yet to come. Repeating this word multiple times also ingrains the problem at hand—the journalists—into the minds of the audience, which is a constant reminder that Luce's real argument hasn't started yet and prepares the audience for the argument that Luce has yet to make. Luce also repeats "infinite" throughout the first paragraph. Using this word emphasizes the unlimited possibilities that journalists could write about besides untrue stories that captivate readers. By repeating this word, Luce successfully ingrains this concept into the minds of the audience, which allows them to be reminded of this important concept throughout Luce's introduction, and eventually allows the audience to be more mindful of this issue when Luce begins to make her argument that the American press is failing because of the lack of journalistic integrity. Luce repeats "the pursuit...of truth" throughout her speech. This key phrase introduces the audience to the fact that they should pursue truth in their writing and not sensationalist stories. The constant repetition of this argument allows the audience to be pre-exposed to Luce's main argument in her introduction which eventually allows the audience to absorb Luce's argument when she starts the main part of her speech.

Luce's verb choice and placement emphasizes the importance of writing truthfully in journalism and therefore convinces her audience to write with integrity. In the third paragraph, Luce uses verbs at the beginning of each clause. She says, "There is no audience...more revolted by a speaker who tried to fawn on it, butter it up, exaggerate its virtues, play down its faults." By placing verbs at the beginning of each clause, Luce emphasizes the wrongdoings of these actions made by journalists in order to have newsworthy stories. The strong connotation of these verbs also emphasizes the extremeness of the measures most journalists take when writing a story. The emphasis on journalists' actions makes the audience aware of their mistakes and establishes a foundation on which they are able to correct their wrongdoings. By making the audience aware of this, Luce invokes guilt in the audience which makes them more susceptible to be influenced by Luce's argument that journalists should have integrity when writing stories. This guilt sets up a foundation—which is the audience's ability to be persuaded—and makes it flexible when it is exposed to other's opinions. This flexibility in the audience's beliefs allows Luce to set up her argument in her introduction.

Luce's ability to capture an audience's attention to convince them to write truthfully and mold their opinions on her argument was successful because she incorporated rhetorical devices such as repetition of important words and phrases and verb choice and placement.

Sample Student Argument Essay

By Emma Perkins
Boulder High School
Boulder, Colorado

Responding to Question 3 from the 2005 Released Exam, this essay
evaluates the pros and cons of requiring rich people to donate all their
spending on luxuries to overseas aid organizations.

For a world so advanced in the areas of science and technology, and a
world that is starting to tackle the many injustices faced by people around
the world, it can be frustrating to note how little progress has been made
in addressing the disparities between what we call the "first" and "third"
worlds. While some people in the first world struggle with the decision of
whether to buy a Lamborghini or a Ferrari, people in the third world
struggle to decide between using their time to find food or using that same
time to gather water.

There are, of course, solutions to this issue. Peter Singer for one has
advocated for the wealthy to donate all but what sustains them of their
income to overseas aid organizations. However, like any decision of any
size, there are both pros and cons to this perhaps extreme plan.

On the one hand, implementing programs such as that described above
would undoubtedly improve the current situation. Considering that the
wealthiest 1% of the world's population holds the majority of the world's
wealth, the funds that would be redistributed on this plan are immense—
almost unfathomable. With such extensive financial resources, overseas aid
organizations would have the capabilities to transform entire countries. I
would even go as far as to say that they could transform the entire world
economy. Over time, these organizations could make sure everybody lived
in a house with modern amenities, attended a school with adequate
resources, and had access to safe food and potable water. Over the course
of a few generations, this would give rise to a whole new group of well-
educated individuals from areas that had previously struggled to stay afloat
on an economy sustained by agriculture. In the future, scientific and
technological cooperation would happen on a global scale, not just
between the "first world" countries.

However, for all the advantages of this plan for the redistribution of the
world's wealth, there are still some significant drawbacks. What if the
wealthy won't cooperate? What if corruption emerges in overseas aid
companies that are being flooded with trillions of dollars? How much
money is needed for the basic requirements of life? How do we define the

basic requirements of life? What if we have the money but the world just doesn't have enough natural resources? These are all questions that beg to be answered in the context of the redistribution of the world's wealth. I can say with 99% certainty, that a good portion of the wealthiest people all the way through the middle classes is not going to jump at the chance to give away significant fractions of their incomes. This means that political devices would have to be put in place to collect the funds. This too has issues though, in most developed countries citizens vote for their governmental officials, so widespread dissent towards a policy could very well result in the election of a government that wouldn't follow through with the plan of redistribution of wealth. Let's say, for arguments sake, that the funds can be collected, then what? Requirements of life can be defined as simply as food, water, and shelter, but surely we don't mean for everybody to be living in a straw hut. That's why we're collecting funds in the first place. Then there's the question of natural resources. Unfortunately, natural resources are a limited commodity, and considering that we are already starting to run out just supporting the world's current status of some developed and some underdeveloped countries, it is a VERY real possibility that our planet simply doesn't have the resources to support upwards of seven billion people with a middle class lifestyle. There are many calculators you can find on the internet that will tell you that even if everybody lived an extremely conservationist middle-class lifestyle, we would still need as many as three or four earths to support our current population, which, I'll remind you is growing exponentially. As hard of a pill as it may be to swallow, it very well might be that no matter what we do, what plans we implement, we cannot achieve a world where everybody can enjoy a comfortable lower-middle to middle-class lifestyle.

In the end, as well-intentioned as Singer's plan may be, I cannot find myself compelled to support it. While there is no doubt that something must be done to improve the current situation, and cut down on the gap between the "first" and "third" worlds, the logistical and political issues of the plan for the redistribution of the world's wealth mean that it cannot ultimately be successful.

PART

4

RESEARCH PAPER

CHAPTER 13

Writing a Research Paper

Research actually means the careful investigation of a subject in order to discover or revise facts, theories, or applications. Your purpose is to demonstrate how other researchers approach a problem, how you synthesize their most useful ideas, and how you treat that problem yourself. A good research paper subtly blends your ideas and synthesizes the attitudes or findings of others. In research writing, you are dealing with ideas that are already in the public domain, but you are also contributing to knowledge. When *your* ideas—rather than the ideas of others—become the center of the research process, writing a research paper becomes dynamic instead of static.

Consider the following tasks as research ideas:

- Evaluating critical responses to a best-selling novel, a book of poetry, an album, or an award-winning film
- Analyzing the impact of voter turnout on presidential politics during a recent decade
- Investigating a literary, political, or scientific scandal of the previous century
- Assessing the effectiveness of urban, suburban, and rural schools, comparing specific measures of student success
- Defining a popular dietary or health-related term, examining how it influences consumer behavior when shopping for food
- Examining how media outlets use social networking websites to deliver content to audiences in target demographics

How would a professional researcher view these projects? First, the researcher sees a subject as a *problem* rather than a mere topic. The researcher has the task of developing or testing a hypothesis stemming from the particular problem—for example, whether a vegetarian diet effectively wards off cancer. *Hypothesis formation* is at the heart of professional research.

Second, the researcher often conducts primary as well as secondary research. *Primary research* relies on analysis and synthesis of texts, letters, manuscripts, and other materials, whether written, visual, or aural. *Secondary research* relies on sources that comment on the primary sources. For example, a critic's commentary on *Citizen Kane* or a historian's analysis of a presidential election would be secondary sources; the film itself or a speech delivered by the president would be primary sources. Because primary sources are not necessarily more reliable than secondary sources, you must always evaluate the reliability of both types of material. Critics can misinterpret, and experts often disagree, forcing you to weigh evidence and reach your own conclusions.

Third, all researchers face deadlines. Confronted with deadlines, professional researchers learn to *telescope* their efforts in order to obtain information quickly. Common strategies include networking (using personal and professional contacts as well as guides to organizations), browsing or searching online, conducting bibliographical searches, and turning to online databases, annotated bibliographies (listing articles on the topic with commentaries on each item), and specialized indexes (focusing on a particular field or discipline). Other strategies include consulting review articles, which evaluate other resources, and browsing through current journals and periodicals (which may provide useful background as well as the most current thinking about the topic).

Finally, good researchers recognize that they cannot confine their search for evidence to one subject area, such as history or physics. Much professional researching cuts across academic subjects and disciplines. The interdisciplinary nature of many research projects creates special problems for the researcher, especially in the use of bibliographical materials, which tend to be subject-oriented. Such research is not beyond your talents and abilities. Learn not only how to use library and electronic sources selectively and efficiently, but also how to view the world outside your library and computer as a vast laboratory to be used fruitfully in order to solve your research problems.

Navigating the Research Process

The research process involves thinking, searching, reading, writing, and rewriting. The process of researching and composing moves back and forth over a series of activities, and the actual act of writing remains unique to the individual researcher. Regardless of a writer's experience, he or she can benefit from thinking about the research process as a series of several interrelated phases.

Phases in the Research Process

Phase I: Defining Your Objective

1. Choose a *researchable* topic.

2. Identify a *problem* inherent in the topic that gives you the reason for writing about the topic.

3. Examine the *purpose* of or the *benefits* to be gained from conducting research on the topic.

4. Think about the assumptions, interests, and needs of your *audience*.

5. Decide how you are going to *limit* your topic.

6. Establish a working *hypothesis* to guide and control the scope and direction of your research.

Phase 2: Locating Your Sources

1. Decide on your *methodology*—the types or varieties of primary and secondary research you plan to conduct. Determine the method of collecting data.

2. Explore your library's online catalog (a utility that lets you search its holdings and databases to which it subscribes) to *determine the viability of your topic*, including how much secondary research has been done on your topic and whether your hypothesis is likely to stand up.

3. Develop a *tentative working bibliography*, a file listing sources that seem relevant to your topic.

4. Review your bibliography, and *reassess your topic and hypothesis*.

Phase 3: Gathering and Organizing Data

1. *Obtain your sources*, taking notes on all information related directly to your thesis.

2. Analyze and organize your information. Design a *preliminary outline* with a *tentative thesis* if your findings support your hypothesis.

3. *Revise your thesis* if your findings suggest alternative conclusions.

Phase 1: Defining Your Objective

The first step in research writing is to select a topic that promises an adventure for you in the realm of ideas and that will interest, if not excite, your audience while meeting the expectations and requirements of your assignment.

You can maximize time and effort if you approach the research project as a problem to be investigated and solved, a controversy to take a position on, or a question to be answered. As a basis, you need a strong hypothesis or working thesis (which may be little more than a calculated guess). The point of your investigation is to identify, illustrate, explain, argue, or prove that thesis. Develop a hypothesis before you actually begin to conduct research; otherwise, you will discover that you are simply reading in or about a topic, instead of reading toward the objective of substantiating your thesis or proposition.

Of course, before you can formulate a hypothesis, you need to start with a general idea of what subject you want to explore, what your purpose is going to be, and how you plan to select and limit a topic from your larger subject area.

Formulating a Hypothesis

A topic will lead to a researchable hypothesis if it does the following:

- Meets the demands of your assignment
- Strongly interests you
- Engages knowledge you already possess
- Raises questions that will require both primary and secondary research to answer
- Provokes you toward an opinion or argument

To help you find and limit a research topic, try the following strategies:

- *Reflect on the assignment.* If your teacher gave you a specific written assignment—even if it does not include a specific topic—review the assignment with an eye toward keywords that indicate the purpose of your research work. Highlight or underline key verbs such as *solve, argue, find, discover,* or *present.* Write out questions for your teacher, and either ask the questions in class or arrange for a conference with her or him.

- *Ask questions.* Ask yourself, in writing, a series of specific questions about your subject, combining related questions. Phrase questions in such a way as to pose problems that demand answers. Then try to determine which topic best fits the demands of the assignment.

- *Prewrite and brainstorm.* Idea generation strategies such as prewriting and brainstorming can help you determine what you already know or believe about an assigned topic. If your assignment is to research gender roles in popular culture, for example, you might begin by brainstorming on how male characters were depicted in the last three movies you saw. For more on prewriting strategies, see Chapter 2.

- *Do some background reading.* Your teacher will probably assign a research topic that has something to do with the content of your class. Review the assigned readings for your course as well as your own notes. If your teacher has provided a bibliography, consult a few of those sources as well. Although the purpose of your background reading is to generate ideas, you should still use the note-taking strategies discussed in the following pages to ensure that you give proper credit later for any ideas you use from this preliminary reading.

Throughout, keep in mind that your purpose is to solve a *specific* problem, shed light on a *specific* topic, state an opinion on a *specific* controversy, or offer *specific* proofs or solutions. Your audience does not want a welter of general information, a bland summary of the known and the obvious, or free associations or meditations on an issue or problem. You know that your audience wants answers; consequently, a way to locate your ideal topic is to ask questions about it.

Phase 2: Locating Your Sources

Begin locating your sources as early as possible for a number of reasons. First, research takes time and patience. Second, you most likely will have to share sources with other students working on similar projects. Some sources are not available online, even through library databases, and some print sources only have one copy or are not in the library. Third, your library may not have access to every source you need; when this is the case, you will have to depend on interlibrary loan services (in which your library borrows the source temporarily or obtains photocopies or scans of it), which can take additional time.

If you have a sufficiently narrowed topic and a working hypothesis, you should know what type of information will be most useful for your report. Not all information on a topic is relevant, of course; with a hypothesis, you can distinguish between useful and irrelevant material.

To use your time efficiently, you have to *streamline* your method for collecting data. Most research writing relies heavily on secondary research material available in libraries or online. To develop a preliminary list of sources, go directly to general reference works or a list of sources or reserved readings provided by your professor. If you already have some knowledge about the subject, begin with resources that permit you to find a continuing series of articles and books on a single issue—

specifically, periodical indexes, newspaper indexes, and online catalogs. Again, you should be moving as rapidly as possible from the general to the specific.

Should You Begin Your Research Online?

The immense capabilities of the Internet make it tempting to begin your search for information online via a commercial search engine. If your research topic demands very contemporary and localized knowledge (a current political campaign, a recent medical breakthrough, a trend in popular culture), beginning your search online can be optimal. This method can also be useful for background reading and idea generating. However, traditional research—both academic and professional—is generally more productive and efficient if begun via a library's online catalog. Commercial search engines usually generate somewhat limited returns when research topics require you to provide deeper contexts and backgrounds, or when primary and secondary sources are restricted to academic journals and databases. Although we begin our discussion of locating sources with guidelines for searching online, only you can determine the most efficient and effective way of beginning your research.

Finding Online Materials

Depending on your topic, there are subject-specific online pages that link you to everything you could want, including both primary and secondary sources. *Findlaw* is a good example for law-related content; most of the sciences and many of the liberal arts have useful pages like this. The UC-Berkeley Library suggests also using subject directories (whose subject-specific contents are supplied by humans rather than computer programs), such as *academicinfo.net,* to look for academic resources. Once you have located a URL (universal resource locator) for a site on the Web, go directly to that location. The end of the address is one indication of the kind of location you will reach. Some of the most popular domain extensions include:

> .org = nonprofit organizations, including professional groups
> .edu = colleges, universities, and other educational institutions
> .com = businesses and commercial enterprises
> .gov = government branches and agencies
> .mil = branches of the military
> .net = major computer networks
> .tv = video content
> .museum = museums
> .info = informational sites
> .store = retail businesses
> .web = sites about the World Wide Web
> .coop = cooperative organizations
> .int = international organizations
> .pro = credentialed professionals

Domain extensions can also include the website's country of origin (like .au for Australia or .uk for United Kingdom). New domain extensions are created often to accommodate the ever-expanding volume of Web content. Keep in mind, though, that the domain extension is but the initial way to identify the content of a site. For example, some museums use the .museum extension, while others use .org; still others are part of universities and therefore use .edu. Some .com sites offer both commerce and information, just as some .org sites sell products or services. A careful evaluation of the contents and research about the organization responsible for the site's maintenance are called for before you rely on a source to help prove your hypothesis.

If you need to search the Internet for sources, try using a search engine like Google, using keywords. Given the enormous number of websites and their component pages, you need to select your search terms carefully so that you locate reasonable numbers of pertinent sources.

A Web page often supplies links to other useful sites, separately or as hyperlinked text. If you click on the link, usually distinguished from plain text by formatting or color, you can go directly to that related site. For example, the sites *www.ntis.gov* and *www.data.gov*, sponsored by the federal government, include links to federal databases and a keyword search that can lead to particular resources.

Following a chain of links requires you to assess whether each link seems reliable and current. This kind of research can take a great deal of time, especially if you explore each link and then follow it to the next. As you move from link to link, keep your hypothesis in mind so that you are not distracted from your central purpose.

Evaluating Online Sources

▶ Is the author identified? Is the site sponsored by a reputable business, agency, or organization? Does the site supply information so that you can contact the author or the sponsor?

▶ Does the site provide information comparable to that in other reputable sources, including print sources?

▶ Does the site seem accurate and authoritative or quirky and idiosyncratic?

▶ Does the site seem unbiased, or is it designed to promote a particular business, industry, organization, political position, or philosophy?

▶ Does the site supply appropriate, useful links? Do these links seem current and relevant? Do most of them work? Does the site document sources for the information it supplies directly?

▶ Has the site been updated or revised recently?

▶ Does the site seem carefully designed? Is it easy and logical to navigate? Are its graphics well integrated and related to the site's overall purpose or topic? Is the text carefully edited?

Look beyond conventional online sources too. Streaming media, like webcasts (television and radio content) and podcasts (downloadable media files), can be gleaned for information, as can professional blogs (Web-based journals or commentaries written by content experts) and professional bulletin boards (sites where users can post and exchange content-specific information). Before using open source (wikis) and casual networking sites as sources for your paper, however, always ask your teacher for his/her policy. The content from such sites can be problematic because you cannot always verify its accuracy or the authority of the person who posted it, and sources for the posted information often are not cited correctly (if at all).

Using the Library's Online Catalog

The library's catalog lists information by author, title, subject, and keyword. Of the four, the subject listings are the best place to look for sources, but they are not necessarily the place to start your research. Begin by determining what your library offers. For instance, the online catalog may include all library materials or only holdings acquired fairly recently. The catalog also may or may not supply up-to-date information because books may take several years to appear in print. Thus you may need to turn to separate indexes of articles, primary documents, and online materials for the most current material. Remember also that when you search by subject, you are searching the subject fields that are assigned by the cataloger. This differs from a keyword search in which the researcher—you, the writer—selects key terms that describe the research situation and enters them into a search engine that will find these terms anywhere within the item record—whether they happen to be in the title, comments, notes, or subject fields.

If your library does have a consolidated online system, you may have immediate access to materials available regionally and to extensive online databases. You may be able to use the same terminal to search for books shelved in your own library, materials available locally through the city or county library, and current periodicals listed in specialized databases. Such access can simplify and consolidate your search.

Subject indexing can be useful when you are researching a topic around which a considerable body of information and analysis has already developed. Identify as many keywords or relevant subject classifications as possible. Use these same terms as you continue your search for sources, and add additional terms identified in the entries you find. Alternatively, select one of the titles you feel is most closely related to your subject, and pull up that record, which may yield fruitful links, directing you to other materials that have been assigned the same headings.

Checking General Reference Sources

General reference sources include encyclopedias, dictionaries, handbooks, atlases, biographies, almanacs, yearbooks, abstracts, and annual reviews of scholarship within a field. Many of these sources are available both in print and online. Begin your search for these sources in your library's reference room. General reference sources can be useful for background reading and for an introduction to your topic. The bibliographies they contain (such as those that end articles in an encyclopedia) are generally limited, however, and frequently out-of-date. Professional researchers do not rely exclusively on general reference sources to solve research problems, and neither should you.

Searching Indexes and Databases

Electronic and print indexes and databases include up-to-date articles in journals, magazines, and newspapers. Indexes usually list materials that you will then need to locate. Some databases, however, may include complete texts of articles or even books. Ask a reference librarian how to access materials on microfiche, microfilm, CD-ROM, or online. If you need historical information or want to trace a topic back in time, however, you may need to use print indexes as well because electronic sources may date back only a few years or cover only a certain number of years.

The indexes and databases listed here are just a few of the many resources that are widely available. Some are general; others are specialized by discipline or field. Such indexes supply ready access to a wide array of useful materials, including articles, books, newspaper stories, statistics, and government documents. Ask the librarian in the reference area or the catalog area whether these are available in print or online.

Electronic and Print Indexes and Databases

General Resources

- *American Statistics Index*
- *Congressional Information Service Index*
- *Expanded Academic Index*
- *FirstSearch Catalog*
- *Magazine Index*
- *National Newspaper Index*
- *New York Times Index*

Specialized Resources

- *Applied Science and Technology Index*
- *Biological and Agricultural Index*
- *Business Periodicals Index*
- *Education Index*
- *ERIC (Educational Resources Information Center)*
- *General Business File*
- *Humanities Index*
- *Index Medicus or Medline*
- *MLA (Modern Language Association) International Bibliography*
- *PsychLit or PsycINFO*
- *Public Affairs Information Service (PAIS)*
- *Social Sciences Index*

Each index or database restricts the sources it lists in specific ways, based on the particular topics covered or the types of sources included. For example, the *MLA International Bibliography* lists books, journals, articles, websites, and other publications. Besides books and articles, however, it includes essays or chapters collected in a book, conference papers, films, recordings, and other similar sources, but it does not list summaries or encyclopedia articles. Its primary subjects include literary criticism, literary themes and genres, linguistics, and folklore. Thus you can search for an author's name, a title, a literary period, or subjects as varied as hoaxes, metaphysical poetry, and self-knowledge, all in relation to studies in modern languages and literature. This bibliography is available online and is updated regularly during the year.

As your search progresses and your hypothesis evolves, you will find resources even more specifically focused on your interests.

Evaluating Print Sources

▶ Is the author a credible authority? Does the book cover, preface, or byline indicate the author's background, education, or other publications? Do other writers refer to this source and accept it as reliable? Is the publisher or publication reputable?

▶ Does the source provide information comparable to that in other reputable sources?

▶ Does the source seem accurate and authoritative, or does it make claims that are not generally accepted?

▶ Does the source seem unbiased, or does it seem to promote a particular business, industry, organization, political position, or philosophy?

▶ Does the source supply notes, a bibliography, or other information to document its sources?

▶ If the source has been published recently, does it include current information? Are its sources current or dated?

▶ Does the source seem carefully edited and printed?

Using Nonprint Sources

In the library and online, you have access to potentially useful nonprint materials of all kinds—videos, DVDs, CD-ROMs, films, slides, works of art, records of performances, microfiche, microfilm, or other sources that might relate to your topic. When you search for these sources, you may find them in your library's main catalog or in a separate listing. In the catalog entry, be sure to note the location of the source and its access hours, especially if they are limited. If you need a projector or other equipment to use the material, ask the reference librarian where you go to find such equipment.

Developing Field Resources

You may want to *interview* an expert, *survey* the opinions of other students, *observe* an event or situation, or examine it over a long period of time as a *case study*. Ask your teacher's advice as you design questions for an interview or a survey or procedures for a short- or long-term observation. Also be sure to find out whether you need permission to conduct this kind of research on campus or in the community.

The questions you ask will determine the nature and extent of the responses that you receive; as a result, your questions should be developed after you have established clear objectives for your field research. You also need to plan how you will analyze the answers before, not after, you administer the questionnaire or conduct the interview. Once you have drafted interview or survey questions, test them by asking your friends or classmates to respond. Use these preliminary results to revise any ambiguous questions and to test your method of analysis. If you are an observer, establish in advance what you will observe, how you will record your observations, and how you will analyze them. Get permission, if needed, from the site where you will conduct your observation. Your field sources can help you expand your knowledge of the topic, see its applications or discover real-world surprises, or locate more sources, whether print, electronic, or field.

Using Visuals in Your Paper

Some of the nonprint sources you consult in your research might be useful to include, rather than just cite or refer to, in your own final paper. Technology has made it very easy to cut and paste visuals from sources into your own work, as well as to create and incorporate your own visuals. Be sure that when you incorporate other visuals into your paper (or when you create a visual, such as a graph or chart, that draws on data from another source) you correctly and completely cite the source of the visual data. A caption that briefly describes the visual and gives its source information is not always sufficient; be sure to check what your teacher or style guide (MLA, APA, etc.) stipulates.

Using Nonprint Sources in Online Versions of Your Paper

You can enhance your paper's content not only with visuals, but also with other media or resources. If you are submitting your project electronically or posting it online, you could create hyperlinks to electronic versions of primary and secondary sources. Hyperlinks are also useful when you need to link to electronic sources like audio or video files or when you want to make supplemental information on a topic or keyword available to be viewed by readers at their discretion. Occasionally you might also embed a feature like a YouTube clip in your project; however, be careful not to violate any copyright laws.

In order to gain expert information, you may wish to contact an informed individual directly by e-mail, following up on contact information supplied at a website or through other references. If your topic is of long-term interest to you and you have plenty of time to do your research, you may want to join a *listserv* or *e-mail conference*, a group of people interested in a particular topic, whose messages are sent automatically to all participants. Exchanges among those interested in a topic may also be posted on a *bulletin board server* or a *newsgroup,* where you can read past and ongoing messages and exchanges. The information you receive from others may be very authoritative and reliable, but it may also represent the biased viewpoint of the individual. Assess it carefully by comparing it with information from other sources, print as well as electronic.

Considerations in Using Nonprint Sources

▶ Is a nonprint source the most effective and useful way to present data? For example, if your paper is researching the ways in which photojournalists depict presidential candidates, you will probably want to include sample photographs in your paper. If your topic is trends in voter turnout, you might consult charts and graphs in your research but describe in words the evidence from those visuals rather than reproduce them in your paper. The reverse can also be true: If a source contains great quantities of data, arranging it in an appropriate graph or chart can help readers understand much complex information at a glance. Also, carefully constructed charts and graphs can help communicate across language and cultural barriers.

▶ Can the source be easily reproduced? What kinds of technology will you need to capture an image, import it into your text, and print it legibly (and, if necessary, in color)? What capabilities will your audience need to access a visual? For example, if you are submitting a paper electronically, remember that large visual files can take a long time to download. Also, your audience might need plug-ins, add-ins, or specific programs to view videos or listen to audio files.

▶ Have you gathered and noted all of the necessary source information, so that you can provide context (and, if necessary, a caption) for the visual as well as accurate bibliographical citation?

Preparing a Working Bibliography

The purpose of compiling a working bibliography is to keep track of possible sources, to determine the nature and extent of the information available, to provide a complete and accurate list of sources to be presented in the paper, and to make preparing the final bibliography much easier. Include in your working bibliography all sources that you have a hunch will be potentially useful. After all, you may not be able to obtain all the items listed, and some material will turn out to be useless, repetitious, or irrelevant to your topic. Such entries can easily be eliminated at a later stage when you prepare your final bibliography.

One way to simplify the task of preparing your final *Works Cited* or *References* section is to use a standard form for your working bibliography, whether you use cards or computer entries. The models given later in this chapter are based on two guides, abbreviated as MLA and APA. The *MLA Handbook* (New York: The Modern Language Association of America, 2016; 8th ed.) is generally followed for humanities classes, such as language arts and foreign languages. Teachers in the social sciences, natural sciences, education, and business are likely to favor the style presented in the *Publication Manual of the American Psychological Association* (Washington, D.C.: American Psychological Association, 2010; 6th ed.). Because the preferred form of citation of sources varies considerably from field to field, check with your teacher to determine which of these two formats they prefer or if they recommend another style. Follow any specific directions from a teacher carefully.

As you locate relevant sources, take down complete information on each item on a 3 × 5 note card, or start a bibliographic file on your computer. Complete information, properly recorded, will save you the trouble of having to scurry back to the library or back to a Web page for missing data when compiling your final bibliography. Be sure to list the source's call number and location in the library or its URL or DOI (digital object identifier); then you can easily find the material once you are ready to begin reading and relocate it if you need to refer to it again. When preparing bibliography cards for entries listed in annotated bibliographies, citation indexes, and abstracts, you might want to jot down notes from any pertinent summaries that are provided. Complete a separate card or file entry for each item that you think is promising.

Once you begin to build a bibliographic database, you can refer to your listings and supplement them each time you are assigned a paper.

Information for a Working Bibliography

Record the following information for a book:

1. Name(s) of author(s)
2. Title of book, italicized
3. Place of publication
4. Publisher's name
5. Date of publication
6. Call number or location in library
7. URL or DOI and date of access online

SAMPLE BOOK BIBLIOGRAPHY

Author: Taranto, Gina
Title of book: *Discourse Adjectives*
Place of publication: New York
Publisher's name: Routledge
Date of publication: 2006
Call number: P273.T372006

Record the following information for an article in a periodical:

1. Name(s) of author(s)

2. Title of article, in quotation marks

3. Title of periodical, italicized

4. Volume number or issue number

5. Date of publication

6. Page numbers on which article appears

7. Call number or location in library

8. URL or DOI and date of access online

SAMPLE PERIODICAL BIBLIOGRAPHY

Author's first name: Erin

Author's last name: Minear

Title of article: "Music and the Crisis of Meaning in *Othello*"

Title of periodical: *Studies in English Literature 1500–1900*

Volume number: 49

Date of publication: Spring 2009

Page numbers of article: 355-70

URL: www.jstor.org/journal/studengllite1500

Date of access online: 15 August 2018

Reassessing Your Topic

After you have compiled your working bibliography, take the time to reassess the entire project before you get more deeply involved in it. Analyze your bibliography cards or files carefully to determine whether you should proceed to the next stage of information gathering.

Your working bibliography should send out signals that help you shape your thinking about the topic. The dominant signal should indicate that your topic is neither too narrow nor too broad. Generally, a bibliography of 10–15 promising entries for a 1,500-word paper indicates that your topic might be properly limited at this stage. A listing of only 3 or 4 entries signals that you must expand the topic or consider discarding it. Conversely, a listing of 100 entries warns that you might be working yourself into a research swamp.

Another signal from your working bibliography should help you decide whether your hypothesis is on target or could be easily recast to make it more precise. Entry titles, abstracts, and commentaries on articles are excellent sources of confirmation. If established scholarship does not support your hypothesis, it would be best to discard your hypothesis and begin again.

Finally, the working bibliography should provide signals about the categories or parts of your research. Again, titles, abstracts, and commentaries are useful. In other words, as you compile the entries, you can begin to think through the problem and to perceive contours of thought that will dictate the organization of the paper even before you begin to do detailed research. Your working bibliography should be filled with such signals.

Phase 3: Gathering and Organizing Data

If your working bibliography confirms the value, logic, and practicality of your research project, you can move to the next phase of the research process: taking notes and organizing information. Information shapes and refines your thinking; you move from an overview to a more precise understanding, analysis, and interpretation of the topic. By the end of this third phase, you should be able to transform your hypothesis into a thesis and your assembled notes into an outline.

Plagiarism and Intellectual Property

In this phase of the research process, it is especially critical that you maintain a clear distinction between ideas, opinions, information, and words from other sources and your interpretation of that information. *Plagiarism,* or the illicit appropriation of content and ideas, can result from sloppy note taking or poor study habits. Taking care to summarize, paraphrase, and quote from sources with scrupulous care—as well as ensuring that you have given yourself enough time to consider your argument and write your paper—will go a long way toward avoiding plagiarism. The temptation to plagiarize is especially keen in an age when essays can easily be purchased online and when primary and secondary source information can be cut and pasted at the click of a button into your work. Be aware that such behavior in the classroom may result in a failing grade, suspension, or worse. In the professional world, plagiarism can even result in the loss of a job, the destruction of a reputation, and criminal charges. Plagiarism is a kind of theft. What a plagiarist steals is called, in legal terms, *intellectual property*—the ideas, opinions, inventions, and discoveries in which another writer or researcher has invested considerable time and resources. When you are unsure of whether or how to give credit to another source, *always* assume that you should give credit (and ask your teacher for help with citation guidelines).

Evaluating Sources

As you move into the third phase, begin by skimming your source material to sort out the valuable sources from the not-so-valuable ones. For a book, check the table of contents and index for information on your topic; then determine whether the information is relevant to your problem. For an article, see if the abstract or topic sentences in the body of the essay confirm your research interests. The guidelines on the next page can help you determine if a source will be useful.

> ▶ Is it directly relevant to your topic?
>
> ▶ Does it discuss the topic extensively, uniquely, and authoritatively?
>
> ▶ Does it bear on your hypothesis, supporting, qualifying, or contradicting it?
>
> ▶ Does it present relatively current information, especially for research in the social and natural sciences?
>
> ▶ Does it meet the criteria for credibility discussed in "Evaluating Online Sources" (page 666) and "Evaluating Print Sources" (page 669)?

Taking Notes

After you have a core of valuable material, you can begin to read these sources closely and take detailed notes. Skillful note taking—be it on your computer or mobile device, in a notebook, or on note cards—requires a subtle blend of active reading skills. It is not a matter of recording all the information available or simply copying long quotes. You want to select and summarize the general ideas that will form the outline of your paper, record specific evidence to support your ideas, and copy exact statements you plan to quote for evidence or interest. You also want to add your own ideas and evaluation of the material. All the notes you take must serve the specific purpose of your paper as stated in your hypothesis. It is essential that you record source information for *every* note that you take, whether that note is a summary, a paraphrase, or a direct quotation.

Guidelines for Taking Notes About Your Topic

1. Write the author's last name, the title of the source, and the page number at the top of each card or entry. (Complete information on the source should already be recorded on a card or in a file.)

2. Record only one idea or a group of closely related facts on each card or in each entry.

3. List a subtopic at the top of the card or entry. This will permit you to arrange your cards or entries from various sources into groups, and these groups can then serve as the basis of your outline.

4. List three types of information: (*a*) summaries of material, (*b*) paraphrases of material, in which you recast the exact words of the author, and (*c*) direct quotations, accurately transcribed.

5. Add your own ideas at the bottom of the card or following specific notes.

Summarizing

When you write a *summary* of a source, you focus on its main points and restate them in your own words. Summary notes can be especially helpful to remind you, as you draft, of sources that you might want to revisit and look at more closely. Summaries can also be introduced into the body of your essay, especially in an argument research paper, to provide additional information and support for your thesis. Here is an example of a primary source text and a student's summary:

Primary Source: Elliott, Carl. "Humanity 2.0." *The Wilson Quarterly (1976-),* **vol. 27, no. 4, 2003, pp. 13–20. JSTOR, www.jstor.org/stable/40260800.**

> Even technologies that unambiguously provide enhancements will raise issues of social justice not unlike those we currently face with ordinary medical technologies (wealthy Americans, for example, get liver transplants, while children in the developing world die from diarrhea). We live comfortably with such inequities, in part because we have so enthusiastically embraced an individualistic ethic. But to an outsider, a country's expenditure of billions of dollars on liposuction, face-lifts, and Botox injections while many of its children go without basic health care might well seem obscene.

Student Summary

> **Topic label:** "Transhumanism" and bioethics
> **Author of article:** Elliott
> **Relevant pages/URL:** www.jstor.org/stable/40260800
> Bioethicist and philosopher Carl Elliott defines "transhumanism" and describes a conference of "transhumanists" that he attended. As a bioethicist, Elliott argues that we need to pay attention to the ethical implications of the medical "enhancements" currently practiced or being developed that might contribute to the "transhumanist" goal of creating perfect human beings. In particular, our society's emphasis on developing medical technologies to make us more beautiful or intelligent at the expense of those less fortunate is especially disturbing.

Paraphrasing

A *paraphrase* focuses on one specific point or piece of information in an article and restates it in your words. Writing a paraphrase of a source can help you to better understand it. When you paraphrase, follow the original writer's argument but do not mimic the writer's sentence structure or simply replace keywords with synonyms. In unacceptable paraphrases, the sentence structure of the original is imitated, and synonyms replace the original terms (for example, *scandalous* for *obscene*). In acceptable paraphrases, key terms from the original source are directly quoted, and the source argument is rephrased in the student's terms.

👎 Unacceptable Paraphrase

"Transhumanism" and bioethics

Elliott

www.jstor.org/stable/40260800

Even procedures designed for cosmetic purposes raise controversies over fairness (rich people get transplants while poor children die from basic diseases). Americans are fine with these inequalities because our culture values the individual. To non-Americans, the money we spend on plastic surgery even though many American children lack health insurance probably appears scandalous.

👍 Acceptable Paraphrase

"Transhumanism" and bioethics

Elliott

www.jstor.org/stable/40260800

Elliott points out that our culture already seems to overlook the injustice of some individuals spending a great deal of money on cosmetic surgery (or "enhancements") while many lack access to basic health care. Elliott describes this as a uniquely American "Individualist ethic" but points out that other cultures might see this inequality as "obscene." By extension, the willingness of the transhumanist movement to explore medical "enhancements" that will only benefit a very few wealthy people is also, ethically, "obscene."

As these examples demonstrate, an acceptable paraphrase shows that the researcher is genuinely engaged with the source's *argument*—not just the words—and has thought about how this particular component of the argument supports the original author's thesis. The summary and paraphrase are introduced with signal phrases, which include the name of the source and an action verb (*says, suggests, acknowledges, maintains,* etc.). Signal phrases help your reader discern what comes from you and what comes from a source. They can also signal your tone, or attitude, toward the source.

Quoting

When the language of source material is essential to understanding its argument, *quotation* is the most effective strategy. When you quote directly from a source, put quotation marks around the material that you are selecting.

👍 Acceptable Quotation

"Transhumanism" and bioethics

Elliott

www.jstor.org/stable/40260800

"But to an outsider, a country's expenditure of billions of dollars on liposuction, face-lifts, and Botox injections while many of its children go without basic health care might well seem obscene."

When you have completed all your research, organize your notes under the various subtopics or subheadings that you have established. Now, by reviewing your notes and assessing the data, you should be able to transform the calculated guess that was your hypothesis into a much firmer thesis. Focus on your thesis by stating it at the top of the page where you are working on your outline. If possible or desirable, try to combine some subtopics and eliminate others so that you have three to five major categories for analysis and development. You are now ready to develop an outline for the essay.

Designing an Outline

Because you must organize a lot of material in a clear way, an outline is especially valuable in a research essay. Spend as much time as is reasonable drafting an outline. Begin by creating a rough outline that simply lists your general subheadings and their supporting data. Next, work more systematically through your notes and fill in the rough outline with as much detail as possible, developing each point logically and in detail. If you are required to submit an outline with your research paper, you should begin to develop a full, formal outline at this stage. Such an outline would be structured like this:

I.
    A.
    B.
        1.
        2.
        3.
            a.
            b.
II.

Use Roman numerals for your most important points, capital letters for the next most important points, Arabic numbers for supporting points, and lowercase letters for pertinent details or minor points. If you are including visuals such as photographs or graphics, include them in the outline as well.

Phase 4: Writing and Submitting the Paper

As you enter the fourth and final phase of the research process, keep in mind that a research paper is a formal essay, not a rag-tag compilation of notes. You should be prepared to take your research effort through several increasingly polished versions, most likely at least a rough draft, a revised draft, and a final manuscript.

Writing the Rough Draft

For your rough draft, concentrate on filling in the gaps in your outline. Take the time to rearrange your notes in the topic order that your outline assumes. In this way, you will be able to integrate notes and writing more efficiently and effectively.

Even as you adhere to your formal outline in beginning the rough draft, you should be open to alternate possibilities and prospects for presenting ideas and information. Although your primary task in writing a first draft is to rough out the shape and content of your paper, the flow of your ideas will often be accompanied by self-adjusting operations of your mind, all aimed at making your research effort even better than you thought it could be at the outline stage.

Whether you incorporate quotations from your notes into the rough draft is a matter of preference. Some writers prefer to transcribe quotations and paraphrases at this point in order to save time at a later stage. Other writers copy and insert these materials directly from entries in a computer file for notes. Still others believe that their thought processes are interrupted by having to write out summarized, quoted, and paraphrased material and to design transitions between their own writing and the transcribed material. They simply write "insert" in the draft with a reference to the appropriate notes. Whatever your strategy, it is essential that you keep track of the sources of summarized, quoted, and paraphrased material so that you can properly cite the sources and avoid plagiarism.

The need to integrate material from several sources will test your reasoning ability during the writing of the rough draft. For any given subtopic in your outline, you will be drawing together information from a variety of sources. To an extent, your outline will tell you how to arrange some of this information. At the same time, you must contribute your own commentary, arrange details in an effective order, and sort out conflicting claims and interpretations. A great deal of thinking as well as writing goes into the design of your first draft. You are not involved in a dull transcription of material when writing the rough draft of a research paper. Instead, you are engaged in a demanding effort to think your way through a problem of considerable magnitude, working in a logical way from the introduction and the statement of your thesis, through the evidence, to the outcome or conclusion that supports everything that has come before.

Revising the Draft

In the rough draft, you thought and wrote your way through the problem. Now you must rethink and rewrite in order to give better form and expression to your ideas. Use the guidelines outlined on the next page to approach your revision.

Consider every aspect of your paper, from the most general to the most specific. Look again at the overall organization, key topics, paragraphs, and sentences; read through for clarity of expression and details of grammar, punctuation, and spelling. A comprehensive revision effort will result in a decidedly more polished version of your paper.

▶ Does your title illuminate the topic of the essay and capture the reader's interest?

▶ Have you created the proper tone to meet the expectations of your audience?

▶ Does your opening paragraph hook the reader? Does it clearly establish and limit the topic? Is your thesis statement clear, limited, and interesting?

▶ Does the order of body paragraphs follow the order of your thesis? Do all the body paragraphs support your thesis? Is there a single topic and main idea for each paragraph? Do you achieve unity, coherence, and proper development? Is there sufficient evidence in each paragraph to support the main idea?

▶ Are there clear and effective transitions linking your ideas within and between paragraphs?

▶ Have you selected the best strategies to meet the demands of the assignment and the expectations of your audience?

▶ Are your assertions clearly stated, defined, and supported? Do you use sound logic and avoid faulty reasoning? Do you acknowledge other people's ideas properly? Do you use signal phrases to introduce your sources when summarizing, paraphrasing, and quoting? Are all of your summaries, paraphrases, and quotations appropriately cited?

▶ Is your conclusion strong and effective?

▶ Are your sentences grammatically correct? Have you avoided errors in the use of verbs, pronouns, adjectives, and prepositions? Have you corrected errors of agreement?

▶ Are your sentences complete? Have you corrected all fragments, comma splices, and fused sentences?

▶ Have you varied your sentences effectively? Have you employed clear coordination and subordination? Have you avoided awkward constructions?

▶ If you include visual information, do you provide adequate context? Is the placement of the visual logical? Is the visual clearly reproduced?

▶ For an electronic paper, if you include hyperlinks, are they clearly and appropriately placed in the text? Are the hyperlinks active? Do they connect to the correct files or pages?

▶ Are all words spelled correctly? Do your words mean what you think they mean? Are they specific? Are they concrete? Is your diction appropriate to college writing? Is your language free of clichés, slang, jargon, and euphemism? Do you avoid needless abstractions? Is your usage sound?

▶ Have you carefully attended to such mechanical matters as apostrophes, capitals, numbers, and word divisions?

▶ Does your manuscript conform to acceptable guidelines for submitting printed or online work?

Preparing the Final Manuscript

Leave time in your research effort to prepare a neat, clean, attractively designed manuscript. Store all of your files (notes, drafts, and final version) on a backup flash drive or external hard drive, and print a duplicate copy of the paper. Submit a neat, clear version, and keep the copy. Consult your teacher for the desired format, and carefully follow the guidelines for manuscript preparation in your final version. Look also at the sample research paper later in this chapter, which illustrates how to present the final version of a paper in accordance with MLA style.

Documenting Sources

Documentation is an essential part of any research paper. Documenting your sources throughout the paper and in a Works Cited or References section tells your audience just how well you have conducted your research. It offers readers the opportunity to check on authorities, do further reading, and assess the originality of your contribution to an established body of opinion. Neglect of proper documentation can lead to charges of plagiarism.

Quotations, paraphrases, and summaries obviously require credit, for they are the actual words or the theories or interpretations of others. Paraphrases and summaries also frequently offer statistics or data that are not well known, and this type of information requires documentation as well. Facts in a controversy (facts open to dispute or to varying interpretations) also fall within the realm of documentation. Visual information (maps, graphics, and photos) also require documentation, even if they show common knowledge (such as a map of Japan). Video and audio sources (like music files and podcasts), and even conversations, lectures, and e-mails, require documentation.

Materials that Require Documentation

- Direct quotations

- Paraphrased material

- Summarized material

- Any key idea or opinion adapted and incorporated into your paper

- Specific data (whether quoted, paraphrased, or tabulated in graphs, charts, lists, or tables)

- Visual media like illustrations, maps, photographs, or screenshots

- Disputed facts

Parenthetical documentation—briefly identifying sources within parentheses in the text—is the most common method of indicating sources. The purpose of a parenthetical citation is to identify a source briefly yet clearly enough that it can be located in the list of references at the end of the paper. In MLA style, the author's last name and the page number in the source are included. APA style uses the author's last name and the year of publication; page numbers are included primarily for direct quotations. Then complete information is listed, alphabetically by author or title (if a source has no specific author), in the Works Cited or References section following the text of the paper. The bibliographic information you have collected should provide you with the details needed for the preparation of both parenthetical documentation and a list of sources.

General Guidelines for Parenthetical Documentation

1. Give enough information so that the reader can readily identify the source in the Works Cited (MLA) or References (APA) section of your paper.

2. Supply the citation information in parentheses placed where the material occurs in your text.

3. Give the specific information required by the documentation system you are using, especially when dealing with multivolume works, editions, newspapers, and legal documents.

4. Make certain that the sentence containing the parenthetical documentation is readable and grammatically correct.

With your parenthetical documentation prepared, turn your attention next to a final Works Cited or References section. To prepare this list of sources, simply transcribe those bibliography cards or entries that you actually used to write your paper, following the appropriate format. In the following sections, you will find examples of MLA and APA documentation forms. Use these examples to help you cite your sources efficiently and clearly.

General Guidelines for Preparing a List of Sources

1. Use the title Works Cited (MLA) or References (APA).

2. Include only works actually cited in the research paper unless directed otherwise by your teacher.

3. Arrange all works alphabetically according to author's last name or according to the title of a work if there is no author. Ignore *A*, *An*, or *The* when you are alphabetizing.

4. Begin each entry at the left margin. Indent everything in an entry that comes after the first line by five spaces or ½ inch (MLA style) or by five to seven spaces (following APA style for students) unless your teacher directs otherwise.

5. Double-space every line, both between and within sources.

6. Punctuate with periods after the three main divisions in most entries—author, title, and publishing information.

MLA (Modern Language Association) Documentation

Make it as clear as possible to your reader where a source begins (with a signal phrase) and ends (with a parenthetical citation) in your paper. When you cannot provide specific parenthetical information (such as when a source does not have page numbers), make it as easy as possible for your reader to find the citation on your Works Cited page by including key identification elements like the source's name within the sentence. The following examples illustrate how to cite some of the most common sources in the text and in the list of Works Cited at the end of a paper.

MLA Parenthetical Documentation

Book

A basic MLA in-text citation includes the author's last name and the page number (for sources that use numbered pages), identifying exactly where the quotation or information is located. This in-text citation leads readers to an entry on the Works Cited page, which provides more complete information about the source.

> In the conclusion, he offers a gruesome description of the dying man's physical and emotional struggles (Tolstoy 1252–53).

If the author's name is included in the text, it does not need to be repeated in the citation.

> Garcia Marquez uses another particularly appealing passage as the opening of the story (105).

If citing a quotation longer than four typed lines, set it off from the text of the paper and indented one-half inch (1/2") from the left margin. Double-space the quote and move the period before the parenthetical citation.

Work with Three or More Authors

If you mention the authors' names in your sentence narrative, you may include all the last names or write just the first author's name followed by "and others." In the parenthetical citation, however, include only the first author's name followed by *et al.*

> Most political revolutions have been instigated by people in the middle class (Bentley et al. 634).

Work Without an Author

Use the full title of the work if it is brief; if the title is longer, however, use a shortened version, beginning with the word you will use to alphabetize the work on the Works Cited page.

> *Computerworld* has developed a thoughtful editorial on the issue of government and technology ("Uneasy Silence" 54).

Work in an Anthology

Use the name of the author of the quotation, not the editor of the anthology.

> The narrator describes it as "a big, squarish frame house that had once been white, decorated with cupolas and spires and scrolled balconies in the heavily lightsome style of the seventies, set on what had once been our most select street" (Faulkner 449).

More Than One Work in a Single Parenthetical Reference

> Multiple studies conducted since 2000 indicate that educating children as young as six about healthy eating and exercising habits reduces the incidents of childhood obesity by 30% (Mickelson 105; Waller and Jackson 45).

Common or Classical Literature

If an often-studied literary work exists in multiple editions, readers may need more information than just a page number if they have a different edition than the one you used. Including the chapter number helps them locate your source more easily.

> After Billy's violent death, Sonny feels "that he [is] the only person in town" (McMurtry 277; ch. 26).

Quoting Dialog from a Play

Use Arabic numbers to cite the act, scene, and line numbers from the play, unless your teacher tells you to do otherwise.

> Shakespeare makes use of the classic anagnorisis, or recognition of one's tragic flaw, in the play when Hamlet tells Horatio he has learned to "Let be" (5.2.209).

Line Number(s) for Poem or Song Lyrics

For the first quote, you may use the notation "line" or "lines" and the line number(s); afterward, use only the line number(s).

> Owen is particularly adept at using onomatopoeia to reinforce the persona's terror as he watches a fellow soldier's suffering: "In all my dreams, before my helpless sight, // He plunges at me, guttering, choking, drowning" (lines 15–16). Even the phrase "Gas! Gas!" imitates the insidious hissing sound of the mustard gas as it is released from the shell (9).

Citation for Visuals (Map, Graph, Chart, Photograph, etc.)

The label *Fig. 1* and caption of the medium should be placed below it, flush with the left margin. Figures should be numbered sequentially, and captions should be used to describe their contents; source information should follow the figure.

> Fig. 1. "Malaria: Geographic Distribution," map from Centers for Disease Control and Prevention, 2004, www.cdc.gov/malaria/about/distribution.html.

Parenthetical Citations for Online Sources

Sometimes PDF files of articles and online versions of printed journals label the article's pages to correspond to the printed version, so use them if they are provided. Sometimes a source without page numbers will provide numbered screens, paragraphs, sections, chapters, or references, so use them to help your reader locate your sources. MLA parenthetical citation does not use a comma to separate the author's name from the page number (as does APA), but it does use commas to separate the author's name from the paragraph, section, or reference number. Most online sources, however, do not have page numbers for easy parenthetical citation. In that case, use the author's name or the title of the article or Web page.

(Markus, par. 15) (Markus, sec. 3) (Markus) ("The H Bomb") (CNN.com)

MLA List of Works Cited

Following your paper, list the references you have cited in alphabetical order on a separate page titled "Works Cited." See the Works Cited page of the sample paper later in this chapter for an illustration of how you should prepare this page. Use the following sample entries to help you format your references in MLA style. Pay special attention to full names of authors, abbreviated names of publishers, details of punctuation, and other characteristic features of MLA citations.

Book with One or Two Authors

Note the punctuation and use of italics in the basic entry for a book.

Reynolds, David S. *John Brown, Abolitionist.* Knopf, 2005.

Locker, Kitty, and Donna Kienzler. *Business and Professional Communication.* McGraw-Hill, 2017, p. 123.

Book with Three or More Authors

Bentley, Jerry H., et al. *Traditions and Encounters: A Global Perspective on the Past.* 6th ed., McGraw-Hill, 2017.

Work Without an Author

Sir Gawain and the Green Knight. Translated by Bernard O'Donoghue, Penguin, 2006.

Work or Chapter in an Edited Book or Anthology

Sher, Ira. "Nobody's Home." *Paraspheres: Extending Beyond the Spheres of Literary and Genre Fiction,* edited by Rusty Morrison and Ken Keegan, Omnidawn, 2006, pp. 303–10.

Work Translated from Another Language

> Eco, Umberto. *On Literature.* Translated by Martin McLaughlin, Harcourt, 2004.

Article in a Scholarly Journal

Include the volume number (if available) and issue number (if available), followed by the year and the pages of the entire article.

> Robson, Mark. "The Ethics of Anonymity." *Modern Language Review,* vol. 103, no. 2, 2008, pp. 350–63.

Article in a Magazine or Newspaper

Include the day, month, year, and page numbers. If no author is listed, begin with the article's title. If an article in a magazine or newspaper does not continue on consecutive pages, follow the page number on which it begins with a plus sign.

> Orlean, Susan. "The It Bird." *The New Yorker,* 28 Sept. 2009, pp. 26–31.

> Skidmore, Sarah. "New Coupons Mean Users Clip Less." *Times* [Shreveport], 30 Aug. 2009, pp. 11A+.

Works Cited Entries for Online Sources

List the author, the title of the document/specific page (in quotes), and the title of the website (in italics), as well as any translator, editor, and entity responsible for the site's upkeep, and the date of the electronic publication or last update. Include the URL for the Web location. Use only the "www" address and eliminate "http://." For electronic articles, when a DOI is available, use that instead of the URL. You may conclude with the date on which you visited the website, but this step is no longer mandatory unless your teacher requires it.

Book Accessed Via an Electronic Database

> Joseph, Jay. *The Missing Gene: Psychiatry, Heredity, and the Fruitless Search for Genes.* Algora, 2006. *Questia,* www.questia.com/library/120093671/the-missing-gene-psychiatry-heredity-and-the-fruitless. Accessed 26 Aug. 2018.

Journal Article Accessed Via an Online Database

> Taylor, Daniel J., et al. "The Role of Sleep in Predicting College Academic Performance: Is It a Unique Predictor?" *Behavioral Sleep Medicine*, vol. 11, no. 3, 2013, pp. 159–72. *NCBI,* doi:10.1080/15402002.2011.602776. Accessed 11 Jul. 2017.

Magazine or Newspaper Article Accessed Online

> Rosen, Jeffrey. "Forced into a Gun Debate." *Time,* 26 Apr. 2007, www.content.time.com/time/magazine/article/0,9171,1615186,00.html.

Document or Individual Page on a Website

Latham, Ernest. "Conducting Research at the National Archives into Art Looting, Recovery, and Restitution." *The National Archives Library,* National Archives and Records Administration, Sept. 2009, www.archives.gov/research/holocaust/articles-and-papers/symposium-papers/conducting-research-art-looting.html.

Blog Post

Mehta, Seema. "Two Swine Flu Clinics Open Today for Uninsured and At-Risk L.A. County Residents." *L.A. Now,* 23 Oct. 2009, 10:45 p.m., latimesblogs.latimes.com/lanow/2009/10/uninsured-atrisk-begin-receiving-swine-flu-vaccines-at-county-health-clinics.html.

CD, LP, MP3, or Other Sound Recording

What you want to emphasize determines how you will cite the source (e.g., a performer, a conductor, composer, etc.). Song titles are placed in quotation marks, while the entire compilation (album, in whatever format) is italicized.

Basie, Count. "Sunday at the Savoy." *88 Basie Street,* Pablo Records, 1984.

Film

Start with any actor, producer, director, or other person whose work you wish to emphasize. Otherwise, simply begin with the title of the film itself.

The Lovely Bones. Produced and directed by Peter Jackson, performances by Saoirse Ronan, Mark Wahlberg, and Rachel Weisz, Dreamworks, 2009.

Programs on Radio or Television

You can cite the entire series (title in italics), a specific episode (title in quotation marks), and you can focus on a particular individual's performance or contribution.

"Wee Small Hours." *Mad Men,* created by Dahvi Waller and Matthew Weiner, directed by Scott Hornbacher, performance by Jon Hamm, season 3, episode 9, AMC, 2009.

Interview

Poehler, Amy. *Inside the Actor's Studio,* interview by James Lipton, Bravo, 21 Sept. 2009.

Webcast or Web-Based Video

"Nobody Knows the Trouble They've Seen: Close Combat in Iraq." *YouTube,* uploaded by nickwalnut, 18 Feb. 2018, www.youtube.com/watch?v=yzsMkOnPxKk

Map or Other Visual Media

"The Origins of Human Beings." *Atlas of African-American History*, by James Ciment, Facts-Infobase, 2007, p. 2. Map.

Artwork

Include the title of the work (in italics), the year of completion (*n.d.* if unknown), and the location of the artwork.

Rodin. *Torso of a Young Woman*. 1910, Musée Rodin, Paris.

Email

Burnett, Jack. "Re: Best Nutrition for Bodybuilding." Received by David Tebbe, 11 Sept. 2018.

APA (American Psychological Association) Documentation

The samples below show how to use APA style for citing a source in the text and in the References section at the end of a paper.

APA Parenthetical Documentation

The basic APA parenthetical citation includes the author's last name and the date of publication, information generally sufficient to identify the source in the reference list. Although researchers in the social sciences often cite works as a whole, you should add the page number to identify exactly where a quotation or other specific information is located. If the source is not paginated (e.g., a website), use paragraph numbers or headings to help your reader find the information. Consider that the danger of not using some sort of citation (like the author/year or page number) at the end of a paraphrased passage is that your reader may not be able to separate the outside source from your ideas. If the author's name (or the year) is included in the text, it does not need to be repeated in the citation.

Direct Quotation with Author Name in Internal Citation

One argues that "for the most part, Justice Scalia's opinion for the majority of the Supreme Court in *Heller* is a solid presentation of textual arguments and historical evidence for interpreting the Second Amendment broadly to protect non-military use of guns" (Rostron, 2009, p. 386).

Direct Quotation with Author Name in Signal Phrase

Rostron (2009) maintained that "for the most part, Justice Scalia's opinion for the majority of the Supreme Court in *Heller* is a solid presentation of textual arguments and historical evidence for interpreting the Second Amendment broadly to protect non-military use of guns" (p. 386).

How to Use a Page or Paragraph Number with a Paraphrase

Clarke (2005) maintained that the lackluster response of FEMA after Hurricane Katrina can be traced in part to the Bush administration's lack of support for the Department of Homeland Security (p. 38).

The city's most current traffic flow analysis (McPherson, 2008) proposed two alternatives (pp. 45–53).

In 2008, Wyatt compared the costs and benefits of both designs (Conclusion section, para. 12).

APA List of References

As you examine the following examples, notice how capitalization, italics, punctuation, and other features change with the type of source noted. Note also that authors' names are listed with last names first, followed by initials only. Although the entries in an APA reference list follow very specific patterns, references in your paper—to titles, for instance—should use standard capitalization (that is, only the first word of titles and subtitles). Similarly, the word *and* should be spelled out in your paper even though the ampersand (&) is used with authors' and editors' names in parenthetical citations and References entries. Note that the names of months (in periodical and online citations) are spelled out, not abbreviated. For updated examples and further guidance on APA style, see the American Psychological Association website at *www.apastyle.org*.

Book

> Wodarski, J. S. (2009). *Behavioral medicine: A social worker's guide*. New York, NY: Routledge.

Work in an Edited Book

Do not put the title of the work/chapter in quotation marks.

> Fox, J. J., & Gable, R. A. (2004). Functional behavior assessment. In R. B. Rutherford, Jr., M. M. Quinn, & S. R. Mathur (Eds.), *Handbook of research in emotional and behavioral disorders* (pp. 143–62). New York, NY: Guilford Press.

Electronic Version of a Printed Book

The URL takes the place of the publisher information. Do not use a period after a URL.

> Cameron, S. (2009). *The economics of hate* [Electronic version]. Retrieved from http://ezproxy.lsus.edu:2194/Reader/

Article in a Journal with Pagination by Volume

Use initial caps for all important words in the titles of journals, magazines, and newspapers. Include the volume in italics.

> Stansel, D. (2008). Local government investment and long-run economic growth. *Journal of Social, Political and Economic Studies, 34*, 244–259.

Article in a Journal with Pagination by Issue

Include both the volume (in italics) and the issue number (in parentheses).

> Boulden, W. T. (2008). Evaluation of the advancing young adult learning project. *Adult Basic Education and Literacy Journal 2*(1), 3–12.

Article from an Electronic Journal

Many online scholarly sources now include a digital object identifier (DOI), a series of symbols, letters, and numbers that help the reader identify and locate the source. When the DOI is available, include it in your citation; it takes the place of the publisher information or the URL where you accessed the article. Check out *www. doi.org* for more information or *www.crossref.org* to look up an article's DOI. When citing an article accessed on a subscription database, do not include the name of the database in your entry.

> Baggio, G. (2008, December). Processing temporal constraints: An ERP study. *Language learning, 58*, 35–55. doi:10.1111/j.1467-9922.2008.00460.x

Article in a Magazine

If the publication includes a month, season, or specific date, list it after the year. Do not abbreviate. For online articles, include the URL of the magazine's home page, not a direct link to the article.

> Searcy, W. A., & Nowicki, S. (2008, March/April). Bird song and the problem of honest communication. *American Scientist, 96*(2), 114–121.

> Underwood, Anne. (2008, April 14). Ten fixes for the planet. *Newsweek, 151*(15), 52–56.

> Beinart, P. (2008, June 26). The war over patriotism. *Time.* Retrieved from http://www.time.com

Article in a Daily Newspaper

Use p. or pp. to indicate page numbers. If the article continues to another page that is not consecutive, list all the pages (pp. A24, A27).

> Thompson, G. (2009, February 12). Report faults homeland security's efforts on immigration. *The New York Times*, p. A24.

> Miller, C. C. (2009, July 22). Marketing small businesses with Twitter. *The New York Times.* Retrieved from http://www.nytimes.com

Blog

> Siemens, G. (2009, September 18). Re: Untangling the web [Web log post]. *Elearnspace.org.* Retrieved from http://www.elearnspace.org/blog

Podcast or Webcast

> Star talk: Apollo 40th anniversary (2009, July 31) [Audio podcast]. Retrieved from http://www.discovermagazine.com

Images—Maps, Photographs, Tables, Charts

US Geological Survey (Cartographer). (2009). Maps of recent earthquake activity in California-Nevada [Seismic activity map]. Retrieved from http://quake.usgs.gov/recenteqs/latestfault.htm

The sample paper that follows shows how one student correctly incorporated appropriate sources into a research paper in order to prove her thesis.

Clara Lee

Professor Paul Smith

Writing Workshop II

5 September 2017

The Courage of Intimacy:

Movie Masculinity

Mike Newell's 1997 film *Donnie Brasco* begins and

ends with an extreme close-up of Johnny Depp's eyes.

Shot in wide-screen so that the eyes literally span the

entire screen, the image is a black-and-white snapshot that

appears during the opening credits and returns as a full-

color close-up at the end of the movie. Depp's lustrous

eyes are large and black and beautiful, and gazing at them

up close gives the viewer a surprisingly intimate sensation.

Even within the conventional narrative that makes up

the body of the movie, they become noticeably important;

Web-site critic Rob Blackwelder observes that "Depp has

[the central conflict of the movie] in his eyes in every

scene," and Susan Wloszczyna of *USA Today* notes, "It's

all in the eyes. Depp's intense orbs focus like surveillance

cameras, taking in each crime and confrontation. He's

Side annotations

- Header: Last name and page number ½ inch below top of page ▶
- Heading should be 1 inch below top of page ▶
- Title centered; defines topic ▶
- All lines should be double-spaced, including heading and title ▶
- All margins should be 1 inch ▶
- Opening interests reader with detail from film ▶
- Paragraph indented ½ inch or 5 spaces ▶
- Quotation from electronic source ▶
- Support from print source ▶

sucked into the brutal, bullying lifestyle, and so are we"

(28). The close-up image at the beginning and end is one

of the few instances in which the film draws blatant

attention to its own style, but the device calls attention to

the film's central focus, its constant probing into the

character at the center of the movie.

Somehow, without restricting the film to a first-person

narration by Depp's undercover FBI agent, the audience

comes to identify with him and understand the many

pressures increasing inside his head simply by watching

his eyes. They reflect his watchfulness, his uncertainty, his

frustration, and his guilt—all without drawing too much

attention to himself from his unsuspecting wiseguy

companions. He is guarded with his words, causing his

closest Mafioso friend to remark, "You never say anything

◄ Quotation from film

without thinking about it first." His quietness invites

viewers to read his looks and expressions, to become

intimately acquainted with a character who constantly has

to hide part of himself from the people around him, until

they can virtually feel every twinge of fear or regret that

the character feels. Seeing this man trapped in situations

◄ Thesis stated

in which he faces crisis after crisis, unwillingly alienated

from his family and eventually his employers, trying only

to protect the people he loves, viewers can ultimately

recognize him as a more sensitive, struggling, and

courageous hero than those celebrated in the past.

Fig. 1—Johnny Depp in the title role of *Donnie Brasco*, directed by Mike Newell, Sony, 1997.

Over the decades, Hollywood has glorified the gruff

masculinity of actors from Humphrey Bogart to Sylvester

Stallone. Joan Mellen notes in her 1977 book *Big Bad*

Wolves: Masculinity in the American Film that in traditional

Hollywood films, especially the stoic action films of the

1970s, "physical action unencumbered by effeminate

introspection is what characterizes the real man" (5). In

the 1990s, it seems that much changed; introspection

became a central part of leading-male roles. We can see

this clearly in the character-driven films of 1997 alone,

which won accolades for such intimate roles as Robert

Duvall's tormented evangelical preacher in *The Apostle,* Matt Damon's emotionally needy genius and Robin Williams's mourning therapist in *Good Will Hunting,* and the unemployed guys struggling over issues like impotence and child custody in *The Full Monty.*

◄ Other examples noted

Thoughtfulness, vulnerability, and the ability to handle relationships became virtual requirements for the male "hero" in the 1990s. The old-fashioned masculinity of characters played by Clint Eastwood or John Wayne in the past has come to be regarded as emotionally repressed and overly macho.

◄ Background tied to thesis

Archive Photos/Getty Images

Fig. 2—John Wayne, the epitome of mid-20th century masculinity

The change is partly cyclical. Mellen cites the 1930s and 1950s as eras in film in which leading men were given greater depth. She says, "Despite the limitations imposed by a repressive society [in the fifties], film recovered for men an individual self with a distinctive identity and a flourishing ego" (191–92). Actors like Marlon Brando and James Dean, in particular, played insecure, emotionally torn rebels who express tenderness in their relationships with women and with other men. However, in the sixties, "as the Vietnam War progressed . . . maleness itself appeared under siege and in need of defense," and "traumatic events of the sixties induced the Hollywood hero to tighten up, reveal as little about himself as possible, and to find comfort in his own recalcitrance" (248–49).

Things scarcely got better when "glorification of the vigilante male [became] the dominant masculine myth of the seventies" (295) with films like *Dirty Harry* and *Taxi Driver*. Mellen notes, "In the seventies film, people are allowed no option: they must meet force with force" (307). Following two decades of grim testosterone, there was a definite reaction in the bubble gum pop culture of the eighties, with flashy cartoon violence starring Sylvester Stallone or Arnold Schwarzenegger presenting highly

Clarification added in brackets ▶

Quotation with page numbers ▶

Ellipses for words omitted ▶

Quotations and summary from source ▶

unrealistic images of masculinity, and lighter portrayals like Marty McFly and Indiana Jones gaining in popularity. By the nineties, American audiences were no longer taking tough guy masculinity seriously, leading to a trend of ironic humor in action films from *True Lies* to *Independence Day.* It is doubtful that Will Smith would have been a favorite action hero before the 1990s.

However, the crucial underlying shift in American culture is the debilitation of the conventional white male hero in a country he once monopolized. Trends in society within the past forty years have led to greater freedom for women, minorities, and homosexuals, and as pride and power among these groups increased, there has been a backlash against the white male. The hero of the 1990s has to prove that he is sensitive and completely respectful of every group mentioned above in order to remain sympathetic, forcing his previous role of unquestioned dominance to change drastically. In addition, now that women are going to work and less is expected of men in terms of being the provider and protector of the family and society, more is expected of them in their personal relationships. As noted in 1996 by Sylvester Stallone, a fitting symbol of the old macho masculinity who tried to

◄ Transition back to present day

change his image to a more sensitive one, "I think the leading man of the future will be one who is beleaguered by the need to constantly define on film the male-female relationship." He also notes, "People want to nurture the underdog. The day of the strongman is over" (94). The themes of inefficacy in society, sensitivity in relationships, and a reaction to the old strongman ideal show up clearly in *Donnie Brasco*.

In the movie, FBI agent Joe Pistone, alias Donnie Brasco, goes undercover in the belief that he is on the side of law and order, with the simple goal of booking some major criminals; instead he finds a bunch of endearing but disturbingly violent men who become his closest companions for several years. Particularly perplexing is his relationship with Benjamin "Lefty" Ruggiero, the trod-upon hit man whose thirty years of faithful service are rewarded with dirty-work assignments while younger wiseguys are promoted over him. Lefty is the one who notices Donnie and recruits him into the organization, and from the start his faith in Donnie is clear; as Pistone smugly reports to a contact early in the movie, "I got my hooks in this guy." However, Pistone's smugness wears off as Lefty repeatedly invites him into his home, confides in him with his

---

Sidebar annotations:

Quotation from published interview ▶

Analysis of film ▶

Plot summary and interpretation ▶

Character analysis ▶

complaints and his dreams, and says unexpectedly one day

waiting in the hospital where his own son is in the E.R. for a

drug overdose, "I love you, Donnie."

It is appropriate that the fictional Donnie Brasco is an

orphan, because Lefty essentially becomes a surrogate

father to him. Pistone, concerned for Lefty's fate, becomes

more and more reluctant to "pull out" of his undercover

assignment, revealing Donnie Brasco as a spy and leaving

the blame (and death sentence) on Lefty. At one point he

stops meeting his FBI contacts because they are pressuring

him to pull out. Instead, he lets himself take on his mob

alter ego more and more, tearing both his professional and

personal lives apart.

In a way, the film is an interesting commentary on how

ideals have changed, because it is set in the 1970s, the last

decade of the full-fledged he-man hero, but made with a

1990s ideology. Because it is based on a book by the real

agent Joe Pistone, who is currently living under the

Witness Protection Program, one might think the portrayal

would be strictly fact-based and would not be affected by

the obsession with the sensitive male; but of course, one

must never underestimate the power of filmmakers in any

era to interpret their material with their own contemporary

vision (note the portrayal of the Three Musketeers as aging and vulnerable in the 1998 screen adaptation of *The Man in the Iron Mask;* the 1970s version of the same book depicted the Musketeers as brash and irreverent).

There is plenty of traditional macho posturing in the Mafia sequences of *Donnie Brasco,* but director Mike Newell places special emphasis on Pistone's sensitive relationship with Lefty Ruggiero, his mentor in the mob, and on his imperiled relationship with his wife, turning *Donnie Brasco* into "a relationship movie . . . about conflict of loyalty" ("Donnie Brasco"). Newell, a British director most famous for his vastly different romantic comedy *Four Weddings and a Funeral,* also boasted about *Donnie Brasco*'s "'absolutely novel point of view about the Mob,'" focusing on "'the lowest rung, the have-nots'" (Schickel et al.), rather than the rich and powerful men at the top so often depicted in mob movies. The film focuses on the soulful side of a male protagonist in a genre in which sensitivity is rare.

In fact, *Donnie Brasco* has been recognized as an evolutionary step in the genre of gangster films. *Time* calls it a "neo-Scorsesian study of lowlife Mob life," and says that it "rises above the mire of its shopworn genre by showing the cracks in its characters' armor" (Schickel et

Electronic source cited by authors' names only

al.). Conventional gangster films usually depict the rise and fall of a charismatic criminal. The gangster movies of the thirties and forties featured fast-talking tough guys like James Cagney and Humphrey Bogart; Francis Ford Coppola's 1972 epic *The Godfather,* which revived the genre, depicted the same glamour, ruthlessness, and power of the Mafia, on an even greater romanticized scale. But after a spate of stylized mob movies in the previous thirty years, many reviewers of *Donnie Brasco* welcomed a new approach in a genre that was growing old and stale. Put another way, *Donnie Brasco* is the film that finally brings its genre into the nineties by replacing its tough, glamorous hero with a real guy who can't live up to the stereotypes.

◄ Contrasts lead back to thesis

Almost in direct response to the ideal of masculinity presented in the past, Newell shows that although at first Pistone is doing everything right—fitting perfectly into his undercover persona, doing top-rate work for the FBI, and sending checks home regularly to his family—he cannot "be the man in the f—kin' white hat" that he thought he could be, as he puts it late in the movie. He knows how impossible it is to fulfill his male responsibilities in all three of his very different worlds after he has ditched the

◄ Analysis of main character

FBI, almost lost his marriage, and realized that his undercover work, once revealed, will be the cause of Lefty's death. He has failed his own expectations of himself to save the day and make everything right. The contemporary audience recognizes the realism of the situation. As Stallone states in his interview, "The male is [only] the illusion of the protector and guardian, . . . [b]ecause in this day and age, there is no security he can offer" (94). By now the audience realizes that a hero cannot always save the day in a conventional sense. In an odd way, viewers even appreciate his failure because it has knocked all of his arrogance out of him and left only an exposed, vulnerable character.

A contemporary audience can especially relate to the issues of family breakdown, recognizing in Donnie's situation the roots of the culture of estrangement and divorce which is so widespread today. Violating the conventional lone male gangster/cop figure, Joe Pistone has not only a wife but three small daughters hidden away in suburbia, and he can't tell them anything about his job without putting them at risk. His visits home are less and less frequent, sometimes months apart, due to the consuming nature of his "job." Although viewers can see from the start the tenderness and love he has for his wife

and daughters, his prolonged absences and broken

promises (he misses his daughter's first Communion) lead

to intensifying arguments between him and his wife. As

she constantly reminds him, his job is tearing their home

apart, and not knowing what he is doing makes it all the

more unbearable. Pistone knows, as his identification with

the Mafia grows deeper and deeper, that his involvement

has serious consequences for his family, and this

mounting pressure becomes impossible to resolve when

weighed against the life of Lefty Ruggiero.

◀ Analysis of relationships with other characters

Regarding the role of women in Mafia movies, Mellen

points out that "well into the seventies the male protagonist

of films from *The Godfather* (I or II) to *Serpico* uses women

solely to discard them" (327). Wives in *The Godfather* are

cheated on, lied to, and in one case, violently beaten. At a

pivotal moment at the end of the movie, the wife of Michael

Corleone tearfully asks him if he has ordered the death of

his sister's husband, and he looks directly into her eyes and

lies, saying he did not. She smiles and believes him. Her

character is, in fact, constantly under the thumb of her

husband who misleads her, ignores her, and coerces her

into marrying him after not contacting her for over a year.

◀ Contrasting example

She and the other women in the movie are not once consulted or listened to, no matter how much their husbands' actions affect their lives.

Donnie Brasco could have been made in precisely the same way. Pistone's wife Maggie is, after all, left at home for months at a time while her husband is off doing his job for the FBI. However, Newell makes the relationship between them a pivotal storyline in the movie. Repeatedly in the course of the narrative, interrupting the Mafia sequences, the audience sees Pistone call or visit home, reinforcing his identity as a husband and father. Viewers also note the progression as his relationship begins to sour. The lowest point comes when Pistone shows up at his home in the middle of the night to retrieve a bag containing $3 million in cash and confronts Maggie, who has found it and hidden it. When she tells him that he has become "like one of them," he strikes her, and both recoil in surprise, less shocked at the blow than at the realization of what their marriage has become. At this critical moment, he tries to tell her the truth. He awkwardly explains the situation with Lefty and his fear of being responsible for his death. He tells her that he is not sure of what is right anymore. He tells her, "I'm not like them.

Contrasting example related to film ▶

Incident from film substantiates interpretation ▶

Quotation from film ▶

I am them." It is evident that the troubles of Pistone's

marriage hurt himself as much as his wife, and in a sense,

dealing with them takes more courage than risking his life

as an undercover agent in the Mafia. The film treats this

relationship delicately, and the woman here is not merely

discarded or lied to, but confronted and confided in, with

her concerns presented as clearly as his own.

What makes Pistone's situation so compelling is that

he starts out believing that he can be one of the traditional

"solitary heroes who solve all problems for themselves"

(Mellen 23) and instead comes up against situations that ◄ Source identified in citation

are too difficult to handle. Joe Pistone slaps his wife, not to

exert his male dominance, but because he has lost control.

When he tries to make things right, he doesn't sweep her ◄ Detail from film supports interpretation

into his arms (and probably have his way with her, in the

true tradition of male heroes); he is almost frightened to

make a move and instead makes a gesture—kissing the

back of her head—to try and reestablish the emotional (not

sexual) intimacy between them. In his early scenes with

Lefty, Pistone is noticeably on his guard and detached

from the affection Lefty is developing for him; later, when

he has the opportunity to be promoted within the ranks of

the mob and Lefty feels betrayed, Pistone tries to express

his devotion by visiting him at the hospital where his son

has overdosed. When Lefty orders him to leave, he refuses.

These gestures are some of Pistone's most heroic acts,

at least as Newell presents it. Although he is given a medal

and a check for $500 at the end of the movie for his

undercover work (which is enough to secure scores of

convictions), his feelings about it are clearly mixed; his

loyalty to the FBI has been disintegrating as he has lost

faith in their good guy/bad guy rhetoric, and his primary

concern—Lefty's safety—is now uncertain. His success in

infiltrating a group of depressed Brooklyn wiseguys is now

a cause for guilt. Pistone's ambivalence and impotence are

"like a version of *Death of a Salesman* . . . about a man at

the end of his tether and at the end of his time, realizing

that his whole life [has come] down to the point, really, of

a cheap [reward], but set in mob terms" (Newell).

Return to detail used in first
paragraph ▶

It is at this point at the end of the movie, as Pistone

accepts his reward and his wife tells him it's all over, that

Newell returns to the extreme close-up of Depp's eyes,

and the audience sees how troubled they are. Viewers are

left with that image, indicating that Newell intended for

them to leave the theater asking themselves what it was all

for—whether doing his job was really the right thing or not. True to life, there is no easy, happy ending, in which a man can die in battle or save the day and thus fulfill his "masculine" duties. What matters, however, as viewers return to that close-up, is that they have seen Joe Pistone/Donnie Brasco's vulnerability and his devotion within his relationships. If he feels confused or uncertain at the end, it is because he has faced these emotional issues, which are far more subtle than the challenges related to his job. The audience has seen him show more courage in his private struggles than John Wayne ever did out on the frontier and can applaud him for that.

Like many films, *Donnie Brasco* is a cultural reflection of its makers and the audience, who were trying to come to grips with the changing view of the white male's place in society since the 1970s. By 1999, the sensitive, flawed hero was joined by what Chris Holmlund calls the "macho [man] in crisis," who acts out his frustrations in movies like *Fight Club* and *Magnolia* (229). Holmlund echoes the argument of social critic Susan Bordo that things like "cosmetic surgery and androgynous fashion were turning masculinity into a fluid, problematic category" for American men at the cusp of the 21st century (229), and that violence seemed to be a

◄ Return to thesis

natural antidote to the confusion. She notes, however, that such violence has been used ironically by some filmmakers as an acknowledgment that traditional expressions of masculinity are "mere performance" (229).

Within a few years, however, a version of the straightforward hero of yore came roaring back in reaction to the anger and fear Americans felt after the terrorist attacks on 11 September 2001. In those first few years after 9/11, Susan Faludi observed "a powerful resurgence in traditional sex roles and a glorification of he-man virility as embodied by [John] Wayne, the ur-savior of virtuous but helpless damsels in distress." She points to Steven Spielberg's 2005 film *War of the Worlds* as an example of how American films tried to reshape and reclaim masculinity in the mid-2000s: "'It's some bizarre, weirdly out-of-proportion fixation, . . . an exaltation of American masculinity in an intergalactic crisis'" (qtd. in Cohen). The terror and anger the nation experienced as a result of 9/11 felt nearly that epic to most Americans for years, but with the diminishing sense of panic by the end of the decade, American films have turned an eye toward other kinds of masculinity.

Relates to modern cinema ▶

Since 2007, writers and directors seem to have adopted a near-schizophrenic approach to capturing the changing idea of modern American masculinity on film. Romantic

comedies have offered up a new kind of hero: the pasty,

overweight underachiever; and with ticket sales soaring for

such films, the less-than-heroic leading man is suddenly in

vogue in virtually every film genre in Hollywood. More than

ever, hapless men, incapable of or unwilling to assume the

alpha-male stance, have come to symbolize masculinity in

American films. Christopher Goodwin bemoans this "sorry

state of masculinity in American movies today" and points

out that even action heroes are "schlub[s] . . . pathetic, if

well-meaning, losers [who] inevitably end up with the hottest

chicks." He blames the trend, born in films like *Forgetting*

Sarah Marshall and *Knocked Up,* in part on "wish fulfillment

for most men, who can't imagine scoring so high" and on the

acceptance of everyone's inner "nerd" (8). In looking at the ◄ Paraphrase

proliferation of comedic "schlemiel" protagonists, David

Buchbinder also touches on traditional masculinity as

"performance" and explores whether the schlemiel is

popular because he is indicative of men who refuse to live by

such artificial constraints (235) or because he makes them

feel more capable when measured against him (236).

    This Hollywood portrayal of masculinity perhaps

signals a paradigm shift in how women see men and,

more important, how they see themselves. Guy Garcia says that the American man's identity crisis is thanks to the emergent power of women. He claims that as women make strides in education and the business world, men are struggling with "the very definition of what it means to be a man" (185). Garcia believes that Americans enjoy "shows like *Ice Road Truckers* and *Deadliest Catch,* which glorify men who do dangerous, physically demanding jobs, [and which] have struck a nostalgic chord in the zeitgeist" (185). Perhaps to rage against this emotional paralysis, some filmmakers are introducing a new level of brutality in dramatic films and shifting the focus from the traditional hero onto a sinister figure, who would normally be identified as the antagonist. Ong Sor Fern cites two examples of films that concentrate on sadistic antiheroes, *There Will Be Blood* and *No Country for Old Men*. Fern muses, "It is tempting, even inevitable, to infer that this current obsession with strong male figures has something to do with the lack of [them] in America today." Buchbinder also sees films that promote traditional masculinity as Hollywood's "nostalgic" attempt to pacify "a certain hysteria, an anxiety on the part of at least some men that a familiar form of masculinity may be fading"

(243). In the age of the metrosexual, the popularity of these testosterone-fueled escapades is an attempt to rehabilitate our definition of masculinity and reclaim a portion of the power white men felt during the days of *Dirty Harry*.

Given Mellen's assertion of the cyclical pattern of masculinity in American cinema, though, we can only hope that it won't be long before we see a renaissance of the enlightened hero, at his best when he is true-to-life, flawed so we can identify with him but not so flawed that we spend our time laughing at his ineptitude. We need the occasional stoic cowboy or renegade cop, but sometimes we really want a hero we can admire and emulate because he is able to triumph in the end despite his personal struggles. Such a depiction of masculinity would be a welcome alternative to the two extreme portraits that permeate American films today. Perhaps if we could agree on what masculinity means in 21st-century America, we wouldn't need to turn every good guy into one of Goodwin's "schlubs," nor would we need to bathe in the glorified violence of the antihero who rages against his social and cultural impotence. We could once again celebrate the personal triumphs of our Donnie Brascos, who can be both human and heroic.

Works Cited

Blackwelder, Rob. "Donnie Brasco." *SPLICEDwire Film Review and Feature Content Services*, www.splicedwire.com/97reviews/donnie.html.

Buchbinder, David. "Enter the Schlemiel: The Emergence of Inadequate or Incompetent Masculinities in Recent Film and Television." *Canadian Review of American Studies,* vol. 38, no. 2, 2008, pp. 227–45. *Project Muse,* muse.jhu.edu/article/251556/pdf.

Cohen, Patricia. "Towers Fell, and Attitudes Were Rebuilt: An Interview with Susan Faludi." *The New York Times,* 27 Sept. 2007, late ed., p. B10, www.nytimes.com/2007/09/27/arts/design/27falu.html.

Donnie Brasco. Directed by Mike Newell, performance by Johnny Depp, Tristar, 1997.

Fern, Ong Sor. "There Will Be Masculinity: Two Oscar-Nominated Films Look at What It Means to Be a Man in the Context of American Society." *The Straits Times.com,* 14 Feb. 2008.

Garcia, Guy. "Men: The New Misfits." *Fortune,* 13 Oct. 2008, pp. 185–6.

Begins new page; Title 1 inch below top of page and centered ▶

All lines double-spaced, including title and entries ▶

Entries in alphabetical order ▶

First line at margin; Next lines indented ½ inch or 5 spaces ▶

Article title in quotation marks ▶

Goodwin, Christopher. "Enter the Flat Pack: The Sorry State of Masculinity in American Movies." *Times Online* [London], 27 Apr. 2008, Culture sec., p. 8, www.thetimes.co.uk/article/the-sorry-state-of-masculinity-in-american-movies-stlndsgwlhr.

Holmlund, Chris. "1999: Movies and Millennial Masculinity." *American Cinema in the 1990s: Themes and Variations,* edited by Chris Holmlund, Rutgers UP, 2008, pp. 225–48.

Mellen, Joan. *Big Bad Wolves: Masculinity in American Film.* Pantheon, 1977.

Newell, Mike. "Donnie Brasco-Mike Newell Interview." *YouTube,* uploaded by Buzzati, 30 June 2007, www.youtube.com/watch?v=neDvCIbM5wY.

Schickel, Richard, et al. "Depp Charge." *Time,* 3 Mar. 1997, content.time.com/time/magazine/article/0,9171,986001,00.html.

Stallone, Sylvester. "The Masculine Mystique." *Esquire,* Dec. 1996, pp. 89–96.

Wloszczyna, Susan. "*Donnie Brasco*: A High Point for Lowlifes." *USA Today,* 28 Feb. 1997, p. 1D.

◄ Book title italicized

◄ Video title in quotation marks

PART

5

AP LANGUAGE AND COMPOSITION PRACTICE EXAM

SECTIONS AT A GLANCE

Section I—Multiple Choice

Section II—Free Response
- Synthesis Essay
- Analysis Essay
- Argument Essay

Section I—Multiple Choice

⏱ **1 hour** • **Number of Questions: 45**

Directions: This part consists of selections from prose works and draft passages. Questions relate to content, form, style, and revision. After reading each passage, choose the best answer to each question.

Note: Pay particular attention to the requirement of questions that contain the words NOT or EXCEPT.

Questions 1-13 refer to the passage below.
(The following passage is from a psychology book published in the twentieth century.)

The shortcomings of modern fairy stories highlight the elements which are most enduring in traditional fairy tales. Tolkien describes the facets which are necessary in a good fairy tale as fantasy, recovery, escape, and
5   consolation—recovery from deep despair, escape from some great danger, but, most of all, consolation. Speaking of the happy ending, Tolkien stresses that all complete fairy stories must have it. It is a sudden joyous 'turn.' . . . However fantastic or terrible the
10   adventure, it can give to child or man that hears it, when the 'turn' comes, a catch of breath, a beat and lifting of the heart, near to tears.[45]

How understandable, then, that when children are asked to name their favorite fairy tales, hardly any
15   modern tales are among their choices.[46] Many of these new tales have sad endings, which fail to provide the escape and consolation which the fearsome events in the fairy tale make necessary, to strengthen the child for meeting the vagaries of his life. Without such
20   encouraging conclusions, the child, after listening to the story, would feel that there is indeed no hope of extricating himself from the despairs of his life.

In the traditional fairy tale, the hero is rewarded and the evil person meets his well-deserved fate, thus
25   satisfying the child's deep need for justice to prevail. How else can a child hope that justice will be done to him, who so often feels unfairly treated? And how else can he convince himself that he must act correctly, when he is so sorely tempted to give in to the asocial
30   proddings of his desires? Chesterton once remarked that some children with whom he saw Maeterlinck's play *The Blue Bird* were dissatisfied "because it did not end with the Day of Judgment, and it was not revealed to the hero and the heroine that the Dog had
35   been faithful and the Cat faithless. For children are innocent and love justice, while most of us are wicked and naturally prefer mercy."[47]

One may rightly question Chesterton's belief in the innocence of children, but he is absolutely correct
40   in observing that the appreciation of mercy for the unjust, while characteristic of a mature mind, baffles

the child. Furthermore, consolation not only requires, but is the direct result of, justice (or, in the case of adult listeners, mercy) being done.

45   It seems particularly appropriate to a child that exactly what the evildoer wishes to inflict on the hero should be the bad person's fate—as the witch in "Hansel and Gretel" who wants to cook children in the oven is pushed into it and burned to death, or the

50 usurper in "The Goose Girl" who names and suffers her own punishment. Consolation requires that the right order of the world is restored; this means punishment of the evildoer, tantamount to the elimination of evil from the hero's world—and then

55 nothing stands any longer in the way of the hero's living happily ever after.

45 J.R.R. Tolkien, *Tree and Leaf* (Boston: Houston Mifflin, 1965).
46 Mary J. Collier and Eugene L. Gaier, "Adult Reactions to Preferred Childhood Stories," *Child Development*, vol. 29 (1958).
47 G.K. Chesterton, *Orthodoxy* (London: John Lane, 1909).
Maurice Maeterlinck, *The Blue Bird* (New York: Dodd, Mead, 1911).

1. In the passage, the author contrasts traditional and modern fairy tales primarily to
    A) show the difference between modern and traditional stories
    B) elaborate on the child's need for justice and distaste for mercy
    C) criticize the cruel nature of traditional tales
    D) develop an argument in favor of more lenient stories for children
    E) demonstrate his broad knowledge of children's literature and its applicability to modern psychology

2. The author's primary purpose of the first paragraph (lines 1-12) is to
    A) establish himself as knowledgeable in the field of psychology
    B) call attention to Tolkien's work and cite him as an expert
    C) argue that all fairy tales have four necessary components in order to be included in the genre
    D) encourage readers to consider all aspects of analysis when reading fairy tales
    E) explain Tolkien's framework as a useful mechanism for analyzing fairy tales

3. In the final paragraph of the passage, the author uses exemplification to
    A) offer abstract theories that apply to the analysis the author has provided
    B) connect his analysis back to the first paragraph's listing of "facets"
    C) prove that children are capable of enjoying fairy tales that do not follow the framework established by Tolkien
    D) provide concrete examples of fairy tales that satisfy a child's understanding of the world
    E) entertain the reader by referencing stories they are sure to remember from childhood

4. The speaker's use of dashes in the final paragraph contributes most to
   A) providing a sense that the piece has not been thoroughly edited
   B) offering a series of definitions necessary to understand the speaker's meaning
   C) connecting the stories to the analysis proffered
   D) suggesting that the speaker is unsure of the outcome
   E) implying that he does not know how to express his beliefs

5. Which of the following best describes the relationship between the first and second paragraphs?
   A) The first paragraph presents a noted expert, while the second paragraph offers the unqualified opinions of the author.
   B) The first paragraph outlines a cause, and the second paragraph details the effect.
   C) The first paragraph establishes a framework for analysis, and the second paragraph applies that framework in a general sense to modern fairy tales.
   D) The second paragraph provides a process that could remedy the problems introduced in the first paragraph.
   E) The second paragraph describes concrete applications of the theory proposed in the first paragraph.

6. Words such as *evildoer* (line 46) and *usurper* (line 50) in the final paragraph imply which of the following about the author?
   A) The author believes that children are essentially bad and must be punished to become fully realized as adults.
   B) The author suggests that children should only be allowed to read positive fairy tales to protect them from the harsh realities of some stories.
   C) The author recognizes that children perceive the world as existing in binary opposition.
   D) The author believes that children must be exposed to both good and evil in order to develop an understanding of the world.
   E) The author indicates that children do not like fairy tales in which the "bad" character wins.

7. Which of the following best describes the rhetorical function of the last sentence of the second paragraph?
   A) Describes a process that must be followed
   B) Offers an extrinsic solution to an intrinsic problem
   C) Employs parallelism to convince the reader of the author's position
   D) Draws a conclusion after establishing a problematic situation
   E) Defines a cause after considering the effect

8. Based on the information provided in the notes, it can be inferred that
   A) all research conducted on this subject occurred during the twentieth century
   B) the author prefers books to journals
   C) many writers have already done considerable research on the analysis of fairy tales
   D) the author has conducted research from using primary and secondary texts
   E) fairy tale analysis has only been conducted by researchers in Great Britain and the United States

9. In paragraph four, the effect of the parenthetical information is to
   A) define a familiar term within a rhetorical context
   B) provide a clear counterargument to the information that has preceded it
   C) state directly an additional claim
   D) offer a concession to a previously stated argument
   E) qualify a concept, providing clarification

10. The passage is primarily about
    A) the literary interpretation of fairy tales
    B) children's psychological reaction to fairy tales
    C) the importance of writing and reading traditional fairy tales
    D) the hero's journey
    E) the superiority of reading fairy tales when compared to watching them performed on stage

11. The author's chief strategy in lines 38-42 ("One may . . . the child.") is to
    A) offer a concession as he makes a further claim
    B) prove an expert wrong
    C) directly claim the opposite of the conventional wisdom
    D) provide an accepted truism as complementary to his own analysis
    E) introduce an expert who agrees with his findings

12. In the context of the passage as a whole, the final paragraph serves to
    A) provide specific examples as evidence of the author's claims
    B) show how fairy tales in general agree with the author's analysis
    C) draw a conclusion from a body of evidence
    D) introduce an idea that will be proven in the next paragraph
    E) examine in detail an analytical situation that cannot be proven with the author's framework

13. Which of the following best describes the function of the third paragraph (lines 23–37)?
    A) Forces readers to question their existing assumptions about the topic
    B) Offers an example in support of the claim made in the previous paragraph
    C) Provides a transition to the next phase of analysis
    D) Explains the source of the author's exigence
    E) Establishes a claim then offers logical evidence in support of that claim

(The following passage is from a scientific article published in the twenty-first century.)

Earthquake early warning (EEW) systems rapidly
detect and characterize ongoing earthquakes in real
time to provide advance warnings of impending
ground motion. They use the information contained in
5 the early parts of the typically low-amplitude ground
motion waveforms to estimate the ensuing and
potentially large-amplitude ground motion. Because
EEW alert information can be transmitted faster than
seismic wave propagation speed, such ground motion
10 warnings may arrive at a target site before the strong
shaking itself, thereby providing invaluable time for
both people and automated systems to take actions to
mitigate earthquake-related injury and losses. These
actions might range from simple procedures like
15 warning people to get themselves to a safe location to
complex automated procedures like halting airport
takeoffs and landings (1). There are, however, basic
seismological principles that provide physical bounds
on how quickly an alert can be issued, how early a
20 user can receive a warning before strong shaking
arrives, and how accurately the strength of that
shaking can be estimated. Here, we address the first
two questions to establish the ultimate time
performance that a physically realistic EEW system
25 can achieve. This issue of how much advance warning
an EEW alert can provide for specific levels of ground
motion (that is, timeliness) has not been previously
addressed, leaving both user expectations and overall
system performance poorly defined.
30   EEW systems are in operation in many parts of
the world to provide warnings to populations at high
seismic hazard. Mexico has successfully been
operating an EEW system since 1991 (SASMEX) (2)
that alerts upon the occurrence of a large earthquake,
35 thereby implying some level of ground motion but
without quantitatively predicting it. In contrast, the
Japan Meteorological Agency (JMA) EEW system
that has been operating since 2007 (3) and the
ShakeAlert EEW system being developed for the west
40 coast of the United States (4) estimate the location and
magnitude of an earthquake, which are used in a
ground motion prediction equation (GMPE) to
calculate expected ground shaking; if the expected
ground motion is greater than a threshold that some
45 user has specified, that user is alerted. The JMA
system provides alerts to a subprefecture whenever
ground motions are expected to exceed JMA intensity
4 within that subprefecture; typically, initial alerts are
issued to subprefecture(s) closest to the epicenter, and
50 more distant regions are alerted if the area affected
grows, as the rupture evolves and magnitude estimates

are updated. The JMA system has issued hundreds of alerts, including alerts sent to several million people during the 2011 M9.0 Tohoku earthquake (5).

55   Existing estimates of the timeliness of EEW alerts are based on the assumption that either the final rupture size and extent is known immediately (6, 7) or the final magnitude of an earthquake can be determined from recordings of just several seconds of

60 the initial P wave (8, 9). However, others have argued that warning time will be limited because the final magnitude of an earthquake is undetermined at the time of nucleation (10–13). This argument is based on theoretical considerations (14) and observational

65 studies suggesting that the earliest phase arrivals of larger earthquakes are indistinguishable from small earthquakes (15–18). More recently, Meier et al. (19) demonstrated that small and large ruptures have indistinguishable onsets by examining recordings from

70 a large data set of shallow crustal earthquakes ($4 \leq M \leq 8$), suggesting that rupture onsets are not diagnostic of final rupture size.

REFERENCES AND NOTES

1. S. Wu, J. L. Beck, T. H. Heaton, ePAD: Earthquake probability-based automated decisionmaking framework for earthquake early warning. *Comput. Aided Civ. Inf.* **28**, 737–752 (2013).
2. J. M. Espinosa-Aranda, A. Cuellar, A. Garcia, G. Ibarrola, R. Islas, S. Maldonado, F. H. Rodriguez, Evolution of the Mexican Seismic Alert System (SASMEX). *Seismol. Res. Lett.* **80**, 694–706 (2009).
3. M. Hoshiba, K. Iwakiri, N. Hayashimoto, T. Shimoyama, K. Hirano, Y. Yamada, Y. Ishigaki, H. Kikuta, Outline of the 2011 off the Pacific coast of Tohoku Earthquake (M_w 9.0): Earthquake early warning and observed seismic intensity. *Earth Planets Space* **63**, 7 (2011).
4. M. D. Kohler, E. S. Cochran, D. Given, S. Guiwits, D. Neuhauser, I. Henson, R. Hartog, P. Bodin, V. Kress, S. Thompson, C. Felizardo, J. Brody, R. Bhadha, S. Schwarz, Earthquake early warning ShakeAlert system: West coast wide production prototype. Seismol. Res. Lett. 89, 99–107 (2017).
5. Y. Fujinawa, Y. Noda, Japan's earthquake early warning system on 11 March 2011: Performance, shortcomings, and changes. *Earthquake Spectra* **29**, S341–S368 (2013).
6. T. H. Heaton, A model for a seismic computerized alert network. *Science* **228**, 987–990 (1985).
7. M. A. Meier, How "good" are real-time ground motion predictions from earthquake early warning systems. *J. Geophys. Res.* **122**, 5561–5577 (2017).
8. R. M. Allen, Probabilistic warning times for earthquake ground shaking in the San Francisco Bay Area. *Seismol. Res. Lett.* **77**, 371–376 (2006).
9. A. Zollo, M. Lancieri, S. Nielsen, Earthquake magnitude estimation from peak amplitudes of very early seismic signals on strong motion records. *Geophys. Res. Lett.* **33**, L23312 (2006).
10. H. Kanamori, Real-time seismology and earthquake damage mitigation. *Annu. Rev. Earth Planet. Sci.* **33**, 195–214 (2005).
11. P. Rydelek, S. Horiuchi, Earth science: Is earthquake rupture deterministic? *Nature* **442**, E5–E6 (2006).
12. P. Rydelek, C. Wu, S. Horiuchi, Comment on "Earthquake magnitude estimation from peak amplitudes of very early seismic signals on strong motion records" by Aldo Zollo, Maria Lancieri, Stefan Nielsen. *Geophys. Res. Lett.* **34**, L20302 (2007).
13. S. Yamamoto, P. Rydelek, S. Horiuchi, C. Wu, H. Nakamura, On the estimation of seismic intensity in earthquake early warning systems. *Geophys. Res. Lett.* **35**, L07302 (2008).

14. T. Sato, H. Kanamori, Beginning of earthquakes modeled with the Griffith's fracture criterion. Bull. *Seismol. Soc. Am.* **89**, 80–93 (1999).

15. J. Mori, H. Kanamori, Initial rupture of earthquakes in the 1995 Ridgecrest, California sequence. *Geophys. Res. Lett.* 23, 2437–2440 (1996).

16. W. L. Ellsworth, G. C. Beroza, Observation of the seismic nucleation phase in the Ridgecrest, California, earthquake sequence. *Geophys*. Res. Lett. **25**, 401–404 (1998).

17. D. Kilb, J. Gomberg, The initial subevent of the 1994 Northridge, California, earthquake: Is earthquake size predictable? *J. Seismol.* **3**, 409–420 (1999).

18. T. Uchide, S. Ide, Scaling of earthquake rupture growth in the Parkfield area: Self-similar growth and suppression by the finite seismogenic layer. *J. Geophys. Res.* **115**, B11302 (2010).

19. M.A. Meier, J. P. Ampuero, T. H. Heaton, The hidden simplicity of subduction megathrust earthquakes. *Science* **357**, 1277–1281 (2017).

14. In the context of the passage, the word *mitigate* (line 13) can be best explained to mean
   A) appease
   B) lessen
   C) intercede
   D) weaken
   E) resolve

15. The first sentence of the passage, "Earthquake . . . ground motion." (lines 1-4), functions to
   A) present the author's opinion as to the importance of the technology
   B) propose the need for the adoption of new technology
   C) define the technology described in the article
   D) introduce refinements to an existing understanding of a technology
   E) suggest that adoption of technology may be too hasty

16. The references and notes provided for the article suggest all EXCEPT:
   A) The topic has been studied in a variety of countries.
   B) The topic has been addressed by several different scientific organizations.
   C) Researchers began considering this phenomenon in 1985.
   D) The research has been reported predominantly by academic journals.
   E) California has been a location of considerable research.

17. In paragraph 3, the author offers references 10-13 primarily to
   A) provide additional information related to the P wave
   B) introduce theoretical considerations regarding larger earthquakes
   C) suggest that research conducted from 2005-2008 has since been disproven
   D) acknowledge the disagreement that exists among experts regarding timeline analysis
   E) offer a definitive source for discussions of nucleation

18. What is the main focus addressed by the article?
   A) warning people to get themselves to a safe location (line 15)
   B) complex automated procedures like halting airport takeoffs and landings (lines 16-17)
   C) basic seismological principles that provide physical bounds (lines 17-18)
   D) how quickly an alert can be issued and how early a user can receive a warning before strong shaking arrives (lines 19-21)
   E) how accurately the strength of that shaking can be estimated (lines 21–22)

19. Between the first and second paragraphs, the author shifts from
    A) defining terminology to recognizing locations in the world where the technology has been developed
    B) identifying uses of the technology to describing its impact when used
    C) providing important research guidelines to recognizing the limitations of the technology
    D) analyzing seismological principles to applying those principles
    E) introducing the purpose of the paper to identifying specific examples of the technology's current usage

20. Taken as a whole, the passage is best described as
    A) a narrative account of earthquake survival
    B) a press release for an early warning system that will soon be available
    C) a description of an ongoing debate within the scientific community
    D) an article written for science teachers to provide current research
    E) a discussion of current research in a specific scientific field

21. The series of notes in paragraph 3 serves to
    A) reference other experts within the scientific community to establish the groundwork for continuing research
    B) establish varying positions that exist within the scientific community
    C) provide readers with source material to use for further study
    D) show that other experts have agreed with the author's findings
    E) counter claims from those who believe that seismic activity does not exist

22. Which statement best describes the main idea of paragraph two?
    A) Countries do not agree on the best type of EEW to use.
    B) Developing countries lag industrialized countries in this technology.
    C) Many different EEW systems are already in existence and have been in use for many years.
    D) The JMA system in Japan is the most successful system in the world.
    E) The United States lags the rest of the world in this technology.

23. The beginning of paragraph three marks a shift from
    A) a discussion of Japan's EEW system to a mention of specific timelines
    B) non-research related information to research-related information
    C) theoretical discussion to concrete application of research
    D) specific solutions to generalizations of the problem being addressed
    E) a description of systems in deployment around the world to an overview of scientific research

24. What problem might researchers consider when discussing the "theoretical considerations" cited in line 64?
    A) Theoretical considerations cannot be proven.
    B) The observational studies are contrary to the theoretical considerations.
    C) Most modern studies do not agree with these theoretical considerations.
    D) Only one research article is cited, and that article is from 1999.
    E) The study does not include seismic analysis.

25. In context, the noun *rupture*, repeated in the passage, most clearly means
    A) break
    B) fault
    C) burst
    D) sever
    E) capture

Questions 26-30 are based on the following passage.

The passage below is a draft.

(1) Transportation issues plague millions of Americans who simply seek to arrive at work or school on time and without wasting the better part of their day commuting. (2) Traffic issues present some of the biggest problems confronting cities today, and these issues are getting worse in part due to the perpetuation of urban sprawl.

(3) As American cities expand, replacing farmland or forests with subdivisions, more roads must be built to alleviate traffic problems and allow people to commute even farther than before. (4) Additionally, wherever more homes are built, services inevitably follow. (5) These new schools, hospitals, and malls require even more roads, causing the whole process to start over again in what seems to be a perpetual circle.

(6) Some countries have enacted zoning laws to counteract urban sprawl and traffic congestion, limiting the amount of farmland that can be sold for housing developments and prioritizing building up instead of out. (7) By emphasizing the construction of public transportation and bike paths to get vehicles off the roads and rewarding people for car-pooling, these countries have significantly incentivized commuters to be smarter and more creative as they contemplate their transportation choices.

(8) In the Netherlands and Belgium, for example, people are not allowed to drive into major cities; instead, they are required to park on the outskirts of town and take buses into the city. (9) In Amsterdam, almost every road has bike lanes and almost everyone has a bicycle. (10) In Spain, residents of Barcelona, one of the world's most densely populated urban areas, enjoy the city's public transportation and "pedestrianized" streets—narrow mazes between four-to-seven-story buildings that lead to neighborhood cafes under shade trees.

(11) There is no question that transportation in the United States has become problematic. (12) The only question is this: How will we confront the looming dilemma? (13) It's time for the United States to follow these and similar practices of urban growth.

26. Which of the following sentences, if placed before sentence 1, would both capture the audience's interest and provide the most effective introduction to the topic of the paragraph?
    A) Some 250 million vehicles are driven each day in the United States.
    B) For the first time in human history, most people live in urban areas.
    C) Nearly 7 million police-reported motor vehicle crashes occurred in the United States in 2018.
    D) The time Americans spend in gridlock to and from congested urban areas equates to 35 workdays and $87 billion a year in lost productivity.
    E) The average American driver over his or her lifetime will drive enough miles to travel to the moon and back *three times*.

27. The writer wants to add a phrase at the beginning of sentence 6 (reproduced below), adjusting the capitalization as needed, to set up a comparison with the idea discussed in paragraph 2.

    Some countries have zoning laws to counteract urban sprawl and traffic congestion. . .

    Which of the following choices best accomplishes this goal?
    A) Furthermore,
    B) For example,
    C) Similarly,
    D) By contrast,
    E) In fact,

28. The writer wants to add the following sentence to the passage to provide additional explanation.

    New urbanization strategies break away from rings of superhighways and instead focus on a high-density neighborhood approach.

    Where would the sentence best be placed?
    A) Before sentence 6
    B) After sentence 6
    C) After sentence 7
    D) After sentence 8
    E) After sentence 9

29. In the fifth paragraph (sentences 11-13), the writer wants to add a concession and rebuttal. Which of the following claims would best achieve this purpose?
    A) The highway system the United States uses today to connect suburbs with core cities functions perfectly well, so there's no need to change it.
    B) Attempts to make Americans give up their suburbs and vehicles will go nowhere.
    C) Regaining time and productivity lost from traffic congestion is well worth the effort of limiting urban sprawl.
    D) It would be extremely costly for the United States to remove highways running through major cities, but it could be done.
    E) Americans might think limiting urban sprawl and traffic congestion is too difficult, but strategies used in other countries are successful and are utilized already in some U.S. cities.

30. The writer wants to add more information to the fourth paragraph (sentences 8-10) to support the main argument of the paragraph. All of these pieces of evidence help achieve this purpose EXCEPT which one?
    A) When one is not worried about finding a parking spot, a whole new appreciation of the cityscape opens up.
    B) By walking and biking, city dwellers also experience better health and cleaner air.
    C) The price of gasoline will eventually limit the luxury of driving long distances to work.
    D) Local hubs provide a sense of connectedness among neighbors in high-density urban areas.
    E) These strategies are underscored by the necessity of efficient and affordable mass transit.

Questions 31-36 are based on the following passage.

The passage below is a draft.

(1) During the 1300s and 1400s, an intellectual movement emerged in Italy and gradually spread across Europe, bringing about expanded commerce, increased wealth, and renewed interest in learning and art. (2) Ushering in an era marked both by a growth in scientific knowledge and a profusion in artistic development and expression, a single career dramatically demonstrates the power of this movement—the career of Italian scientist and artist Leonardo da Vinci.

(3) A driven man of unbounded curiosity, Leonardo was acknowledged as a genius in many fields, producing notebooks that contain notes, drawings, and diagrams covering a wide range of interests, from the movement of water and the mechanics of flight to the study of light. (4) In his own lifetime he was referred to as "the divine Leonardo," and his supporters had endless faith in his creativity and his capacity to accomplish the seemingly impossible. (5) Indeed, with so many interests and skills Leonardo struggled with attending to all of his many projects; instead, he was known to jump from one to another with such frequency that many remained unfinished. (6) Only a few of his paintings were actually completed, and his sculptures exist only in the written records of his contemporaries. (7) Living in distrust of intellectual competitors, he wrote his scientific studies backwards with his left hand so that reading them required a mirror in order to conceal his ideas from prying eyes. (8) Perhaps he was, as one biographer described him centuries after his death, a man who awoke too early in darkness while those around him remained asleep.

(9) Leonardo began work on the *Mona Lisa* around 1503. (10) Also known as La Gioconda, Mona Lisa was the wife of Francesco del Giocondo. (11) The painting's subject presents a direct gaze and mysterious smile that have fascinated art aficionados for centuries. (12) Additionally, the juxtaposition of light and shadow creates a dreamlike quality, augmenting the painting's mysterious charm. (13) In the style of the period, Mona Lisa lacks eyebrows, creating the idea that her forehead is unusually and dramatically high. (14) She sits calmly with hands folded casually, in front of a far-distant landscape of mountains, valleys, and rivers.

(15) Arguably the world's most famous portrait, the *Mona Lisa* clearly had special meaning for Leonardo since he continued working on it for the rest of his life. (16) Leonardo refused to part with the painting, which he perpetually claimed was unfinished. (17) It was an excuse he used until the day he died in 1519.

31. Consider sentence 2 (reproduced below). Which of the following versions of the sentence offers a clear, defensible thesis statement?

Ushering in an era marked both by a growth in scientific knowledge and a profusion in artistic development and expression, a single career dramatically demonstrates the power of this movement—the career of Italian scientist and artist Leonardo da Vinci.

A) (as it is now)
B) This era, that of Renaissance humanism, was marked by a growth in scientific knowledge and a profusion in artistic development and expression and is dramatically demonstrated by the work of Italian scientist and artist Leonardo da Vinci.
C) Often remembered as an eclectic inventor and brilliant artist, Leonardo da Vinci was a member of this movement.
D) Leonardo da Vinci's artistic achievements offer a glimpse into this movement, providing a singular example of an artist whose work has stood the test of time.
E) Although some might argue that ideals of Renaissance humanism are too complex to be distilled into a discussion of a single adherent, the life and artistic career of Leonardo da Vinci present a compelling argument for the artistic contributions of the movement.

32. The author wants to add a phrase at the beginning of sentence 6 (reproduced below), adjusting the capitalization as needed, to expand upon the idea discussed in sentence 5.

Only a few of his paintings were actually completed, and his sculptures exist only in the written records of his contemporaries.

Which of the following choices best accomplishes this goal?
A) Furthermore,
B) For example,
C) Similarly,
D) By contrast,
E) In fact,

33. Consider sentence 7 (reproduced below). Which of the following versions of the sentence most clearly and effectively conveys the author's ideas?

Living in distrust of intellectual competitors, he wrote his scientific studies backwards with his left hand so that reading them required a mirror in order to conceal his ideas from prying eyes.

A) (as it is now)
B) Distrustful of intellectual competitors, he wrote his scientific studies backwards with his left hand so that reading them required a mirror in order to conceal his ideas from prying eyes.
C) Distrustful of intellectual competitors and with a desire to conceal his ideas from prying eyes, Leonardo wrote his scientific studies backwards with his left hand so that reading them required a mirror.
D) Living in distrust of intellectual competitors, so that reading them required a mirror, he wrote his scientific studies backwards with his left hand in order to conceal his ideas from prying eyes.
E) Living in distrust of intellectual competitors, he wrote his scientific studies backwards with his left hand in order to conceal his ideas from prying eyes so that reading them required a mirror.

34. Which of the following sentences should be added to the opening paragraph in order to provide sufficient background information for students reading this passage in a college-level introductory world history class?
    A) Leonardo is oft-revered as one of the most important painters of the Italian Renaissance.
    B) This movement, better known as Renaissance humanism, combined the philosophical study known as utilitarianism with medieval scholasticism.
    C) Although Leonardo is best remembered as an artist, his scientific achievements are even more compelling than his artwork.
    D) As a humanist, Leonardo was ahead of his time, accomplishing more than anyone else.
    E) (do not add any of these)

35. Which of the following changes is most appropriate in order to maintain the tone of the passage?
    A) In sentence 11, change "aficionados" to "lovers" to uphold an intimate tone.
    B) In sentence 12, change "juxtaposition" to "contrast" to sustain a straightforward tone.
    C) In sentence 13, change "idea" to "illusion" to maintain a scholarly tone.
    D) In sentence 14, change "casually" to "strictly" to present a formal tone.
    E) (none of these)

36. Which of the following sentences provides the best claim to add as a topic sentence at the beginning of paragraph 3?
    A) (as it is now)
    B) The *Mona Lisa* is considered one of the most brilliant works ever created in the art world, and there are several reasons why.
    C) Leonardo was benefited by many important patrons, who became the objects of his most famous paintings.
    D) Perhaps no single work is more indicative of Leonardo's greatness than the attention to detail and the artistic genius embodied by the *Mona Lisa*.
    E) In addition to his many scientific discoveries and important inventions, Leonardo is known as a portrait painter.

Questions 37-45 are based on the following passage.
The passage below is a draft.

(1) Dotting the American landscape, Big Box stores, most of which are part of national chains, are usually housed in huge, warehouse-type buildings and carry a wide variety of goods that are sold at rock-bottom prices. (2) Proponents of Big Box stores—and they are many—cite the low price of goods to the consumer as the main benefit of these stores. (3) Certainly, for people living on a low or fixed income, the low prices these stores offer are a boon that may allow them to buy products they otherwise would not be able to afford. (4) Additionally, the vast size of the stores and the huge inventory they carry often allow a "one-stop shopping" experience that simplifies and streamlines shopping for busy consumers. (5) This saves time and may help support the environment by saving gas used for driving between stores. (6) In short, people perceive that they are getting good value for their money at a Big Box store, and in some ways, their perceptions are right.

(7) However, Big Box stores also have their detractors. (8) These opponents point out that items sold in Big Box stores are cheap because most are produced overseas by workers who get extremely low wages—wages far below what an American could live on (for example, $1–$2/hour). (9) Some people insist that although this wage is low by United States standards, it raises the standard of living for impoverished people in developing nations. (10) Others see this as unfair exploitation of cheap foreign labor.

(11) U.S. workers in Big Box stores are also often poorly paid, earning so little they may not earn enough to support their families. (12) Employees in many Big Box stores are paid at or just above the minimum wage. (13) So even though the stores do use local labor, their workers are not paid enough to invigorate a local economy, instead producing negative economic effects that ripple throughout the community. (14) Low-wage workers often do not have the money to spend in other local businesses; therefore, local restaurants, movie theaters, service providers, and others may see their businesses decline—losing money or even having to close.

(15) Loss of local customers affects the incentives for entrepreneurs to open new businesses. (16) If existing businesses are being shuttered because they cannot compete on price or variety with the Big Box stores, what chance has a new venture to compete with such huge retail establishments? (17) And there is little likelihood that a Big Box store will buy goods from a local start-up company instead of its far cheaper overseas suppliers.

(18) In societal terms, Big Box stores rarely help local communities, since the benefits they pass on to consumers in terms of low prices have been shown to undermine locally owned, or "mom and pop," stores. (19) These small shops simply cannot compete with the vast buying power—and resulting low per-unit cost—of the national chain stores. (20) Sometimes by choice, sometimes by necessity, local consumers choose to shop at a Big Box store, starving the "mom and pop" store of needed business. (21) As Big Box stores have proliferated, small locally owned stores have gone out of business, becoming increasingly rare throughout the country. (22) In many communities, "Main Street" is now lined with the shuttered storefronts of what once were locally owned stores, forcing consumers to go to the vast Big Box store at or near the mall miles away from the city center.

(23) Some view the demise of the "mom and pop" store as a necessary outgrowth of robust competitive capitalism, and it is true that market competition caused this decline. (24) The Mom and Pop who owned the "mom and pop" store spent the money they made in the community, probably shopping at other locally owned stores. (25) In contrast, the Big Box stores generally do not invest their profits in the communities in which they are found. (26) Instead, the profits from the Big Box store are channeled away from the local community and into the distant coffers at the corporation's headquarters. (27) Local money spent yields no local benefit. (28) The issue is complex, but the warning is clear: Consumers need to be aware of how and where they spend money affects their local economy.

37. Which of the following sentences, if placed after sentence 1, would clarify the definition of a Big Box store and provide the most effective introduction to the topic of the paragraph?
   A) Although these stores may vary regionally, some of the most widely recognized stores include Walmart and Target, which, combined, account for more than 8,000 stores.
   B) While Big Box prices are good, many people avoid shopping in these stores due to a fear of crowds.
   C) Many Big Box stores also have a significant online presence, encouraging shoppers to move their shopping off the grid.
   D) According to Walmart's corporate website, 75 percent of managers began their careers as hourly employees.
   E) Contributing to a national debt crisis, Big Box stores tempt consumers into spending billions of dollars—hundreds of billions to be exact.

38. The writer wants to add additional evidence to bolster the claim made in paragraph 3 (sentences 11-14). Which of the following sentences, if added after sentence 12, best meets this goal?
   A) The federal minimum wage, which is set at $7.25, has not been raised since 2009.
   B) Some areas have a mandatory minimum wage that is set higher than the federal minimum wage.
   C) Some economists argue that raising the minimum wage will create jobs by infusing more money into the economy.
   D) In fact, a person working full time at minimum wage will earn slightly more than the federal poverty guideline for a single person household, but will earn significantly below that guideline for a household with even one child.
   E) (none of these)

39. The writer originally wrote this as a draft of an essay for a college course, but now would like to submit it as an op-ed to a local newspaper in a community where a Big Box store is considering locating. Which of the following changes should the writer consider making?
   A) (no changes)
   B) Provide additional information on economic initiatives in the state.
   C) Incorporate jobs data from the local chamber of commerce or economic development authority.
   D) Interview the CEO of the Big Box store opening in the community.
   E) Offer a personal perspective as someone who enjoys shopping in Big Box stores.

40. The writer wants to add more information to the fourth paragraph (sentences 15-17) to support the main argument of the paragraph. All of the following pieces of evidence help achieve this purpose EXCEPT which one?

A) One of the most important factors of opening any new retail establishment is market analysis, and markets that are saturated by Big Box stores are seldom attractive for small business owners.

B) Often, the announcement of a Big Box retailer opening a new store in an area sounds a death knell for pre-existing "mom and pop" establishments, who know they will not be able to compete on pricing.

C) In addition to the higher price of purchasing from smaller, local manufacturers, Big Box stores often choose to order in large quantities for higher discounts—placing orders that cannot be met in size by smaller manufacturers.

D) Local manufacturing operations are at a distinct disadvantage when competing with large scale manufacturers because the cost of both raw materials and labor is higher for smaller companies.

E) Big Box stores may offer many jobs, but the jobs are not the highly sought-after jobs that exist in such areas as the technology sector.

41. Consider the passage as a whole. Which of the following revisions of sentence 6 (reproduced below) offers a clear, defensible thesis statement for this passage?

In short, people perceive that they are getting good value for their money at a Big Box store, and in some ways, their perceptions are right.

A) (as it is now)

B) Although some people do not approve of Big Box stores, they offer the best value for consumers.

C) In addition to providing an overall positive value proposition, Big Box stores are good for the economy.

D) While consumers may perceive that Big Box stores provide the best value for their money, additional indicators of a healthy economy complicate this perception.

E) Big Box stores, while good for the economy, prove problematic for issues of international trade.

42. The writer has decided to rewrite sentence 16 (reproduced below) as a declarative sentence rather than as a question. Which of the following versions most clearly conveys the writer's argument?

If existing businesses are being shuttered because they cannot compete on price or variety with the Big Box stores, what chance has a new venture to compete with such huge retail establishments?

A) Big Box stores force "mom and pop" shops out of business, proving that no new business can survive when they are present.

B) When entrepreneurs see existing businesses being driven out of business because they cannot compete with Big Box stores, they have little incentive to take on the risk of beginning new ventures.

C) It is the business model of the Big Box store to prevent any new small businesses from being started in communities they have overtaken; therefore, new small businesses stand no chance of success.

D) New ventures are never viable in areas with Big Box stores, which shutter local businesses by driving down prices to unmatchable levels.

E) (do not add any of these)

43. The writer wishes to offer an alternative perspective to that provided in sentence 23 (reproduced below).

    Some view the demise of the "mom and pop" store as a necessary outgrowth of robust competitive capitalism, and it is true that market competition caused this decline.

    Which of the following sentences best achieves the writer's objective?

    A) Others argue that market competition is not to blame.
    B) "Mom and pop" stores have simply outlived their usefulness in an era marked by cyber-shopping.
    C) Yet there are others who point out the hidden costs in this trend.
    D) Still others argue that capitalism itself is the problem.
    E) Capitalism, however, does not explain downturns in consumer spending.

44. The writer wants to add information to sentence 12 (reproduced below) to provide additional explanation.

    Employees in many Big Box stores are paid at or just above the minimum wage.

    Which sentence would best clarify the argument associated with the information provided by the writer?

    A) (as it is now)
    B) Employees in many Big Box stores are paid at or just above the minimum wage, which is set at the federal level and sometimes altered by local communities.
    C) While employees in many Big Box stores are paid at or just above the minimum wage, many leave their Big Box experience to open businesses of their own.
    D) Because employees in many Big Box stores are paid at or just above the minimum wage, prices are kept low enough for them to able to shop where they work.
    E) Although employees in many Big Box stores are paid at or just above the mandated minimum wage, critics argue that this is not a living wage, leaving many hourly employees at or below the poverty level.

45. In the fourth paragraph (sentences 15-17), the writer wants to add a concession and rebuttal. Which of the following claims would best achieve this purpose if added at the end of the paragraph?
    A) However, the fact that overseas products are cheaper simply means that American manufacturers are not doing their part to promote small business engagement.
    B) Telling people where they must shop will simply not work; those who wish to shop at Big Box stores will simply drive a little further.
    C) Reining in the Big Box stores and promoting local businesses will help both the U.S. manufacturing sector and small businesses.
    D) While some might say that the outlook is impossibly bleak for small business owners, community development agencies in many areas have successfully bolstered small businesses through publicity engagements and economic incentives.
    E) Supporting small businesses must be a communitywide effort, with consumers committed to ridding themselves both of predatory merchants and imported products.

Section II
Free-Response Questions
⏱ **2 hours, 15 minutes | 3 Questions**

Question 1: Synthesis

Suggested reading time: 15 minutes
Suggested writing time: 40 minutes

A debate rages between teenagers and parents and educators: How much sleep do teens actually need? Teens may argue that adequate sleep, while a precious commodity, is unattainable when faced with homework, part-time jobs, and extracurricular engagements. Parents and educators counter that rest is a necessity in order to optimize learning and development. As part of this debate, experts have questioned the best time to start and end the high school day for teenagers.

Carefully read the following six sources, including the introductory information for each source. Then synthesize information from at least three sources into a cohesive, well-written essay that evaluates the factors a school system should consider when deciding the best time to start the school day for high school students.

You may refer to the sources by their titles (Source A, Source B, etc.) or by the descriptions provided in parentheses.

Source A (American Academy of Sleep Medicine)
Source B (Crist)
Source C (Graph CDC)
Source D (Pignolet and Moore)
Source E (Graph Sleep and College GPA)
Source F (Hinton)

Academy of Sleep Medicine. "Review Suggests that Teens Benefit from Later High School Start Times." Press release. Dec. 14, 2016. Available from: https://aasm.org.

The following is from a press release issued by the American Academy of Sleep Medicine, a scientific nonprofit organization.

A review of the scientific literature by a workgroup composed of representatives from the American Academy of Sleep Medicine, Centers for Disease Control and Prevention, Sleep Research Society, and American Academy of Dental Sleep Medicine found that later high school start times are associated with positive outcomes among teens, including longer weekday sleep durations and reduced vehicular accident rates.

Results of a systematic review and meta-analysis of 18 peer-reviewed studies published prior to April 2016 show that sleep durations on school nights increased by an average of about 19 minutes when school started up to 60 minutes later, and total sleep time on school nights was about 53 minutes longer when the delayed school start time was more than 60 minutes later. Delayed high school start times also were associated with reduced motor vehicle accident rates, less subjective daytime sleepiness, and lower differences between sleep durations on school and weekend nights.

"Our review intended to bring some rigor to evaluating how later school start times affect various aspects of high school student health and performance," stated lead author Timothy I. Morgenthaler, MD, past president of the American Academy of Sleep Medicine and professor of medicine at Mayo Clinic in Rochester, Minnesota. "Many people believe that school start times are one of the big reasons students do not get enough sleep; a CDC study found that 85.6 percent of U.S. high schools started before 8:30 a.m., which is the earliest time recommended by the American Academy of Pediatrics. Because of this, there is a push to move school start times later."

The review is published in the Dec. 15 issue of the Journal of Clinical Sleep Medicine.

To promote optimal health, the American Academy of Sleep Medicine recommends that adolescents between the ages of 13 and 18 years should sleep 8 to 10 hours per 24 hours on a regular basis. However, CDC data show that about 69 percent of high school students sleep less than 8 hours on an average school night. According to the American Academy of Sleep Medicine, a natural shift in the timing of the body's internal "circadian" clock occurs during puberty, causing most teens to have a biological preference for a late-night bedtime, which can conflict with early school start times.

"Our nation's future is literally dependent upon the physical, mental, and educational excellence of our high school students," said Morgenthaler. "The most recent national surveys show that less than one third of high school students get enough sleep as recommended by the leading national authorities. This is of concern since inadequate sleep has been linked to worsened mental health, decreased ability to learn, increased obesity rates, increased motor vehicle accidents, and even increased substance abuse." . . .

Although the review found somewhat mixed support for the assertion that delaying school start times improved grades or standardized test scores, it did find that later school start times may be associated with a decrease in tardiness or truancy. Delayed school start times also may be associated with better behavioral health.

SOURCE B

The following is an article from a national news source.

When high schools start at 8:30 a.m. or later, attendance rates and graduation rates improve, according to a new study.

The study backs previous research that says additional sleep boosts psychological, behavioral and academic benefits for teens.

"So much research explains the impact of insufficient sleep on suicide, substance abuse, depression, auto accidents and more," said lead study author Pamela McKeever of Central Connecticut State University in New Britain.

"This connects the dots between the world of science and education," she told Reuters Health. "Through this, educators and parents can see how lack of sleep impacts the school indicators that we use to measure student success."

McKeever and colleague Linda Clark looked at school start times, graduation rates and attendance rates for 30,000 students in 29 high schools across seven states. They found that two years after a delayed start was implemented at these high schools, average attendance rates and graduation rates had increased several percentage points.

For example, the average graduation completion rate was 79 percent before the delayed start was implemented, and it was 88 percent afterward.

"This doesn't only impact our high school students. This impacts all of society," McKeever said. "As graduation rates improve, young adults experience less hardship after graduation, a lower chance of incarceration and a higher chance of career success."

Delayed bell times could close the achievement gap as well, McKeever and Clark wrote in Sleep Health, the journal of the National Sleep Foundation. When schools start later, students in lower socioeconomic categories are more likely to get to the bus on time. When they arrive at school on time, they're more likely to stay in class and graduate.

"When kids miss a bus early in the morning and that's their only form of transportation, they miss class and then soon the credits," said Kyla Wahlstrom of the University of Minnesota in Minneapolis, who wasn't involved with this study. "People don't understand the link between early wakeup times and graduation rates, but it's that direct."

Since the late 1990s, Wahlstrom and other researchers have suggested that delayed high school start times may help students. In 2014, she and her colleagues reported that in a three-year study with 9,000 students in eight public high schools across three states, attendance rates increased with a start time of 8:35 a.m. or later.

In December, the American Academy of Sleep Medicine advised that later school start times could improve sleep, reduce car accidents and reduce sleepiness. The American Academy of Pediatrics also recommends 8:30 a.m. as the earliest time to begin school.

But school policies have yet to change nationwide. The U.S. Centers for Disease Control and Prevention (CDC) reports that in 42 states, 75-100 percent of public schools start before 8:30 a.m.

Teens are "driven by biology to go to sleep later, and there's not much we can do about that, but school start times are the main reason they get up when they do," said Anne Wheaton, an epidemiologist at the CDC in Atlanta, in email to Reuters Health. Wheaton wasn't involved with this study.

A limitation of the study is that many variables affect attendance and graduation rates. Changes at the school level, such as different teachers, policies and the surrounding community itself, could affect students and their ability to complete class credits, extracurricular activities and afterschool jobs. Also, the data didn't measure sleep time or indicate whether students slept more due to delayed start times.

"The debate about school start time and adolescent sleep patterns has been going on for a number of years," said Mary Carskadon of the Sleep for Science Research Lab at Brown University in Providence, Rhode Island, who wasn't involved with this study.

"Efforts to delay the school bell are more likely to succeed best when parents and the teens themselves use better choices," she told Reuters Health by email. "This includes having a set bedtime and limiting arousing activities in the evening."

SOURCE C

U.S. Department of Health and Human Services, Centers for Disease Control and Prevention. "Recommended Hours of Sleep Per Day." How Much Sleep, March 2, 2017, www.cdc.gov/sleep/about_sleep/how_much_sleep.html.

The following graph uses data from the Centers for Disease Control and Prevention.

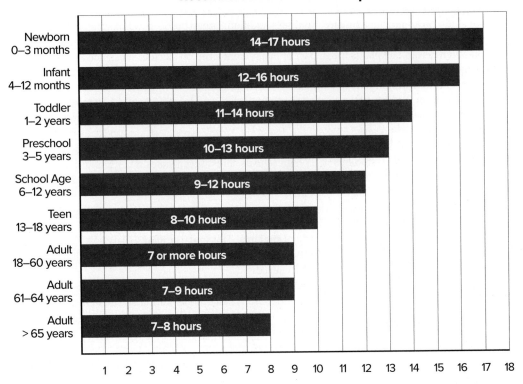

Recommended Hours of Sleep

Age Group	Recommended
Newborn 0–3 months	14–17 hours
Infant 4–12 months	12–16 hours
Toddler 1–2 years	11–14 hours
Preschool 3–5 years	10–13 hours
School Age 6–12 years	9–12 hours
Teen 13–18 years	8–10 hours
Adult 18–60 years	7 or more hours
Adult 61–64 years	7–9 hours
Adult > 65 years	7–8 hours

Sources: Centers for Disease Control and Prevention, National Sleep Foundation, American Academy of Sleep Medicine https://www.cdc.gov/sleep/about_sleep/how_much_sleep.html

SOURCE D

The following is from a national newspaper.

A year after this Memphis suburb decided to start middle- and high-school classes a bit later in the morning in hopes of improving student achievement, none of the seven other districts in the county have found the motivation to change.

As California considers a first-of-its kind bill to outlaw a school day starting before 8:30 a.m., school districts across 19 states have later start times this school year than last, according to the nonprofit advocacy group Schools Start Later.

Shelby County school leaders cite the cost, logistics and an overall lack of interest as factors why they're not changing. Some schools in each district start as early as 7 a.m. CT in spite of mountains of recent studies and lobbying from medical groups on the benefits of starting school no earlier than 8:30 a.m.

Germantown residents also aren't uniformly convinced their expensive change—$500,000 for this school year—was for the better.

"I'm not seeing any bright, shiny, happy kids kicking their heels together," Houston High Principal Kyle Cherry said.

The change in Germantown came through grassroots efforts, driven by parents incensed that some children riding the bus had to wake up as early as 5:45.

Cole Bowden, 16, of Germantown and a student at Houston High, started school 45 minutes later this past year, shifting to a 7:45 bell and pushing the end of school from 2 p.m. to 2:45. The rising junior doesn't like that it pushes his wrestling practice further into the afternoon, leaving less time for homework or a job.

But his sister, 14-year-old Paige Bowden, loved being able to start eighth-grade classes at 8 a.m. at Houston Middle School. . . .

When Germantown's district took shape in early 2014, a number of parents saw the opportunity to change something that had long bothered them, the 7 a.m. start time at Houston middle and high schools.

Parents came in droves to speak at board meetings about pushing back the time. But that spurred others to speak out in favor of the early time, citing after-school activities and jobs that would be affected if school started later.

Linda Fisher, the current board chairwoman and one of the founding members of the board, said early concerns were over finances.

At the time, schools in the district started at 7, 8 and 9 a.m. Pushing them all back would make elementary schools start too late, so more schools would have to start at the same time, requiring more buses and bus drivers.

The district has a contract with Durham School Services for its transportation, and as part of that it shares buses with Collierville Schools. The contract included a clause that if one district altered its start times, affecting their ability to share buses, that district would have to cover the increased costs for both school systems.

The board balked at a price tag in the hundreds of thousands of dollars, voting 3-2 against changing the times. They promised to review the issue the following year.

Parental voices intensified, and the district held meetings for parents, teachers and school leaders. The second vote was unanimous: Starting in the 2016-17 year, no school started before 7:45 a.m.

"I think everybody definitely was in agreement that it was the best decision for our students," Fisher said. "It was the financial aspect that held it off a year."

The total cost was about $1 million over the two remaining years of the contract with Durham and Collierville. That includes $350,000 paid to Collierville for the effect on its bus schedule. While that part of the cost goes away after the contract terminates at the end of this school year, Germantown will still have $200,000 to $300,000 in extra transportation costs each year in a district with fewer than 6,000 students. . . .

St. George's Independent School, which has a high school in Collierville, Tenn., but offers shuttles for students from almost 15 miles away in East Memphis, changed last year from an 8 a.m. start time to 8:30. Head of School Ross Peters said the move was a response to research saying the 8:30 time is healthier but was also a way to make the school as accessible as possible for students who live farther away. Instead of pushing back the end of the day, the school made class periods during the day longer and fewer, removing transitional time between classes, Peters said.

SOURCE E

Taylor, Daniel J., et al. "The Role of Sleep in Predicting College Academic Performance: Is It a Unique Predictor?" Behavioral Sleep Medicine, vol. 11, no. 3, 2013.

The following is from a scientific journal.

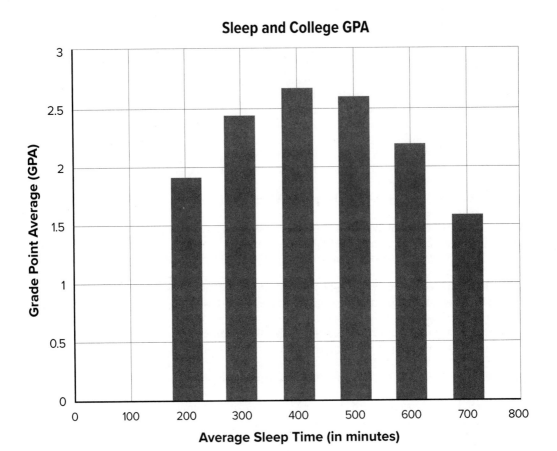

Source: Taylor, Daniel J., et al. "The Role of Sleep in Predicting College Academic Performance: Is It a Unique Predictor?" *Behavioral Sleep Medicine*, Volume 11, Issue 3, 2013.

SOURCE F

Hinton, Marva. "Later School Start Times for Teenagers Get Another National Endorsement." Text first appeared on Edweek.org on 4/21/2017. Reprinted with permission from Education Week.

The following is from a blog that appeared on the website of a professional publication for principals and teachers.

Another national organization of health-care professionals has come out in favor of school start times no earlier than 8:30 a.m. for middle and high school students.

The American Academy of Sleep Medicine (AASM) has now made the same recommendation as the American Academy of Pediatrics, the Centers for Disease Control and Prevention, the American Medical Association, and several other national organizations.

The AASM made its recommendation through a position statement, which was published this month in the Journal of Clinical Sleep Medicine.

The statement reads in part, "During adolescence, internal circadian rhythms and biological sleep drive change to result in later sleep and wake times. As a result of these changes, early middle school and high school start times curtail sleep, hamper a student's preparedness to learn, negatively impact physical and mental health, and impair driving safety."

AASM stresses that a lack of proper sleep is associated with many problems for students including poor school performance, obesity, increased depressive symptoms, and increased risk of car accidents.

Dr. Nathaniel F. Watson is the lead author of the AASM statement and the group's immediate past president. He's also a professor of neurology at the University of Washington.

AASM recommends that adolescents get eight to 10 hours of sleep per night. But that can be difficult when school starts before 8:30 a.m. Simply going to bed earlier is not a viable option for most teenagers. During adolescence, changes occur in the circadian rhythms of teens making it difficult for them to fall asleep before 11 p.m.

The group's policy statement includes statistics showing most teenagers are not getting enough sleep:

- Nearly 70 percent of high school students in the United States sleep seven hours or less on school nights;
- Only 23 percent sleep eight hours, while only 2 percent sleep 10 hours or more.

Watson said he hopes the AASM taking a stand will encourage more school boards around the country to adopt later school start times for middle and high school students.

"We're concerned about adolescent health and well-being," said Watson. "The evidence has continued to mount regarding the issue of the negative impact of early bell times on adolescent health."

One of the biggest dangers is sleepy teens getting behind the wheel of a car.

"The research shows younger people are more susceptible to the effects of drowsiness when driving," said Watson. "When you consider the problem of drowsy driving and fall-asleep crashes, it's this younger group of drivers, these novice drivers, who are most susceptible to being affected by this."

Statistics provided by the AASM show crash rates for teen drivers decline by 17 percent following a school start time delay of one hour.

Beyond Later Bell Times

Watson adds that morning bell times of 8:30 a.m. and later won't solve all of adolescents' sleep problems.

For schools that do push start times back, the AASM recommends that practices or other school-related events also don't take place before 8:30 a.m.

Watson also stresses that students and their parents have a role to play.

He has the following tips for healthy adolescent sleep:

- Consistent bedtimes and wake times both during the week and on the weekends
- A consistent bedtime routine
- No caffeine after 2 p.m.
- No exercise or eating right before bed
- Turn off all screens in the wind-down time before bed.

Question 2: Rhetorical Analysis

Suggested writing time: 40 minutes

With strong transcendentalist tendencies, Walt Whitman (1819-1892) is best known as the American poet who published *Leaves of Grass* in 1855. The following excerpt is from the preface to that work. Read the excerpt carefully. Then write an essay in which you analyze the choices Whitman makes to characterize the United States. Support your analysis with references to the text.

In your response you should do the following:
- Respond to the prompt with a claim that establishes a line of reasoning.
- Select and use evidence to develop and support your line of reasoning.
- Develop commentary that explains the relationship between the evidence and your claim, demonstrating an understanding of the rhetorical situation.
- Use appropriate grammar and punctuation in communicating your argument.

America does not repel the past or what it has
produced under its forms or amid other politics or the
idea of castes or the old religions . . . . accepts the
lesson with calmness . . . is not so impatient as has
5 been supposed that the slough still sticks to opinions
and manners and literature while the life which served its
requirements has passed into the new life of the
new forms . . . perceives that the corpse is slowly
borne from the eating and sleeping rooms of the house
10 . . . perceives that it waits a little while in the door . . .
that it was fittest for its days . . . that its action has
descended to the stalwart and wellshaped heir who
approaches . . . and that he shall be fittest for his days.
    The Americans of all nations at any time upon the
15 earth, have probably the fullest poetical nature. The
United States themselves are essentially the greatest
poem. In the history of the earth hitherto the largest
and most stirring appear tame and orderly to their
ampler largeness and stir. Here at last is something in
20 the doings of man that corresponds with the broadcast
doings of the day and night. Here is not merely a
nation but a teeming nation of nations. Here is action
untied from strings necessarily blind to particulars and
details magnificently moving in vast masses. Here is
25 the hospitality which forever indicates heroes . . . .
Here are the roughs and beards and space and
ruggedness and nonchalance that the soul loves. Here
the performance disdaining the trivial unapproached in
the tremendous audacity of its crowds and groupings
30 and the push of its perspective spreads with crampless
and flowing breadth and showers its prolific and
splendid extravagance. One sees it must indeed own
the riches of the summer and winter, and need never
be bankrupt while corn grows from the ground or the
35 orchards drop apples or the bays contain fish or men
beget children upon women.
    Other states indicate themselves in their deputies
. . . . but the genius of the United States is not best or
most in its executives or legislatures, nor in its

40 ambassadors or authors or colleges or churches or
parlors, nor even in its newspapers or inventors . . . but
always most in the common people. Their manners
speech dress friendship—the freshness and candor of
their physiognomy—the picturesque looseness of their
45 carriage . . . their deathless attachment to freedom—
their aversion to anything indecorous or soft or
mean—the practical acknowledgment of the citizens
of one state by the citizens of all other states—the
fierceness of their roused resentment— their curiosity
50 and welcome of novelty—their self-esteem and
wonderful sympathy—their susceptibility to a slight—
the air they have of persons who never knew how it
felt to stand in the presence of superiors—the fluency
of their speech—their delight in music, the sure
55 symptom of manly tenderness and native elegance of
soul . . . their good temper and open handedness—the
terrible significance of their elections—the President's
taking off his hat to them, not they to him—these too
are unrhymed poetry. It awaits the gigantic and
60 generous treatment worthy of it.

The largeness of nature or the nation were
monstrous without a corresponding largeness and
generosity of the spirit of the citizen. Not nature nor
swarming states nor streets and steamships nor
65 prosperous business nor farms nor capital nor learning
may suffice for the ideal of man . . . nor suffice the
poet. No reminiscences may suffice either. A live
nation can always cut a deep mark and can have the
best authority the cheapest . . . namely from its own
70 soul. This is the sum of the profitable uses of
individuals or states and of present action and
grandeur and of the subjects of poets.—As if it were
necessary to trot back generation after generation to
the eastern records! As if the beauty and sacredness of
75 the demonstrable must fall behind that of the mythical!
As if men do not make their mark out of any times! As
if the opening of the western continent by discovery
and what has transpired since in North and South
America were less than the small theatre of the antique
80 or the aimless sleepwalking of the middle ages! The
pride of the United States leaves the wealth and finesse
of the cities and all returns of commerce and
agriculture and all the magnitude of geography or
shows of exterior victory to enjoy the breed of full
85 sized men or one full sized man unconquerable and
simple.

Preface to *Leaves of Grass* by Walt Whitman. Brooklyn, New York: 1855.

Question 3: Argument Essay

Suggested writing time: 40 minutes

For centuries, philosophers have questioned the human quest for power. Are all humans subject to the corrupting influence of power, or are some able to remain morally upright even within its grasp?

"Power tends to corrupt and absolute power corrupts absolutely. Great men are almost always bad men, even when they exercise influence and not authority. . . ." —Lord Acton

"Much that passes as idealism is disguised hatred or disguised love of power." —Bertrand Russell

"Most people can bear adversity. But if you wish to know what a man really is, give him power." —Robert G. Ingersoll (also attributed to Abraham Lincoln)

Consider the nature of power and its influence on the individual. Then write an essay in which you take a position on the impact of the quest for power on the individual.

In your response you should do the following:
- Respond to the prompt with a claim that establishes a line of reasoning.
- Select and use evidence to develop and support your line of reasoning.
- Develop commentary that explains the relationship between the evidence and your claim, demonstrating an understanding of the rhetorical situation.
- Use appropriate grammar and punctuation in communicating your argument.

Sources:
–From "Letter to Archbishop Mandell Creighton" by Lord Acton (John Emerich Edward Dalberg), April 5, 1887. https://history.hanover.edu/courses/excerpts/165acton.html
–Bertrand Russell--Nobel Lecture. NobelPrize.org. Nobel Media AB 2018. Wed. 31 Oct 2018. https://www.nobelprize.org/prizes/literature/1950/russell/lecture/
–From *Reminiscences of Abraham Lincoln by Distinguished Men of His Time*. Allen Thorndike Rice, editor. Harper & Brothers Publishers, 1909, p. 427.

Glossary of Rhetorical Terms

A

Abstract/concrete patterns of language reflect an author's word choice. Abstract words (for example, *wisdom, power,* and *beauty*) refer to general ideas, qualities, or conditions. Concrete words name material objects and items associated with the five senses—words like *rock, pizza,* and *basketball.* Both abstract and concrete language are useful in communicating ideas. Generally, you should not be too abstract in writing. It is best to employ concrete words, naming things that can be seen, touched, smelled, heard, or tasted in order to support generalizations, topic sentences, or more abstract ideas.

Acronym is a word formed from the first or first few letters of several words, as in OPEC (Organization of Petroleum Exporting Countries).

Action in narrative writing is the sequence of happenings or events. This movement of events may occupy just a few minutes or extend over a period of years or centuries.

Alliteration is the repetition of initial consonant sounds in words placed closely next to each other, as in "her *t*ears *t*raced a *t*rail of *t*orment." Prose that is highly rhythmical or "poetic" often makes use of this method.

Allusion is a literary, biographical, or historical reference, whether real or imaginary. It is a "figure of speech" (a fresh, useful comparison) employed to illuminate an idea.

Analogy is a form of comparison that uses a clear illustration to explain a difficult idea or function. It is unlike a formal comparison in that its subjects of comparison are from different categories or areas. For example, an analogy likening "division of labor" to the activity of bees in a hive makes the first concept more concrete by showing it to the reader through the figurative comparison with the bees.

Analysis is a method of exposition in which a subject is broken up into its parts to explain their nature, function, proportion, or relationship. Analysis thus explores connections and processes within the context of a given subject. (See *causal analysis* and *process analysis.*)

Anaphora is the repetition of the same word(s) at the beginning of successive lines or sentences for tonal or poetic effect. For example, President Lincoln used anaphora in "We cannot dedicate, we cannot consecrate, we cannot hallow, this ground."

Anecdote is a brief, engaging account of some incident, often historical, biographical, or personal. As a technique in writing, anecdote is especially effective in creating interesting essay introductions and also in illuminating abstract concepts in the body of the essay.

Antecedent in grammar is the word, phrase, or clause to which a pronoun refers. In writing, antecedent also refers to any happening or thing that is prior to another or to anything that logically precedes a subject.

Antithesis is the balancing of one idea or term against another for emphasis.

Antonym is a word whose meaning is opposite to that of another word.

Aphorism is a short, pointed statement expressing a general truism or an idea in an original or imaginative way. Marshall McLuhan's statement that "the medium is the message" is a well-known contemporary aphorism.

Archaic language is vocabulary or usage that belongs to an earlier period and is old-fashioned today. The word *thee* for *you* is an archaism still in use in certain situations.

Archetypes are special images or symbols that, according to Carl Jung, appeal to the total racial or cultural understanding of a people. Such images or symbols as the mother archetype, the cowhand in American film, a sacred mountain, or spring as a time of renewal tend to trigger the "collective unconscious" of the human race.

Argumentation is a formal variety of writing that offers reasons for or against something. Its goal is to persuade or convince the reader through logical reasoning and carefully controlled emotional appeal. Argumentation as a formal mode of writing contains many properties that distinguish it from exposition. (See *assumption, deduction, evidence, induction, logic, persuasion, proposition,* and *refutation.*)

Assonance is defined generally as likeness or rough similarity of sound. Its specific definition is a partial rhyme in which the stressed vowel sounds are alike but the consonant sounds are unlike, as in *late* and *make.* Although more common to poetry, assonance can also be detected in highly rhythmic prose.

Assumption in argumentation is anything taken for granted or presumed to be accepted by the audience and therefore unstated. Assumptions in argumentative writing can be dangerous because the audience might not always accept the idea implicit in them. (See *begging the question.*)

Audience is that readership toward which an author directs his or her essay. In composing essays, writers must acknowledge the nature of their expected readers—whether specialized or general, minimally educated or highly educated, sympathetic or unsympathetic toward the writer's opinions, and so forth. Failure to focus on the writer's true audience can lead to confusion in language and usage, presentation of inappropriate content, and failure to appeal to the expected reader.

B

Balance in sentence structure refers to the assignment of equal treatment in the arrangement of coordinate ideas. It is often used to heighten a contrast of ideas.

Begging the question is an error or a fallacy in reasoning and argumentation in which the writer assumes as a truth something for which evidence or proof is actually needed.

C

Causal analysis is a form of writing that examines causes and effects of events or conditions as they relate to a specific subject. Writers can investigate the causes of a particular effect or the effects of a particular cause or combine both methods.

Basically, however, causal analysis looks for connections between things and reasons behind them.

Characterization is the creation of people involved in the action. It is used especially in narrative or descriptive writing. Authors use techniques of dialogue, description, reportage, and observation in attempting to present vivid and distinctive characters.

Chronology or chronological order is the arrangement of events in the order in which they happened. Chronological order can be used in such diverse narrative situations as history, biography, scientific process, and personal account. Essays that are ordered by chronology move from one step or point to the next in time.

Cinematic technique in narration, description, and occasionally exposition is the conscious application of film art to the development of the contemporary essay. Modern writers often are aware of such film techniques as montage (the process of cutting and arranging film so that short scenes are presented in rapid succession), zoom (intense enlargement of subject), and various forms of juxtaposition, and use these methods to enhance the quality of their essays.

Classification is a form of exposition in which the writer divides a subject into categories and then groups elements in each of those categories according to their relationships with one another. Thus a writer using classification takes a topic, divides it into several major groups, and then often subdivides those groups, moving always from larger categories to smaller ones.

Cliché is an expression that once was fresh and original but that has lost much of its vitality through overuse. Because expressions like "as quick as a wink" and "blew her stack" are trite or common today, they should be avoided in writing.

Climactic ordering is the arrangement of a paragraph or essay so that the most important items are saved for last. The effect is to build slowly through a sequence of events or ideas to the most critical part of the composition.

Coherence is a quality in effective writing that results from the careful ordering of each sentence in a paragraph and each paragraph in the essay. If an essay is coherent, each part will grow naturally and logically from those parts that come before it. Following careful chronological, logical, spatial, or sequential order is the most natural way to achieve coherence in writing. The main devices used in achieving coherence are transitions, which help connect one thought with another.

Colloquial language is conversational language used in certain types of informal and narrative writing but rarely in essays, business writing, or research writing. Expressions like "cool," "bro," or "I hear you" often have a place in conversational settings. However, they should be used sparingly in essay writing for special effects.

Comparison/contrast as an essay pattern treats similarities and differences between two subjects. Any useful comparison involves two items from the same class. Moreover, there must be a clear reason for the comparison or contrast. Finally, there must be a balanced treatment of the various comparative or contrasting points between the two subjects.

Conclusions are the endings of essays. Without a conclusion, an essay would be incomplete, leaving the reader with the feeling that something important has been left out. There are numerous strategies for conclusions available to writers: summarizing main points in the essay, restating the main idea, using an effective quotation, offering the reader the climax to a series of events, returning to the beginning and echoing it, offering a solution to a problem, emphasizing the topic's significance, or setting a new frame of reference by generalizing from the main thesis. A conclusion should end the essay in a clear, convincing, emphatic way.

Concrete (See *abstract/concrete.*)

Conflict in narrative writing is the clash or opposition of events, characters, or ideas that makes the resolution of action necessary.

Connotation/denotation are terms specifying the way a word has meaning. Connotation refers to the "shades of meaning" that a word might have because of various emotional associations it calls up for writers and readers alike. Words like *patriotism, pig,* and *rose* have strong connotative overtones to them. Denotation refers to the "dictionary" definition of a word—its exact meaning. Good writers understand the connotative and denotative value of words and control the shades of meaning that many words possess.

Context is the situation surrounding a word, group of words, or sentence. Often the elements coming before or after a certain confusing or difficult construction will provide insight into the meaning or importance of that item.

Coordination in sentence structure refers to the grammatical arrangement of parts of the same order or equality in rank.

D

Declarative sentences make a statement or assertion.

Deduction is a form of logic that begins with a generally stated truth or principle and then offers details, examples, and reasoning to support the generalization. In other words, deduction is based on reasoning from a known principle to an unknown principle, from the general to the specific, or from a premise to a logical conclusion. (See *syllogism.*)

Definition in exposition is the extension of a word's meaning through a paragraph or an entire essay. As an extended method of explaining a word, this type of definition relies on other rhetorical methods, including detail, illustration, comparison and contrast, and anecdote.

Denotation (See *connotation/denotation.*)

Description in the prose essay is a variety of writing that uses details of sight, sound, color, smell, taste, and touch to create a word picture and to explain or illustrate an idea.

Development refers to the way a paragraph or an essay elaborates or builds upon a topic or theme. Typical development proceeds either from general illustrations to specific ones or from one generalization to another. (See *horizontal/vertical.*)

Dialogue is the reproduction of speech or conversation between two or more persons in writing. Dialogue can add concreteness and vividness to an essay and can also help reveal character. A writer who reproduces dialogue in an essay must use it for a purpose and not simply as a decorative device.

Diction is the manner of expression in words, choice of words, or wording. Writers must choose vocabulary carefully and precisely to communicate a message and also to address an intended audience effectively; this is good diction.

Digression is a temporary departure from the main subject in writing. Any digression in the essay must serve a purpose or be intended for a specific effect.

Discourse (forms of) relates conventionally to the main categories of writing—narration, description, exposition, and argumentation. In practice, these forms of discourse often blend or overlap. Essayists seek the ideal fusion of forms of discourse in the treatment of their subject.

Division is that aspect of classification in which the writer divides some large subject into categories. Division helps writers split large and potentially complicated subjects into parts for orderly presentation and discussion.

Dominant impression in description is the main impression or effect that writers attempt to create for their subject. It arises from an author's focus on a single subject and from the feelings the writer brings to that subject.

E

Editorializing is to express personal opinions about the subject of the essay. An editorial tone can have a useful effect in writing, but at other times an author might want to reduce editorializing in favor of a better balanced or more objective tone.

Effect is a term used in causal analysis to describe the outcome or expected result of a chain of happenings.

Emphasis indicates the placement of the most important ideas in key positions in the essay. As a major principle, emphasis relates to phrases, sentences, and paragraphs—the construction of the entire essay. Emphasis can be achieved by repetition, subordination, careful positioning of thesis and topic sentences, climactic ordering, comparison and contrast, and a variety of other methods.

Episodic relates to that variety of narrative writing that develops through a series of incidents or events.

Essay is the name given to a short prose work on a limited topic. Essays take many forms, ranging from personal narratives to critical or argumentative treatments of a subject. Normally, an essay will convey the writer's personal ideas about the subject.

Etymology is the origin and development of a word—tracing a word back as far as possible.

Evidence is material offered to support an argument or a proposition. Typical forms of evidence are facts, details, and expert testimony.

Example is a method of exposition in which the writer offers illustrations in order to explain a generalization or a whole thesis. (See *illustration.*)

Exclamatory sentences in writing express surprise or strong emotion.

Exigence refers to the issue or situation that prompts a writer to write now.

Expert testimony as employed in argumentative essays and in expository essays is the use of statements by authorities to support a writer's position or idea. This method often requires careful quotation and acknowledgment of sources.

Exposition is a major form of discourse that informs or explains. Exposition is the form of expression required in much college writing, for it provides facts and information, clarifies ideas, and establishes meaning. The primary methods of exposition are *illustration, comparison and contrast, analogy, definition, classification, causal analysis,* and *process analysis* (see entries).

Extended metaphor is a figurative comparison that is used to structure a significant part of the composition or the whole essay. (See *figurative language* and *metaphor.*)

F

Fable is a form of narrative containing a moral that normally appears clearly at the end.

Fallacy in argumentation is an error in logic or in the reasoning process. Fallacies occur because of vague development of ideas, lack of awareness on the part of writers of the requirements of logical reasoning, or faulty assumptions about the proposition.

Figurative language as opposed to literal language is a special approach to writing that departs from what is typically a concrete, straightforward style. It is the use of vivid, imaginative statements to illuminate or illustrate an idea. Figurative language adds freshness, meaning, and originality to a writer's style. Major figures of speech include *allusion, hyperbole, metaphor, personification,* and *simile* (see entries).

Flashback is a narrative technique in which the writer begins at some point in the action and then moves into the past in order to provide crucial information about characters and events.

Foreshadow is a technique that indicates beforehand what is to occur at a later point in the essay.

Frame in narration and description is the use of a key object or pattern—typically at the start and end of the essay—that serves as a border or structure for the substance of the composition.

G

General/specific words are the basis of writing, although it is wise in college composition to keep vocabulary as specific as possible. General words refer to broad categories and groups, whereas specific words capture with force and clarity the nature of the term. General words refer to large classes, concepts, groups, and emotions; specific words are more particular in providing meanings. The distinction between general and specific language is always a matter of degree.

Generalization is a broad idea or statement. All generalizations require particulars and illustrations to support them.

Genre is a type or form of literature—for example, short fiction, novel, poetry, or drama.

Grammatical structure is a systematic description of language as it relates to the grammatical nature of a sentence.

H

Horizontal/vertical paragraph and essay development refers to the basic way a writer moves either from one generalization to another in a carefully related series of generalizations (horizontal) or from a generalization to a series of specific supporting examples (vertical).

Hortatory style is a variety of writing designed to encourage, give advice, or urge to good deeds.

Hyperbole is a form of figurative language that uses exaggeration to overstate a position.

Hypothesis is an unproven theory or proposition that is tentatively accepted to explain certain facts. A working hypothesis provides the basis for further investigation or argumentation.

Hypothetical examples are illustrations in the form of assumptions that are based on the hypothesis. As such, they are conditional rather than absolute or certain facts.

I

Identification as a method of exposition refers to focusing on the main subject of the essay. It involves the clear location of the subject within the context or situation of the composition.

Idiomatic language is the language or dialect of a people, region, or class—the individual nature of a language.

Ignoring the question in argumentation is a fallacy that involves the avoidance of the main issue by developing an entirely different one.

Illustration is the use of one or more examples to support an idea. Illustration permits the writer to support a generalization through particulars or specifics.

Imagery is clear, vivid description that appeals to the sense of sight, smell, touch, sound, or taste. Much imagery exists for its own sake, adding descriptive flavor to an essay. However, imagery (especially when it involves a larger pattern) can also add meaning to an essay.

Induction is a method of logic consisting of the presentation of a series of facts, pieces of information, or instances in order to formulate or build a likely generalization. The key is to provide prior examples before reaching a logical conclusion. Consequently, as a pattern of organization in essay writing, the inductive method requires the careful presentation of relevant data and information before the conclusion is reached at the end of the paper.

Inference involves arriving at a decision or opinion by reasoning from known facts or evidence.

Interrogative sentences are sentences that ask or pose a question.

Introduction is the beginning or opening of an essay. The introduction should alert the reader to the subject by identifying it, set the limits of the essay, and indicate what the thesis (or main idea) will be. Moreover, it should arouse the reader's interest in the subject. Among the devices available in the creation of good introductions are making a simple statement of thesis; giving a clear, vivid description of an important setting; posing a question or series of questions; referring to a relevant historical event; telling an anecdote; using comparison and contrast to frame the subject; using several examples to reinforce the statement of the subject; and presenting a personal attitude about a controversial issue.

Irony is the use of language to suggest the opposite of what is stated. Writers use irony to reveal unpleasant or troublesome realities that exist in life or to poke fun at human weaknesses and foolish attitudes. In an essay there may be verbal irony, in which the result of a sequence of ideas or events is the opposite of what normally would be expected. A key to the identification of irony in an essay is our ability to detect where the author is stating the opposite of what he or she actually believes.

Issue is the main question upon which an entire argument rests. It is the idea that the writer attempts to prove.

J

Jargon is special words associated with a specific area of knowledge or a particular profession. Writers who employ jargon either assume that readers know specialized terms or take care to define terms for the benefit of the audience.

Juxtaposition as a technique in writing or essay organization is the placing of elements—either similar or contrasting—close together, positioning them side by side in order to illuminate the subject.

L

Levels of language refer to the kinds of language used in speaking and writing. Basically, there are three main levels of language—formal, informal, and colloquial. Formal English, used in writing or speech, is the type of English employed to address special groups and professional people. Informal English is the sort of writing found in newspapers, magazines, books, and essays. It is popular English for an educated audience but still more formal than colloquial (conversational) English. Colloquial English is spoken (and occasionally written) English used in conversations with friends, employees, and peer group members; it is characterized by the use of slang, idioms, ordinary language, and loose sentence structure.

Linear order in paragraph development means the clear line of movement from one point to another.

Listing is a simple technique of illustration in which facts or examples are used to support a topic or generalization.

Logic as applied to essay writing is correct reasoning based on induction or deduction. The logical basis of an essay must offer reasonable criteria or principles of thought, present these principles in an orderly manner, avoid faults in reasoning, and result in a complete and satisfactory outcome in the reasoning process.

M

Metaphor is a type of figurative language in which an item from one category is compared briefly and imaginatively with an item from another category. Writers use such implied comparisons to assign meaning in a fresh, vivid, and concrete way.

Metonymy is a figure of language in which a thing is not designated by its own name but by another associated with or suggested by it, as in "The Supreme Court has decided" (meaning the judges of the Supreme Court have decided).

Mood is the creation of atmosphere in descriptive writing.

Motif in an essay is any series of components that can be detected as a pattern. For example, a particular detail, idea, or image can be elaborated upon or designed to form a pattern or motif in the essay.

Myth in literature is a traditional story or series of events explaining some basic phenomenon of nature; the origin of humanity; or the customs, institutions, and religious rites of a people. Myth often relates to the exploits of gods, goddesses, and heroes.

N

Narration as a form of essay writing is the presentation of a story in order to illustrate an idea.

Non sequitur in argumentation is a conclusion or inference that does not follow from the premises or evidence on which it is based. The non sequitur thus is a type of logical fallacy.

O

Objective/subjective writing refers to the attitude that writers take toward their subject. When writers are objective, they try not to report their personal feelings about the subject; they attempt to be detached, impersonal, and unbiased. Conversely, subjective writing reveals an author's personal attitudes and emotions. For many varieties of college writing, such as business or laboratory reports, term papers, and literary analyses, it is best to be as objective as possible. But for many personal essays in composition courses, the subjective touch

is fine. In the hands of skilled writers, the objective and subjective tones often blend.

Onomatopoeia is the formation of a word by imitating the natural sound associated with the object or action, as in *buzz* or *click*.

Order is the arrangement of information or materials in an essay. The most common ordering techniques are *chronological order* (time in sequence), *spatial order* (the arrangement of descriptive details), *process order* (a step-by-step approach to an activity), *deductive order* (a thesis followed by information to support it), and *inductive order* (evidence and examples first, followed by the thesis in the form of a conclusion). Some rhetorical patterns, such as comparison and contrast, classification, and argumentation, require other ordering methods. Writers should select those ordering principles that permit them to present materials clearly.

Overstatement is an extravagant or exaggerated claim or statement.

P

Paradox is a statement that seems to be contradictory but actually contains an element of truth.

Paragraph is a unit in an essay that serves to present and examine one aspect of a topic. Composed normally of a group of sentences (one-sentence paragraphs can be used for emphasis or special effect), the paragraph elaborates an idea within the larger framework of the essay and the thesis unifying it.

Parallelism is a variety of sentence structure in which there is balance or coordination in the presentation of elements. "I came, I saw, I conquered" is a standard example of parallelism, presenting both pronouns and verbs in a coordinated manner. Parallelism can appear in a sentence, a group of sentences, or an entire paragraph.

Paraphrase as a literary method is the process of rewording the thought or meaning expressed in something that has been said or written before.

Parenthetical refers to giving qualifying information or explanation. This information normally is marked off or placed within parentheses.

Parody is ridiculing the language or style of another writer or composer. In parody, a serious subject tends to be treated in a nonsensical manner.

Periphrasis is the use of many words where one or a few would do; it is a roundabout way of speaking or writing.

Persona is the role or characterization that writers occasionally create for themselves in a personal narrative.

Personification is giving an object, a thing, or an idea lifelike or human characteristics, as in the common reference to a car as "she." Like all forms of figurative language, personification adds freshness to description and makes ideas vivid by setting up striking comparisons.

Persuasion is the form of discourse, related to argumentation, that attempts to move a person to action or to influence an audience toward a particular belief.

Point of view is the angle from which a writer tells a story. Many personal and informal essays take the *first-person* (or "I") point of view, which is natural and fitting for essays in which the author wants to speak in a familiar way to the reader. On the other hand, the *third-person* point of view ("he," "she," "it," "they") distances the reader somewhat from the writer. The third-person point of view is useful in essays in which the writers are not talking exclusively about themselves, but about other people, ideas, and events.

Post hoc, ergo propter hoc in logic is the fallacy of thinking that a happening that follows another must be its result. It arises from a confusion about the logical causal relationship.

Process analysis is a pattern of writing that explains in a step-by-step way how something is done, how it is put together, how it works, or how it occurs. The subject can be a mechanical device, a product, an idea, a natural phenomenon, or a historical sequence. However, in all varieties of process analysis, the writer traces all important steps, from beginning to end.

Progression is the forward movement or succession of acts, events, or ideas presented in an essay.

Proportion refers to the relative emphasis and length given to an event, an idea, a time, or a topic within the whole essay. Basically, in terms of proportion, the writer gives more emphasis to a major element than to a minor one.

Proposition is the main point of an argumentative essay—the statement to be defended, proved, or upheld. It is like a *thesis* (see entry) except that it presents an idea that is debatable or can be disputed. The *major proposition* is the main argumentative point; *minor propositions* are the reasons given to support or prove the issue.

Purpose is what the writer wants to accomplish in an essay. Writers having a clear purpose will know the proper style, language, tone, and materials to utilize in designing an effective essay.

R

Refutation in argumentation is a method by which writers recognize and deal effectively with the arguments of their opponents. Their own argument will be stronger if they refute—prove false or wrong—all opposing arguments.

Repetition is a simple method of achieving emphasis by repeating a word, a phrase, or an idea.

Rhetoric is the art of using words effectively in speaking or writing. It is also the art of literary composition, particularly in prose, including both figures of speech and such strategies as *comparison and contrast, definition,* and *analysis.*

Rhetorical question is a question asked only to emphasize a point, introduce a topic, or provoke thought, but not to elicit an answer.

Rhythm in prose writing is a regular recurrence of elements or features in sentences, creating a patterned emphasis, balance, or contrast.

S

Sarcasm is a sneering or taunting attitude in writing, designed to hurt by evaluating or criticizing. Basically, sarcasm is a heavy-handed form of *irony* (see entry). Writers should try to avoid sarcastic writing and to use more acceptable varieties of irony and satire to criticize their subject.

Satire is the humorous or critical treatment of a subject in order to expose the subject's vices, follies, stupidities, and so forth. The intention of such satire is to reform by exposing the subject to comedy or ridicule.

Sensory language is language that appeals to any of the five senses—sight, sound, touch, taste, or smell.

Sentimentality in prose writing is the excessive display of emotion, whether intended or unintended. Because sentimentality can distort the true nature of a situation or an idea, writers should use it cautiously, or not at all.

Series as a technique in prose is the presentation of several items, often concrete details or similar parts of grammar such as verbs or adjectives, in rapid sequence.

Setting in narrative and descriptive writing is the time, place, environment, background, or surroundings established by an author.

Simile is a figurative comparison using *like* or *as*.

Slang is a kind of language that uses racy or colorful expressions associated more often with speech than with writing. It is colloquial English and should be used in essay writing only to reproduce dialogue or to create a special effect.

Spatial order in descriptive writing is the careful arrangement of details or materials in space—for example, from left to right, top to bottom, or near to far.

Specific words (See *general/specific words.*)

Statistics are facts or data of a numerical kind, assembled and tabulated to present significant information about a given subject. As a technique of illustration, statistics can be useful in analysis and argumentation.

Style is the specific or characteristic manner of expression, execution, construction, or design of an author. As a manner or mode of expression in language, it is the unique way each writer handles ideas. There are numerous stylistic categories—such as literary, formal, argumentative, and satiric—but ultimately, no two writers have the same style.

Subjective (See *objective/subjective.*)

Subordination in sentence structure is the placing of a relatively less important idea in an inferior grammatical position to the main idea. It is the designation of a minor clause that is dependent upon a major clause.

Syllogism is an argument or form of reasoning in which two statements or premises are made and a logical conclusion is drawn from them. As such, it is a form of deductive logic—reasoning from the general to the particular. The *major premise* presents a quality of class ("All writers are mortal"). The *minor premise* states that a particular subject is a member of that class ("Ernest Hemingway was a writer"). The conclusion states that the qualities of the class and the member of the class are the same ("Hemingway was mortal").

Symbol is something—normally a concrete image—that exists in itself but also stands for something else or has greater meaning. As a variety of figurative language, the symbol can be a strong feature in an essay, operating to add depth of meaning and even to unify the composition.

Synonym is a word that means roughly the same as another word. In practice, few words are exactly alike in meaning. Careful writers use synonyms to vary word choice without ever moving too far from the shade of meaning intended.

Syntax is sentence structure. A writer can use a variety of sentence types—long and complex, short and simple, or even placing the subject and verb at the end—to achieve different effects.

T

Theme is the central idea in an essay; it is also termed the *thesis*. Everything in an essay should support the theme in one way or another.

Thesis is the main idea in an essay. The *thesis sentence,* appearing early in the essay (normally somewhere in the first paragraph) serves to convey the main idea to the reader in a clear and emphatic manner.

Tone is the writer's attitude toward his or her subject or material. An essay writer's tone may be objective, subjective, comic, ironic, nostalgic, critical, or a reflection of numerous other attitudes. Tone is the voice that writers give to an essay.

Topic sentence is the main idea that a paragraph develops. Not all paragraphs contain topic sentences; often the topic is implied.

Transition is the linking of ideas in sentences, paragraphs, and larger segments of an essay in order to achieve *coherence* (see entry). Among the most common techniques to achieve smooth transitions are (1) repeating a key word or phrase, (2) using a pronoun to refer to a key word or phrase, (3) relying on traditional connectives such as *thus, however, moreover, for example, therefore, finally,* or *in conclusion,* (4) using parallel structure (see *parallelism*), and (5) creating a sentence or paragraph that serves as a bridge from one part of an essay to another. Transition is best achieved when a writer presents ideas and details carefully and in logical order.

U

Understatement is a method of making a weaker statement than is warranted by truth, accuracy, or importance.

Unity is a feature in an essay whereby all material relates to a central concept and contributes to the meaning of the whole. To achieve a unified effect in an essay, the writer must design an effective introduction and conclusion, maintain consistent tone or point of view, develop middle paragraphs in a coherent manner, and above all stick to the subject, never permitting unimportant or irrelevant elements to enter.

Usage is the way in which a word, phrase, or sentence is used to express a particular idea; it is the customary manner of using a given language in speaking or writing.

V

Vertical (See *horizontal/vertical.*)

Voice is the way you express your ideas to the reader, the tone you take in addressing your audience. Voice reflects your attitude toward both your subject and your readers. (See *tone.*)